D0205908

Church and State in America

CHURCH AND STATE IN AMERICA

A Bibliographical Guide

The Civil War
to the Present Day

EDITED BY

John F. Wilson

GP

GREENWOOD PRESS
NEW YORK · WESTPORT, CONNECTICUT · LONDON

Library of Congress Cataloging-in-Publication Data
(Revised for vol. 2)

Church and state in America.

Includes indexes.
Contents: v. 1. The Colonial and early national
periods—v. 2. The Civil War to the present day.
1. Church and state—United States—Bibliography.
2. United States—Church history—Bibliography.
I. Wilson, John Frederick.
Z7776.72.C48   1986   016.322′1′0973   85-31698
ISBN 0-313-25236-X (lib. bdg. : v. 1 : alk. paper)
ISBN 0-313-25914-3 (lib. bdg. : v. 2 : alk. paper)

Library of Congress Catalog Card Number: 85-31698
ISBN: 0-313-25236-X (v. 1)
ISBN: 0-313-25914-3 (v. 2)

First published in 1987

Greenwood Press, Inc.
88 Post Road West, Westport, Connecticut 06881

Printed in the United States of America

The paper used in this book complies with the
Permanent Paper Standard issued by the National
Information Standards Organization (Z39.48-1984).

10   9   8   7   6   5   4   3   2   1

Contents

Introduction   vii
John F. Wilson

1. Church-State Issues in the Period of the Civil War   1
William F. Deverell

2. Church-State Issues in Reconstruction and the Culture of the Southern States   33
Gardiner H. Shattuck, Jr.

3. Social Justice in an Industrial Society   67
Mark S. Massa

4. Immigration and Urbanization: Changing Patterns of Religious and Cultural Authority   107
Richard Hughes Seager

5. Church and State at the Turn of the Century: Missions and Imperialism, Bureaucratization, and War, 1898–1920   143
James D. Beumler

6. Church-State Issues in the Twenties and Thirties   185
Richard D. Horn

7. America Emerges as a World Power: Religion, Politics, and Nationhood, 1940–1960   225
James D. Beumler

8. Religion and the Nation: 1960 to the Present   263
David Harrington Watt

9. Religion and Education: 1870 to the Present   301
   John W. Lowe, Jr.

10. Religion and Law in the United States: 1870 to the
    Present   339
    Winnifred F. Sullivan

11. Women and Religion in America, 1870–1920   373
    Elizabeth B. Clark

   Index   427

   Contributors   453

Introduction

John F. Wilson

This volume of bibliographical studies and its predecessor are among the earliest publications sponsored by the Project on Church and State located at Princeton University. The Project's goal is to meet the need for responsible literature, written from historical or comparative perspectives, on the relations between the spheres of religion and politics broadly defined, with particular reference to the United States. Existing publications are uneven in coverage and quality, a situation created by fitful scholarly attention to this subject in recent decades. Guided by a steering committee of historians, the Project has commissioned, in addition to these two bibliographical volumes, a number of book-length studies, a legal casebook, and an overall survey. The hope is that this small library will be a starting point for further inquiry and will give readers of all kinds a better understanding of the American past and present, and even of the future, where this particular question is concerned. The Project has designed a broad approach to its goal, one that is deliberately critical rather than prescriptive. The object is to encourage serious reflection about these important issues rather than to advocate a particular position in the current political climate.

In the introduction to the first volume, I suggested that our common uses of the words "church" and "state" are often too narrow. "Church" fails to denote the religious dimensions of the culture to be found outside formal denominations—themselves increasingly plural—while "state" glosses over the complexities of our political life, a system of many levels and divided powers in which, additionally, many quasi-governmental roles are played by private agencies. The use of the word "state" is as misleading as that of "church" because American political reality departs from the European "state" to which the term was first applied in much the same way that American religious reality departs from the classical European definition of "church."

Moreover, to define these issues by the terms church and state deprives them of their dynamic quality. These issues play a disturbing role in the political culture, one that is not encompassed by the more static significance of the conventional definition. The full implications of relations between church and state are better understood if the topic is defined less in terms of institutions than in terms of authority, and how patterns of authority characterize the society. These volumes make use of this more inclusive definition and therefore incorporate a much broader range of literature than would be relevant under the concept of church and state which primarily focuses on institutions.

The first volume covers the subject from the colonial settlements to the middle of the nineteenth century. The second takes the story from the Civil War to the present day. The majority of the chapters are devoted to historical periods. In addition, chapters on education, law, and gender relations respectively appear in both volumes. Each chapter consists of a critical essay and a listing of selected books, journal articles, primary sources, a few dissertations, and other relevant materials. The emphasis is on works of the last twenty-five years, with the addition of older publications that remain important. The authors of these chapters are current graduate students or young faculty members whose specialized studies afford them particular knowledge of a given period or topic.

The essays in both bibliographical volumes vary in form according to their contents. Some make use of significant internal divisions in both text and listings, for example, while others do not. Some use footnotes to specify general points while others incorporate all references into the text. In a few chapters, particular figures or publications are treated as representative, whereas the majority are characterized by more straightforward analysis. Certain bibliographic citations appear in more than one chapter since each essay is intended to be a relatively complete guide to its subject. The repetition serves both to underline the interrelatedness of many of the topics and to highlight the fact that only a few authors have approached the subject from our viewpoint. In spite of these variations, as stated in the first volume, the purpose underlying each chapter remains the same: to lead the reader into the primary and secondary literature that bears on the church-state issue in its broadest definition in the context of American culture. Because of this inclusive perspective, we believe both volumes will have wide use among those interested in the more general study of American religion and culture, as well as among specialists in church-state questions.

This second volume presented certain challenges. For instance, the first four chapters stand in a special relationship to each other. The initial chapter on the Civil War suggests how that event precipitated profound changes in the thinking of Americans about their political and religious institutions. One outcome of the war was a persistent regional subculture—the South—that for virtually a century embodied a distinctive view of religion and its relationship to the broader society including governing institutions. The Civil War was also followed by a remarkable double transformation of American society more generally. One driving force was industrialization, linked to the growth of cities and the decline of agriculture. These essentially social changes occasioned distinctive responses by religious leaders and institutions—as well as countervailing critiques. A second was immigration on a vast scale. So many new cultural and religious traditions came with the immigrants that the consequent shifts in patterns of interaction largely recast the culture. In dealing with these questions, the first four essays in this volume and their associated listings are more intricately interrelated than any others of the essentially period-defined chapters in either volume.

With regard to the chapters on the most recent period another factor should be mentioned. Secondary literature has not yet developed for the contemporary period, or, to be more precise, the line between primary and secondary sources is elusive. In these chapters the authors have attempted to respond to this problem and make clear to the reader how it influences use of the sources they cite.

Finally, the nature of the material covered in the specialized topical chapters in this volume placed certain constraints on the authors. For instance, the chapter on women in American religion ends in 1920 because by the First World War the nineteenth-century ideal of domesticity, on which women had relied for their public as well as their private persona and which had depended so much on their spirituality, was no longer their most representative image. Women's religion became a more private matter as they sought their public identity in political activities and participation in the labor force. The later historiography reflects this change, concentrating more on women's institutional church affiliations than on the political and social dimensions of their spirituality. For this reason the essay on family and gender does not attempt to address the new casting of issues which occurred in our generation except as it has contributed to the significant reinterpretation of preceding periods.

The subject of education also presents us with a special problem in the twentieth century. Indeed church-state issues have largely come to national prominence in conflicts over schooling. These issues have concerned both rights deriving from religious background in the context of publicly funded schools and demands for public support of religiously founded and maintained schools. The chapter concerned with education is largely organized in terms of those issues which have been resolved in the courts, especially federal courts, because so much relevant literature has been generated as a result of the related decisions. This approach, inevitable though it is, unfortunately has the effect of underemphasizing the significant changes in education brought about, for instance, by the growing importance of science and technology, or the need for an awareness of other cultures as our globe seems to contract. Although these changes have refashioned the place of formal schooling in the society in ways that are of great significance for church-state issues, their implications for the respective roles of religion and education have not yet been systematically plumbed. It is an important task for the coming generation of scholarship.

Finally, the author of the topical chapter on law has had to deal with the remarkable expansion of relevant literature occasioned by the explosion of litigation on church-state issues in both state and federal courts. Any selection from that literature is necessarily restricted and therefore partial. For the purposes of this project an essay of use to the general reader seemed called for rather than one narrowly focused on technical issues. We trust the essay presented here will enable lay people to locate both the more specialized legal commentary and interpretive material as well as the kind of writing about law and religion that goes beyond the narrowest legal questions to include reflection on politics, law, and society.

As this bibliographical component comes to completion, the Project's emphasis turns to other aspects of the endeavor. The casebook, *The Believer and the Powers that Are*, by John T. Noonan, Jr., has recently been published. The individual studies, both on specific periods in the American experience and on related topics in other societies, will begin to appear in the near future. Finally, the overall survey of the church-state issue in American culture will follow. All of these publications are intended to promote a deeper and better informed approach to an issue as vital today as it ever has been in our society, an issue that gives no sign of decreasing in importance over the coming decades.

The members of the steering committee for the Project have been involved with the bibliographical component from the outset: Robert T. Handy, professor emeritus at Union Theological Seminary; Stanley N. Katz, president of the American Council of Learned Societies and formerly professor of the history of law at Princeton University; and Albert J. Raboteau, my colleague at Princeton, have helped to bring these volumes to completion in many and critically important ways. James D. Beumler, who has contributed two chapters to this volume, also assisted us throughout in using to advantage current computer technology. Lorraine Fuhrmann, administrator of the Department of Religion at Princeton, has tirelessly attended to the complex practical details of the management of the Project. Most significant, Yoma Ullman,

who serves as overall coordinator of the Project, has orchestrated completion of this second volume as she did the first. Her unstinting commitment of
time, and dedicated attention to subject matter, has left us all deeply in her
debt. Without her collaboration, the Project could not have hoped to achieve
this kind of publication. The Project on Church and State has been financed
through a generous grant from the Lilly Endowment. Dr. Robert W. Lynn,
Senior Vice President for Religion, has taken a strong interest in our work,
and we greatly value his continuing counsel and intellectual stimulation.

Church and State in America

Church-State Issues in the Period of the Civil War

William F. Deverell

Leo Pfeffer, in his influential examination of church-state issues in American history, *Church, State, and Freedom,* wrote that "the church in America has always been knee deep in politics" (p. 198). And while the whole of American history can be characterized by an energetic involvement of religious groups in affairs of state, large and small, there can be little doubt that the height of such activity occurred during the period dominated by the Civil War. For nothing in American political history has so captivated the church as the issues of that era: a vociferous battle of words debating the sinfulness or godliness of slavery, a retributive, bloody, fratricidal war in which both sides claimed God's favor, and a widespread belief that out of carnage would come the fulfillment of Christ's millennial promise.

But this church involvement in the politics of the Civil War is invariably difficult to unravel and analyze. The scholar attempting to study "church-state issues in the period of the Civil War" faces no simple task. The naturally complex relationship between the "church" and the "state" becomes even more muddled by the events and emotions of war. The ever-present difficulties inherent in precisely defining a "church-state issue" magnify the challenge.

For the purposes of the following essay, which introduces the bibliography that follows, "church-state issues" will encompass several shades of meaning. First, the traditional: we will note instances where the arbitrary boundaries set to separate "church" from "state" have been crossed—or crossed just enough to elicit contemporary or historiographical comment or controversy. In other words, this essay will address works that discuss historical moments when the integrity of the church has been threatened by the state (and vice versa) in a manner contrary to the constitutional provisions which oppose integration of church and state. An example of such an issue, and one with a growing historiographical literature to which we shall return, would be

the office of military chaplain. Did the development of the chaplaincy in the
Civil War represent a weakening of the institutional independence of church
and state?

By and large, however, this essay will focus on a historiographical discussion of works that study the relationship between two categories less rigid
than "church" and "state." Scholarship that examines the common ground
between religion and politics in the Civil War era will be addressed. For it is
this mixture of the spiritual and the secular that promises most to the student
attempting to understand that era. If characterized by any one feature, it is
notable for a fascinating melding of patriotism and piety; the American
church has never been more deeply involved in politics.

Scholars of the Civil War have long sought to understand the roots of the
sectional conflict through study of events and circumstances that predate the
war by years, decades, even generations. Recent scholarship has examined
the coming of the war in light of fractures within Protestant denominations in
antebellum America. In his book *Broken Churches, Broken Nation*, C. C.
Goen illuminates the antebellum era by a careful study of the conflicts that
various Protestant denominations faced in the two decades prior to the war.
Goen emphasizes the importance of religion to antebellum America, but he
does not argue that a strict causal relationship existed between the cleaving
of religious bodies and the cleaving of the nation. His point in the book is that
questions of nineteenth-century group beliefs—an important realm of inquiry
to Civil War scholars—"cannot be answered fully without taking into account the role of the churches—particularly the large evangelical denominations with national constituencies—as significant influences on public opinion and popular feeling" (p. 5).

As a prelude, Goen stresses the role that religion and the church played in
fostering American nationalism. By emphasizing the country's God-given role
in history, its "providential design," Protestant clergy explicitly paired "the
Kingdom of God with the American republic" (p. 41). At the same time, the
denominational organizations themselves tied the nation's sections together
beneath banners of common purpose, practice, and belief. Goen reminds us
that the Methodist Episcopal Church, for instance, "was the most extensive
national institution in antebellum America other than the federal government" (p. 57).

The corrosiveness of the slavery issue, however, exposed dangerous weaknesses in the foundation of American nationalism. In 1837, the Presbyterian
church underwent an Old School/New School division largely due to disagreements over slavery (the New School would divide again twenty years
later). The Methodist and Baptist churches followed with sectional cleavages
in 1844 and 1845. Goen highlights these denominational splits and argues

convincingly that, as religion and the churches played a vital role in the creation of American nationalism, both were perhaps no less important to the creation of nationalism's reverse: disunion. In a sense, Goen echoes John C. Calhoun, who pointed out before the Senate in 1850 that the Union was surely imperiled: the strong, binding ties of religion and denominational loyalty had begun to snap.

Goen blames the Protestant leadership for failing to wrestle effectively with the awesome problem of slavery. In their support of the institution, at times nothing short of impassioned, southern preachers sought justification from the Bible and stridently denounced their northern counterparts for meddling in southern and secular affairs. For their part, ever mindful of the taint of "radicalism" and "abolitionism," many northern preachers defended their apathy by stressing the clergy's duty to remain in the world but not of it. Even those who used the pulpit to oppose slavery—and there were many— did not grasp the massive sociological impact of the institution. To them, slavery was the sin of the individual slaveholder against God and the individual slave. Redemption would follow the penitent act of manumission. Slavery could be abolished—one slave at a time—only when the slaveholder was convinced of his sin; his conscience and godliness alone could move him to act.

In addition to their ineffective response to slavery, Goen charges that northern and southern preachers failed to hear the warning bells of disunion. Both sections downplayed the significance of the denominational schisms. Some preachers actually praised the divisions as peaceful solutions to sectional conflict. Goen chastises the clergy for failing to recognize the denominational splits for what they were: early, ominous, and significant representations of serious rents in the national fabric.

Some critics have written that Goen overemphasizes the influence of the Protestant schisms, making them miniature dress rehearsals for secession and the Civil War. They point out that the war did not immediately follow the church divisions; sectional animosities hardened for more than a decade. Others believe that the real and symbolic significance of religion to the coming of the Civil War (especially the importance of the breakdown of denominational unity) is extremely difficult to assess.

In *The South and the North in American Religion*, Samuel S. Hill, Jr., a distinguished scholar of southern religion, suggests it is "impossible, and unnecessary" to determine the extent to which religion promoted antebellum sectional disaffection (p. 69). Hill's purpose in this work and in two superb overviews which he edited, *Encyclopedia of Religion in the South* and *Religion in the Southern States*, is to highlight the distinctiveness of southern religion. Hill characterizes the antebellum estrangement of northern and southern churches as an increasing alienation exacerbated by the slavery issue. But, he argues, to imagine that northern and southern churches were once a unified whole would be to ignore differences magnified—not caused— by slavery. Hill stresses the private nature of southern religion, a brand of Protestantism that emphasized the nurturing of the individual Christian within the prescribed and fairly rigid boundaries of church influence. Unlike northern Protestantism, which took a great interest in secular affairs, southern Protestantism generally remained cloistered behind the walls of its churches.

Why this difference existed is not at all clear. Some scholars have proposed complex theological arguments in partial explanation. Richard E. Beringer and his fellow authors in their recent book *Why the South Lost the Civil War* suggest that the South believed in a different conception of the Christian millennium (an argument we will address later). Others argue that southern reluctance to mix matters secular and sacred, at least in some Protestant denominations, sprang from a defensive reaction to the activities of northern abolitionist evangelicals. In other words, ecclesiastical doctrine which restricted the boundaries of church influence (e.g., churches, northern and southern alike, ought have no relationship with purely civil matters, especially slavery) was bound to further discredit the abolitionist efforts of northern churches.

Yet some historians dispute the idea that antebellum southern churches shunned public involvement; on the contrary, they see a southern tendency to involve the church actively in civil affairs. In "From Theocracy to Spirituality: The Southern Presbyterian Reversal on Church and State," Jack P. Maddex examines the antebellum behavior of one southern Protestant denomination. The Presbyterians, he writes, "did not teach absolute separation of religion from politics, or even church from state" (p. 438). Proslavery advocates, with Presbyterian blessing if not actual sponsorship, used the pulpit to support slavery and express distaste for the meddling North. Such activity, Maddex claims, could hardly constitute anything other than an energetic mixing of matters political with matters religious. Not until after the war did southern Presbyterians embrace the doctrine which opposed secular involvement. Further, Maddex claims that scholars have misinterpreted leading theologian James Henley Thornwell of South Carolina as a strict church and state separationist when, in fact, he enthusiastically championed the role of God in affairs of state and section. Readers may wish to consult two other essays by Maddex that examine the relationship between southern Christianity and proslavery ideology: "Proslavery Millennialism: Social Eschatology in Antebellum Southern Calvinism" and "'The Southern Apostasy' Revisited: The Significance of Proslavery Christianity." For additional analysis of Thornwell, see H. Shelton Smith's essay, "The Church and the Social Order in the Old

South as Interpreted by James Henley Thornwell." For further insight into the social attitudes of southern Protestants, see John Lee Eighmy's *Churches in Cultural Captivity* and Anne C. Loveland's *Southern Evangelicals and the Social Order.*

Few scholars dispute the idea that northern Protestantism actively sought to correct the moral and religious shortcomings of society at large—a mission that, because it invariably brought the church into the political arena, blurred the distinction between the secular and the purely spiritual. Northern Protestantism's societal stewardship is ably discussed in Clifford S. Griffin's book *Their Brothers' Keepers.* Antebellum northern reform movements, backed as they often were by Yankee Protestants, exuded a vigorous Christian energy. The Beringer volume ascribes this enthusiasm for widening the church's social and political activity to the northern conception of the millennium, Christ's promised return to earth. Northern Protestants, its authors suggest, ardently believed that the millennium would occur only after Christians acted to perfect society. This "postmillennialist" doctrine neatly explained the importance of Christian work in the world: the millennial age, Christ's long earthly reign, would arise out of the energetic labors of the faithful. Accordingly, northern Protestants set about perfecting their world through a myriad of reform crusades: abolitionism, temperance movements, children's aid societies, labor reform, and many others.

Insight into northern Protestantism and social reform, especially abolitionism, can be gained by consulting several excellent books and articles. Charles C. Cole, Jr., introduced the subject in his standard study *The Social Ideas of Northern Evangelists, 1826–1860.* Also important are Timothy L. Smith's *Revivalism and Social Reform* and John W. Kuykendall's *Southern Enterprize.* "Northern Missionary Activities in the South, 1846–1861," by Fletcher Melvin Green, is a useful complement to Kuykendall's work. John R. McKivigan's recent book *The War against Proslavery Religion: Abolitionism and the Northern Churches, 1830–1865* provides a thorough, deeply researched analysis of the complex role northern churches played in the equally complex abolitionist movement. James Fulton Maclear's "The Evangelical Alliance and the Antislavery Crusade" should also be consulted. A fine study of abolitionism's links to the broader culture is Lawrence J. Friedman's book *Gregarious Saints: Self and Community in American Abolitionism, 1830–1870.* George M. Frederickson's *The Black Image in the White Mind: The Debate on Afro-American Character and Destiny, 1817–1914* is a superb study of the racial attitudes, perceptions, and prejudices that enveloped nineteenth-century America. Studies of individual churchmen can also be very helpful. Bertram Wyatt-Brown analyzes abolitionism, religion, and politics through the actions of Lewis Tappan in *Lewis Tappan and the Evan-*

gelical War against Slavery; similar in purpose is William Gravely's book *Gilbert Haven, Methodist Abolitionist: A Study in Race, Religion, and Reform, 1850–1880.* John B. Boles examines the left flank of early nineteenth-century Methodism in his article "John Hersey: Dissenting Theologian of Abolitionism, Perfectionism, and Millennialism." The northern commitment to antislavery, or lack thereof, is commented upon in essays analyzing the views of powerful northern preacher Horace Bushnell by Howard A. Barnes, Charles C. Cole, Jr., and Sydney E. Ahlstrom.

As described in *Why the South Lost the Civil War,* the southern Protestant church was far less apt to become involved in extensive social or political activity largely because it did not subscribe to a postmillennialist conception that both justified and demanded good works. Southern Protestants, the various contributors argue, generally adhered to a "premillennialist" faith: a belief that Christ would return to earth before the advent of the glorious millennial age, and by that return would inaugurate the millennium. As such, the labors of good Christians on earth were relatively unimportant: Christ alone could perfect human society. Reinforcing this understanding was the increasingly defensive southern posture regarding slavery: because the institution was divinely affirmed (southerners were ever quick to voice biblical justifications of slavery), southern society was already perfect in the eyes of God.

Students of American millennialism should first consult the work of James H. Moorhead. His book *American Apocalypse: Yankee Protestants and the Civil War, 1860–1869* is the best study of northern millennial faith during the war. In addition, Moorhead has recently written two valuable overview essays: "Between Progress and Apocalypse: A Reassessment of Millennialism in American Religious Thought, 1800–1880" and "Millennialism." An important complement to Moorhead's scholarship is William A. Clebsch's *Christian Interpretations of the Civil War.* Ernest Lee Tuveson's *Redeemer Nation: The Idea of America's Millennial Role* is also helpful, especially the sixth chapter, "The Ennobling War." James F. Maclear's "The Republic and the Millennium" provides a more general description of American millennialism, as does Clebsch's book *From Sacred to Profane America: The Role of Religion in American History.*

Despite their seemingly different millennial conceptions, both the North and the South, prompted by the coming of the Civil War, began to align frightening political developments with millennial hopes and fears. The dissolution of the Union, or perhaps a cataclysmic fratricidal war—the closest the nation had ever approached Armageddon—might just introduce the millennium. As the decade of the 1850s brought one ominous political crisis after another—the hopelessly fragile "armistice" of the Compromise of 1850,

Bleeding Kansas, the Dred Scott decision, John Brown's raid—pulpits in both sections rang with odd jeremiads of despair and disguised hope. Yes, the North, or the South, or the entire nation, would pay dearly for her sins at the retributive hands of an angry God. But perhaps God's terrible justice would purify America, and he would lead the victorious into the age of the millennium and the Second Coming.

Northern Protestantism, in particular, resonated with the belief that the coming of the Civil War coincided with the coming of the millennium. Certainly the apocalyptic vision inherent in Harriet Beecher Stowe's *Uncle Tom's Cabin* or Julia Ward Howe's "The Battle Hymn of the Republic" (with its millennial prophesy: "Mine eyes have seen the glory of the coming of the Lord") bears testimony to this faith. Accordingly, northerners mobilized as enthusiastic warriors in the service of God. In Moorhead's words: "What makes the 1860s especially interesting is the sheer intensity and virtual unanimity of Northern conviction that the Union armies were hastening the day of the Lord—indeed that the war was not merely one sacred battle among many but was the climactic test of the redeemer nation and its millennial role" (*American Apocalypse*, p. x). The fact that overtly "moral" or "religious" aims (such as the abolition of slavery) were distinctly absent from the initial northern war effort appears strikingly paradoxical. How then could the war possibly be seen as a religious crusade? How could Horace Bushnell declare in the midst of the conflict that "we associate God and religion with all that we are fighting for" (quoted in Barnes, "The Idea That Caused a War," p. 81)?

As Moorhead brilliantly suggests, northerners simply recast the political and military objectives of the Union as the definitive Christian struggles of the age. The sins of individuals, northerner and southerner alike, were inextricably linked to the sins of the nation; all were to be purged in the bloody trial. But to keep America's millennial promise alive, the Union had to prevail. Once the war had broken out, "[northern] Protestants hopelessly confused the weapons of the saints with the Union's military power and awaited the first signs of the millennium in the exploits of the Army of the Potomac" (*American Apocalypse*, p. x).

The South also placed God in the center of the conflict. Many students of the Civil War have noted that Julia Ward Howe's paean to God's guardianship over the Union could easily have been a patriotic devotional in the South. In other words, southerners linked God and religion to their war effort no less directly than the North. Southerners may not have believed as strongly as northerners that the war would bring about the millennium, but southern churches and churchgoers loyally supported the Confederacy nonetheless. Such loyalty is the common theme in nearly all studies of southern churches and southern religion during the Civil War. As James W. Silver writes, the "church as a whole compiled an enviable record of unwavering support of and devotion to the Confederate government" (*Confederate Morale*, p. 63). Similarly, Emory M. Thomas notes in *The Confederate Nation* that "among all the institutions in Southern life, perhaps the Church most faithfully served the Confederate army and nation" (*Confederate Nation*, p. 246).

But such faithful support was not merely institutional. Southern preachers (like their northern counterparts) explicitly aligned their section's cause with God's plans. In this way, southern religion was an integral part of the Confederate war effort. Confederate President Jefferson Davis, writes Thomas, "realized as a matter of personal piety and public policy that the Confederate cause required God on the Southern side" (*Confederate Nation*, p. 245). And "for those Southerners who believed they were God's people and that the Confederacy was part of God's plan, it was a matter of simple semantics to identify religion with politics and patriotism" (Silver, *Confederate Morale*, p. 42).

For insight into the complex role of religion in the Confederacy, readers should perhaps consult general studies of southern religion before focusing on more specific denominational or regional questions. *Religion in the Southern States: A Historical Study* and *Encyclopedia of Religion in the South*, both edited by Samuel S. Hill, Jr., are excellent introductions, as is Charles H. Lippy's *Bibliography of Religion in the South. Religion in the Old South*, by Donald G. Mathews, is a superb analysis of the role of religion in the antebellum South; see also the essays in *Religion in the South*, edited by Charles Reagan Wilson, and "Religion, Society and Culture in the Old South: A Comparative View," by Dickson D. Bruce, Jr.

The best single study of religion as a bulwark to the Confederacy remains James Silver's excellent monograph *Confederate Morale and Church Propaganda*. Beringer and his collaborators in *Why the South Lost the Civil War* devote several chapters and an equal number of provocative assertions to the role of religion in the Confederacy. Unfortunately, Joseph Blount Cheshire's *The Church in the Confederate States* is now too dated to be of much use. Two of W. Harrison Daniel's many essays are especially helpful in this connection: "Southern Protestantism and Secession," in which he points out the catalytic role of Lincoln's election in strengthening southern church support of the Confederacy, and "Protestantism and Patriotism in the Confederacy," which complements Silver's monograph (as does Willard E. Wight's "The Churches and the Confederate Cause").

Studies which analyze specific denominations during the war are uneven in quality and vary in degree of usefulness. This aspect of southern (and northern) religious history deserves works of greater synthesis. Several of the more penetrating studies include "The Presbyterians and the Sectional Conflict," by J. Treadwell Davis; *The Sectional Crisis and Northern Methodism*, by Donald G. Jones; "The Reaction of the Protestant Episcopal Church in Virginia to the Secession Crisis," by Leonard I. Sweet; and three essays by W. Harrison Daniel: "Virginia Baptists, 1861–1865"; "The Southern Baptists in the Confederacy"; and "A Brief Account of the Methodist Episcopal Church, South in the Confederacy." Clarence E. Walker's *A Rock in a Weary Land: The African Methodist Episcopal Church During the Civil War and Reconstruction* is a thorough study of the Civil War activities of an important black church. Two older essays by Edgar Legare Pennington are still useful: "The Confederate Episcopal Church in 1863" and, especially, "The Organization of the Protestant Episcopal Church in the Confederate States of America." William Warren Sweet's 1912 book *The Methodist Episcopal Church and the Civil War*, though obviously dated, is nonetheless useful for factual reference. Benjamin J. Blied's book *Catholics in the Civil War*, though helpful, may prove difficult to find. Lewis G. Vander Velde's *The Presbyterian Churches and the Federal Union, 1861–1869* is a fifty-year-old classic that still merits consultation. Bertram W. Korn has studied Jewish participation in and reaction to the Civil War; see especially his book *American Jewry and the Civil War*. Harry Simonhoff's *Jewish Participants in the Civil War* is also helpful.

There are many excellent general denominational histories that are useful in identifying various denominational doctrines and practices. Presbyterianism, in particular, has received a great deal of scholarly attention. Ernest Trice Thompson's three-volume study *Presbyterians in the South* is extremely thorough; see also his book *The Spirituality of the Church: A Distinctive Doctrine of the Presbyterian Church in the United States*. An interesting and ambitious study is Elwyn Allen Smith's book *The Presbyterian Ministry in American Culture: A Study in Changing Concepts, 1700–1900*. A good denominational history of Methodism is Frederick A. Norwood's *The Story of American Methodism: A History of the United Methodists and Their Relations*. For insight into the Baptist denomination, see Robert G. Torbet's *A History of the Baptists*.

As we have seen, southern clergy were as a rule fiercely loyal to the Confederacy; preachers encouraged their congregations to see divine guidance and blessing in secession and war. But a handful of church leaders were noticeably less supportive of the Confederacy than their congregations. In the Confederacy proper, this rare situation generally occurred in isolated geographical pockets of unionist sentiment, such as the hill country of Tennessee. For a description of the ostracism of pro-Union preachers in the South, see W. Harrison Daniel's "Protestant Clergy and Union Sentiment in the Confederacy."

Not surprisingly, many such conflicts between congregations and their

clergy existed in the border states, where political loyalties vacillated be-
tween allegiance to the Union one moment and the Confederacy the next.
Some parishes had pro-Confederate congregations and unionist preachers,
others the reverse. Maryland, in particular, seems to have been especially
afflicted by divided political loyalties within her churches. Nelson Waite
Rightmyer addresses these problems in "The Church in a Border State—
Maryland," as does Richard R. Duncan in "Maryland Methodists and the Civil
War." Duncan and Edward N. Todd analyze the role of Bishop William Robinson Whittingham, a unionist who led the Maryland diocese of the Episcopal
church during the war. In one celebrated case, the pro-Confederate rector at
one of Whittingham's parishes refused to comply with his order calling for a
special day of thanksgiving after the Union victory at Gettysburg (see Duncan's "Bishop Whittingham, the Maryland Diocese, and the Civil War" and
"Bishop Whittingham, Mount Calvary Church, and the Battle of Gettysburg,"
edited by Edward N. Todd). In an important essay, Louis Weeks and James C.
Hickey examine divided political loyalties within the Walnut Street Presbyterian Church in Louisville, Kentucky. Out of the conflict, which outlasted
the Civil War, eventually came a Supreme Court decision "which established
the modern view of the relation between the civil courts and connectional
church bodies in the United States" (Weeks and Hickey, " 'Implied Trust,' " p.
459). Bruce T. Brown further examines the debate on church involvement in
politics in his essay "Grace Church, Galesburg, Illinois, 1864–1866: The Supposed Neutrality of the Episcopal Church During the Years of the Civil War."
Brown suggests that the members of Grace Church who opposed the melding
of church and state were likely to be pro-southern copperheads who were
unhappy with the church's decided pro-Union bent. In other words, their
opposition to bringing politics into the church itself sprang from a deeply
political motivation. Unless the church could be politically prosouthern, it
ought not to be political at all.

By far the sharpest conflicts within churches and between churches and
civil authorities—conflicts often expressed in the explicit terms of church-
state controversy—occurred in areas of the South governed by the Union
army of occupation. Several scholarly works address these conflicts. Despite
its title, which suggests a work of greater breadth, Paul G. Ashdown's essay
"Commission From a Higher Source: Church and State in the Civil War"
examines a small incident that occurred in occupied Tennessee when Samuel
Ringgold, rector of Trinity Church in Clarksville, defied occupation orders
and buried a Confederate soldier. The Reverend Alfred A. Watson of St.
James Church in Wilmington, North Carolina, saw his church sacked and
turned into a military hospital when he refused to offer prayers for President
Abraham Lincoln. Watson's refusal was expressed partly as an aversion to

mixing matters of church and state, but he was also obeying church doctrine. The prayer book of his Episcopal parish no longer had references to the United States and her civil servants; following secession, all such passages referred to the Confederate States of America (see John Nicolson's article "'To Mock My Maker'—A Civil War Letter on Freedom of Conscience"). Milan J. Kedro analyzes the Pine Street church "incident" in St. Louis during the war years in "The Civil War's Effect upon an Urban Church: The St. Louis Presbytery under Martial Law." The Reverend Samuel McPheeters refused to support fast days proclaimed either by Lincoln or the Presbyterian General Assembly. Accordingly, Union military officials banished him from the state of Missouri. The case eventually reached Lincoln; he rescinded the banishment order, choosing instead to see the McPheeters case as an affair of the church, not the state.

Increasing scholarly attention has focused on the nature of the military chaplaincy in both the Confederacy and the Union. Wartime religious ministry to soldiers could seemingly pose problems of a church-state nature. Could the state sponsor religious instruction for its men in uniform? In fact, the Civil War military chaplain found his position difficult not because he transgressed any theoretical boundaries, but because his government made so few provisions for his livelihood. The military chaplain, in both the Union and the Confederacy, was caught in the unenviable niche of being not wholly a man of the cloth, not wholly a man in uniform. As often as not, soldiers perceived the chaplain as a nuisance. Thorough general studies of the chaplaincy include Roy J. Honeywell's *Chaplains of the United States Army; Military Chaplains: From a Religious Military to a Military Religion*, edited by Harvey Cox; and two works by Herman A. Norton, *Struggling for Recognition*, and *Rebel Religion: The Story of Confederate Chaplains*. Bell Irvin Wiley's "'Holy Joes' of the Sixties: A Study of Civil War Chaplains" is somewhat dated but nonetheless useful. The same is true for James W. Silver's "The Confederate Preacher Goes to War." W. Harrison Daniel's essay "An Aspect of Church and State Relations in the Confederacy: Southern Protestantism and the Office of Army Chaplain" describes the discrimination and poor conditions faced by most Confederate chaplains. Daniel also notes the contribution of a handful of Confederate "fighting parsons," those chaplains who ministered to the soldiers in camp and fought alongside them in battle. Rollin W. Quimby's essays also portray the difficulties military chaplains faced from nearly all quarters; see his "Congress and the Civil War Chaplaincy" and "The Chaplain's Predicament." Quimby's interesting essay "Recurrent Themes and Purposes in the Sermons of the Union Army Chaplain" examines the homiletic tradition of Union sermons. John W. Blassingame's brief article "Negro Chaplains in the Civil War" describes the small but nonetheless important role played by black chaplains in the Union forces. Bertram W. Korn examines the virtually non-existent Jewish chaplaincy in two perceptive essays: "Congressman Clement L. Valladingham's Championship of the Jewish Chaplaincy in the Civil War" and "Was There a Confederate Jewish Chaplain?" Willard E. Wight describes the Confederacy's attempt to enlist Catholic chaplains in "The Bishop of Natchez and the Confederate Chaplaincy"; see also his "Bishop Verot and the Civil War." Less scholarly studies of the chaplaincy, though still useful, include those of Charles F. Pitts, Sidney J. Romero, and David B. Sabine.

The Union generally relied more on institutions than on individual chaplains to minister to the religious needs of its soldiers. Both the Christian Commission and the Sanitary Commission sent delegates to battlefield camps. Federal sponsorship of these agencies seems to indicate that the government was not uneasy about sponsoring religious instruction. For insight into the Christian Commission, see James O. Henry's "The United States Christian Commission," and "The Civil War Diary of a Christian Minister," edited by Leo P. Kibby. William Quentin Maxwell's *Lincoln's Fifth Wheel* is a thorough study of the Sanitary Commission.

Regardless of the agency of instruction, chaplains on both sides (like their home front counterparts) preached that the war was just in God's eyes. To fight was correct; to die was Christian sacrifice in the highest sense. Soldiers accepted such teaching with mixed reactions. Except for battlefield conversions and spurts of revivalism, the Civil War soldier was generally no more nor less religious than his civilian contemporaries. His religiosity has been the subject of many competent discussions. Silver's *Confederate Morale and Church Propaganda* is again an excellent introduction, as are the social histories of Michael Barton (*Goodmen: The Character of Civil War Soldiers*) and Bell Irvin Wiley (*The Life of Johnny Reb, the Common Soldier of the Confederacy* and *The Life of Billy Yank, the Common Soldier of the Union*). E. M. Boswell's "Rebel Religion," Sidney J. Romero's *Religion in the Rebel Ranks,* and Edgar Legare Pennington's "The Confederate Episcopal Church and the Southern Soldiers" are general overviews. W. Harrison Daniel's "Southern Protestantism and Army Missions" describes the role that missionaries played in sharing the work of Confederate chaplains. His essay "The Christian Association: A Religious Society in the Army of Northern Virginia" analyzes the importance of that religious organization in the Confederate ranks; see also the essay by John Shepard, Jr., "Religion in the Army of Northern Virginia." Robert Partin presents a case study of Confederate religion in "The Sustaining Faith of an Alabama Soldier." Efforts to obtain Bibles are described in W. Harrison Daniel's "Bible Publication and Procurement in the Confederacy." G. MacLaren Brydon analyzes the Confederate

version of the Book of Common Prayer in "The 'Confederate Prayer Book' ";
see also Fletcher Melvin Green's essay on Confederate literacy in *Democracy
in the Old South and Other Essays*.

Perhaps the most religiously inclined of all Civil War soldiers were pacifists who found themselves in uniform or who fought enlistment require-
ments out of religious conviction. Civil War pacifism deserves greater study,
but there are several good introductions to the subject. Edward Needles
Wright's 1931 study, *Conscientious Objectors in the Civil War*, is thorough
but now dated. Patrick Sowle and Richard L. Zuber analyze the wartime
difficulties faced by North Carolina Quakers in, respectively, "The Quaker
Conscript in Confederate North Carolina" and "Conscientious Objectors in
the Confederacy: The Quakers of North Carolina." The Confederacy made
legal provisions in 1862 for Quakers and other conscientious objectors to
avoid military service upon payment of a three hundred dollar fee or the
enlistment of a substitute. David Edwin Harrell, Jr., examines the Mexican
War and Civil War pacifism of a small religious group in "Disciples of Christ
Pacifism in Nineteenth Century Tennessee." Samuel Horst's *Mennonites in
the Confederacy: A Study in Civil War Pacifism* describes the Mennonite
and Dunker (Church of the Brethren) opposition to the war.

As the Confederacy's military fortunes dimmed in the middle years of the
Civil War, a series of revivals swept through the Confederate army. Both
Emory M. Thomas in *The Confederate Nation: 1861–1865* and Charles Reagan Wilson in *Baptized in Blood: The Religion of the Lost Cause, 1865–1920*
describe this phenomenon. Not unlike other revivals throughout American
history, the Confederate revivals signaled profound anxiety amongst those
who participated. Certainly part of that anxiety was due to the tide of the war;
Union forces were seemingly gaining the upper hand over the poorly supplied
rebels. But some scholars argue that southern religion itself may have been
partly to blame. Unlike scholars (for example, Silver in *Confederate Morale*
and Daniel in "Southern Protestantism and Army Missions") who have argued that southern religion strengthened discipline and morale among Confederate troops, these historians suggest that southern religion hurt the Confederate war effort. The southern practice of linking religious devotion so
explicitly to specific political objectives may have blunted the Confederacy's
military effectiveness when those objectives seemed increasingly difficult to
attain.

The authors of *Why the South Lost the Civil War* argue that "the South's
religious views served as a trap for Confederate will" (Beringer et al., p. 98).
These scholars suggest that as southerners believed God supported their
region and its social system, they naturally had faith that he would guide the
Confederacy to victory in the Civil War. Yet as the momentum of the war

began to turn in favor of the Union, the South began to doubt itself. Initial battlefield reverses could be explained away as the result of God's displeasure regarding a lack of southern commitment to the rigors of sectional conflict. The South could regain God's favor by increased aggressiveness on the battlefield (a Confederate trait substantiated by Civil War military historiography). But as losses multiplied, southerners began to suspect that God was perhaps not on their side at all. Their cause was then not only unjust, it was terrifyingly ungodly. By intertwining religious faith with military fortune, the South left itself in a psychologically precarious position. As long as the Confederate army won battles, religion was a powerful builder of discipline and morale. But as the war turned in the Union's favor in 1863, more and more southerners became "gradually convinced that God willed they should not win" (Beringer et al., p. 102). Such a realization would have obvious effects on the Confederacy's ability to wage war.

Beringer and his co-authors argue that guilt, as both the crucial component of southern Protestantism and a powerful feature of southern society at large, was at the root of this peculiar situation. So important and so destructive were the enervating effects of guilt and religion that "both of them," these scholars write, "must constitute key words in the lexicon of those who would isolate the causes of the Confederate defeat" (Beringer et al., p. 361). For additional analysis of the prevalence of guilt in southern society and religion, see Bertram Wyatt-Brown's book *Southern Honor: Ethics and Behavior in the Old South*, and *The Ruling Race: A History of American Slaveholders*, by James Oakes.

Such a provocative and complex thesis is no doubt difficult to prove. But it is clear that Civil War–era northern religion was not centered so exclusively on guilt as southern religion. For one, northerners were not fighting to preserve a guilt-inducing institution (Oakes writes convincingly of slaveholder guilt in *The Ruling Race*). In addition, northern society could lay claim to a powerful brand of "civil religion" that, because of its nationalizing influence, helped further legitimate the cause of the Union. By far the most important feature of this civil religion was Abraham Lincoln.

Perhaps the greatest of all American political figures, Lincoln has also been called "the religious center of American history" (see Melvin B. Endy, Jr., "Abraham Lincoln," p. 229). His Christ-like martyrdom in the Union cause, complete with all the symbolism that assassination on Good Friday can conjure, has etched for him a permanent place in the history of American religion. But that role is as complex as it is crucial. How are we to assess the abiding influence of this man who, serving simultaneously as the nation's highest political and, arguably, most important religious figure, so thoroughly embodied the Civil War–era mixture of church and state?

An older, yet nonetheless important, tradition of Lincoln scholarship sought to analyze Lincoln's own religious views and ideas. This category includes such classic studies as William E. Barton's *The Soul of Abraham Lincoln* and *Lincoln and the Preachers* by Edgar D. Jones. Examinations such as these confirm that Abraham Lincoln was indeed a deeply religious man, imbued with a profound sense of God and possessed of both a powerful understanding of Christianity and an uncanny knowledge of the Bible.

But such analyses, concerned as they are with pointed investigation of Lincoln's personal religion, fail to assess the larger question of Lincoln's religious role in the deepest political crisis the nation has ever faced. For insight into this, we must turn to broader and more recent studies.

Any inquiry into Abraham Lincoln's religious role in the Civil War (and American history in general) should perhaps begin with Robert N. Bellah's seminal article "Civil Religion in America." Bellah's essay discusses the religious aspects of American political history; he notes that "the separation of church and state has not denied the political realm a religious dimension" (p. 3). This dimension is American civil religion, a concept that embodies the religious features of nationalism and nationhood. At the risk of oversimplifying an extremely complex theory, American civil religion may be viewed as a set of shared beliefs about American nationalism, largely religious in formulation and expression, yet mediating between the distinct categories of religion and politics. For instance, references to God in political speeches and protocol are common, generally uncontested expressions of civil religion. They are recognized as serving an important, if minor, nationalizing function which is true to the American tradition of allying God with the nation; hence, they are tacitly confirmed as uncontroversial.

Parenthetically, efforts by activist Civil War–era Christians to pass a constitutional amendment affirming God's guidance over America were not successful. Such an attempt somehow transgressed the accepted perimeters of civil religion and strayed into a realm where church combined with state to an unacceptable degree; see the essays of Morton Borden, "The Christian Amendment," and Jon C. Teaford, "Toward a Christian Nation: Religion, Law and Justice Strong."

Lincoln is the most important figure in the history of American civil religion, Bellah argues, because of the nationalizing role he played during America's ultimate crisis. "The Civil War raised the deepest questions of national meaning," he writes. "The man who not only formulated but in his own person embodied its meaning for Americans was Abraham Lincoln" (p. 9).

There are several books and essays that further address the importance of Lincoln to northern nationalism and civil religion. Among these are: Glen E.

Thurow, *Abraham Lincoln and American Political Religion;* Elton True-blood, *Abraham Lincoln: Theologian of American Anguish;* Hans J. Morgenthau and David Hein, *Essays on Lincoln's Faith and Politics;* Melvin B. Endy, Jr., "Abraham Lincoln and American Civil Religion: A Reinterpretation"; and William J. Wolf, *The Religion of Abraham Lincoln.* These studies have several features in common: each attempts to assess Lincoln's religious or civil religious role in the conflict through exegesis of his speeches and writings, and each accepts the assumption that that role was vital to the Union's survival.

Lincoln believed that the Civil War was divine punishment for nationwide complicity in the sin of slavery. Yet such a belief did not produce the enervating guilt that we have noted in the Confederacy. Lincoln never doubted the value of the Union; he believed that the North could rise above sin, always with God's help, and purge human bondage from the nation—a position he moved to gradually, but inexorably, as the war progressed. At times, Lincoln wondered as to God's purpose, as he did in his Meditation on the Divine Will and in the Second Inaugural Address. Yet he recognized and placed faith in the power of God to forge a new and better America through the trial of the Civil War. Through fast day proclamations and through days of thanksgiving, Lincoln humbly allied the cause of the Union with God's purpose, providing for the North the intertwined objectives of preserving the sacred fabric of the Union and waging war in the service of the Lord.

The South had no spokesman of Lincoln's power and charisma. Moreover, unlike the North, it had no strong tradition of civil religion and was unable to construct one that was viable from its own resources. Insofar as Confederate civil religion existed, it was a weak antidote to the guilt that harassed the South. The subsequent theological justification of Confederate defeat enshrined in the "Lost Cause" ideology paradoxically created a civil religion around an abortive nation. This would play an important role only in the New South.

By contrast, the North's (and specifically Abraham Lincoln's) ability to produce a powerful brand of civil religion provided the Union with nationalistic grist to sustain it through the war years. The importance of Lincoln to this civil religion can hardly be overestimated. In life, Lincoln, whom Sydney Ahlstrom has called a "theologian of democracy," gave voice and power to northern civil religion and expressed the perseverance of the Union. His death was perhaps no less important; James Moorhead has written that Lincoln's assassination "symbolized the expiation of the national sins, and his blood—the token of every drop drawn by the sword during four years of war—purchased a new and perfect nationality for the American people" (*American Apocalypse,* p. 175).

BIBLIOGRAPHY

Ahlstrom, Sydney E. "History, Bushnell and Lincoln." Church History 30 (June 1961), 223-230.

Ahlstrom, Sydney E. "Religion, Revolution and the Rise of Modern Nationalism: Reflections on the American Experience." Church History 44 (December 1975), 492-504.

Ahlstrom, Sydney E. A Religious History of the American People. New Haven: Yale University Press, 1972.

Albrecht, Robert C. "The Theological Response of the Transcendentalists to the Civil War." New England Quarterly 38 (March 1965), 21-34.

Ashdown, Paul G. "Commission from a Higher Source: Church and State in the Civil War." Historical Magazine of the Protestant Episcopal Church 48 (September 1979), 321-330.

Barnes, Howard A. "The Idea That Caused a War: Horace Bushnell Versus Thomas Jefferson." Journal of Church and State 16 (Winter 1974), 73-84.

Barton, Michael. Goodmen: The Character of Civil War Soldiers. University Park: Pennsylvania State University Press, 1981.

Barton, William E. The Soul of Abraham Lincoln. New York: G.H. Doran, 1920.

Basler, Roy P., ed. The Collected Works of Abraham Lincoln. 9 vols. New Brunswick, N.J.: Rutgers University Press, 1953.

Bearden, Robert E. L., Jr. "The Episcopal Church in the Confederate States." Arkansas Historical Quarterly 4 (Winter 1945), 269-275.

Bellah, Robert N. The Broken Covenant: American Civil Religion in Time of Trial. New York: Seabury Press, 1975.

Bellah, Robert N. "Civil Religion in America." _Daedalus_ 96 (Winter 1967), 1-21.

Beringer, Richard E.; Hattaway, Herman; Jones, Archer; and Still, William N., Jr. _Why the South Lost the Civil War_. Athens: University of Georgia Press, 1986.

Blassingame, John W. "Negro Chaplains in the Civil War." _Negro History Bulletin_ 27 (October 1963), 24, 23.

Blied, Benjamin J. _Catholics in the Civil War_. Milwaukee, by the author, 1945.

Boles, John B. "John Hersey: Dissenting Theologian of Abolitionism, Perfectionism, and Millennialism." _Methodist History_ 14 (July 1976), 215-234.

Boller, Paul F., Jr. "Religion and the U.S. Presidency." _Journal of Church and State_ 21 (Winter 1979), 5-22.

Borden, Morton. "The Christian Amendment." _Civil War History_ 25 (June 1979), 156-167.

Boswell, E. M. "Rebel Religion." _Civil War Times Illustrated_ 11 (October 1972), 26-33.

Brown, Bruce T. "Grace Church, Galesburg, Illinois, 1864-1866: The Supposed Neutrality of the Episcopal Church During the Years of the Civil War." _Historical Magazine of the Protestant Episcopal Church_ 46 (June 1977), 187-208.

Brown, Lawrence L., ed. "Documentary History of the American Church. Views of the Bishops of Ohio and Louisiana upon the Secession of the Southern States and Its Effects upon the Ecclesiastical Allegiance of the Dioceses." _Historical Magazine of the Protestant Episcopal Church_ 31 (September 1962), 288-302.

Bruce, Dickson D., Jr. "Religion, Society and Culture in the Old South: A Comparative View." _American Quarterly_ 26 (October 1974), 399-416.

Bryan, T. Conn. "The Churches in Georgia during the Civil War." _Georgia Historical Quarterly_ 33 (December 1949), 283-302.

Brydon, G. MacLaren. "The 'Confederate Prayer Book.'" _Historical Magazine of the Protestant Episcopal Church_ 17 (December 1948), 339-344.

Brydon, G. MacLaren. "The Diocese of Virginia in the Southern Confederacy." _Historical Magazine of the Protestant Episcopal Church_ 17 (December 1948), 384-410.

Burger, Nash Kerr. "The Diocese of Mississippi and the
    Confederacy." Historical Magazine of the Protestant
    Episcopal Church 9 (March 1940), 52-77.

Cash, Wilbur J. The Mind of the South. New York: Knopf, 1941.

Cheshire, Joseph Blount. The Church in the Confederate States.
    New York: Longmans, Green, and Co., 1912.

Clebsch, William A. Christian Interpretations of the Civil
    War. Philadelphia: Fortress, 1969. Reprinted from Church
    History 30 (June 1961), 212-222.

Clebsch, William A. From Sacred to Profane America: The Role
    of Religion in American History. New York: Harper & Row,
    1968.

Clebsch, William A. "Stephen Elliot's View of the Civil War."
    Historical Magazine of the Protestant Episcopal Church 31
    (March 1962), 7-20.

Cole, Charles C., Jr. "Horace Bushnell and the Slavery
    Question." New England Quarterly 23 (March 1958), 19-30.

Cole, Charles C., Jr. The Social Ideas of the Northern
    Evangelists, 1826-1860. New York: Columbia University
    Press, 1954.

Connelly, Thomas L., and Bellows, Barbara. God and General
    Longstreet: The Lost Cause and the Southern Mind. Baton
    Rouge: Louisiana State University Press, 1982.

Cox, Harvey, ed. Military Chaplains: From a Religious Military
    to a Military Religion. New York: American Report Press,
    1971.

Crewdson, Robert L. "Bishop Polk and the Crisis in the Church:
    Separation or Unity?" Historical Magazine of the Protestant
    Episcopal Church 52 (March 1983), 43-51.

Cushman, Joseph D., Jr. "The Episcopal Church in Florida
    During the Civil War." Florida Historical Quarterly 38
    (April 1960), 294-301.

Daniel, W. Harrison. "An Aspect of Church and State Relations
    in the Confederacy: Southern Protestantism and the Office of
    Army Chaplain." North Carolina Historical Review 36
    (January 1959), 47-71.

Daniel, W. Harrison. "Bible Publication and Procurement in the
    Confederacy." Journal of Southern History 24 (May 1958),
    191-201.

Daniel, W. Harrison. "A Brief Account of the Methodist Episcopal Church, South in the Confederacy." *Methodist History* 6 (January 1968), 27-41.

Daniel, W. Harrison. "Chaplains in the Army of Northern Virginia: A List Compiled in 1864 and 1865 by Robert L. Dabney." *Virginia Magazine of History and Biography* 71 (July 1963), 327-340.

Daniel, W. Harrison. "The Christian Association: A Religious Society in the Army of Northern Virginia." *Virginia Magazine of History and Biography* 69 (January 1961), 93-100.

Daniel, W. Harrison. "Protestant Clergy and Union Sentiment in the Confederacy." *Tennessee Historical Quarterly* 23 (September 1964), 284-290.

Daniel, W. Harrison. "Protestantism and Patriotism in the Confederacy." *Mississippi Quarterly* 24 (Spring 1971), 117-134.

Daniel, W. Harrison. "The Southern Baptists in the Confederacy." *Civil War History* 6 (December 1960), 389-401.

Daniel, W. Harrison. "Southern Presbyterians in the Confederacy." *North Carolina Historical Review* 44 (July 1967), 231-255.

Daniel, W. Harrison. "Southern Protestantism and Army Missions in the Confederacy." *Mississippi Quarterly* 17 (Fall 1964), 179-191.

Daniel, W. Harrison. "Southern Protestantism and Secession." *Historian* 29 (May 1967), 391-408.

Daniel, W. Harrison. "Southern Protestantism and the Negro, 1860-1865." *North Carolina Historical Review* 41 (July 1964), 338-359.

Daniel, W. Harrison. "Virginia Baptists, 1861-1865." *Virginia Magazine of History and Biography* 72 (January 1964), 94-114.

Davis, J. Treadwell. "The Presbyterians and the Sectional Conflict." *Southern Quarterly* 8 (January 1970), 117-134.

Degler, Carl. *Place Over Time: The Continuity of Southern Distinctiveness*. Baton Rouge: Louisiana State University Press, 1977.

Donald, David. *Lincoln Reconsidered: Essays on the Civil War Era*. New York: Knopf, 1956.

Donald, David. *The Nation in Crisis, 1861-1877*. New York: Appleton-Century-Crofts, 1969.

Donald, James M. "Bishop Hopkins and the Reunification of the Church." _Historical Magazine of the Protestant Episcopal Church_ 47 (March 1978), 73-91.

Duncan, Richard R. "Bishop Whittingham, the Maryland Diocese, and the Civil War." _Maryland Historical Magazine_ 61 (December 1966), 329-347.

Duncan, Richard R. "Maryland Methodists and the Civil War." _Maryland Historical Magazine_ 59 (December 1964), 350-368.

Dunham, Chester H. _The Attitude of the Northern Clergy Toward the South, 1860-1865_. Toledo, Ohio: Gray Company, 1942.

Dunstan, William E., III. "The Episcopal Church in the Confederacy." _Virginia Cavalcade_ 19 (Spring 1970), 5-15.

Eaton, Clement. _A History of the Old South: The Emergence of a Reluctant Nation_. 3d ed. New York: Macmillan, 1975.

Eaton, Clement. _A History of the Southern Confederacy_. New York: Macmillan, 1954.

Eaton, Clement. _The Waning of the Old South Civilization, 1860-1880's_. Athens: University of Georgia Press, 1968.

Eighmy, John Lee. _Churches in Cultural Captivity: A History of the Social Attitudes of Southern Baptists_. Edited by Samuel S. Hill, Jr. Knoxville: University of Tennessee Press, 1972.

Endy, Melvin B., Jr. "Abraham Lincoln and American Civil Religion: A Reinterpretation." _Church History_ 44 (June 1975), 229-241.

Erickson, Gary Lee. "Lincoln's Civil Religion and the Lutheran Heritage." _Lincoln Herald_ 75 (Winter 1973), 158-171.

Fehrenbacher, Don E., ed. _Manifest Destiny and the Coming of the Civil War, 1840-1861_. New York: Appleton-Century-Crofts, 1970.

Fowler, Arlene L. "Chaplain D. Eglinton Barr: A Lincoln Yankee." _Historical Magazine of the Protestant Episcopal Church_ 45 (December 1976), 435-438.

Frederickson, George M. _The Black Image in the White Mind: The Debate on Afro-American Character and Destiny, 1817-1914_. New York: Harper & Row, 1971.

Frederickson, George M. _The Inner Civil War: Northern Intellectuals and the Crisis of the Union_. New York: Harper & Row, 1968.

Friedman, Lawrence J. Gregarious Saints: Self and Community in American Abolitionism, 1830-1870. New Rochelle, N.Y.: Cambridge University Press, 1982.

Goen, C[larence] C. Broken Churches, Broken Nation: Denominational Schisms and the Coming of the American Civil War. Macon, Ga.: Mercer University Press, 1985.

Gravely, William. Gilbert Haven, Methodist Abolitionist: A Study in Race, Religion, and Reform, 1850-1880. Nashville: Abingdon, 1973.

Green, Fletcher Melvin. Democracy in the Old South and Other Essays. Edited by J. Isaac Copeland. Nashville: Vanderbilt University Press, 1969.

Green, Fletcher Melvin. "Northern Missionary Activities in the South, 1846-1861." Journal of Southern History 21 (May 1955), 147-172.

Greninger, Edwin T. "Thanksgiving: An American Holiday." Social Science 54 (Winter 1979), 3-15.

Griffin, Clifford S. Their Brothers' Keepers: Moral Stewardship in the United States, 1800-1865. New Brunswick, N.J.: Rutgers University Press, 1960.

Handy, Robert T. A Christian America: Protestant Hopes and Historical Realities. New York: Oxford University Press, 1971.

Harrell, David Edwin, Jr. "Disciples of Christ Pacifism in Nineteenth Century Tennessee." Tennessee Historical Quarterly 21 (September 1962), 263-274.

Harris, Donnell R. "The Gradual Separation of Southern and Northern Baptists, 1845-1907." Foundations 7 (April 1964), 130-144.

Hassler, William W. "Religious Conversion of General Dorsey Pender, C.S.A." Historical Magazine of the Protestant Episcopal Church 33 (June 1964), 171-178.

Heathcote, Charles W. The Lutheran Church and the Civil War. New York: Fleming H. Revell, 1919.

Henry, James O. "The United States Christian Commission in the Civil War." Civil War History 6 (December 1960), 374-388.

Hill, Samuel S., Jr. The South and the North in American Religion. Athens: University of Georgia Press, 1980.

Hill, Samuel S., Jr. Southern Churches in Crisis. New York: Holt, Rinehart and Winston, 1967.

Hill, Samuel S., Jr., ed. Encyclopedia of Religion in the
    South. Macon, Ga.: Mercer University Press, 1984.

Hill, Samuel S., Jr., ed. Religion in the Southern States: A
    Historical Study. Macon, Ga.: Mercer University Press,
    1983.

Holifield, E. Brooks. The Gentlemen Theologians: American
    Theology in Southern Culture, 1795-1860. Durham, N.C.: Duke
    University Press, 1978.

Honeywell, Roy J. Chaplains of the United States Army.
    Washington, D.C.: Office of the Chief of Chaplains,
    Department of the Army, 1958.

Horst, Samuel. Mennonites in the Confederacy: A Study in Civil
    War Pacifism. Scottdale, Pa.: Herald Press, 1967.

Howe, Mark DeWolfe. The Garden and the Wilderness: Religion
    and Government in American Constitutional History. Chicago:
    University of Chicago Press, 1965.

Hughes, Richard T. "A Civic Theology for the South: The Case
    of Benjamin M. Palmer." Journal of Church and State 25
    (Autumn 1983), 447-467.

Johnson, Thomas Scott. "Letters from a Civil War Chaplain."
    Journal of Presbyterian History 46 (September 1968), 219-
    235.

Jones, Donald G. The Sectional Crisis and Northern Methodism:
    A Study in Piety, Political Ethics, and Civil Religion.
    Metuchen, N.J.: Scarecrow Press, 1979.

Jones, Edgar D. Lincoln and the Preachers. New York: Harper &
    Row, 1948.

Kedro, Milan J. "The Civil War's Effect upon an Urban Church:
    The St. Louis Presbytery under Martial Law." Missouri
    Historical Society Bulletin 27 (April 1971), 173-193.

Keller, Ralph A. "Methodist Newspapers and the Fugitive Slave
    Law: A New Perspective for the Slavery Crisis in the North."
    Church History 43 (September 1974), 319-339.

Kibby, Leo P., ed. "The Civil War Diary of a Christian
    Minister: The Observations of Eri Baker Hulbert, United
    States Christian Commission Delegate, while Assigned with
    the Army of the James, February-March, 1865." Journal of
    the West 3 (April 1964), 221-232.

Kleppner, Paul J. "Lincoln and the Immigrant Vote: A Case of
    Religious Polarization." Mid-America 48 (July 1966), 176-
    195.

Korn, Bertram W. _American Jewry and the Civil War_. Philadelphia: Jewish Publication Society of America, 1951.

Korn, Bertram W. "Congressman Clement L. Vallandigham's Championship of the Jewish Chaplaincy in the Civil War." _American Jewish Historical Quarterly_ 53 (December 1963), 188-191.

Korn, Bertram W. "Was There a Confederate Jewish Chaplain?" _American Jewish Historical Quarterly_ 53 (September 1963), 63-69.

Korn, Bertram W., ed. "The Jews of the Confederacy." _American Jewish Archives_ 13 (April 1961), 3-90.

Korn, Bertram W., ed. "The Jews of the Union." _American Jewish Archives_ 13 (November 1961), 131-230.

Kuykendall, John W. _Southern Enterprize: The Work of National Evangelical Societies in the Antebellum South_. Westport, Conn.: Greenwood, 1982.

LaFontaine, Charles V. "God and Nation in Selected U.S. Presidential Inaugural Addresses, 1789-1945: Part One." _Journal of Church and State_ 18 (Winter 1976), 39-60.

LaFontaine, Charles V. "God and Nation in Selected U.S. Presidential Inaugural Addresses, 1789-1945: Part Two." _Journal of Church and State_ 18 (Autumn 1976), 503-520.

Lefler, Hugh T. "Thomas Atkinson, Third Bishop of North Carolina." _Historical Magazine of the Protestant Episcopal Church_ 17 (December 1948), 422-434.

Linder, Robert D. "Civil Religion in Historical Perspective: The Reality That Underlies the Concept." _Journal of Church and State_ 17 (Autumn 1975), 399-422.

Lippy, Charles H., ed. _Bibliography of Religion in the South_. Macon, Ga.: Mercer University Press, 1985.

Lipscomb, Oscar H. "Catholics in Alabama, 1861-1865." _Alabama Review_ 20 (October 1967), 278-288.

Littell, Franklin Hamilton. _From State Church to Pluralism: A Protestant Interpretation of Religion in American History_. Garden City, N.Y.: Doubleday, 1962.

London, Lawrence F. "The Literature of the Church in the Confederate States." _Historical Magazine of the Protestant Episcopal Church_ 17 (December 1948), 345-355.

Loveland, Anne C. _Southern Evangelicals and the Social Order, 1800-1860_. Baton Rouge: Louisiana State University Press, 1980.

Lucey, William L., ed. "The Diary of Joseph B. O'Hagen, S.J., Chaplain of the Excelsior Brigade." Civil War History 6 (December 1960), 402-409.

McCardell, John. The Idea of a Southern Nation: Southern Nationalists and Southern Nationalism, 1830-1860. New York: Norton, 1969.

McKivigan, John R. The War against Proslavery Religion: Abolitionism and the Northern Churches, 1830-1865. Ithaca, N.Y.: Cornell University Press, 1984.

Maclear, James Fulton. "The Evangelical Alliance and the Antislavery Crusade." Huntington Library Quarterly 42 (Spring 1979), 141-164.

Maclear, James Fulton. "The Republic and the Millennium." In The Religion of the Republic, edited by Elwyn A. Smith, 183-216. Philadelphia: Fortress, 1971.

Maclear, James Fulton. "'The True American Union' of Church and State: The Reconstruction of the Theocratic Tradition." Church History 28 (March 1959), 41-62.

Macmillan, Margaret B. "Michigan Methodism in the Civil War." Methodist History 3 (January 1965), 26-38.

McMurtrie, Douglas C., ed. Lincoln's Religion. Chicago: Black Cat, 1936.

McPherson, James M. Ordeal by Fire: The Civil War and Reconstruction. New York: Knopf, 1982.

MacVicar, Barbara McClung. "Southern and Northern Methodism in Civil War California." California Historical Society Quarterly 40 (December 1961), 327-342.

Maddex, Jack P. "From Theocracy to Spirituality: The Southern Presbyterian Reversal on Church and State." Journal of Presbyterian History 54 (Winter 1976), 438-458.

Maddex, Jack P. "Proslavery Millennialism: Social Eschatology in Antebellum Southern Calvinism." American Quarterly 31 (Spring 1979), 46-62.

Maddex, Jack P. "'The Southern Apostasy' Revisited: The Significance of Proslavery Christianity." Marxist Perspectives 2 (Fall 1979), 132-141.

Marty, Martin E. Righteous Empire: The Protestant Experience in America. New York: Dial Press, 1970.

Mathews, Donald G. Religion in the Old South. Chicago: University of Chicago Press, 1977.

Maxwell, William Quentin. <u>Lincoln's Fifth Wheel: The Political History of the United States Sanitary Commission</u>. New York: Longmans, Green and Co., 1956.

Mead, Sidney E. "Abraham Lincoln's 'Last, Best Hope of Earth': The American Dream of Destiny and Democracy." <u>Church History</u> 23 (March 1954), 3-16.

Mead, Sidney E. <u>The Lively Experiment: The Shaping of Christianity in America</u>. New York: Harper & Row, 1963.

Mitchell, Joseph. "Southern Methodist Newspapers During the Civil War." <u>Methodist History</u> 11 (January 1973), 20-39.

Monroe, Haskell. "South Carolinians and the Formation of the Presbyterian Church in the Confederate States of America." <u>Journal of Presbyterian History</u> 42 (December 1964), 219-243.

Monroe, Haskell. "Southern Presbyterians and the Secession Crisis." <u>Civil War History</u> 6 (December 1960), 351-360.

Moorhead, James H. <u>American Apocalypse: Yankee Protestants and the Civil War, 1860-1869</u>. New Haven: Yale University Press, 1978.

Moorhead, James H. "Between Progress and Apocalypse: A Reassessment of Millennialism in American Religious Thought, 1800-1880." <u>Journal of American History</u> 71 (December 1984), 524-542.

Moorhead, James H. "Millennialism." In <u>Encyclopedia of Religion in the South</u>, edited by Samuel S. Hill, Jr. Macon, Ga.: Mercer University Press, 1984.

Morgenthau, Hans J., and Hein, David. <u>Essays on Lincoln's Faith and Politics</u>. Vol. 4 of <u>American Values Projected Abroad</u>, edited by Kenneth W. Thompson. Lanham, Md.: University Press of America, 1983.

Murph, David R. "Abraham Lincoln and Divine Providence." <u>Lincoln Herald</u> 73 (Spring 1971), 8-15.

Murphy, Dubose. "The Protestant Episcopal Church in Texas during the Civil War." <u>Historical Magazine of the Protestant Episcopal Church</u> 1 (June 1932), 90-101.

Murphy, Dubose. "The Spirit of a Primitive Fellowship: The Reunion of the Church." <u>Historical Magazine of the Protestant Episcopal Church</u> 17 (December 1948), 435-448.

Murphy, Robert J. "Catholic Church in the United States during the Civil War Period, 1852-1866." <u>American Catholic Historical Society of Philadelphia Records</u> 39 (December 1928), 272-346.

Neely, Mark E., Jr. "Lincoln and 'Civil Religion.'" Lincoln
    Lore, no. 1657, 1976.

Nichols, Roy F. Religion and American Democracy. Baton Rouge:
    Louisiana State University Press, 1959.

Nicolson, John. "'To Mock My Maker'--A Civil War Letter on
    Freedom of Conscience." Historical Magazine of the
    Protestant Episcopal Church 41 (March 1972), 67-76.

Niebuhr, Reinhold. "The Religion of Abraham Lincoln." In
    Lincoln and the Gettysburg Address: Commemorative Papers,
    edited by Allan Nevins. Urbana: University of Illinois
    Press, 1964.

Norton, Herman A. Rebel Religion: The Story of Confederate
    Chaplains. St. Louis: Bethany Press, 1961.

Norton, Herman A. "Revivalism in the Confederate Armies."
    Civil War History 6 (December 1960), 410-424.

Norton, Herman A. Struggling for Recognition. The United
    States Army Chaplaincy, vol. 2, 1791-1865. Washington,
    D.C.: Office of the Chief of Chaplains, Department of the
    Army, 1977.

Norton, Wesley. "The Role of a Religious Newspaper in Georgia
    During the Civil War." Georgia Historical Quarterly 48
    (June 1964), 125-146.

Norwood, Frederick A. The Story of American Methodism: A
    History of the United Methodists and Their Relations.
    Nashville: Abingdon, 1974.

Oakes, James. The Ruling Race: A History of American
    Slaveholders. New York: Knopf, 1982.

Oates, Stephen B. With Malice Toward None: The Life of Abraham
    Lincoln. New York: Harper & Row, 1977.

Paludan, Phillip S. "The American Civil War Considered as a
    Crisis in Law and Order." American Historical Review 77
    (October 1972), 1013-1034.

Parish, Peter J. "The Instruments of Providence: Slavery,
    Civil War, and the American Churches." In The Church and
    War: Papers Read at the Twenty-First Summer Meeting and the
    Twenty-Second Winter Meeting of the Ecclesiastical History
    Society, edited by W. J. Shiels. Oxford: Basil Blackwell,
    1983.

Parker, Harold M., Jr. "The Independent Presbyterian Church
    and Reunion in the South, 1813-1863." Journal of
    Presbyterian History 50 (Summer 1972), 89-110.

Partin, Robert. "The Sustaining Faith of an Alabama Soldier."
     Civil War History 6 (December 1960), 425-438.

Pennington, Edgar Legare. "Bishop Stephen Elliot and the
     Confederate Episcopal Church." Georgia Review 4 (Fall
     1950), 233-247.

Pennington, Edgar Legare. "The Confederate Episcopal Church
     and the Southern Soldiers." Historical Magazine of the
     Protestant Episcopal Church 17 (December 1948), 356-383.

Pennington, Edgar Legare. "The Confederate Episcopal Church in
     1863." South Carolina Historical and Genealogical Magazine
     52 (January 1951), 5-16.

Pennington, Edgar Legare. "The Organization of the Protestant
     Episcopal Church in the Confederate States of America."
     Historical Magazine of the Protestant Episcopal Church 17
     (December 1948), 308-338.

Pfeffer, Leo. Church, State, and Freedom. Boston: Beacon
     Press, 1953.

Pitts, Charles F. Chaplains in Gray: The Confederate
     Chaplains' Story. Nashville: Broadman, 1957.

Quimby, Rollin W. "The Chaplain's Predicament." Civil War
     History 8 (March 1962), 25-37.

Quimby, Rollin W. "Congress and the Civil War Chaplaincy."
     Civil War History 10 (September 1964), 246-259.

Quimby, Rollin W. "Recurrent Themes and Purposes in the
     Sermons of the Union Army Chaplain." Speech Monographs 31
     (November 1964), 425-436.

Raboteau, Albert J. Slave Religion: The "Invisible
     Institution" in the Antebellum South. New York: Oxford
     University Press, 1978.

Randall, James G. Lincoln the President, Springfield to
     Gettysburg. New York: Dodd, Mead & Co., 1946.

Richey, Russell E., and Jones, Donald G., eds. American Civil
     Religion. New York: Harper & Row, 1974.

Rightmyer, Nelson Waite. "The Church in a Border State--
     Maryland." Historical Magazine of the Protestant Episcopal
     Church 17 (December 1948), 411-421.

Romero, Sidney J. "The Confederate Chaplain." Civil War
     History 1 (June 1955), 127-140.

Romero, Sidney J. "Louisiana Clergy and the Confederate Army."
     Louisiana History 2 (Summer 1961), 277-300.

Romero, Sidney J. _Religion in the Rebel Ranks_. Lanham, Md.: University Press of America, 1983.

Rose, Willie Lee. _Rehearsal for Reconstruction: The Port Royal Experiment_. Indianapolis: Bobbs-Merrill, 1964.

Sabine, David B. "The Fifth Wheel: The Troubled Origins of the Chaplaincy." _Civil War Times Illustrated_ 19 (May 1980), 14-23.

Shattuck, Gardiner H., Jr. "A Shield and Hiding Place: The Religious Life of the Civil War Armies." Ph.D. diss., Harvard University, 1985.

Shepard, John, Jr. "Religion in the Army of Northern Virginia." _North Carolina Historical Review_ 25 (July 1948), 341-376.

Silver, James W. _Confederate Morale and Church Propaganda_. Tuscaloosa, Ala.: Confederate Publishing Co., 1957.

Silver, James W. "The Confederate Preacher Goes to War." _North Carolina Historical Review_ 33 (October 1956), 499-509.

Simonhoff, Harry. _Jewish Participants in the Civil War_. New York: Arco Publishing, 1963.

Smith, Elwyn Allen. _The Presbyterian Ministry in American Culture: A Study in Changing Concepts, 1700-1900_. Philadelphia: Westminster, 1962.

Smith, H. Shelton. "The Church and the Social Order in the Old South as Interpreted by James Henley Thornwell." _Church History_ 7 (June 1938), 115-124.

Smith, H. Shelton. _In His Image, But . . . Racism in Southern Religion 1780-1910_. Durham, N.C.: Duke University Press, 1972.

Smith, H. Shelton; Handy, Robert T.; and Loetscher, Lefferts A. _American Christianity_. 2 vols. New York: Scribner, 1963.

Smith, Timothy L. _Revivalism and Social Reform: American Protestantism on the Eve of the Civil War_. 1957. Reprint. New York: Harper & Row, 1965.

Somkin, Fred. "Scripture Notes to Lincoln's Second Inaugural." _Civil War History_ 27 (June 1981), 172-173.

Sowle, Patrick. "The Quaker Conscript in Confederate North Carolina." _Quaker History_ 56 (Autumn 1967), 90-105.

Stange, Douglas C. "United for Sovereignty and Freedom: Unitarians and the Civil War." _Proceedings of the Unitarian Universalist Historical Society_ 19 (1980-81), 16-38.

Stewart, Charles J. "Civil War Preaching." In _Preaching in American History_, edited by DeWitte Holland, 184-205. Nashville: Abingdon, 1968.

Stokes, Anson Phelps. _Church and State in the United States_. 3 vols. New York: Harper & Brothers, 1950.

Stowe, Walter H. "A Study in Conscience: Some Aspects of the Relations of the Clergy to the State." _Historical Magazine of the Protestant Episcopal Church_ 19 (December 1950), 301-323.

Strout, Cushing. _The New Heavens and the New Earth: Political Religion in America_. New York: Harper & Row, 1974.

Sweet, Leonard I. "The Reaction of the Protestant Episcopal Church in Virginia to the Secession Crisis: October, 1859 to May, 1861." _Historical Magazine of the Protestant Episcopal Church_ 41 (June 1972), 137-151.

Sweet, William Warren. _The Methodist Episcopal Church and the Civil War_. Cincinnati: Methodist Book Concern Press, 1912.

Teaford, Jon C. "Toward a Christian Nation: Religion, Law and Justice Strong." _Journal of Presbyterian History_ 54 (Winter 1976), 422-437.

Thomas, Emory M. _The Confederate Nation: 1861-1865_. New York: Harper & Row, 1979.

Thompson, Ernest Trice. _Presbyterians in the South_. 3 vols. Richmond, Va.: John Knox, 1963-1974.

Thompson, Ernest Trice. _The Spirituality of the Church: A Distinctive Doctrine of the Presbyterian Church in the United States_. Richmond, Va.: John Knox, 1961.

Thompson, Robert E. _History of the Presbyterian Churches in the United States_. New York: Scribner, 1907.

Thurow, Glen E. _Abraham Lincoln and American Political Religion_. Albany, N.Y.: State University of New York Press, 1976.

Todd, Edward N., ed. "Bishop Whittingham, Mount Calvary Church, and the Battle of Gettysburg." _Maryland Historical Magazine_ 60 (September 1965), 325-328.

Torbet, Robert G. _A History of the Baptists_. Philadelphia: Judson, 1950.

Trueblood, Elton. _Abraham Lincoln: Theologian of American Anguish_. New York: Harper & Row, 1973.

Tucker, Glenn. "Was Lincoln a Converted Christian?" _Lincoln Herald_ 78 (Fall 1976), 102-108.

Turner, Thomas Reed. _Beware the People Weeping: Public Opinion and the Assassination of Abraham Lincoln_. Baton Rouge: Louisiana State University Press, 1982.

Tuveson, Ernest Lee. "The Enobling War." Chap. 6 in _Redeemer Nation: The Idea of America's Millennial Role_. Chicago: University of Chicago Press, 1968.

Vander Velde, Lewis G. _The Presbyterian Churches and the Federal Union, 1861-1869_. Cambridge: Harvard University Press, 1932.

Vandiver, Frank E. _Jefferson Davis and the Confederate State_. Oxford: Clarendon Press, 1964.

Walker, Arthur L. "Three Alabama Baptist Chaplains, 1861-1865." _Alabama Review_ 16 (July 1963), 174-184.

Walker, Clarence E. _A Rock in a Weary Land: The African Methodist Episcopal Church During the Civil War and Reconstruction_. Baton Rouge: Louisiana State University Press, 1982.

Ward, Gordon W., Jr. "The Formation of the Lutheran General Synod, South, During the Civil War." _Lutheran Quarterly_ 13 (May 1961), 132-154.

Watkins, Richard H. "The Baptists of the North and Slavery, 1856-1860." _Foundations_ 13 (October-December 1970), 317-333.

Weeks, Louis, and Hickey, James C. "'Implied Trust' for Connectional Churches: _Watson v. Jones_ Revisited." _Journal of Presbyterian History_ 54 (Winter 1976), 459-470.

Wight, Willard E. "The Bishop of Natchez and the Confederate Chaplaincy." _Mid-America_ 39 (April 1957), 67-72.

Wight, Willard E. "Bishop Verot and the Civil War." _Catholic Historical Review_ 47 (July 1961), 153-163.

Wight, Willard E. "The Churches and the Confederate Cause." _Civil War History_ 6 (December 1960), 361-373.

Wiley, Bell Irvin. "'Holy Joes' of the Sixties: A Study of Civil War Chaplains." _Huntington Library Quarterly_ 16 (May 1953), 287-304.

Wiley, Bell Irvin. _The Life of Billy Yank, the Common Soldier of the Union_. Indianapolis: Bobbs-Merrill, 1952.

Wiley, Bell Irvin. The Life of Johnny Reb, the Common Soldier of the Confederacy. Indianapolis: Bobbs-Merrill, 1943.

Williams, Robert J. "Slavery and Patriotism: New Jersey Methodists During the Civil War." Methodist History 21 (July 1983), 192-206.

Wilson, Charles Reagan. Baptized in Blood: The Religion of the Lost Cause, 1865-1920. Athens: University of Georgia Press, 1980.

Wilson, Charles Reagan. "The Religion of the Lost Cause: Ritual and Organization of the Southern Civil Religion, 1865-1920." Journal of Southern History 46 (May 1980), 219-238.

Wilson, Charles Reagan, ed. Religion in the South. Jackson: University Press of Mississippi, 1985.

Wilson, Edmund. "Abraham Lincoln: The Union as Religious Mysticism." In Eight Essays. New York: Doubleday, 1954.

Wolf, William J. The Religion of Abraham Lincoln. New York: Seabury Press, 1963.

Wright, Edward Needles. Conscientious Objectors in the Civil War. 1931. Reprint. New York: A. S. Barnes and Company, 1961.

Wyatt-Brown, Bertram. Lewis Tappan and the Evangelical War against Slavery. Cleveland: Press of Case Western Reserve University, 1969.

Wyatt-Brown, Bertram. Southern Honor: Ethics and Behavior in the Old South. New York: Oxford University Press, 1982.

Zuber, Richard L. "Conscientious Objectors in the Confederacy: The Quakers of North Carolina." Quaker History 67 (Spring 1978), 1-19.

2

Church-State Issues in Reconstruction and the Culture of the Southern States

Gardiner H. Shattuck, Jr.

WHITE CHRISTIANITY IN THE ANTEBELLUM PERIOD

Writing to his father a few months before the outbreak of the Civil War, Charles C. Jones, Jr., of Georgia expressed despair as he considered the irreconcilable differences that divided the North from the South. The consensus of beliefs and attitudes that once had yoked the American people together had been dissipated, he thought, by the impact of divergent secular and religious trends in the first half of the nineteenth century. Jones believed that there were actually two American races, "which, although claiming a common parentage, have been so separated by climate, by morals, and by religion, . . . that they cannot longer exist under the same government" (Myers, *Children of Pride*, p. 648). Although the religious heritage of the majority of southerners and northerners was represented by the broad consensus of evangelical Protestantism, this tradition had broken apart in America in the debates over slavery in the early nineteenth century, and its regional components had diverged since then. By 1861, Christians of both sections were denouncing the churches of the other section as riddled with corruption, and praising their own religious bodies for maintaining a humble and godly spirit, the essence of the gospel.

The most important theoretical disagreement between religion in the North and religion in the South in the nineteenth century concerned, in fact, the proper relationship of church and state and the responsibility of the churches for the morals of their society. The religious defense of slavery that developed in the South after 1830 was based on the premise that the encouragement of personal conversion and individual piety, not the restructuring of society, was the only legitimate activity of the Christian church. Because of pressure from northern evangelicals to force southerners to eradicate slavery in their states, southern Christians formulated a doctrine advocating the strict non-interference of ecclesiastical institutions in political affairs. In order to manage their worldly business without outside interference, many evangelicals in the South argued that the church had no right at all to involve itself with the "things which are Caesar's." While the state had a God-given sanction simply to govern society, the church had a similar sanction, they reasoned, to superintend the spiritual sphere alone.

Presbyterian minister James Henley Thornwell of South Carolina best expressed these ideas for southerners when he formulated the concept that became known as "the doctrine of the spirituality of the church." Too many Americans, Thornwell feared, regarded the church as an organization constituted to undertake moral reform and wage war on every type of human ill, whether civil, social, or political. Thornwell conceded that the church, limited to its own appropriate sphere, might affect the general interests of citizens and contribute to the moral progress of humanity, but he denied that the church as an institution ought to be concerned with the promotion of secular well-being. The church, he believed, had no business constructing society afresh, rearranging the class structure, or changing any outward political forms. In Thornwell's mind, it was theoretically impossible for the Christian faith to have a social relevance. Church and society were "as planets moving in different orbits, and unless each is confined to its own track, the consequences may be as disastrous . . . as the collision of different spheres in the world of matter" (*Collected Writings*, 4:449).

Not only theory and theology, but also social factors shaped the particular ways in which churchmen viewed the relationship of religion and culture in the South. In the tightly knit and orderly villages of Puritan New England, the church had held a position that was central to the everyday life of the region, and as a consequence vigorously upheld a theory that buttressed its existing civil responsibilities. The social position of the churches in the South, however, was always very different from that in the North. There had been few towns during the colonial period, and the population of the South was mainly scattered throughout the countryside. The establishment of Anglicanism in the southern colonies had been feeble, resisted even by many Anglican laymen, and the church had played only a minor role before the Revolution. When southern evangelicalism arose at the end of the eighteenth century, moreover, its identity was determined in part by its opposition to the prevailing secular culture. Since many evangelicals held a low social rank anyway, they were not interested in maintaining the solidarity of the larger society.

Despite the emergence of evangelical Protestantism as the religious consensus of the southern people in the nineteenth century, its ideology never really outgrew this early social heritage. The South became more unified in its political, cultural, and religious thought as it moved toward the revolt against the North, but the ethic that dominated southern churches remained private and individualistic. The churches could well afford to promote their asocial moral code, though, for in a society as homogeneous as theirs, a willingness to accept the status quo presupposed that evangelical Protestantism would always exert a tight but indirect control over the larger culture. The clergymen who formulated the social ethic for Christians in the South still looked to each person's own internal restraints as the principal means by which society would be undergirded and maintained.

There are several excellent books that illuminate the development of evangelicalism in the South before the Civil War. Bertram Wyatt-Brown's *Southern Honor* demonstrates how southern Christians sometimes felt at odds with their culture, while at the same time devising means to accommodate themselves to it. Donald G. Mathews's masterful study, *Religion in the Old South*, provides a synthetic analysis of the varied religious forces at work in the South prior to the war, and E. Brooks Holifield's equally fine work, *The Gentlemen Theologians*, discusses how the clergy adapted their theology to the realities of southern culture. John W. Kuykendall's *Southern Enterprize* describes the incursion of northern evangelicals into the antebellum South, and their attempts to reshape that region in a Yankee mold. Anne C. Loveland's *Southern Evangelicals and the Social Order* is a superior, sympathetic work on the thought of southern churchmen who attempted to grapple (sometimes against their own will) with reform activities. H. Shelton Smith's *In His Image, But . . .* provides an extended study of the impact of white racism on church life in the South from colonial times to the early twentieth century. Finally, Jack P. Maddex's articles on southern Christianity ("Proslavery Millennialism" and " 'The Southern Apostasy' Revisited") attempt to correct prevailing historiographic patterns regarding the religious defense of slavery. Maddex argues that "proslavery Christianity" was not a superficial defensive posture forged by southern theologians only in the 1830s, but actually represented a legitimate, long-standing expression of the class ideology of the Old South—an outlook that ran counter to the libertarian norm prevailing in the rest of the United States.

RELIGION AND THE LOST CAUSE

In 1866, Edward A. Pollard coined the phrase (*The Lost Cause*) that became the byword for those who attempted to perpetuate the ideals of the antebellum South in the post–Civil War period. Politicians, soldiers, poets, novelists, journalists, and clergymen rallied to defend their section, and expressed with eloquence the frustrations of southerners about defeat, poverty, and the social upheaval they had been forced to endure. Religious ideology proved to be an essential element in the mythmaking about the Lost Cause. Clergy, eager to vindicate their people, sought to show how the South had actually emerged the *moral* victor in the war, and saw in the defeat of the Confederacy universal lessons about redemption in the midst of suffering. Abram Ryan, a Roman Catholic priest and former army chaplain, for example, wrote prolifically on this theme. "Calvaries and crucifixions take deepest hold on humanity," Ryan wrote, and "the sufferings of the right are graven deepest on the chronicle of nations." Although "crowns of roses" worn by conquerors had always faded, "crowns of thorns" inflicted upon the conquered alone have endured (*Poems*, pp. 27–28, and passim). The debasement of the South symbolized, therefore, God's enduring love for the southern people.

William Porcher DuBose, a Confederate officer ordained to the Episcopal ministry near the end of the war, and later a prominent theologian, discussed in his autobiography the profound effect that the southern defeat had had upon his religious development. One night in camp, while he contemplated the hopelessness of the Confederate cause, DuBose felt absolutely alone; at that moment of his deepest depression, he underwent an experience of conversion. "Without home or country, or any earthly interest or object before me," he wrote, "I redevoted myself wholly and only to God, and to the work and life of His Kingdom" (*Turning Points in My Life*, pp. 49–50). DuBose believed that the war had forced him to realize for the first time how only divine truth was secure, and how—with the failure of the southern struggle for independence—the church remained as the only institution that could maintain the ideals for which the Old South stood.

For many years after Appomattox, southern churchmen continually reminded Americans of the spiritual benefits that adversity provided. Although temporal prosperity made men arrogant and seduced them into believing that they did not need God, hardship taught forbearance and Christian humility. William Faulkner's novel *The Unvanquished* poignantly depicts the atmosphere that southern Christians envisioned as existing in their region at the conclusion of the war. Faulkner described Brother Fortinbride, a lay preacher and former soldier who, as the conflict drew to a close and defeat confronted the South, knew there was no further chance that God would give victory to the Confederate armies. Fortinbride counseled his people to turn their attention instead to religion, for only there would they find hope for renewal. Contrasting the infidelity of the victorious North with the faithful piety of the South, Fortinbride believed that "victory without God is mockery and delusion, but . . . defeat with God is not defeat" at all (pp. 154–155). The theme of religious victory in the midst of temporal defeat provided a seductive figure of strength to a demoralized southern society.

The willingness to use this image of defeat helped make the southerners' message more attractive to a northern audience, and aided the process by which North and South were eventually reconciled to each other after the war. The idea of a spiritual victory arising out of defeat was at the heart of the Christian message, and never threatened the temporal dominance of the North. Clerical spokesmen for the Lost Cause admitted their earthly defeat, but shifted the focus for southern superiority to another plane altogether. These writers dared to tell the successful North that success was not really that important, and asked northerners to appreciate instead the virtues of failure. The formulation of this religious myth and its acceptance in the North, further- more, was one element in a wider literary movement at the end of the century. Northerners, indeed, showed a marked desire to imbibe stories about quaint southern folkways and regionalisms. As Douglas Southall Freeman com- mented in 1939, "the Confederates who lost the war in the field . . . in the realm of letters [won] the peace" (*The South to Posterity*, p. x).

Christian spokesmen for the South moralized against the evils of northern society and pointed with pride to their own provincial culture, untouched by the spirit of the modern age. Only in the churches in the South, they said, were there still men and women who practiced true piety, and resisted the forces of worldliness and irreligion that were at large in the nation as a whole. Although they had been defeated in the war, white southerners re- joiced that they had not lost the simple piety of antebellum days. Religious apologists for the South used both the relative isolation of their region from the hustle and bustle of the North and the alleged aloofness of the southern churches from the vagaries of social change as reasons for the enduring moral strength of the defeated Confederacy. Defeat in the Civil War and the southerners' consequent preoccupation with self-justification, therefore, did not force the collapse of the religious tradition of the South, but helped instead to rejuvenate it.

Central to the southerners' argument regarding their own righteousness was the contention that the Confederate army had been a special bearer of evangelical Christianity during the period of the war. Clergymen attempted to justify the South's war for independence by glorifying the faith of the Con- federate fighting man. Many Confederate generals were extolled as paragons of heroism and honor, and the faith and military brilliance for which they were famous seemed irrefutable evidence of the moral purity of the Confede- rate cause. Ex-Confederate chaplains such as Robert Lewis Dabney, who wrote about Stonewall Jackson's military exploits and religious character (in *Life and Campaigns of Lieut.-Gen. Thomas J. Jackson*); J. William Jones, who described the positive effect of Robert E. Lee's faith on the morale of his army (in *Personal Reminiscences, Anecdotes, and Letters of Gen. Robert E.*

Lee, Life and Letters of Robert Edward Lee, and "The Morale of the Confederate Army"); and Randolph Harrison McKim, who demonstrated that a Christ-
like Lee had accepted defeat with grace and forgiveness (in *In Memoriam:
Good Men a Nation's Strength* and *The Soul of Lee*), believed that southern
soldiers remained virtuous and morally triumphant despite losing the war.

Two other books elaborated on these themes, and are crucial for understanding the religious mood of the South after Appomattox. In *A Narrative of
the Great Revival Which Prevailed in the Southern Armies,* William W. Bennett chronicled the religious life of the Confederate army, and argued that
southerners should take heart from that experience. Bennett, who during the
war had headed the Soldier's Tract Association of the Methodist Episcopal
Church, South, actively promoted the image of the Confederate army as a
religious force. He believed that the southern army camp had been "a school
of Christ," and that the "moral miracles" that had occurred there were the
greatest of all history and "truly 'the silver lining' to the dark and heavy
cloud" of the war (pp. 16, 73, 230, and 426–427). Appearing in 1887, a decade
after Bennett's work, moreover, J. William Jones's *Christ in the Camp; or,
Religion in Lee's Army* proved to have an even more profound influence on
the South. Jones demonstrated that soldiers in the Army of Northern Virginia
were religious as well as military heroes. As much a collection of universal
lessons about morality as an actual history of the Confederacy, *Christ in the
Camp* was upbeat and beguiling, and concentrated on describing how the
postwar strength of the southern churches had derived from the spiritual
invigoration that the men had received during their army service.

Not only clergymen, but also lay leaders wrote passionately about the faith
of the southern fighting man. *The Land We Love,* a journal edited by D. H. Hill,
a prominent Presbyterian layman and former Confederate general, was in-
stituted specifically to advance the ideology of the Lost Cause. Hill on several
occasions linked southern piety with the supposed moral superiority of the
Confederate soldiers. Generals like Clement Evans (ordained a Methodist
minister in 1866) and John Brown Gordon (converted during the war) held
key positions among groups that formulated the ideology of the Lost Cause.
In his *Reminiscences of the Civil War,* Gordon discussed at length how
religion had prepared soldiers to endure the hardships they suffered in the
Reconstruction era. Former soldiers of lower rank than Gordon or Evans
wrote as well about the religious life of the Confederate camp. Carlton Mc-
Carthy's *Detailed Minutiae of Soldier Life in the Army of Northern Virginia*
and Robert Stiles's *Four Years Under Marse Robert* told of the profound
effect of religious revivals on the southern soldiers. As these writings demonstrated, religion stood at the heart of the southern mythology about the Civil
War.

Although there is substantial primary literature documenting the role of religion in shaping the myth of the Lost Cause, worthwhile secondary accounts analyzing those developments have only begun to appear in the past decade. No longer concerned with either mindlessly justifying or excoriating the nineteenth-century clerical apologists of the Lost Cause, historians of the South are now able to look with insight and even sympathy at the religious elements that bolstered postwar southern culture, and gave hope in an otherwise disheartening time. The best modern account of late-nineteenth-century southern religion is Charles Reagan Wilson's *Baptized in Blood: The Religion of the Lost Cause,* a landmark work that examines the Lost Cause as a type of civil religion. The religion of the Lost Cause, expressed in civic and ecclesiastical events that called to mind the southerners' experience during the war, created a new common identity for the South after the destruction of the social structures of the antebellum period. Two other important books illustrating the centrality of religion in the culture of the South are Thomas L. Connelly's *The Marble Man: Robert E. Lee and His Image in American Society* and *God and General Longstreet: The Lost Cause and the Southern Mind* (co-written with Barbara L. Bellows). Rollin Osterweis's *The Myth of the Lost Cause* provides a useful overview of the development of the "Lost Cause" idea. John A. Simpson's "The Cult of the 'Lost Cause,'" Michael M. Cass's "Charles C. Jones, Jr. and the 'Lost Cause,'" and Charles Reagan Wilson's "Bishop Thomas Frank Gailor: Celebrant of Southern Tradition" and "The Religion of the Lost Cause: Ritual and Organization of the Southern Civil Religion" are short pieces about the weaving of religious elements into the Lost Cause myth.

RECONSTRUCTION AND THE BLACK CHURCHES

Besides forcing southerners to make these ideological responses to their defeat, the Civil War had profound practical consequences for church life in the South. The first problem with which southern Christians had to contend was the threat to the integrity of their ecclesiastical organizations. Nothing was more immediately disruptive, of course, than the sheer physical destruction suffered by the churches while the Union armies ravaged the southern states. The war's catastrophic impact upon church life in the South is amply documented by W. Harrison Daniel's article on "The Effects of the Civil War on Southern Protestantism." The war prevented churches from holding scheduled meetings and dramatically reduced church membership as more and more southern men were forced into military service. Daniel believes that the preoccupation with wartime matters had a thoroughly debilitating influence upon the church. The popular notion that "people turn to the church in time of war," he concludes, simply was not true in the South. Fully one-third of the membership of Baptist and Methodist churches was lost in the areas most touched by military activity during the conflict.

A most egregious impingement of secular authority upon the churches occurred whenever a region in the South came under federal control. Local inhabitants then were customarily directed to subscribe to an oath of allegiance to the United States government. Southern clergymen, who often occupied prominent and influential positions within their communities, were especially susceptible to harassment. Episcopal clergy were placed in an extremely difficult position, since the Book of Common Prayer required them to pray for "all in civil authority." After the secession of the southern states and the formation of a Confederate Episcopal Church, the Prayer Book had been altered so that southern Episcopalians could pray only for Confederate officials. Clergy who continued to pray for Confederate leaders in Union-occupied towns, therefore, could easily be condemned as disloyal. Although southern clergymen argued that military officials had no right to interfere in matters that belonged strictly to the spiritual sphere, many ministers (most notably Richard Wilmer, Episcopal bishop of Alabama) were barred temporarily from functioning ecclesiastically. Although no modern secondary work examines this church-state conflict in any great detail, Walter H. Stowe briefly discusses it in his article, "A Study in Conscience."

Related to this attempted incursion against the independence of the southern churches was a mission undertaken by northern church leaders for the purpose of placing their clergy in pulpits in the South. Many in the North believed that the southerners' revolt had made the South a legitimate missionary field, where northerners might not only evangelize the newly freed blacks, but also teach white southerners tenets of the "true" Christianity that only northern churchmen knew. Following in the wake of their victorious armies, northern clergymen (most notably Methodists) occupied pulpits in major southern cities. This action, viewed at first as a temporary expedient for defeating the rebellion, was later justified as an unprecedented opportunity to "reconstruct" the southern church. Yankee churchmen prepared to establish beachheads of Christian piety in the defeated South, and eradicate the moral darkness that two centuries of human slavery had allegedly cast upon that region. Numerous ministers, missionaries, and teachers traveled southward to instruct whites and blacks in the fundamentals of Christian civilization: frugality, fidelity, sobriety, self-control, and proper love of country.

There are many accounts that describe the northern missionary efforts in the South after the war. Augustus Field Beard, *A Crusade of Brotherhood: A History of the American Missionary Association* and H. Paul Douglass,

Christian Reconstruction in the South are older, laudatory chronicles of this work, while Joe M. Richardson, *Christian Reconstruction*, provides a modern, scholarly analysis of the American Missionary Association. John Eaton's *Grant, Lincoln, and the Freedmen* is a firsthand account by a Union chaplain who worked with blacks during the war. Ralph E. Morrow's *Northern Methodism and Reconstruction* for many years provided the best discussion of the invasion of the South by northern churchmen, while Donald G. Jones's more recent *The Sectional Crisis and Northern Methodism* is a corrective to Morrow's interpretation of the northerners' missionary activities as vindictive and politically motivated. William Gravely, *Gilbert Haven, Methodist Abolitionist*, recounts the career of a northern minister who, convinced that the outcome of the Civil War had prepared America for the planting of "Christian democracy" in the South, was prominent in the mission to erect such a religious commonwealth there. William S. McFeely's excellent monograph, *Yankee Stepfather*, explores the religious basis that inspired the work of O. O. Howard and many members of the Freedmen's Bureau. And three recent books illuminate the important role of education and the work of northern women in the mission to southern blacks: Robert C. Morris, *Reading, 'Riting, and Reconstruction;* Jacqueline Jones, *Soldiers of Light and Love;* and Elizabeth Jacoway, *Yankee Missionaries in the South*

Despite the very disruptive effects of the incursion of northern churchmen into the South, the greatest change in the southern churches occurred as a result of the emancipation of the native, southern blacks. After the war, blacks withdrew in large numbers from previously unified (though unequal) ecclesiastical bodies, and formed their own churches. Although northern missionaries gave them significant financial aid and encouragement, the free blacks usually did not need that prodding, since the unwillingness of southern whites to associate with them and their desire to exercise leadership were enough to prompt an exodus from the white-controlled churches. The best short description of the division of the churches after 1865 is Kenneth K. Bailey's "The Post-Civil War Racial Separations in Southern Protestantism."

Southern whites viewed the departure of blacks with some ambivalence. Although they feared that emancipation might force a certain amount of social mingling between the races in the churches, they also recognized that the complete withdrawal of blacks from the white churches meant the loss of a valuable controlling influence over their ex-slaves. Despite the efforts of some white southern defenders of black aspirations, most white southerners believed that equality between the races should be recognized no more in the church than in civil society. Among the few southerners who turned their backs on the racism of their fellow whites, and based their advocacy of racial reform on religious values, Atticus G. Haygood, the Methodist bishop of

Georgia (*Our Brothers in Black*), and George W. Cable (*The Silent South*) are the best known.

For most blacks in the postwar period, the church continued to be the same essential forum of leadership and self-expression that it had been during slavery. An older historiographic view that dismissed the slaves' religion only as an opiate for their earthly pains or as a heavy-handed attempt by whites to control their bondsmen is now recognized as a distortion of black religious history. Although slaves often heard a truncated version of the gospel from whites, the similarity in theology and ecclesiology of the new black denominations suggests that the biracial worship experiences of the antebellum period still had a significant impact on blacks. Black ministers, as the most educated and articulate members of their communities, assumed prominent roles during the first few years of freedom. Preachers, such as Henry M. Turner of the African Methodist Episcopal Church, held key positions in both church and state during the Reconstruction era. Whites also looked to some of the less militant black ministers to discipline the freedmen and disabuse them of any extravagant notions about the meaning of their recent emancipation.

W. E. B. DuBois's *The Souls of Black Folk* was the first among older studies of black religious life. DuBois argued that religion provided comfort and hope to people who were often comfortless and hopeless, and enabled blacks to withstand (as much as was possible) the assaults of white oppression. DuBois developed this theme more fully in his *The Negro Church*. After DuBois, the next academic study of the black churches was undertaken by Carter G. Woodson in *The History of the Negro Church* (now in a third edition). E. Franklin Frazier's short but influential book, *The Negro Church in America*, suggests that Christianity gave new social cohesion to slaves after they had been physically removed from their African heritage. Eugene D. Genovese, *Roll, Jordan, Roll*, Albert J. Raboteau, *Slave Religion*, John W. Blassingame, *The Slave Community*, and Lawrence W. Levine, *Black Culture and Black Consciousness*, all provide differing, though complementary, interpretations about the centrality of religious experience in the lives of slaves. Willie Lee Rose's *Rehearsal for Reconstruction* and Leon F. Litwack's *Been in the Storm So Long* are two studies that discuss the continuing importance of the church for the ex-slaves right after emancipation, while Joel Williamson, *The Crucible of Race*, is a comprehensive study that analyzes southern religion within the broad cultural context of white attitudes on race in the late nineteenth century.

SOCIAL ISSUES IN THE NEW SOUTH

Historians have often viewed southern evangelicalism as simply a "culture religion," shaped by and subservient to the dominant social ideology of the

South. This thesis is examined in detail in John Lee Eighmy's important monograph on the social attitudes of Southern Baptists, *Churches in Cultural Captivity*. In many ways, that interpretation is correct, for few southern churchmen ever directly challenged the fundamental ethos of their society either before or after the war. Yet on some social issues that impinged prominently on southern life, church members did take positions that, they thought, ran counter to their culture. The New South period was not simply a time of pusillanimous adaptation, but one of confrontation as well.

Principal among these social issues was the so-called "liquor question." Although the South was probably the heaviest drinking section of the country up to 1860, this had changed dramatically by the end of the century, when complicity in the making, sale, or consumption of alcoholic beverages came to be regarded as a reprehensible evil. Baptists and Methodists, of course, gave themselves passionately to organized efforts to control the liquor business. While the prohibition of intoxicants received the greatest attention from church people, southern Christians vigorously condemned as well the sins of gambling, Sabbath desecration, dancing, theatrical performing, and novel reading (to name but a few). Church members were even willing to enlist the support of the government in legislating and enforcing their moral reforms—a fact that in many ways contradicted the traditional southern opposition to church-state cooperation and seemed to belie the notion of an entirely "spiritual" church.

Did the willingness of southern Christians to become involved in some moral crusades absolutely contradict, then, the stereotyped image of a spiritualized church? Rufus B. Spain's work, *At Ease in Zion*, probably provides the best answer to this question. Spain concluded that the Southern Baptists, both as a denomination and as individuals, were more involved in political affairs after 1865 than they had been before the Civil War. The informal relationship of white evangelical Protestantism and southern society was now stronger than ever, and had worn away some of the formal, ideological barriers that once had been erected between church and state during the slavery controversy. Southern Baptists adhered to the doctrine of church-state separation insofar as direct aid to church institutions was concerned, but looked to the state in increasingly greater degrees to help in achieving certain moral and religious ends.

Looking at the relationship of religion and southern culture in a positive light, scholars in recent years have discovered in the South advocates of the social gospel as well. While the proponents of social Christianity were at all times a distinct minority, there still were church members who challenged the common assumption that Christians must espouse only an individualistic ethic. Methodists, and especially Methodist women working through the home missionary channels of their denomination, were usually the most consistent supporters of programs that advanced the material needs of southerners. In the introduction to his excellent study, *The Social Gospel in the South*, John P. McDowell briefly surveys the literature on social Christianity in the late nineteenth century. He notes not only that standard histories of the social gospel in the North have completely ignored the activity for reform in the southern churches, but also that historians of the South itself have failed to account for such influence in their own work. Although McDowell's conclusions about the prevalence of a southern social gospel have not found wholehearted acceptance in the scholarly community, his careful analysis of the mission work of Methodist women does help to dispel the notion that southern religion had no concern at all for social reform.

The influence of Protestantism and southern culture on one another has been heatedly discussed ever since the period about which McDowell writes. Indeed, the presence of progressive critics decrying the lack of a social ethic in their churches suggests the extent to which a social ethic *did* exist at least in the minds of a few southerners. The negative commentary of some southerners about their region may perhaps have obscured the practical work that individuals were accomplishing at the end of the century. Edgar Gardner Murphy, an Episcopal clergyman from Alabama and a leading proponent of child labor legislation (*Problems of the Present South*), for instance, was a key representative of social Christianity, who blamed southern Protestantism for an inadequate response to new social issues arising at the end of the century. Ralph E. Luker has studied Murphy and the relationship of religion and reform in *A Southern Tradition in Theology and Social Criticism* and "The Social Gospel and the Failure of Racial Reform."

A number of other historians also have looked behind the cant regarding supposedly unresponsive churches, and have indicated ways in which southern Christians attempted to respond (albeit often inadequately) to social changes. Anne Firor Scott's article on "Women, Religion and Social Change in the South" shows how Protestant women turned to missionary activities in the 1870s. Freed from the responsibilities of managing plantations, these women immersed themselves instead in home missionary ventures of a moral and social nature. Further important examples of this shifting perspective in scholarship are Frederick A. Bode's "Religion and Class Hegemony: A Populist Critique in North Carolina" and *Protestantism and the New South;* J. Wayne Flynt's "Dissent in Zion," "Southern Baptists and Reform," and " 'Feeding the Hungry and Ministering to the Broken Hearted' "; Jacquelyn Dowd Hall's *Revolt Against Chivalry* (on the women's campaign against lynching); and Dale E. Soden's "The Social Gospel in Tennessee."

In conjunction with this uncovering of the work of those who applied their religious faith to reform, even some of the secular rhetoric of the period must be examined in a new light. Certainly, Henry Grady's idea of a "New South" contained themes consistent with American civil religion, and invoked transcendent notions about American republicanism. Optimistic young southerners like Grady attempted to draw the South out of isolation and back into the mainstream of American civic life. While some southerners idealized the Old South, and appealed to values and virtues that supposedly had been lost, others clamored for commerce and credit from the North, and expressed a willingness to accept the changes that had occurred in their land. They envisioned a region of racial peacefulness and a stable economic order in step with the rest of the United States.

As Paul M. Gaston explains in his fine book on *The New South Creed*, Grady and his colleagues tried to transcend the ruin suffered in the war, and appealed to northerners with a kind of gospel in which they hoped *all* Americans would believe. In the famous speech (*The New South*) by which his movement was named, Grady professed gratitude that God had defeated the old southern order, and had swept slavery away forever from American soil. He praised both the Puritan and the Cavalier, who together had formed and fashioned the American nation, and who were representative symbols for both parts of the country. Above all, Abraham Lincoln had been the quintessence, Grady thought, of the Puritan and of the Cavalier, and had embodied all the best elements of the two regional cultures. Lincoln died not simply as a northern hero, but as a martyr for the universal ideals on which the United States had first been founded.

HISTORIOGRAPHY AND GENERAL STUDIES

The history of the nineteenth-century South has always represented a symbolic battleground over which scholars of varying political affiliations have fought in the twentieth century. Many American historians in the first half of the twentieth century accepted at face value the myths that white southerners had fashioned about themselves in the century before. Expressed in the harsh indictments of William Dunning and his students against the excesses of Republican Reconstruction (e.g., Dunning, *Essays on the Civil War and Reconstruction*), or in the optimistic themes of national reconciliation advanced by "New South" historians such as Paul H. Buck (*The Road to Reunion*), celebration of the South's recovery after the Civil War, and acceptance of the racial and social status quo in that region, were widespread in historical scholarship until the 1950s. Although war and reconstruction had shattered the economic structure of the South, and given political control for a while to a debased segment of the southern population (so the story went), the moral qualities of the true leaders of the southern people had enabled the South to rebound from near ruin, and regain a position from which it could again influence national political affairs.

This point of view was rarely challenged during the first half of our century. Gradually, however, a small group of revisionist historians began to give a new direction to the study of the periods of Reconstruction and the New South. After the appearance of C. Vann Woodward's *Origins of the New South* in 1951, Marxists, blacks seeking historical vindication, skeptical white southerners, and northern neo-abolitionists came to challenge many previously accepted interpretations of the history of the South. (This historiographic turn has been adeptly studied by historians such as Kenneth M. Stampp, *The Era of Reconstruction;* Paul M. Gaston, " 'The New South' "; Carl N. Degler, "Rethinking Post-Civil War History"; and Sheldon Hackney, "*Origins of the New South* in Retrospect.") The critics of the older historiography gained further strength, moreover, from the civil rights movement of the 1960s, when most Americans were forced to reexamine southern mores and social customs. Seen in a new way, the northern crusade to reconstruct the South after 1865 seemed as proper and as high-minded as the similar work undertaken a hundred years later, while the "redemption" of the southern states by native whites in the 1870s was no longer viewed as a praiseworthy effort, but instead appeared as a sordid tale, containing elements of betrayal, decline, and—above all—racism. Standard historical interpretations of the postwar South, therefore, were in large measure reversed during the late 1950s and early 1960s.

By the mid-1970s, North and South had again made peace, symbolized most prominently by the election of a southerner as President. Not only the embarrassed recognition of northern liberals that their region was guilty of racial discrimination as blatant as any then present in the South, but also a conservative backlash against alleged favoritism to minorities bespoke a renewed rapprochement and understanding between southerners and northerners. Historical scholarship has in some measure mirrored these trends, and seems once more to have found estimable qualities in the culture and religion of the South. In recent years, there has been a discernible shift away from earlier attempts to find villains and culprits to blame for the events of Reconstruction. Instead, many scholars have realized how Reconstruction was just one of the failures that America has experienced in the course of its history. Southern history projects a tragic, pessimistic image that now seems recognizable in the history of the United States as a whole.

Although scholars certainly recognize that the period of southern history after 1865 is hardly attractive by standards respected in democratic civilizations, most acknowledge that not every southerner was wholly benighted or reactionary. The ideals that led northerners to reconstruct the fallen South may simply have been unattainable anywhere in America at that time. A new generation of "post-revisionist" historians thus tries not to be judgmental when it laments Reconstruction as a lost opportunity to accomplish genuine social change in the South. These historians attribute this failure as much to the inability of northern Republicans to overcome their latent racism as to the intransigent conservatism of southern Democrats. Dan T. Carter (*When the War Was Over*), for example, insists that the abortive attempts of white southerners to reestablish their political dominance after the war may actually have been the most constructive course open to them at that time. And Michael Perman notes explicitly that his recent book approaches Reconstruction "not in terms of why it failed but of how it worked" (*The Road to Redemption*, p. xiii).

Simultaneous with this renascence of interest in southern history, the study of southern religion has also appeared as a respectable field of scholarly inquiry. John B. Boles has recently sketched the historiography of this subject in "Evangelical Protestantism in the Old South." With the exception of a few pioneering works, such as Hunter Farish's *The Circuit-Rider Dismounts*, most studies of religion in the South prior to the 1960s, Boles concludes, were basically either bland filiopietistic or denominational histories. Even when Henry May praised the "recovery" of American religious history in 1964, he did not mention a single title on southern religion. Virtually every major work on religious developments in post–Civil War America until the mid-1960s concentrated on the North and the attempts by northern churches to face industrialization and social disruption in their cities. Only in the past few years have historians begun to "recover" as well the religious history of the South.

As C. Vann Woodward persuasively and eloquently argued in *The Burden of Southern History*, irony has always been inherent in the history of the South. Forced to struggle with the experience of tragedy and defeat in a rich and successful nation, southerners after the Civil War saw their history stand in sharp contrast to that of the victorious North. No scholar of American Christianity has better appropriated the idea of southern distinctiveness and used it to examine the religious differences between the two sections of the country than Samuel S. Hill, Jr. Since the publication of his *Southern Churches in Crisis* in 1966, Hill has been a major figure in promoting the serious, scholarly study of southern religion, and his work demonstrates well the significance of southern religion in both creating and preserving the regional particularity of the South. His *The South and the North in American Religion*, moreover, is an especially fine comparison of the northern and southern churches in the nineteenth century. Short and well argued, this book highlights the social attitudes of the churches in the two regions as illustrative of one, very basic, difference between religious life in the North and in the South.

Given such clear regional dissimilarities, therefore, why have religious historians for so long assumed that only a single motif could explain all Christian developments in America—a motif that might be labeled "by Puritanism possessed"? Jerald C. Brauer asks this rhetorical question in a recent article, "Regionalism and Religion in America," for he believes that new studies on southern religion have rendered doubtful certain major assumptions regarding the development of Christianity in the United States. It is no longer possible to generalize exclusively within the interpretive framework of white, northern religious history. Christians in the South, white and black, never shared the northern (i.e., Puritan) "vision of a Christian America, a righteous empire, a conviction of steady progress in the coming of the Kingdom," the idea of the entire nation "united under God standing for God's will in history" (pp. 367–368). The southern religious world view was for the most part more fatalistic and otherworldly than that of most northern Protestants.

In order to understand the religious situation in the South from 1865 to 1900, one must consult both general overviews of the historical period and standard religious histories of the North at that time. For the history of Reconstruction and the New South eras, the following works provide excellent and comprehensive introductions: James M. McPherson, *Ordeal By Fire: The Civil War and Reconstruction;* James G. Randall and David Herbert Donald, *The Civil War and Reconstruction;* C. Vann Woodward, *Origins of the New South;* and Clement Eaton, *The Waning of the Old South Civilization.* For the religious history of the latter half of the nineteenth century, see especially Paul A. Carter, *The Spiritual Crisis of the Gilded Age;* Ronald C. White and C. Howard Hopkins, *The Social Gospel;* T. J. Jackson Lears, *No Place of Grace;* James H. Moorhead, *American Apocalypse;* and Anson Phelps Stokes, *Church and State in the United States.*

Many biographies of prominent nineteenth-century ministers furnish essential documentation for the study of the interaction between religion and culture. Although Baptists and Methodists were by far the most numerous of all southern church members, Presbyterians and Episcopalians comprised a significant portion of the literate and politically dominant class in the South. Thus, writings by these spokesmen of the Episcopal and Presbyterian churches remain extant and available to scholars out of proportion to the membership figures of their churches. The biographies and autobiographies of the following denominational leaders provide valuable insights into how the leading mainline clergy (unrepresentative though they may be of the whole body of southern Christians) envisioned the relationship of church and state: Baptists, like James Petigru Boyce, John Albert Broadus, George Boardman Taylor, and James B. Taylor; Methodists, like James Osgood Andrews, Oscar P. Fitzgerald, and George Foster Pierce; Presbyterians, like Robert Lewis Dabney, John L. Girardeau, Moses Drury Hoge, Richard McIlwaine, and Benjamin Morgan Palmer; and Episcopalians, like Ellison Capers, Stephen Elliott, Thomas F. Gailor, James Hervey Otey, William Nelson Pendleton, Anthony Toomer Porter, and Richard Hooker Wilmer.

Important studies of groups outside this Protestant mainstream are few. Although Roman Catholics have been a significant factor in urban areas, along the Gulf Coast of Texas and Mississippi, and in Louisiana, most scholarly work on Roman Catholicism in the South has been in the field of diocesan, state, and local studies only. *Catholics in the Old South* (edited by Randall W. Miller and Jon L. Wakelyn) is the best book about the antebellum period, but nothing of comparable quality has been written on the church after the Civil War. Jews, who made up less than 1 percent of the population of the South, and who were virtually invisible outside of a few major cities, are represented by two collections of essays that have merit. *Jews in the South* (edited by Leonard Dinnerstein and Mary Dale Palsson) and *"Turn to the South"* (edited by Nathan M. Kaganoff and Melvin I. Urofsky) both handle this subject matter with great insight.

Finally, two very recent secondary works provide indispensable, general introductions to southern religion. Any serious study of this field must now begin with Samuel Hill's *Encyclopedia of Religion in the South* and Charles H. Lippy's *Bibliography of Religion in the South*. These works point perceptively to the numerous avenues by which scholars are analyzing this broad topic at the present time. They are the essential reference tools for anyone who is interested in examining in depth any aspect of the study of southern religious history.

BIBLIOGRAPHY

1. WHITE CHRISTIANITY IN THE ANTEBELLUM PERIOD

Bruce, Dickson D., Jr. "Religion, Society and Culture in the Old South: A Comparative View." American Quarterly 26 (October 1974), 399-416.

Holifield, E. Brooks. The Gentlemen Theologians: American Theology in Southern Culture, 1795-1860. Durham, N.C.: Duke University Press, 1978.

Holifield, E. Brooks. "Thomas Smyth: The Social Ideas of a Southern Evangelist." Journal of Presbyterian History 51 (Spring 1973), 24-39.

Kuykendall, John W. Southern Enterprize: The Work of National Evangelical Societies in the Antebellum South. Westport, Conn.: Greenwood, 1982.

Loveland, Anne C. Southern Evangelicals and the Social Order, 1800-1860. Baton Rouge: Louisiana State University Press, 1980.

Maddex, Jack P. "From Theocracy to Spirituality: The Southern Presbyterian Reversal on Church and State." Journal of Presbyterian History 54 (Winter 1976), 438-457.

Maddex, Jack P. "Proslavery Millennialism: Social Eschatology in Antebellum Southern Calvinism." American Quarterly 31 (Spring 1979), 46-62.

Maddex, Jack P. "'The Southern Apostasy' Revisited: The Significance of Proslavery Christianity." Marxist Perspectives 2 (Fall 1979), 132-141.

Mathews, Donald G. Religion in the Old South. Chicago: University of Chicago Press, 1977.

Myers, Robert Manson, ed. The Children of Pride: A True Story
    of Georgia and the Civil War. New Haven: Yale University
    Press, 1972.

Silver, James W. Confederate Morale and Church Propaganda.
    New York: Norton, 1967.

Smith, H. Shelton. "The Church and the Social Order in the Old
    South as Interpreted by James Henley Thornwell." Church
    History 7 (June 1938), 115-124.

Smith, H. Shelton. In His Image, But . . . : Racism in
    Southern Religion, 1780-1910. Durham, N.C.: Duke University
    Press, 1972.

Thompson, Ernest Trice. The Spirituality of the Church: A
    Distinctive Doctrine of the Presbyterian Church in the
    United States. Richmond: John Knox, 1961.

Thornwell, James Henley. The Collected Writings of James
    Henley Thornwell. 4 vols. Edited by John B. Adger and John
    L. Girardeau. Richmond: Presbyterian Committee of
    Publication, 1871-1873.

Wyatt-Brown, Bertram. Southern Honor: Ethics and Behavior in
    the Old South. New York: Oxford University Press, 1982.

2. RELIGION AND THE LOST CAUSE

Primary

Bennett, William W. A Narrative of the Great Revival Which
    Prevailed in the Southern Armies During the Late Civil War
    Between the States of the Federal Union. Philadelphia:
    Claxton, Remsen & Haffelfinger, 1877.

Cheshire, Joseph B. The Church in the Confederate States: A
    History of the Protestant Episcopal Church in the
    Confederate States. New York: Longmans, Green, 1912.

Confederate Veteran. 1893-1932. Nashville, Tenn.

Cooke, John Esten. Stonewall Jackson: A Military Biography;
    with an Appendix by J. William Jones, Containing Personal
    Reminiscences, and a Full Account of the Ceremonies
    Attending the Unveiling of Foley's Statue, Including the
    Oration by Moses D. Hoge. New York: D. Appleton, 1876.

Dabney, Robert Lewis. A Defence of Virginia, and Through Her
    of the South. New York: E. J. Hale & Son, 1867.

Dabney, Robert Lewis. _Life and Campaigns of Lieut.-Gen. Thomas J. Jackson_. New York: Blelock and Co., 1866.

Dixon, Thomas, Jr. _The Clansman: An Historical Romance of the Ku Klux Klan_. New York: Doubleday, Page, 1905.

Dixon, Thomas, Jr. _The Leopard's Spots: A Romance of the White Man's Burden, 1865-1900_. New York: Doubleday, Page, 1902.

DuBose, William P. _Turning Points in My Life_. New York: Longmans, Green, 1912.

Gordon, John Brown. _Reminiscences of the Civil War_. New York: Scribner, 1903.

Jackson, Mary Anna. _Memoirs of Stonewall Jackson by His Widow_. Louisville: Prentice Press, 1895.

Jones, J. William. _Army of Northern Virginia Memorial Volume_. Richmond: J. W. Randolph & English, 1880.

Jones, J. William. _Christ in the Camp; or, Religion in Lee's Army_. Richmond: B. F. Johnson & Co., 1887.

Jones, J. William. _Life and Letters of Robert Edward Lee, Soldier and Man_. New York: Neale Publishing Co., 1906.

Jones, J. William. "The Morale of the Confederate Army." In _Confederate Military History_, edited by Clement A. Evans, vol. 12, 117-193. Atlanta: Confederate Publishing Company, 1899.

Jones, J. William. _Personal Reminiscences, Anecdotes, and Letters of Gen. Robert E. Lee_. New York: D. Appleton, 1875.

Land We Love. 1866-1869. Charlotte, N.C.

McCarthy, Carlton. _Detailed Minutiae of Soldier Life in the Army of Northern Virginia, 1861-1865_. Richmond: B. F. Johnson Publishing Co., 1899.

McKim, Randolph Harrison. _In Memoriam: Good Men a Nation's Strength_. Baltimore: John Murphy & Co., 1870.

McKim, Randolph Harrison. _The Motives and Aims of the Soldiers of the South in the Civil War_. Nashville: United Confederate Veterans, 1904.

McKim, Randolph Harrison. _A Soldier's Reflections: Leaves from the Diary of a Young Confederate._ New York: Longmans, Green, 1910.

McKim, Randolph Harrison. _The Soul of Lee_. New York: Longmans, Green, 1918.

Pendleton, William Nelson. "Personal Recollections of General Lee." Southern Magazine 15 (December 1874), 603-636.

Pollard, Edward A. The Lost Cause: A New Southern History of the War of the Confederates. New York: E. B. Treat & Co., 1866.

Ryan, Abram Joseph. Poems: Patriotic, Religious, Miscellaneous. Baltimore: John B. Piet, 1880.

Ryan, Abram Joseph. Selected Poems of Father Ryan. Edited by Gordon Weaver. Jackson: University and College Press of Mississippi, 1973.

Southern Historical Society Papers. 1876-1959. Richmond, Va.

Stiles, Robert. Four Years Under Marse Robert. New York: Neale Publishing Co., 1903.

Wharton, Henry M. White Blood: A Story of the South. New York: Neale Publishing Co., 1906.

Secondary

Aaron, Daniel. The Unwritten War: American Writers and the Civil War. New York: Oxford University Press, 1975.

Cass, Michael M. "Charles C. Jones, Jr. and the 'Lost Cause.'" Georgia Historical Quarterly 55 (Summer 1971), 222-233.

Clebsch, William A. Christian Interpretations of the Civil War. Philadelphia: Fortress, 1969.

Connelly, Thomas L. The Marble Man: Robert E. Lee and His Image in American Society. Baton Rouge: Louisiana State University Press, 1977.

Connelly, Thomas L., and Bellows, Barbara L. God and General Longstreet: The Lost Cause and the Southern Mind. Baton Rouge: Louisiana State University Press, 1982.

Faulkner, William. Absalom, Absalom! 1936. Reprint. New York: Random House, Vintage Books, 1972.

Faulkner, William. The Unvanquished. 1934. Reprint. New York: Random House, Vintage Books, 1965.

Freeman, Douglas Southall. The South to Posterity: An Introduction to the Writing of Confederate History. New York: Scribner, 1939.

Hobson, Fred. Tell About the South: The Southern Rage to Explain. Baton Rouge: Louisiana State University Press, 1983.

Luker, Ralph E. "The Crucible of Civil War and Reconstruction
    in the Experience of William Porcher DuBose." South
    Carolina Historical Magazine 83 (January 1982), 50-71.

Osterweis, Rollin G. The Myth of the Lost Cause, 1865-1900.
    Hamden, Conn.: Archon Books, 1973.

Overy, David H. "When the Wicked Beareth Rule: A Southern
    Critique of Industrial America." Journal of Presbyterian
    History 48 (Summer 1970), 130-142.

Pressly, Thomas J. Americans Interpret Their Civil War. New
    York: Free Press, 1962.

Simkins, Francis B. "Robert Lewis Dabney, Southern
    Conservative." Georgia Review 18 (Winter 1964), 393-407.

Simpson, John A. "The Cult of the 'Lost Cause.'" Tennessee
    Historical Quarterly 34 (Winter 1975), 350-361.

Warren, Robert Penn. The Legacy of the Civil War: Meditations
    on the Centennial. New York: Random House, 1961.

Weaver, Richard M. The Southern Tradition at Bay: A History of
    Postbellum Thought. Edited by George Core and M. E.
    Bradford. New Rochelle, N.Y.: Arlington House, 1968.

Wilson, Charles Reagan. Baptized in Blood: The Religion of the
    Lost Cause, 1865-1920. Athens: University of Georgia Press,
    1980.

Wilson, Charles Reagan. "Bishop Thomas Frank Gailor: Celebrant
    of Southern Tradition." Tennessee Historical Quarterly 38
    (Fall 1979), 322-331.

Wilson, Charles Reagan. "The Religion of the Lost Cause:
    Ritual and Organization of the Southern Civil Religion,
    1865-1920." Journal of Southern History 46 (May 1980), 219-
    238.

Wilson, Charles Reagan. "Robert Lewis Dabney: Religion and the
    Southern Holocaust." Virginia Magazine of History and
    Biography 89 (January 1981), 79-89.

Wilson, Edmund. Patriotic Gore: Studies in the Literature of
    the Civil War. New York: Oxford University Press, 1966.

3. RECONSTRUCTION AND THE BLACK CHURCHES

Primary

American Missionary. 1865-1900. New York.

Beard, Augustus Field. <u>A Crusade of Brotherhood: A History of</u> <u>the American Missionary Association</u>. Boston: Pilgrim Press, 1909.

Cable, George W. <u>The Silent South</u>. New York: Scribner, 1885.

Douglass, H. Paul. <u>Christian Reconstruction in the South</u>. Boston: Pilgrim Press, 1909.

Eaton, John. <u>Grant, Lincoln, and the Freedmen: Reminiscences</u> <u>of the Civil War</u>. New York: Longmans, Green, 1907.

Haygood, Atticus G. <u>Our Brothers in Black</u>. Nashville: Southern Methodist Publishing House, 1881.

Hopkins, Alphonso A. <u>The Life [of] Clinton Bowen Fisk</u>. 1888. Reprint. New York: Negro Universities Press, 1969.

Rust, Richard Sutton. <u>The Freedmen's Aid Society of the</u> <u>Methodist Episcopal Church</u>. New York: Tract Department [of the Methodist Episcopal Church, 1880].

Tourgee, Albion W. <u>Bricks Without Straw: A Novel</u>. 1888. Reprint. Edited by Otto H. Olsen. Baton Rouge: Louisiana State University Press, 1969.

Tourgee, Albion W. <u>A Fool's Errand</u>. 1879. Reprint. Edited by John Hope Franklin. Cambridge: Harvard University Press, Belknap Press, 1961.

Washington, Booker T. <u>Up From Slavery: An Autobiography</u>. Boston: Houghton, Mifflin, 1901.

Secondary

Armstrong, Warren Bruce. "Union Chaplains and the Education of the Freedmen." <u>Journal of Negro History</u> 52 (April 1967), 104-115.

Bailey, Kenneth K. "The Post-Civil War Racial Separations in Southern Protestantism: Another Look." <u>Church History</u> 46 (December 1977), 453-473.

Blassingame, John W. <u>The Slave Community: Plantation Life in</u> <u>the Antebellum South</u>. rev. and enl. ed. New York: Oxford University Press, 1979.

Daniel, W. Harrison. "The Effects of the Civil War on Southern Protestantism." <u>Maryland Historical Magazine</u> 69 (Spring 1974), 44-63.

Daniel, W. Harrison. "Virginia Baptists and the Negro, 1865-1902." <u>Virginia Magazine of History and Biography</u> 76 (July 1968), 340-363.

Drake, Richard B. "Freedmen's Aid Societies and Sectional
    Compromise." Journal of Southern History 29 (May 1963),
    175-186.

DuBois, W. E. B. Black Reconstruction in America. 1935.
    Reprint. Cleveland: World Publishing Company, 1962.

DuBois, W. E. B. The Souls of Black Folk: Essays and Sketches.
    Chicago: McClung & Co., 1903.

DuBois, W. E. B., ed. The Negro Church. Atlanta: The Atlanta
    University Press, 1903.

Frazier, E. Franklin. The Negro Church in America. New York:
    Schocken, 1964.

Genovese, Eugene D. Roll, Jordan, Roll: The World the Slaves
    Made. New York: Pantheon, 1974.

Gravely, William. Gilbert Haven, Methodist Abolitionist: A
    Study in Race, Religion, and Reform, 1850-1900. Nashville:
    Abingdon, 1973.

Griffin, Clifford S. Their Brothers' Keepers: Moral
    Stewardship in the United States, 1800-1865. New Brunswick,
    N.J.: Rutgers University Press, 1960.

Jacoway, Elizabeth. Yankee Missionaries in the South: The Penn
    School Experiment. Baton Rouge: Louisiana State University
    Press, 1980.

Jones, Donald G. The Sectional Crisis and Northern Methodism:
    A Study in Piety, Political Ethics and Civil Religion.
    Metuchen, N.J.: Scarecrow, 1979.

Jones, Jacqueline. Soldiers of Light and Love: Northern
    Teachers and Georgia Blacks, 1865-1873. Chapel Hill:
    University of North Carolina Press, 1980.

Levine, Lawrence W. Black Culture and Black Consciousness:
    Afro-American Folk Thought from Slavery to Freedom. New
    York: Oxford University Press, 1977.

Litwack, Leon F. Been in the Storm So Long: The Aftermath of
    Slavery. New York: Knopf, 1979.

McFeely, William S. Yankee Stepfather: General O. O. Howard
    and the Freedmen. New Haven: Yale University Press, 1968.

Moorhead, James H. American Apocalypse: Yankee Protestants and
    the Civil War, 1860-1869. New Haven: Yale University Press,
    1978.

Morris, Robert C. Reading, 'Riting, and Reconstruction: The
    Education of Freedmen in the South, 1861-1870. Chicago:
    University of Chicago Press, 1981.

Morrow, Ralph E. Northern Methodism and Reconstruction. East
    Lansing: Michigan State University Press, 1956.

Paris, Peter J. The Social Teaching of the Black Churches.
    Philadelphia: Fortress, 1985.

Perman, Michael. Reunion Without Compromise: The South and
    Reconstruction, 1865-1868. Cambridge: Cambridge University
    Press, 1973.

Raboteau, Albert J. Slave Religion: The "Invisible
    Institution" in the Antebellum South. New York: Oxford
    University Press, 1978.

Reimers, David. White Protestantism and the Negro. New York:
    Oxford University Press, 1965.

Richardson, Joe M. Christian Reconstruction: The American
    Missionary Association and Southern Blacks, 1861-1890.
    Athens: University of Georgia Press, 1986.

Richardson, Joe M. "'Labor is Rest to Me Here in This the
    Lord's Vineyard': Hardy Mobley, Black Missionary During
    Reconstruction." Southern Studies 22 (Spring 1983), 5-20.

Roark, James L. Masters Without Slaves: Southern Planters in
    the Civil War and Reconstruction. New York: Norton, 1977.

Rose, Willie Lee. Rehearsal for Reconstruction: The Port Royal
    Experiment. Indianapolis: Bobbs-Merrill, 1964.

Sefton, James E. The United States Army and Reconstruction,
    1865-1877. Westport, Conn.: Greenwood, 1980.

Stampp, Kenneth M., and Litwack, Leon F., eds. Reconstruction:
    An Anthology of Revisionist Writings. Baton Rouge:
    Louisiana State University Press, 1969.

Stanley, A. Knighton. The Children Is Crying:
    Congregationalism Among Black People. New York: Pilgrim
    Press, 1979.

Stowe, Walter H. "A Study in Conscience: Some Aspects of the
    Relations of the Clergy to the State." Historical Magazine
    of the Protestant Episcopal Church 19 (December 1950), 301-
    323.

Sweet, William Warren. "Methodist Church Influence in Southern
    Politics." Mississippi Valley Historical Review 1 (March
    1915), 546-560.

Trelease, Allen W. White Terror: The Ku Klux Klan Conspiracy
    and Southern Reconstruction. New York: Harper and Row,
    1971.

Vander Velde, Lewis G. The Presbyterian Churches and the
    Federal Union, 1861-1869. Cambridge: Harvard University
    Press, 1932.

Walker, Clarence E. A Rock in a Weary Land: The African
    Methodist Episcopal Church During the Civil War and
    Reconstruction. Baton Rouge: Louisiana State University
    Press, 1982.

Warnock, Henry Y. "Prophets of Change: Some Southern Baptist
    Leaders and the Problem of Race, 1900-1921." Baptist
    History and Heritage 7 (July 1972), 172-183.

Washington, Joseph R. Black Religion: The Negro and
    Christianity in the United States. Boston: Beacon Press,
    1964.

Williamson, Joel. The Crucible of Race: Black/White Relations
    in the American South Since Emancipation. New York: Oxford
    University Press, 1984.

Woodson, Carter G. The History of the Negro Church. 3d ed.
    Washington, D.C.: Associated Publishers, 1972.

Woodward, C. Vann. Reunion and Reaction: The Compromise of
    1877 and the End of Reconstruction. Boston: Little, Brown,
    1951.

4.   SOCIAL ISSUES IN THE NEW SOUTH

Bailey, Hugh Coleman. Edgar Gardner Murphy, Gentle
    Progressive. Coral Gables, Fla.: University of Miami Press,
    1968.

Bode, Frederick A. Protestantism and the New South: North
    Carolina Baptists and Methodists in Political Crisis, 1894-
    1904. Charlottesville: University Press of Virginia, 1975.

Bode, Frederick A. "Religion and Class Hegemony: A Populist
    Critique in North Carolina." Journal of Southern History 38
    (August 1971), 417-438.

Eighmy, John Lee. Churches in Cultural Captivity: A History of
    the Social Attitudes of Southern Baptists. Edited by Samuel
    S. Hill, Jr. Knoxville: University of Tennessee Press,
    1972.

Eighmy, John Lee. "Religious Liberalism in the South During the Progressive Era." Church History 38 (September 1969), 359-372.

Farish, Hunter Dickinson. The Circuit-Rider Dismounts: A Social History of Southern Methodism, 1865-1900. 1938. Reprint. New York: Da Capo, 1969.

Flynt, J. Wayne. "Dissent in Zion: Alabama Baptists and Social Issues, 1900-1914." Journal of Southern History 35 (November 1969), 523-542.

Flynt, J. Wayne. "'Feeding the Hungry and Ministering to the Broken Hearted': The Presbyterian Church in the United States and the Social Gospel, 1900-1920." In Religion in the South, edited by Charles Reagan Wilson, 83-137. Jackson: University Press of Mississippi, 1985.

Flynt, J. Wayne. "Southern Baptists and Reform: 1890-1920." Baptist History and Heritage 7 (October 1972), 211-224.

Gaston, Paul M. The New South Creed: A Study in Southern Mythmaking. New York: Knopf, 1970.

Grady, Henry. The New South: Writings and Speeches of Henry Grady. Edited by Mills Lane. Savannah, Ga.: Beehive Press, 1971.

Grantham, Dewey W. Southern Progressivism: The Reconciliation of Progress and Tradition. Knoxville: University of Tennessee Press, 1983.

Hall, Jacquelyn Dowd. Revolt Against Chivalry: Jessie Daniel Ames and the Women's Campaign Against Lynching. New York: Columbia University Press, 1979.

Harrell, David Edwin. A Social History of the Disciples of Christ. 2 vols. Nashville: Disciples of Christ Historical Society, 1966-1973.

Hill, Samuel S., Jr., et al. Religion and the Solid South. Nashville: Abingdon, 1972.

Luker, Ralph E. "The Social Gospel and the Failure of Racial Reform, 1877-1898." Church History 46 (March 1977), 80-99.

Luker, Ralph E. A Southern Tradition in Theology and Social Criticism, 1830-1930: The Religious Liberalism and Social Conservatism of James Warley Miles, William Porcher DuBose and Edgar Gardner Murphy. New York: E. Mellen, 1984.

McDowell, John P. The Social Gospel in the South: The Woman's Home Mission Movement in the Methodist Episcopal Church, South, 1886-1939. Baton Rouge: Louisiana State University Press, 1982.

Murphy, Edgar Gardner. Problems of the Present South: A
    Discussion of Certain of the Educational, Industrial and
    Political Issues in the Southern States. New York:
    Macmillan, 1904.

Newton, John C. Calhoun. The New South and the Methodist
    Episcopal Church, South. Baltimore: King Brothers, 1887.

Pope, Liston. Millhands and Preachers: A Study of Gastonia.
    New Haven: Yale University Press, 1942.

Scott, Anne Firor. "Women, Religion and Social Change in the
    South." In Religion and the Solid South, edited by Samuel
    S. Hill, Jr., et al., 92-121. Nashville: Abingdon, 1972.

Smith, Timothy L. Revivalism and Social Reform: American
    Protestantism on the Eve of the Civil War. Baltimore: Johns
    Hopkins University Press, 1980.

Soden, Dale E. "The Social Gospel in Tennessee: Mark Allison
    Matthews." Tennessee Historical Quarterly 41 (Summer 1982),
    159-170.

Spain, Rufus B. At Ease in Zion: A Social History of Southern
    Baptists, 1865-1900. Nashville: Vanderbilt University
    Press, 1967.

White, Ronald C., and Hopkins, C. Howard. The Social Gospel:
    Religion and Reform in Changing America. Philadelphia:
    Temple University Press, 1976.

Wilson, Charles Reagan, ed. Religion in the South. Jackson:
    University Press of Mississippi, 1985.

5.   HISTORIOGRAPHY AND GENERAL STUDIES

Primary

Manuscript Locations

Church Historical Society. Episcopal Theological Seminary of
    the Southwest, Austin, Tex.

Disciples of Christ Historical Society. Nashville, Tenn.

Duke University Library. Durham, N.C.

Emory University Library. Atlanta, Ga.

Historical Foundation of the Presbyterian and Reformed
    Churches. Montreat, N.C.

South Caroliniana Library. Library of the University of South
    Carolina, Columbia, S.C.

Southern Baptist Convention. Dargan-Carver Library, Nashville,
    Tenn.

Southern Historical Collection. Library of the University of
    North Carolina at Chapel Hill, N.C.

Union Theological Seminary Library. Richmond, Va.

University of the South Library. Sewanee, Tenn.

Vanderbilt University Library. Nashville, Tenn.

Virginia Historical Society. Richmond, Va.

Journals

Central Presbyterian. 1865-1900. Richmond, Va.

Christian Advocate. 1865-1900. Nashville, Tenn.

Christian Index. 1865-1900. Atlanta, Ga.

Christian Observer. 1865-1900. Louisville, Ky.

Home Monthly. 1866-1873. Nashville, Tenn.

Quarterly Review of the Methodist Episcopal Church, South.
    1865-1888, and 1894-1900. Nashville, Tenn.

Religious Herald. 1865-1900. Richmond, Va.

Sewanee Review. 1892-1900. Sewanee, Tenn.

Southern Bivouac. 1882-1887. Louisville, Ky.

Southern Christian Advocate. 1865-1900. Charleston, S.C.

Southern Churchman. 1865-1900. Richmond, Va.

Southern Methodist Review. 1888-1894. Nashville, Tenn.

Southern Presbyterian. 1865-1900. Milledgeville, Ga., etc.

Southern Presbyterian Review. 1865-1885. Columbia, S.C.

Southern Review. 1867-1879. Baltimore, Md.

Ecclesiastical Reports

Methodist Episcopal Church, South. Journal of the General
    Conference. 1866-1900.

Presbyterian Church in the United States. Minutes of the General Assembly. 1866-1900.

Southern Baptist Convention. Proceedings. 1865-1900.

Books

American Church History Series. 13 vols. New York: Christian Literature Co., 1893-1897.

Blackburn, George A. The Life Work of John Girardeau. Columbia, S.C.: State Company, 1916.

Broadus, John A. Memoir of James Petigru Boyce. New York: A. C. Armstrong and Son, 1893.

Capers, Walter B. The Soldier-Bishop: Ellison Capers. New York: Neale Publishing Co., 1912.

Caskey, Thomas W. Caskey's Last Book, Containing an Autobiographical Sketch of His Ministerial Life, with Essays and Sermons. Edited by B. F. Manire. Nashville: Messenger Pub. Co., 1896.

Elliott, Stephen. Sermons by Stephen Elliott. New York: Pott and Amery, 1867.

Fitzgerald, Oscar P. Fifty Years: Observations--Opinions-- Experiences. Nashville: Publishing House of the Methodist Episcopal Church, South, 1903.

Gailor, Thomas F. Some Memories. Kingsport, Tenn.: Southern Publishers, 1937.

Girardeau, John L. Sermons by John L. Girardeau. Edited by George A. Blackburn. Columbia, S.C.: State Company, 1907.

Green, William M. Memoir of Rt. Rev. James Hervey Otey. New York: James Pott, 1885.

Hoge, Peyton H. Moses Drury Hoge: Life and Letters. Richmond: Presbyterian Committee of Publication, 1899.

Johnson, Thomas Cary. The Life and Letters of Benjamin Morgan Palmer. Richmond: Presbyterian Committee of Publication, 1906.

Johnson, Thomas Cary. The Life and Letters of Robert Lewis Dabney. Richmond: Presbyterian Committee of Publication, 1903.

Lee, Susan P. Memoirs of William Nelson Pendleton, D.D. Philadelphia: J. B. Lippincott Company, 1893.

McIlwaine, Richard. Memories of Three Score Years and Ten.
    New York: Neale Publishing Co., 1908.

Porter, Anthony Toomer. Led On! Step by Step: Scenes from
    Clerical, Military, Educational, and Plantation Life in the
    South, 1828-1898. New York: G. P. Putnam's Sons, 1898.

Robertson, Archibald T. Life and Letters of John Albert
    Broadus. Philadelphia: American Baptist Publication
    Society, 1901.

Smith, George Gilman. The Life and Letters of James Osgood
    Andrews. Nashville: Publishing House of the Methodist
    Episcopal Church, South, 1882.

Smith, George Gilman. The Life and Times of George Foster
    Pierce. Sparta, Ga.: Hancock Publishing Company, 1888.

Taylor, George Boardman. Life and Times of James B. Taylor.
    Philadelphia: Bible and Publication Society, 1872.

Taylor, George Braxton. Life and Letters of Rev. George
    Boardman Taylor, D.D. Lynchburg, Va.: J. P. Bell Company,
    1908.

Whitaker, Walter C. Richard Hooker Wilmer: A Biography.
    Philadelphia: George W. Jacobs & Co., 1907.

Wilmer, Richard Hooker. The Recent Past from a Southern
    Standpoint: Reminiscences of a Grandfather. New York: T.
    Whittaker, 1887.

                           Secondary

Bailey, Kenneth K. Southern White Protestantism in the
    Twentieth Century. New York: Harper and Row, 1964.

Baker, Robert A. Relations Between Northern and Southern
    Baptists. New York: Arno Press, 1980.

Baker, Robert A. The Southern Baptist Convention and Its
    People. Nashville: Broadman Press, 1974.

Baker, Tod A.; Steed, Robert P.; and Moreland, Laurence W.,
    eds. Religion and Politics in the South: Mass and Elite
    Perspectives. New York: Praeger, 1983.

Boles, John B. "Evangelical Protestantism in the Old South:
    From Religious Dissent to Cultural Dominance." In Religion
    in the South, edited by Charles Reagan Wilson, 13-34.
    Jackson: University Press of Mississippi, 1985.

Boles, John B. "Religion in the South: A Tradition Recovered."
    Maryland Historical Magazine 77 (December 1982), 388-401.

Brauer, Jerald C. "Regionalism and Religion in America."
     Church History 54 (September 1985), 366-378.

Buck, Paul H. The Road to Reunion, 1865-1900. Boston: Little,
     Brown, 1947.

Carter, Dan T. When the War Was Over: The Failure of Self-
     Reconstruction in the South, 1865-1867. Baton Rouge:
     Louisiana State University Press, 1985.

Carter, Paul A. The Spiritual Crisis of the Gilded Age.
     DeKalb: Northern Illinois University Press, 1971.

Cash, Wilbur J. The Mind of the South. Garden City, N.Y.:
     Doubleday, 1954.

Dabbs, James McBride. Haunted By God. Richmond: John Knox,
     1972.

Daniel, W. Harrison. "Virginia Baptists and the Myth of the
     Southern Mind, 1865-1900." South Atlantic Quarterly 73
     (Winter 1974), 85-98.

Degler, Carl N. The Other South: Southern Dissenters in the
     Nineteenth Century. New York: Harper and Row, 1974.

Degler, Carl N. Place Over Time: The Continuity of Southern
     Distinctiveness. Baton Rouge: Louisiana State University
     Press, 1977.

Degler, Carl N. "Rethinking Post-Civil War History." Virginia
     Quarterly Review 57 (Spring 1981), 250-267.

Dinnerstein, Leonard, and Palsson, Mary Dale, eds. Jews in the
     South. Baton Rouge: Louisiana State University Press, 1973.

Dunning, William Archibald. Essays on the Civil War and
     Reconstruction and Related Topics. 1897. Reprint.
     Freeport, N.Y.: Books for Libraries Press, 1971.

Eaton, Clement. The Waning of the Old South Civilization,
     1860-1880's. Athens: University of Georgia Press, 1968.

Gaston, Paul M. "The 'New South.'" In Writing Southern
     History: Essays in Historiography in Honor of Fletcher M.
     Green, edited by Arthur S. Link and Rembert W. Patrick, 316-
     336. Baton Rouge: Louisiana State University Press, 1965.

Hackney, Sheldon. "Origins of the New South in Retrospect."
     Journal of Southern History 38 (May 1972), 191-216.

Hill, Samuel S., Jr. The South and the North in American
     Religion. Athens: University of Georgia Press, 1980.

Hill, Samuel S., Jr. _Southern Churches in Crisis_. New York:
    Holt, Rinehart and Winston, 1966.

Hill, Samuel S., Jr., ed. _Encyclopedia of Religion in the_
    South. Macon, Ga.: Mercer University Press, 1984.

Hill, Samuel S., Jr, ed. _Religion in the Southern States: A_
    Historical Study. Macon, Ga.: Mercer University Press,
    1983.

Kaganoff, Nathan M., and Urofsky, Melvin I., eds. _"Turn to the_
    South": Essays on Southern Jewry. Charlottesville:
    University of Virginia Press, 1979.

Kurtz, Ernest. "The Tragedy of Southern Religion." _Georgia_
    Historical Quarterly 66 (Summer 1982), 217-247.

Lears, T. J. Jackson. _No Place of Grace: Antimodernism and the_
    Transformation of American Culture, 1880-1920. New York:
    Pantheon, 1981.

Lippy, Charles H. _Bibliography of Religion in the South_.
    Macon, Ga.: Mercer University Press, 1985.

McKinney, John C., and Thompson, Edgar T., eds. _The South in_
    Continuity and Change. Durham, N.C.: Duke University Press,
    1965.

McPherson, James M. _Ordeal By Fire: The Civil War and_
    Reconstruction. New York: Knopf, 1982.

Miller, Randall W., and Wakelyn, Jon L., eds. _Catholics in the_
    Old South: Essays on Church and Culture. Macon, Ga.: Mercer
    University Press, 1983.

Perman, Michael. _The Road to Redemption: Southern Politics,_
    _1869-1879_. Chapel Hill: University of North Carolina Press,
    1984.

Poteat, Edwin M., Jr. "Religion in the South." In _Culture in_
    the South, edited by W. T. Couch, 248-269. Chapel Hill:
    University of North Carolina Press, 1935.

Randall, James G., and Donald, David Herbert. _The Civil War_
    and Reconstruction. 2d ed., rev. Lexington, Mass.: Heath,
    1969.

Reed, John Shelton. _The Enduring South: Subcultural_
    Persistence in Mass Society. Lexington, Mass.: Heath, 1971.

Reed, John Shelton. _One South: An Ethnic Approach to Regional_
    Culture. Baton Rouge: Louisiana State University Press,
    1982.

Simkins, Francis Butler. _The Everlasting South_. Baton Rouge:
     Louisiana State University Press, 1963.

Stampp, Kenneth M. _The Era of Reconstruction, 1865-1877_. New
     York: Knopf, 1965.

Stokes, Anson Phelps. _Church and State in the United States_.
     3 vols. New York: Harper and Brothers, 1950.

Tate, Allen. "Remarks on the Southern Religion." In _I'll Take
     My Stand: The South and the Agrarian Tradition_, 155-175.
     1930. Reprint. Baton Rouge: Louisiana State University
     Press, 1977.

Thompson, Ernest Trice. _Presbyterians in the South_. 3 vols.
     Richmond: John Knox, 1963-1974.

Weisenburger, Francis P. _Ordeal of Faith: The Crisis of
     Church-Going America, 1865-1900_. New York: Philosophical
     Library, 1959.

Woodward, C. Vann. _The Burden of Southern History_. rev. ed.
     Baton Rouge: Louisiana State University Press, 1968.

Woodward, C. Vann. _Origins of the New South, 1877-1913_. Vol.
     9 of _A History of the South_. 1951. [rev. ed.] Baton
     Rouge: Louisiana State University Press, 1971.

Yance, Norman A. _Religion Southern Style; Southern Baptists
     and Society in Historical Perspective_. Macon, Ga.: Mercer
     University Press, 1978.

3

Social Justice in an Industrial Society

Mark S. Massa

In the half century between Appomattox and the outbreak of World War I the process of industrialization, long viewed as an integral component in the American construction of an earthly millennial kingdom, emerged as a problematic area in the culture. Both the massive expansion of industrial technology on an unprecedented scale, and the cultural upheaval that ensued in the attempt to meet the new industrial needs, aroused widespread fears that the social and spiritual bases of American civilization itself were under siege. The replacement of communal, small-scale patterns of personal and economic interaction with impersonal, associational relationships dependent on one's task in the new industrial system, accompanied by the widespread labor unrest, violent strikes, and financial panics that marked the period, engendered a time of confusion and of painful social and spiritual adjustments in almost every area of American culture.

The complex interaction of church and state in America after the Civil War was precipitated in large part by the cultural challenges posed by this rapid industrialization, challenges that resulted in broad-based movements seeking social justice in an emerging corporate society. These reform movements, issuing from various parts of the culture (churches, political parties, and the new "social sciences," for example), attempted to realize a vision of social and economic justice that had inhered in America's largely Protestant culture since at least the First Great Awakening of the eighteenth century.

The relative importance of secular and religious impulses (broadly conceived) in these reform efforts remained fairly stable throughout the period under consideration; it was *where* they manifested themselves within the culture that provides the tension and the drama for the following essay. By the outbreak of the First World War, reform impulses that claimed the prerogatives of cultural hegemony emerged increasingly from the new "corporate state" rather than from the evangelical Protestant "voluntary establishment"

(Robert T. Handy, *Christian America*) that had claimed such hegemony for nearly two centuries. Indeed, the nascent corporate state of the twentieth century (Robert H. Wiebe, *Search for Order*, and James Weinstein, *The Corporate Ideal*) would come to attract and embody most of the religious impulses dedicated to achieving social justice previously centered in church-related institutions and movements. It is this story—the transfer of cultural authority for achieving social justice in an industrial society from ecclesiastical institutions and movements to secular, political institutions and movements, now exercising "religious" prerogatives within the culture—that provides the interpretive framework for the following essay.

The best general introductions to the complex social and intellectual challenges facing American culture between 1875 and 1920 remain the older seminal works by Arthur M. Schlesinger ("Critical Period"), Sidney E. Mead ("American Protestantism"), Samuel P. Hayes (*Response to Industrialization*), and Richard Hofstadter (*Age of Reform*). While all of these works reveal the historiographic agenda of their time (the first two in focusing on the ecclesiastical dilemmas of mainline Protestantism to the exclusion of other religious traditions, and the latter two in analyzing both the threats and the responses of the period largely in terms of Hofstadter's theory of "status strain" experienced by the northern middle class), they remain cogent and masterful studies offering the reader a sophisticated introduction to the complex forces that challenged the existing cultural relationships between church and state in Gilded Age America.

More recently, historians have nuanced and deepened our understanding of the cultural challenges engendered by industrialization, and of the resulting movements for social justice, by analyzing the political pretensions of religious groups claiming cultural hegemony, as well as uncovering the profoundly religious impulses that fueled many of the secular movements for political and industrial reform. Robert Handy's magisterial study of the long-term issues that defined the mainstream religious experience in America (*Christian America*) places the social and political search for social justice within a broader religious cultural vision; Paul A. Carter's study of the interaction of religious and secular forces that defined the crises of the period (*Spiritual Crisis*) weaves together the disparate stories from various strands of the culture; John L. Thomas (*Alternative America*) offers a convincing account of the religious impulses that inspired the political and literary careers of populists Henry George, Edward Bellamy, and Henry Demarest Lloyd; John D. Buenker and his collaborators in *Progressivism* present that critical movement as a moral and religious, as well as a political, response to industrialism, while Robert M. Crunden studies the profoundly religious concerns of Jane Addams, John Dewey, Albion Small, and other progressive intellectuals who worked for political, social, and industrial reform (*Ministers of Reform*).

The earliest and most-studied institutional response to the challenges of industrialization emerged from within those Protestant churches that had long claimed cultural hegemony and social responsibility for American culture, a response that has been collectively labeled "the social gospel" (see part 1, section a of the bibliographical listings). In reality a congeries of theological and ecclesiastical movements dedicated to making religiously meaningful the traumatic emergence of a corporate, industrial society, the social gospel sought to make the older, individualistic gospel of evangelical Protestantism more relevant to new needs by emphasizing the *social* implications of religion found in the Hebrew prophets and in the teachings of the historical Jesus. Its most vocal advocates—Josiah Strong, Washington Gladden, Richard T. Ely, and Walter Rauschenbusch—called for a new, more radical, rethinking of the gospel to bring social and industrial institutions, no less than individuals, under the law of love.

While this new social Christianity clearly emerged from *within* an ancient and venerable evangelical Protestant tradition of cultural leadership (seen most clearly in the career of Josiah Strong), it nonetheless represented a substantially new development, seeking corporate answers to the new corporate challenges of industrialization. The secular political and industrial spheres, the advocates of the new social Christianity announced, constituted the raw materials out of which the Kingdom of God itself was to be fashioned, making the political arena, no less than the churchly, the scene of God's presence and invitation. Thus the earliest voluntary associations dedicated to addressing the new industrial problems to achieve political influence emerged from within the Protestant establishment: the Eight-Hour League, the Church Association for the Advancement of the Interests of Labor, the campaign of the Reverend Charles Parkhurst against Tammany Hall, the political crusade of the National Council of Congregational Churches for a federal Children's Bureau, and the Men and Religion Forward Movement.

The story of the politically active social Christianity that sponsored these reform groups has been recounted in a number of important publications; the best narrative introductions, however, remain the pioneering studies by C. Howard Hopkins, Aaron I. Abell, and Henry F. May. Hopkins's *Rise of the Social Gospel* and Abell's *Urban Impact*, published in 1940 and 1943 respectively, constituted the earliest critical reviews of the social gospel, and remain among the best. May's *Protestant Churches and Industrial America* has provided a much-borrowed hermeneutical device that has shaped subsequent analysis of the movement: May divided the social gospel movement into three related but distinct wings to explain the complex social and political response of mainstream Protestantism to the industrial crisis.

Conservative social Christianity, May's "right wing" of the social gospel, emerged seamlessly from the millennial, revivalistic evangelicalism of the antebellum Protestant mainstream, and never challenged the dominant individualistic tone that characterized the older piety; it nonetheless opened its vast audience to the pleas for social reform made by political and industrial leaders. At least since the publication of Timothy L. Smith's *Revivalism and Social Reform* in 1957, the exploration of the evangelical roots of the social gospel has become historiographically fashionable, leading to a number of recent studies of this conservative, but popular and widespread, form of the social gospel. Philip D. Jordan ("Evangelical Social Gospel") and Paul R. Meyer ("Strong's Thought"), offer perceptive essays on the Evangelical Alliance and its central American figure, Josiah Strong, illustrating the important connection between conservative social and cultural movements like the Alliance and the popular commitment to social reform that characterized church-state relations of the period. Likewise, the popular impact of the Christian social novel, arguably the most effective form for spreading social and political reform ideas, has been explored by Billie Barnes Jensen ("Social Gospel Experiment"), Grier Nicholl ("Minister"), and James H. Smylie ("Sheldon's *In His Steps*").

The radical religious impulse toward social reform embodied in the Christian socialism of William D. P. Bliss and George D. Herron—May's "left wing" of the social gospel—was the most politically active form of the social gospel in both legislative and union efforts, seeking to reconstruct both society and the church along lines that would meet the needs of industrial workers more effectively. While remaining numerically small, Christian socialism exerted political and social pressure far beyond its numbers through advocacy groups like the Union Reform League, the Social Reform Union and, most notably, the Society of Christian Socialists. Detailed studies of the political and cultural impact of these groups have yet to be undertaken, although an excellent introduction to their work remains James Dombrowski's 1936 monograph (*Early Days*); Robert Handy's essays on "Christianity and Socialism in America" and "Herron and the Kingdom Movement" provide important critical and scholarly addenda to that earlier work. The articles of Robert Crunden ("George D. Herron") and Richard B. Dressner ("Bliss's Christian Socialism") offer the best recent historiographic treatments of the practical efforts of the two major figures in the movement to Christianize an industrializing culture.

The best study of the "progressive social Christianity" that May defined as the central wing of the movement is Robert Handy's *The Social Gospel*, an edited collection of works by Gladden, Ely, and Rauschenbusch, with important biographical and bibliographical commentaries by the author. The biographies by Dores Sharpe (*Rauschenbusch*) and Jacob Dorn (*Gladden*) provide important information about the reform efforts of both central figures. Sharpe's older study of Rauschenbusch retains something of the hagiographic, although it offers valuable biographical information about that figure's sophisticated critique of capitalism in favor of industrial democracy. Jacob Dorn's *Washington Gladden* remains the most informative biography in the area, and offers a balanced and well-researched portrait of that social gospeler's efforts to mediate in industrial strikes, to politicize the National Council of Congregational Churches on labor issues, and to bring industrial reform issues generally before the churchgoing electorate.

"The Social Creed of the Churches," a Methodist statement of social commitment adopted by the Federal Council of Churches in 1908, was arguably the most culturally influential and politically effective of the institutional social gospel efforts to effect political reform on industrial issues, lending the considerable popular prestige of the Federal Council to influencing public opinion on reform. Both Donald K. Gorrell ("Federation for Social Service") and Ralph L. Pearson ("Internationalizing") offer cogent studies of the important role which the creed played in forming the popular reaction to industrial and labor issues.

Paul A. Carter (*Decline and Revival*) and Robert Moats Miller (*Protestantism and Social Issues*) have documented the continued ecclesiastical commitment to industrial and labor reform after World War I, the date traditionally assigned for the demise of the social gospel. As evidence they cite the important role played by the Interchurch World Movement in the great steel strike of 1919 (see also Charles Harvey, "Rockefeller and Interchurch"), the influence of Reinhold Niebuhr and other members of the League of Christian Socialists in the political and economic discussions of the interwar years, and the influential legislative campaigns of the Federal Council of Churches against the open-shop "American Plan," against the twelve-hour day in the steel industry, and for the Child Labor Amendment to the Constitution.

Recent historiography has also revised older presuppositions (classically expressed in W. A. Visser 't Hooft, *Background*) that informed much of the earlier study of the social gospel. It has questioned the uniqueness of the social gospel as an American phenomenon (William R. Hutchison, "Americanness"); it has traced the important personal and institutional ties that linked the religious movement for industrial reform to American political movements, especially to Progressivism (Robert M. Crunden, "George D. Herron"; Sidney Fine, "Forerunner of Progressivism"; Ferenc M. Szasz, "Progressive Clergy");

and it has nuanced the story of social reform by viewing the social gospel from the vantage of those outside its decision-making elite: the urban poor (Nathan I. Huggins, *Protestants Against Poverty*), blacks (Ralph E. Luker, "Failure of Racial Reform"), and northern and southern women (Janet F. Fishburn, *The Fatherhood of God* and John Patrick McDowell, *Social Gospel in the South,* respectively). A full-scale study of the social gospel incorporating these important but neglected stories into the narrative history remains to be written, although Ronald C. White and C. Howard Hopkins's *Social Gospel* has adumbrated a satisfying overarching schema in a collection of edited primary sources.

The very success of the social gospel's message within the mainline American churches—centered on a "Kingdom of God theology" that stressed the continuity of the sacred and the secular—thus ironically contributed to the "secularization" of the religious search for social justice. If the ecclesiastical and governmental instrumentalities were *partners* in the quest for social justice in human society (Samuel Zane Batten, *The Christian State*), then both the church and the state provided equally legitimate spheres for religious activity aimed at realizing the social ethics of Jesus. The religious vision of a just political and social order, advanced with such urgency and cogency by the social gospel, soon found ready supporters outside the Protestant mainstream, and even outside the ecclesiastical sphere entirely. Indeed, the advocates of a social Christianity who sought the destruction of the wall separating "sacred" and "secular" areas of life succeeded far better than they knew.

By the end of the nineteenth century, both the Catholic and the Jewish communities in America had broadened and reshaped the mainstream (Protestant) quest for social justice by seeking a larger role in the legislative and juridical processes that defined church-state relations in the emerging industrial culture (part 1, section b). The new political and social activism that resulted was due in part to the large numbers from both immigrant religious communities in the industrial working class; but it was also due to venerable traditions of social teaching evinced in papal social encyclicals and in the prophetic commitment to social justice, a commitment of special importance in the American tradition of Reform Judaism.

The Jewish social gospel—that socially active version of Reform Judaism preached by Isaac Wise, David Einhorn, and Kaufmann Kohler, and embodied in the Pittsburgh Platform—is especially important in considering legislative efforts relating to labor arbitration, workers' compensation, and the formation of labor unions. Egal Feldman's study ("Social Gospel and the Jews") has outlined important areas where further research in this largely neglected field would be most fruitful. But given the overwhelming working-class character of American Judaism during the critical period of industrialization (1865–1917), the most penetrating studies of Jewish political and social activism have tended to focus, not on the Reform Jewish tradition of social thought, but rather on the immigrant labor movement, especially on the garment workers' unions, where Jews quickly gained important leadership roles.

A conservative, European-based social philosophy put American Catholics out of step with liberal industrial reform efforts in the pre-1880 period, but during the last decade of the century a distinctive Catholic social gospel took shape in response to radically new social and industrial conditions. Large-scale participation of Catholics in labor organizations like the Knights of Labor; the new liberal, clerical leadership of James Gibbons, John Ireland, and Edward McGlynn; and the publication in 1891 of the papal social encyclical *Rerum Novarum*, all enabled American Catholics to recast their conservative, individualistic response to the problems of industrialization into a new industrial and political activism. No longer feeling themselves to be aliens in a strange land, Catholic "Americanist" leaders offered a distinctively Catholic social gospel (Gibbons, "The Church and the Republic") to coreligionists ready to contribute to the religious quest for a just society.

The best of the institutional histories narrating the considerable legislative efforts of American Catholics in this period are James E. Roohan's work on *Catholics and the Social Question* and Donald Gavin's study of the National Conference of Catholic Charities from 1910 to World War I. Roohan's work documents the growing awareness among church leaders of the inadequacy of the charity phase of reform, while Gavin offers a more detailed and satisfying account of the most important official agency of the Catholic social gospel.

Aaron Abell, in two important studies (*American Catholicism and Social Action* and a collection of edited primary sources, *American Catholic Thought*), sought to relate Catholic social and political reform efforts to larger social and industrial patterns. Both of these works remain the best introductions to Catholic reform efforts, surpassed in the literature only by a much briefer but historiographically more sophisticated essay offered by Jay P. Dolan ("Towards A Social Gospel"). Dolan's essay, the best single interpretive treatment of the subject, provides an excellent introduction to more detailed studies of Catholic political and legislative reform efforts: to David J. O'Brien's superb study of Catholic involvement and support in the New Deal's efforts at industrial and social reform (*Catholics and Social Reform*); to Philip Gleason's perceptive, revisionist work on the conservative German Catholic community and its involvement in the political and industrial order (*Conservative*

Reformers); to Francis L. Broderick's biography (*Right Reverend New Dealer*) of John Ryan, the most influential figure involved in Catholic social reform, whose studies of the American economic system formed the basis for the epochal *Bishops' Program of Social Reconstruction.*

The most prophetic movement for industrial and political reform to emerge from within the American Catholic church was the Catholic Worker Movement, which championed labor's cause in numerous political and legislative battles. William D. Miller's studies of both the Worker movement itself (*A Harsh and Dreadful Love*) and of its most important figure, Dorothy Day, offer important details, but lack both critical distance and a scholarly apparatus. Mel Piehl's superb study of the movement (*Breaking Bread*) provides both a lucid history of its efforts for social reform and a provocative framework for understanding subsequent Catholic radicalism, utilizing the radical movement within the Protestant social gospel (Christian socialism) as a model for understanding its Catholic analogue.

Charles J. Tull's study of the most controversial Catholic figure involved in the political and economic crusades of depression-age America, *Father Coughlin and the New Deal,* has offered a fine narrative account of that priest's radio crusade for social and industrial reform, and of Coughlin's ambiguous relationship with New Deal economic legislation, although Alan Brinkley's work (*Voices of Protest*) provides the most satisfying analysis of Coughlin's National Union for Social Justice, an organization that wielded considerable political power during the early Roosevelt era.

The history of the American labor movement illustrates both the ubiquity of the religious impulse in social and political movements for industrial reform, and the complexity of church-state relationships during the industrializing era (part 1, section c). The explicit "mission to labor" undertaken by mainline churchmen (Gladden, *Working People*), as well as the more diffuse, non-institutional religious impulses within the labor movement operating apart from (and to some extent opposed to) institutional religion (*Mother Jones Speaks*), witness to the perduring power of the prophetic vision of social justice in a secularizing industrial culture. But those self-same spiritual energies that found expression in the labor movement, and the highly charged religious imagery that marked the rhetoric of labor leaders, also witness to a subtle but significant shift in the relative importance of secular and political (over against ecclesiastical) institutions as the locus for reform energies and as the vehicle for prophetic witness within the culture.

Liston Pope in *Millhands and Preachers* offered the classic study documenting the fears of mainline ecclesiastical churchpeople that institutional religion was losing its working-class constituency, fears that account in part for the ecclesiastical mission to the emerging labor movement. Similarly, the fear of precisely such an eventuality among the largely working-class Catholic population constituted the central theme in the story offered by Henry J. Browne of the role of Catholic leaders, especially of James Gibbons, in supporting early unionizing efforts (*Knights of Labor*). More recently, the works of Neil Betten (*Catholic Activism* and "Urban Catholicism") have offered a similar "ecclesiastical fear of Marx" interpretation for many of the Catholic efforts among the labor movement.

Far more important to the labor missionaries of the mainline churches than these cultural and political fears, however, was the ancient Judeo-Christian commitment to social justice, a commitment that transcended sacred/secular boundaries. George H. Nash ("Charles Stelzle") and John L. Shover ("Gladden and Labor") have explored the efforts of two of the more important labor missionaries to politicize the institutionally religious on labor issues and to catechize non-institutional Christians within the labor movement. Nash's study of Stelzle (the "apostle of labor"), especially, brings together political, industrial, and ecclesiastical concerns in a successful synthesis. A. David Bos's study of Gladden's battles against nativist fears ("Gladden Versus Anti-Catholicism"), so closely linked to that figure's labor efforts, similarly offers a new approach to issues concerning the interplay of religion and culture that combines the social gospel, labor history, and ecumenical studies.

Aaron Abell's study of the American reception of the papal social encyclical *Rerum Novarum*, which officially declared the Roman Catholic church's commitment to social and industrial reform ("Reception of Leo XIII's Encyclical"), remains essential reading (forty years later) for understanding the American Catholic labor crusade, a crusade that combined catechesis, political lobbying, and an overt mission to union leaders. Henry J. Browne ("Terence Powderly") and David J. O'Brien ("Catholics and Organized Labor"), in two classic essays, have recounted the important and intimate discussions between labor leaders and church officials, during the 1880s and 1930s respectively, that led to important, indeed decisive, ecclesiastical political support in the strikes, boycotts, and unionizing efforts that marked those two critical decades.

The notable success of the Catholic mission to labor was due in significant measure to the efforts of "labor priests" like Peter Yorke, Cornelius O'Leary, and, most famously, Peter Dietz, who mediated between the economic, industrial concerns of union workers and the political, social, and ecclesiastical concerns of church leaders. Joseph F. Brusher's engaging account of Yorke (*Consecrated Thunderbolt*—an excellent study despite its title), William B. Flaherty's essay on O'Leary and the Knights of Labor ("Clergyman and Labor

Progress"), and Mary Harrita Fox's classic study of Dietz (*Labor Priest*), provide valuable historical data.

Jewish efforts for social justice have been more satisfactorily documented in this area than in any other, perhaps because of the widespread Jewish support for, and participation in, the labor movement. Hyman Berman ("Jewish Labor Movement") has provided a discerning if narrowly focused account of the unionizing efforts of Jews in the "needle trades," resulting in the organization of Jewish fraternal labor orders. More satisfying in their consideration of broader political and cultural issues are the studies by Selig Perlman ("America and Jewish Labor Movement") and J. B. S. Hardman ("Jewish and Non-Jewish Influences"), which offer sophisticated critical studies of the American and foreign political, economic, and industrial influences that shaped the Jewish labor movement, and of the resulting cultural impact of that movement on America. Elias Tcherikower's monographic study of the *Early Jewish Labor Movement*, while more detailed and documented than the work of Hardman and Perlman, fails to achieve their broad scope and critical sophistication.

Perhaps the most famous and dramatic instance of the interaction of religion and labor was the Interchurch World Movement's Commission of Inquiry, headed by a Methodist bishop, Francis McConnell, that investigated the 1919 steel strike. The report of the commission, which found for the strikers and against the United States Steel Corporation, was widely viewed at the time, and generally has been viewed since, as a significant moral and popular victory for the churches, legitimizing in the eyes of the labor movement ecclesiastical claims to cultural hegemony. Walter W. Benjamin ("McConnell and the Great Steel Strike") and Philip C. Ensley ("Interchurch Movement and the Steel Strike") offer useful studies of the commission, while Eldon Ernst's larger study (*Moment of Truth*), if making somewhat broader historical claims for the decisiveness of the dramatic series of events, nonetheless provides valuable detailed information on central labor and religious figures involved in the strike and the commission.

Balancing, and to some extent supplanting, this earlier historiographic preoccupation with ecclesiastical involvement in labor issues, however, is a growing body of scholarly literature that traces the broader, non-institutional religious impulses that informed the rhetoric, symbolism, and drawing power of the labor movement, studies that have emerged since Herbert Gutman's seminal article on "Protestantism and the Labor Movement." Gutman illustrated both in that essay and in his more recent *Work, Culture and Society* that diffuse, non-institutional, religious impulses linked the crusade-like character of the labor movement with earlier evangelical reform efforts, whose spiritual fervor was not replicated in secular groups like labor unions. Much of the scholarly literature since Gutman has documented this important shift in cultural authority, offering case studies of the most notable figures involved in labor issues. Among the best of these studies are John R. Aiken and James R. McDonnell's study of "Rauschenbusch and Labor Reform," illustrating how the labor movement rejected the liberal piety of the social gospel as preached by Rauschenbusch as "hopelessly middle-class," while incorporating much of its rhetoric and religious imagery into the movement's political and social crusades. Likewise, Theresa Corcoran has illustrated how Vida Scudder ("Scudder and the Lawrence Textile Strike") appropriated explicitly religious principles into her political efforts to end a disastrous textile strike.

The cultural upheaval following the Civil War, engendered by industrialization as well as by new demographic and intellectual challenges, led to painful schisms within America's previously united evangelical establishment. If part of that establishment came to support the new socialized gospel as the most effective means for retaining cultural (and thus political) hegemony in the emerging industrial society, a significant number of evangelicals rejected its corporate spirituality and ostensibly "secular theology" as a betrayal of the faith once delivered, whatever its effectiveness in retaining political and social influence for the churches. These new defenders of the "old-time religion" sought to recapture evangelicalism's earlier hegemonic status by emphasizing its revivalistic, individualistic features. Conservative evangelical leaders like Isaac M. Haldeman (*Professor Rauschenbusch*) evinced an ambivalent attitude to the pluralist, "post-Protestant" culture emerging in America. Haldeman and his fellow conservatives claimed *true* insider status in American culture while betraying profound fears of marginalization as outsiders in an industrialized corporate state. Their conservative evangelical piety failed to recapture the social and political halls of power, and their fate, marked by social and political marginalization as well as by intellectual and emotional disaffection with the course of mainstream America, was emblematic of the shift of cultural authority marking the period (part 2).

George M. Marsden, in the best single study of religious conservatism between the Civil War and the Scopes trial (*Fundamentalism and American Culture*), has offered the most convincing interpretation of the conservative Protestant social and political response to industrial society, a response of profound ambivalence from former insiders now excluded from the religious, political, and cultural mainstream. Thus Marsden sees as constituent, related parts of the same complex story the individualistic, world-renouncing piety of Dwight L. Moody, the evangelical commitment to social reform and political activism expressed in groups like the International Christian Workers Association with their "Holy Spirit in Life and Work" conferences, and the

industrial schools and institutional churches of Stephen Tyng, Russell Conwell, and George A. Gordon.

The best bibliographic introduction to the complex issues surrounding the
conservative evangelical response to industrialism are the essays of Robert
R. Mathieson ("Evangelicals and the Age of Reform"), George Marsden ("The
Gospel of Wealth"), James F. Findlay (Preface, *Moody*), and Donald W.
Dayton (*Evangelical Heritage*). These are penetrating and balanced evalua-
tions of the historical literature published since Timothy Smith's and William
McLoughlin's earlier seminal works.

Perhaps the most complex issue addressed by this literature involves the
question of the "great reversal," that point at which evangelicals turned away
from their older social and political activism toward cultural and political
quietism. First studied at length by sociologist David Moberg (*Great Reversal*),
this issue has been addressed in a number of recent works: Norris Magnuson
(*Salvation in the Slums*) has documented the massive efforts of evangelical
missions to reach the lives of the industrial poor in the 1870s and 1880s;
Timothy P. Weber (*Living in the Shadow*) offers cogent evidence against the
traditional allegation that premillennialists were inherently apolitical and
predisposed to antireform sentiments; Ferenc Szasz (*Divided Mind*), less
convincingly, sees the years from 1901 to 1917 as a time of triumph for
conservative evangelicals, during which they sponsored large campaigns for
social and industrial reform; Robert D. Linder ("Resurgence") sees a significant return to social and political activism on the part of evangelicals after
1925.

The challenges posed by industrialism to the largely agrarian culture of
nineteenth-century America effected changes in the political and legal life of
the nation that proved to be as dramatic as those in its re-
ligious/denominational life. Indeed, due in part to the massive, culture-wide
scale of the new challenges, social and industrial reform impulses that had
previously found their locus within denominationally bounded institutions
and movements, deriving from them much of their fervor and social legitimization, increasingly came to be expressed in political and social reform movements that sought broader, nondenominational, bases of support (part 3).

Social and political movements like the Farmers' Alliance, the People's
party, and the congeries of figures and movements known collectively as
Progressivism, grew out of and drew upon impulses as profoundly religious
as those expressed in the various forms of the social gospel. But if these
quasi-religious political movements continued to draw on earlier evangelical
impulses and rhetoric, the heaven they envisioned resembled more the cor-

porate state than the Kingdom of God. The social and political reforms sponsored by the new science of sociology likewise grew largely out of traditional
religious concerns, and many, if not most, of its early practitioners viewed
their efforts as overtly ministerial and missionary; but by the early twentieth
century sociologists were offering their data for reformist platforms in em-
phatically secular terms, viewing the promise of a better society as a legitimate end in itself. The rhetoric, symbols, and ideals of the prohibition
crusade have long been recognized as both implicitly and explicitly religious;
what has only recently been appreciated is the degree to which that ostensibly retrograde political movement incorporated both religious and progressive concerns into its work, seeking legal and political reforms which
would enable people to choose more easily the morally good, and industrially
safe, path.

The major political, economic, and industrial reform crusades of the first
two decades of the twentieth century were thus direct heirs of earlier nineteenth-century movements, inheriting their implicitly religious rhetoric and
symbols. But the economic and political goals of these newer movements
came to be expressed in ever more secular, non-theological language, focusing on the state itself, rather than the church, as the best vehicle for achieving
the ancient vision of social justice.

The people of the American West and the South were especially hard hit
when the process of industrialization shattered their rural, agrarian culture.
The socio-political response of these areas was a "peoples' movement" most
commonly known as populism, the "Great Third Party" of the 1890s (part 3,
section a). It would be difficult to overemphasize the degree to which this
political movement retained the atmosphere and energy of earlier religious
crusades. Drawn from the earlier Farmers' Alliance and Grange movements,
and from the works of urban intellectuals like Edward Bellamy, Henry
George, and Henry Demarest Lloyd, populism was endowed with an explicitly religious language and symbolic world view, so that its political rallies
were likened, by both supporters and opponents, to camp meetings, its organizational structure was consciously copied from Methodist church government, and its local meetings invariably opened with "Jesus, Lover of my
Soul."

But the legislative and economic crusades undertaken by the People's
party elicited only partial support from denominations fearful of political
radicalism; and if this did not appreciably weaken the religious flavor of the
resulting political battles, it did lead committed populists to define their
political and economic crusades apart from, and to some extent opposed to,

denominational concerns. Populism thus emerged as the first secular political movement dedicated to addressing the social problems caused by industrialization.

The classic work dealing with the social and political reform efforts that arose in response to the industrial challenges of the period, of which populism was an important but by no means solitary example, is Richard Hofstadter's *Age of Reform*, which reviews such efforts between the Civil War and World War II. Hofstadter's book remains even today the historiographical benchmark for subsequent scholarly studies, and his work provides valuable historical and bibliographical information on the major figures, issues, and political campaigns that marked the age. But Hofstadter has been widely criticized by scholars for advancing a now largely discredited hermeneutical framework of "status strain" for explaining the reform efforts of this period, and his treatment of populism must be balanced by other accounts of the movement, among the best of which remain the classic studies of Samuel Hayes (*Response to Industrialization*) and John D. Hicks (*The Populist Revolt*).

Hicks's work, the pioneering study of populism, remains in many respects the most satisfying and balanced introduction to the movement, although his book has more recently been expanded and nuanced by Carleton Beals (*The Great Revolt*) and Norman Pollack (*The Populist Response*), both of whom offer good narrative accounts. These works can be supplemented by a number of recent studies of populism that address the complex nature of the movement's political campaigns: Peter H. Argersinger ("Pentecostal Politics") offers a convincing interpretation of Kansas populism as both a "movement of religious people and a religious movement of the people" (p. 24), fulfilling socially the structural and functional roles of the quiescent evangelical churches in the face of widespread social evil. Karel D. Bicha ("A Common Pietism") has suggestively argued that what bound the "prairie radicals" of populism together was less a political platform than the common religious experience of pietistic Protestantism, an experience that was social rather than theological, and which thus endowed the campaigns of the People's party with a spiritual legitimization previously confined to ecclesiastical movements.

Demographic studies linking populist voting patterns to denominational affiliation have sought to document the specific ways in which religion affected political behavior. Both pioneering works in this area—the studies by Richard Jensen (*Winning of the Midwest*) and by Paul Kleppner (*Cross of Culture*)—utilize a problematic methodological distinction between religious "liturgicals" (Jensen) or "ritualists" (Kleppner) on the one hand and "pietists" on the other, to trace the influence of religious belief on voting behavior. Both Jensen and Kleppner argue that the populist "gospel" was closely tied to an evangelical, pietist background, thus linking their work, distantly, to that of Hofstadter. Building on the earlier scholarship of Jensen and Kleppner, Robert W. Cherny (*Populism, Progressivism*) has convincingly demonstrated how religious affiliation provided the organizational pattern for political behavior in Nebraska between 1885 and 1918, in the process adumbrating a new model for church-state interaction during the industrializing era: Cherny integrates in a more sophisticated and critical manner than Jensen or Kleppner the concerns of intellectual history with demographic methods to uncover how ethno-religious beliefs provided, not just a standard of behavior for Sunday mornings, but also a way of organizing the social patterns that profoundly affected political behavior.

Recent studies in intellectual history, focused on populist theoreticians like Edward Bellamy and Henry George, and on populist political leaders like William Jennings Bryan, have likewise uncovered the intimate interaction between religious and political reform impulses as these were played out in the populist movement (see especially Eileen W. Lindner's "Redemptive Politic of Henry George"). Perhaps the best single study of this religio-political interaction in the populist intellectual tradition is John L. Thomas's *Alternative America*, an intriguing analysis of the adversary tradition of American political and social reform as that tradition was manifested in the careers of Bellamy, George, and Lloyd. Building on older studies that documented the religious motivations for social reform among these seminal populist thinkers (Joseph L. Blau, "Bellamy's Religious Motivation for Reform," and Fred Nicklason, "Henry George: Social Gospeller"), Thomas sees the populism advocated by these three writers of the most important apologias for the populist cause (*Looking Backward, Progress and Poverty*, and *Wealth Against Commonwealth*, respectively) as "a blend of producerist advice and Christian ethics, not so much political directive as moral imperative to restore the vitality of the faithful" (p. 312). Thomas's introduction to the 1967 reprint of Bellamy's work likewise provides a valuable interpretive framework within which to read that tract.

The single most important political figure in the populist pantheon was William Jennings Bryan, the "Political Evangelist" as Paolo E. Coletta labeled him. Coletta's biography, focused on Bryan's "pre-Fundamentalist" political career, provides an excellent narrative account of the Great Commoner's populist campaigns, but must be supplemented by Paul W. Glad's broader if less critical study (*The Trumpet Soundeth*). Glad's work, although lacking Coletta's scholarly apparatus, nonetheless reveals more clearly a man for whom politics, social reform, and religion were inextricably joined. The 1896 populist presidential campaign, the political event that is the focus for Jenson and Kleppner as well as for Coletta and Glad, provides an especially dramatic national event through which to understand the nexus of religious, political, and reformist impulses that underlay the populist cause. George B. Tindall's *Populist Reader,* which includes speeches delivered by Bryan and other populist leaders during that important presidential campaign, offers some interesting selections illustrating this multileveled crusade.

The Progressive Era reveals in dramatic fashion the profoundly religious sources of the legal and political search for social justice undertaken by the "state" in the industrializing era, as well as the complex interaction of spiritual, legislative, and bureaucratic energies in the cause of social and economic reform between the last decade of the nineteenth century and the American entry into war in 1917 (part 3, section b). As both John Buenker (*Urban Liberalism*) and J. Joseph Huthmacher ("Urban Liberalism") have convincingly argued, progressivism was less an organized movement than a congeries of reformers and movements that supported "good government" causes like municipal reform, the referendum, and the recall, and that militated for the replacement of the ideology of laissez-faire with the cultural ideal of a responsible social and economic order enforced by the state. These disparate reform impulses received a collective identity and designation from the Progressive party, which in turn lent its name to the first dozen years or so of the present century.

But if most historians agree as to the movement's designation, they have differed sharply on how to approach the reform tradition that ostensibly united it: Richard Hofstadter (*Age of Reform*) sees the movement as, at heart, a revolt against the new industrial discipline, led by the "victims of an upheaval in status" caused by industrial organization. Samuel Hayes (*Response to Industrialization*), and Robert Wiebe (*Search for Order*) have proposed revisionist variations on this "organizational synthesis" approach, presenting more complex sociological models and stressing the interaction of industrialism and urbanism in creating the progressive ethos. And in an intriguing variation on this "flight to corporatism" interpretation, James Weinstein (*The Corporate Ideal*) posits the business community itself as the proud parent of the powerful if sometimes unruly offspring that grew up to become the positive state.

But the various social, political, and economic reforms which the disparate progressivist groups called upon the state to sponsor were as intimately related to the older evangelical reform agenda as to an emerging "modern" organizational ethos. That portion of the middle class that had supported "social Christianity" recognized similar reformist impulses in the municipal crusades of Samuel "Golden Rule" Jones in Toledo and of Washington Gladden on the Columbus (Ohio) city council, as well as in Theodore Roosevelt's

"Square Deal" and "Bull Moose" platforms, impulses made explicit in the 1912 Progressive party theme song "Onward Christian Soldiers," and in Roosevelt's own call to action, "We stand at Armageddon and we battle for the Lord." For this politically powerful and socially concerned section of the middle class, progressivism provided a convenient ideological bridge for connecting the increasingly secular quest for social justice in a pluralist society with earlier, explicitly religious, reform crusades.

David W. Noble (*Paradox of Progressive Thought*) has demonstrated the continuing belief in moral absolutes, in spiritual progress, and in theism within an evolutionary framework, that characterized the thinking of progressives like Jane Addams, Frederic Howe, and Woodrow Wilson. Likewise, William McLoughlin's essay on "Pietism and the American Character" and Dewey W. Grantham's on "The Progressive Era and the Reform Tradition" have noted the degree to which the legislative and legal crusades undertaken by political leaders during the progressive period resulted from the union of older, evangelical reform impulses with newer emphases on scientific organization and "rational technique" in the cause of social justice. Similarly, Clyde Griffen's "The Progressive Ethos" and Jean B. Quandt's "Secularization of Postmillennialism" present progressivism as essentially a "postmillennial ethos," delivering the "sensitive conscience of American Protestantism during its most expansive and optimistic era" (Griffen, p. 148) into the safekeeping of the state. Both argue convincingly that the progressive appeal for political and social reform was effective among Americans with no predisposition toward reform precisely because its vision and rhetoric derived from the Protestant values so pervasive among the native-born; both likewise argue that the juxtaposition of practical, piecemeal approaches to political and social reform with a religious, semi-pietistic vision of democracy—both of which elements characterized the positions of a significant number of progressives—constitutes the most satisfactory test for membership in that notoriously amorphous fellowship.

The joint effort of John Buenker, John Burnham, and Robert Crunden entitled simply *Progressivism* provides the most sophisticated and balanced treatment of the various emphases that informed the progressive ethos. These three scholars organize their respective essays around the thesis that the progressive alignment on political and social issues constituted a shifting coalition of diverse interests whose fragility was evinced in their plan to meet the *corporate* challenges of industrialization, urbanization, and immigration with legislation that sought to improve *individual* morality. Thus the progressive agenda witnessed to both the convergence of an older, individualistic religious ethos with the new political need to meet the corporate challenges of industrialization, and to the inherent tension between the concern for the common voter and the corporate vision that characterized the movement generally.

More recently Robert Crunden has expanded his essay in the above work into a full-length and engaging but somewhat overargued study of the religious impulses behind the social and political reform platforms of Jane Addams, Robert LaFollette, Theodore Roosevelt, Woodrow Wilson, and other progressive political crusaders (*Ministers of Reform*). Along similar lines, Jean Quandt's study of the works of Frederic Howe, John Dewey, Franklin Giddings, and other progressive intellectuals (*From the Small Town to the Great Community*) argues that the small-town, evangelical Protestant background of many of the "progressive communitarians" provided the communitarian ideal sought in much of the progressive legislative reform effort.

Since the work of Hugh C. Bailey (*Liberalism in the New South*), Kenneth K. Bailey (*Southern White Protestantism*) and John Lee Eighmy ("Religious Liberalism in the South"), scholars have explored the previously ignored economic and political reform traditions of the South, traditions embodied in a distinctively regional form of progressivism. E. Charles Chatfield ("Southern Sociological Congress") and J. Wayne Flynt ("Southern Baptists and Reform") have documented the ways in which evangelical impulses found expression in such southern reform efforts as the Prison Reform Association, the Child Labor Committee, the Southern Methodist and Southern Baptist Temperance Leagues, and, especially, in the Southern Sociological Congress. Scholarly consideration of the latter organization reveals the unmistakable influence of social gospel ideas on the progressive movement of that area, and the ways in which legislative and political efforts claimed the religious legitimacy of earlier evangelical crusades. Merwin Swanson's study of the Country Life Movement has explored how many of the reform ideals and programs originating in urban, industrial contexts were broadened to transform rural and southern churches into community centers, part of whose social and political function was to militate for local public health legislation, for the promotion of scientific agricultural techniques, and for municipal and state legislative reforms.

Studies of the major progressive political and social leaders are voluminous, but among those most helpful in tracing the complex interaction of religio-cultural impulses in the political and legal battles of the period are Arthur S. Link's study of Woodrow Wilson ("Presbyterian in Government") and John C. Farrell's monograph on Jane Addams (*Beloved Lady*), both of which provide excellent introductions to the complex social and personal tensions that brought disparate reform impulses together in the lives of these two important figures. The bibliographies (annotated and otherwise) in the works of Buenker et al., Crunden, Chandler, and Davis provide excellent introductory guides to major works dealing with church-state issues in the lives of Theodore Roosevelt, Charles Evans Hughes, Robert LaFollette, and other progressive political figures.

Long before the passage of the Volstead Act, the "dry crusade" spoke the language of social and humanitarian amelioration dear to the hearts of American social and religious reformers (part 3, section c). At least since the Age of Jackson, temperance movements had campaigned with abolitionism, prison reform, woman's rights, and child labor legislation for a reformation of American society along the lines of a millennial vision. Indeed, with the founding of the Prohibition party and the Anti-Saloon League after the Civil War, the explicitly religious and the explicitly political components of that vision joined forces to effect tangible legislative embodiment. Both populist and progressive political leaders recognized a kindred discourse in prohibition rhetoric, and the social gospel granted the temperance impulse official status in 1912, when the Social Creed of the Churches was amended to include an explicit commitment to the "protection of the individual and of society from the economic and moral waste of the liquor traffic."

But it was the "great experiment" launched by the Eighteenth Amendment that offered the clearest and most dramatic instance of the confluence of religious, social, and political reform ideals in concrete legislative form. The passage of that amendment in 1919 witnessed to the close cooperation between religious and secular reform groups to abolish the liquor traffic, thus eliminating, it was commonly believed, the primary cause of political vice, economic inefficiency, moral dissoluteness, and industrial accidents.

For thirty years after the repeal of the amendment in 1933, an entire generation of scholars viewed the prohibition interlude as a sanctimonious interference with basic individual liberties by church people crossing the line into state issues, and as an eccentric preoccupation with an issue that was, at best, marginal to the real problems of a rapidly industrializing and urbanizing society. This historiographic line became, in fact, quite sophisticated, as evinced in Joseph Gusfield's *Symbolic Crusade*. Gusfield utilized Hofstadter's "status strain" interpretive framework to present the temperance movement as essentially a symbolic crusade, through which middle-class Protestants sought to assert (symbolically) their cultural hegemony in a post-Protestant culture. In a similar manner, Andrew Sinclair (*Prohibition*) interpreted that movement, in the phrase Hofstadter used in the preface, as the "final assertion of the rural Protestant mind against an urban, polyglot culture" (p. ix). John Buenker ("Illinois and Prohibition") likewise posited social and religious status strain issues as the heart of the prohibition struggle in Illinois, documenting his thesis with a demographic study of the ethno-religious backgrounds of legislators and their constituents. For these scholars, the prohibition experiment was indeed the result of religious influences in the political sphere—inappropriate influences whose destruction of the wall between church and state resulted in political and social disaster.

But a number of recent studies have revised these earlier interpretations in significant ways; among the best are the works of James H. Timberlake (*Prohibition and the Progressive Movement*), John Burnham ("New Perspectives"), and K. Austin Kerr ("Organizing for Reform"). These revisionist scholars have rescued the prohibition crusade and the temperance movement from their previous association with bigoted cranks, and have (largely successfully) fought to place them within the venerable social reform tradition, a tradition wherein religious and social reformers worked cooperatively for political redress to industrially inspired ills.

Timberlake argued that the overwhelming political support given to prohibition by the progressives was largely because they perceived it as a scientific remedy to many of the problems of industrial society: as an attack on the monopolistic tendencies of the liquor industry; as an attempt to eliminate a major cause of industrial accidents and worker inefficiency; and as a concrete way of preventing irrational economic behavior by both workers and employers. And while Timberlake's study failed to do full justice to the religious impulses in the prohibition movement, neglecting as well the positive role played by immigrants and non-Protestants, it nonetheless signaled a significant shift in historiographic temper: the religious and the progressive reformist impulses of the age were no longer necessarily opposed, and the "retrograde" prohibition movement itself now appeared in a new light.

Like Timberlake, Kerr noted that the application of scientific bureaucratic techniques to the problems of industrialization—an important characteristic of the progressive program—was central to the organization and political tactics of the largely ecclesiastically sponsored and clerically led Anti-Saloon League, a group that achieved considerable political power in several states. John Burnham's essay ties the religious reform impulses in the prohibition movement together with progressive concerns regarding the increasing use of machinery in industry: the intemperate worker, once merely inefficient, now became a menace both to himself and to others. Among the most engaging features of Burnham's article is his analysis of the conclusions drawn from Martha Bruere's famous 1927 industrial survey, which documented how prohibition had substantially improved working conditions among low-income Americans.

Norman Clark (*Deliver Us From Evil*) offers a synthetic interpretation of prohibition as a rational response to a genuine social evil, a response in which middle-class Protestants took the leading role. But Clark fails to consider the non-Protestant movements that aided the political fight, movements like the Catholic Total Abstinence Union described by Jean Bland (*Hibernian Crusade*), for whom crusading for temperance was as Catholic as going to Sunday mass.

In many respects Jack S. Blocker's account of the movement (*Retreat From Reform*) offers the most satisfying synthetic treatment incorporating much of recent scholarship. Blocker interprets the prohibition movement as a largely urban crusade dedicated to bringing moral order to a socially and culturally divided society, a crusade inspired by religious impulses but also incorporating wider reform traditions. Blocker argues that prohibitionism initially appealed to both evangelically inclined professional people and to former populists on explicitly religious grounds, and that it achieved in leaders like Frances Willard a broader constituency through offering its program as a viable alternative to socialism.

Ruth B. Bordin's superb study of the Women's Christian Temperance Union (WCTU) (*Women and Temperance*) offers a discerning account of the most politically active and effective woman's organization of the nineteenth century, and begins to fill a critical gap in the historiography in this area. Indeed, given the crucial political importance of women in the temperance and prohibition movements through pressure groups like the WCTU, further studies of the political efforts of women's home missionary and reformatory societies are badly needed.

Biographies of major figures in the temperance and prohibition movements are plentiful, although they often display uncritical hagiographic tendencies. Among the more perceptive studies are Virginius Dabney's detailed but underdocumented study (*Dry Messiah*) of James Cannon, the Methodist bishop who played a controversial role in the political campaigns of the Anti-Saloon League, and Mary Earhart's perceptive study (*From Prayers to Politics*) of Frances Willard, the woman who fashioned the WCTU into a vigorous advocacy organization for women's rights, social reform, and progressivist legislation.

The political and social reform crusades of the industrializing era that sought a more humane and equitable society were chiefly concerned with finding out the truth about how society worked, and on the basis of that knowledge sponsoring legislative programs for meeting the needs of a newly emerging corporate society. But by the end of the nineteenth century, the increased concern over the application of "rational technique" and scientific standards to the study of social problems and their amelioration had led to the emergence, out of a largely amateur and ministerial area of study, of the new "social sciences," now ostensibly independent of the ministry and organized along standardized, professional lines (part 3, section d). Indeed, many social reformers (both clerical and lay) felt that such a move toward empirical standards by these young sciences would increase their political utility in furthering legislative and judicial reform efforts. Especially in the cases of the new sciences of sociology and economics, however, the line between the ministerial and the scientific character of the profession remained unclear for several decades, during which time cleric-scientists like Francis Greenwood Peabody regularly published "sociological reports" offering a "scientific" basis for ameliorative legislation, while secular social scientists like the "St. Augustine of the American cult of science," Lester Frank Ward, formulated the basic pattern of the American concept of the planned society with the fervor (and the rhetoric) of a theologian.

The essays of Dorothy Ross, "The Development of the Social Sciences," and of Russell R. Dynes, "Sociology as a Religious Movement," provide the best brief introductions to the complex impulses that influenced the early years of the social sciences, especially as those impulses sought ameliorative legislation for social evils. John Rutherford Everett's study of the economic thought of John Bates Clark, Richard T. Ely, and Simon N. Patten (*Religion in Economics*), published four decades ago, still remains the best monographic introduction to the various forces that influenced the emergence of economics as a profession, especially as those forces fought for supremacy in the American Economic Association (AEA). Alfred W. Coats's more recent study ("First Two Decades") provides important details about the political battles that preoccupied the AEA, and is a valuable supplement to Everett's work, although a more comprehensive modern study of this important organization is needed.

The social scientists who most clearly united religious, political, and organizational ideals in their work for society—Ely, Patten, and Ward—have been the objects of numerous studies. Ralph Henry Gabriel's magisterial study of American intellectual history (*Course of American Democratic Thought*) remains the best narrative introduction to the place of these social scientists in the cultural nexus of the Gilded Age, and to their important roles in attempting to provide the scientific data for the legislative and legal reforms of the period; Everett's multiple study, and the individual studies of Daniel M. Fox (*Discovery of Abundance*) and Benjamin G. Rader (*The Academic Mind and Reform*) are less synthetic but more focused.

The emergence of sociology out of the new interest in "social ethics" promoted by Francis Peabody at Harvard and William B. Greene at Princeton Seminary has been described by David B. Potts ("Social Ethics at Harvard") and William H. Swatos ("Faith of Our Fathers"), while J. Graham Morgan ("Sociology and the Social Gospel") has documented the close relation between the social and legislative crusades of the churches and the beginnings of academic sociology. Dorothy Ross's work on G. Stanley Hall (*Psychologist as Prophet*) and R. Jackson Wilson's study of both Hall and James Mark Baldwin (*In Quest of Community*) similarly emphasize the religious impulses informing the social planning and legislative campaigns of social scientists committed to providing data for the construction of a more just society.

BIBLIOGRAPHY

1. ECCLESIASTICAL CLAIMS TO CULTURAL AUTHORITY

a. The Social Gospel

Primary Sources

Batten, Samuel Zane. The Christian State: Democracy and Christianity. Philadelphia: Griffith and Rowland, 1909.

Bliss, William D. P. Encyclopedia of Social Reform. New York: Funk & Wagnalls, 1897.

Ely, Richard T. The Social Aspects of Christianity. New York: T. Y. Crowell & Co., 1889.

Ely, Richard T. The Social Law of Service. New York: Eaton & Mains, 1896.

Gladden, Washington. Applied Christianity: Moral Aspects of Social Questions. Boston: Houghton, Mifflin, 1887.

Herron, George D. The Christian Society. Chicago: Fleming H. Revell, 1894.

Herron, George D. The Christian State: A Political Vision of Christ. New York: T. Y. Crowell and Co., 1895.

Rauschenbusch, Walter. Christianity and the Social Crisis. New York: Macmillan, 1907.

Rauschenbusch, Walter. Christianizing the Social Order. Boston: Pilgrim Press, 1912.

Rauschenbusch, Walter. A Theology for the Social Gospel. New York: Macmillan, 1917.

Sheldon, Charles. In His Steps. New York: Burt Co., 1896.

Strong, Josiah. <u>Our Country; Its Possible Future and Its Present Crisis</u>. New York: American Home Missionary Society, 1885.

Ward, Harry F., ed. <u>The Social Creed of the Churches</u>. New York: Easton & Mains, 1914.

Secondary Works

Abell, Aaron I. <u>The Urban Impact on American Protestantism, 1865-1900</u>. Cambridge: Harvard University Press, 1943.

Carter, Paul A. <u>The Decline and Revival of the Social Gospel</u>. Ithaca, N.Y.: Cornell University Press, 1954.

Carter, Paul A. <u>The Spiritual Crisis of the Gilded Age</u>. DeKalb: Northern Illinois University Press, 1971.

Cross, Robert D. <u>The Church and the City, 1865-1900</u>. Indianapolis: Bobbs-Merrill, 1967.

Crunden, Robert M. "George D. Herron in the 1890's: A New Frame of Reference for the Progressive Era." <u>Annals of Iowa</u> 42 (Fall 1973), 81-113.

Dombrowski, James. <u>The Early Days of Christian Socialism in America</u>. New York: Columbia University Press, 1936.

Dorn, Jacob. <u>Washington Gladden: Prophet of the Social Gospel</u>. Athens: Ohio State University Press, 1967.

Dressner, Richard B. "William Dwight Porter Bliss's Christian Socialism." <u>Church History</u> 47 (March 1978), 66-82.

Fine, Sidney. "Richard T. Ely, Forerunner of Progressivism, 1880-1901." <u>Mississippi Valley Historical Review</u> 37 (March 1951), 599-624.

Fishburn, Janet F. <u>The Fatherhood of God and the Victorian Family: A Study of the Social Gospel in America</u>. Philadelphia: Fortress, 1981.

Gorrell, Donald K. "The Methodist Federation for Social Service and the Social Creed." <u>Methodist History</u> 13 (January 1975), 3-32.

Handy, Robert T. <u>A Christian America: Protestant Hopes and Historical Realities</u>. 2d ed. New York: Oxford University Press, 1984.

Handy, Robert T. "Christianity and Socialism in America, 1900-1920." <u>Church History</u> 21 (March 1952), 39-54.

Handy, Robert T. "George D. Herron and the Kingdom Movement." <u>Church History</u> 19 (June 1950), 97-115.

Handy, Robert T., ed. The Social Gospel in America, 1870-1920.
    New York: Oxford University Press, 1966.

Harvey, Charles. "John D. Rockefeller and the Interchurch
    World Movement, 1919-1920." Church History 51 (June 1982),
    198-209.

Hopkins, C. Howard. The Rise of the Social Gospel in American
    Protestantism. New Haven: Yale University Press, 1940.

Hudson, Winthrop, ed. Walter Rauschenbusch: Selected Writings.
    New York: Paulist Press, 1984.

Huggins, Nathan I. Protestants Against Poverty: Boston's
    Charities, 1879-1900. Westport, Conn.: Greenwood, 1971.

Hutchison, William R. "The Americanness of the Social Gospel."
    Church History 44 (September 1975), 367-381.

Hutchison, William R. The Modernist Impulse in American
    Protestantism. Cambridge: Harvard University Press, 1976.

Jensen, Billie Barnes. "A Social Gospel Experiment in
    Newspaper Reform: Charles M. Sheldon and the Topeka Daily
    Capital." Church History 33 (March 1964), 74-83.

Jordan, Philip D. "Ecumenism, Nationalism and an Evangelical
    Social Gospel, 1883-1900." Chap. 6 in The Evangelical
    Alliance for the United States of America, 1847-1900. New
    York: E. Mellen, 1982.

King, William M. "The Biblical Basis of the Social Gospel."
    In The Bible and Social Reform, edited by Ernest R. Sandeen.
    Philadelphia: Fortress, 1982.

Luker, Ralph E. "The Social Gospel and the Failure of Racial
    Reform, 1877-1898." Church History 46 (March 1977), 80-99.

McDowell, John Patrick. The Social Gospel in the South: The
    Woman's Missionary Movement in the Methodist Episcopal
    Church, South. Baton Rouge: Louisiana State University
    Press, 1982.

Mann, Arthur. Yankee Reformers in the Urban Age. Cambridge:
    Harvard University Press, Belknap Press, 1954.

May, Henry F. The Protestant Churches and Industrial America.
    New York: Harper & Brothers, 1949.

Mead, Sidney E. "American Protestantism Since the Civil War:
    From Americanism to Christianity." Chap. 9 in The Lively
    Experiment: The Shaping of Christianity in America. New
    York: Harper & Row, 1963.

Meyer, Donald B. The Protestant Search for Political Realism, 1919-1941. Berkeley and Los Angeles: University of California Press, 1960.

Meyer, Paul R. "The Fear of Cultural Decline: Josiah Strong's Thought About Reform and Expansion." Church History 42 (September 1973), 396-405.

Miller, Robert Moats. American Protestantism and the Social Issues, 1919-1939. Westport, Conn.: Greenwood, 1958.

Muller, Dorothea. "The Social Philosophy of Josiah Strong: Social Christianity and American Progressivism." Church History 28 (June 1959), 183-200.

Nicholl, Grier. "The Image of the Protestant Minister in the Christian Social Novel." Church History 37 (September 1968), 319-334.

Niebuhr, H. Richard. The Kingdom of God in America. 1935. Reprint. Camden, Conn.: Shoestring, 1956.

Pearson, Ralph L. "Internationalizing the Social Gospel: The Federal Council of Churches and European Protestantism, 1914-1925." Historical Magazine of the Protestant Episcopal Church 52 (September 1983), 275-292.

Schlesinger, Arthur M. "A Critical Period in American Religion, 1875-1900." Massachusetts Historical Society, Proceedings 64 (1930-32), 523-546.

Sharpe, Dores. Walter Rauschenbusch. New York: Macmillan, 1942.

Smylie, James H. "Sheldon's In His Steps: Conscience and Discipleship." Theology Today 32 (April 1975), 32-45.

Szasz, Ferenc M. "The Progressive Clergy and the Kingdom of God." Mid-America 55 (January 1973), 3-20.

Visser 't Hooft, W. A. The Background of the Social Gospel in America. Haarlem, The Netherlands: H. D. Tjeenk Willink & Zoom, 1928.

White, Ronald C., and Hopkins, C. Howard. The Social Gospel: Religion and Reform in Changing America. Philadelphia: Temple University Press, 1976.

b. Newer Cultural Claims:
The Catholic and Jewish Quest for Social Justice

Primary Sources

Bishops' Program of Social Reconstruction: A General Review of
the Program and Survey of Remedies. Washington, D.C.:
National Catholic Welfare Council, 1920.

Coughlin, Charles. A Series of Lectures on Social Justice.
Royal Oak, Mich.: Radio League of the Little Flower, 1935.

Day, Dorothy. Houses of Hospitality. New York: Sheed & Ward,
1939.

Gibbons, James Cardinal. "The Church and the Republic." North
American Review 189 (March 1909), 321-336.

Ryan, John A. Social Reconstruction. New York: Macmillan,
1920.

Ryan, John A., and Millar, Moorehouse F. X. The State and the
Church. New York: Macmillan, 1922.

Secondary Works

Abell, Aaron I. American Catholicism and Social Action: A
Search for Social Justice, 1865-1950. Notre Dame, Ind.:
University of Notre Dame Press, 1963.

Abell, Aaron I., ed. American Catholic Thought on Social
Questions. Indianapolis: Bobbs-Merrill, 1968.

Brinkley, Alan. Voices of Protest: Huey Long, Father Coughlin
and the Great Depression. New York: Knopf, 1982.

Broderick, Francis L. Right Reverend New Dealer: John A. Ryan.
New York: Macmillan, 1963.

Cowett, Mark. "Rabbi Morris Newfield and the Social Gospel:
Theology and Societal Reform in the South." American Jewish
Archives 34 (April 1982), 52-79.

Dolan, Jay. "Towards A Social Gospel." Chap. 12 in The
American Catholic Experience, A History from Colonial Times
to the Present. Garden City, N.Y.: Doubleday, 1985.

Feldman, Egal. "The Social Gospel and the Jews." American
Jewish Historical Quarterly 58 (March 1969), 308-322.

Gavin, Donald. The National Conference of Catholic Charities,
1910-1916. Milwaukee: Bruce Publishing Co., 1962.

Gleason, Philip. The Conservative Reformers: German-American Catholics and the Social Order. Notre Dame, Ind.: University of Notre Dame Press, 1968.

Miller, William D. Dorothy Day, A Biography. San Francisco: Harper & Row, 1982.

Miller, William D. A Harsh and Dreadful Love: Dorothy Day and the Catholic Worker Movement. New York: Liveright, 1973.

O'Brien, David J. American Catholics and Social Reform: The New Deal Years. New York: Oxford University Press, 1968.

Piehl, Mel. Breaking Bread: The Catholic Worker and the Origin of Catholic Radicalism. Philadelphia: Temple University Press, 1982.

Roohan, James E. American Catholics and the Social Question, 1865-1900. New York: Arno Press, 1976.

Tull, Charles J. Father Coughlin and the New Deal. Syracuse, N.Y.: Syracuse University Press, 1965.

c. The Claims of Religion and the Labor Movement

Primary Sources

Ely, Richard T. Studies in the Evolution of Industrial Society. New York: Macmillan, 1903.

Gladden, Washington. Working People and Their Employers. New York: Funk & Wagnalls, 1885.

Interchurch World Movement. Commission of Inquiry, Interchurch World Movement. Report on the Steel Strike of 1919. New York, 1920.

Jones, Mother. Mother Jones Speaks. Collected Writings and Speeches. Edited by Philip S. Foner. New York: Monad Press, 1983.

Keane, John J. "The Encyclical Rerum Novarum." American Catholic Quarterly Review 16 (July 1891), 595-611.

Ryan, John A. A Living Wage. New York: Macmillan, 1906.

Stelzle, Charles. The Gospel of Labor. New York: Fleming H. Revell, 1912.

Secondary Works

Abell, Aaron I. "The Reception of Leo XIII's Labor Encyclical in America, 1891-1919." Review of Politics 7 (October 1945), 464-495.

Aiken, John R., and McDonnell, James R. "Walter Rauschenbusch and Labor Reform: A Social Gospeller's Approach." Labor History 11 (Spring 1970), 131-150.

Benjamin, Walter W. "Bishop Francis J. McConnell and the Great Steel Strike of 1919-1920." In A Miscellany of American Christianity, edited by Stuart Henry, 22-47. Durham, N.C.: Duke University Press, 1963.

Berman, Hyman. "A Cursory View of the Jewish Labor Movement: An Historiographic Survey." American Jewish Historical Quarterly 52 (December 1962), 79-97.

Betten, Neil. Catholic Activism and the Industrial Worker. Gainesville: University Presses of Florida, 1976.

Betten, Neil. "Urban Catholicism and Industrial Reform, 1937-1940." Thought 44 (Fall 1969), 434-450.

Bos, A. David. "Washington Gladden Versus Anti-Catholicism." Journal of Ecumenical Studies 18 (Spring 1981), 281-292.

Browne, Henry J. The Catholic Church and the Knights of Labor. Washington, D.C.: Catholic University of America Press, 1949.

Browne, Henry J. "Terence V. Powderly and the Church-Labor Difficulties of the Early 1880s." Catholic Historical Review 32 (April 1946), 1-27.

Brusher, Joseph F. Consecrated Thunderbolt: Father Yorke of San Francisco. Hawthorne, N.J.: Joseph F. Wagner, 1973.

Corcoran, Theresa. "Vida Scudder and the Lawrence Textile Strike." Essex Institute Historical Collections 115 (July 1979), 183-195.

Cronin, Bernard. Father Yorke and the Labor Movement in San Francisco. Washington, D.C.: Catholic University of America Press, 1943.

Ensley, Philip C. "The Interchurch World Movement and the Steel Strike of 1919." Labor History 13 (Spring 1972), 217-230.

Ernst, Eldon. Moment of Truth for Protestant America. Missoula: University of Montana Press, 1974.

Flaherty, William B. "The Clergyman and Labor Progress: Father Cornelius O'Leary and the Knights of Labor." Labor History 10 (Spring 1970), 175-189.

Fox, Mary Harrita. Peter E. Dietz, Labor Priest. Notre Dame, Ind.: University of Notre Dame Press, 1953.

Gutman, Herbert. "Protestantism and the Labor Movement: The Christian Spirit in the Gilded Age." American Historical Review 72 (October 1966), 74-101.

Gutman, Herbert. Work, Culture and Society in Industrializing America. New York: Knopf, 1977.

Hardman, J. B. S. "The Jewish Labor Movement in the United States: Jewish and Non-Jewish Influences." American Jewish Historical Quarterly 52 (December 1962), 98-132.

Nash, George H. "Charles Stelzle: Apostle to Labor." Labor History 11 (Spring 1970), 151-174.

O'Brien, David J. "American Catholics and Organized Labor in the 1930s." Catholic Historical Review 52 (October 1966), 323-349.

Perlman, Selig. "America and the Jewish Labor Movement: A Case of Mutual Illumination." American Jewish Historical Quarterly 46 (March 1957), 221-232.

Pope, Liston. Millhands and Preachers: A Study of Gastonia. New Haven: Yale University Press, 1942.

Shover, John L. "Washington Gladden and the Labor Question." Ohio Historical Quarterly 68 (October 1959), 335-352.

Tcherikower, Elias. The Early Jewish Labor Movement in the United States. Translated by Aaron Antonovsky. New York: YIVO Institute, 1961.

2. THE DECLINE OF CULTURAL AUTHORITY: EVANGELICALS AND THE AGE OF REFORM

Primary Sources

The King's Business: Proceedings of the World's Convention of Christians at Work and Seventh Annual Convention of Christian Workers in the United States. Boston, 1892.

Haldeman, Isaac M. Professor Rauschenbusch's "Christianity and the Social Crisis." New York: Cook, n.d.

Pierson, Arthur T. Forward Movements of the Past Half-Century. New York: Funk & Wagnalls, 1903.

Secondary Works

Dayton, Donald W. Discovering an Evangelical Heritage. New York: Harper & Row, 1976.

Findlay, James F. Dwight L. Moody, American Evangelist, 1837-
    1899. Chicago: University of Chicago Press, 1969.

Lears, T. J. Jackson. No Place of Grace: Antimodernism and the
    Transformation of American Culture, 1880-1920. New York:
    Pantheon, 1981.

Linder, Robert D. "The Resurgence of Evangelical Social
    Concern, 1925-75." In The Evangelicals, edited by David F.
    Wells and John D. Woodbridge. Nashville: Abingdon, 1975.

McLoughlin, William G. The American Evangelicals, 1800-1900.
    New York: Harper & Row, 1968.

McLoughlin, William G. Modern Revivalism: Charles Grandison
    Finney to Billy Graham. New York: Ronald Press, 1959.

McLoughlin, William G. Revivals, Awakenings and Reform: An
    Essay on Religion and Social Change, 1607-1977. Chicago:
    University of Chicago Press, 1978.

Magnuson, Norris. Salvation in the Slums: Evangelical Social
    Work, 1865-1920. Metuchen, N.J.: Scarecrow, 1977.

Marsden, George M. Fundamentalism and American Culture. New
    York: Oxford University Press, 1980.

Marsden, George M. "The Gospel of Wealth, the Social Gospel
    and the Salvation of Souls in 19th Century America." Fides
    et Historia 5 (Fall 1972), 10-21.

Mathieson, Robert R. "Evangelicals and the Age of Reform,
    1870-1930." Fides et Historia 16 (Fall 1985), 74-85.

Moberg, David. The Great Reversal: Evangelism versus Social
    Concern. Philadelphia: Lippincott, 1972.

Sizer, Sandra S. Gospel Hymns and Social Religion: The
    Rhetoric of Nineteenth Century Revivalism. Philadelphia:
    Temple University Press, 1978.

Smith, Timothy L. Revivalism and Social Reform in Mid-
    Nineteenth Century America. Nashville: Abingdon, 1957.

Szasz, Ferenc M. The Divided Mind of Protestant America, 1880-
    1930. University: University of Alabama Press, 1982.

Weber, Timothy P. Living in the Shadow of the Second Coming:
    American Premillennialism, 1875-1925. New York: Oxford
    University Press, 1979.

Weisberger, Bernard A. They Gathered at the River. Chicago:
    Quadrangle, 1958.

3. CULTURAL AUTHORITY AND THE RISE OF THE CORPORATE STATE

a. Populism and the Search for Social Justice

Primary Sources

Bellamy, Edward. Looking Backward, 2000-1887. 1888. Reprint.
Cambridge: Harvard University Press, 1967.

Donnelly, Ignatius L. Caesar's Column. Chicago: F. J. Schulte
& Co., 1890.

George, Henry. The Condition of Labor: An Open Letter to Pope
Leo XIII. New York: U.S. Book Co., 1891.

George, Henry. Progress and Poverty; An Inquiry Into the Cause
of Industrial Depressions. New York: Lovell, Gestefeld &
Co., 1879.

Lloyd, Henry Demarest. Wealth Against Commonwealth. New York:
Harper & Brothers, 1894.

Secondary Works

Argersinger, Peter H. "Pentecostal Politics in Kansas:
Religion, the Farmers' Alliance, and the Gospel of
Populism." Kansas Quarterly 1 (Fall 1969), 24-35.

Beals, Carleton. The Great Revolt and Its Leaders. London:
Abelard and Schuman, 1968.

Bicha, Karel D. "Prairie Radicals: A Common Pietism." Journal
of Church and State 18 (Winter 1976), 79-94.

Blau, Joseph L. "Bellamy's Religious Motivation for Social
Reform: A Review Article." Review of Religion 21 (March
1957), 156-166.

Cherny, Robert W. Populism, Progressivism and the
Transformation of Nebraska Politics, 1894-1903. Lincoln:
University of Nebraska Press, 1981.

Coletta, Paolo E. William Jennings Bryan, vol. 2, Political
Evangelist, 1860-1908. Lincoln: University of Nebraska
Press, 1965.

Glad, Paul W. The Trumpet Soundeth: William Jennings Bryan and
His Democracy, 1896-1912. Lincoln: University of Nebraska
Press, 1960.

Hicks, John D. The Populist Revolt. Minneapolis: University
of Minnesota Press, 1931.

Hofstadter, Richard. The Age of Reform: From Bryan to FDR.
     New York: Knopf, 1955.

Jeansonne, Glen. "Preacher, Populist and Propagandist: The
     Early Career of Gerald K. Smith." Biography 2 (Fall 1979),
     303-327.

Jensen, Richard. The Winning of the Midwest: Social and
     Political Conflict, 1888-1896. Chicago: University of
     Chicago Press, 1971.

Kleppner, Paul. The Cross of Culture: A Social Analysis of
     Midwestern Politics, 1850-1900. New York: Free Press, 1970.

Lindner, Eileen W. "The Redemptive Politic of Henry George:
     Legacy of the Social Gospel." Ph.D. diss., Union
     Theological Seminary, 1985.

Nicklason, Fred. "Henry George: Social Gospeller." American
     Quarterly 22 (Fall 1970), 649-664.

Nugent, Walter T. K. The Tolerant Populists: Kansas Populism
     and Nativism. Chicago: University of Chicago Press, 1963.

Pollack, Norman. The Populist Response to Industrial America.
     Cambridge: Harvard University Press, 1962.

Smith, Willard H. "William Jennings Bryan and the Social
     Gospel." Journal of American History 53 (June 1966), 41-60.

Thomas, John L. Alternative America: Henry George, Edward
     Bellamy, Henry Demarest Lloyd and the Adversary Tradition.
     Cambridge: Harvard University Press, Belknap Press, 1983.

Thomas, John L. Introduction to Looking Backward: 2000-1887,
     by Edward Bellamy. 1888. Reprint. Cambridge: Harvard
     University Press, 1967.

Tindall, George B. A Populist Reader. New York: Harper & Row,
     1966.

b. Progressivism and Social Justice

Primary Sources

Addams, Jane. Twenty Years at Hull House. New York:
     Macmillan, 1910.

Baker, Roy Stannard. American Chronicle. The Autobiography of
     Ray Stannard Baker. New York: Scribner, 1945.

Ely, Richard T. Ground Under Our Feet; An Autobiography. New
     York: Macmillan, 1938.

Gladden, Washington. The Cosmopolis City Club. New York:
    Century Co., 1893.

Howe, Frederic C. The Confessions of a Reformer. New York:
    Scribner, 1925.

Secondary Works

Bailey, Hugh C. Liberalism in the New South: Southern Social
    Reformers and the Progressive Movement. Coral Gables, Fla.:
    University of Miami Press, 1969.

Bailey, Kenneth K. Southern White Protestantism in the
    Twentieth Century. New York: Harper & Row, 1965.

Barnard, John. From Evangelicalism to Progressivism at Oberlin
    College, 1866-1917. Columbus: Ohio State University Press,
    1969.

Buenker, John D. Urban Liberalism and Progressive Reform. New
    York: Scribner, 1973.

Buenker, John D.; Burnham, John C.; and Crunden, Robert M.
    Progressivism. Cambridge, Mass.: Schenkman Publishing
    Company, 1977.

Chandler, Alfred D. "The Origins of Progressive Leadership."
    In Letters of Theodore Roosevelt, edited by Elting E.
    Morrison, vol. 8, 1462-1465. Cambridge: Harvard University
    Press, 1954.

Chatfield, E. Charles. "The Southern Sociological Congress:
    Organization of Uplift." Tennessee Historical Quarterly 19
    (Spring 1960), 328-347.

Crunden, Robert M. Ministers of Reform. The Progressives'
    Achievement in American Civilization, 1889-1920. New York:
    Basic, 1982.

Davis, Allen F. Spearheads for Reform: The Social Settlements
    and the Progressive Movement. New York: Oxford University
    Press, 1967.

Eighmy, John Lee. "Religious Liberalism in the South During
    the Progressive Era." Church History 38 (September 1969),
    359-372.

Farrell, John C. Beloved Lady: A History of Jane Addams' Ideas
    on Reform and Peace. Baltimore: Johns Hopkins University
    Press, 1967.

Flynt, J. Wayne. "Southern Baptists and Reform: 1890-1920."
    Baptist History and Heritage 7 (October 1972), 211-224.

Grantham, Dewey W. "The Progressive Era and the Reform Tradition." Mid-America 46 (October 1964), 227-251.

Griffen, Clyde. "The Progressive Ethos." In The Development of an American Culture, edited by Stanley Coben and Lorman Ratner. 2d ed. New York: St. Martin, 1983.

Hayes, Samuel P. The Response to Industrialization, 1885-1914. Chicago: University of Chicago Press, 1957.

Huthmacher, J. Joseph. "Urban Liberalism and the Age of Reform." Mississippi Valley Historical Review 49 (September 1962), 231-241.

Link, Arthur S. "Woodrow Wilson, Presbyterian in Government." In Calvinism and the Political Order, edited by George L. Hunt. Philadelphia: Westminster, 1965.

McLoughlin, William G. "Pietism and the American Character." American Quarterly 17 (Summer 1965), 163-186.

Noble, David W. The Paradox of Progressive Thought. Minneapolis: University of Minnesota Press, 1958.

Quandt, Jean B. From the Small Town to the Great Community: The Social Thought of the Progressive Intellectuals. New Brunswick, N.J.: Rutgers University Press, 1970.

Quandt, Jean B. "Religion and Social Thought: The Secularization of Postmillennialism." American Quarterly 25 (Fall 1973), 390-409.

Swanson, Merwin. "The Country Life Movement and the American Churches." Church History 46 (September 1977), 358-373.

Weinstein, James. The Corporate Ideal in the Liberal State, 1900-1918. Boston: Beacon Press, 1968.

Wiebe, Robert H. The Search for Order, 1877-1920. New York: Hill & Wang, 1967.

c. Politics, Religion and Prohibition

Primary Sources

Bruere, Martha Bensley. Does Prohibition Work? A Study of the Operation of the Eighteenth Amendment Made By the National Federation of Settlements. New York: Harper & Brothers, 1927.

Cherrington, E. H. The Evolution of Prohibition in the United States of America. Westerville, Ohio: American Issue Press, 1920.

Peabody, Francis Greenwood. The Liquor Problem: A Summary of
     Investigations Conducted by the Committee of Fifty, 1893-
     1903. Boston, 1905.

Willard, Frances. Glimpses of Fifty Years: The Autobiography
     of an American Woman. Chicago: Women's Christian Temperance
     Publication Association, 1889.

                        Secondary Works

Bland, Jean. Hibernian Crusade: The Story of the Catholic
     Total Abstinence Union of America. Washington, D.C.:
     Catholic University of America Press, 1951.

Blocker, Jack S. Retreat From Reform: The Prohibition Movement
     in the United States, 1890-1913. Westport, Conn.:
     Greenwood, 1976.

Bordin, Ruth B. Women and Temperance: The Quest for Power and
     Liberty, 1873-1900. Philadelphia: Temple University Press,
     1981.

Buenker, John D. "The Illinois Legislature and Prohibition,
     1907-1919." Journal of the Illinois State Historical
     Society 62 (Winter 1969), 363-384.

Burnham, John C. "New Perspectives on the Prohibition
     'Experiment' of the 1920s." Journal of Social History 2
     (Fall 1968), 51-68.

Clark, Norman. Deliver Us From Evil: An Interpretation of
     American Prohibition. New York: Norton, 1976.

Dabney, Virginius. Dry Messiah: The Life of Bishop Cannon.
     New York: Knopf, 1949.

Earhart, Mary. Frances Willard: From Prayers to Politics.
     Chicago: University of Chicago Press, 1967.

Gusfield, Joseph. Symbolic Crusade: Status Politics and the
     American Temperance Movement. Urbana: University of
     Iliinois Press, 1963.

Kerr, K. Austin. "Organizing for Reform: The Anti-Saloon
     League and Innovation in Politics." American Quarterly 32
     (Spring 1980), 37-53.

Sinclair, Andrew. Prohibition, The Era of Excess. Boston:
     Little, Brown, 1962.

Timberlake, James H. Prohibition and the Progressive Movement,
     1900-1912. Cambridge: Harvard University Press, 1963.

d. Reform, Religion and the Rise of the Social Sciences

Primary Sources

Commons, John R. Social Reform and the Church. New York: T. Y. Crowell, 1894.

Ely, Richard T. Ground Under Our Feet. New York: Macmillan, 1938.

Mathews, Shailer. "Christian Sociology." American Journal of Sociology 1 (1895), 182-194, 359-380, 457-472, 604-617, 711-784; 2 (1896), 108-117, 274-287, 416-432.

Patten, Simon N. The Social Basis of Religion. New York: Macmillan, 1911.

Rauschenbusch, Walter. "The Stake of the Church in the Social Movement." American Journal of Sociology 3 (July 1897), 18-30.

Small, Albion. The Meaning of Social Science. Chicago: University of Chicago Press, 1910.

Small, Albion. "The Significance of a Sociology for Ethics." In Decennial Publications of the University of Chicago, Investigations Representing the Departments. First and second series. Chicago: University of Chicago Press, 1903.

Taylor, Graham. "The Social Function of the Church." American Journal of Sociology 5 (November 1899), 305-321.

Secondary Works

Coats, Alfred W. "The First Two Decades of the American Economic Association." American Economic Review 50 (September 1960), 555-574.

Dynes, Russell R. "Sociology as a Religious Movement." American Sociologist 9 (November 1974), 169-176.

Everett, John Rutherford. Religion in Economics: A Study of John Bates Clark, Richard T. Ely and Simon N. Patten. New York: King's Crown Press, 1946.

Fox, Daniel M. The Discovery of Abundance: Simon N. Patten and the Transformation of Social Theory. Ithaca, N.Y.: Cornell University Press, 1967.

Furner, Mary O. Advocacy and Objectivity: A Crisis in the Professionalization of American Social Science, 1865-1905. Lexington: University Press of Kentucky, 1975.

Gabriel, Ralph Henry. The Course of American Democratic Thought. New York: Ronald Publishing Co., 1940.

Morgan, J. Graham. "The Development of Sociology and the
    Social Gospel in America." Sociological Analysis 30 (Spring
    1969), 42-53.

Potts, David B. "Social Ethics at Harvard, 1881-1931." In
    Social Sciences at Harvard, 1860-1920, edited by Paul H.
    Buck. Cambridge: Harvard University Press, 1965.

Rader, Benjamin G. The Academic Mind and Reform: The Influence
    of Richard T. Ely in American Life. Lexington: University
    Press of Kentucky, 1966.

Ross, Dorothy. "The Development of the Social Sciences." In
    The Organization of Knowledge in Modern America, edited by
    Alexandra Oleson and John Voss, 107-138. Baltimore: Johns
    Hopkins University Press, 1979.

Ross, Dorothy. G. Stanley Hall: The Psychologist as Prophet.
    Chicago: University of Chicago Press, 1972.

Swatos, William H. "The Faith of Our Fathers: On the
    Christianity of Early American Sociology." (bibliography)
    Sociological Analysis 44 (Spring 1983), 33-52.

Thompson, Alan. "Prophetic Religion and the Democratic Front:
    The Mission of Harry F. Ward." Radical Religion 5, no. 1
    (1980), 29-36.

Wilson, R. Jackson. In Quest of Community: Social Philosophy
    in the United States, 1860-1920. New York: Wiley,
    1968.

4

Immigration and Urbanization: Changing Patterns of Religious and Cultural Authority

Richard Hughes Seager

Sidney Mead, when referring to the relationship between the Protestant churches and the state (*Nation with the Soul of a Church*), observed that the church-state relationship was best described as a conflict between the claims of particular religious traditions and a highly generalized theology associated with the American nation—the "religion of the Republic." This is a useful model when considering the dynamics of immigration and the broadly cultural dimension of the church-state question. In the course of the nineteenth century, an estimated thirty-five million immigrants brought cultural and religious systems to the United States that were distinct from, if not alien to, the established patterns of American civilization. In the process, Old World cultural values were transplanted, adjusted, and to varying degrees transformed into what Will Herberg (*Protestant-Catholic-Jew*) called "the American Way of Life."

A second useful model was developed by Louis Hartz in *The Founding of New Societies*. Hartz emphasized the importance of the charter group of English dissidents who, by establishing the original cultural patterns of American society, became the core culture that determined the ground rules for subsequent immigrants. In *The Liberal Tradition*, Hartz argued that these original patterns evolved into a society having the capacity to absorb conservative values into a conformist mass culture. Hartz's thesis presented a problem central to the dynamics of immigration: how was the immigrant community to adjust to the American environment and at the same time maintain its group identity?

In the immigrants' encounter with American culture, primary authority rested with the pattern of cultural arrangements and ideals that throughout the century had been given an explicitly religious value by native Protestant churches. But a second locus of authority was also influential: the folkways and religious traditions of migrating peoples. Throughout the great migrations these two authorities were in conflict. The cultures and religions of the immigrant had the venerable authority of tradition; American civilization, and with it the Protestant American tradition, had the more determinative authority that dictated the ground rules for successful adaptation to the American way of life.

When World War I and the restriction of immigration cut the flow of new immigrants, however, the question of authority gradually shifted. Tensions between folk heritage and American mores, between the immigrant groups and the Protestant core culture, faded. In communities of immigrant descent, strains of Old World cultural and religious values persisted together with New World idealism, liberal patterns of associational life, and American nationalism. What had once been a question of a conflict between cultural and religious authorities became recast in terms of a challenge facing America: how to maintain social and national unity while being an ethnically and religiously pluralistic society and a cultural mosaic.

PROTESTANT CORE CULTURE

The American Protestant core culture posited by Louis Hartz was infused by a highly dynamic religious idealism that has been described in various ways. Historian Rowland T. Berthoff ("Peasants and Artisans") characterized it as a classically inspired republicanism energized by evangelical zeal; Nathan O. Hatch (*Sacred Cause*) described it in terms of "civil millennialism" originating in the revolutionary era; Ernest L. Tuveson (*Redeemer Nation*) explored the fusion of Christian doctrine and Enlightenment progressivism as the dominant form of religious nationalism well into the twentieth century. Standard interpretations of the relationship between Protestant churches and American culture by Henry F. May ("The Religion of the Republic"), Sidney E. Mead (*The Lively Experiment*), Winthrop S. Hudson (*The Great Tradition*), and Robert T. Handy (*A Christian America*) indicate that throughout the nineteenth century Protestantism remained the dominant religious influence in shaping the ideals of American society. Separation of church and state; freedom of religion; voluntary and democratic institutions; a capitalistic, industrial economy; competitive individualism; and Anglo-Saxon traditions were understood to be elements in the quest for a millennial society. Recent interpretations of the major conservative (George M. Marsden, *Fundamentalism*) and liberal (William R. Hutchison, *The Modernist Impulse*) camps in American Protestantism add theological depth to this fundamental identification of Protestant religion and American civilization.

Moral idealism, with its roots in the Protestant heritage, reinforced the proprietary relationship between Protestantism and American culture. D. H.

Meyer, in *The Instructed Conscience*, argues that a secularized morality and piety underlay both evangelical reformism and nineteenth-century aestheticism, and formed the basis for a national ethic. John G. Sproat (*Best Men*) and Arthur Mann (*Yankee Reformers*) emphasize the role of genteel moralism in the reform crusades of the Gilded Age. Paul S. Boyer, in *Urban Masses*, argues that progressive reformers attempted to replicate the cultural ideals of the antebellum social order in the sprawling cities of the late nineteenth century. For a discussion of the evolution of a genteel cultural style that was influential with the traditional elite, the rising middle class, and the emerging caste of commercial magnates, see Stow Persons, *The Decline of Gentility*. Howard Mumford Jones, in his *Age of Energy*, presents a panoramic interpretation of the transformation of this traditional idealism into an authoritative force underlying commerce, industry, education, philosophy, and the arts. Kermit Vanderbilt (*Charles Eliot Norton*), John Henry Raleigh (*Matthew Arnold*), and *American Renaissance*, published by the Brooklyn Museum, outline the way in which a trans-Atlantic, Anglophilic taste for cosmopolitan high culture was embraced by the upper and middle classes.

At the end of the century, the liberal theological aspirations of the mainline Protestant churches, the aesthetic ideals of the genteel classes, the political and economic values of American society, and the millennial hopes for a Christian republic found a concrete expression in the idealized urban landscape of the World's Columbian Exposition. The Exposition was a symbol of cultural unity (Reid Badger, *Great American Fair*) and a fulfillment of the quest for a celestial city (David F. Burg, *Chicago's White City*). Recent commentators have been more critical. For Alan Trachtenberg (*Incorporation of America*), the Exposition was a latter-day "city on a hill" that embodied a covert alliance between industrial capitalism, the state, and the traditional aesthetics of a cultural elite; it created an illusion of unity in a society torn by social unrest. For Robert W. Rydell (*Visions of Empire*), the Exposition was a concrete expression of the racist hierarchies implicit in the Anglo-Saxons' self-identification as a chosen people.

The real American city was often the arena for the difficult encounter between immigrants and the American way of life. Thomas L. Philpott (*The Slum and the Ghetto*) recounts the attempts of the middle class to respond to the disruption of city life caused by immigration and industrialism. Sam Bass Warner, in his *Streetcar Suburbs*, analyzes neighborhood and class fragmentation in the expanding city. His *Urban Wilderness* surveys the transformation of urban forms, with special attention to immigrant neighborhoods and the activities of philanthropic charities. For a comparison of social and economic mobility, with attention to the influence of the religious backgrounds of blacks, Catholics, Jews, and the Yankees who "stood on the shoulders" of previous generations, see Stephan Thernstrom's *The Other Bostonians* and a book he wrote with Richard Sennett, *Nineteenth Century Cities.*

Throughout the course of the century, optimistic, cosmopolitan hopes were mirrored by outbursts of xenophobic alarm. John Higham's *Strangers in the Land* remains the best interpretive treatment of the alternating confidence and despair over America's capacity to assimilate immigrant groups; nativism, racism, anti-Catholicism, and anti-Semitism waxed and waned throughout the century. Ray Allen Billington's *Protestant Crusade* and David Brion Davis's "Some Themes of Counter-Subversion" treat the fear of Catholics in the antebellum years; for anti-Catholicism and the American Protective Association at the end of the century consult Donald L. Kinzer's *An Episode in Anti-Catholicism.* For an introduction to American anti-Semitism, see Leonard Dinnerstein, *Anti-Semitism in the United States* and John Higham, *Send These to Me.* For a comprehensive compendium of hypotheses about American anti-Semitism, see Melvin M. Tumin, *An Inventory and Appraisal.* Robert K. Murray (*Red Scare*), William Preston (*Aliens and Dissenters*), and Stanley Coben ("A Study in Nativism") examine the antiradicalism that emerged between the turn of the century and the twenties ostensibly in response to Bolshevism, labor agitation, and the leftist sentiments and divided national loyalties of immigrants. For a recent introduction to the ideas espoused by late-nineteenth-century radicals, see Aileen S. Kraditor, *Radical Persuasion.* Sally M. Miller's *Radical Immigrants* presents a more general survey of immigrant radicalism from Owenite socialism to scientific socialists at the turn of the century.

Concerted efforts were made to educate the immigrant in American social, political, and economic ideals. Edward G. Hartmann's *The Movement to Americanize the Immigrant* remains the best interpretive study of the idealism and fear that resulted in the Americanization crusade of the World War I era. Gerd Korman (*Industrialization, Immigrants, and Americanizers*) highlights the efforts to promote "100 percent Americanization" through industrial education. Robert L. Buroker ("From Voluntary Association to Welfare State") charts the transformation of Protestant voluntary organizations into agencies of the welfare state. In a different vein, Helen Lefkowitz Horowitz (*Culture and the City*) recounts the efforts of Chicago philanthropists to institutionalize the cultural ideals of the genteel tradition in museums, libraries, and art associations, and of social activists to encourage cultural uplift in Chicago settlement houses. Elizabeth Lee and Kenneth A. Abbott ("Chinese Pilgrims"), Philip D. Jordan ("Immigrants, Methodists"), John B. MacNab ("Bethlehem Chapel"), Lionel U. Rideout ("The Church, the Chinese, and the Negroes"), Paula K. Benkart ("Changing Attitudes"), Robert H. Seager ("Some Denominational Reactions"), and Paul William Walasky ("Entertainment of Angels") assess the varied missionary activities of Protestant churches that were directed toward immigrant groups. Lawrence B. Davis's *Immigrants, Baptists, and the Protestant Mind* is a full-length study of a church's "cycle of response" to the immigrant; American Baptists moved from providential hopes for the conversion of immigrants, through fear and paternalism when faced with indifference, to an acceptance of diversity and a renewed interest in conversion from a "cosmopolitan" or assimilative point of view.

Racist ideas about national origin often informed the response to the immigrant. Richard Hofstadter (*Social Darwinism*), Mark H. Haller (*Eugenics*), Thomas F. Gossett (*Race: The History of an Idea*), and Robert C. Bannister (*Social Darwinism: Science and Myth*) attend to the idea of race in its relationship to scientific theories that were current during the nineteenth century. Barbara M. Solomon's *Ancestors and Immigrants*, a study of the founding of the influential Immigration Restriction League, underscores the way in which traditional genteel values were transformed into a scientific ideology of race when Boston's elite lost its sense of authority in the face of a radical social and cultural change. Edward Norman Saveth's *American Historians and the European Immigrants* remains a valuable study of the complex mixture of idealism and cultural arrogance that was implicit in the concept of the city, frontier, or Anglo-Saxon institutions as a melting pot. For a recent survey of the development of the idea of the melting pot over the course of the century, see Richard Conant Harper, *The Course of the Melting Pot Idea to 1910*.

Saveth's account also examines the emergence of the scholarly study of American immigration. Since the 1920s several generations of historians, led by Karl Wittke, Marcus Hansen, and Oscar Handlin, have turned the field of immigration history into a rich and immense field of study. For standard surveys of American immigration, see Henry S. Commager's *Immigration and American History*, Leonard Dinnerstein and David M. Reimers's *Ethnic Americans*, Maldwyn A. Jones's *American Immigration*, and Philip A. M. Taylor's *Distant Magnet*. For helpful bibliographic essays that provide an orientation to the field, see Robert D. Cross ("How Historians Have Looked at Immigrants") and Rudolph J. Vecoli ("European Americans: From Immigrants to Ethnics").

Due to the enormous variety of the national groups that took part in the great migrations of the nineteenth century, this discussion is confined to representative nationalities: literature concerned, in particular, with the Chinese, black migrants to the northern cities, and the Scandinavians, together with studies of ethnic communities as related to Catholicism and Judaism. Throughout the discussion, particular attention will be given to the encounter between ethnic religions and cultures on the one hand and the core culture on the other, and the persistence of national identity as a factor that coexisted with Americanization.

CHINESE MIGRATIONS

During the last half of the nineteenth century, the Chinese population rose from an estimated four thousand in 1850 to over one hundred thousand by the end of the century. Their experience was more traumatic than that of European migrants; anti-Chinese race prejudice was more virulent. Even so, Chinese institutions were gradually transformed by American civilization, while at the same time the Chinese retained a vital connection with the homeland.

In *Bitter Strength*, Gunther P. Barth argues that anti-Chinese prejudice was a product of Yankee fears that authoritarian Asian traditions threatened the founding of an ideal egalitarian society in mid-century California. Barth pays special attention to the assistance given to the Chinese by the early Protestant Home Missions. Stuart Creighton Miller (*Unwelcome Immigrant*) emphasizes the stereotypes of the Chinese as idolatrous, servile, morally diseased, and anti-progressive. For the perception of the Chinese as a public health menace, see Joan B. Trauner, "Medical Scapegoats." Differing perspectives on the role of the labor question are discussed in Isabella Black ("American Labour"), Ping Chiu (*Chinese Labor*), Delber L. McKee (" 'The Chinese Must Go!' ") and Alexander P. Saxton's more interpretive *Indispensable Enemy*. An examination of the methods and motives of the leaders of the organized drive to exclude the Chinese is found in Elmer C. Sandmeyer's *The Anti-Chinese Movement in California.*

Community studies emphasize different aspects of the way in which Chinatown life preserved ethnic distinctiveness even as the Chinese became increasingly involved in American culture. In *Longtime Californ'*, Victor G. Nee and Brett de Bary Nee analyze the historical development of Chinese associational life through interviews and oral history; in "Chinatowns in the Delta," George Chu studies agricultural communities in Sacramento, California from an economic point of view. Ivan H. Light's "From Vice District to Tourist Attraction" examines the "embourgeoisement" of urban Chinatowns as they became entertainment zones for Caucasian tourists by the 1930s. There are few historical treatments of Confucian kinship religion in the United States. An analysis of the transplantation of clan, language association groups, benevolent organizations, and secret societies is found in Stanford M. Lyman's *The Asians in the West*, his *Structure of Chinese Society*, and in H. M. Lai's "The Chinese." As in the case of other immigrant groups, the authority of Chinese associations tended to erode with the second generation. For a brief discussion of the Chinese temple in America, the Chinese-American church as a "hybrid institution," and the competition between American and Chinese values, see Rose Hum Lee, *The Chinese in the United States.*

Political events at the turn of the century made contact with the mainland important for the development of Chinese-American identity. Members of Chinese secret societies in America supported revolutionary change in China as a strategy for enhancing their own status, while revolutionary sentiments in China encouraged Chinese-Americans to embrace progressive American values. For the importance of this continuity of trans-Pacific identification with the Chinese mainland see Shih-shan H. Tsai's *China and the Overseas Chinese* and Linda Pomerantz's "The Chinese Bourgeoisie."

BLACK MIGRATIONS NORTH

In the decades from roughly 1890 to 1930, an estimated one and a half million southern blacks migrated to northern cities to find an urban Promised Land. The religious traditions and folkways of this largely rural population were transformed by the dynamic, industrial, urban environment. One consequence was that new forms of religion emerged. In addition, when the promise of the cities proved to be limited and the idealism of the North qualified by racial exclusivism, Pan-Africanist religious ideas helped to create an alternative American identity for many urban blacks.

Literature on the "great migration" is based on dated but authoritative classics which have been recently reprinted. Carter G. Woodson's *Century of Negro Migration* remains a basic introduction to migratory trends. His *History of the Negro Church*, Benjamin E. Mays and Joseph W. Nicholson's *The Negro's Church*, and St. Clair Drake and Horace Cayton's *Black Metropolis* contain early assessments of the impact of the migration on black urban religion in the North. E. Franklin Frazier and C. Eric Lincoln's assessment of blacks as forming a "nation within a nation" (*The Negro Church*) remains influential. Recent works by Stanley Lieberson (*A Piece of the Pie*) and Daniel M. Johnson and Rex R. Campbell (*Black Migration*) study the problem of job competition with other migrant groups and immigration demographics respectively. Florette Henri's *Black Migration: The Movement North* directs brief attention to the transformation of southern religion in the context of an increasingly urbanized way of life among migrant blacks.

Recent community studies also discuss different aspects of religion within broader studies of black urban life. James Borchert's *Alley Life* includes an anthropological assessment of the stabilizing influence of informal religion, folkways, and associations among poor blacks in Washington, D.C. In her *Black Migration and Poverty*, Elizabeth H. Pleck notes that rural folkways were strengthened in Boston as blacks gained access to elements of the urban scene; access did not include, however, a corresponding rise in economic mobility. Gilbert Osofsky in *Harlem: The Making of a Ghetto* notes the influential role of the churches in the creation of community through their involvement in Harlem real estate. Allan H. Spear in *Black Chicago* describes the way in which separatist churches, YMCA's, fraternal lodges, and other associations helped to lay the foundation for the segregated twentieth-century ghetto. Seth M. Scheiner's "The Negro Church" is a brief survey of black urban religion in this period that reiterates the older view of the relative decline of black churches, a fact he attributes to their decentralized, congregational authority.

Decline or not, churches remained among the most authoritative black urban institutions. Richard Bardolph, in *The Negro Vanguard*, argues that the black church served as a training ground for both business and religion and he discusses prominent members of the leadership elite. An account of the religious, political, and social activities of prominent clerics of the era is found in Randall K. Burkett and Richard Newman's *Black Apostles* and William M. Welty's *Black Shepherds*. Arthur Huff Fauset's *Black Gods* remains a useful early study of the dialectic between Africanism and Protestantism in urban "storefront cults." See also Elmer T. Clark's *The Small Sects* and Ira E. Harrison's "The Store Front Church." For a critical assessment of the relationship between small black religious groups and established black and white churches, see Joseph R. Washington, *Black Sects and Cults*. Unpublished dissertations dealing with specific storefront groups and blacks in the various established denominations can be found in Ethel L. Williams and Clifton F. Brown's *Howard University Bibliography*.

Gayraud S. Wilmore (*Black Religion*), along with other commentators, argues that Marcus Garvey's black nationalism and Pan-Africanist movement epitomized the mood of the black masses when the promise of the North went unfulfilled in the twenties. Edmund D. Cronon's biography, *Black Moses*, and Theodore G. Vincent's *Black Power* are basic scholarly treatments of Garvey. Tony Martin's more recent *Race First* studies the ideological and organizational challenges surmounted by Garvey's Universal Negro Improvement Association. Randall K. Burkett's *Black Redemption* discusses the views of prominent established church leaders on the Garvey movement. In his *Garveyism as a Religious Movement*, Burkett portrays Garvey as "the foremost black theologian of the early twentieth century." Garvey's program was a compound of Anglo-Catholic doctrine and rite, traditional black biblicism that focused on Africa as the Promised Land, and American civil religion. Even as urban blacks first struggled to merge into the American cultural mainstream at about the time of the Harlem Renaissance, black masses looked beyond the United States for an alternative identity. Ethnic self-identification coexisted with the persistent efforts of blacks to find a satisfying place in the American way of life.

Immigrants of European nationality, while faced with enormous challenges, did not encounter the extreme forms of race prejudice experienced by blacks and Chinese. Patterns of associational life were established to replicate Old World forms; they served as buffers between the immigrant and the dominant society, but underwent decline as the process of Americanization progressed. Ties to traditional culture and religion persisted as folk elements in an ethnic tradition or as more powerful alternative identities that coexisted with Americanization.

SCANDINAVIAN LUTHERAN IMMIGRANTS

Among Scandinavian immigrants, with their religious heritage in Lutheran national churches, a pattern emerged that was similar to that among immigrant Catholics and Jews. Earlier migrants, who had made adjustments to the American environment, struggled with newer immigrants who attempted to keep Old World traditions alive. Yet by the turn of the century when new immigration waned, older patterns of association declined and the national and ecclesiastical traditions became increasingly Americanized.

Ulf Beijbom's *Swedes in Chicago* is an excellent demographic study of the many secular and religious associations that supported a Swedish enclave in Chicago—"the Swedish Promised Land"—during the middle of the century. Sture Lindmark (*Swedish America*) focuses on the attempts of the Swedes to maintain their culture in the first decades of the twentieth century. Essays in James Iverne Dowie and Ernest M. Espelie's *Swedish Community in Transition* discuss the early Lutheran church, Americanization conflicts in the Augustana Synod, and the decline of a syncretistic Swedish-American culture after World War I. A. William Hoglund, in his *Finnish Immigrants*, pays special attention to the proliferation of Finnish choral groups, mutual aid societies, libraries, and churches and the efforts of Finns both to maintain their heritage and to seek ties to the broader culture. With restriction of immigration, Finnish associations began a precipitous decline in the 1920s. Dorothy B. Skaardal's excellent study, *The Divided Heart*, based on Scandinavian novels, essays, and magazines, discusses the waning of attempts to preserve cultural heritage and corporate self-identity, and the emergence of a pragmatic and individualistic ethic more in tune with the American environment.

A number of historians of religion have studied the Americanization process in the Lutheran churches. For an excellent survey of the theological and language debates, the restraints on rapid Americanization due to the influence of new immigrants, and the checkered attempts to organize folk heritage societies as a way to maintain a connection between religion and national culture, see Enok Mortensen, *The Danish Lutheran Church*. G. Everett Arden's *Augustana Heritage* recounts the conservative influence of Swedish pietists on the Augustana Synod and its Americanization during World War I. Paul P. Nyholm (*Americanization of the Danish Lutheran Churches*) describes the waning of the Danish language church, the Americanization of rites, feasts, and hymns, and the church's movement toward fraternal union with other national churches. Ralph J. Jalkanen's *Faith of the Finns* is a collection of essays discussing topics such as the influence of Finnish revivals on the American church, the transformation of the Suomi Synod from a religious to an ethnic community, and American influences on church architecture. E. Clifford Nelson and Eugene L. Fevold (*The Lutheran Church*) recount similar themes, describing "Americanized church work" and a "Janus-faced church"—both traditionalist and modernist—as the Norwegians emerged from a Lutheran "ghetto" circa World War I. For an assessment of the persistence of ethnicity and the assimilation of Scandinavians and other "white ethnics" into the core culture, see Charles H. Anderson, *White Protestant Americans*.

ROMAN CATHOLIC MIGRATIONS

The idea of a Janus-faced church is also applicable to Roman Catholicism, particularly in the nineteenth century, when efforts to Americanize the immigrants caused local, national, and international controversy. There were two distinct, but related, dimensions to the struggle. The first was a series of conflicts between Catholic coreligionists over whether to preserve national religious practices in immigrant communities in the United States or to unify Catholic communities in an Americanized church. The second question had to do with the religious meaning of Americanization. In this case the central, monarchical authority of Rome came into direct conflict with the idealistic, progressive, and future-oriented values of America.

Tensions among the national churches began early in the nineteenth century and lasted well into the early decades of the twentieth. Thomas T. McAvoy's "Formation of the Catholic Minority" is a brief introduction to the early relations between Anglo-American and French Catholics, the formation of a liberal elite, and the emergence of the Irish as church leaders in the antebellum decades. Oscar Handlin's *Boston's Immigrants* is an older, pioneering study of the conflicts among the French, Irish, and Yankee communities during the first half century of the Irish migrations, conflicts that left

Boston a divided city. For a more extensive treatment of the submergence of the early liberal Catholic culture of Boston and the emergence of the institutional church dominated by the Irish and preoccupied by the problem of Americanizing the immigrant, see Donna Merwick, *Boston Priests*.

For a treatment of Irish community life spanning ten generations, see Dennis Clark, *The Irish in Philadelphia*. Church and parochial school played a vital part in the creation of an Irish subculture that served as a protective wall, a barrier to risk-taking, and a caretaking support structure before the emergence of the welfare state. The ideal of a Catholic enclave first took shape in response to concerns that Catholic immigrants would be absorbed by the Protestant culture that surrounded them. Jay P. Dolan's *Immigrant Church* recounts the antebellum consolidation of Catholic power in New York. Both the Irish and the German minorities were bound into a single church that formed a bulwark against Protestant culture. This unifying and protective strategy laid the foundation for Catholic relations with the rest of American society well into the twentieth century.

German Catholics made vigorous efforts to retain their national heritage and special religious practices. In *Immigrant Milwaukee*, Kathleen Neils Conzen describes the creation of an antebellum German community that included Lutherans and Jews. The Catholic church, in particular, played an early and active role in the creation of an organizational network that gave a wider cultural life to the community. Early arrivals in Milwaukee, Germans quickly established an enduring German-American identity in the community. Colman J. Barry, in *The Catholic Church and German Americans*, examines the efforts of German Catholics to gain Vatican recognition as a distinct national church in America, the efforts of the Americanizers to mold them into a uniform church, and the climactic controversy that centered on Peter Paul Cahensly and the question of the viability of a German language church in the United States. As with other immigrant communities, successful adaptation to American culture called into question the legitimacy and utility of organizations based on Old World nationalities. Philip Gleason's *The Conservative Reformers* is an account of how German Catholics transformed an older national organization—the Central Verein—into a socially activist, but doctrinally conservative reform group in order to give German ethnic organizations a new rationale during the progressive age.

The experience of the Poles gives an indication of the complex relationship between the Americanist tendencies of the church leadership and the aspirations of national minorities to maintain traditional religious and culture practices. Thomas I. Monzell, in "The Catholic Church and the Americanization of the Polish Immigrant," argues that the church played a vital and valuable role in helping Poles adjust to the American environment. Victor R. Greene, in *For*

God and Country, makes a distinction between a prochurch party that supported the American church leadership and a nationalist party that worked to maintain Polish national traditions. Controversy began over the question of parish control; by the end of the century it had issued in a national debate that fostered a sense of Polish-American ethnic self-consciousness among both elites and masses. Anthony J. Kuzniewski's *Faith and Fatherland* describes the particularly complex situation facing Poles in Milwaukee: to what degree did Poles have to sacrifice national tradition in order to gain leadership positions in a regional church dominated by Germans and a national church led by the Irish?

The estimated four million Italian immigrants who arrived between 1880 and 1920 have been the subject of a variety of studies. Humbert S. Nelli's *Italians in Chicago* focuses on the high mobility in Italian communities. Neighborhoods were "beachheads"; community organizations, the Italian language press, and churches were "interim" institutions that served to mediate Old World traditions to the new demands of the American environment. More recent studies by Virginia Yans-McLaughlin (*Family and Community*) and John W. Briggs (*Italian Passage*) have emphasized the stability of Italian neighborhoods where Old World kinship patterns, family life, and institutions could be replicated, at least in part, in the American environment. All three studies give attention to the Italian encounter with the Protestant missions and welfare agencies, and discuss the significance of local churches. Rudolph J. Vecoli ("Contadini in Chicago," "Prelates and Peasants") focuses on the persistence of distinct Italian religious traditions such as the devotion to saints, *feste,* and the *corno* used for protection against the evil eye; he calls into question the success of the Americanizing goals of the Irish church. For a more interpretive and sociological view of Italian parishes, see Silvano M. Tomasi, *Piety and Power.* Italian parishes in New York presided over the change from the old communal life to the associational society of the United States. They were agents of both ethnic solidarity and group assimilation; they forced the issue of pluralism within the American Catholic church and provided a link between local and universal loyalties.

While one face of Catholicism was concerned with adjusting the immigrant to American life, the other was concerned with conservative and traditional Catholic leadership in Rome. The "Americanist heresy" of the late nineteenth century was a flash point for theological, ecclesiastical, and ethnic conflicts that emerged in public debate in America and abroad.

Standard accounts of the controversy are Thomas T. McAvoy's *Americanist Heresy* and Robert D. Cross's *Emergence of Liberal Catholicism.* Fraternization with Protestants, receptivity to science, democracy, and American nationalism, and an enthusiasm for the progressive idealism of the age were factors in a controversy sufficiently vague to be recalled as "the phantom heresy." For recent works that draw more precise attention to doctrinal issues, see David P. Killen, "Americanism Revisited" and Thomas E. Wangler, "The Birth of Americanism." For accounts of the efforts of American liberals to mediate the situation in Rome and the position of conservatives in the United States respectively, see Gerald P. Fogarty, *The Vatican and the Americanist Crisis* and Robert E. Curran, *Michael Augustine Corrigan.* The best brief analysis of the theological issue and its relationship to the question of national minorities is Chapter 11 of Jay P. Dolan's *The American Catholic Experience.* In Dolan's view, Americans emerged from the papal condemnation of Americanism with a dual loyalty: "100 percent Roman" and "100 percent American," conservative in theology and religion, but progressive in many social and political ideals. For an important sequel to this development, see William M. Halsey's *Survival of American Innocence.* Halsey argues that conservative neo-Thomist theology, along with genteel moralism and idealism, became the mainstay of the Catholic ghetto mentality well into the 1940s.

Dolan's *Catholic Experience* offers a far richer analysis of American Catholicism than older standard surveys. One-third of the book is dedicated to the cultural, liturgical, and social life of immigrant minorities, the emergence of the progressive leadership from the early Anglo-Catholic elite, and the "Romanizing" of the church at the turn of the century. Dolan concludes his account with the church's newly emerging liberalism and pluralism in the 1980s, but notes the problematic relationship between Americans and the traditionalist, if charismatic, leadership of the church in Rome.

JUDAISM AND IMMIGRATION

In contrast to the Roman Catholics, the decentralized authority of the Jewish community allowed for greater latitude in adjusting to the American environment. The Reform tradition, in particular, embraced American civilization, reinterpreted Judaism in terms of American national ideals, and became an influential and successful part of dynamic urban culture in the middle of the nineteenth century. However, the turn-of-the-century "new immigration" was crucial for the development of twentieth-century Judaism. Central and Eastern European culture, religious orthodoxies, radical social ideas, and Zionism reshaped American Judaism. Reform, Conservative, and Orthodox Judaism became constituent elements of twentieth-century Judaism, sharing together an identification with Israel and the international diaspora community.

Marc D. Angel's "The Sephardim" recounts the efforts of the earliest Spanish and Portuguese Jewish community to sustain itself in the course of later Jewish immigration. Sefton D. Temkin's "A Century of Reform Judaism" is an excellent introduction to the theological conflicts between moderate and radical reformers in the mid–nineteenth century and the encounter between the Reform tradition and the East European immigrants at the turn of the century. Leon A. Jick's *Americanization of the Synagogue* is a good introduction to early liberalizing tendencies among American Jews. For a series of essays on worship, ritual, and the nature of the Reform movement, see Joseph L. Blau, *Reform Judaism.* Benny Kraut's *From Reform Judaism to Ethical Culture* is a recent account of Felix Adler's Ethical Culture Society as a "model of apostasy" and an early form of Jewish secularism. Kraut's two articles, "Francis E. Abbot" and "Judaism Triumphant" are fascinating accounts of the gulf that persisted between Reform Judaism and Unitarians despite their shared commitment to a liberal, universalist, religious agenda. The best historical treatment of Conservative Judaism is Moshe Davis's *Emergence of Conservative Judaism,* which contains an excellent introductory chapter on the formative influence of Protestantism on American Judaism. Surveys by Nathan Glazer, *American Judaism,* and Joseph Blau, *Judaism in America,* remain brief, useful, interpretive introductions to the varied strands of the Jewish tradition from a historical and sociological perspective.

Oscar Handlin's *Adventures in Freedom* is a survey of Judaism that focuses on the broader cultural problems of adjustment to the U. S. environment. In *The Promised City,* Moses Rischin offers a pioneering community study of New York's East Side that, while paying little attention to institutional religion, treats the social idealism of the East European migrants as secularized Judaism and the labor movement as an Americanizing force. The value of Rischin's work has been enhanced through a recent reexamination by a new generation of scholars ("A Re-Examination") in the journal *American Jewish History.* Arthur A. Goren's *New York Jews* recounts the ambitious and controversial effort to build an independent organizational structure for the Jewish community within New York City. For a richly descriptive interpretation of the "bi-culturism" of New York's Yiddish culture, see Irving Howe, *World of Our Fathers.* Fueled by the desire to found a commonwealth, the Yiddish community created an ethnic enclave whose institutions, such as the Yiddish and labor presses, served as a vehicle to enhance group identity, yet at the same time helped to Americanize the East European Jews.

There are numerous studies of Jewish community life in other cities. Standard treatments such as Stuart E. Rosenberg's *Community in Rochester,* Lloyd Gartner's *Jews of Cleveland,* and Max Vorspan and Lloyd P. Gartner's *Jews of Los Angeles* chart the development of local Jewish synagogues and other associations, the upward mobility of the Reform Jewish community, and the encounter between the Reform community and the East European immigrant. More interpretive historical treatments are Steven Hertzberg's *Strangers Within the Gate City,* which recounts the early emergence of a Jewish elite during the reconstruction of Atlanta, and Jeffrey S. Gurock's *When Harlem Was Jewish,* which focuses on the complex patterns of interaction between the established Jewish community of New York and the new immigrants in the creation of Harlem. Rudolph Glanz's *Studies in Judaica Americana* contains essays on varied aspects of mid-century Jewish culture including the relations between Jews and other German migrant groups, the role of the Jewish peddler, and the rise of Jewish clubs. Trade books rather than scholarly accounts, Stephen Birmingham's *The Grandees* and *"Our Crowd"* describe the extraordinary economic and cultural accomplishments of the Sephardic and Reform German elites respectively.

A multifaceted Zionist movement was among the most important influences on American Judaism to develop as a result of the migrations. A collection of essays edited by Isidore S. Meyer *(Early History)* focuses on a number of individuals and locales important to Zionism's first promotion in the United States. Marnin Feinstein's *American Zionism* is a detailed account of the founding of the first American branch of *Hoveve Zion* in 1884, the impact of the East European migrations on the movement, and its growth in the early twentieth century. Naomi W. Cohen *(American Jews and the Zionist Idea)* emphasizes the distinctiveness of American Zionism; unlike their European counterparts, American Zionists had a dual faith in both the Zionist ideal and the American national tradition. Yonathan Shapiro *(Leadership)* discusses Zionism as an ideology of group survival and identity and notes the important part both spiritual and restorationist ideals played in the process of Americanization. Melvin I. Urofsky *(American Zionism)* begins his analysis at the onset of World War I and discusses the Americanization of the movement to the Holocaust.

A number of articles provide an excellent orientation to the relationship between Judaism and U.S. civilization. For a brief overview of Judaism cast in terms of the frontier thesis as utilized by Willam Warren Sweet, see Abraham J. Karp, "What's American about American Jewish History." An equally helpful introduction is found in Moses Rischin, "The Jews and the Liberal Tradition," in which alternative interpretations are offered in rejoinders by Stanley Falk and Abraham Karp. For a contrasting and critical assessment of American Judaism as "hegemonic" and "philistine liberalism," see Ben Halpern, "The Roots of American Jewish Liberalism."

In his recent book *Haven and Home,* Abraham Karp presents a rich cultural and religious history of the Jews in America that is a valuable supplement to the surveys by Handlin, Glazer, and Blau. Karp emphasizes the confident

Americanization of the Jews and their equally confident sense of their distinctiveness as a unique people. Jews, he concludes, have a "dual identity" in a land of ethnic diversity. Charles S. Liebman's *Ambivalent American Jew* provides a more conflict-oriented analysis of American Judaism; Jews are "torn" between two commitments, America and the history and people of their tradition.

In the decades on either side of 1900, as the Americanization process was transforming the religion and culture of the immigrant, the core culture dominated by Protestant Yankees was also undergoing massive structural change. With the consolidation of the urban industrial system, the waning of idealistic modes of thought, and the revolt against closed systems (John Higham, "Reorientation of American Culture"), America fully entered into the pragmatic spirit of the twentieth century. Capitalist, consumer culture transformed the collective symbols of American civilization into consumable goods (Trachtenberg, *Incorporation of America*); therapeutic values, rather than religious traditions, increasingly defined human experience (T. J. Jackson Lears, *No Place of Grace*). Intellectual historian Henry May (*End of Innocence*) saw the collapse of the authoritative idealism of Victorian custodians of culture in the first decades of the twentieth century; church historian Robert Handy (*A Christian America*) described the same era as the second disestablishment of the Protestant tradition.

Rowland Berthoff (*An Unsettled People*, "The American Social Order") argues that the immigrant played an important role in the process of transforming American culture. The great migrations helped to destroy the old communal order formed in the colonial and early national periods; a new communal order that incorporated the immigrant was constructed, a process that reached its culmination in the New Deal. Nathan Glazer ("The Immigrant Groups and American Culture") concurs; Glazer notes that, with the demise of the old authoritative high culture, a popular culture of great vibrancy and diversity—in large measure a contribution of the immigrant—was ascendant. It is at this point that Oscar Handlin, in his *The American People in the Twentieth Century*, begins his discussion of the complex interplay of Americanism, nationalism, ethnicity, and the forces of cultural unity and diversity in the twentieth century.

With the waning of explicitly racist ideologies, the demise of a clearly authoritative core culture, and the fundamental Americanization of the immigrant, the question of authority changed. Interpreters of the immigrant experience recast the issue of Protestant religion and culture versus immigrant traditions in terms of a variety of theoretical descriptions that centered on the persistence, or absence, of an enduring ethnicity in descendants of immigrant stock in a racially, religiously, and culturally pluralist America.

An introduction to basic concepts is helpful. Philip Gleason ("American Identity and Americanization") provides an historical survey of the development of the melting pot, Americanizing, and pluralist models of American culture. Michael Novak's "Pluralism: A Humanistic Perspective" is an excellent if moderate statement of the "new pluralist" ideals of the 1960s. Oscar Handlin ("Historical Perspectives") describes ethnic groups as enduring membership pools in which personal identity is forged and out of which individuals negotiate with the common culture. Milton M. Gordon ("Assimilation in America") makes the distinction between the easily achieved acculturation of the immigrant to social and economic roles and the far more problematic assimilation of deeply felt personal values to American norms. Variants of Gordon's hypothesis are found throughout the interpretive literature on the immigrant experience.

Will Herberg's concept of the triple melting pot in *Protestant-Catholic-Jew* has been extremely influential as a model for interpreting contemporary American religion. According to Herberg, ethnicity has given way to group identification in terms of the three major traditions, all of which hold a fourth in common: a highly generalized and secularized faith that embraces the democratic, individualistic, and pragmatic optimism which is a constituent part of the religion of "the American Way of Life." An equally influential but contrasting analysis of ethnic groups in modern America was offered by Nathan Glazer and Daniel P. Moynihan in *Beyond the Melting Pot.* According to them, ethnicity remains a vital part of American life; ethnic groups have been transformed into "interest groups" that continue to mediate between the needs of particular communities and the broader society. Church historians have also attempted to elucidate the continuing relationship between ethnic and religious identities. Martin E. Marty ("Ethnicity: The Skeleton of Religion") examines contemporary models such as tribalism, secularity, and civil religion in terms of the relationships among religion, ethnicity, and an American common life. Timothy L. Smith ("Religious Denominations as Ethnic Communities") argues that, while the question of nationality among descendants of immigrants has ceased to be an issue, differences persist in terms of religion, ethnicity, and, in the last analysis, collective psychology. This literature on ethnicity and religion expands the discussion well beyond the late nineteenth and early twentieth centuries. It attempts to understand persistent tensions in contemporary society resulting from the melding of the idealistic, nationalistic spirit forged in the American Protestant tradition with the values, aspirations, and historical experience of the millions of people whose roots in the United States are inextricably linked to the era of the great migrations.

BIBLIOGRAPHY

PROTESTANT CORE CULTURE

Badger, Reid. The Great American Fair: The World's Columbian
    Exposition and American Culture. Chicago: Nelson-Hall,
    1979.

Bannister, Robert C. Social Darwinism: Science and Myth in
    Anglo-American Social Thought. Philadelphia: Temple
    University Press, 1979.

Benkart, Paula K. "Changing Attitudes of Presbyterians Towards
    Southern and Eastern European Immigrants, 1880-1914."
    Journal of Presbyterian History 49 (Spring 1971), 222-245.

Billington, Ray Allen. The Protestant Crusade, 1800-1860: A
    Study of the Origins of American Nativism. New York:
    Macmillan, 1938.

Boyer, Paul S. Urban Masses and Moral Order in America, 1820-
    1920. Cambridge: Harvard University Press, 1978.

Brooklyn Museum. American Renaissance, 1876-1917. Brooklyn,
    N.Y.: Brooklyn Museum, 1979.

Burg, David F. Chicago's White City of 1893. Lexington:
    University Press of Kentucky, 1976.

Buroker, Robert L. "From Voluntary Association to Welfare
    State: The Illinois Immigrant's Protective League, 1908-
    1926." Journal of American History 58 (December 1971), 643-
    660.

Coben, Stanley. "A Study in Nativism: The American Red Scare
    of 1919-20." Political Science Quarterly 79 (March 1964),
    52-75.

Davis, David Brion. "Some Themes of Counter-Subversion: An Analysis of Anti-Masonic, Anti-Catholic, and Anti-Mormon Literature." Mississippi Valley Historical Review 47 (September 1960), 205-224.

Davis, Lawrence B. Immigrants, Baptists, and the Protestant Mind in America. Urbana: University of Illinois Press, 1973.

Dinnerstein, Leonard, comp. Anti-Semitism in the United States. New York: Holt, Rinehart, Winston, 1971.

Gossett, Thomas F. Race: The History of an Idea in America. Dallas: Southern Methodist University Press, 1963.

Haller, Mark H. Eugenics: Hereditarian Attitudes in American Thought. New Brunswick, N.J.: Rutgers University Press, 1963.

Handy, Robert T. A Christian America: Protestant Hopes and Historical Realities. New York: Oxford University Press, 1971.

Harper, Richard Conant. The Course of the Melting Pot Idea to 1910. New York: Arno Press, 1980.

Hartmann, Edward G. The Movement to Americanize the Immigrant. New York: Columbia University Press, 1948.

Hartz, Louis. The Founding of New Societies: Studies in the History of the United States, Latin America, South Africa, Canada, and Australia. New York: Harcourt, Brace, World, 1964.

Hartz, Louis. The Liberal Tradition in America: An Interpretation of American Political Thought Since the Revolution. New York: Harcourt, Brace, 1955.

Hatch, Nathan O. The Sacred Cause of Liberty: Republican Thought and the Millennium in Revolutionary New England. New Haven: Yale University Press, 1977.

Higham, John. "Immigration." In The Comparative Approach to American History, edited by C. Vann Woodward, 91-105. New York: Basic, 1968.

Higham, John. "The Reorientation of American Culture in the 1890s." In The Origins of Modern Consciousness, edited by John Weiss. Detroit: Wayne State University Press, 1965.

Higham, John. Send These to Me: Jews and Other Immigrants in Urban America. New York: Atheneum, 1975.

Higham, John. *Strangers in the Land: Patterns of American Nativism, 1860-1925*. New Brunswick, N.J.: Rutgers University Press, 1955.

Hofstadter, Richard. *Social Darwinism in American Thought*. Boston: Beacon Press, 1955.

Horowitz, Helen Lefkowitz. *Culture and the City: Cultural Philanthropy in Chicago from the 1880's to 1917*. Lexington: University Press of Kentucky, 1976.

Hudson, Winthrop S. *The Great Tradition of the American Churches*. New York: Harper and Row, 1953.

Hutchison, William R. *The Modernist Impulse in American Protestantism*. Cambridge: Harvard University Press, 1976.

Jones, Howard Mumford. *The Age of Energy: Varieties of American Experiences, 1865-1915*. New York: Viking, 1971.

Jordan, Philip D. "Immigrants, Methodists, and a 'Conservative' Social Gospel, 1865-1908." *Methodist History* 17 (October 1978), 16-43.

Kinzer, Donald L. *An Episode in Anti-Catholicism: The American Protective Association*. Seattle: University of Washington Press, 1964.

Korman, Gerd. *Industrialization, Immigrants, and Americanizers: The View from Milwaukee, 1866-1921*. Madison: State Historical Society of Wisconsin, 1967.

Kraditor, Aileen S. *The Radical Persuasion, 1890-1917: Aspects of the Intellectual History and the Historiography of Three American Radical Organizations*. Baton Rouge: Louisiana State University Press, 1981.

Lears, T. J. Jackson. *No Place of Grace: Antimodernism and the Transformation of American Culture, 1880-1920*. New York: Pantheon, 1981.

Lee, Elizabeth, and Abbott, Kenneth A. "Chinese Pilgrims and Presbyterians in the United States, 1851-1977." *Journal of Presbyterian History* 55 (Summer 1977), 125-144.

McBride, Paul W. "Peter Roberts and the YMCA Americanization Program, 1907-World War I." *Pennsylvania History* 44 (April 1977), 145-162.

MacNab, John B. "Bethlehem Chapel: Presbyterians and Italian Americans in New York City." *Journal of Presbyterian History* 55 (Summer 1977), 145-160.

Mann, Arthur. *Yankee Reformers in the Urban Age*. Cambridge: Harvard University Press, Belknap Press, 1954.

Marsden, George M. Fundamentalism and American Culture: The Shaping of Twentieth-Century Evangelicalism, 1870-1925. New York: Oxford University Press, 1980.

May, Henry F. The End of Innocence: A Study of the First Years of Our Own Times, 1912-1917. New York: Knopf, 1959.

May, Henry F. "The Religion of the Republic." In Ideas, Faiths, and Feelings: Essays on American Intellectual and Religious History, 1952-1982. New York: Oxford University Press, 1983.

Mead, Sidney E. The Lively Experiment: The Shaping of Christianity in America. New York: Harper and Row, 1963.

Mead, Sidney E. The Nation with the Soul of a Church. New York: Harper and Row, 1975.

Meyer, D. H. The Instructed Conscience: The Shaping of a National Ethic. Philadelphia: University of Pennsylvania Press, 1972.

Miller, Sally M. The Radical Immigrants. New York: Twayne, 1974.

Murray, Robert K. Red Scare: A Study in National Hysteria, 1919-1920. Minneapolis: University of Minnesota Press, 1955.

Persons, Stow. The Decline of Gentility. New York: Columbia University Press, 1973.

Philpott, Thomas L. The Slum and the Ghetto: Neighborhood Deterioration and Middle Class Reform, Chicago, 1880-1930. New York: Oxford University Press, 1978.

Preston, William. Aliens and Dissenters: Federal Suppression of Radicals, 1903-1933. Cambridge: Harvard University Press, 1963.

Raleigh, John Henry. Matthew Arnold and American Culture. Berkeley: University of California Press, 1957.

Rideout, Lionel U. "The Church, the Chinese, and the Negroes in California, 1849-1893." Historical Magazine of the Protestant Episcopal Church 28 (June 1959), 115-138.

Rydell, Robert W. All the World's a Fair: Visions of Empire at American International Expositions, 1876-1916. Chicago: University of Chicago Press, 1984.

Saveth, Edward Norman. American Historians and the European Immigrants, 1875-1925. New York: Columbia University Press, 1948.

Seager, Robert H. "Some Denominational Reactions to the Chinese in California, 1856-1892." Pacific Historical Review 28 (February 1959), 49-66.

Solomon, Barbara M. Ancestors and Immigrants: A Changing New England Tradition. Cambridge: Harvard University Press, 1956.

Sproat, John G. The Best Men: Liberal Reformers in the Gilded Age. New York: Oxford University Press, 1968.

Thernstrom, Stephan. The Other Bostonians: Poverty and Progress in the American Metropolis, 1880-1970. Cambridge: Harvard University Press, 1973.

Thernstrom, Stephan, and Sennett, Richard. Nineteenth Century Cities: Essays in the New Urban History. New Haven: Yale University Press, 1969.

Trachtenberg, Alan. The Incorporation of America: Culture and Society in the Gilded Age. New York: Hill and Wang, 1982.

Tumin, Melvin M. An Inventory and Appraisal of Research on American Antisemitism. New York: Freedom Books, 1961.

Tuveson, Ernest L. Redeemer Nation: The Idea of America's Millennial Role. Chicago: University of Chicago Press, 1968.

Vanderbilt, Kermit. Charles Eliot Norton: Apostle of Culture in a Democracy. Cambridge: Harvard University Press, Belknap Press, 1959.

Walasky, Paul William. "The Entertainment of Angels: American Baptists and Assimilation, 1890-1925." Foundations 19 (Fall 1976), 346-360.

Warner, Sam Bass. Streetcar Suburbs: The Process of Growth in Boston, 1870-1900. Cambridge: Harvard University Press and MIT Press, 1962.

Warner, Sam Bass. The Urban Wilderness: A History of the American City. New York: Harper and Row, 1972.

CHINESE MIGRATIONS

Barth, Gunther P. Bitter Strength: A History of the Chinese in the United States, 1850-1870. Cambridge: Harvard University Press, 1964.

Black, Isabella. "American Labour and Chinese Immigration." Past and Present 25 (July 1963), 59-76.

Chinn, T. W.; Lai, H. M.; and Choy, Philip D. A History of the
     Chinese in California: A Syllabus. San Francisco: Chinese
     Historical Society of America, 1969.

Chiu, Ping. Chinese Labor in California, 1850-1880: An
     Economic Study. Madison: State Historical Society of
     Wisconsin, 1963.

Chu, George. "Chinatowns in the Delta: The Chinese in the
     Sacramento-San Joaquin Delta, 1870-1960." California
     Historical Society Quarterly 49 (March 1970), 21-37.

Coolidge, Mary R. Chinese Immigrants. 1909. Reprint.
     Taipei: Ch'eng-wen Publishing Co., 1968.

Lai, H. M. "The Chinese." In Harvard Encyclopedia of American
     Ethnic Groups, edited by Stephan Thernstrom. Cambridge:
     Harvard University Press, Belknap Press, 1980.

Lee, Rose Hum. The Chinese in the United States of America.
     Hong Kong: Hong Kong University Press, 1960.

Light, Ivan H. "From Vice District to Tourist Attraction: The
     Moral Career of American Chinatowns, 1880-1940." Pacific
     Historical Review 43 (August 1974), 367-394.

Lyman, Stanford M. The Asians in the West. Social Sciences
     and Humanities Publications, no. 4. Reno: University of
     Nevada, 1970.

Lyman, Stanford M. Chinese Americans. New York: Random House,
     1974.

Lyman, Stanford M. "Conflict and the Web of Group Affiliation
     in San Francisco's Chinatown, 1850-1910." Pacific
     Historical Review 43 (November 1974), 473-499.

Lyman, Stanford M. The Structure of Chinese Society in
     Nineteenth Century America. Port Washington, N.Y.:
     Associated Faculty Press, 1984.

McKee, Delber L. "'The Chinese Must Go!' Commissioner General
     Powderly and Chinese Immigration, 1897-1902." Pennsylvania
     History 44 (January 1977), 37-51.

Melendy, H. Brett. The Oriental Americans. New York: Twayne,
     1972.

Miller, Stuart Creighton. The Unwelcome Immigrant: The
     American Image of the Chinese, 1785-1882. Berkeley:
     University of California Press, 1969.

Nee, Victor G., and Nee, Brett de Bary. Longtime Californ': A
     Documentary Study of an American Chinatown. New York:
     Pantheon, 1973.

Pomerantz, Linda. "The Chinese Bourgeoisie and the Anti-
Chinese Movement in the United States, 1850-1905."
Amerasian Journal 11 (January 1984), 1-33.

Sandmeyer, Elmer C. The Anti-Chinese Movement in California.
1939. Reprint. Urbana: University of Illinois Press, 1973.

Saxton, Alexander P. The Indispensable Enemy: Labor and the
Anti-Chinese Movement in California. Berkeley: University
of California Press, 1971.

Trauner, Joan B. "The Chinese as Medical Scapegoats in San
Francisco, 1870-1905." California History 57 (Spring 1978),
70-87.

Tsai, Shih-shan H. China and the Overseas Chinese in the
United States, 1868-1911. Fayetteville: University of
Arkansas Press, 1983.

                    BLACK MIGRATIONS NORTH

Bardolph, Richard. The Negro Vanguard. New York: Rinehart and
Co., 1959.

Borchert, James. Alley Life in Washington: Family, Community,
Religion, and Folklife in the City, 1850-1970. Urbana:
University of Illinois Press, 1980.

Burkett, Randall K. Black Redemption: Churchmen Speak for the
Garvey Movement. Philadelphia: Temple University Press,
1978.

Burkett, Randall K. Garveyism as a Religious Movement: The
Institutionalization of a Black Civil Religion. ATLA
Monograph Series, no. 13. Metuchen, N.J.: Scarecrow, 1978.

Burkett, Randall K., and Newman, Richard, eds. Black Apostles:
Afro-American Clergy Confront the Twentieth Century.
Boston: G. K. Hall, 1978.

Clark, Elmer T. The Small Sects in America. New York:
Abingdon-Cokesbury, 1949.

Cronon, Edmund D. Black Moses: The Story of Marcus Garvey and
the Universal Negro Improvement Association. Madison:
University of Wisconsin Press, 1955.

Drake, St. Clair, and Cayton, Horace. Black Metropolis: A
Study of Negro Life in a Northern City. 3d ed. New York:
Harcourt, Brace, 1970.

Essien-Udom, E. U. "Garvey and Garveyism." In America's Black
    Past: A Reader in Afro-American History, edited by Eric
    Foner. New York: Harper and Row, 1970.

Fauset, Arthur Huff. Black Gods of the Metropolis: Negro
    Religious Cults of the Urban North. 1944. Reprint.
    Philadelphia: University of Pennsylvania Press, 1971.

Frazier, E. Franklin, and Lincoln, C. Eric. The Negro Church
    in America. New York: Schocken, 1974.

Harrison, Ira E. "The Store Front Church as Revitalization
    Movement." In The Black Church in America, edited by Hart
    M. Nelsen. New York: Basic, 1971.

Hellwig, David J. "The Afro-American and the Immigrant, 1880-
    1930: A Study of Black Social Thought." Ph.D. diss.,
    Syracuse University, 1973.

Henri, Florette. Black Migration: The Movement North, 1900-
    1920. Garden City, N.Y.: Doubleday, Anchor Books, 1975.

Johnson, Daniel M., and Campbell, Rex R. Black Migration in
    America: A Social Demographic History. Durham, N.C.: Duke
    University Press, 1981.

Lieberson, Stanley. A Piece of the Pie: Black and White
    Immigrants Since 1880. Berkeley: University of California
    Press, 1980.

Martin, Tony. Race First: The Ideological and Organizational
    Struggles of Marcus Garvey and the Universal Negro
    Improvement Association. Westport, Conn: Greenwood, 1976.

Mays, Benjamin E., and Nicholson, Joseph W. The Negro's
    Church. 1933. Reprint. New York: Arno Press, 1969.

Moses, Wilson J. The Golden Age of Black Nationalism, 1850-
    1925. Hamden, Conn.: Archon Books, 1978.

Osofsky, Gilbert. Harlem: The Making of a Ghetto: Negro New
    York, 1890-1930. New York: Harper and Row, 1968.

Pleck, Elizabeth H. Black Migration and Poverty: Boston, 1865-
    1900. New York: Academic Press, 1979.

Scheiner, Seth M. "The Negro Church and the Northern City,
    1890-1930." In Seven on Black: Reflections on the Negro
    Experience in America, edited by William G. Shade and Roy C.
    Herrenkohl. Philadelphia: Lippincott, 1969.

Scheiner, Seth M. Negro Mecca: A History of the Negro in New
    York City, 1865-1920. New York: New York University Press,
    1965.

Spear, Allan H. Black Chicago: The Making of the Negro Ghetto,
1890-1920. Chicago: University of Chicago Press, 1967.

Vincent, Theodore G. Black Power and the Garvey Movement.
Berkeley: Ramparts, 1971.

Washington, Joseph R. Black Sects and Cults. Garden City,
N.Y.: Doubleday, 1972.

Welty, William M. Black Shepherds: A Study of the Leading
Negro Clergymen in New York City, 1900-1940. Ann Arbor:
University Microfilms, 1970.

Wilmore, Gayraud S. Black Religion and Black Radicalism.
Garden City, N.Y.: Doubleday, 1972.

Woodson, Carter G. A Century of Negro Migration. 1918.
Reprint. New York: Russell and Russell, 1969.

Woodson, Carter G. History of the Negro Church. 1921.
Reprint. Washington, D.C.: Associated Publishers, 1972.

SCANDINAVIAN LUTHERAN IMMIGRANTS

Anderson, Charles H. White Protestant Americans: From National
Origin to Religious Group. Englewood Cliffs, N.J.: Prentice
Hall, 1970.

Arden, G. Everett. Augustana Heritage: A History of the
Augustana Lutheran Church. Rock Island, Ill.: Augustana
Press, 1963.

Beijbom, Ulf. Swedes in Chicago: A Demographic and Social
Study of the 1846-1880 Immigration. Translated by Donald
Brown. Stockholm: Laromedselsforlagen, 1971.

Dowie, James Inverne, and Espelie, Ernest M., eds. The Swedish
Immigrant Community in Transition: Essays in Honor of Dr.
Conrad Bergendoff. Rock Island, Ill.: Augustana Historical
Society, 1963.

Hoglund, A. William. Finnish Immigrants in America, 1880-1920.
Madison: University of Wisconsin Press, 1960.

Jalkanen, Ralph J., ed. The Faith of the Finns: Historical
Perspectives on the Finnish Lutheran Church in America.
East Lansing: Michigan State University Press, 1972.

Lindberg, Duane R. Men of the Cloth and the Social-Cultural
Fabric of the Norwegian Ethnic Community in North Dakota.
New York: Arno Press, 1980.

Lindmark, Sture. _Swedish America, 1914-32: Studies in Ethnicity with an Emphasis on Illinois and Minnesota_. Studia Historica Upsaliensia 37. Stockholm: Laromedselsforlagen, 1971.

Mortensen, Enok. _The Danish Lutheran Church in America_. Philadelphia: Board of Publications, Lutheran Church in America, 1967.

Nelson, E. Clifford, and Fevold, Eugene L. _The Lutheran Church Among Norwegian Americans: A History of the Evangelical Lutheran Church_. 2 vols. Minneapolis, Minn.: Augsburg Publishing House, 1960.

Nyholm, Paul P. _The Americanization of the Danish Lutheran Churches in America: A Study in Immigrant History_. Copenhagen, Denmark: Institute for Danish Church History, 1963.

Skaardal, Dorothy B. _The Divided Heart: Scandinavian Immigrant Experience Through Literary Sources_. Lincoln: University of Nebraska Press, 1974.

ROMAN CATHOLIC MIGRATIONS

Abramson, Harold J. "Ethnic Diversity within Catholicism: A Comparative Analysis of Contemporary and Historical Religion." _Journal of Social History_ 4 (Summer 1971), 359-388.

Barry, Colman J. _The Catholic Church and German Americans_. Washington, D.C.: Catholic University of America Press, 1953.

Barton, Josef J. _Peasants and Strangers: Italians, Rumanians, and Slovaks in an American City, 1890-1950_. Cambridge: Harvard University Press, 1975.

Birmingham, Stephen. _Real Lace: America's Irish Rich_. New York: Harper and Row, 1973.

Briggs, John W. _An Italian Passage: Immigrants to Three American Cities, 1890-1930_. New Haven: Yale University Press, 1978.

Clark, Dennis. _The Irish in Philadelphia: Ten Generations of Urban Experience_. Philadelphia: Temple University Press, 1973.

Conzen, Kathleen Neils. _Immigrant Milwaukee, 1836-1860: Accommodation and Community in a Frontier City_. Cambridge: Harvard University Press, 1976.

Cordasco, Francesco, ed. Protestant Evangelism Among Italians in America. New York: Arno Press, 1975.

Cross, Robert D. The Emergence of Liberal Catholicism in America. Cambridge: Harvard University Press, 1958.

Cross, Robert D., ed. The Church and the City, 1865-1910. Indianapolis, Ind.: Bobbs-Merrill, 1967.

Curran, Robert E. Michael Augustine Corrigan and the Shaping of Conservative Catholicism in America, 1878-1902. New York: Arno Press, 1978.

Dolan, Jay P. The American Catholic Experience. Garden City, N.Y.: Doubleday, 1985.

Dolan, Jay P. The Immigrant Church: New York's Irish and German Catholics, 1815-65. Baltimore: Johns Hopkins University Press, 1975.

Fogarty, Gerald P. The Vatican and the Americanist Crisis: Denis J. O'Connell, American Agent in Rome, 1885-1903. Rome: Universita Gregoriana, 1974.

Gleason, Philip. The Conservative Reformers: German-American Catholics and the Social Order. Notre Dame, Ind.: University of Notre Dame Press, 1968.

Gleason, Philip. "An Immigrant Group's Interest in Progressive Reform: The Case of the German-American Catholics." American Historical Review 73 (December 1967), 367-379.

Greene, Victor R. For God and Country: The Rise of Polish and Lithuanian Ethnic Consciousness in America, 1860-1910. Madison: State Historical Society of Wisconsin, 1975.

Halsey, William M. The Survival of American Innocence: Catholicism in an Era of Disillusionment, 1920-1940. Notre Dame, Ind.: University of Notre Dame Press, 1980.

Handlin, Oscar. Boston's Immigrants: A Study in Acculturation. Cambridge: Harvard University Press, Belknap Press, 1959.

Juliani, Richard N. "Italians and Other Americans: The Parish, the Union, and the Settlement House." In Perspectives in Italian Immigration and Ethnicity, edited by Silvano M. Tomasi. New York: Center for Migration Studies, 1977.

Kessner, Thomas. The Golden Door: Italian and Jewish Immigrant Mobility in New York City, 1880-1915. New York: Oxford University Press, 1977.

Killen, David P. "Americanism Revisited: John Spalding and Testem Benevolentiae." Harvard Theological Review 66 (October 1973), 413-454.

Kuzniewski, Anthony J. Faith and Fatherland: The Polish Church War in Wisconsin, 1896-1918. Notre Dame, Ind.: University of Notre Dame Press, 1980.

Linkh, Richard M. American Catholicism and the European Immigrants, 1900-1924. New York: Center for Migration Studies, 1975.

McAvoy, Thomas T. The Americanist Heresy in Roman Catholicism, 1895-1900. Notre Dame, Ind.: University of Notre Dame Press, 1963.

McAvoy, Thomas T. "The Formation of the Catholic Minority in the United States, 1820-1860." In Religion in American History: Interpretive Essays, edited by John M. Mulder and John F. Wilson. Englewood Cliffs, N.J.: Prentice-Hall, 1978.

Merwick, Donna. Boston Priests, 1848-1910: A Study of Social and Intellectual Change. Cambridge: Harvard University Press, 1973.

Miller, Randall M., and Marzik, Thomas D. Immigrants and Religion in Urban America. Philadelphia: Temple University Press, 1977.

Monzell, Thomas I. "The Catholic Church and the Americanization of the Polish Immigrant." Polish-American Studies 26 (January-June 1969), 1-15.

Nelli, Humbert S. Italians in Chicago, 1880-1930: A Study in Ethnic Mobility. New York: Oxford University Press, 1970.

Orsi, Robert Anthony. The Madonna of 115th Street: Faith and Community in Italian Harlem, 1880-1950. New Haven: Yale University Press, 1985.

Potter, George W. To the Golden Door: The Story of the Irish in Ireland and America. Westport, Conn.: Greenwood, 1960.

Sewry, Charles L. "Infallibility, the American Way, and Catholic Apologetics." Journal of Church and State 15 (Spring 1973), 293-302.

Shannon, William V. The American Irish. 2d ed. New York: Macmillan, 1966.

Thomas, William I., and Znaniecki, Florian. The Polish Peasant in Europe and America. 2 vols. 1927. Reprint. New York: Dover, 1958.

Tomasi, Silvano M. Piety and Power: The Role of Italian Parishes in the New York Metropolitan Area, 1880-1930. New York: Center for Migration Studies, 1975.

Vecoli, Rudolph J. "The Contadini in Chicago: A Critique of
The Uprooted." Journal of American History 51 (December
1964), 404-417.

Vecoli, Rudolph J. "Prelates and Peasants: Italian Immigrants
and the Catholic Church." Journal of Social History 2
(Spring 1969), 217-268.

Wangler, Thomas E. "The Birth of Americanism: 'Westward the
Apocalyptic Candlestick.'" Harvard Theological Review 65
(July 1972), 415-436.

Yans-McLaughlin, Virginia. Family and Community: Italian
Immigrants in Buffalo, 1880-1930. Ithaca, N.Y.: Cornell
University Press, 1977.

JUDAISM AND IMMIGRATION

Angel, Marc D. "The Sephardim of the United States: An
Exploratory Study." American Jewish Year Book 74 (1973),
77-138.

Birmingham, Stephen. The Grandees: America's Sephardic Elite.
New York: Harper and Row, 1971.

Birmingham, Stephen. "Our Crowd": The Great Jewish Families of
New York. New York: Harper and Row, 1967.

Blau, Joseph L. Judaism in America: From Curiosity to Third
Faith. Chicago: University of Chicago Press, 1976.

Blau, Joseph L. Reform Judaism: A Historical Perspective. New
York: KTAV, 1973.

Cohen, Naomi W. American Jews and the Zionist Idea. New York:
KTAV, 1975.

Davis, Moshe. The Emergence of Conservative Judaism: The
Historical School in Nineteenth Century America.
Philadelphia: Jewish Publication Society of America, 1963.

Feinstein, Marnin. American Zionism, 1884-1904. New York:
Herzl Press, 1965.

Gartner, Lloyd P. The History of the Jews of Cleveland.
Cleveland: Western Reserve Historical Society, 1978.

Glanz, Rudolf. Studies in Judaica Americana. New York: KTAV,
1970.

Glazer, Nathan. American Judaism. 2d ed. Chicago: University
of Chicago Press, 1972.

Goren, Arthur A. New York Jews and the Quest for Community: The Kehillah Experiment, 1908-1922. New York: Columbia University Press, 1970.

Gurock, Jeffrey S. When Harlem Was Jewish, 1870-1930. New York: Columbia University Press, 1979.

Halpern, Ben. "The Roots of American Jewish Liberalism." American Jewish Historical Quarterly 66 (December 1976), 190-214.

Handlin, Oscar. Adventures in Freedom: Three Hundred Years of Jewish Life in America. New York: McGraw-Hill, 1954.

Hertzberg, Steven. Strangers Within the Gate City: The Jews of Atlanta, 1845-1915. Philadelphia: Jewish Publication Society of America, 1978.

Howe, Irving. World of Our Fathers. New York: Harcourt Brace Jovanovich, 1976.

Jick, Leon A. The Americanization of the Synagogue, 1820-1870. Hanover, N.H.: University Press of New England, 1976.

Karp, Abraham J. Haven and Home: A History of the Jews in America. New York: Schocken, 1985.

Karp, Abraham J. "What's American About American Jewish History: The Religious Scene." American Jewish Historical Quarterly 52 (June 1963), 283-294.

Kraut, Benny. "Francis E. Abbot: Perceptions of a Nineteenth Century Religious Radical on Jews and Judaism." In Studies in the American Jewish Experience, edited by Jacob Marcus and Abe Peck. Cincinnati: American Jewish Archives, 1981.

Kraut, Benny. From Reform Judaism to Ethical Culture: The Religious Evolution of Felix Adler. Cincinnati: Hebrew Union College Press, 1979.

Kraut, Benny. "Judaism Triumphant: Isaac Meyer Wise on Unitarianism and Liberal Christianity." Association for Jewish Studies Review 78 (1982-83), 179-230.

Liebman, Charles S. The Ambivalent American Jew: Politics, Religion, and Family in American Jewish Life. Philadelphia: Jewish Publication Society of America, 1973.

Meyer, Isidore S., ed. Early History of Zionism in America. New York: American Jewish Historical Society and Theodor Herzl Foundation, 1958.

"A Re-Examination of a Classic Work in American Jewish History: Moses Rischin's The Promised City, Twenty Years Later." American Jewish History 73 (December 1983), 133-204.

Rischin, Moses. "The Jews and the Liberal Tradition in
    America." _American Jewish Historical Quarterly_ 51
    (September 1961), 4-29.

Rischin, Moses. _The Promised City: New York's Jews, 1870-1914_.
    Cambridge: Harvard University Press, 1962.

Rosenberg, Stuart E. _The Jewish Community in Rochester, 1843-
    1925_. New York: American Jewish Historical Society and
    Columbia University Press, 1954.

Shapiro, Yonathan. _Leadership of the American Zionist
    Organization, 1897-1930_. Urbana: University of Illinois
    Press, 1971.

Swichkow, Louis J., and Gartner, Lloyd P. _The History of the
    Jews of Milwaukee_. Philadelphia: Jewish Publication Society
    of America, 1963.

Temkin, Sefton D. "A Century of Reform Judaism in America."
    American Jewish Year Book 74 (1973), 3-75.

Urofsky, Melvin I. _American Zionism from Herzl to the
    Holocaust_. Garden City, N.Y.: Doubleday, Anchor Books,
    1975.

Vorspan, Max, and Gartner, Lloyd P. _History of the Jews of Los
    Angeles_. San Marino, Calif.: Huntington Library, 1970.

BIBLIOGRAPHIES AND BIBLIOGRAPHIC ESSAYS

Brickman, William W. _The Jewish Community in America: An
    Annotated and Classified Bibliographical Guide_. New York:
    Benjamin Franklin, 1977.

Buenker, John D., and Burkel, Nicholas C. _Immigration and
    Ethnicity: A Guide to Information Sources_. Detroit: Gale,
    1977.

Cordasco, Francesco. _The Immigrant Woman in North America: An
    Annotated Bibliography of Selected References_. Metuchen,
    N.J.: Scarecrow, 1985.

Cordasco, Francesco. _The Italian-American Experience: An
    Annotated and Classified Bibliographical Guide, with
    Selected Publications of the Casa Italiana Educational
    Bureau_. New York: Benjamin Franklin, 1974.

Cordasco, Francesco. Italians in the United States: An
Annotated Bibliography of Doctoral Dissertations Completed
at American Universities, with a Handlist of Selected
Published Bibliographies, Related Reference Materials, and
Guide Books for Italian Emigrants. Fairview, N.J.: Junius
Press, 1981.

Cordasco, Francesco, comp. Italian Americans: A Guide to
Information Sources. Detroit: Gale, 1978.

Cordasco, Francesco, and Alloway, David N. American Ethnic
Groups, The European Heritage: A Bibliography of Doctoral
Dissertations Completed at American Universities. Metuchen,
N.J.: Scarecrow, 1981.

Cross, Robert D. "How Historians Have Looked at Immigrants to
the United States." International Migration Review 7
(Spring 1974), 4-13.

Ellis, John Tracy, and Trisco, Robert. A Guide to American
Catholic History. 2d ed. Santa Barbara, Calif.: ABC-Clio,
1982.

Glazer, Nathan. "The Immigrant Groups and American Culture."
Yale Review 48 (Spring 1959), 382-397.

Gurock, Jeffrey S. American Jewish History: A Bibliographical
Guide. New York: Anti-Defamation League of the B'nai
B'rith, 1983.

Hoglund, A. William. Immigrants and Their Children in the
United States: A Bibliography of Doctoral Dissertations
1885-1982. New York: Garland Publishing Co., 1986.

Hune, Shirley. Pacific Migration to the United States: Trends
and Themes in Historical and Sociological Literature. RIIES
Bibliographic Studies, no. 2. Washington, D.C.: Smithsonian
Institution, 1977.

Marcus, Jacob R., ed. An Index to Scientific Articles on
American Jewish History. Publication of the American Jewish
Archives, no. 7. New York: KTAV, 1971.

Miller, Elizabeth W. The Negro in America: A Bibliography. 2d
ed. Cambridge: Harvard University Press, 1970.

Mortensen, Enok. Danish-American Life and Letters: A
Bibliography. Des Moines, Iowa: Committee of Publications
of the Danish Evangelical Lutheran Church in America, 1945.

Rogers, Daniel. "American Historians and East Asian
Immigrants." Pacific Historical Review 43 (November 1974),
449-472.

Rogers, Daniel. "North American Scholarship and Asian
    Immigrants, 1974-1979." Immigration History Newsletter 11
    (May 1979), 8-11.

Thernstrom, Stephan. Harvard Encyclopedia of American Ethnic
    Groups. Cambridge: Harvard University Press, Belknap Press,
    1980.

Tomasi, Silvano M., and Stibili, Edward C. Italian-Americans
    and Religion: An Annotated Bibliography. New York: Center
    for Migration Studies, 1978.

Vecoli, Rudolph J. "European Americans: From Immigrants to
    Ethnics." International Immigration Review 6 (Winter 1972),
    403-434.

White, Joseph M. "Historiography of Catholic Immigrants and
    Religion." Immigration History Newsletter 14 (November
    1982), 5-11.

Williams, Ethel L., and Brown, Clifton F. The Howard
    University Bibliography of African and Afro-American
    Religious Studies with Locations in American Libraries.
    Wilmington, Del.: Scholarly Resources, 1977.

THEORETICAL REFLECTIONS AND SURVEYS

Berthoff, Rowland T. "The American Social Order: A
    Conservative Hypothesis." American Historical Review 65
    (April 1960), 495-514.

Berthoff, Rowland T. "Peasants and Artisans, Puritans and
    Republicans: Personal Liberty and Communal Equality in
    American History." Journal of American History 69 (December
    1982), 579-598.

Berthoff, Rowland T. An Unsettled People: Social Order and
    Disorder in American History. New York: Harper and Row,
    1971.

Commager, Henry S., ed. Immigration and American History:
    Essays in Honor of Theodore C. Blegen. Minneapolis:
    University of Minnesota Press, 1961.

Dinnerstein, Leonard, and Reimers, David M. Ethnic Americans:
    A History of Immigration and Assimilation. New York: Dodd,
    Mead, 1975.

Fishman, Joshua A. Language Loyalty in the United States: The
    Maintenance and Perpetuation of Non-English Mother Tongues
    by American Ethnic and Religious Groups. Janua Linguarum,
    Series Maior 21. The Hague: Mouton, 1966.

Glazer, Nathan, and Moynihan, Daniel P. Beyond the Melting
   Pot: The Negroes, Puerto Ricans, Jews, Italians, and Irish
   of New York City. Cambridge, Mass.: MIT Press, 1963.

Gleason, Philip. "American Identity and Americanization." In
   Harvard Encyclopedia of American Ethnic Groups, edited by
   Stephan Thernstrom. Cambridge: Harvard University Press,
   Belknap Press, 1980.

Gleason, Philip. "The Melting Pot: Symbol of Fusion or
   Confusion?" American Quarterly 16 (Spring 1964), 20-46.

Gordon, Milton M. Assimilation in American Life: The Role of
   Race, Religion, and National Origins. New York: Oxford
   University Press, 1964.

Gordon, Milton M. "Assimilation in America: Theory and
   Reality." Daedalus 90 (Spring 1961), 263-285.

Handlin, Oscar. The American People in the Twentieth Century.
   Cambridge: Harvard University Press, 1954.

Handlin, Oscar. "Historical Perspectives on the American
   Ethnic Group." Daedalus 90 (Spring 1961), 220-232.

Herberg, Will. Protestant-Catholic-Jew: An Essay in American
   Religious Sociology. Garden City, N.Y.: Doubleday, 1955.

Jones, Maldwyn A. American Immigration. Chicago: University
   of Chicago Press, 1960.

Marty, Martin E. "Ethnicity: The Skeleton of Religion in
   America." Church History 41 (March 1972), 5-21.

Novak, Michael. "Pluralism: A Humanistic Perspective." In
   Harvard Encyclopedia of American Ethnic Groups, edited by
   Stephan Thernstrom. Cambridge: Harvard University Press,
   Belknap Press, 1980.

Powell, James H. The Concept of Cultural Pluralism in American
   Social Thought, 1915-1965. Ann Arbor: University
   Microfilms, 1972.

Smith, Timothy L. "New Approaches to the History of
   Immigration in Twentieth Century America." American
   Historical Review 71 (July 1966), 1265-1279.

Smith, Timothy L. "Religious Denominations as Ethnic
   Communities: A Regional Case Study." Church History 35
   (June 1966), 207-226.

Taylor, Philip A. M. The Distant Magnet: European Immigration
   to the U.S.A. New York: Harper and Row, 1971.

5

Church and State at the Turn of the Century: Missions and Imperialism, Bureaucratization, and War, 1898–1920

James D. Beumler

The first two decades of the twentieth century were critical in the development of church-state issues in American public life. They were years marked by large-scale immigration and many religiously inspired attempts at social reform, both covered in the two preceding chapters of this volume. These years were also marked by other events and processes of lasting impact on American church-state relations that require separate consideration. Two of these were international, and in them religion played a crucial role—the era of foreign missions (the 1890s through the 1910s) and the First World War. In both, clergy were important national leaders, political actions were justified to the public in the language of religion, and the political actors themselves thought of their work in religious terms. In another major development, religious groups at the turn of the century began to organize at national levels in a bureaucratization that would allow churches to interact with the state and other modern corporate entities in an entirely new way.

These three topics—missions and their relation to imperialism in the years surrounding the Spanish-American War, the bureaucratization of religion, and the place of religion in World War I—are the focus of this essay and accompanying bibliography. The bibliography's items are arranged, like the essay, under the headings "Missionaries and Expansionists," "Bureaucratization," and "World War I." Preceding these is a listing of books and articles under the heading "General Perspectives on Religion in the Period" that provides the reader with an appreciation of the larger religious and historical background within which these chosen events and processes unfolded and where their examination must begin.

GENERAL PERSPECTIVES ON RELIGION IN THE PERIOD

America in 1898, though undergoing substantial change, was still very much a Protestant nation. Attempts to find a unifying theme in the religious aspects of the United States at the turn of the century have focused on the development of religious liberalism. All of the events and changes outlined in this essay occurred in the context of a growth of liberal theology which Henry P. Van Dusen, one of its earliest historical interpreters, described in a 1936 article (reissued in 1978) as "the child of the late nineteenth-century outlook, and of the evangelical experience" ("A Half-Century of Liberal Theology," p. 348). From the former parent, religion took on such characteristics as devotion to truth, deference to science, tentativeness as to the possibility of metaphysical certainty, and an emphasis on continuity between the natural and the divine. From the latter, evangelicalism, the creative impulse in religion drew convictions about the authority of Christian experience and the centrality of Jesus Christ, a loyalty to the historic faith and a missionary compassion.

Although the numbers of those who fully embraced liberal theology and the closely related social gospel were limited, the new undogmatic religious attitude, with its accommodation to modern thought and society, deeply permeated the culture. Winthrop S. Hudson's article "The Methodist Age in America" sheds light on how this was possible by explaining the contours of evangelicalism and by emphasizing how Americans' religious attitudes had come in the nineteenth century to resemble Methodism in terms of favoring good works and mission activity over theological disputation and doctrinal rigidity. As for the evolution of Van Dusen's "nineteenth-century outlook," Paul A. Carter's *The Spiritual Crisis of the Gilded Age* nicely traces out the adoption of modern beliefs about science, creation, and evolution and their relation to religion during the years leading up to 1895.

Another approach to the study of religious liberalism is to focus on its leaders, a cadre of Protestant clergy noted particularly for their contribution to public life in the causes of progressivism, economic justice amidst widespread industrialization, child labor and municipal reforms, and in the debates over imperialism. The emergence of an elite corps of reform-minded clergy with such a high degree of public influence has led historians to explore the sources of that development. Some interpreters of the culture, among them Richard Hofstadter, have seen this process as the result of a decline in religion and particularly in ministerial status. In this view the clergy's challenge to the status quo was a bid for renewed standing motivated by self-interest. Representing an alternative position, William R. Hutchison has categorized this reading of religious change as simplistic in an article entitled "Cultural Strain and Protestant Liberalism." He argues instead that wider changes in the culture and commonalities in the religious family histories of a whole generation of intelligent evangelicals better explain the formation of the religious liberals.

Whatever the sources of religious liberalism, it provided the context for the era's interactions between church and state and religion and society. It was the precondition to the missionary impulse toward expansion, to ecclesiastical bureaucratization, and to the dominant attitudes of religion during World War I. Mission to the rest of the world was most forcefully undertaken given a theological conviction that the world was subject to improvement. The antidogmatic turn in theology made ecumenism possible and ecclesiastical restructuring easier. Even the close identification of many religious leaders in World War I with the allied cause in the "war to end all wars" is better understood with reference to the progressive notion of history promoted by ministers and politicians alike. Throughout the period, in its debates, movements, and processes, a coming of the Kingdom of God loomed large.

In addition to Van Dusen's highly readable introduction to liberal theology cited above, there are a number of other works which explore the subject. The intellectual history of liberal theology has been treated in great depth and detail by Hutchison in *The Modernist Impulse in American Protestantism* and in *Errand to the World: American Protestant Thought and Foreign Missions*. The political and cultural impact of the period's heightened religious liberalism has been assessed by Kenneth Cauthen in *The Impact of American Religious Liberalism*, by Henry F. May in *Protestant Churches and Industrial America*, and by C. Howard Hopkins in *The Rise of the Social Gospel in America, 1865–1915*. Its continuing impact is the focus of books by Robert Moats Miller and Donald B. Meyer. From the period itself come a variety of works that provide a flavor of the prevailing intellectual mood. Glenn Gaius Atkins's *Religion in Our Times* is a perceptive volume looking back on a life lived within the liberal religious tradition. The change in conception of church-state issues over the period is evident in the distance between Isaac Amada Cornelison's *The Relation of Religion to Civil Government in the United States of America: A State Without a Church, But Not Without a Religion* written in 1895 and William H. P. Faunce's immediately postwar *The New Horizon of State and Church*, yet the degree to which church and state were allied throughout the period was the subject of critical postwar reflections in John J. Burke's "The Historical Attitude of the Church Toward Nationalism" and William Adams Brown's *The Church in America* and *Church and State in Contemporary America*. In an effort to demonstrate the distinctiveness of religious liberalism's contribution to American culture, Henry May contrasts it with the complacency of Protestantism in the years immediately after the Civil War: "In 1876 Protestantism presented a massive, almost unbroken front in its defense of the social status quo. Two decades later social criticism had penetrated deeply into each major church"

(*Protestant Churches and Industrial America*, p. 91). While May is quite correct in identifying the first shift from defense of the status quo to a liberalism critical of American society, a further shift also took place, making liberal religion itself complacent. William Adams Brown was to lament after World War I of his colleagues that "in the heat of the struggle the judgment of many a minister did not conspicuously rise above that of the average citizen. The Universal note, so signally sounded by Israel's prophets in times of similar crises, was less in evidence than we could have desired" (*The Church in America*, p. 97). For good or ill, religious liberalism would be a persistent force in the shaping of developments in church-state relations for years to come, and a particularly potent one in the first decades of the twentieth century.

MISSIONARIES AND EXPANSIONISTS

In 1889 a young Republican congressman from Massachusetts named Henry Cabot Lodge wrote:

Our relations with foreign nations today fill but a slight place in American politics, and excite generally only a languid interest. We have separated ourselves so completely from the affairs of other people that it is difficult to realize how large a place they occupied when the government was founded (quoted in Hofstadter and Hofstadter, *Great Issues*, p. 171).

There was one great exception to this situation: the involvement of Americans in foreign missions. Consequently, when the nature of American activities overseas changed over the next decade, and Hawaii, Cuba, and the Philippines became household words, the increased attention Americans paid to foreign affairs was influenced by their experience with missions. In retrospect it seems inevitable that religion and statecraft, missionary and expansionist objectives, should have become inextricably intertwined in these years.

In terms of actually holding colonial possessions, the United States arguably never went the imperialist route. But if one accepts William Langer's definition of imperialism as "the rule or control, political or economic, direct or indirect, of one state, nation or people over other similar groups, or perhaps one might better say the disposition, urge or striving to establish such rule or control" (*The Diplomacy of Imperialism*, p. 67), then America has been at times imperialistic, and some of its Christians particularly so. And yet the words "imperialist" and "imperialism" are laden with so many shades of meaning that a word of further definition is in order. In the historical context of the 1890s and early 1900s, proponents of the extension of American economic, political, or military power abroad thought of themselves as "expansionists," while their opponents labeled them as "imperialists" and their program as "imperialism." Because the relevant historiography uses it, we will employ the term "imperialism" as the analytical category for the issue, and use "expansionists" as the term for people favoring an enlarged American role in other lands.

Though now more than thirty years old, the most probing attempt to interpret the phenomenon of American foreign missions is still Paul A. Varg's "Motives in Protestant Missions, 1890–1917." Recognizing the limits of knowledge about human motivation that the historian faces, Varg maintains that it nevertheless remains one of the central questions about the whole missionary enterprise. Why, he asks, should the American people have accepted "the Christianization of far-off lands as one of the most laudable of all human enterprises"? (p. 68) Paying special attention to China, the central focus of American missionary activity in its most popular phase, Varg concludes that the initial motivation was the revivalism of Dwight L. Moody that had captured the hearts of a generation of young men and women. Moody's revivalism, although centered on the salvation of one's own soul, was also highly evangelical; always present was a concern for the souls of others, lest they be lost. China was the largest single reservoir of unsaved souls and so China was the place the soul-savers went. Around the turn of the century, however, the theology of the damnation of the heathen fell out of fashion. While missionaries themselves continued for some years to be motivated principally by a concern for souls, many supporters of those missionaries began to be offended by the old beliefs. Humanitarian concern for the welfare of the Chinese people—eliminating foot-binding, ignorance, and poverty—became the new, more publicly popular motivation for support of the missionary impulse, paralleling a similar transformation of religious motivation toward social concern at home.

Varg also examines the relation between business and political imperialism and missions. Again he finds a complex picture. In China, American merchants saw missionaries as meddlers and hopeless zealots. Missionaries, for their part, "held that business men as a group had no sympathy with missionary aims and that their behavior reflected unfavorably upon Christianity" (p. 73). But if in the field there was mutual distrust, then on the home front there was tremendous business support for the missionary crusade. Varg found no instance of a missionary justifying his work by the expanded trade or political opportunity it would provide, but did find that many of the movement's supporters would have agreed with the journalist who happily reported, "every missionary is a salesman for the manufactures of Christendom" (p. 74). Nevertheless Varg concludes that the concept of the missionary enterprise as merely a tool of the middle-class exploitation of what would later come to be called the third world lacks support as a general thesis.

William Hutchison has picked up this last theme in his article "A Moral Equivalent For Imperialism: Americans and the Promotion of 'Christian Civilization,' 1880–1910." He interprets the years from 1880 to 1910 as ones in which American liberals and revivalists attempted a conquest of the world not only for Christ but also for "Christian Civilization." For Hutchison, as for Varg, the missions were not simply a tool of exploitation, although they could play that role. Hutchison sees the turn-of-the-century missionary effort as drawing more on the world-renovating social aspect of liberal social Christian activism and less on the individualistic and voluntaristic elements of American Christianity than had been usual in American missionary activity. This in turn meant that the liberals' nonsectarian, nondoctrinal outlook opened the way for enterprises of social salvation overseas, but in a way that could not help but be marked by Western techniques and Western cultural assumptions.

Other interpreters of the American missionaries are not so sure as Hutchison and Varg that the activity was undertaken with good intentions even if tainted by cultural assumptions. Though on balance he sees Methodist missionaries as honest and sincere, Kenneth M. MacKenzie finds too many examples of missionary imperialism to be sanguine about the relation of the one enterprise to the other. In *The Robe and the Sword*, he amasses substantial evidence to show that while the Methodist church did not consciously promote American imperialism, it did help develop a rationale to make imperialism palatable. Unlike Varg or Hutchison, MacKenzie identifies numerous missionaries who sincerely believed that "missions paid." An example was the Reverend John B. McGuffin, who suggested that once converted, the heathen were useless to Christian civilization until they were also converted to the "expensive standard of Christian living" and began wearing "Christian apparel" in homes filled with pictures, carpets, and musical instruments. The commercial gain from evangelism was after all, in McGuffin's view, no more than the scriptures had guaranteed: "Godliness is profitable unto all things, having the promise of that which now is, and of that which is to come" (p. 15).

MacKenzie's book also examines the ways in which missionaries functionally contributed to imperialism, confirming Lord Salisbury's dictum, "First the missionary, then the consul, then the general" (p. 22). However, Mackenzie is careful to distinguish what the Methodists did from what they thought they were doing as he follows the attitudes of church leaders, organizations, and periodicals through the years leading up to 1900. With the highest of ideals, the Methodists opposed European-style imperialism but supported American expansionism. In their eyes expansion was different because it was benevolent and only exercised for the benefit of the whole brotherhood of nations. In MacKenzie's view, this of course led to foreign domination. But ironically, because of the hospitals and schools and orphanages the missionary impulse brought with it, and because of the knowledge of, and respect for, other peoples that years of missionary contact brought Americans, MacKenzie is able to conclude that, given a climate of American external aggression, the Methodist church "helped to make American imperialism benevolent in fact as in word" (p. 116).

Similar conclusions are reached by Jerry Israel in "The Missionary Catalyst: Bishop James W. Bashford and the Social Gospel in China," and Graeme S. Mount in "The Presbyterian Church in the U.S.A. and American Rule in Puerto Rico, 1898–1917." Margaret E. Crahan tells the story of how Methodist missionaries to Cuba, because they saw themselves as bearers of a superior culture, were most successful with the Cuban middle class in "Religious Penetration and Nationalism in Cuba: U.S. Methodist Activities, 1898–1958." And Michael C. Reilly's article on Charles Henry Brent documents how an Episcopal bishop could, in the mission field, be both a firm advocate of American paternalism and a liberal on social issues.

All of the preceding interpretations of the link between missions and imperialism, while critical in varying degrees, nonetheless understand the missionary impulse as benevolent. For a completely different view of American missionary activity, one can go to Emilio Pantojas García who, in his article "La Iglesia Protestante y La Americanización de Puerto Rico: 1898–1917" openly distrusts missionary motivations. He argues that the attempted "Americanization" of Puerto Rico was, not only in practice but also by intent, the result of American Protestant missionaries' aims to de-Hispanicize and de-Catholicize the island's inhabitants.

Another aspect of church-state relations bound up with the American missionary efforts involved Protestant and Roman Catholic tensions. In both the Philippines and in Mexico, Protestant missionaries sought the protection of the government for their efforts to "Christianize" already Christian people. Kenton J. Clymer's article "Methodist Missionaries and Roman Catholicism in the Philippines, 1899–1916" makes it clear that so far as early Methodist missionaries were concerned, Catholicism had made Filipinos better than pagans, but only just. The same charges about Catholicism were made in Mexico as Karl M. Schmitt's "American Protestant Missionaries and the Diaz Regime in Mexico: 1876–1911" reveals. Protestant missionaries used a variety of labels to describe Catholicism, including "Christless religion," "baptized paganism," "a mercenary religion," and "an enemy of the Bible" (p. 255). Schmitt's treatment of the way in which American missionaries brought with them to foreign lands the expectation of religious toleration is particularly perceptive, for it provides a key to understanding how the missionaries could regard the Mexican dictatorship known as the Porfiriato as an enlightened, progressive regime, and how indeed many American church representatives viewed the governments under which they conducted their activity as good to the extent that they were left unmolested or positively encouraged. Frank T. Reuter's *Catholic Influence in American Colonial Policies, 1898–1904* describes how most Roman Catholic–Protestant tensions were actually handled by the State Department overseas. He finds that the tensions were usually resolved in favor of the preexisting Roman Catholic state church and that the U.S. government never used its colonial powers to give exclusive sanction to the activities of Protestant missionaries—much to the dismay of the missionaries, who apparently left their devotion to separation of church and state at home when they went off to formerly Spanish lands.

The involvement of religion with the issue of imperialism was not, however, limited to missionary activity. Clergy and church members were also engaged in the great debate over expansionism. Indeed one of the first and greatest proponents of expansion was none other than Josiah Strong, Congregationalist minister and head of the Evangelical Alliance, who declared in his 1885 bestseller, *Our Country:*

Long before the thousand millions are here, the mighty centrifugal tendency, inherent in this [Anglo-Saxon] stock and strengthened in the United States, will assert itself. Then this race of unequaled energy, with all the majesty of numbers and the might of wealth behind it—the representative, let us hope, of the largest liberty, the purest Christianity, the highest civilization—having developed peculiarly aggressive traits calculated to impress its institutions upon mankind, will spread itself over the earth. If I read not amiss, this powerful race will move down upon Mexico, down upon Central and South America, out upon the islands of the sea, over upon Africa and beyond. And can any one doubt that the result of this competition of races will be the "survival of the fittest"? (p. 161)

A glimpse of Strong at work in pursuit of this manifest destiny in the context of a foreign policy crisis is provided by James Eldin Reed's article entitled, "American Foreign Policy, the Politics of Missions and Josiah Strong, 1890–1900." Reed is able to conclude that Strong was at once a "humanitarian and an aggressive nationalist, an internationalist and a jingo." Moreover, he uses the case of Strong's involvement with Turkish-Armenian affairs of no direct political or economic consequence to the United States to argue forcefully that missions were an independent source of expansionism, not a mere excuse for imperialism.

One of the earliest secondary works written on the expansionist debate that still repays reading is J. W. Pratt's *Expansionists of 1898*. A later account of particular value is Ernest May's *American Imperialism: A Speculative Essay*. May focuses on the question of why America in 1898 departed from a traditional anticolonial stance in favor of an imperialist course by eagerly gathering up new "possessions" in the context of the Spanish-American War, and then within literally months, reversed course again by refusing to become a colonial power. Placing geopolitical realities aside, May tries to answer his question by analyzing the role of "opinion leaders," among them Protestant clergy, in shaping effective public opinion.

Winthrop Hudson's brief article, "Protestant Clergy Debate the Nation's Vocation, 1898–1899," also assesses the clergy's role as opinionmakers during the period of debate surrounding the Spanish-American War and its aftermath. In doing so, Hudson intentionally pursues May's thesis by examining the role of the clergy in greater detail. Although he recognizes the part played by some ministers in providing the pious justification for imperialism and colonialism—necessary because "Americans never learned to do wrong knowingly" (p. 110)—he also sees others as critical opinion leaders for the anti-imperialist side. The clergy were particularly well represented among those who believed that it was necessary to liberate Cuba from Spanish rule and atrocities, but that American colonies were inconsistent with the ideals of the American republic. Hudson's treatments of Lyman Abbott and Henry Van Dyke are particularly effective. At his hand they were, respectively, figures who were publicly sucked into and staunchly resisted the colonialist cause. Other capable portraits of opponents of imperialism are rendered by Robert L. Beisner's *Twelve Against Empire*.

Much has been written linking American Protestants to expansionism, but a sense of American manifest destiny extended also to Roman Catholics as two articles by Thomas E. Wangler demonstrate. In "The Birth of Americanism: 'Westward the Apocalyptic Candlestick'" Wangler describes how in the last years of the nineteenth century "a myth or faith" was born in the American Catholic community that American Catholicism had a providential role to play in the world and in the church universal. Subscribers to this "faith" held that God was replacing the old with a new world; Europe was in decline and the United States was rising to take its place in the progress of civilization. The church would need to reform; what better source for a prototype church than the prototypical new nation? Thus, American Catholicism had a missionary role to parallel its Protestant counterpart, but its role was to be exercised not so much in foreign mission fields as in a grand demonstration project in the United States and in convincing the European church to modernize. Wangler discusses how this new gospel was brought to Europe in his second article "American Catholic Expansionism, 1886–1894." In great detail, Wangler uncovers how the Americanists, as they came to be known, skillfully penetrated the European Catholic press and planted articles favorable to their point of view and promoted their plans. In consequence these men, Bishops John Ireland and John Keane, Monsignor Denis O'Connell and James Cardinal Gibbons, successfully controlled—for a time—what Rome knew about America and what Americans knew about the Vatican. All of this was done in the service of promoting American-style Roman Catholicism at home and abroad, but taken together with Protestant expansionism it raises a question: what was it about the American self-conception, ideology, and character at this period that led to the nearly universal conviction that America had something to offer everyone and everywhere?

One answer to this question is to suggest that the sense of duty to "inferior" peoples, and the sense that America had something to give those peoples cannot be understood apart from the Social Darwinism that was so influential in late nineteenth-century thought. As Richard Hofstadter makes clear in his *Social Darwinism in the United States, 1860–1915*, this ideology, with its application of "survival of the fittest" to human races and nations, made a great impact even on the thinking of the Protestant leaders who decried the name of Darwin for its association with the anathematized theory of evolution.

Another way to view the American faith in expansionism is to follow the lead of the economic historians who have seen that one of its sources may well have been the very success that market capitalism had brought to America. Americans had seen their lives change before their eyes, especially after the Civil War. For them, railroads, telegraphs, telephones, ready-made clothing, Sears and Roebuck's and Montgomery Ward's catalogs all represented a much better standard of living and way of life and they were anxious to share it with the rest of the world. They could not understand how a consumer goods lifestyle might not be as welcome to other people, and they were blind even at home as to the costs of an industrialized world and the economic disparity engendered between nations producing raw materials and those producing manufactured goods. Or perhaps Americans understood the disparities quite well and simply concluded that their own welfare was more important than that of less-developed peoples called "markets." Both interpretations have been offered to elucidate the larger issues presented by American economic expansionism. Two of the most searching analyses in this vein are by William Appleman Williams (*The Tragedy of American Diplomacy*) and David M. Potter (*People of Plenty*). Potter captures well how abundance has forged a distinctive American character while Williams translates those ideals into the tragically unattainable goals of American international relations.

BUREAUCRATIZATION

Directly related to mission and empire was the bureaucratic transformation taking place in and among America's religious bodies at the turn of the century. When John R. Mott, founder of the Student Volunteer Movement and guiding light of the Young Men's Christian Association proclaimed as his ideal "The Evangelization of the World in This Generation," the goal naturally required organization of missionary activity on a new, grand, and inter-denominational scale. But the transformation of theologically and ecclesiologically related networks of local churches into modern denominations complete with national staffs, million-dollar budgets, commissioned field workers in dozens of countries, and unparalleled lobbying power involved more than simply organizing to meet the imperatives of his objective.

The participants in the institutional transformation were themselves aware that vast changes were taking place. Together with the historians that followed them, they left a richly descriptive body of literature documenting the new nationalized denominations and the process of bureaucratization. The assessment of what such bureaucratization meant to American life and culture, however, is a task which remains largely undone. We must therefore be content to examine the current state of knowledge about the events themselves, look at some of the more significant interpretations offered to date, and then suggest models to be borrowed from the social sciences to further the analytical process.

The Roman Catholic church's Americanist crisis mentioned earlier worked profound structural effects on that church in America. In addition to Thomas Wangler's articles on Americanism, articles by Jay P. Dolan and Robert F. McNamara along with books by Robert D. Cross and Gerald P. Fogarty are helpful in following this process. Jay Dolan's article, "A Catholic Romance With Modernity," describes how the liberalism of the 1890s was followed by a conservative backlash. The substance of that reaction is covered in Robert McNamara's "Bernard McQuaid's Sermon on Theological Americanism." On June 25, 1899, McQuaid, bishop of Rochester, New York, preached a sermon asserting that Americanism was a real danger because it was characterized by ecumenical activities, support of public education, agitation against the ban on Catholic membership in non-Catholic fraternal organizations, and encouragement of Catholic participation in non-Catholic churches and unions. This brought to a head the controversy over Americanism, precipitated Pope Leo XIII's letter *Testem Benevolentiae* condemning it, and, in McNamara's view, set the tone for Catholic church-state relations with the American nation for the next twenty years. Moreover, the reaction to the papal letter among non-Catholics was overwhelmingly negative according to Samuel J. Thomas in "The American Periodical Press and the Apostolic Letter 'Testem Benevolentiae'" and fostered antipathy toward the Pope.

Whether the liberal Catholicism of the Americanists was actually derailed by papal condemnation has been questioned by Neil T. Storch in "John Ireland's Americanism After 1899." He finds that Ireland continued to be a thoroughgoing Americanist even after supposed suppression. Similar findings are reached in Robert Cross's *The Emergence of Liberal Catholicism in America* and Gerald Fogarty's *The Vatican and the Americanist Crisis.* Fogarty further argues in *The Vatican and the American Hierarchy* that the major effect of *Testem Benevolentiae* was not to stop liberal Catholicism in its tracks, but rather to frustrate for a time national solidarity and cooperation among the American bishops. In place of interdiocesan cooperation, a form of ecclesiastical organization and development that Fogarty calls Romanization took root in the American church. To meet the needs of his see, each bishop and archbishop in America had to have his own patron in Rome to advance his interests. Since this development coincided with a period of peak Roman Catholic immigration which necessitated a vast expansion of the diocesan infrastructure of hospitals, schools, churches, and charities, bureaucratization took on a localized character. Each archdiocese became a system almost unto itself. This form of organization would prevail until the American hierarchy renewed cooperation at the national level in the context of World War I.

The Protestant denominations were also caught up in bureaucratic change and rationalization, though on a more national basis than the Catholic church. Paul D. Brewer discusses centralization in the Southern Baptist Convention, a denomination known for its distrust of hierarchy, from the late nineteenth century onward in "The State Convention: Is It Headquarters?" Steven T. Henderson's "Social Action in a Conservative Environment" makes it clear that even Southern Baptists, despite their "fanatical commitment to the evangelization of individuals," were swept up by the social gospel vision of the hour to organize for social action in the years following 1908 (p. 245). Two articles by Robert A. Baker, "The Cooperative Program in Historical Perspective" and "The Magnificent Years, (1917–1931)," outline a progressive era in the Southern Baptist Convention and document the rationalization of denominational financing in the early 1920s.

In the Methodist Church, commitment to the "Social Creed" (an official statement of faith cast in terms of social gospel beliefs) called forth an organization, the Methodist Federation for Social Service, described at length in Walter G. Muelder's *Methodism and Society in the Twentieth Century* and assessed more briefly by Donald K. Gorrell in "The Methodist Federation for Social Service and the Social Creed." Creighton Lacy's book on Frank Mason North is also informative. In other churches, the lure of foreign missions proved to be the catalyst for bureaucratic reorganization into more centralized authorities that could speak to both governments and the church itself with one voice. Such was the case in the northern Presbyterian Church under the leadership of Robert E. Speer and also, surprisingly, in the Mennonite church (see Theron F. Schlabach, "The Humble Become 'Aggressive Workers': Mennonites Organize for Missions, 1880–1910").

Even on the fringe of Protestantism, among the Mormons and Jehovah's Witnesses, the charismatic leadership of the nineteenth century was being replaced by the professional leadership of the twentieth. Thomas G. Alexander evaluates the rationalization of Mormon leadership in the years between 1890 and 1930 in Weberian terms in " 'To Maintain Harmony': Adjusting to External and Internal Stress, 1890–1930." Michael Quinn identifies the principal agent of that transformation as the Spanish-American War in "The Mormon Church and the Spanish-American War: An End to Selective Pacifism." Quinn describes how the current prophet at the time of the war, Brigham Young, Jr., opposed the war but was himself opposed by other church leaders who had "come to recognize national authority as supreme in such matters." The Jehovah's Witnesses, meanwhile, are seen as a living critique of American denominations and denominationalism, but also as subject to the pressures of American life and history by Edward Abrahams in "The Pain of the Millennium: Charles Taze Russell and the Jehovah's Witnesses, 1879–1916."

In addition to the organizational activity occurring inside the Protestant denominations, this was a period of peak development of cooperation between the denominations. The older organizations of the Protestant complex (which were based on the membership of individual Christians) continued to exist for the most part. The YMCA and the Student Volunteer Movement continued to grow under the leadership of John R. Mott, whose story is told in Basil Mathews's *John R. Mott, World Citizen,* and in two books by C. Howard Hopkins, *John R. Mott: 1865--1955* and *History of the Y.M.C.A. in North America.* Some newer movements received increased support during these years including the movement for national prohibition and the American Red Cross. Other, older elements of the evangelical establishment experienced a decline in fortunes, including the Evangelical Alliance and, to a lesser extent, the American Bible and American Tract societies. The real innovation in ecumenical life was the growth of coordination between denominations at an official level, for as Robert T. Handy has explained, "The informal devices which the denominations had founded for cooperation in the previous century were not proving adequate to the demands of the new one, especially in the effort to deal seriously with the burgeoning cities at home and with difficult missionary problems abroad" (*A Christian America*, p. 147).

And so the Protestant denominations began to found, and officially participate in, cooperative institutions beyond the denomination out of a conviction that the problems the churches were called to face were beyond the scope of any one church or any collectivity of Christian individuals. In this way the social gospel's fundamental tenet that the causes and cures of social ills were corporate led to a fundamental restructuring of the Protestant conception of the church and in turn to the birth of a host of ecumenical organizations. In 1893 the group that became permanent in 1911 as the Foreign Missions Conference of North America first met, and in 1902 the agency later known as the Missionary Education Movement of the United States and Canada was created. Meanwhile, in 1908, the Home Missions Council was formed. Its history has been recounted by Robert Handy in *We Witness Together: A History of Cooperative Home Missions*. Finally, there was the Federal Council of Churches of Christ in America, which was planned in 1905 and was brought into being in 1908, representing twenty-nine different communions. The expectations of the denominations for the new council were high but so were the stakes. A 1910 Presbyterian General Assembly report warned: "There must be a combination of the churches—a united, persistent effort to lift society, in both Church and State, or the Republic is doomed" (quoted in Handy, *A Christian America*, p. 150). The Federal Council's early years are recounted by Charles S. MacFarland (*Christian Unity in the Making*), are placed in the context of nearly three-quarters of a century of ecumenical work by Samuel McCrea Cavert (*Church Cooperation and Unity in America*), and are analyzed by John Abernathy Smith ("Ecclesiastical Politics and the Funding of the Federal Council of Churches").

Not every plan for ecumenical organization and action that was proposed during these years was a success, however. Two articles by Charles E. Harvey, "John D. Rockefeller, Jr., and the Interchurch World Movement of 1919–1920," and "Speer Versus Rockefeller and Mott, 1910–1935" tell how Robert Speer stood against the ever more bureaucratic and centralized ideals of large-scale organization favored by Mott and promoted by Rockefeller. Speer defended denominational integrity and drew a line beyond which American Protestantism was not prepared to move in pursuit of political influence. Eldon G. Ernst picks up the story in *Moment of Truth for Protestant America: Interchurch Campaigns Following World War One* and describes what happened when the Interchurch World Movement tried to spread American religion abroad—it foundered, like Woodrow Wilson's attempt to export American democracy through the League of Nations.

American Judaism also underwent a major period of organizational development that enabled it to act on a supracongregational level. Reform Judaism had already begun to organize its institutional life; its rabbis met in 1869 and again in 1885 to formulate and publish statements of the Reformed theological position, its synagogues were gathered into the Union of American Hebrew Congregations in 1873, and its rabbinate was organized into the Central Conference of American Rabbis in 1889. In 1898, the other forms of Judaism which had taken root in American soil, particularly through recent waves of eastern European immigration, also began to form national organizations. In that year the Union of Orthodox Jewish Congregations was founded. In 1902 the Union of Orthodox Rabbis was established and Conservative Judaism received a great boost when a reorganized Jewish Theological Seminary in New York City began operations under the presidency of the famous scholar Solomon Schecter. Schecter went on in 1913 to found the United Synagogue of America, the central Conservative body, and Conservative rabbis established their own organization, the Rabbinical Assembly of America, in 1919. Most of the national bodies of American Judaism owe their origins to these first years of the twentieth century. Again, as in Protestantism, these can be seen as key years for denominational bureaucratic organization.

The organizational history of the Reform movement has been analyzed by Steven A. Fox in "On the Road to Unity" and by Maurice N. Eisendrath in "The Union of American Hebrew Congregations." The formative years in the organization of Conservative Judaism, 1910 to 1913, are covered by Herbert Rosenblum in "Ideology and Compromise." Louis Bernstein's "Generational Conflict in American Orthodoxy" is a fine case study of how ethnicity interacted with denominational organizing activity. Bernstein recounts how the Union of Orthodox Rabbis was founded in 1902 by rabbis born and trained in Europe and how Americanization of the rabbinate led to the organization in 1926 of the Rabbinate Council of America, a separate organization for English-speaking rabbis within Orthodoxy.

The first decades of the twentieth century were also ones in which Zionism both divided and united the American Jewish community and led to the creation of lasting pan-Jewish institutions such as the American Jewish Congress. An interesting article in this regard is Gary P. Zola's "Reform Judaism's Pioneer Zionist: Maximilian Hellor." Other cooperative efforts are addressed in Marc Lee Raphael's "Federated Philanthropy in an American Jewish Community: 1904–1948" and Melvin I. Urofsky's "Stephen Wise: The Last of the Superstars."

If in these years, as has been argued, bureaucratization developed in all religious communities, naturally affecting the way those communities related to the larger culture, how is this phenomenon to be explained? Some interpreters from within the guild of church historians have approached the question, though none with complete success. Sidney E. Mead in an influential article, "Denominationalism: The Shape of Protestantism in America," argued in 1954 that the shape of the modern denomination was presaged by the nineteenth-century voluntary societies, the American Board of Commissioners for Foreign Missions, the American Home Mission Society, the Bible Society, the Tract Society, the American Sunday School Union, the Temperance Society, the Colonization and Anti-Slavery societies, the YMCA and the Student Volunteers Movement. Mead writes: "The genius of these movements is the same as that of the individual denominations, namely, to instrument certain defined objectives, in this case of such nature and extent as to enlist the support of individuals in many different denominations" (p. 302). Mead further emphasizes that these societies were not formed by denominations in cooperation, but by voluntary associations of individuals crossing denominational lines and constituting "superdenominations." Though initially these groups were what one now might call single-issue interest groups, or even affinity groups, many of them came to have a life of their own. Thus, as Mead notes, the "Y" had as its original goal the evangelization of uprooted men. It built libraries, reading rooms, inexpensive hotels, and recreational and other facilities as a means to that end, but as belief in simple evangelization declined the facilities themselves became ends for the program, "until today the primary appeal of the 'Y' is likely to be as a community welfare organization somewhat embarrassed by its earlier evangelistic emphasis" (p. 305). The ability of these groups to outlive their original objectives and even to challenge the role of churches in public life was to some a blessing and to others a curse, but it virtually assured that the next stage in organizational development would not rely on religious individuals to create autonomous entities, but rather look to religious bodies to represent themselves in ever more public ways. With the Federal Council a new ecumenical emphasis on mission to society was begun. The Council represented churches, not individuals, and its purpose was both unity and social service. Mead leaves his analysis here, but one may deduce from his work that this new social ecumenism was possible only because churchly activity had moved away from exclusively saving individual souls in individual churches and because the denominations had sufficiently internalized this transformation to see themselves as complex organizations, engaged in a wide range of publishing, educational, and missionary enterprises. Thus redefined, the denominations found it possible and desirable to cooperate as entities to do the things they already believed that churches should do.

Another attempt to grapple with the experience of denominational organization is offered in a collection of essays edited by Russell E. Richey, *Denominationalism*. Besides offering perceptive comments in introductions to the book's various sections and reprinting the Mead essay cited above, Richey reproduces two excellent articles by Timothy L. Smith that are applicable to the bureaucratic changes of the early twentieth century: "Congregation, State, and Denomination: The Forming of the American Religious Structure" and "Religious Denominations as Ethnic Communities: A Regional Case Study." In the second, Smith explains the denomination as "a structural super-organization designed to give guidance, support, and discipline to local congregations." He notes that it was born of necessity and not out of a design to meet some "high doctrine of 'denominationalism.'" He adds that "the fulfillment of its functions required, however, a specific rationale, a permanent structure, and a leadership dedicated not only to serving the congregations but to perpetuating both the larger institution and their own place in it" (*Denominationalism*, pp. 195–196). By seeing that a supracongregational organization has its own bureaucratic imperatives, Smith's analysis comes as close to a structural and functional view of religious bureaucracy as any that has been offered by historians of American religion, but for those concerned with how the bureaucratization of religion affected the American church-state equation it still leaves something to be desired.

Outside the fold of American religious history, however, the field of sociology offers some studies that may shed light on the phenomenon of bureaucratization within religion. At a theoretical level, Paul DiMaggio and Walter Powell have suggested in "The Iron Cage Revisited: Institutional Isomorphism and Collective Rationality in Organizational Fields" that institutions developed in different fields within a culture in the same period will assume remarkably similar forms. This, together with what is known from case studies about American government and business in the late nineteenth and early twentieth centuries, tends to suggest that religious bureaucratization stemmed, at least in part, from the bureaucratization and rationalization of other parts of society. In an age of trusts, collectives, and corporations, it is not surprising that religion might reorganize itself on parallel and complementary lines. Social histories of bureaucratization include Alfred Chandler's *The Visible Hand: The Managerial Revolution in American Business*, and Stephen Skowronek's *Building a New American State: The Expansion of National Administrative Capacities, 1877–1920*. Articles from related areas that provide suggestive models for the study of religious bureaucratization are William G. Roy's "The Politics of Bureaucratization and the U.S. Bureau of Corporations," Jon C. Teaford's "State Administrative Agencies and the Cities of 1890–1920," and Richard L. McCormick's discussion of the origins of the modern bureaucratic state entitled "The Discovery that Business Corrupts Politics: A Reappraisal of the Origins of Progressivism." One effort to apply a cross-disciplinary perspective to the issue is found in Ben Primer's *Protestants and American Business Methods.*

The sociologically oriented literature also includes an article by Eric Woodrum, "Towards a Theory of Tension in American Protestantism," which, following Max Weber, offers a model for understanding the tensions to be observed in nineteenth- and twentieth-century Protestantism. The model argues that conflicts over "mission" reflect differences in secular accommodations between laity, parish clergy, and supracongregational staff. These differences are seen as structural; they derive from the social location of the parties in the conflict. Additionally, the outcomes of disputes are seen as resulting from informal domination of power structures by religious professionals. Woodrum's model is particularly pertinent to the study of organization and change in turn-of-the-century American religion, for this was a period of deep and lasting changes in the structures of ecclesiastical power and tremendous expansion in the ranks of clergy not based in the parish. The rise of the religious bureaucrat, no less than the rise of the government bureaucrat, must be located in these years. Before 1900, religious leaders who became notable public figures came overwhelmingly from the pulpits of prominent churches. Afterwards they came increasingly from the ranks of denominational executives.

The advantages of studying denominational transformation in order to understand turn-of-the-century church-state relations also become evident when one sees how closely American religion and American politics were linked. Though early theorists of voting behavior discounted the relationship in favor of issue-oriented, informed-voter interpretations of political behavior, the consensus now sees religious and ethnic conflict as at the very heart of American political life of the time. As Paul Kleppner describes the current view in his "Religion, Politics, and the American Polity, a Dynamic View of Relationships": "the two major parties mobilized the support of distinctive— but mutually antagonistic—coalitions of ethnoreligious groups. Party differences were expressions of these irreconcilable ethnoreligious conflicts; elections became the secular analogs of religious wars; and most citizens came to see party-candidate alternatives as all-or-nothing options" (p. 351–352). This view has been especially influential in understanding the differences among religious groups on the issue of temperance, which was translated into a legislative program during this period with great success. For more on temperance and the battle for prohibition see Charles S. Merz's legislative history, *The Dry Decade,* and Joseph R. Gusfield's fine interpretive account, *Symbolic Crusade: Status Politics and the American Temperance*

Movement, which casts the movement as the attempt of a declining Protestant establishment to reassure itself on its preeminent leadership in the nation. A related issue—sabbath-keeping—receives interesting treatment by Steven Riess in "Professional Sunday Baseball: A Study in Social Reform, 1892–1934" and by Benjamin Kline Hunnicutt in "The Jewish Sabbath Movement in the Early Twentieth Century."

The view that religious belief and political affiliation and action were intimately linked also finds expression in the work of Richard Jensen, whose *The Winning of the Midwest, 1888–96* argues that for the purposes of assessing political behavior among late-nineteenth-century American Christians the relevant distinction is between "pietists" and "liturgicals." Among the pietists he counts Methodists, Quakers, (New School) Presbyterians, Disciples, Northern Baptists, Congregationalists, and English and Scandinavian Lutherans. The liturgical groups were Roman Catholics, (Old School) Presbyterians, Episcopalians, and German Lutherans. The pietists, because of their emphasis on personal experience of Christ and on Arminian theology, tended to be politically disposed toward progressive reforms and reformist politics. The liturgicals, who believed that spontaneous religiosity was dangerous and needed to be constrained by creeds and priests, rituals and theologians, favored the conservative politics of order, social control, and deference to authorities and "one's betters." Jensen's argument, though at some points overdrawn, is sufficiently subtle to explain the affinity between social gospel optimism about the Kingdom of God and reformist politics, and how the evangelicals who became antiprogressive fundamentalists in the early twentieth century deserve to be classified as liturgicals for their pessimism about human potential and their doctrinal rigidity.

But if Jensen, Gusfield, and Kleppner have made persuasive cases for understanding political differences and conflicts, the differences can be exaggerated. As Sydney E. Ahlstrom reminds readers of his *Religious History of the American People,* in the 1896 election a vote for either candidate would have endorsed a self-identified evangelical for president. Ahlstrom goes on to argue that the politics of the period cannot be understood apart from the core Protestantism that was shared by most of America. Similarly, Robert Dallek has argued in his "National Mood and American Foreign Policy" that the foreign policy of the United States during the whole of our period, 1898 to 1920, is best understood as reflecting the evangelical faith and ideals of Theodore Roosevelt and Woodrow Wilson—themselves representatives of two opposing parties—which appropriately reflected the progressive-evangelical ideals of the men who voted for them.

If the interpretation of the causes and meaning of some areas of religious bureaucratization awaits additional effort by historians, the potential of such study to illuminate political and social change appears large. Moreover, scholars have already given considerable attention to the topic as it relates to World War I. Those organizations are best considered in the context of the war.

WORLD WAR I

Considering the role of religion in World War I involves a return to themes considered earlier in this essay, for as William E. Leuchtenburg has eloquently argued:

American entrance into the war cannot be seen apart from the American sense of mission. The United States believed that American moral idealism could be extended outward, that American Christian democratic ideals could and should be universally applied. . . . The culmination of a long political tradition of emphasis on sacrifice and decisive moral combat, the war was embraced as that final struggle where the righteous would do battle for the Lord (*The Perils of Prosperity*, p. 34).

And if America participated in the First World War with a nearly religious conviction that it had entered on the side of God and civilization, writing about the place of religion in the war has had to come to terms, explicitly or implicitly, with that conviction.

The earliest historiography about religion and the war was produced by two writers with decidedly partisan agendas. When Michael Williams wrote his book *American Catholics and the War* in 1921, his principal concern was to counter nativism and to show that Catholics had been loyal to America in its moment of need. His history therefore tends to focus on the degree of Catholic support for the war. Missing from his account is any sense that Catholics were reluctant to see the war come. Instead what emerges is a picture of American Catholics engaged in a holy war side by side with their countrymen.

The earliest historical account of Protestants and the war was Ray H. Abrams's *Preachers Present Arms*, first published in 1933. Abrams's description of the Protestant crusade against the Kaiser and the Central Powers quickly became the accepted version of the period and even Dorothy Dohen's *Nationalism and American Catholicism* was written using Abrams's perspective. Yet Abrams wrote as a pacifist concerned to show the clergy at their most unreflective and militaristic. His version of the war, though colorful, well-documented, and still chilling to read over fifty years later, is so single-minded as also to lack balance.

To correct the biases of previous historiography and, for the first time, bring together data from Protestant, Catholic, and occasionally Jewish sources, is the achievement of John F. Piper, Jr.'s *The American Churches in World War I*, published in 1985. Piper stresses the diversity of responses to the war. He finds outright, unquestioning supporters, reluctant participants, and firmly committed pacifists throughout the churches. More importantly, he goes beyond the rhetoric of publicly announced positions to describe in detail the organizational and practical activities of service chaplains, the government, the churches, and quasi-church organizations in the training camps and on the battlefields. Through Piper's eyes, the religious aspect of the war appears partly as unbridled rhetoric, but mostly as organizations stumbling over one another to improve camp life's morals and conditions, as fund drives, and as churches engaged in providing sacraments to servicemen.

Although Piper's account is probably destined to become the definitive history of the relation of organized religion to the war, other items in the present bibliography highlight particular aspects of the conflict and deserve to be singled out for special attention. The first of these are the materials on Catholicism and the war. Aaron I. Abell's *American Catholicism and Social Action* is probably the best overall introduction to themes in the period. The desire to respond to the religious needs of the war effort on a par with the Protestant Federal Council of Churches worked an organizational miracle on the Roman Catholic church. The creation of an official national body of American Catholics in the middle of the war, the National Catholic War Council, eventually led to the development of institutions through which Catholics still interact officially with larger American society—the U.S. Catholic Conference and the National Conference of Catholic Bishops. The history of that creation and subsequent evolution under the leadership of John J. Burke, John A. Ryan, and James Cardinal Gibbons is well told in two articles by Elizabeth McKeown, "The National Bishops' Conference" and "Apologia for an American Catholicism." Wartime writing by these church leaders themselves, Burke's "Special Catholic Activities in War Service," Gibbons's *Catholic Loyalty*, and Ryan's "Freedom of Speech in Wartime," make it clear that Catholic involvement in the war cause was more nuanced than the picture presented by Williams. All three men's lives are the subject of biographies: John B. Sheerin's *Never Look Back: The Career and Concerns of John J. Burke*, John Tracy Ellis's *The Life of James Cardinal Gibbons*, and Francis L. Broderick's *Right Reverend New Dealer: John A. Ryan.*

The materials on Protestants and the war focus largely on individuals, both advocates of the war and its opponents, but also on religious movements for pacifism. Among the more interesting of the outright Protestant supporters of the war cause were a modernist theologian, Shailer Mathews, and a fundamentalist revival preacher, Billy Sunday, the subject of a fine biography, *Billy*

Sunday Was His Real Name by William G. McLoughlin, Jr. Mathews's *Patriotism and Religion* makes a strident case for war from the perspective of a just war for progress in civilization. Sunday, as usual, put the issue more graphically, telling his audiences:

I tell you it is Bill against Woodrow, Germany against America, Hell against Heaven. . . . Either you are loyal or you are not, you are either a patriot or a black-hearted traitor. . . . All this talk about not fighting the German people is a lot of bunk. They say that we are fighting for an ideal. Well, if we are we will have to knock down the German people to get it over (quoted in Piper, p. 11).

The background of Protestant support for the war cannot be understood apart from the idealistic example of the child of the manse who led the country, Woodrow Wilson. Particularly helpful in this regard is John M. Mulder's *Woodrow Wilson: The Years of Preparation*. Also not to be overlooked are the books of Wilson's foremost interpreter, Arthur S. Link, including *Wilson: Campaigns for Progressivism and Peace, 1916–1917, Wilson: The New Freedom,* and an edited volume, *The Impact of World War I.*

Protestants also included a number of prominent pacifists who would become heroes to later generations of American peace movement members. These included Norman Thomas, Kirby Page, Jane Addams, and A. J. Muste. Norman Thomas wrote of the experiences of World War I pacifists in *The Conscientious Objector in America* in 1923, and is also the focus of a biography by Murray B. Seidler, *Norman Thomas, Respectable Rebel.* Kirby Page left behind a book entitled *The Sword or the Cross,* and A. J. Muste's writings have been collected by Nat Hentoff in *The Essays of A. J. Muste.* More generally the story of the war's pacifists has been told in Horace C. Peterson and Gilbert C. Fite's *Opponents of War, 1917–1918,* Peter Brock's *Pacifism in the United States From the Colonial Era to the First World War,* Charles Chatfield's *For Peace and Justice: Pacifism in America, 1914–1941,* and C. Roland Marchand's *The American Peace Movement and Social Reform, 1898–1918.*

One group of pacifists whose experience of the war was particularly difficult were the Mennonites, whose sympathies were doubly suspect for their belief in nonresistance and their German ancestry. Kansas was the site of a great deal of tension between Mennonites and their neighbors over the war, as is documented in Herbert L. Pankratz's "The Suppression of Alleged Disloyalty in Kansas During World War I," Margaret Entz's "War Bond Drives and the Kansas Mennonite Response," and two articles by James C. Juhnke, "Mob Violence and Kansas Mennonites in 1918," and "The Victories of Nonresistance: Mennonite Oral Tradition and World War I." In related cases,

Allan Teichroew has edited records from federal surveillance of Mennonites in "Military Surveillance of Mennonites in World War I," and Ted Joseph has written "The United States vs. S. H. Miller: The Strange Case of a Mennonite Editor Being Convicted of Violating the 1917 Espionage Act."

The long-term effects of the war on American religion, life, and culture, though probably not as profound as the effects on Europe, were far-reaching. The suppression of pacifists and free speech at home during the war was instrumental in the growth of a civil liberties movement. This case has been argued by Harry N. Scheiber in *The Wilson Administration and Civil Liberties, 1917–1921* and by Donald Johnson in *The Challenge of American Freedoms: World War I and the Rise of the American Civil Liberties Union*. The stories of the horrors of mustard gas, trench warfare, and widespread disease brought back by American soldiers after the war made pacifists of many of those who had supported the war wholeheartedly during the conflict. As prominent an advocate as Harry Emerson Fosdick, who had summoned Americans to fight in such books as *The Challenge of the Present Crisis* and *Finishing the War*, would reject all war with regret and disgust in the 1920s. The growth of postwar disillusionment into the broad-based peace movement of the 1930s is properly the concern of another chapter in this volume, yet as Darrel E. Bigham has argued in "War as Obligation in the Thought of American Christians, 1898–1920," the experience of the war ushered in the end of an era. The duty to serve in the nation's wars, the manifest destiny of the United States, the making of the world "safe for democracy," none of these would ever again be so simply accepted. Never would they go so widely unquestioned.

BIBLIOGRAPHY

GENERAL PERSPECTIVES ON RELIGION IN THE PERIOD

Atkins, Glenn Gaius. _Religion in Our Times_. New York: Round Table Press, 1932.

Averill, Lloyd J. _American Theology in the Liberal Tradition_. Philadelphia: Westminster, 1967.

Bennett, John C., ed. _The Church Through Half a Century_. New York: Scribner, 1936.

Brauer, Jerald C. _Protestantism in America_. Philadelphia: Westminster, 1953.

Brown, William Adams. _Church and State in Contemporary America_. New York: Scribner, 1936.

Brown, William Adams. _The Church in America_. New York: Macmillan, 1922.

Buckham, John W. _Progressive Religious Thought in America: A Survey of the Enlarging Pilgrim Faith_. Boston: Houghton Mifflin, 1919.

Burke, John J. "The Historical Attitude of the Church Toward Nationalism." _Catholic Historical Review_ 14, no. 2 (1928), 69-80.

Carter, Paul A. _The Spiritual Crisis of the Gilded Age_. DeKalb: Northern Illinois University Press, 1971.

Cauthen, Kenneth. _The Impact of American Religious Liberalism_. New York: Harper and Row, 1962.

Cornelison, Isaac Amada. The Relation of Religion to Civil
    Government in the United States of America: A State Without
    a Church, But Not Without a Religion. New York: Putnam,
    1895.

Faunce, William H. P. The New Horizon of State and Church.
    New York: Macmillan, 1918.

Garrison, Winfred E. The March of Faith: The Story of Religion
    in America Since 1865. New York: Harper and Brothers, 1933.

Hopkins, C. Howard. The Rise of the Social Gospel in America,
    1865-1915. New Haven: Yale University Press, 1940.

Hudson, Winthrop S. "The Methodist Age in America." Methodist
    History 12, no. 3 (1974), 3-15.

Hutchison, William R. "Cultural Strain and Protestant
    Liberalism." American Historical Review 76, no. 2 (1971),
    386-411.

Hutchison, William R. Errand to the World: American Protestant
    Thought and Foreign Missions. Chicago: University of
    Chicago Press, 1987.

Hutchison, William R. The Modernist Impulse in American
    Protestantism. Cambridge: Harvard University Press, 1976.

May, Henry F. Protestant Churches and Industrial America. New
    York: Harper and Brothers, 1949.

Meyer, Donald B. The Protestant Search for Political Realism,
    1919-1941. Berkeley: University of California Press, 1960.

Miller, Robert Moats. American Protestantism and Social
    Issues, 1919-1939. Chapel Hill: University of North
    Carolina Press, 1958.

Van Dusen, Henry P. "A Half-Century of Liberal Theology."
    Religion in Life 47, no. 3 (1978), 343-360.

                 MISSIONARIES AND EXPANSIONISTS

Beaver, R. Pierce. Ecumenical Beginnings in Protestant World
    Missions: A History of Comity Work. New York: Nelson, 1962.

Beisner, Robert L. Twelve Against Empire: The Anti-
    Imperialists, 1898-1900. New York: McGraw-Hill, 1968.

Best, Gary Dean. "The Jewish 'Center of Gravity,' and
    Secretary Hay's Romanian Notes." American Jewish Archives
    32, no. 1 (1980), 23-34.

Clymer, Kenton J. "Methodist Missionaries and Roman
    Catholicism in the Philippines, 1899-1916." Methodist
    History 18, no. 3 (1980), 171-178.

Clymer, Kenton J. "Religion and American Imperialism:
    Methodist Missionaries in the Philippine Islands, 1899-
    1913." Pacific History Review 49, no. 1 (1980), 29-50.

Crahan, Margaret E. "Religious Penetration and Nationalism in
    Cuba: U.S. Methodist Activities, 1898-1958." Revista
    Interamericana 8, no. 2 (1978), 204-224.

Dallek, Robert. "National Mood and American Foreign Policy: A
    Suggestive Essay." American Quarterly 34, no. 4 (1982),
    339-361.

Dennis, James S. Christian Missions and Social Progress: A
    Sociological Study of Foreign Missions. 3 vols. New York:
    Fleming H. Revell, 1897-1906.

Dulles, Foster Rhea. America's Rise to World Power, 1898-1954.
    New York: Harper and Brothers, 1954.

Fairbank, John King. "Assignment for the '70's." American
    Historical Review 74, no. 3 (1969), 876-879.

Grabill, Joseph L. "The 'Invisible' Missionary: A Study in
    American Foreign Relations." Journal of Church and State
    14, no. 1 (1972), 93-105.

Hofstadter, Richard. The Age of Reform: From Bryan to F.D.R.
    New York: Random House, Vintage Books, 1960.

Hofstadter, Richard. Social Darwinism in the United States,
    1860-1915. Philadelphia: University of Pennsylvania Press,
    1945.

Hofstadter, Richard, and Hofstadter, Beatrice K. Great Issues
    in American History: From Reconstruction to the Present Day,
    1864-1981. New York: Random House, Vintage Books, 1982.

Hudson, Winthrop S. "Protestant Clergy Debate the Nation's
    Vocation, 1898-1899." Church History 42, no. 1 (1973), 110-
    118.

Hughes, Arthur J. "'Amazin' Jimmy and A Mighty Fortress Was
    Our Teddy': Theodore Roosevelt and Jimmy Carter, The
    Religious Link." Presidential Studies Quarterly 9, no. 1
    (1979), 80-83.

Hutchison, William R. "A Moral Equivalent For Imperialism:
    Americans and the Promotion of 'Christian Civilization,'
    1880-1910." Indian Journal of American Studies 13, no. 1
    (1983), 55-68.

Israel, Jerry. "The Missionary Catalyst: Bishop James W.
    Bashford and the Social Gospel in China." Methodist History
    14, no. 1 (1975), 24-43.

Jordan, Philip D. The Evangelical Alliance for the United
    States of America, 1847-1900: Ecumenism, Identity and the
    Religion of the Republic. Lewiston, N.Y.: E. Mellen, 1982.

Jordan, Philip D. "Immigrants, Methodists and a 'Conservative'
    Social Gospel, 1865-1908." Methodist History 17, no. 1
    (1978), 16-43.

Kline, Lawrence O. "Monitoring the Nation's Conscience: A
    Perspective on Methodism and American Society." Methodist
    History 12, no. 4 (1974), 44-62.

Langer, William. The Diplomacy of Imperialism, 1890-1902. New
    York: Knopf, 1951.

Latourette, Kenneth Scott. "Colonialism and Missions:
    Progressive Separation." Journal of Church and State 7, no.
    3 (1965), 330-349.

Latourette, Kenneth Scott. A History of Christian Missions in
    China. New York: Macmillan, 1929.

Latourette, Kenneth Scott. A History of the Expansion of
    Christianity. 7 vols. New York: Harper and Brothers, 1937-
    1945.

Laubach, Frank Charles. The People of the Philippines, Their
    Religious Progress and Preparation for Spiritual Leadership
    in the Far East. New York: George H. Doran Company, 1925.

MacKenzie, Kenneth M. The Robe and the Sword: The Methodist
    Church and the Rise of American Imperialism. Washington,
    D.C.: Public Affairs Press, 1961.

Magan, Percy T. Imperialism Versus the Bible, the
    Constitution, and the Declaration of Independence; or, the
    Peril of the Republic of the United States. Battle Creek,
    Mich.: National Cooperative Library Association and Pub.
    Co., 1899.

Marty, Martin E. Righteous Empire: The Protestant Experience
    in America. New York: Dial Press, 1970.

May, Ernest R. American Imperialism: A Speculative Essay. New
    York: Atheneum, 1968.

Metallo, Michael V. "Presbyterian Missionaries and the 1911
    Chinese Revolution." Journal of Presbyterian History 62,
    no. 2 (1984), 153-168.

Meyer, Paul R.   "The Fear of Cultural Decline: Josiah Strong's
     Thought About Reform and Expansion."   Church History 42, no.
     3 (1973), 396-405.

Mount, Graeme S.   "The Presbyterian Church in the U.S.A. and
     American Rule in Puerto Rico, 1898-1917."   Journal of
     Presbyterian History 57, no. 1 (1979), 51-64.

Muller, Dorothea R.   "Josiah Strong and American Nationalism: A
     Reevaluation."   Journal of American History 53, no. 3
     (1966), 487-503.

Ninkovich, Frank.   "Ideology, the Open Door and Foreign
     Policy."   Diplomatic History 6, no. 2 (1981), 185-208.

Ogle, Arthur Bud.   "Above the World: William Jennings Bryan's
     View of the American Nation in International Affairs."
     Nebraska History 61, no. 2 (1980), 153-171.

Ottman, Ford C.   Imperialism and Christ.   New York: C. C. Cook,
     1912.

Pantojas García, Emilio.   "La Iglesia Protestante y La
     Americanización de Puerto Rico: 1898-1917."   Revista de
     Ciencias Sociales 18, nos. 1-2 (1974), 97-122.

Piper, John F., Jr.   "Robert E. Speer: Christian Statesman in
     War and Peace."   Journal of Presbyterian History 47, no. 3
     (1969), 201-225.

Potter, David M.   People of Plenty: Economic Abundance and the
     American Character.   Chicago: University of Chicago Press,
     1954.

Pratt, J. W.   Expansionists of 1898.   Baltimore: Johns Hopkins
     Press, 1936.

Quinn, D. Michael.   "The Mormon Church and the Spanish-American
     War: An End to Selective Pacifism."   Pacific History Review
     43, no. 3 (1974), 342-366.

Reed, James Eldin.   "American Foreign Policy, the Politics of
     Missions and Josiah Strong, 1890-1900."   Church History 41,
     no. 2 (1972), 230-245.

Reilly, Michael C.   "Charles Henry Brent: Philippine Missionary
     and Ecumenist."   Philippine Studies 24, no. 3 (1976), 303-
     325.

Reuter, Frank T.   Catholic Influence in American Colonial
     Policies, 1898-1904.   Austin: University of Texas Press,
     1967.

Russell, C. Allyn. "William Jennings Bryan: Statesman--
    Fundamentalist." Journal of Presbyterian History 53, no. 2
    (1975), 93-119.

Schmitt, Karl M. "American Protestant Missionaries and the
    Diaz Regime in Mexico: 1876-1911." Journal of Church and
    State 25, no. 2 (1983), 253-277.

Sinclair, John H., ed. Protestantism in Latin America: A
    Bibliographical Guide. Pasadena, Calif.: William Carey
    Library, 1976.

Speer, Robert E. The New Opportunity of the Church. New York:
    Macmillan, 1919.

Speer, Robert E. Papers. Speer Library of Princeton
    Theological Seminary, Princeton, N.J.

Strong, Josiah. Expansion, Under New World-Conditions. New
    York: Baker and Taylor, 1900.

Strong, Josiah. Our Country: Its Possible Future and its
    Present Crisis. New York: American Home Missionary Society,
    1885.

Swift, Morrison Isaac. Expansion for the Sake of God, Love and
    Civilization. Los Angeles: Ronbroke Press, 1900.

Thomas, Ivor. "Baptist Anti-Imperialist Voice: George Horr and
    The Watchman." Foundations 18, no. 4 (1975), 340-357.

Tuveson, Ernest Lee. Redeemer Nation: The Idea of America's
    Millennial Role. Chicago: University of Chicago Press,
    1968.

Varg, Paul A. Missionaries, Chinese and Diplomats: The
    American Protestant Missionary Movement in China, 1890-1952.
    Princeton, N.J.: Princeton University Press, 1958.

Varg, Paul A. "Motives in Protestant Missions, 1890-1917."
    Church History 23, no. 1 (1954), 68-82.

Walasky, Paul Williams. "The Entertainment of Angels: American
    Baptists and Americanization, 1890-1925." Foundations 19,
    no. 4 (1976), 346-360.

Wangler, Thomas E. "American Catholic Expansionism, 1886-
    1894." Harvard Theological Review 75, no. 3 (1982), 369-
    393.

Wangler, Thomas E. "The Birth of Americanism: 'Westward the
    Apocalyptic Candlestick.'" Harvard Theological Review 65,
    no. 4 (1972), 415-436.

Williams, William Appleman. _The Tragedy of American Diplomacy_.
    Cleveland: World Publishing Co., 1959.

Woods, Randall B. "Terrorism in the Age of Roosevelt: The Miss
    Stone Affair, 1901-1902." _America Quarterly_ 31, no. 4
    (1979), 478-495.

                        BUREAUCRATIZATION

Abrahams, Edward. "The Pain of the Millennium: Charles Taze
    Russell and the Jehovah's Witnesses, 1879-1916." _American
    Studies_ 18, no. 1 (1977), 57-70.

Ahlstrom, Sydney E. _A Religious History of the American
    People_. 2 vols. New Haven: Yale University Press, 1972.

Alexander, Thomas G. "'To Maintain Harmony': Adjusting to
    External and Internal Stress, 1890-1930." _Dialogue: A
    Journal of Mormon Thought_ 15, no. 4 (1982), 44-58.

Baker, Robert A. "The Cooperative Program in Historical
    Perspective." _Baptist History and Heritage_ 10, no. 3
    (1975), 169-176.

Baker, Robert A. "The Magnificent Years, (1917-1931)."
    Baptist History and Heritage 8, no. 3 (1973), 144-157.

Barnes, William Wright. _The Southern Baptist Convention, 1845-
    1953_. Nashville, Tenn.: Broadman, 1954.

Bernstein, Louis. "Generational Conflict in American
    Orthodoxy: The Early Years of the Rabbinical Council of
    America." _American Jewish History_ 69, no. 2 (1979), 226-
    233.

Blau, Joseph L., ed. _Reform Judaism: A Historical Perspective_.
    New York: KTAV, 1973.

Brewer, Paul D. "The State Convention: Is It Headquarters?"
    Baptist History and Heritage 14, no. 3 (1977), 41-51.

Broderick, Francis L. _Right Reverend New Dealer: John A. Ryan_.
    New York: Macmillan, 1963.

Brown, William Adams. _Toward a United Church: Three Decades of
    Ecumenical Christianity_. New York: Scribner, 1946.

Cavert, Samuel McCrea. _The American Churches in the Ecumenical
    Movement: 1900-1968_. New York: Association Press, 1968.

Cavert, Samuel McCrea, ed. Church Cooperation and Unity in America: A Historical Review, 1900-1970. New York: Association Press, 1970.

Chandler, Alfred. The Visible Hand: The Managerial Revolution in American Business. Cambridge: Harvard University Press, 1977.

Cross, George. "Federation of the Christian Churches in America--An Interpretation." American Journal of Theology 23, no. 2 (1919), 129-145.

Cross, Robert D. The Emergence of Liberal Catholicism in America. Cambridge: Harvard University Press, 1958.

Cuddy, Edward. "Pro-Germanism and American Catholicism, 1914-1917." In Catholicism in America, edited by Philip Gleason, 92-100. New York: Harper and Row, 1970.

DiMaggio, Paul, and Powell, Walter. "The Iron Cage Revisited: Institutional Isomorphism and Collective Rationality in Organizational Fields." American Sociological Review 82 (1977), 929-964.

Dolan, Jay P. "A Catholic Romance With Modernity." Wilson Quarterly 5, no. 4 (1981), 120-133.

Douglass, Harlan Paul. Church Unity Movements in the United States. New York: Institute of Social and Religious Research, 1934.

Douglass, Harlan Paul, and Brunner, Edmund deS. The Protestant Church as a Social Institution. New York: Harper and Brothers, 1935.

Dulles, Foster Rhea. The American Red Cross: A History. New York: Harper and Brothers, 1950.

Dyer, Thomas G. "Aaron's Rod: Theodore Roosevelt, Tom Watson, and Anti-Catholicism." Research Studies 44, no. 1 (1976), 60-68.

Egan, Maurice Francis, and Kennedy, John B. The Knights of Columbus in Peace and War. New Haven, Conn.: The Knights of Columbus, 1920.

Eisendrath, Maurice N. "The Union of American Hebrew Congregations: Centennial Reflections." American Jewish Historical Quarterly 63, no. 2 (1973), 138-159.

Ellis, John Tracy. The Life of James Cardinal Gibbons. 2 vols. Milwaukee: Bruce Publishing Company, 1952.

Ernst, Eldon G. Moment of Truth for Protestant America: Interchurch Campaigns Following World War One. Missoula, Mont.: Scholars Press, 1974.

Federal Council of Churches of Christ in America. Records, 1894-1952. Record Group 18, Records of the National Council of Churches of Christ. Presbyterian Historical Society, Philadelphia, Pa.

Fogarty, Gerald P. The Vatican and the American Hierarchy from 1870 to 1965. Stuttgart: Hiersemann, 1982.

Fogarty, Gerald P. The Vatican and the Americanist Crisis: Denis J. O'Connell, American Agent in Rome, 1885-1903. Rome: Universita Gregoriana, 1974.

Fox, Steven A. "On the Road to Unity: The Union of American Hebrew Congregations and American Jewry, 1873-1903." American Jewish Archives 32, no. 2 (1980), 145-193.

Friesel, Evyatar. "Jacob H. Schiff Becomes a Zionist: A Chapter in American-Jewish Self-Definition, 1907-1917." Studies in Zionism 5 (1982), 55-92.

Furner, Mary O. Advocacy and Objectivity: A Crisis in the Professionalization of American Social Science, 1865-1905. Lexington: University Press of Kentucky, 1975.

Gorrell, Donald K. "The Methodist Federation for Social Service and the Social Creed." Methodist History 13, no. 2 (1975), 3-32.

Gusfield, Joseph R. Symbolic Crusade: Status Politics and the American Temperance Movement. Urbana: University of Illinois Press, 1963.

Handy, Robert T. A Christian America: Protestant Hopes and Historical Realities. 2d ed. New York: Oxford University Press, 1984.

Handy, Robert T. "Christianity and Socialism in America, 1900-1920." Church History 21 (March 1952), 39-54.

Handy, Robert T. We Witness Together: A History of Cooperative Home Missions. New York: Friendship Press, 1956.

Harvey, Charles E. "John D. Rockefeller, Jr., and the Interchurch World Movement of 1919-1920: A Different Angle on the Ecumenical Movement." Church History 51, no. 2 (1982), 198-209.

Harvey, Charles E. "Speer Versus Rockefeller and Mott, 1910-1935." Journal of Presbyterian History 60, no. 3 (1982), 283-299.

Henderson, Steven T. "Social Action in a Conservative
    Environment: The Christian Life Commission and Southern
    Baptist Churches." Foundations 23, no. 3 (1980), 245-251.

Hopkins, C. Howard. History of the Y.M.C.A. in North America.
    New York: Association Press, 1951.

Hopkins, C. Howard. John R. Mott: 1865-1955. Grand Rapids:
    Eerdmans, 1979.

Hunnicutt, Benjamin Kline. "The Jewish Sabbath Movement in the
    Early Twentieth Century." American Jewish History 69, no. 2
    (1979), 196-225.

Hutchinson, John A. We Are Not Divided. New York: Round Table
    Press, 1941.

Jensen, Richard. "Religion, Morality and American Politics."
    Journal of Libertarian Studies 6, nos. 3-4 (1982), 321-332.

Jensen, Richard. The Winning of the Midwest, 1888-96.
    Chicago: University of Chicago Press, 1971.

Kaganoff, Nathan M., and Katz-Hyman, Martha B. "Judaica,
    American." American Jewish History 69, no. 4 (1980), 509-
    527.

Kauffman, Christopher F. Faith and Fraternalism: The History
    of the Knights of Columbus, 1882-1982. New York: Harper and
    Row, 1982.

King, William R. History of the Home Missions Council, With
    Introductory Outline History of Home Missions. New York:
    Home Missions Council, 1930.

Kleppner, Paul. "Religion, Politics, and the American Polity,
    a Dynamic View of Relationships." Journal of Libertarian
    Studies 6, nos. 3-4 (1982), 349-358.

Lacy, Creighton. Frank Mason North: His Social and Ecumenical
    Mission. Nashville: Abingdon, 1967.

Leonard, Bill J. "A History of the Baptist Laymen's Movement."
    Baptist History and Heritage 13, no. 1 (1978), 35-44.

Lynch, Frederick. The Christian Unity Movement in America.
    London: James Clark and Co., 1922.

McCormick, Richard L. "The Discovery that Business Corrupts
    Politics: A Reappraisal of the Origins of Progressivism."
    American Historical Review 86, no. 2 (1981), 147-174.

Macfarland, Charles S. Across the Years. New York: Macmillan,
    1936.

Macfarland, Charles S. Christian Unity in the Making: The First Twenty-Five Years of the Federal Council of the Churches of Christ in America, 1905-1930. New York: The Federal Council of Churches of Christ in America, 1948.

Macfarland, Charles S., ed. The Churches of Christ in Council. New York: Missionary Education Movement, 1917.

McKeown, Elizabeth. "Apologia for an American Catholicism: The Petition and Report of the National Catholic Welfare Council to Pius XI, April 25, 1922." Church History 43, no. 4 (1974), 415-428.

McKeown, Elizabeth. "The National Bishops' Conference: An Analysis of Its Origins." Catholic Historical Review 66, no. 4 (1980), 565-583.

McNamara, Robert F. "Bernard McQuaid's Sermon on Theological Americanism." Records of the American Catholic Historical Society of Philadelphia 90 (March-December 1979), 23-32.

Marsden, George M. Fundamentalism and American Culture: The Shaping of Twentieth Century Evangelicalism, 1870-1925. New York: Oxford University Press, 1980.

Mathews, Basil. John R. Mott: World Citizen. New York: Harper and Brothers, 1934.

Mayo, Katherine. That Damn "Y". Boston: Houghton Mifflin, 1920.

Mead, Sidney E. "Denominationalism: The Shape of Protestantism in America." Church History 23, no. 4 (1954), 291-321. Reprinted in Sidney E. Mead, The Lively Experiment, New York: Harper and Row, 1963.

Merz, Charles S. The Dry Decade. Garden City, N.Y.: Doubleday, Doran, and Co., 1931.

Morse, Hermann N. Toward a Christian America: The Contribution of Home Missions. New York: Council of Women for Home Missions and Missionary Education Movement, 1935.

Muelder, Walter G. Methodism and Society in the Twentieth Century. Nashville: Abingdon, 1961.

Niebuhr, H. Richard. The Kingdom of God in America. New York: Harper and Brothers, 1959.

North, Frank Mason. Papers. In the possession of Eric M. North.

O'Grady, John. Catholic Charities in the United States. Washington, D.C.: National Council of Catholic Charities, 1930.

O'Toole, James M. "'That Fabulous Churchman': Toward a Biography of Cardinal O'Connell." Catholic Historical Review 70, no. 1 (1984), 28-44.

Piper, John F., Jr. "Father John J. Burke, C.S.P., and the Turning Point in American Catholic History." Records of the American Catholic Historical Society of Philadelphia 92 (March-December 1981), 101-113.

Primer, Ben. Protestants and American Business Methods. Ann Arbor, Mich.: UMI Research Press, 1979.

Raphael, Marc Lee. "Federated Philanthropy in an American Jewish Community: 1904-1948." American Jewish History 68, no. 2 (1978), 147-162.

Rausch, David A. "Protofundamentalism's Attitude Toward Zionism, 1878-1918." Jewish Social Studies 43, no. 2 (1981), 137-152.

Rauschenbusch, Walter. A Theology for the Social Gospel. New York: Macmillan, 1917.

Richey, Russell E., ed. Denominationalism. Nashville: Abingdon, 1977.

Riess, Steven. "Professional Sunday Baseball: A Study in Social Reform, 1892-1934." Maryland Historian 4, no. 2 (1973), 95-108.

Rosenblum, Herbert. "Ideology and Compromise: The Evolution of the United Synagogue Constitutional Preamble." Jewish Social Studies 35, no. 1 (1973), 18-31.

Rosenthal, Jerome C. "A Fresh Look at Louis Marshall and Zionism, 1900-1912." American Jewish Archives 32, no. 2 (1980), 109-118.

Routh, Porter. "The Role of the Executive Committee of the Southern Baptist Church." Baptist History and Heritage 11, no. 4 (1976), 194-203.

Roy, William G. "The Politics of Bureaucratization and the U.S. Bureau of Corporations." Journal of Political and Military Sociology 10, no. 2 (1982), 183-199.

Ryan, John A. Social Doctrine in Action: A Personal History. New York: Harper and Brothers, 1941.

Schlabach, Theron F. "The Humble Become 'Aggressive Workers': Mennonites Organize for Missions, 1880-1910." Mennonite Quarterly Review 52, no. 2 (1978), 113-126.

Sharpe, Dores R. Walter Rauschenbusch. New York: Macmillan, 1942.

Sheerin, John B. Never Look Back: The Career and Concerns of
    John J. Burke. New York: Paulist Press, 1975.

Skowronek, Stephen. Building a New American State: The
    Expansion of National Administrative Capacities, 1877-1920.
    Cambridge: Harvard University Press, 1982.

Smith, John Abernathy. "Ecclesiastical Politics and the
    Funding of the Federal Council of Churches." Church History
    43, no. 3 (1974), 350-365.

Smith, Timothy L. "Congregation, State, and Denomination: The
    Forming of the American Religious Structure." William and
    Mary Quarterly, 3d ser., 25, no. 2 (1968), 155-176.
    Reprinted in Denominationalism, edited by Russell E. Richey.
    Nashville: Abingdon, 1977.

Smith, Timothy L. "Religious Denominations as Ethnic
    Communities: A Regional Case Study." Church History 35, no.
    2 (1966), 207-226. Reprinted in Denominationalism, edited
    by Russell E. Richey. Nashville: Abingdon, 1977.

Storch, Neil T. "John Ireland's Americanism After 1899: The
    Argument from History." Church History 51, no. 4 (1982),
    434-444.

Teaford, Jon C. "State Administrative Agencies and the Cities
    of 1890-1920." American Journal of Legal History 25, no. 3
    (1981), 223-248.

Thomas, Samuel J. "The American Periodical Press and the
    Apostolic Letter 'Testem Benevolentiae.'" Catholic
    Historical Review 62, no. 4 (1976), 408-423.

Timberlake, James H. Prohibition and the Progressive Movement,
    1900-1920. Cambridge: Harvard University Press, 1963.

Tuerk, Richard. "Jacob Riis and the Jews." New York
    Historical Society Quarterly 63, no. 3 (1979), 178-201.

Urofsky, Melvin I. "Stephen Wise: The Last of the Superstars."
    Present Tense 6, no. 4 (1979), 21-26.

VanderMeer, Philip R. "Religion, Society, and Politics: A
    Classification of American Religious Groups." Social
    Science History 5, no. 1 (1981), 3-24.

Wangler, Thomas E. "A Bibliography of the Writings of
    Archbishop John J. Keane." Records of the American Catholic
    Historical Society of Philadelphia 89, nos. 1-4 (1978), 60-
    73.

Wiley, S. Wirt. History of Y.M.C.A.-Church Relations in the
    United States. New York: Association Press, 1944.

Woodrum, Eric. "Towards a Theory of Tension in American
   Protestantism." Sociological Analysis 39, no. 3 (1978),
   219-227.

Zabriskie, Alexander C. Bishop Brent: Crusader for Christian
   Unity. Philadelphia: Westminster, 1948.

Zola, Gary P. "Reform Judaism's Pioneer Zionist: Maximilian
   Hellor." American Jewish History 73, no. 4 (1984), 375-397.

                        WORLD WAR I

Abell, Aaron I. American Catholicism and Social Action. Notre
   Dame, Ind.: University of Notre Dame Press, 1960.

Abell, Aaron I. "The Catholic Church and Social Problems in
   the World War I Era." Mid-America 30, no. 3 (1948), 139-
   151.

Abrams, Ray H. Preachers Present Arms. New York: Round Table
   Press, 1933.

Anthony, Alfred Williams. "Some Compensations of War."
   Missionary Review of the World 41 (November 1918), 811-817.

The Army and Religion. New York: Associated Press, 1920.

Auerbach, Jerold S. "Woodrow Wilson's 'Predictions' to Frank
   Cobb: Words Historians Should Doubt Ever Got Spoken."
   Journal of American History 54, no. 4 (1967), 608-617.

Bainton, Roland H. Christian Attitudes Toward War and Peace.
   New York: Abingdon, 1960.

Batten, Samuel Z., ed. The Moral Meaning of the War.
   Philadelphia: American Baptist Publication Society, 1919.

Bigham, Darrel E. "War As Obligation in the Thought of
   American Christians, 1898-1920." Peace and Change 7, nos.
   1-2 (1981), 45-58.

Bishirsian, Richard J. "Croly, Wilson and the American Civil
   Religion." Modern Age 23, no. 1 (1979), 33-38.

Bowman, Rufus, D. The Church of the Brethren and War, 1708-
   1941. Elgin, Ill.: Brethren Publishing House, 1944.

Brock, Peter. Pacifism in the United States From the Colonial
   Era to the First World War. Princeton, N.J.: Princeton
   University Press, 1968.

Brown, William Adams. Papers. Library of Union Theological
    Seminary, New York.

Burke, John J. "Special Catholic Activities in War Service."
    Annals of the American Academy of Political and Social
    Science 79 (1918), 213-220.

Chambers, Frank P. The War Behind the War, 1914-1918. New
    York: Harcourt, Brace and Company, 1939.

Chatfield, Charles. For Peace and Justice: Pacifism in
    America, 1914-1941. Knoxville: University of Tennessee
    Press, 1971.

Chrystal, William G. "Reinhold Niebuhr and the First World
    War." Journal of Presbyterian History 55, no. 3 (1977),
    285-298.

Curti, Merle E. Peace or War: The American Struggle, 1636-
    1936. New York: Norton, 1936.

Daniels, Josephus. The Wilson Era: Years of War and After,
    1917-1923. Chapel Hill: University of North Carolina Press,
    1946.

Davidson, Charles N., Jr. "George Arthur Buttrick:
    Christocentric Preacher and Pacifist." Journal of
    Presbyterian History 53, no. 1 (1975), 143-167.

Dohen, Dorothy. Nationalism and American Catholicism. New
    York: Sheed and Ward, 1967.

Durham, Weldon B. "'Big Brother' and the 'Seven Sisters': Camp
    Life Reforms in World War I." Military Affairs 42, no. 2
    (1978), 57-60.

Eddy, George Sherwood. The Right to Fight: The Moral Grounds
    of War. New York: Association Press, 1918.

Entz, Margaret. "War Bond Drives and the Kansas Mennonite
    Response." Mennonite Life 30, no. 3 (1975), 4-9.

Faunce, William H. P. Religion and War. New York: Abingdon,
    1918.

Fosdick, Harry Emerson. The Challenge of the Present Crisis.
    Philadelphia: American Baptist Publishing Society, 1917.

Fosdick, Harry Emerson. Finishing the War. New York:
    Association Press, 1919.

Fosdick, Harry Emerson. The Living of These Days. New York:
    Harper and Brothers, 1956.

Fosdick, Raymond B. <u>Chronicle of a Generation, An</u>
    <u>Autobiography</u>. New York: Harper and Brothers, 1958.

Fosdick, Raymond B. "The War and Navy Departments' Commission
    on Training Camp Activities." <u>Annals of the American</u>
    <u>Academy of Political and Social Science</u> 79 (1918), 130-142.

Gibbons, James Cardinal. <u>Catholic Loyalty</u>. New York: Paulist
    Press, 1917.

Hartzler, Jonas S. <u>Mennonites in the World War</u>. Scottdale,
    Pa.: Mennonite Publishing House, 1922.

Hentoff, Nat, ed. <u>The Essays of A. J. Muste</u>. Indianapolis:
    Bobbs-Merrill, 1967.

Hershberger, Guy F. <u>War, Peace, and Nonresistance</u>. Scottdale,
    Pa.: Herald Press, 1944.

Hicks, Granville. "The Parsons and the War." <u>American Mercury</u>
    10, no. 2 (1927), 129-142.

Johnson, Donald. <u>The Challenge of American Freedoms: World War</u>
    <u>I and the Rise of the American Civil Liberties Union</u>.
    Lexington: University Press of Kentucky, 1963.

Joseph, Ted. "The United States vs. S. H. Miller: The Strange
    Case of a Mennonite Editor Being Convicted of Violating the
    1917 Espionage Act." <u>Mennonite Life</u> 30, no. 3 (1975), 14-
    18.

Juhnke, James C. "Mob Violence and Kansas Mennonites in 1918."
    <u>Kansas Historical Quarterly</u> 43, no. 3 (1977), 334-350.

Juhnke, James C. "The Victories of Nonresistance: Mennonite
    Oral Tradition and World War I." <u>Fides et Historia</u> 7, no. 1
    (1977), 19-25.

Kerby, William J. Papers. Archives of the Catholic University
    of America, Washington, D.C.

Kerby, William J. "Re-Education by War." <u>Catholic World</u> 106,
    no. 1 (1918), 451-461.

Lancaster, James L. "The Protestant Churches and the Fight for
    Ratification of the Versailles Treaty." <u>Public Opinion</u>
    <u>Quarterly</u> 21, no. 4 (1967), 597-619.

Leuchtenburg, William E. <u>The Perils of Prosperity, 1914-1932</u>.
    Chicago: University of Chicago Press, 1958.

Link, Arthur S. <u>Wilson: Campaigns for Progressivism and Peace,</u>
    <u>1916-1917</u>. Princeton, N.J.: Princeton University Press,
    1965.

Link, Arthur S. Wilson: The New Freedom. Princeton, N.J.:
  Princeton University Press, 1956.

Link, Arthur S., ed. The Impact of World War I. New York:
  Harper and Row, 1969.

Lynch, Frederick. President Wilson and the Moral Aims of the
  War. New York: Fleming H. Revell Company, 1918.

McConnell, Francis J. Democratic Christianity. New York:
  Macmillan, 1919.

Macfarland, Charles S., ed. The Churches of Christ in Time of
  War. New York: Missionary Education Movement, 1917.

Mackenzie, William Douglas. Christian Ethics in the World War.
  New York: Association Press, 1918.

McLoughlin, William G., Jr. Billy Sunday Was His Real Name.
  Chicago: University of Chicago Press, 1955.

McNeal, Patricia. "Origins of the Catholic Peace Movement."
  Review of Politics 35, no. 3 (1975), 346-374.

Marchand, C. Roland. The American Peace Movement and Social
  Reform, 1898-1918. Princeton, N.J.: Princeton University
  Press, 1973.

Mathews, Shailer. Patriotism and Religion. New York:
  Macmillan, 1918.

Mecklin, John E. "The War and the Dilemma of the Christian
  Ethic." American Journal of Theology 23, no. 1 (1919), 14-
  40.

Miller, Albert R. H. The Church and War. St. Louis, Mo.:
  Bethany Press, 1931.

Miller, Robert Moats. Harry Emerson Fosdick: Preacher, Pastor,
  Prophet. New York: Oxford University Press, 1985.

Moellering, Ralph L. Modern War and the American Churches.
  New York: American Press, 1956.

Moody, Paul D. "The Precedent of the First World War." In
  Religion of Soldier and Sailor, edited by Willard L. Sperry.
  Cambridge: Harvard University Press, 1945.

Morgan, David T. "The Revivalist as Patriot: Billy Sunday and
  World War I." Journal of Presbyterian History 51, no. 2
  (1973), 199-215.

Mulder, John M. Woodrow Wilson: The Years of Preparation.
  Princeton, N.J.: Princeton University Press, 1978.

National Catholic War Council. Archives. Library of the
    Catholic University of America, Washington, D.C.

Page, Kirby. The Sword or the Cross. Chicago: Christian
    Century Press, 1921.

Pankratz, Herbert L. "The Suppression of Alleged Disloyalty
    in Kansas During World War I." Kansas Historical Quarterly
    42, no. 3 (1976), 277-307.

Peterson, Horace C., and Fite, Gilbert C. Opponents of War,
    1917-1918. Madison: University of Wisconsin Press, 1957.

Piper, John F., Jr. The American Churches in World War I.
    Athens: Ohio Unversity Press, 1985.

Rihbany, Abraham M. Militant America and Jesus Christ.
    Boston: Houghton Mifflin, 1917.

Ryan, John A. "Freedom of Speech in Wartime." Catholic World
    106, no. 2 (1918), 577-588.

Scheiber, Harry N. The Wilson Administration and Civil
    Liberties, 1917-1921. Ithaca, N.Y.: Cornell University
    Press, 1960.

Seabrook, John H. "Bishop Manning and World War I."
    Historical Magazine of the Protestant Episcopal Church 36,
    no. 4 (1967), 301-321.

Seidler, Murray B. Norman Thomas, Respectable Rebel.
    Syracuse, N.Y.: Syracuse University Press, 1961.

Slosson, Preston W. The Great Crusade and After, 1914-1928.
    New York: Macmillan, 1939.

Sneath, E. Hershey, ed. Religion and the War. New Haven: Yale
    University Press, 1918.

Speer, Robert E. The Christian Man, the Church and the War.
    New York: Macmillan, 1918.

Speer, Robert E. "The Church and the World Today." Missionary
    Review of the World 40, no. 9 (1917), 667-673.

Speer, Robert E. "Looking Through the War Clouds." Missionary
    Review of the World 41, no. 1 (1918), 11-15.

Teichroew, Allan, ed. "Military Surveillance of Mennonites in
    World War I." Mennonite Quarterly Review 53, no. 2 (1979),
    95-127.

Thomas, Norman. The Conscientious Objector in America. New
    York: B. W. Huebsch, 1923.

Thompson, James J., Jr. "Southern Baptists and Post-war
    Disillusionment, 1918-1920." <u>Foundations</u> 21, no. 2 (1978),
    113-122.

Tippy, Worth M. <u>The Church and the Great War</u>. New York:
    Fleming H. Revell Company, 1918.

Van Kirk, Walter W. <u>Religion Renounces War</u>. New York:
    Willett, Clark and Co., 1934.

Williams, Michael. <u>American Catholics and the War</u>. New York:
    Macmillan, 1921.

6

Church-State Issues
in the Twenties and Thirties

Richard D. Horn

Taken together, the twenties and thirties in American history present a panorama of great swings and shifts in politics and society. Prosperity collapsed into the worst depression in American history and then returned with the Second World War. National prohibition finally triumphed in the Eighteenth Amendment only to die in the Twentieth. At first, nativism carried the day with immigration restriction and the revived Ku Klux Klan trumpeted its "Americanism," but then ethnic Americans found unprecedented political strength in the Roosevelt coalition. Organized labor seemed dead in the water after the failure of the strikes of 1919; by the late thirties it was booming and rapidly on its way to becoming a mainstream, legitimate force in American life. Radicalism too, whether imported or homegrown, seemed moribund early in the period, but revived by the mid-thirties, only to be reduced again to impotence by the end of the decade. The Wilsonian interlude in the Republican-dominated polity quickly ended and the Democratic party itself began to collapse in the early twenties; yet with the help of the depression, the Democrats swept to power and established the liberal state. Throughout this period, Americans continued to desert the country for the city, and the development of mass culture accelerated.

These nearly tidal movements often involved crucial questions for the relationship between church and state, which the literature in this bibliography reflects. This literature, moreover, has undergone some shifts of its own. Much of it, especially those items written before approximately 1970, took its viewpoint from the liberalism that emerged from the thirties. Understandably, this historiography often charted the progress of society out of intolerance, fanaticism, and divisive utopianism into tolerance, broad-mindedness, relativism, and consensual pragmatism. In the last decade and a half, the heavy criticism of liberalism from first the New Left and then the New Right has opened the study of this period to other viewpoints more sympathetic to groups and ideas formerly considered atavistic, simple-minded, authoritarian, and pathological. The student of church-state relations in this period must examine the literature on both sides of the divide. While the postliberal historiography is less whiggish, it has hardly abolished the categories and concerns of its predecessors, especially in topics involving the populist movements of the twenties. Explaining the intensity and rancor of some of the quarrels of this period remains a difficult task, even when one is not burdened with a theory of progress.

This essay breaks into five parts. The first deals with issues and movements which that liberal historiography consigned to the backwaters of history: prohibition, nativism, fundamentalism and anti-evolution agitation, the Klan and protofascist movements. Most of these topics fall within the early part of our period, to the mid-twenties. The next two discuss the literature about the relationship of mainline Protestantism and Catholicism to social reform and the New Deal. The fourth section deals with church-state issues in foreign policy. The fifth section discusses the existing gaps in the literature.

Much of the best general introductory writing on this period is two decades old and needs revision. For the most recent attempt at a synthetic narrative, see Barry D. Karl, *The Uneasy State: The United States From 1915 to 1945*. The standard histories of the twenties are William E. Leuchtenburg, *The Perils of Prosperity*, and John D. Hicks, *The Republican Ascendancy*. On the thirties, there is still nothing more interesting and readable than Arthur M. Schlesinger, Jr., *The Age of Roosevelt*, but it is yet unfinished, the third volume ending in 1937. Leuchtenberg's *Franklin D. Roosevelt and the New Deal* is a good, one-volume narrative.

An overview to the intellectual history of the twenties is provided by Roderick Nash, *The Nervous Generation*. Exceptionally detailed introductions to intellectuals and social thought in this period, with invaluable pointers to primary sources, are Edward A. Purcell, Jr., *The Crisis of Democratic Theory*, and Richard H. Pells, *Radical Visions and American Dreams*. Both provide a secular perspective for assessing the importance of Catholic and Protestant neo-orthodoxy.

SPECTACLES OF THE FADING PROTESTANT HEGEMONY: PROHIBITION, FUNDAMENTALISM, THE KLAN, AND THE BROWN SCARE

In his landmark book of 1955, *The Age of Reform*, Richard Hofstadter presented an interpretation of the twenties which dominated the literature until quite recently. After the First World War, he argued, the progressive-populist reform coalition broke up in disillusionment and the final fruit of this coalition, prohibition, substituted "peevishness" for reform (p. 290). Cut off from mainline urban progressivism, the rural populists had no counterbalance to their tendencies toward intolerance, racism, paranoia, and fanaticism. The results were militant and anti-urban fundamentalism, the flowering of the Ku Klux Klan, and the collapse of the Democratic party. The futile and almost pathetic last years of William Jennings Bryan symbolized these destructive and backward tendencies.

In the last decade or two, social historians investigating the nineteenth century in America have displayed the interconnectedness of Protestant evangelism, moral reform, and the growth of middle-class society in such a way that it is now possible to view the twenties in a longer time frame. Thus the events of the decade may now be seen as the winding down of the nineteenth-century Protestant project of creating a Christian-capitalist order, rather than a backward-looking orgy of repression. This was largely Robert T. Handy's thesis in *A Christian America*, when he suggested that the twenties saw the disintegration of a century-old dream. In keeping with this perspective, recent work on fundamentalism and the Klan has pointed out the appeal of these movements to urban middle-class elements. And with populism having recently been rehabilitated as an authentic revival of republican ideology (see Lawrence Goodwyn's *Democratic Promise: The Populist Moment in America*), it has become a respectable ancestor for other movements of protest in the twenties and thirties, which had themselves been labeled protofascist. Still, the urgency and violence—real and rhetorical—of the controversies of the twenties limit any attempt to explain them away easily. Indeed, the revulsion which liberal historians felt for what they thought to be repressive and reactionary movements expressed the real problems those movements posed for an open society.

On prohibition and the twenties, Charles Merz's 1931 history, *The Dry Decade*, is still respected and highly useful as a narrative. But his argument that repeal of prohibition was an inevitable result of a popular uprising against government repression, similar to the ending of Reconstruction after the Civil War, now appears simplistic and antiquated. The classic study in the Hofstadter style is Andrew Sinclair's *Era of Excess*. Sinclair argues that the entire battle over prohibition was marked by fanaticism on both sides; that the drys abhorred saloons partly because they competed with churches in the business of consolation; that prohibition became a lightning rod for all complaints about modern society. The Volstead Act, for Sinclair, was the last victory of rural resentment over urban modernism, "the Corn Belt over the conveyor belt." The prohibition movement foundered on its own excesses, outlawing even light wine and beer, and left its most enduring legacy in the establishment of organized crime.

Perhaps the most able reply to Sinclair's argument has come from Norman H. Clark, in both a study of prohibition in Washington State, and a general interpretive essay on the history of the whole movement from its roots in the nineteenth century. In his Washington study, Clark relies on voting statistics to show that prohibition indeed drew strong rural support, but relied equally on the votes of the urban middle class, in a reaction not so much to modernism as to an older American bogeyman, the ethnic, largely Catholic working class. The upper echelons of urban and commercial society led the movement for repeal, in a response to the Great Depression and the political corruption and violence which accompanied prohibition enforcement. In a sense, the Protestant middle class grew tired of paying the price for a reform which it had largely sponsored in the first place. In *Deliver Us From Evil*, Clark takes a much broader approach, sweeping in the findings of many local studies, in an overview sympathetic to the spirit of moderate prohibitionism. Taking seriously the problems of public drunkenness and alcoholism, Clark credits the prohibition movement with the permanent elimination of the saloon from American life. The forces behind repeal were complicated, but grew from the powerful reshaping of the modern, secular consciousness brought about by consumerism and the mass media. The American ideal of stewardship collided with the growing ethic of personal liberation, and the battle was played out in such arenas as the movies, which increasingly portrayed drinking as acceptable and even admirable.

An important contribution to this argument comes from Sean Dennis Cashman. His essentially narrative history, based on criminal records, gives full play to the appeal of the romance of bootlegging and organized crime. While quite unsympathetic to the wets, Cashman supports Clark's thesis through devoting part of his work to an examination of the imagery of the movies.

If Clark's large-scale structural explanation for the failure of prohibition is essentially correct, it yet poses an immense problem for further historical interpretation. How could such a massive and deep change in American society have occurred within the space of a decade? The prohibition movement was powerful enough in 1919 to force ratification of an amendment to the Constitution, something which opponents of child labor, however numerous, popular, and eloquent, could not do. Yet by 1933 prohibition's opponents were strong enough to return the blow with the Twenty-first Amendment. This problem has been the concern of David E. Kyvig and others in a recent monograph and a set of symposium papers.

Kyvig has shown that the opponents of the prohibition amendment organized in the mid-twenties and successfully played upon American fears of government intervention in private life. Antiprogressives, the opponents of prohibition later turned against the New Deal in such associations as the

Liberty League. Kyvig and his associates have illuminated the political frame-work of repeal, but have not banished all anomalies. Why a movement which successfully employed antistatist rhetoric to overturn a constitutional amend-ment found so little success in fighting New Deal legislation with the same weapon is a mystery.

Without a doubt, prohibition and its repeal together present a knot which those who would understand church-state issues in the twentieth century must try to untangle. If the Nineteenth Amendment represented a triumph of a Protestant-progressive coalition, then the Twenty-first Amendment repre-sented that coalition's demise. The failure of prohibition may be a key to understanding some other aspects of the disintegration of the Protestant hegemony.

Prohibition provided the clearest issue of nationwide importance on which religious partisans could align. There is no doubt that it played a major part in the 1924 Democratic National Convention, in which delegates pledged to Al Smith—avowedly wet and Catholic to boot—and William Gibbs McAdoo—dry but unwilling to denounce the Klan—struggled for days until turning in exhaustion to John W. Davis on the 103rd ballot. Likewise, when Smith won the nomination in 1928, alcohol and Smith's religion became major issues in his campaign against Herbert Hoover. Interpretations of the meaning of that election have spilled over into larger questions about the importance of prohibition and Catholicism as general political issues throughout the period.

In *The Politics of Provincialism*, David Burner provides the best single volume on the politics of the period, from the liberal perspective. Burner argues that the Democratic party's coalition came apart in 1920 over a variety of problems, some of which involved nativism and prohibitionism, but which added up to a rural-urban split. Although the twin issues of prohibition and the Klan split the party in 1924, by the next election John J. Raskob and Franklin Roosevelt had built up the elements of a successful rural-urban coalition which Al Smith squandered by playing the part of a "Gotham cock-ney." While his religion and wet stand both hurt him, his city-slicker image could hardly have overcome the Republican majority in prosperous times. For a lively narrative account of the election, see Edmund A. Moore, *A Catholic Runs for President*.

Against Burner's rural-urban dichotomy, Allan J. Lichtman has marshaled an impressive display of statistics and multivariate analysis to show that Smith's Catholicism was the single most important issue in the election. He goes further to argue that the Protestant-Catholic split ran right through twentieth-century American politics, but surfaced only in the elections of 1928 and 1960. In these findings, Lichtman has been supported by the local studies of G. Michael McCarthy, William Foy Lisenby, Barbara C. Wingo, and

John L. Shover, all of whom see the election of 1928 as exposing deep divisions along explicitly religious lines, Protestants against Catholics.

After prohibition, perhaps the most obvious expression of the fading Protestant hegemony was the fundamentalist movement and its vocal attack on modernism, particularly the teaching of evolutionary theory. Historians writing in the liberal tradition have attempted to treat this movement fairly, but have begun from the assumption that such widely different heroes of fundamentalism as the violent minister J. Frank Norris, the politician Bryan, and the Princeton conservative theologian J. Gresham Machen shared a deep mistrust of everything new and urban. For a good example of this approach, see Norman K. Furniss's *The Fundamentalist Controversy*.

More recently, Timothy P. Weber, Ernest R. Sandeen, and George M. Marsden have pointed out the roots of twentieth-century fundamentalism in American evangelicalism and the development of premillennialist thought in the late nineteenth century. Marsden in particular has argued that American fundamentalism arose as a reaction within the mainstream of American evangelical reform to the rise of Protestant liberalism at the turn of the century. According to Marsden, the widely accepted project of creating a Protestant American economy and polity—the impetus behind so much of American moral reform—split into two or more movements in the twentieth century. One side moved to the left in liberal theology and the more radical aspects of the social gospel; the other defended literal interpretation of the Bible and personal holiness, including crusades against personal sins like drinking, gambling, and dancing. That is, fundamentalism was as much a reaction to modernism within the churches as to modernity without. In this light it is interesting to turn back to Stewart G. Cole's 1931 study of fundamentalism, which largely concerns itself with theological issues and battles within the major denominations and is still an excellent guide to doctrinal politics.

Although Marsden's interpretation puts fundamentalism back into the context of mainstream American Protestantism, it dodges key problems of the twenties. Why, for instance, should a movement so dedicated to theological dispute and intrachurch action have gone out into the political world on a quixotic chase after evolutionism? Why should such a movement have been so quick to stigmatize itself with the outlandish spectacle of the Scopes trial? To some extent Marsden has avoided these questions by not investigating the inherently theatrical side of early twentieth-century revivalism. One should supplement Marsden with C. Allyn Russell's *Voices of Fundamentalism* for a clearer view of the range of fundamentalist behavior, from moderates to extremists, from scholars to ranters. Russell's work is a set of short biographical portraits of J. Frank Norris, John Roach Straton, William Bell Riley, J. C. Massee, J. Gresham Machen, William Jennings Bryan, and Clarence Macartney.

As yet no consensus exists on the social nature of the fundamentalist movement of the twenties. John M. Werly has returned to a theme from Hofstadter and asserted that premillennialists practiced the "paranoid style," along with others like Huey Long and Father Coughlin, and provide a clear link to more recent hucksters of conspiracy theories in and out of the evangelical movement. Leon McBeth supports Marsden's reading of fundamentalism, pointing out that fundamentalists could not capture the Southern Baptist Convention in the twenties simply because there was no appreciable modernist force within the denomination against which to rail. Gregory H. Singleton has shown that San Francisco Protestants of Anglo-Saxon origin tended to split along socioeconomic lines over fundamentalism, with successful managers and professionals remaining in the established churches and less successful, marginal middle-class members joining fundamentalist splinter groups. Finally, Joel A. Carpenter has insisted that fundamentalism in the twenties was no particular reaction to modernism, but part of a continuous tradition from the mid-nineteenth century down to the present.

Of the anti-evolution crusade and the Scopes trial itself, there is a large and sufficiently self-explanatory literature. How William Jennings Bryan came to be involved in this movement, and his motives, political and religious, are dealt with in biographical studies by Lawrence W. Levine, Ferenc Morton Szasz, and Paolo E. Coletta. They generally agree that Bryan was sincere in both his anti-evolutionism and his political reformism, and did not pay very much attention to either the scientific or theological aspects of his position. Growing ever surer that evolutionism would dissolve the moral glue of society, he remained a liberal in political terms—insofar as he called for greater democratic control over business—while being a conservative in religious terms.

On the severity and importance of the fundamentalist-modernist struggle over evolution and related issues beyond the Scopes trial, the historical record is inconclusive. On the one hand, religiously motivated enthusiasts led attacks on educators and called for anti-evolution laws in several states. On the other hand, most of these attacks failed in their immediate objectives. Willard B. Gatewood's *Preachers, Pedagogues and Politicians*, is one of the most complete accounts of a statewide battle, in North Carolina, where moderate forces prevailed over strong attacks. Gatewood has also edited a collection of opposing viewpoints on evolution and the relationship of religion and science in the period entitled *Controversy in the Twenties*.

Only a little less spectacular than anti-evolutionism, and a good deal more worrisome, were the outbreaks of nativist movements and legislation, especially the enormous popularity of the Ku Klux Klan. For the history of nativism in America, including the anti-Semitism of Henry Ford, the restriction of immigration in 1924, and the revival of the Klan, see John Higham's definitive account, *Strangers in the Land.* See also Robert K. Murray, *Red Scare.* There are no recent secondary studies of the role of religion in nativism after World War I generally, but useful information can be gleaned from Robert Moats Miller's *American Protestantism and Social Issues,* especially with respect to the response to lynchings, segregation in the South, and the resurgent Klan. See also the articles by Edward Cuddy and Elaine Fain on anti-Catholicism, and Niel M. Johnson on the response of the Missouri Synod to a law banning the use of the German language.

Shortly after the end of World War I, the Ku Klux Klan, refounded partly as a fraternal organization and partly as a money-making scheme in 1915, spread rapidly and widely over most of the United States and parts of Canada. Although the Klan was formally only a fraternal order, it invaded the political realm in many states; its members engaged in frequent acts of violence and intimidation; its secret powers were so respected and feared that at first neither the major Protestant denominations nor the Democratic party dared to pass resolutions condemning the order by name. But after a peak of presumed power in 1924, the Klan faded quickly, being widely denounced by press and church, until by the thirties it could hardly be considered more than a fringe group on the far right of American politics.

About the resurgent Klan there has been abundant writing. Precisely what the connection between the Klan and organized churches consisted in is hard to say. Clearly, the Klan exploited religious symbols and enlisted local pastors and church services for recruiting, possibly with the connivance or at least the tolerance of higher ecclesiastical authorities. The Klan made its connection to Protestantism and prohibition explicit. For a glimpse into the mind of the second Imperial Wizard, see Hiram Wesley Evans, "The Klan's Fight for Americanism." Once the public outcry against the Klan had fairly begun, however, support for the movement from clergy and press quickly dried up, and general denunciation became the fashion.

Because the revived Klan was essentially a loosely organized network of local organizations connected by commission-seeking membership salesmen (Kleagles), it adapted itself remarkably well to local issues and politics. The most complete account of the movement, David M. Chalmers's *Hooded Americanism,* covers the growth of the Klan in every state in which it had a significant organization, and stresses its fraternal, reforming side, without ignoring the sporadic, almost spontaneous violence which accompanied its spread. Kenneth T. Jackson, *The Ku Klux Klan in the City,* challenges the Hofstadterian notion that the Klan was simply a movement of rural resentment. Studying the Klan in nine midwestern and southern cities, Jackson argues that the Klan had a wide socioeconomic base, an urban leadership, the tacit support of the clergy at first, and a less violent nature than legend suggests.

A small flood of local studies show that the Klan focused on issues of local political corruption, law enforcement, and moral laxity—everything from bootlegging to divorce—and generally employed politics more than violence in attempts to take control of local governments from people who were perceived as corrupt and criminal (and alien). The most recent of these studies, Robert Alan Goldberg's *Hooded Empire*, argues that the success of the Klan in Colorado was not due to the postwar economic depression, black urban immigration, the red scare, or ethnic infiltration into WASP neighborhoods—all factors which Jackson has cited. Rather, Goldberg writes, the Klan was a kind of good-government movement, responding to rises in crime and prostitution, with no official policy of terror.

The Klan remains a problem for the student of church-state issues, because none of these studies denies that violence, anti-Semitism, anti-Catholicism, and generalized intolerance accompanied the rise of the Klan everywhere. And the widespread clerical involvement in the movement is well documented. Without a doubt, the Klan is part of the larger story of the attenuation of the impulse toward a Protestant social order in America. The fact that such a movement provided a means for general complaints about modern immorality and disorder to express themselves in violent xenophobia and anti-Semitism may lead us to draw uncomfortable parallels to fascist movements in Europe in the same period.

Indeed, there were several outgrowths of the fundamentalist movement, broadly construed, which blossomed into quasi-fascist movements. These are the topic of an excellent recent volume by Leo P. Ribuffo, *The Old Christian Right*. In it he examines the lives and careers of William Dudley Pelley, founder of the Silver Legion; Gerald B. Winrod, a dispensational premillennialist who founded the Defenders of the Christian Faith; and Gerald L. K. Smith, a minister who tried to inherit the mantle of Huey Long. Ribuffo locates them firmly in the context of premillennialism, prohibitionism, and anti-Semitism which produced others like them, and argues that for such people, the anxieties of the twenties did not mysteriously melt away with the arrival of the New Deal. Rather, the expanded power of the central government and the repeal of the Eighteenth Amendment confirmed their worst misgivings about the modern world. Pelley, Winrod, and Smith each ultimately found their way to anti-Semitism, charging Jews with a worldwide conspiracy. But Ribuffo refuses to take this trio seriously as true American fascist threats, since their following was always tiny, their strategies for gaining power so ill-considered, and their ultimate suppression so quick and easy once the federal government cracked down in wartime. In fact, Ribuffo proffers the intriguing suggestion that the late thirties saw a "brown scare," initiated from the left, vigorously prosecuted by the federal government, and fully as unwarranted as either of the great red scares.

The name most often mentioned in connection with religion and fascism, moreover, was not that of any Protestant fundamentalist but that of a Catholic, Father William Coughlin, the radio priest of Royal Oak, Michigan, and founder of the National Union for Social Justice. Coughlin proceeded from early support of the New Deal to a fixation with monetary reform, through a short-lived attempt to form a third party in the 1936 election, to a spell of anti-Semitism, before being silenced in 1942 as the result of a deal struck by the Justice Department and his own superiors in the church. At the height of his popularity, he was heard by an enormous, nationwide audience and feared as a potential American Hitler by otherwise sober members of both major parties. There is no dearth of secondary literature about Coughlin, ranging from John L. Spivak's rabid *Shrine of the Silver Dollar*—itself a primary document of the brown scare—to a sympathetic biography based in part upon interviews with Coughlin himself, Sheldon Marcus's *Father Coughlin*. Most useful are Charles J. Tull's *Father Coughlin and the New Deal* and Alan Brinkley's *Voices of Protest*. Brinkley argues that both Father Coughlin and Huey Long partook of the populist traditions of local protest against overwhelming centralized power. In an appendix dedicated to the relationship of Long and Coughlin to fascism, Brinkley concludes that one's judgment hinges on the murky definitions of fascism itself. Neither Coughlin nor Long showed any sympathy for Italy or Germany nor did they propose any great myth of national destiny and the state. Rather, they posed local democracy against "the interests," and their somewhat fluid plans could accept moves to the right and the left.

PROTESTANTISM MIRED AND MOVING

While one wing of the Protestant reform impulse turned to the pursuit of a Christian society based on abstinence and biblical inerrancy, another wing, variously called modernism or liberalism, entered a period of prolonged testing and transformation. The different routes of social gospel advocates through these two decades make fascinating reading and no two are exactly alike. A. J. Muste moved from pacifism through labor organization to a period of revolutionary socialism, before returning to pacifism by World War II. Along the way he left the ministry and then returned. Norman Thomas left the pulpit for good to become the perennial standard-bearer of the Socialist party. Harry Ward moved steadily into the orbit of the Soviet Union. Reinhold Niebuhr drifted into a short flirtation with Marxism, but became a founding father of

American neo-orthodox theology and postwar liberalism, and one of the most famous men of his times.

Churchmen imbued with the spirit of prewar progressivism and the social gospel began the twenties with high, overinflated hopes for "Christianizing the Social Order"—Walter Rauschenbusch's phrase. The first fruits of this hopefulness were the two reports of the Interchurch World Movement's inquiry into the steel strike of 1919. But the movement soon bogged down in the prosperity and nonpolitics of the twenties, split into several factions over both social and denominational issues, and was in many ways far less prepared for the events of the Great Depression and the New Deal than its Catholic counterpart.

The fate of the social gospel in these two decades is the subject of three major works closely related to the post–New Deal liberal tradition that cover different aspects of this period. Paul A. Carter's *The Decline and Revival of the Social Gospel*, part narrative, part analysis, chronicles the course of social reformism in those Protestant denominations which had been known for their social gospel orientation before the First World War. Robert Moats Miller's *American Protestantism and Social Issues* is a series of linked essays on the response, in church councils, church journals and magazines, and sermons, to social issues from lynching and the Klan to the New Deal and the coming of war. Donald B. Meyer's *The Protestant Search for Political Realism* deals almost exclusively with the theology of thinkers and reflective councils in this period, in a history of ideas and their implications. Each has its own distinctive strengths and weaknesses. Together they provide a composite history of the relation of religion to liberal social thought in the mainline Protestant denominations, with the necessary exception of Lutheranism.

Carter's study serves as a readable history of the whole period, moving from the doldrums in which reform-inclined ministers found themselves in the twenties to the challenges to their optimism which the depression and the rise of totalitarianism posed. He shows how the movement split over prohibition, pacifism, and the status of the blacks in the South, how frustrations over the low status of pastors and the failures of immodestly conceived programs to Christianize the social order helped usher in acceptance of the neo-orthodoxy of Reinhold Niebuhr. But he maintains that the end result was a revived movement for social reform within the Protestant churches, a movement which for all practical purposes resembled the old social gospel.

Miller's essays address one major, central problem: how Protestant churchmen (mostly ministers, editors, and members of commissions) could combat the structural conservatism of their denominations and the lethargy of rank-and-file laymen, and speak and act for the churches on important social questions. Miller concludes that on nearly every major issue, a significant minority of ministers stood to the left of their laymen and that the religious press did speak up frequently, even in the darkest days of the twenties. These conclusions hold for the major Protestant denominations, with the partial exception of the Lutheran sects, whose modernist movement had always been small. At the same time, he argues, the social position of Protestantism as the religion of the privileged, powerful, and contented always militated against much meaningful church action, especially before the Great Depression. Dedicated ministers might ram manifestoes through councils and editorial boards, but their churches had no obligation and little inclination to listen or to act upon such statements. Miller's work deals forthrightly with a recurrent question in interpreting church-state relations: who is the church? What his account lacks in overall continuity and depth, it gains in political awareness, in its pictures of Protestant churches simultaneously rooted and stirring.

The largest, most thorough, and most challenging study of this era is Donald B. Meyer's *The Protestant Search for Political Realism*, a study of the twists and turns of the theology and politics of social gospel reformers from Walter Rauschenbusch through Reinhold Niebuhr (into the forties). Meyer contends that the social gospel was rebuffed in its appeals to labor, business, and the church. The hope of Christianizing the social order was repeatedly disappointed in the decade of prosperity and then shattered into many splinters in the depression. He firmly locates Reinhold Niebuhr's *Moral Man and Immoral Society* and *Interpretation of Christian Ethics* at the center of the challenge to the social gospel. By the end of the thirties, Niebuhr's political realism dominated, but the tremendous success of the New Deal blunted the starkness of his dichotomies.

Meyer's book is both immensely difficult and immensely important. It is weighed down by reified ideas and "churchy" terms which take on portentous, but vague meaning—"witness," "prophets," "the passion"—and most of all by its basic assumption that the neo-orthodox separation of the ideal church from sinful society was the goal toward which the social gospel was somehow stumbling. After all, this book, like so many from the fifties and sixties, was written in an era and an academy dominated by Niebuhr. But these shortcomings are outweighed by the careful analysis given to the changing views of a group of highly individualistic thinkers, such as Sherwood Eddy, Kirby Page, Francis McConnell, A. J. Muste, and Harry Ward. Reinhold Niebuhr and Walter Rauschenbusch receive special attention. Finally, the book is an excellent guide to source materials from this period.

The dominant figure of this era in the relationship of Protestantism to social and political action was and is Reinhold Niebuhr, an ambitious German-American midwestern pastor, protégé of Sherwood Eddy, and a founder of interest groups from the Fellowship for a Christian Social Order to Americans for Democratic Action. His intellectual odyssey from early social gospel activism and support of World War I to the near-Marxism of *Moral Man,* to the full-blown neo-orthodoxy of *The Nature and Destiny of Man* can easily be appreciated from examining his major writings, some of which are listed here. And of course there is an enormous body of secondary literature about him, relevant and recent portions of which are also listed. In this reviewer's opinion, Richard Wightman Fox's *Reinhold Niebuhr* is very nearly definitive. Fox manages to place Niebuhr in a more complex historical and personal context than previous writers, and along the way revises the conventional wisdom about this restless spirit. Crucial to understanding Niebuhr, Fox argues, is his origin as a German-speaking American, his search for as wide a pastoral role in society as possible, and his near infatuation with British socialism. Fox sensitively describes the dialectical relationship Reinhold had with his younger brother, the Yale theologian H. Richard Niebuhr. The portrait of Reinhold which emerges from Fox's account is of a man much less sure of himself, far less radical than the conventional portrait would have him, quick to criticize sloppy thinking, reacting to events as much as working out ideas, rushing into print with half-formed thoughts, and probably not so deep a thinker as his brother. Niebuhr's interest in Marxism is balanced by his Deweyan side. Fox's biography can be usefully supplemented by Ronald H. Stone's *Prophet to Politicians* for a full appreciation of Niebuhr's immense influence in the political world.

Other major studies of figures in the liberal wing of Protestantism in this period include; on H. Richard Niebuhr, James W. Fowler, *To See the Kingdom;* Robert Moats Miller's recent biography of Harry Emerson Fosdick; Jo Ann Oviman Robinson's biography of A. J. Muste; and biographies of Norman Thomas by Harry Fleischman and Murray B. Seidler. For further secondary work on the far left of this movement, see the articles by Eugene P. Link and Matthew John Fennero on Harry Ward and his circle, and J. Petryshyn on Albert Edward Smith, a Canadian Methodist pastor who joined the Communist party.

Besides the works of Reinhold Niebuhr, one may profitably examine a large body of primary sources. Francis J. McConnell and Sherwood Eddy have written autobiographies. The works by McConnell, Muste, Douglas Clyde Macintosh, and Shailer Mathews in this bibliography are included for their relative availability, and should be considered an introduction to a much wider literature.

Of course, as Robert Moats Miller is at pains to point out, the overwhelming majority of Protestant clergy and laity were neither fundamentalist nor liberal activists. Not enough work has been done in exposing the relationship of

Protestantism and business boosterism in the twenties. Businessmen consciously used the language of religion in justification of their callings, most notoriously Henry Ford, who once compared building a factory to building a church and working in such a factory to worshiping in it. Given current interest in civil religion in America, it should not be long before there is a full-length study. In the interim, there are two articles by William T. Doherty, Jr., which point out the interrelationship of businesses and churches as churches began to run more like businesses and businessmen appropriated religion to suit their ideology. James A. Neuchterlein has written on the religious ethos of business made explicit in the bestseller of the twenties, Bruce Barton's *The Man Nobody Knows*. Barton's book cast Christ as a successful businessman, and although the book is in the tradition of other, older advice books which mix moral sermons with commercial tips, it has been often cited as the prime example of Babbittry in the twenties. There are also valuable insights in the works already cited by Robert Moats Miller and Paul A. Carter.

In general, the southern denominations of Protestantism seem to have been less vulnerable to the virus of the social gospel. David M. Reimers, in *White Protestantism and the Negro*, and John Lee Eighmy, in *Churches in Cultural Captivity*, argue that the traditional acquiescence of white Protestant churches to first slavery and then Jim Crow made them extremely cautious on all social issues. Not until after World War II did the consensus of silence begin to break down. Kenneth K. Bailey, in *Southern White Protestantism in the Twentieth Century*, suggests that southern Protestantism did make some changes in its basically conservative social views, but did so quite slowly and quietly. James J. Thompson, Jr., in *"Tried as by Fire": Southern Baptists and the Religious Controversies of the 1920s*, gives an account of the controversies which rocked this denomination and may have preoccupied its attention to the exclusion of the social gospel.

A group of articles by John Marszalek, R. Douglas Brackenridge, and Randolph Meade Walker suggest that the role of black clergy in the South during this time was one of mediation and conciliation, working for what they could reasonably expect to gain for blacks, in the manner of Booker T. Washington. If a group of recent articles by Mollie C. Abernathy, Jacquelyn Dowd Hall, Lawrence L. Brown, and Arnold Shankman can be read as pointing toward any generalizations, then the most radical force for social reform in the South—particularly concerning the abolition of lynching and chivalric codes of violence—consisted of women working within the denominations.

Of special interest to those curious about the fruits of neo-orthodox radicalism in the South is Thomas M. Jacklin's "Mission to the Sharecroppers," which paints a somber picture of an attempt by northern theologians, including Reinhold Niebuhr, to fund two large cooperative farms for displaced sharecroppers. Theory and practice, it seems, did not mesh very well.

CATHOLICISM AND SOCIAL ACTION: NEW DEALERS, LABOR ORGANIZERS, ASCETICS, AND AGRARIANS

At the end of World War I, the Catholic attempt at social reconstruction closely paralleled the Protestant. An early, ambitious pronouncement on widespread social reform, by a group of bishops, raised antipathy among much of the clergy and laity. For Catholic liberals the twenties were a time of stagnation and frustration, with conservative forces pointing to nativism and hysteria against left-wingers as good reasons for toning down proposals for social reconstruction. A compact band of labor liberals, led by the indefatigable John A. Ryan and William Dietz, continued to press for basic labor standards, such as maximum hours and minimum wage laws and child-labor bans.

Unlike their counterparts in the Protestant social gospel movement, however, liberal Catholics were intellectually preadapted for many of the major legislative enactments of the New Deal, especially the National Industrial Recovery Act (NIRA), the Agricultural Adjustment Act (AAA), and the Wagner Act. This was in large part due to the encouragement provided by the encyclical of Pope Pius XI, generally called *Quadragesimo Anno* (May 1931). In his pronouncement, an amplification of Leo XIII's 1891 labor encyclical, *Rerum Novarum*, the pope suggested that workers and capitalists within each industry should form cooperative councils to fix just prices and wages, with aid but not control to proceed from the state. He defended the right of workers to organize into unions, not so much for the sake of striking but to negotiate on issues of common interest. This proposal, strikingly similar to John A. Ryan's interpretation of *Rerum Novarum* in the *Bishops' Program of Social Reconstruction* (developed by the National Catholic War Council in 1919), predisposed many Catholics to look kindly upon the industrial codes of the National Recovery Administration. Likewise, the firm restatement of papal approval for labor organization combined with first the NIRA and then the Wagner Act in encouraging such diverse Catholic efforts as the Association of Catholic Trade Unions and the ascetic Catholic Worker movement of Dorothy Day and Peter Maurin. Catholic agrarian theorists initially hailed the AAA as the first step toward reestablishing the rural, integrated life.

Catholic activism in the New Deal stemmed from more than the similarity of papal and presidential encyclicals. Catholic voters formed an important bloc for Roosevelt and the Democratic party, and FDR was careful to cultivate this support. Toward the coming of World War II this alliance did not essentially fail, but became a good deal more strained as Catholics began to call for stronger action by the government against the anticlerical regimes of Mexico and Loyalist Spain. Furthermore, the ideology of *Quadragesimo Anno* could go only so far with the new general welfare state. The distrust of a strong secular government and outright hostility to anything smelling of socialism, both of which were strong ingredients of both papal and American liberal Catholic thought, drew lines in the dirt beyond which Catholic radicalism would not go.

For general introductions to Catholic liberalism, see Robert D. Cross, *The Emergence of Liberal Catholicism in America*, and Aaron I. Abell, *American Catholicism and Social Action*. Abell has also collected and edited an important group of documents in *American Catholic Thought on Social Questions*, which includes excerpts from the *Bishops' Program*, documents from the rural life movement, and passages from Dorothy Day and Father Coughlin. Two of the most important primary documents of the period are the aforementioned *Bishops' Program*, and the manifesto prepared by the Social Action Department of the National Catholic Welfare Conference (the peacetime sequel to the National Catholic War Council), *Organized Social Justice*, being a response to the invalidation of the NIRA and the AAA by the Supreme Court, and signed by 131 prominent clergy and laymen. John A. Ryan's own memoirs, *Social Doctrine in Action*, hold useful primary documentation. See also his joint publication with Moorhouse F. X. Millar, *The State and the Church*, for their description of the ideal Catholic polity.

The period of retrenchment during the twenties is covered in various books and articles. Philip Gleason, in two long chapters in his history of the German-American Catholic Central Verein, *The Conservative Reformers*, credits the surge of assimilationism and anti-German feeling after World War I with the dampening of the Verein's enthusiasm for labor reform. Donna Thomas shows that a diocesan newspaper could take conservative stands on social issues for fear of nativism in her article, "The Providence *Visitor* and Nativist Issues, 1916–1924." Christopher J. Kauffman's *Faith and Fraternalism: The History of the Knights of Columbus, 1882–1982*, is a commissioned history of the order, but provides information about the attention which the Ku Klux Klan drew from Catholics in general. Francis L. Broderick's biography of John A. Ryan, *The Right Reverend New Dealer*, devotes several chapters to Ryan's struggles within his church for wider support for labor unions and the ill-fated child-labor amendment.

There are several fine studies of the relationship of Catholicism and the New Deal. George Q. Flynn, in *American Catholics and the Roosevelt Presidency, 1932–1936*, credits Catholic electoral support of FDR to the "fortuitous" resemblance of early New Deal legislation to some of the recommendations of

Pius XI's encyclical, and to Roosevelt's open and fervent support of Al Smith in 1924 and 1928. David J. O'Brien, in *American Catholics and Social Reform: The New Deal Years*, suggests that Catholics were ambivalent about the New Deal and generally hamstrung by the encyclicals, fearing both communism and the federal government and spending too much energy on personal moral reform. Lawrence B. DeSaulniers, in *The Response in American Catholic Periodicals to the Crises of the Great Depression, 1930–1935*, tends to support Flynn with a close examination of periodical literature, but does not follow the subject past Roosevelt's first term of office. Thomas E. Blantz has provided a biography of Francis J. Haas, academic, labor mediator, member of the National Labor Relations Board, and eventual bishop of Grand Rapids, in *A Priest in Public Service*. And Broderick's biography of Ryan, indispensable to the whole period, is equally useful here.

There is a growing literature on the Catholic Worker movement, which formed around the urban shelters and the newspaper which Dorothy Day founded and led for four decades. Mel Piehl provides a thorough introduction and interpretation of the movement in *Breaking Bread*. Without oversimplifying the complex roots of the movement in the odd mixture of Day's Greenwich Village anarchism, Maurin's semiroyalist agrarianism, and the ambiguous encyclicals of Pius XI, Piehl argues that the Catholic Worker movement provided a locus for social action which was genuinely both Catholic and radical. The movement germinated several strains of independent radicalism, including the work of the socialist Michael Harrington. Piehl can be usefully supplemented by several biographical studies of Day and Maurin, of which William D. Miller's *Dorothy Day: A Biography* is the foremost.

For an insight into the religious and political philosophy of the Catholic Worker movement, one can do no better than to read the *Catholic Worker* itself. Both Maurin and Day resist theoretical summaries, but in 1936 Paul Hanley Furfey, a theologian deeply involved in the movement, attempted a summa in *Fire on the Earth*.

Related to the Catholic Worker movement but formally independent was the Association of Catholic Trade Unions (ACTU), the subject of Douglas P. Seaton's *Catholics and Radicals*. Seaton argues that the ACTU began by trying to mediate between Marxist radicalism and the kind of organic capitalism embodied in the labor encyclicals. But the movement turned most of its attention to attacking Communists in the CIO, and by the late thirties was spending much more time in red-hunting than in labor-organizing and agitating.

Finally, although there are no book-length studies on the relationship of Catholic neo-orthodox political theory to Catholic social action, Edward A. Purcell, Jr., has devoted two chapters to the development of a Catholic political theory which posited Thomism as the foundation for democracy in the late thirties in his *The Crisis of Democratic Theory.*

CHURCHES AND FOREIGN AFFAIRS: PACIFISM AND ACTIVISM

U.S. foreign policy between the two world wars was characterized by a strong revulsion to arms and intervention of any kind; in fact, the twenties and the thirties were almost unique in American history for their combination of isolationism and pacifism. The pacifist persuasion dominated church-state issues which centered on foreign policy until the very brink of Pearl Harbor. But throughout the thirties, beginning with the Japanese invasion of Manchuria in 1931 and continuing with the Spanish Civil War, the widespread pacifist consensus, Protestant and Catholic, began to shatter into factions over the obvious problems posed by the rise of frankly aggressive, totalitarian states. In addition, clear reports of the mounting persecution of Jews and political dissidents in Germany and Italy challenged both immigration restriction and the isolationism of the Roosevelt administration. Caught between the evils of totalitarianism and war, many Americans were nearly immobilized by indecision.

On pacifism in general, with specific attention to the nondenominational (really Quaker and Protestant) Fellowship of Reconciliation, see John K. Nelson, *The Peace Prophets: American Pacifist Thought, 1919–1941.* Nelson examines in detail the various turns of thought experienced by many of the thinkers who are also analyzed in Donald B. Meyer's *The Protestant Search for Political Realism,* but also gives a good deal of attention to general movements like the "Outlawry of War" in the late twenties, and the Oxford pledge movement. On the particular role of the historic peace churches—Friends, Mennonites, and the Brethren—see Robert Kreider's 1976 article and the documents edited by Donald F. Durnbaugh in *On Earth Peace.* Also of interest is an article by John R. M. Wilson, "The Quaker and the Sword," which discusses Herbert Hoover's Quaker values and his decision to cut back on naval forces rather than the army because of the offensive value of the former and the defensive value of the latter.

The de facto involvement of American missions in the Sino-Japanese War brought pressures to intervene on the American government from 1931 onward. In this context see articles by Frederick B. Hoyt and Robert F. Smylie.

American Catholics participated in the general consensus on pacifism throughout the twenties and much of the thirties, but also became involved in lobbying on foreign policy toward Mexico and Loyalist Spain, both of which had shameful records of anticlerical pogroms. Patricia McNeal, *The American*

Catholic Peace Movement, 1928–1972, shows the continuity of that movement from the consensus of the twenties to the uproar over Vietnam. In a companion study to his earlier book on Catholic support of early New Deal legislation, George Q. Flynn has taken up the story of the relationship of Catholics to Roosevelt's foreign policy in *Roosevelt and Romanism.* Flynn points out that Catholic pressures on Roosevelt were at first rather vague, more in his head—as he contemplated their political clout—than in theirs. Only in 1939, when a desperate pro-Loyalist group in Congress proposed the lifting of sanctions on trade with belligerents in Spain, did American Catholics engage in organized lobbying. In addition, Flynn recounts the furor over Roosevelt's attempts to send a personal representative to the Vatican, and the Protestant attempt to block any formal recognition of Rome as a sovereign state. Wilson D. Miscamble, in "Catholics and American Foreign Policy from McKinley to McCarthy," surveys the available literature on this topic and concludes in support of Flynn that except for blocking the attempted termination of the Spanish embargo, Catholics had little impact on American foreign policy. Nonetheless, the myth of a Catholic influence was very much in the air at the time. No less a figure than Reinhold Niebuhr succumbed to it. The ambivalence of prominent American Catholics like John A. Ryan about intervention against Hitler and Mussolini was so well known that a British report in 1943 predicted that American Catholics would push the Roosevelt administration into postwar isolationism (see Thomas E. Hackey, "The Influence of Roman Catholics and Their Church in American Politics: A British Analysis in 1943"). There are also several relevant chapters in Kauffman's history of the Knights of Columbus which document that order's involvement in the Mexican situation, and in general anticommunist rhetoric in the late thirties and forties.

By far the most disturbing problem of foreign policy in the thirties for historians has been the lack of a strong American response to the destruction of European Jewry under Hitler. Two general works on the problem of immigration restriction and the Holocaust are Henry L. Feingold, *The Politics of Rescue*, and Saul S. Friedman, *No Haven for the Oppressed.* Both blame FDR for lacking commitment to the cause of rescuing the Jews in the face of strong American anti-Semitism. Feingold is more restrained, Friedman more open in condemnation. On anti-Semitism in America during this time see Donald S. Strong, *Organized Anti-Semitism in America: The Rise of Group Prejudice During the Decade, 1930–1940.* Robert W. Ross has shown persuasively that if American Protestants ignored the persecution of the Jews, it was not for lack of attention in the religious press. In his *So It Was True,* he argues that the American Protestant press, especially the *Christian Century,* responded early and frequently to the mounting atrocities, and sought confirmation of all the rumors.

ON THE PERIPHERY? JEWS AND BLACKS

Compared to the rich and deep literature available on most of the mainline
Protestant sects and Catholicism, the available writing on Jewish groups and
blacks is quite thin. Some attention has been paid to the response of American churches to questions such as lynching, civil rights, and the Holocaust,
but still less than one might expect, given the importance of these questions
in American history. And the best works in this area, such as the books by
David M. Reimers and Robert Moats Miller, examine the reactions of dominant bodies rather than the ecclesiastical framework of the oppressed minorities themselves. For a glimpse into Catholic attitudes toward race relations,
see John LaFarge's early statement of Catholic doctrines with respect to race,
Interracial Justice. Also of interest is Donald J. Kemper's account of the
integration of Catholic schools in St. Louis. In the case of Jews, the best
recent work has focused on the unchurched, secular side of Judaism; in the
case of blacks, very little attention has been paid to the church generally, and
especially in the urban setting.

Somewhat peripheral to church-state issues, but vital to understanding
ethnic politics, are two masterful studies by Irving Howe and Arthur Liebman, *World of Our Fathers* and *Jews and the Left*, respectively. Howe's work
is more richly illustrative and evocative of the mood of the lower East Side;
Liebman's effort is more sociological, but compendious on Jewish institutions. Both argue that from the 1890s into the 1930s a combination of factors—some stemming from *shtetl* life in Eastern Europe and some arising
from the urban experience of recent immigrants—encouraged a secular socialism based on Yiddish, which lent East European Jews solidarity and
predisposed them to an intellectualized radicalism. From this ferment came
much of the leadership for the Socialist Party of America, as well as the first
generation of authentic university radicals in American history.

This secular radicalism based on Yiddish culture faded as the Yiddish
language began to disappear. By the thirties, Jewish radicals increasingly had
to choose between radical politics and their Jewishness—represented by the
synagogue rather than Yiddish-language institutions. Thus, Howe and Liebman provide a picture of religious Judaism as a restraining force on radicalism, rather than an active participant in politics. To the extent that they
were politically active, Jews were motivated by their secular ethnic organizations rather than their religious institutions.

Recent articles by Irwin Yellowitz on Morris Hillquit; Deborah Dash Moore
and Marc Lee Raphael on Jewish philanthropy; and David H. Dalin on nonpar-
tisan Jewish Republicans in San Francisco all tend to support the thesis that
the Jewish religious institutions usually acted broadly to restrain involvement

in politics, except for good-government movements. David Brody has argued that Jews in general accepted the consensus on immigration restriction, even in the face of the growing threat to Jewish existence in Europe, well into the thirties. The great exception to the rule may be found in Melvin I. Urofsky's biography of Stephen Wise, a rabbi who founded and led New York's Free Synagogue, preached vigorously on all social and political questions, actively supported progressive legislation, and was America's leading Zionist after Louis Brandeis. Wise's energy, especially in the face of opposition from within and without Judaism, was astonishing. After a long career as a reformer and a Zionist, in the twenties and thirties he spearheaded the attack on Tammany Hall which led to the resignation of Mayor Jimmy Walker, campaigned hard for Smith and Roosevelt, served as a vocal and critical supporter of the New Deal, and fought early and hard for American opposition to Hitler's looming destruction of European Jewry.

The dearth of studies on blacks with respect to church and state in this period is more difficult to explain. There is a smattering of articles, previously cited, on the role of black clergy in the South during these decades, but little or nothing on most issues involving blacks and black churches in the North. The great exception is in the literature about Marcus Garvey, which is presently growing rapidly. Edmund David Cronon's relatively early study, still a good introduction to Garvey and his movement, is being supplemented and gradually supplanted by the publication of the Garvey papers and a forthcoming biography, both under the direction of Robert A. Hill. The religious dimensions of this movement, with its use of symbols, chaplains, and liturgical meeting structure, are the subject of an article by Randall K. Burkett. That the Universal Negro Improvement Association was a potent and at least quasi-religious force in urban black America cannot be doubted, and the current historical interest in it bodes well. But one looks in vain for any work which addresses such issues as the role of black clergy in any of the main social movements of the twenties and thirties.

It is difficult to account for these gaps in the historical record. To some extent, one must consider the possibility that Jewish and black religious institutions were well advised to keep a low profile during such a period of nativism and racism as the twenties, as even the much more powerful Catholic church did until the New Deal. In addition, the New Deal hardly represented a breakthrough for Jews or blacks—when one considers the inactivity of the administration in the face of the Holocaust and continued segregation in the South—and thus there has been no analogue to the whiggish liberal historiography for these two groups. But these are speculations in a void which can be filled only through much more scholarship. Just as in recent years, research into Catholic activism has narrowed an enormous gap in our understanding of the twenties and thirties, so we can expect this void to disappear. But most of the work remains to be done. While the twenties and thirties may have seen the demise of the white Protestant hegemony in the polity, strong vestiges of that hegemony linger in the historiography of the period.

BIBLIOGRAPHY

bbey, Sue Wilson. "Ku Klux Klan in Arizona, 1912-1925."
Journal of American History 14, no. 1 (1973), 10-30.

bell, Aaron I. American Catholicism and Social Action: A Search
for Social Justice, 1865-1950. Garden City, N.Y.: Hanover,
1960.

bell, Aaron I., ed. American Catholic Thought on Social
Questions. Indianapolis: Bobbs-Merrill, 1968.

bernathy, Mollie C. "Southern Women, Social Reconstruction, and
the Church in the 1920's." Louisiana Studies 13, no. 4
(1974), 289-312.

lexander, Charles C. The Ku Klux Klan in the Southwest.
Lexington: University of Kentucky Press, 1965.

lvarez, David J., and True, Edmond J. "Critical Elections and
Partisan Realignment: An Urban Test-Case." Polity 5, no. 4
(1973), 563-576.

ndelson, Robert N. "Msgr. John A. Ryan's Critique of Henry
George." American Journal of Economic Sociology 33, no. 3
(1974), 273-296.

sbury, Herbert. Great Illusion: An Informal History of
Prohibition. Garden City, N.Y.: Doubleday, 1950.

ailey, Kenneth K. Southern White Protestantism in the Twentieth
Century. New York: Harper and Row, 1964.

aker, Alonzo L. "The San Francisco Evolution Debates: June 13-
14, 1925." Adventist Heritage 2, no. 2 (1975), 23-32.

aker, James T. "The Battle of Elizabeth City: Christ and Anti-
Christ in North Carolina." North Carolina Historical Review
54, no. 4 (1977), 393-408.

Barton, Bruce. The Man Nobody Knows: A Discovery of the Real
     Jesus. Indianapolis: Bobbs-Merrill, 1925.

Baum, Gregory. Catholics and Canadian Socialism: Political
     Thought in the Thirties and Forties. New York: Paulist Press,
     1980.

Baumann, Mark K. "John T. Scopes, Leopold and Loeb, and Bishop
     Warren A. Candler." Methodist History 16, no. 2 (1978), 92-
     100.

Baumann, Mark K. "Prohibition and Politics: Warren Candler and
     Al Smith's 1928 Campaign." Mississippi Quarterly 31, no. 1
     (1977-78), 109-118.

Becker, William H. "Reinhold Niebuhr: From Marx to Roosevelt."
     Historian 35, no. 4 (1973), 539-550.

Betten, Neil. "Nativism and the Klan in Town and City:
     Valparaiso and Gary, Indiana." Studies in History and
     Sociology 4, no. 2 (1973), 3-16.

Blantz, Thomas E. A Priest in Public Service: Francis J. Haas
     and the New Deal. Notre Dame, Ind.: University of Notre Dame
     Press, 1982.

Boller, Paul F., Jr. "The Paradox of Freedom: Reinhold Niebuhr'
     Christian Realism." Southwest Review 62, no. 1 (1977), 31-43

Brackenridge, R. Douglas. "Lawrence W. Bottoms: The Church,
     Black Presbyterians and Personhood." Journal of Presbyterian
     History 56, no. 1 (1978), 47-60.

Bradford, Richard H. "Religion and Politics: Alfred E. Smith an
     the Election of 1928 in West Virginia." West Virginia Histor
     36, no. 3 (1975), 213-221.

Brinkley, Alan. Voices of Protest: Huey Long, Father Coughlin
     and the Great Depression. New York: Knopf, 1982.

Broderick, Francis L. The Right Reverend New Dealer: John A.
     Ryan. New York: Macmillan, 1963.

Brody, David. "American Jewry, the Refugees and Immigration
     Restriction." In The Jewish Experience in America, vol. 5,
     At Home in America, edited by Abraham L. Karp. New York:
     KTAV, 1969.

Brown, Lawrence L. "Texas Bishop Vetoes Women Council Delegates
     in 1921." Historical Magazine of the Protestant Episcopal
     Church 48, no. 1 (1979), 93-102.

Buckler, Allen. "The Anti-Evolution Beliefs of William Jennings
     Bryan." Nebraska History 54, no. 4 (1973), 545-559.

Buczek, Daniel S. "Polish American Priests and the American Catholic Hierarchy." Polish American Studies 33, no. 1 (1976), 34-43.

Burkett, Randall K. "Religious Dimensions of the Universal Negro Improvement Association and African Communities League." Afro-Americans in New York Life and History 1, no. 2 (1977), 167-182.

Burner, David. The Politics of Provincialism: The Democratic Party in Transition, 1918-1932. New York: Knopf, 1968.

Calderwood, William. "Religious Reactions to the Ku Klux Klan in Saskatchewan." Saskatchewan History 26, no. 3 (1973), 103-114.

Campbell, Roy. "Gerald B. Winrod vs. the 'Educated Devils.'" Midwest Quarterly 16, no. 2 (1975), 187-198.

Cannistaro, Philip V., and Kovaleff, Theodore P. "Father Coughlin and Mussolini: Impossible Allies." Journal of Church and State 13, no. 3 (1973), 427-443.

Carpenter, Joel A. "Fundamentalist Institutions and the Rise of Evangelical Protestantism, 1929-1942." Church History 49, no. 1 (1980), 62-75.

Carter, Paul A. The Decline and Revival of the Social Gospel: Social and Political Liberation in American Protestant Churches, 1920-1940. Ithaca, N.Y.: Cornell University Press, 1956.

Cashman, Sean Dennis. Prohibition: The Lie of the Land. New York: Free Press, 1981.

Chalmers, David M. Hooded Americanism: The History of the Ku Klux Klan. New York: Franklin Watts, 1981.

Childress, James F. "Reinhold Niebuhr's Critique of Pacifism." Review of Politics 36, no. 4 (1974), 467-491.

Clark, Malcolm, Jr. "The Bigot Disclosed: 90 Years of Nativism." Oregon Historical Quarterly 75, no. 2 (1974), 108-190.

Clark, Norman H. Deliver Us From Evil: An Interpretation of Prohibition. New York: Norton, 1976.

Clark, Norman H. The Dry Years: Prohibition and Social Change in Washington. Seattle: University of Washington Press, 1965.

Clarke, John Henrik, and Garvey, Amy Jaques, eds. Marcus Garvey and the Vision of Africa. New York: Random House, 1974.

Cole, Stewart G. The History of Fundamentalism. New York: R. 1 Smith, 1931.

Coletta, Paolo E. William Jennings Bryan, vol. 3, Political Puritan, 1915-1925. Lincoln: University of Nebraska Press, 1969.

Cronon, Edmund David. "American Catholics and Mexican Anticlericalism, 1933-1936." Mississippi Valley Historical Review 45, no. 2 (1958), 201-230.

Cronon, Edmund David. Black Moses: The Story of Marcus Garvey and the Universal Negro Improvement Association. Madison: University of Wisconsin Press, 1955.

Cross, Robert D. The Emergence of Liberal Catholicism in America. Cambridge: Harvard University Press, 1958.

Cuddy, Edward. "'Are Bolsheviks Any Worse than the Irish?' Ethno-Religious Conflict in America During the 1920's." Eire-Ireland 11, no. 3 (1976), 13-32.

Dalin, David H. "Jewish and Non-Partisan Republicanism in San Francisco, 1911-1963." American Jewish History 68, no. 4 (1979), 492-516.

Day, Dorothy. The Long Loneliness. New York: Harper and Row, 1952.

De Camp, Lyon Sprague. The Great Monkey Trial. Garden City, N.Y.: Doubleday, 1968.

DeSaulniers, Lawrence B. The Response in American Catholic Periodicals to the Crises of the Great Depression, 1930-1935. Lanham, Md.: University Press of America, 1984.

Doherty, William T., Jr. "The Twentieth Century Businessman and Religion." North Dakota Quarterly 47, no. 1 (1979), 67-79.

Doherty, William T., Jr. "The Twentieth Century's Secular Religion." North Dakota Quarterly 47, no. 4 (1979), 54-63.

Durnbaugh, Donald F., ed. On Earth Peace: Discussions on War/Peace Issues between Friends, Mennonites, Brethren, and European Churches, 1935-75. Elgin, Ill.: Brethren Press, 1978.

Eddy, Sherwood. Eighty Adventurous Years: An Autobiography. Ne York: Harper and Brothers, 1955.

Eighmy, John Lee. Churches in Cultural Captivity: A History of the Social Attitudes of Southern Baptists. Knoxville: University of Tennessee Press, 1972.

Ellis, Marc. _Peter Maurin: Prophet in the Twentieth Century_. New York: Paulist Press, 1981.

Ellis, William E. "The Fundamentalist Modernist Schism over Evolution in the 1920's." _Register of the Kentucky Historical Society_ 74, no. 2 (1976), 112-123.

Ensley, Gerald F. "The Social Theology of Francis John McConnell." _Religion in Life_ 45, no. 4 (1976), 482-489.

Evans, Hiram Wesley. "The Klan's Fight for Americanism." _North American Review_ 223 (March-April-May 1926), 33-63.

Fain, Elaine. "Going Public: The Angie Williams Cox Library, the Village of Pardeeville, and the Wisconsin Supreme Court, 1927-1929." _Journal of Library History_ 15, no. 1 (1980), 53-61.

Fax, Elton C. _Garvey: The Story of a Pioneer Black Nationalist_. New York: Dodd, Mead, 1972.

Feingold, Henry L. _The Politics of Rescue: The Roosevelt Administration and the Holocaust, 1938-1945_. New Brunswick, N.J.: Rutgers University Press, 1970.

Fennero, Matthew John. "Social Gospelers and Soviets, 1921-1926." _Journal of Church and State_ 19, no. 1 (1977), 53-73.

Fisher, Albert L. "Mormon Welfare Programs: Past and Present." _Social Science Journal_ 15, no. 2 (1978), 75-100.

Fleischman, Harry. _Norman Thomas: A Biography_. New York: Norton, 1964.

Flynn, George Q. _American Catholics and the Roosevelt Presidency, 1932-1936_. Lexington: University of Kentucky Press, 1968.

Flynn, George Q. _Roosevelt and Romanism: Catholics and American Diplomacy, 1937-1945_. Westport, Conn.: Greenwood, 1976.

Fosdick, Harry E. _Christianity and Progress_. New York: Fleming H. Revell, 1922.

Fowler, James W. _To See the Kingdom: The Theological Vision of H. Richard Niebuhr_. Nashville: Abingdon, 1974.

Fox, Richard Wightman. _Reinhold Niebuhr: A Biography_. New York: Praeger, 1985.

Friedman, Saul S. _No Haven for the Oppressed: United States Policy toward Jewish Refugees, 1938-1945_. Detroit: Wayne State University Press, 1973.

Furfey, Paul Hanley. Fire on the Earth. New York: Macmillan, 1936.

Furniss, Norman K. The Fundamentalist Controversy, 1918-1931. New Haven: Yale University Press, 1954.

Garson, Robert A. "Political Fundamentalism and Popular Democracy in the 1920's." South Atlantic Quarterly 76, no. 2 (1977), 219-233.

Gatewood, Willard B., Jr. Preachers, Pedagogues and Politicians: The Evolution Controversy in North Carolina, 1920-1927. Chapel Hill: University of North Carolina Press, 1966.

Gatewood, Willard B., Jr., ed. Controversy in the Twenties: Fundamentalism, Modernism, and Evolution. Nashville: Vanderbilt University Press, 1969.

Ginger, Ray. Six Days or Forever? Tennessee v. John Thomas Scopes. Boston: Beacon Press, 1958.

Gleason, Philip. The Conservative Reformers: German-American Catholics and the Social Order. Notre Dame, Ind.: University of Notre Dame Press, 1968.

Goldberg, Robert Alan. Hooded Empire: The Ku Klux Klan in Colorado. Urbana: University of Illinois Press, 1981.

Goodwyn, Lawrence. Democratic Promise: The Populist Moment in America. New York: Oxford University Press, 1976.

Gray, Ina Turner. "Monkey Trial--Kansas Style." Methodist History 14, no. 4 (1976), 235-251.

Gripe, Elizabeth Howell. "Women, Restructuring and Unrest in the 1920's." Journal of Presbyterian History 52, no. 2 (1974), 188-199.

Gustafson, Merlin D. "President Hoover and the National Religion." Journal of Church and State 16, no. 1 (1974), 85-100.

Hackey, Thomas E. "The Influence of Roman Catholics and Their Church in American Politics: A British Analysis in 1943." American Benedictine Review 25, no. 1 (1974), 123-136.

Hall, Jacquelyn Dowd. "A Truly Subversive Affair: Women Against Lynching in the Twentieth-Century South." In Women of America: A History, edited by Carol Ruth Bekins and Mary Beth Norton, 360-388. Boston: Houghton Mifflin Company, 1979.

Halsey, William. The Survival of American Innocence: Catholicism in an Era of Disillusionment, 1920-1940. Notre Dame, Ind.: University of Notre Dame Press, 1980.

Handy, Robert T. *A Christian America: Protestant Hopes and Historical Realities*. New York: Oxford University Press, 1971.

Hattery, John W. "The Presidential Campaigns of 1928 and 1960: A Comparison of the *Christian Century* and *America*." *Journal of Church and State* 9, no. 1 (1967), 36-50.

Hentoff, Nat, ed. *The Essays of A. J. Muste*. Indianapolis: Bobbs-Merrill, 1967.

Hicks, John D. *The Republican Ascendancy, 1921-1933*. New York: Harper and Row, 1960.

Higham, John. *Send These to Me: Jews and Other Immigrants in Urban America*. New York: Atheneum, 1975.

Higham, John. *Strangers in the Land: Patterns of American Nativism, 1860-1925*. New Brunswick, N.J.: Rutgers University Press, 1955.

Hill, Robert A., ed. *The Marcus Garvey and Universal Negro Improvement Association Papers*. 2 vols. Berkeley: University of California Press, 1983.

Hofstadter, Richard. *The Age of Reform: From Bryan to F.D.R.* New York: Knopf, 1955.

Hope, Clifford R., Jr. "Strident Voices in Kansas Between the Wars." *Kansas History* 2, no. 1 (1979), 54-64.

Hougland, James G., Jr.; Wood, James R.; and Mueller, Samuel A. "Organizational Goal Submergence: The Methodist Church and the Failure of the Temperance Movement." *Sociology and Social Research* 58, no. 4 (1974), 408-416.

Howe, Irving. *World of Our Fathers*. New York: Simon and Schuster, 1976.

Hoyt, Frederick B. "Protection Implies Intervention: The U.S. Catholic Mission at Kangchow." *Historian* 38, no. 4 (1976), 709-727.

Interchurch World Movement Commission of Inquiry. *Public Opinion and the Steel Strike*. New York: Harcourt, Brace and Company, 1922.

Interchurch World Movement Commission of Inquiry. *Report on the Steel Strike of 1919*. New York: Harcourt, Brace and Howe, 1920.

Jacklin, Thomas M. "Mission to the Sharecroppers: Neo-Orthodox Radicalism and the Delta Farm Venture, 1936-1940." *South Atlantic Quarterly* 78, no. 3 (1979), 302-316.

Jackson, Kenneth T. The Ku Klux Klan in the City, 1915-1930.
    New York: Oxford University Press, 1967.

Janis, Ralph. "Flirtation and Flight: Alternatives to Ethnic
    Confrontation in White Anglo-American Protestant Detroit,
    1880-1940." Journal of Ethnic Studies 6, no. 2 (1978), 1-17.

Jeansonne, Glen. "Preacher, Populist, Propagandist: The Early
    Career of Gerald L. K. Smith." Biography 2, no. 4 (1979),
    303-327.

Jenkins, William D. "The Ku Klux Klan in Youngstown, Ohio: Mora
    Reform in the Twenties." Historian 41, no. 1 (1978), 76-93.

Johnson, Niel M. "The Missouri Synod Lutherans and the War
    Against the German Language." Nebraska History 56, no. 1
    (1975), 137-156.

Karl, Barry D. The Uneasy State: The United States from 1915 to
    1945. Chicago: University of Chicago Press, 1983.

Kauffman, Christopher J. Faith and Fraternalism: The History of
    the Knights of Columbus, 1882-1982. New York: Harper and Row,
    1982.

Kearnes, John. "Utah, Sexton of Prohibition." Utah Historical
    Quarterly 47, no. 1 (1979), 5-21.

Kemper, Donald J. "Catholic Integration in St. Louis, 1935-
    1947." Missouri Historical Review 73, no. 1 (1978), 1-22.

Kreider, Robert. "The Historic Peace Churches' Meeting in 1935.
    Mennonite Life 31, no. 2 (1976), 21-24.

Kyvig, David E. Repealing National Prohibition. Chicago:
    University of Chicago Press, 1979.

Kyvig, David E., ed. Law, Alcohol, and Order: Perspectives on
    National Prohibition. Westport, Conn.: Greenwood, 1985.

LaFarge, John. Interracial Justice. A Study of the Catholic
    Doctrine of Race Relations. New York: American Press, 1937.

Ledbetter, Cal, Jr. "The Antievolution Law: Church and State in
    Arkansas." Arkansas Historical Quarterly 38, no. 4 (1979),
    299-327.

Ledbetter, Patsy. "Defense of the Faith: J. Frank Norris and
    Texas Fundamentalism, 1920-1929." Arizona and the West 15,
    no. 1 (1973), 45-62.

Leuchtenburg, William E. Franklin D. Roosevelt and the New Deal
    1932-1940. New York: Harper and Row, 1963.

Leuchtenburg, William E. The Perils of Prosperity, 1914-1932.
  Chicago: University of Chicago Press, 1958.

Levine, Lawrence W. Defender of the Faith: William Jennings
  Bryan, 1915-1925. New York: Oxford University Press, 1965.

Lichtman, Allan J. Prejudice and the Old Politics: The
  Presidential Election of 1928. Chapel Hill: University of
  North Carolina Press, 1979.

Liebman, Arthur. Jews and the Left. New York: Wiley, 1979.

Link, Eugene P. "Latter Day Christian Rebel: Harry F. Ward."
  Mid-America 56, no. 4 (1974), 221-230.

Lisenby, William Foy. "Brough, Baptist and Bombast: The Election
  of 1928." Arkansas Historical Quarterly 32, no. 2 (1973),
  120-131.

Lotz, Jim. "The Historical and Social Setting of the Antigonish
  Movement." Nova Scotia Historical Quarterly 5, no. 2 (1975),
  99-116.

McBeth, Leon. "Baptist Fundamentalism: A Cultural
  Interpretation." Baptist History and Heritage 13, no. 3
  (1978), 12-19.

McCarthy, G. Michael. "The Brown Derby Campaign in West
  Tennessee: Smith, Hoover, and the Politics of Race." West
  Tennessee Historical Society Papers, no. 27 (1973), 81-98.

McConnell, Francis J. By the Way: An Autobiography. New York:
  Abingdon-Cokesbury, 1952.

McConnell, Francis J. The Christian Ideal and Social Control.
  Chicago: University of Chicago Press, 1932.

McConnell, Francis J. "The Churches and the War Problem."
  Annals of the American Academy of Political and Social Science
  175 (September 1934), 143-149.

Macintosh, Douglas Clyde. Social Religion. New York: Scribner,
  1939.

McKinney, William J., Jr. "H. Richard Niebuhr and the Question
  of Human Society." Religion in Life 43, no. 3 (1974), 362-
  375.

Macnab, John B. "Fosdick at First Church." Journal of
  Presbyterian History 52, no. 1 (1974), 59-77.

McNeal, Patricia. The American Catholic Peace Movement, 1928-
  1972. New York: Arno Press, 1978.

Marcus, Sheldon. _Father Coughlin: The Tumultuous Life of the Priest of the Little Flower_. Boston: Little, Brown, 1973.

Marsden, George M. _Fundamentalism and American Culture: The Shaping of Twentieth Century Evangelicalism, 1870-1925_. New York: Oxford University Press, 1980.

Marszalek, John. "The Black Leader in 1919--South Carolina as a Case Study." _Phylon_ 36, no. 3 (1975), 249-259.

Marty, Martin E. "The Lost Worlds of Reinhold Niebuhr." _American Scholar_ 45, no. 4 (1976), 566-572.

Marty, Martin E. "Reinhold Niebuhr: Public Theology and the American Experience." _Journal of Religion_ 54, no. 4 (1974), 332-360.

Mathews, Shailer. _Christianity and Social Process_. New York: Harper and Brothers, 1934.

Mathews, Shailer. _Jesus on Social Institutions_. New York: Macmillan, 1928.

Mecklin, John Moffatt. _The Ku Klux Klan: A Study of the American Mind_. New York; Harcourt, Brace and Company, 1924.

Merz, Charles. _The Dry Decade_. 1931. Reprint. Seattle: University of Washington Press, 1969.

Mesar, Joe, and Dybdahl, Tom. "The Utopia Park Affair and the Rise of Northern Black Adventists." _Adventist Heritage_ 1, no. 1 (1974), 34-41.

Meyer, Donald B. _The Protestant Search for Political Realism, 1919-1941_. Berkeley: University of California Press, 1961.

Millar, Moorhouse F. X.   "The Origin of Sound Democratic Principles in Catholic Tradition." _Catholic Historical Review_, n.s. 8, no. 1 (1928), 104-126.

Miller, Robert Moats. _American Protestantism and Social Issues, 1919-1939_. Chapel Hill: University of North Carolina Press, 1958.

Miller, Robert Moats. _Harry Emerson Fosdick: Preacher, Pastor, Prophet_. New York: Oxford University Press, 1985.

Miller, William D. _Dorothy Day: A Biography_. San Francisco: Harper and Row, 1982.

Miller, William D. _A Harsh and Dreadful Love: Dorothy Day and the Catholic Worker Movement_. New York: Liveright, 1972.

Miscamble, Wilson D. "Catholics and American Foreign Policy From McKinley to McCarthy: A Historiographical Survey." Diplomatic History 4, no. 3 (1980), 223-240.

Moore, Deborah Dash. "From Kehillah to Federated Philanthropy in New York City, 1917-1933." American Jewish History 68, no. 2 (1978), 131-146.

Moore, Edmund A. A Catholic Runs for President. New York: Ronald Press, 1956.

Murray, Robert K. Red Scare: A Study of National Hysteria, 1919-1920. New York: McGraw Hill, 1964.

Muste, A. J. Non-Violence in an Aggressive World. New York: Harper and Brothers, 1940.

Nash, Roderick. The Nervous Generation: American Thought, 1917-1930. Chicago: Rand McNally, 1970.

National Catholic War Council. The Bishops' Program of Social Reconstruction. A General Review of the Problems and Survey of Remedies. Washington, D.C.: National Catholic War Council, 1920.

National Catholic Welfare Conference. Social Action Department. Organized Social Justice. An Economic Program for the United States Applying Pius XI's Great Encyclical on Social Life. New York: Paulist Press, 1935.

Nelson, John K. The Peace Prophets: American Pacifist Thought, 1919-1941. Chapel Hill: University of North Carolina Press, 1967.

Neuchterlein, James A. "Bruce Barton and the Business Ethos of the 1920's." South Atlantic Quarterly 76, no. 3 (1976), 293-308.

Niebuhr, H. Richard; Miller, Francis; and Pauck, Wilhelm. The Church Against the World. Chicago: Willett, Clark and Company, 1935.

Niebuhr, Reinhold. An Interpretation of Christian Ethics. New York: Harper and Brothers, 1935.

Niebuhr, Reinhold. Moral Man and Immoral Society. New York: Scribner, 1932.

Niebuhr, Reinhold. The Nature and Destiny of Man: A Christian Interpretation. 2 vols. New York: Scribner, 1941-43.

Niebuhr, Reinhold. Reflections on the End of an Era. New York: Scribner, 1934.

Novitsky, Anthony. "Peter Maurin and the Green Revolution."
   Review of Politics 27, no. 1 (1975), 83-103.

Nye, Russell B. "The Thirties: The Framework of Belief."
   Centennial Review 19, no. 2 (1975), 37-58.

O'Brien, David J. American Catholics and Social Reform: The New
   Deal Years. New York: Oxford University Press, 1968.

Osborn, Henry F. Evolution and Religion in Education: Polemics
   of the Fundamentalist Controversy of 1922 to 1926. New York:
   Scribner, 1926.

O'Shaughnessy, Michael J. Man or Money? New York: privately
   printed, 1932.

Patterson, Michael S. "The Fall of a Bishop: James Cannon Versus
   Carter Glass, 1909-1934." Journal of Southern History 39, no.
   4 (1973), 493-518.

Pearson, Alden B., Jr. "A Christian Moralist Responds to War:
   Charles C. Morrison, the Christian Century and the Manchurian
   Crisis, 1931-1933." World Affairs 139, no. 4 (1977), 296-307.

Pells, Richard H. Radical Visions and American Dreams: Culture
   and Social Thought in the Depression Years. New York: Harper
   and Row, 1973.

Petryshyn, J. "From Clergyman to Communist: The Radicalization
   of Albert Edward Smith." Journal of Canadian Studies 13, no.
   4 (1978-79), 61-71.

Piehl, Mel. Breaking Bread: The Catholic Worker and the Origins
   of Catholic Radicalism in America. Philadelphia: Temple
   University Press, 1982.

Pienkos, Donald. "Politics, Religion, and Change in Polish
   Milwaukee, 1900-1930." Wisconsin Magazine of History 61, no.
   3 (1978), 178-209.

Pratt, Norma Fain. "Transitions in Judaism: The Jewish American
   Woman Through the 1930's." American Quarterly 30, no. 5
   (1978), 681-702.

Purcell, Edward A., Jr. The Crisis of Democratic Theory:
   Scientific Naturalism and the Problem of Value. Lexington:
   University Press of Kentucky, 1973.

Racine, Philip N. "The Ku Klux Klan, Anti-Catholicism, and
   Atlanta's Board of Education, 1916-1927." Georgia Historical
   Quarterly 57, no. 1 (1973), 63-75.

Ragsdale, W. B. "Three Weeks in Dayton." American Heritage 26,
   no. 4 (1975), 38-41, 99-103.

Raphael, Marc Lee. "Federated Philanthropy in an American Jewish Community: 1904-1948." American Jewish History 68, no. 2 (1978), 147-169.

Rausch, David A. "Our Hope: An American Fundamentalist Journal and the Holocaust, 1937-1945." Fides et Historia 12, no. 2 (1980), 89-103.

Reimers, David M. White Protestantism and the Negro. New York: Oxford University Press, 1965.

Ribuffo, Leo P. The Old Christian Right: The Protestant Far Right From the Great Depression to the Cold War. Philadelphia: Temple University Press, 1983.

Rice, Dan. "Reinhold Niebuhr and Judaism." Journal of the American Academy of Religion 45, no. 1 (1977), 72.

Richey, Susan. "Comment on the Political Strategy of Christian Pacifists: A. J. Muste, Norman Thomas, and Reinhold Niebuhr." Towson State Journal of International Affairs 11, no. 2 (1977), 111-119.

Riess, Steven. "Professional Sunday Baseball: A Study in Social Reform, 1892-1934." Maryland Historian 4, no. 2 (1973), 95-108.

Roberts, Nancy L. Dorothy Day and the Catholic Worker. Albany: State University of New York Press, 1984.

Robinson, Jo Ann Oviman. Abraham Went Out: A Biography of A. J. Muste. Philadelphia: Temple University Press, 1982.

Ross, Robert W. So It Was True: The American Protestant Press and the Nazi Persecution of the Jews. Minneapolis: University of Minnesota Press, 1980.

Rothwell, David R. "United Church Pacifism, October 1939." Bulletin of the United Church, no. 22 (1973), 36-55.

Russell, C. Allyn. "Mark Allison Mathews: Seattle Fundamentalist and Civic Reformer." Journal of Presbyterian History 57, no. 4 (1979), 446-466.

Russell, C. Allyn. Voices of Fundamentalism: Seven Biographical Studies. Philadelphia: Westminster, 1976.

Russell, C. Allyn. "William Jennings Bryan: Statesman-Fundamentalist." Journal of Presbyterian History 53, no. 2 (1975), 93-119.

Ryan, John A. A Better Economic Order. New York: Harper and Brothers, 1935.

Ryan, John A. Social Doctrine in Action. New York: Harper and
     Brothers, 1941.

Ryan, John A. Social Reconstruction. New York: Macmillan, 1920

Ryan, John A., and Millar, Moorehouse F. X. The State and the
     Church. New York: Macmillan, 1922.

Sandeen, Ernest R. The Roots of Fundamentalism: British and
     American Millenarianism, 1800-1930. Chicago: University of
     Chicago Press, 1970.

Schlesinger, Arthur M., Jr. The Age of Roosevelt. 3 vols.
     Boston: Houghton Mifflin Company, 1957-60.

Scopes, John T., and Presley, James. Center of the Storm:
     Memoirs of John T. Scopes. New York: Holt, Rinehart and
     Winston, 1967.

Seaton, Douglas P. Catholics and Radicals: The Association of
     Catholic Trade Unionists and the American Labor Movement, From
     Depression to Cold War. East Brunswick, N.J.: Associated
     University Presses, 1981.

Seidler, Murray B. Norman Thomas, Respectable Rebel. Syracuse,
     N.Y.: Syracuse University Press, 1967.

Sexton, Robert F. "The Crusade Against Pari-Mutuel Gambling in
     Kentucky: A Study of Southern Progressivism in the 1920's."
     Filson Club Historical Quarterly 50, no. 1 (1976), 47-57.

Shankman, Arnold. "Dorothy Tilly, Civil Rights, and the
     Methodist Church." Methodist History 18, no. 2 (1980), 95-
     108.

Shapiro, Edward S. "Catholic Agrarian Thought and the New Deal.
     Catholic Historical Review 65, no. 4 (1979), 583-599.

Shapiro, Edward S. "The Catholic Rural Life Movement and the Ne
     Deal Farm Program." American Benedictine Review 28, no. 3
     (1977), 307-332.

Sheehan, Arthur. Peter Maurin: Gay Believer. Garden City, N.Y.
     Hanover, 1959.

Shenton, James P. "The Coughlin Movement and the New Deal."
     Political Science Quarterly 73, no. 3 (1958), 352-373.

Shenton, James P. "Fascism and Father Coughlin." Wisconsin
     Magazine of History 44, no. 1 (August 1960), 6-11.

Sher, Julian. White Hoods: Canada's Ku Klux Klan. Vancouver:
     New Star Books, 1983.

Shinn, Roger L. "Realism, Radicalism and Eschatology in Reinhold Niebuhr: A Reassessment." Journal of Religion 54, no. 4 (1974), 409-423.

Shover, John L. "Ethnicity and Religion in Philadelphia Politics, 1924-1940." American Quarterly 25, no. 5 (1973), 499-515.

Simms, Ada. "A Battle in the Air: Detroit's Jews Answer Father Coughlin." Michigan Jewish History 18, no. 2 (1978), 7-13.

Sinclair, Andrew. Prohibition: Era of Excess. Boston: Little, Brown, 1962.

Singleton, Gregory H. "Popular Culture or the Culture of the Populace?" Journal of Popular Culture 11, no. 1 (1977), 254-266.

Smith, Gilbert E. The Limits of Reform: Politics and Federal Aid to Education, 1937-1950. New York: Garland, 1982.

Smith, John S. H. "Cigarette Prohibition in Utah, 1921-23." Utah Historical Quarterly 41, no. 4 (1973), 358-372.

Smylie, Robert F. "John Leighton Stuart: A Missionary in the Sino-Japanese Conflict, 1937-1941." Journal of Presbyterian History 53, no. 3 (1975), 256-276.

Spivak, John L. Shrine of the Silver Dollar. New York: Modern Age Books, 1940.

Stone, Ronald H. Reinhold Niebuhr: Prophet to Politicians. Nashville: Abingdon, 1973.

Strong, Donald S. Organized Anti-Semitism in America: The Rise of Group Prejudice During the Decade 1930-1940. Washington: American Council on Public Affairs, 1941.

Sussman, Warren I. Culture and Commitment, 1929-1945. New York: George Braziller, 1973.

Szasz, Ferenc Morton. The Divided Mind of Protestant America, 1880-1930. University: University of Alabama Press, 1982.

Szasz, Ferenc Morton. "William Jennings Bryan, Evolution and the Fundamentalist-Modernist Controversy." Nebraska History 56, no. 2 (1975), 259-278.

Thomas, Donna. "The Providence Visitor and Nativist Issues, 1916-1924." Rhode Island History 38, no. 2 (1979), 51-62.

Thompkins, Jerry T., ed. D-Days at Dayton: Reflections on the Scopes Trial. Baton Rouge: Louisiana State University Press, 1965.

Thompson, Dennis L. "The Basic Doctrines and Concepts of Reinhold Niebuhr's Political Thought." Journal of Church and State 17, no. 2 (1975), 275-299.

Thompson, James J., Jr. "Tried As By Fire": Southern Baptists and the Religious Controversies of the 1920s. Macon, Ga.: Mercer University Press, 1982.

Thompson, Kenneth W. "Niebuhr as Thinker and Doer." Journal of Religion 54, no. 4 (1974), 424-436.

Toy, Eckhard V., Jr. "The Oxford Group and the Strike of the Seattle Longshoremen in 1934." Pacific Northwest Quarterly 69, no. 4 (1978), 174-184.

Tull, Charles J. Father Coughlin and the New Deal. Syracuse, N.Y.: Syracuse University Press, 1965.

Urofsky, Melvin I. A Voice That Spoke for Justice: The Life and Times of Stephen S. Wise. Albany: State University of New York Press, 1982.

Voskuil, Dennis N. "America Encounters Karl Barth, 1919-1939." Fides et Historia 12, no. 2 (1980), 61-74.

Walker, Randolph Meade. "The Role of the Black Clergy in Memphis During the Crump Era." West Tennessee Historical Society Papers, no. 33 (1979), 29-47.

Ward, Harry. Democracy and Social Change. New York: Modern Age Books, 1940.

Ward, Harry. In Place of Profit. New York: Scribner, 1933.

Wargelin, Raymond W. "Confrontation of Marxist Radicalism with the Finnish Lutheran Church in Finland and on the North American Continent." Lutheran Quarterly 28, no. 4 (1976), 361-377.

Weaver, Bill L. "Kentucky Baptists' Reaction to the National Evolution Controversy, 1922-1926." Filson Club Historical Quarterly 49, no. 3 (1975), 266-275.

Weber, Timothy P. Living in the Shadow of the Second Coming: American Premillennialism, 1875-1925. New York: Oxford University Press, 1979.

Werly, John M. "Premillennialism and the Paranoid Style." American Studies 18, no. 1 (1977), 39-55.

White, Larry. "The Return of the Thief: The Repeal of Prohibition and the Adventist Response." Adventist Heritage 5, no. 2 (1978), 34-47.

Wills, Garry. _Politics and Catholic Freedom_. Chicago: Henry
     Regnery, 1964.

Wilson, John R. M. "The Quaker and the Sword: Herbert Hoover's
     Relations with the Military." _Military Affairs_ 38, no. 2
     (1974), 41-47.

Wingo, Barbara C. "The 1928 Presidential Election in Louisiana."
     Louisiana History 18, no. 4 (1977), 405-415.

Yellowitz, Irwin. "Morris Hillquit: American Socialism and
     Jewish Concerns." _American Jewish History_ 68, no. 2 (1978),
     163-188.

7

America Emerges as a World Power: Religion, Politics, and Nationhood, 1940–1960

James D. Beumler

World War II remade the United States' role in the world and with it the relation of religion to American public life and thought. A nation trying to recover from the greatest economic depression in its history, whose style in foreign affairs was best characterized as isolationist, America was only reluctantly drawn into World War II, notwithstanding a history of selective use of military force when U.S. business interests in Central America and the Caribbean were at stake. America emerged from the war the most powerful nation on earth, in sole possession of the most destructive weapon ever known, confident of its ability to project its might worldwide, and dedicated to interventionist policies in pursuit of such lofty and idealistic goals as world freedom and world peace.

Domestically, the change after the war was even more dramatic. In 1945 there was a shortage of labor, of housing, of meats and durable goods, of school and church buildings. But there was no shortage of hope for the economy, and the Gross National Product quadrupled over its prewar level in the next five years. New families were begun in record numbers and ground was broken for new houses, churches, synagogues, and schools in hundreds of new suburbs ringing the older center cities. Foodstuffs and consumer goods became available again—more than available—cars came in more than just black, major appliances came in more than just white. And there were new products and inventions: commercial television, the transistor, the Univac computer, fluoride toothpaste, chlorophyll gum, and even chlorophyll dogfood. In a myriad of ways, great and small, life was changed. America was now a world power and its people the beneficiaries of unparalleled and widespread economic wealth.

Both of these two grand changes in the American nation and its relation to the world exerted tremendous influence on the dynamic relationship between church and state. Because America was undergoing such crucial transformation, it was inevitable that the role of religion in the nation would also be transformed. In the two decades following 1940 religious thinkers dealt with the morality of war, totalitarian and Communist threats, America's new role as world policeman in Korea, and Supreme Court decisions on First Amendment rights that seemed to strike at the root of the church-state synthesis that had developed slowly in over 160 years of national history. As the fifties ended, they struggled with the meaning and limitations of world power, and probed the changes wrought in the American way of life and character by the very success of the American Dream. They did so in the context of an America changing, both consciously and unconsciously, from a society centered largely in religious and ethnic enclaves to a society that was paradoxically more homogeneous and more openly pluralistic; one which would signal its new degree of acceptance of pluralism in 1960 in a formerly unthinkable act: the election of a Catholic president.

Although the two decades following the outbreak of World War II provided much in the way of activity in the realm of church-state relations and thought, broadly defined, they have still to be deeply explored by historians. Much of the scholarly work done on the period is itself of a piece with the times in which it was written. The analyses offered thus far often appear to be tracts for the times written by interested parties. But this need not thwart the person interested in religion, politics, and American nationhood at mid-century since these tracts for the times provide a wealth of primary material that virtually begs for historical investigation and interpretation. The purpose of this essay, therefore, is not to introduce the great schools of postwar historiography—they have yet to develop—but rather to present the range of events and literature coming out of the period 1940 to 1960, together with those explanations for changes in American religion and public life that have been offered to date.

Reflection among thinkers concerned with religion on nationalism and the nature of the state up until the war was a transatlantic affair with Europe leading the way. Karl Barth's *Church and State* received a small, but appreciative audience in the United States, as did books by W. A. Visser 't Hooft. The freshest and most influential thought came from England in books by Anglican Archbishop William Temple, F. R. Hoare, J. H. Oldham, and Christopher Dawson. Temple's *Citizen and Churchman* and *Christianity and Social Order* sold extraordinarily well and continued to influence American thought long after his death in 1944. He told his readers: "In an age when it is assumed that the Church is concerned with another world than this, and in this with nothing but individual conduct as bearing on prospects in that other world, hardly anyone reads the history of the Church in its exercise of political influence." Americans still hoping for a revival of the social gospel found a spokesman for their views when Temple went on, "It is assumed that the Church exercises little influence and ought to exercise none; it is further assumed that this assumption is self-evident and has always been made by reasonable men. As a matter of fact it is entirely modern and extremely questionable" (*Christianity and Social Order*, pp. 9–10). Dawson produced in 1938 what for many was the definitive theoretical book on church and state of his generation, *Religion and the Modern State*. This Anglo-European influence was directly transmitted to Americans at the 1937 Oxford Universal Christian Conference on Life and Work. There Americans were exposed to Barthian ideas, to Temple himself, and above all to a deeper appreciation of the ecumenical church. As Paul A. Carter characterized the experience of the American delegates to the conference, they went "talking about *our* churches" and went home "talking about the Church" (*Decline and Revival*, p. 195).

In the American context, all of these outside sources fed the "revival of the Social Gospel," as Carter termed it. So too did the work of the late 1930s by American Protestants such as Reinhold Niebuhr, Charles Clayton Morrison, John C. Bennett, Francis J. McConnell, and Harry Ward. Likewise, the liberal Catholic political program for social justice was pushed by its perennial leader John A. Ryan right into the 1940s in such books as *Catholic Principles of Politics*, helping to keep religious thought at least partially focused on religiously motivated activity in public affairs. Such a prior focus was prerequisite to dealing with the moral and political questions in the war that was to follow. Ryan himself, together with Frank Kingdon and Sidney Goldstein, issued in 1938 a volume of essays that prefigured the characteristic American approach both during and immediately after the war to issues of religion, ideology, and conflict—*The Relation of Religion to Communism, Fascism and Democracy*. In it a Roman Catholic, a Protestant, and a Jew found basic agreement as Americans speaking both out of their own religious traditions and out of a shared Western religious and cultural tradition.

When the Second World War officially began for the United States with the Japanese bombing of Pearl Harbor, the American nation found itself with a near-perfect cause for a just war. And yet its religious communities responded with considerably more restraint than they had to the entry of America into the morally more ambiguous First World War. Ray H. Abrams in "The Churches and the Clergy in World War II" notes the subtle shift between the approach of the clergy to the earlier war, when preachers virtually presented arms, and to the later war, when religious support for the cause of the war was tempered by the memory of the horrors of the first conflict and by the intervening years of religious commitment to the causes of peace and pacifism. Mark L. Chadwin's *The Hawks of World War II* also documents the way in which church opinion on participation in the war shifted and gives attention to the roles played by Henry P. Van Dusen and Henry Sloane Coffin and by prominent laypersons including Henry R. Luce and F. P. Miller. Indeed, the churches can be seen to have contributed to the wartime ethos on three distinct fronts. First was the standard war work, with Christian denominations and Jewish organizations contributing more than eight thousand chaplains to the armed forces, and reacting to the threat of Nazism in both pulpit and periodicals. Robert L. Gushwa and Rodger R. Venzke tell the official history of the army's chaplaincy from 1920 to 1945 and 1945 to 1975, respectively. Likewise an authorized history of the navy's Chaplain Corps has been compiled by Clifford M. Drury. The reactions of religious groups to Nazism are nicely surveyed by Frederick K. Wentz in twin articles entitled "American Catholic Periodicals React to Nazism" and "American Protestant Journals and the Nazi Religious Assault."

A second aspect of the wartime ethos was that the issues surrounding religious belief and military service came to occupy the attention of both religious bodies and the government. The historic peace churches (composed of Quakers, Mennonites, and other Anabaptists), once again faced the question, as Albert N. Keim has put it, of "service or resistance." But added to their numbers were those of other faiths, as articles by Patricia McNeal and Michael Young demonstrate with regard to Catholics and Jews, respectively. The number of objectors had been increased in part because of the popular pacifism of the 1930s. As objectors, Jews, Catholics, and Protestants alike often found themselves facing draft boards composed of members of their own faiths who could not understand their objection to service in such a just war. Government policy required those objectors wishing to avoid a prison term to work in an approved alternative public service situation financed by their religious bodies. Many of the larger churches, however, failed to create any provision for this service and instead the churches with historic commitments to pacifism provided the funding for the placement of a great many objectors of all persuasions. The long-term effect of this experience with diversity in response to war can be seen in Umphrey Lee's *The Historic Church and Modern Pacifism* and in Roland H. Bainton's "The Churches and War," both of which were in part designed to argue for tolerance of more than one religious response to the demands of military service and government obligation. The evolution of this issue is described in Joe P. Dunn's "Protestant Church Spokesmen, Universal Military Training, and the Anti-Conscription Campaigns, 1940–1959" and in Lawrence S. Wittner's *Rebels Against War: The American Peace Movement, 1941–1960.*

The third front on which the churches made an impact was in the planning for a world after the war. The most notable arena for this activity was the Federal Council of Churches' Commission on a Just and Durable Peace. The commission was chaired by John Foster Dulles, then a prominent Wall Street lawyer. Dulles, though a minister's son, had evidenced little real interest in religion since leaving his boyhood home. But attending the Oxford Conference changed his mind and he saw ways of infusing world order—an abiding interest ever since his service at the ill-fated Versailles Peace Conference—with a spiritual core. From Oxford forward he was an avid advocate of giving diplomacy a moral base. The Federal Council's commission gave him an outlet for these views and he was joined in his efforts by prominent churchmen such as Henry P. Van Dusen, John C. Bennett, and Reinhold Niebuhr. The report of the commission—which, in light of later events, H. Richard Niebuhr was ironically to suggest should have been called "A Just Endurable Peace"—was a blend of world order utopianism and Christian realism; yet it had one feature rare in ecclesiastical commissions presuming to advise politicians, namely it was in large part adopted as the plan for what became the United Nations. The world order movement is well documented in books by Lyman Bryson and F. Ernest Johnson listed in this bibliography. Dulles's own role in the movement is described in Albert Keim's "John Foster Dulles and the Protestant World Order Movement on the Eve of World War II," in Townsend Hoopes's fine biography, *The Devil and John Foster Dulles*, and in Mark G. Toulouse's more recent *The Transformation of John Foster Dulles*.

With victory in Europe and the Pacific behind the nation in 1945, it seemed there was nothing that American ingenuity could not do. The performance of such a seemingly good and unselfish act as "saving" the world gave America confidence that with good allies it could guarantee perpetual global peace and freedom. The successful contribution of the churches to the war and to the foundation of the United Nations gave them an additional and independent feeling of confidence. For all concerned, the leading issue in the aftermath of a war that had crippled the economies of the other nations of the world—victors and vanquished alike—was the responsible use of America's hegemony.

In the context of church and state interaction overseas, this issue evidenced itself in books with titles like *God and the Nations*, edited by Paul N. Poling, *The Gospel, the Church, and the World* by Kenneth Scott Latourette, and *A Faith for the Nations* by Charles Forman that pleaded for a new missionary effort. Domestically, the churches experienced a surge in confidence. While Robert T. Handy has persuasively argued that the "Protestant era in American life" came to an end in the 1930s, he notes that there was a postwar revival of interest in religion more generally. The percentage of Americans belonging to a church or synagogue steadily increased from 50 percent in 1940 to almost 70 percent in 1960. The exact nature of the so-called "return to religion" was the subject of much scholarly attention and theorizing to which we will return, but the increased interest in churches and in religion in books and on television, when combined with the conviction that America had stood on the morally righteous side of the conflict with the Fascist powers in World War II, produced a sense of religious power within a powerful nation.

The confidence of the era also enabled the creation of the National Council of Churches of Christ in the U.S.A. (NCC), which brought together the Federal Council of Churches and several other interdenominational boards. The Council's inception as an ecumenical body followed by two years that of the World Council of Churches in 1948 and both bodies included Eastern Orthodox churches in their membership. An ecumenical age had been born and the new ecumenical entities spoke to the body politic from a position of assumed strength, as in these words from the NCC's founding message entitled "To the People of the Nation":

The Council has nothing to fear from the times, though it has much to desire of them. . . . The Council stands as a guardian of democratic freedom. The revolutionary truth that men are created free follows from the revelation of God in Jesus Christ, and no person who knows that God as Father has given him all the rights of sonship is likely to remain content under a government which deprives him of basic human rights and fundamental freedoms. The nation may expect in the National Council a sturdy ally of the forces of liberty (NCC, *Christian Faith in Action*, pp. 150–151).

The language of the message is forceful, in places military, and betrays no sense that there is anything that the American people and nation cannot do if properly and spiritually motivated.

America's chance to remake the world in its own image was slowed by the 1949 discovery that the Soviet Union also had atomic weapons and by conflicts over the occupation of Berlin that would deteriorate into the "Cold War" between East and West. Dreams of hegemony were interrupted by nightmares of nuclear terror; and it was here that differences between various religious groups and thinkers were exacerbated in the postwar years. Then, as the nation watched China come under the domination of the Communist forces of Mao Zedong, the cry went up to find out "who lost China." When, in addition, spies operating in America were discovered to have given atomic secrets to the Soviet Union, anticommunism took hold of American life and became a strong presence even within the religious communities.

One of the anticommunist crusade's chief public figures was Senator Joseph McCarthy, a Roman Catholic layman from Wisconsin. Combining a traditional Catholic hostility toward atheistic-totalitarian schemes of government, an equally traditional American nativism, and a vicious disregard for democratic rules of evidence and due process, McCarthy built a potent, though short-lived, political power base. Because for a time after McCarthyism was discredited Catholicism in general was tarred with its brush, the relation between Catholicism and McCarthyism has been one of the more researched questions of the period. Donald F. Crosby's *God, Church, and Flag: Senator Joseph R. McCarthy and the Catholic Church, 1950–1957*, Vincent P. DeSantis's "American Catholics and McCarthyism," and Michael R. Belknap's "Joe Must Go" all examine the topic, while several articles from contemporary periodicals, among them John C. Cort's "Comrades Have a Crisis" and P. J. Gorman's "Catholicism: Safeguard of Democracy," provide a flavor of how strongly the issue was addressed within Catholic circles at the time. McCarthyism's victims and targets, however, were most often Jews and Protestants. In investigations of trade unions, the motion picture industry, and writers, many socialists and former Communists were named by friends and government informants. Partly because many Jews worked in the industries investigated and partly because the traditional Jewish interest in prophetic social justice led them to create or join organizations for radical social change, Jews were disproportionately represented among those named and blacklisted. For this dimension of the Red Scare see Abraham Menes's "Religious and Secular Trends in Jewish Socialism" and Paul Buhle's "Jews and American Communism: The Cultural Question."

The leadership of the major Protestant denominations was also dragged into the confrontation over loyalty and Americanism. In testimony before the House Committee on Un-American Activities (HUAC), on March 26, 1947, J. Edgar Hoover said: "I confess to a real apprehension so long as Communists are able to secure ministers of the Gospel to promote their evil work and espouse a cause that is alien to the religion of Christ and Judaism" (Gaustad, *Documentary History*, p. 489). Against this kind of charge, G. Bromley Oxnam, a Methodist bishop and a president of the World Council of Churches, entered an eloquent protest. Having repeatedly been identified in "unevaluated" HUAC reports released to the public as either a Communist sympathizer or puppet, Oxnam demanded to be heard and both disclaimed sympathy with the communism he opposed because of its atheism and assailed the committee for "procedures that are in effect the rule of men and not of law; procedures subject to the prejudices, passions and political ambitions of Committeemen; procedures designed less to elicit information than to entrap; procedures that cease to be investigation and become inquisition and intimidation" (*I Protest*, p. 153). Another church leader who opposed McCarthy and the anticommunist witchhunt was John Mackay, the president of Princeton Theological Seminary. His controversial "Letter to Presbyterians" and the fallout surrounding the letter are covered in an article by James H. Smylie, "Mackay and McCarthyism, 1953–1954."

The long-range effect of the religious confrontation with communism and anticommunism in the late 1940s and early 1950s can best be seen in the increasing polarization of Protestantism into two schools of thought that divided denominations, seminaries, and even local congregations. One of these might be called "political Protestantism" and the other "conservative Protestantism." The political Protestants tended to support their leaders' right to speak out on public issues. On the other hand, the conservative Protestants advocated that the church attend to spiritual matters and believed that political issues were best left to the consciences of individuals and the formal political process. An exception was made, of course, for expressions of Christian allegiance to the American flag and nation. Nearly every denomination experienced sharp tensions over these issues, and there arose an ongoing debate about the legitimacy of what was then called social action on the part of the churches—a debate that would intensify in the 1960s with the coming of the civil rights and antiwar movements. Key articles and books in the debate included, Dayton D. McKean's "The State, the Church, and the Lobby," John A. Hutchison's *Christian Faith and Social Action*, Luke Eugene Ebersole's *Church Lobbying in the Nation's Capitol*, and William Muehl's *Politics for Christians*. Although historical treatments of the political side of the divide are sorely lacking, three studies of extreme conservative Protestants bear mentioning. They are *The Christian Fright Peddlers* by Brooks R. Walker, *Apostles of Discord* by Ralph Lord Roy, and *The American Far Right* by John Harold Redekop.

America was at a crossroads between high ideals and disappointing results. As usual it was Reinhold Niebuhr who saw the dilemmas most clearly. In his 1952 book, *The Irony of American History*, Niebuhr pointed out the distance between the desires and possibilities of the hour in one broad stroke:

Our age is involved in irony because so many dreams of our nation have been so cruelly refuted by history. Our dreams of a pure virtue are dissolved in a situation in which it is possible to exercise the virtue of responsibility toward a community of nations only by courting the prospective guilt of the atomic bomb. And the irony is increased by the frantic efforts of some of our idealists to escape this hard reality by dreaming up schemes of an ideal world order which have no relevance to either our present dangers or our urgent duties (p. 2).

Indeed, it was Reinhold Niebuhr who stood out during the entire period as both actor and analyst at the point where religion and politics met. Niebuhr's prophetic distrust of both Marxist and secular humanist solutions to the human dilemma and his application of the concept of original sin to both institutions and individuals had featured prominently in his books since *Moral Man and Immoral Society* (1932), particularly in *The Nature and Destiny of Man* (1941–1943) and in *The Children of Light and the Children of Darkness* (1944). But in addition to defining the limits and morally tainted character of individual and collective action, Niebuhr constructively articulated ways in which people could undertake to act responsibly in a morally imperfect world. His *Christianity and Power Politics* (1940) initiated a school of religio-political thought which came to be known as "Christian Realism." Christian Realism in the hands of Niebuhr's liberal colleague John C. Bennett resulted in volumes with such titles as *Christian Realism* or *Christianity and Communism*, the latter of which argued that a realistic assessment of communism would see it as a well-meaning, but misguided effort at achieving the goals of liberal Christianity. Christian Realism was also marshalled in support of conservative foreign policy objectives by John Foster Dulles and later by Michael Novak. Realist thought proved a potent tool for dealing with the ambiguities of the postwar world, but its results were highly dependent on what the moral actor perceived to be real. How great was the Communist threat from within? How benign were Soviet intentions? These questions provided the substance of disagreement amongst Realists. Even Niebuhr himself could be alternately the prophet of peace and the cold warrior. Through the 1950s, for instance, he remained a proponent of nuclear deterrence in such books as *Christian Realism and Political Problems* (1953), *The Irony of American History* (1952), and *The Structure of Nations and Empires* (1959). Yet by the early 1960s he was questioning whether continued acquiescence in a balance of terror might itself be unjust.

The different aspects of Niebuhr's political activities and thought are brought out in studies by Ronald H. Stone and Paul Merkley which stress Niebuhr as liberal prophet and cold warrior, respectively. The best collection of critical articles on Niebuhr remains that of Charles Kegley and Robert W. Bretall. A fine new biography by Richard Wightman Fox supplements June Bingham's older, very personal *Courage to Change;* both depict Niebuhr as a complex man living in complex times. David H. Smith's *The Achievement of John C. Bennett* is the nearest thing available to a biography of Bennett, whose own "Christian Realism: Retrospect and Prospect" is a valuable addition to the literature on Christian Realism.

Christian Realism was not the only source of creative discourse on religion and politics in the 1950s. Driven in part by the anticommunism of the late forties and early fifties, an intellectual examination of the relation between Christianity and democracy took place throughout the decade. The books produced in the lively investigation of the topic included James Hastings Nichols's *Democracy and the Churches*, Samuel Enoch Stumpf's *A Democratic Manifesto*, Winthrop S. Hudson's *The Great Tradition of the American Churches* and "Theological Convictions and Democratic Government," Currin Shields's *Democracy and Catholicism in America*, and *The Churches and the Public*, edited by John Cogley for the then new Center for the Study of Democratic Institutions. Throughout all of this particular literature, one can discern a two-part effort to, on the one hand, defend the loyalty of the churches by showing that Christianity ultimately favored democracy as the purest form of government, and, on the other, to show that American democracy needed religious commitment as its moral lifeblood lest it cease to be truly democratic. All of this is probably best seen in the context of a reaction to McCarthyism and as a way of articulating a reassuring church-state relationship in the modern era, a relationship which stressed the affinity of religion and the American republic for one another while leaving the principle of church-state separation intact.

The nature of separation had become a live issue because the activity of the United States Supreme Court made it one. The legal status of the church-state relationship began to change in 1940 when the free exercise clause of the First Amendment was extended to the states in the ruling of the case of *Cantwell v. Connecticut*. In the same year, however, in *Minersville School District v. Gobitis* the Court turned down the argument made on behalf of the children of Jehovah's Witnesses that the First Amendment protected the right of children not to salute the national flag. The Court had begun to give specific meaning to the free exercise of religion, only seemingly to limit it again later in the same term. Yet, three years later, the Court reversed itself in the nearly identical Jehovah's Witness flag salute case of *West Virginia Board of Education v. Barnette*, the ruling for which weighed patriotism and a civil-religious symbolic act against an unpopular religious belief and found that the Constitution protected the belief. Other cases followed that continued to widen the realm of belief and practice protected by the Constitution, notably *Ballard* and *Girouard*. Then in 1947, in the consideration of *Everson v. Board of Education of Ewing Township*, the Court began a process of narrowing the acceptable limits of state aid to, and entanglement with, religion. The case, together with *McCollum* decided the next year, was notable for interpreting the meaning of the establishment clause of the Constitution in terms of Thomas Jefferson's metaphor of "a wall of separation." *McCollum* used this new judicial principle to outlaw a released time program for religious instruction because of the pressure placed on those students who did not participate. The principle was also used in a series of blue law cases, such as *McGowan v. State of Maryland* and *Braunfeld v. Brown*, to restrict the state from favoring Christianity through Sunday closings and sales prohibitions. And eventually the wall of separation metaphor was applied to the practices of school prayer and Bible reading, beginning with *Engel v. Vitale* in 1962. Yet the Court was not committed to a completely secular state, as Justice William O. Douglas, writing for the majority in *Zorach v. Clauson*, noted when he argued that though "the First Amendment reflects the philosophy that Church and State should be separated," a commonsense approach toward application was called for since "the First Amendment . . . does not say that in every and all respects there shall be a separation of Church and State" (343 U.S. 306 (1952), p. 312). Douglas was also remembered for writing in the same case: "We are a religious people whose institutions presuppose a Supreme Being" (p. 313). The Supreme Court decisions of the 1940s and 1950s were sending out mixed signals to the American people, to say the least. Their effect was to open up the formal question of church-state relations in the United States to fresh debate.

For more on the history and impact of these cases see David R. Manwaring's *Render Unto Caesar*, Theodore Powell's *The School Bus Law*, Myron S. Rudd's "Toward an Understanding of the Landmark Federal Decisions Affecting Relations between Church and State," Frank J. Sorauf's "*Zorach v. Clauson*," and Albert Keim's collection on compulsory education and the Amish.

Speaking directly to the joint issues of the meaning of church-state separation and the relation of American religion to American democracy was the especial forte of John Courtney Murray, a theology professor and Jesuit priest. Beginning in 1942, he questioned his church's traditional position on church-state relations. For centuries the ideal state of Catholic teaching was one in which the state obligated itself to see that its people worshiped God according to correct procedures, granted no rights to erroneous beliefs, and regulated itself according to the divine will as mediated by the teachings of the church. The last major attempt at Roman Catholic accommodation with the religiously plural American state had resulted in the Americanist Crisis and the censuring of the American church by Pope Leo XIII in *Testem Benevolentiae* in 1899. Now another American Catholic set out to show that a state could work for the welfare of all its citizens without compromising the Catholic faith of some of them. While perhaps disappointing in ultimate terms, pluralistic temporal orders were not to be seen as totally useless. Indeed, Murray came to argue that the strength of a system such as the American, where no state church could emerge, was that the church's influence as a moral authority in politics was enhanced because it was not a self-interested party in governments and alliances. Murray's work appeared in article form in such publications as *Religious Education, America, Social Order, Modern Age, The Critic,* and *Theological Studies.* In these articles he appropriated the Founders' ideas concerning the American proposition to a new time, discussing American pluralism, the tensions between civil unity and religious integrity, the vexing issues of censorship and aid to parochial schools, the nature and future of freedom, the morality of war and the legitimacy of the use of force, and the problems of security and risk with reference to Communist imperialism. Leaving no stone unturned, Murray produced some of the most innovative thought on church-state issues in the postwar period. Yet it was in reassessing the relationship of Catholicism to American democracy that he made his greatest contribution, acting as a firm advocate of both:

The question is sometimes raised, whether Catholicism is compatible with American democracy. The question is invalid as well as impertinent; for the manner of its position inverts the order of values. It must, of course, be turned round to read, whether American democracy is compatible with Catholicism. The question, thus turned, is part of the civil question, as put to me. An affirmative answer to it, given under something better than curbstone definition of "democracy," is one of the truths I hold (*We Hold These Truths,* pp. ix–x).

Murray's work in the 1950s laid the groundwork for the most American of the sixteen documents issued by the Second Vatican Council in the 1960s, the *Declaration on Religious Freedom.* The full force of the direction of Murray's earlier efforts was now apparent in the church's resignation of all claims to secular privilege and authority. The only right it still claimed from the state was the right to enjoy with other faiths a "full measure of freedom." Murray himself pronounced the *Declaration,* "the Church's final farewell to the sacred society." Most of Murray's most important essays were collected in *We Hold These Truths* and his thought has been critically treated by Thomas Teel Love.

The twin influences of the changing legal status of church-state arrangements and the communism/democracy debate engendered a new church-state consciousness that was reflected not only in Murray's work, but also in a resurgence of scholarly interest in church and state narrowly defined. The hallmark volume in the new literature produced by scholars in this area was the three-volume work by Anson Phelps Stokes, *Church and State in the United States,* published in 1950. Other important books followed, including Conrad Henry Moehlman's *The Wall of Separation Between Church and*

State, Joseph Martin Dawson's *America's Way in Church, State, and Society*, Loren P. Beth's *The American Theory of Church and State*, Joseph Lecler's *The Two Sovereignties*, Leo Pfeffer's highly textured *Church, State, and Freedom*, Merrimon Cunninggim's *Freedom's Holy Light*, and Jacques Maritain's popular *Man and the State*. In retrospect, additional books, ostensibly focused on church-state issues in other periods and other places, read as the works of scholars searching their distant fields for answers to contemporary problems. Thus, John R. Bodo's argument about "transformationalist" clergy in *The Protestant Clergy and Public Issues, 1812–1848* has everything to do with making the case for religious transformationalist action on public issues in the mid-1950s, Oscar Handlin's *Adventure in Freedom—Three Hundred Years of Jewish Life in America* made the case for contemporary pluralism and tolerance by stressing the benefits that had accrued to American Jews in the past through separation, and Oscar Cullman's *The State in the New Testament* searches for ideological ancestors in a way not dissimilar from the Supreme Court's uses of Thomas Jefferson and James Madison. One other more obvious example of this latter kind of scholarship is Thomas Griffin Sanders's *Protestant Concepts of Church and State*. Finally, *Church and State in Scripture, History and Constitutional Law* by James E. Wood, Jr., E. Bruce Thomson, and Robert T. Miller deserves mention because its publication in 1958 signaled the inception of continuous study of church-state issues at Baylor University. That same year Wood, Thomson, and Miller joined together to produce the first issue of a new scholarly periodical, the *Journal of Church and State*. Events and interest had successfully conspired to create an entire academic subfield in less than a decade and that subfield's activity was all directed at helping American society deal with what Robert T. Handy has so aptly labeled the "second disestablishment."

If historians, law professors, and theologians were turning their scholarly attention to church-state questions, so too the representatives of nearly every major religious body were addressing the issues of the hour from their own perspectives. Arguing that the Roman Catholic church in America had historically been a good citizen, John Tracy Ellis wrote "Church and State in the United States: A Critical Appraisal" for the *Catholic Historical Review* and later went on to write "Church and State: An American Catholic Tradition" for *Catholic Mind*. Meanwhile, Gustave Weigel produced "The Church and the Democratic State" in 1952 at one of the peaks of Roman Catholic concern for that issue. Presbyterian John Mackay represented a somewhat conservative, though not atypical, Reformed position in articles with titles like "Church, State, and Freedom" and "Religion and Government, Their Separate Spheres and Reciprocal Responsibilities." That position was subsequently modified by his encounter with McCarthyism. Lutherans viewed contemporary church-state issues and asked how they fit in with the historic "two swords" doctrine of church and state; see George W. Forell's "Toward a Lutheran View of Church and State" and Ernest Koenker's "Two Realms and the 'Separation of Church and State' in American Society." And finally, as Elmer Neufeld's lengthy article entitled "Christian Responsibility in the Political Situation" demonstrates, even Mennonites were interested in reviewing doctrine on the basis of recent developments.

All in all, the scholars and churches were virtually united in declaring the separation of church and state a particular blessing of the American system of government. America was on the way toward a positive acknowledgment of itself as a religiously pluralistic society. The march toward pluralism, however, entailed definitive resolution of the old issue of Roman Catholic power, allegiance, and distinctness. During the 1950s the society negotiated several aspects of this issue and in doing so put to rest once and for all the widespread anti-Catholicism that had periodically characterized American life. For shorthand, these might be designated Blanshardism, relations with the Vatican, and the faith of candidates for executive office.

Blanshardism is the name that could be given to the activity of Paul Blanshard, businessman, author, founder of Protestants and Other Americans United for Separation of Church and State (POAU), and devout anti-Catholic. His 1949 book *American Freedom and Catholic Power* was a tour de force in the use of official Catholic church documents to argue that Catholicism posed a serious threat to American democracy. The problem, as Blanshard saw it, was the relation between American values and the values of a Romanist hierarchy:

Essentially the Catholic problem in America is what to do with the hierarchy of the Roman Church. The American Catholic *people* have done their best to join the rest of America, but the American Catholic hierarchy, as we shall see in the course of this survey, has never been assimilated. It is still fundamentally Roman in its spirit and directives. It is an autocratic moral monarchy in a liberal democracy (*American Freedom*, pp. 9–10).

After another three hundred pages of laying out his case, Blanshard made his suggestion for solving the Catholic problem:

At least once in our history the American people have thrown off an alien system of control without losing their moral perspective or their sense of respect for their opponents. . . . When the crisis had passed, the American and British people soon realized that their common purposes far outweighed their incidental disagreements. The analogy is not exact, but it contains a suggestion and a hope for the solution of the Catholic problem in the United States (p. 306).

The reaction to Blanshard was divided. To some his nativistic rhetoric expressed their deepest fears. To Roman Catholics, like Francis Cardinal Spellman, Blanshard was a token of a new and vicious wave of bigotry.

American Catholicism itself was changing, however, and the thought and leadership of clerics such as Gustave Weigel and John Courtney Murray, Thomas McAvoy, John Tracy Ellis, Georges Tavard, Daniel Callahan, Bernard Cooke, John Cronin, and Colman Barry and laymen like John Cogley, Matthew Ahmann, George N. Shuster, and Michael Novak make it possible to view the postwar era as one of major intellectual and spiritual renaissance in Catholicism. Blanshard's characterizations of Catholicism appeared to many involved with the rising ecumenism to be a caricature of a Catholicism which no longer existed, if, indeed, it ever had. The embarrassment Blanshard caused his fellow Protestants may have inadvertently contributed to the seriousness of the ecumenical dialogue that began to take shape in the late 1950s. This dialogue is well represented by Thomas Griffin Sanders in "Protestantism, Catholicism and POAU," and a book jointly authored by Robert McAfee Brown and Gustave Weigel, *An American Dialogue—A Protestant Looks at Catholicism and a Catholic Looks at Protestantism*. In time even Blanshard's group took a softer line and became simply Americans United for Separation of Church and State. This transformation is documented in a collection of articles from the organization's magazine entitled *The Best of "Church & State", 1948–1975* and edited by Albert J. Menendez.

Another sticking point in Protestant–Jewish–Roman Catholic relations was the matter of United States representation to the Vatican. After the loss of the Papal States in 1870, the American government had no ambassador to the Vatican. During the Second World War the president maintained a personal representative to the pope, without fanfare and mostly without the objection of the American people. After the war, President Harry Truman saw the political possibilities of pleasing Catholic voters and nominated General Mark Clark to be a full ambassador to the Vatican. Reaction among non-Catholics, however, was surprisingly strong as Protestants, Jews, agnostics, and atheists alike argued that the move represented an unprecedented and unconstitutional recognition of a particular religion. The issue raged on through the 1950s and provides some of the most revealing primary church-state literature of the period. The controversy is well described in Leo Pfeffer's *Church, State, and Freedom*, and by John S. Conway in "Myron C. Taylor's Mission to the Vatican, 1940–1950." Even though in the event the

United States did not open up full diplomatic relations with the Vatican, an awareness that the pope played an important role in international politics served to keep interest in Vatican diplomacy high and in the 1950s a number of books were published to meet that interest, including Robert A. Graham's *Vatican Diplomacy* and Camille Maximilian Cianfarra's *The Vatican and the Kremlin.*

In many ways the presidential election of 1960 signaled that America had finally come to terms with Roman Catholicism. When the possibility that Democrats might nominate John F. Kennedy first emerged, not a few Protestant denominations made it clear that they thought it would be a bad idea. As when Al Smith ran for president in 1928, questions about the candidate's loyalties and fitness for office were raised and there were charges that the nomination had been made to obtain the "Catholic vote." Even the popular Episcopal bishop James Albert Pike made it clear in his book *A Roman Catholic in the White House* that he did not think a Roman Catholic could be fit to hold the office of president. Others suggested that perhaps the time had come to elect a Catholic simply to show that the nation was no longer bigoted. There are several good critical books and articles on the episode including Lawrence H. Fuchs's *John F. Kennedy and American Catholicism* and James S. Wolfe's "The Religious Issue Revisited." Kennedy himself, in an address to the Ministerial Association in Houston in September of 1960, confronted the religious issue and defused it enough to allow his election. The address itself, and its effect, demonstrated what kind of church-state accommodation was acceptable to both Catholics and other voters by 1960. Kennedy expressed the mind of the American people when he said:

I believe in an America where religious intolerance will someday end—where all men and all churches are treated as equal—where every man has the same right to attend or not to attend the church of his choice—where there is no Catholic vote, no anti-Catholic vote, no bloc voting of any kind and where Catholics, Protestants and Jews, both the lay and the pastoral level, will refrain from those attitudes of disdain and division which have so often marred their works in the past, and promote instead the American ideal of brotherhood (*New York Times*, 13 September 1960).

Another religious group which must be figured into the 1950s march toward pluralism were American Jews. The standard account of these years in the history of American Judaism is Nathan Glazer's chapter "The Jewish Revival: 1940–56" in his *American Judaism.* Glazer stressed that the major changes the Jewish community experienced after the war were the movement of Jews toward business and the professions and away from occupations of lower income and lower social status, the decisive embrace of religious Judaism, though usually in the form of Reform or Conservative Judaism, and the rejection of secular quasi-national Jewishness. Glazer adamantly refused to give the credit for the revival in interest in Judaism to the social commentators' favorite explanations: Hitler and Zionism. He concluded instead, "The two greatest events in modern Jewish history, the murder of six million Jews by Hitler and the creation of a Jewish state in Palestine, have had remarkably slight effects on the inner life of American Jewry" (p. 114). From Glazer's point of view, the forces shaping Judaism in the contemporary period were not ideological, but rather sociological. He therefore cast his lot with other sociological interpretations of Judaism such as Marshall Sklare's *Conservative Judaism,* and Harry Gersh's "The New Suburbanites of the 50's." And yet, as Franklin H. Littell would later point out, that the impact of the founding of Israel on America would be so slight also made historical sense, for America had become the chief intellectual, cultural, and financial center of Judaism even before the founding of the state of Israel in 1948. Though American Jews found a special attachment to the Zionist state, Littell concludes, "no substantial number of American Jews has accepted the notion that their citizenship here 'in the diaspora' is either transitory or provisional" (*The Church and the Body Politic,* p. 18).

There were, however, other groups for whom the rebirth of Israel was an event of great significance. Some American Christians, among them certain fundamentalist leaders, saw in the creation of the Jewish state the "restoration of the Jews" prophesied in the New Testament book of Revelation and the fulfillment of one of the steps in the coming of the millennial kingdom of Christ. This kind of expectation and the pro-Israel political alliance formed by American Jews and fundamentalist Christians are well treated in David A. Rausch's article "*Our Hope:* An American Fundamentalist Journal and the Holocaust, 1937–1945." Esther Feldblum has also explored the meaning of the founding of Israel for Christians in her "On the Eve of a Jewish State: American Catholic Responses."

The coming together of Protestants, Catholics, and Jews in a happy and prosperous common culture in the 1950s was for many a dream come true. The revival of interest in religion, celebrated by Henry Link in his 1937 book *The Return to Religion* as a healthy sign that Americans had put away the theological and political squabbling that had stood in the way of enjoying religion's practical blessings, intensified and was heralded in Link's terms by other social commentators. Religion was good because it was good for the family, it made one feel better. Whether it was true made no difference, it worked. But to other observers, the attitude of the Park Forest, Illinois minister who downplayed the spiritual truths he represented and depicted himself as more of a corporate chaplain when interviewed for William Whyte's *Organization Man* betokened a negative aspect in religion on the new suburban frontier.

During the 1950s a great many sociologists and social commentators took it upon themselves to describe the underside of the American Dream as well as its ostensible prosperity. Key texts in this genre include *Organization Man*, David Riesman's *The Lonely Crowd*, *Mass Culture*, edited by Bernard Rosenberg and David Manning White, and C. Wright Mills's *The Power Elite*. All of these studies had something to say about religion and its role in the American way of life, but it was the publication of Will Herberg's *Protestant-Catholic-Jew* in 1955 that brought the issue most acutely to the fore.

Herberg's argument was that American society had been transformed from a collection of small religious/ethnic groups—Swedish Lutherans, German Lutherans, German Jews, East European Jews, etc.—into three great communities, Protestant, Catholic and Jewish. These communities were the result of a triple melting pot that dissolved the distinctiveness that kept people apart. In this sense, then, something positive had been gained. Yet Herberg's argument also had a cutting edge that made him sound like an Old Testament prophet: "Americans fill the houses of worship, but their conceptions, standards, and values, their institutions and loyalties, bear a strangely ambiguous relation to the teachings that the churches presumably stand for" (*Protestant-Catholic-Jew*, p. 286). Though parts of Herberg's analysis and some of his conclusions were later challenged by Michael Novak in *The Rise of the Unmeltable Ethnics*, by Stephen Sharot in "The Three-Generations Thesis and the American Jews," by Sidney E. Mead in "The Post-Protestant Concept and America's Two Religions," and by Patrick Henry in "'And I Don't Care What It Is,'" his work stimulated a number of other thinkers to take a long look at the American way of life, and the American way of religion, in critical terms. Among such efforts were Peter L. Berger's *The Noise of Solemn Assemblies*, Gibson Winter's *The Suburban Captivity of the Churches*, William Miller's "Religion and the American Way of Life," and Thomas T. McAvoy's volume of worthwhile essays entitled *Roman Catholicism and the American Way of Life*.

This conviction that perhaps religion had formed too close a relationship with the dominant American culture would be carried as a major theme into the 1960s; so too would a growing demand for civil rights for black persons. The Second World War had altered America and the way Americans lived and thought and even voted and worshiped, but the changes did not end with the end of the fifties. Instead they had just begun. The stage was set for the sixties.

BIBLIOGRAPHY

Abrams, Ray H. "The Churches and the Clergy in World War II." Annals of the American Academy of Political and Social Science 356 (March 1948), 110-119.

Adams, James L. The Growing Church Lobby in Washington. Grand Rapids: Eerdmans, 1970.

Agar, William Macdonough. Where Do Catholics Stand? New York: Farrar Rinehart, 1941.

Ahlstrom, Sydney E. "Religion and the Rise of Modern Nationalism: Reflections On the American Experience." Church History 44 (December 1975), 492-504.

Alley, Robert S. So Help Me God: Religion and the Presidency, Wilson to Nixon. Richmond, Va.: John Knox, 1972.

Allinsmith, Wesley, and Allinsmith, Beverly. "Religious Affiliation and Political-Economic Attitude--A Study of Eight Major United States Religious Groups." Public Opinion Quarterly 12 (Fall 1948), 377-389.

Almond, Gabriel. The American People and Foreign Policy. New York: Praeger, 1960.

Angell, Robert C. Free Society and Moral Crisis. Ann Arbor: University of Michigan Press, 1958.

Aubrey, Edwin. "Church and State in Contemporary Protestant Thought With Special Reference to the American Scene." Journal of Religion 29 (April 1949), 171-180.

Bainton, Roland H. "The Churches and War: Historical Attitudes Toward Christian Participation." Social Action 15 (January 1945), 2-78.

Barnes, Roswell P. Under Orders: The Churches and Public Affairs. Garden City, N.Y.: Doubleday, 1961.

Barrett, Patricia. Religious Liberty and the American
Presidency--A Study in Church-State Relations. New York:
Herder and Herder, 1963.

Barth, Karl. Church and State. New York: Macmillan, 1939.

Barth, Karl. Die Kirche Zwischen Ost und West. Zollikon-
Zurich: Evangelischer Verlag, A.G., 1949.

Belknap, Michael R. "Joe Must Go." Reviews in American
History 7 (March 1979), 256-261.

Bennett, John C. Christian Ethics and Social Policy. New
York: Scribner, 1946.

Bennett, John C. "Christian Faith and Political Strategy."
Christianity and Crisis, 24 February 1941, 3-6.

Bennett, John C. Christianity and Communism. New York:
Association Press, 1948.

Bennett, John C. Christian Realism. New York: Scribner, 1942.

Bennett, John C. "Christian Realism: Retrospect and Prospect."
Christianity and Crisis, 5 August 1968, 175-190.

Bennett, John C. Christians and the State. New York:
Scribner, 1958.

Bennett, John C. Social Salvation. New York: Scribner, 1935.

Bergendoff, Conrad J. I. "The Lutheran Christian in Church and
State." Lutheran Quarterly 1 (November 1949), 411-424.

Berger, Peter L. The Noise of Solemn Assemblies: Christian
Commitment and the Religious Establishment in America.
Garden City, N.Y.: Doubleday, 1961.

Bernanos, Georges. "Catholics and the Modern State."
Christianity and Crisis, 20 March 1950, 29-30.

Beth, Loren P. The American Theory of Church and State.
Gainesville: University of Florida Press, 1958.

Bingham, June. Courage to Change: An Introduction to the Life
and Thought of Reinhold Niebuhr. New York: Scribner, 1972.

Blanshard, Paul. American Freedom and Catholic Power. Boston:
Beacon Press, 1951.

Blanshard, Paul. God and Man in Washington. Boston: Beacon
Press, 1960.

Bodo, John R. The Protestant Clergy and Public Issues, 1812-
1848. Princeton, N.J.: Princeton University Press, 1954.

Brady, Joseph Hugh. Confusion Twice Confounded: The First
     Amendment and the Supreme Court, An Historical Study.
     South Orange, N.J.: Seton Hall University Press, 1954.

Brown, Robert McAfee, and Weigel, Gustave. An American
     Dialogue--A Protestant Looks at Catholicism and a Catholic
     Looks at Protestantism. Garden City, N.Y.: Doubleday,
     Anchor Books, 1961.

Brunner, Emil. Justice and the Social Order. New York: Harper
     and Brothers, 1945.

Bryson, Lyman, ed. Approaches to World Peace. New York:
     Conference on Science, Philosophy and Religion in Their
     Relation to the Democratic Way of Life, 1944.

Bryson, Lyman, ed. Perspectives on a Troubled Decade:
     Science, Philosophy and Religion 1939-1949. New York:
     Conference on Science, Philosophy and Religion in Their
     Relation to the Democratic Way of Life, 1950.

Buhle, Paul. "Jews and American Communism: The Cultural
     Question." Radical History Review 23 (Spring 1980), 8-33.

Butterfield, Herbert. International Conflict in the Twentieth
     Century. New York: Harper and Brothers, 1960.

Butts, R. Freeman. The American Tradition in Religion and
     Education. Boston: Beacon Press, 1950.

Carter, Paul A. The Decline and Revival of the Social Gospel:
     Social and Political Liberalism in American Protestant
     Churches, 1920-1940. Ithaca, N.Y.: Cornell University
     Press, 1956.

Carter, Paul A. "The Idea of Progress in Most Recent American
     Protestant Thought, 1930-1960." Church History 32 (March
     1963), 75-89.

Cauthen, Kenneth. The Impact of American Religious Liberalism.
     New York: Harper and Row, 1962.

Cavert, Samuel McCrea. "Rethinking the Social Function of the
     Church." Religion in Life 12 (Summer 1943), 344-355.

Center for the Study of Democratic Institutions. Religion and
     American Society: A Statement of Principles. Santa Barbara,
     Calif.: Center for the Study of Democratic Institutions,
     1961.

Chadwin, Mark L. The Hawks of World War II. Chapel Hill:
     University of North Carolina Press, 1962.

Chamberlain, J. Gordon. "The Christian and Action." Union
     Seminary Quarterly Review 7 (January 1952), 27-30.

Cianfarra, Camille Maximilian. The Vatican and the Kremlin. New York: Dutton, 1950.

Cogley, John, ed. The Churches and the Public. Santa Barbara, Calif.: Center for the Study of Democratic Institutions, 1960.

Cohn, Werner. "Jewish Political Attitudes: Their Background." Judaism 8 (Fall 1959), 312-322.

Cole, William A., and Hammond, Phillip E. "Religious Pluralism, Legal Development, and Societal Complexity: Rudimentary Forms of Civil Religion." Journal for the Scientific Study of Religion 13 (June 1974), 177-190.

Connell, Francis J. "Christ the King of Civil Rulers." American Ecclesiastical Review 119 (October 1948), 244-253.

Connell, Francis J. "The Relationship Between Church and State." Jurist 13 (October 1953), 398-414.

Conway, John S. "Myron C. Taylor's Mission to the Vatican, 1940-1950." Church History 44 (March 1975), 85-99.

Cort, John C. "Comrades Have a Crisis." Commonweal 10 (August 1945), 406-408.

Cowan, Wayne H., ed. Facing Protestant-Roman Catholic Tensions. New York: Association Press, 1960.

Crosby, Donald F. God, Church, and Flag: Senator Joseph R. McCarthy and the Catholic Church, 1950-1957. Chapel Hill: University of North Carolina Press, 1978.

Crosby, Donald F. "The Jesuits and Joe McCarthy." Church History 46 (September 1977), 374-388.

Cullman, Oscar. The State in the New Testament. New York: Scribner, 1956.

Cunninggim, Merrimon. Freedom's Holy Light. New York: Harper and Brothers, 1955.

Darby, J. H. "Christianity in the Secular State." Catholic Mind 52 (January 1954), 38-45.

Dawson, Christopher. Religion and the Modern State. New York: Sheed and Ward, 1938.

Dawson, Joseph Martin. America's Way in Church, State, and Society. New York: Macmillan, 1953.

DeSantis, Vincent P. "American Catholics and McCarthyism." Catholic Historical Review 51 (January 1965), 1-30.

Drury, Clifford M., ed. United States Bureau of Naval Personnel: The History of the Chaplain Corps. 5 vols. Washington, D.C.: U.S. Government Printing Office, 1948-1960.

Dunn, Joe P. "Protestant Church Spokesmen, Universal Military Training, and the Anti-Conscription Campaigns, 1940-1959." Proceedings of the South Carolina Historical Association 49 (1979), 41-58.

Ebersole, Luke Eugene. Church Lobbying in the Nation's Capitol. New York: Macmillan, 1951.

Eckardt, A. Roy. The Surge of Piety in America, An Appraisal. New York: Association Press, 1958.

Ellis, John Tracy. "Church and State in the United States: A Critical Appraisal." Catholic Historical Review 38 (October 1952), 285-316.

Ellis, John Tracy. "Church and State: An American Catholic Tradition." Catholic Mind 52 (April 1954), 209-216.

Federal Council of Churches. Report of the Commission on the Relation of the Church to the War in the Light of the Christian Faith. New York: Federal Council of Churches, 1944.

Feldblum, Esther. "On the Eve of a Jewish State: American Catholic Responses." American Jewish Historical Quarterly 64 (December 1974), 99-119.

Fenton, John Clifford. "Toleration and the Church-State Controversy." American Ecclesiastical Review 130 (May 1954), 330-343.

Fenton, John Harold. The Catholic Vote. New Orleans: Hauser Press, 1960.

Ferm, Deane W. "American Protestant Theology, 1900-1970." Religion in Life 44 (Spring 1975), 59-72.

Fey, Harold, and Frakes, Margaret, eds. The Christian Century Reader. New York: Association Press, 1962.

Forell, George W. "Toward a Lutheran View of Church and State." Lutheran Quarterly 5 (August 1953), 280-290.

Forman, Charles. A Faith for the Nations. Philadelphia: Westminster, 1954.

Foster, Finley Milligan. Church and State, Their Relations Considered. New York: Peerless Printing Co., 1940.

Fox, Richard Wightman. Reinhold Niebuhr. New York: Pantheon, 1986.

Fredman, J. George, and Falk, Louis A. Jews in American Wars. New York: Jewish War Veterans of the U.S., 1942.

Fuchs, Lawrence H. John F. Kennedy and American Catholicism. New York: Meredith Press, 1967.

Fuchs, Lawrence H. The Political Behavior of American Jews. Glencoe, Ill.: Free Press, 1956.

Fukuyama, Yoshio. "The American Conscience." In The Search for Identity: Essays on the American Character, edited by Roger Shinn. New York: Harper and Row, 1964.

Furfey, Paul Hanley. "The Churches and Social Problems," Annals of the American Academy of Political and Social Science 256 (March 1948), 101-109.

Gaustad, Edwin Scott, ed. A Documentary History of Religion in America. 2 vols. Grand Rapids: Eerdmans, 1982.

Gerhart, Eugene C. American Liberty and "Natural Law." Boston: Beacon Press, 1953.

Gersh, Harry. "The New Suburbanites of the 50's." Commentary 17 (March 1954), 209-221.

Geyer, Alan F. Piety and Politics: American Protestantism in the World Arena. Richmond, Va.: John Knox, 1963.

Gibbons, Ray. "Christian Accent on Freedom." Social Action 22 (March 1956), 7-21.

Gilby, Thomas. Between Community and Society: A Philosophy and Theology of the State. New York: Longman, Green, 1953.

Glazer, Nathan. American Judaism. Chicago: University of Chicago Press, 1957.

Gordis, Robert. The Root and the Branch: Judaism and the Free Society. Chicago: University of Chicago Press, 1962.

Gorman, P. J. "Catholicism: Safeguard of Democracy." Ave Maria, 21 September 1946, 359-362.

Graham, Robert A. Vatican Diplomacy: A Study of Church and State on the International Plane. Princeton, N.J.: Princeton University Press, 1959.

Greene, Evarts Boutell. Religion and the State--The Making and Testing of an American Tradition. New York: Oxford University Press, 1941.

Gushwa, Robert L. The Best and Worst of Times. The United
     States Army Chaplaincy, vol. 4, 1920-1945. Washington,
     D.C.: Office of the Chief of Chaplains, Department of the
     Army, 1977.

Handlin, Oscar. Adventure in Freedom--Three Hundred Years of
     Jewish Life in America. New York: McGraw-Hill, 1954.

Handy, Robert T. "The Protestant Quest for a Christian
     America." Church History 22 (March 1953), 8-20.

Handy, Robert T. "Realism in Social Christianity." In
     American Christianity, edited by H. Shelton Smith, Robert T.
     Handy, and Lefferts A. Loetscher, vol. 2, ch. xxi. New
     York: Scribner, 1963.

Hanna, Mary T. Catholics and American Politics. Cambridge:
     Harvard University Press, 1979.

Harding, Joan N. "Christianity and Nationalism." Baptist
     Quarterly 14, no. 2 (1952), 125-132.

Harland, Gordon. The Thought of Reinhold Niebuhr. New York:
     Oxford University Press, 1960.

Harper, Elsie. "The Churches and Foreign Policy." Social
     Action 23 (April 1957), 6-17.

Harrison, Paul M. Authority and Power in the Free Church
     Tradition: A Social Case Study of the American Baptist
     Convention. Princeton, N.J.: Princeton University Press,
     1959.

Hartnett, Robert. "Debate with Blanshard." Catholic Mind 48
     (May 1950), 262-270.

Hartnett, Robert. "First Freedom." Thought 23 (December
     1948), 585-591.

Harvard Law School Forum. The Catholic Church and Politics--A
     Transcript of a Discussion on a Vital Issue Presented by the
     Harvard Law School Forum. Cambridge: Harvard Law School
     Forum, 1950.

Hayes, Carlton J. H. "The Church and Nationalism--A Plea for
     Further Study of a Major Issue." Catholic Historical Review
     28 (April 1942), 1-12.

Hayes, Carlton J. H. Nationalism: A Religion. New York:
     Macmillan, 1960.

Henry, Patrick. "'And I Don't Care What It Is': The Tradition-
     History of a Civil Religion Proof-Text." Journal of the
     American Academy of Religion 49 (March 1981), 35-47.

Herberg, Will. _Protestant-Catholic-Jew: An Essay in American Religious Sociology_. Garden City, N.Y.: Doubleday, Anchor Books, 1955.

Hitchcock, James. "The Evolution of the American Catholic Left." _American Scholar_ 43 (Winter 1973-74), 66-84.

Hoare, F. R. _The Papacy and the Modern State_. London: Burns, Oates and Washbourne, 1940.

Hoopes, Townsend. _The Devil and John Foster Dulles_. Boston: Little, Brown, 1973.

Howard University. "The Church, the State and Human Welfare." Addresses by Howard Thurman and John C. Bennett at the 34th Annual Convocation of the School of Religion, Howard University, Nov. 14-16, 1950. Washington, D.C., 1951.

Hudson, Winthrop S. _The Great Tradition of the American Churches_. New York: Harper and Brothers, 1953.

Hudson, Winthrop S. "Theological Convictions and Democratic Government." _Theology Today_ 10 (July 1953), 230-239.

Hughes, Emmet John. _The Church and the Liberal Society_. Princeton, N.J.: Princeton University Press, 1944.

Hughley, J. Neal. _Trends in Protestant Social Idealism_. Freeport, N.Y.: Books for Libraries Press, 1948.

Hutchinson, Paul. _The New Leviathan_. Chicago: Willett, Clark & Company, 1946.

Hutchison, John A. _The Two Cities: A Study of God and Human Politics_. Garden City, N.Y.: Doubleday, 1957.

Hutchison, John A., ed. _Christian Faith and Social Action_. New York: Scribner, 1953.

Hutchison, William R. _American Protestant Thought in the Liberal Era_. New York: Harper and Row, 1968.

Jackson, Barbara W. _Faith and Freedom_. New York: Norton, 1954.

Johnson, Alvin W., and Yost, Frank H. _Separation of Church and State in the United States_. Minneapolis: University of Minnesota Press, 1948.

Johnson, F. Ernest, ed. _World Order: Its Intellectual and Cultural Foundations_. New York: Harper and Brothers, 1944.

Kaye, G., and Szasz, F. M. "Adding 'Under God' to the Pledge of Allegiance." _Encounter_ 34 (Winter 1973), 52-56.

Keehn, Thomas B., and Underwood, Kenneth W. "Protestants in Political Action." Social Action 16 (June 1950), 5-37.

Kegley, Charles, and Bretall, Robert W., eds. Reinhold Niebuhr: His Religious, Social, and Political Thought. New York: Macmillan, 1956.

Keim, Albert N. "John Foster Dulles and the Protestant World Order Movement on the Eve of World War II." Journal of Church and State 21 (Winter 1979), 73-89.

Keim, Albert N. "Service or Resistance? The Mennonite Response to Conscription in World War II." Mennonite Quarterly Review 52, no. 2 (1978), 141-155.

Keim, Albert N., ed. Compulsory Education and the Amish: The Right Not to be Modern. Boston: Beacon Press, 1975.

Kennan, George F. "World Problems in Christian Perspective." Theology Today 16 (July 1959), 155-172.

Kerwin, Jerome G. Catholic Viewpoint on Church and State. Garden City, N.Y.: Hanover House, 1960.

Kerwin, Jerome G. "The Church and the Garrison State." Review of Politics 1 (April 1939), 179-190.

Kliever, Lonnie. H. Richard Niebuhr. Waco, Tex.: Word Press, 1977.

Knight, Frank H. "Intelligence and Social Policy." Ethics 67 (April 1957), 155-169.

Knox, John, ed. Religion and the Present Crisis. Chicago: University of Chicago Press, 1942.

Koenker, Ernest B. "Two Realms and the 'Separation of Church and State' in American Society." Concordia 27 (January 1956), 1-12.

Lambert, Richard D., ed. "Religion in American Society." Annals of the American Academy of Political and Social Science 332 (November 1960), 1-222.

Landis, Judson T. "Social Action in American Protestant Churches." American Journal of Sociology 52 (May 1947), 517-522.

Landon, Harold R., ed. Reinhold Niebuhr: A Prophetic Voice in Our Time. Greenwich, Conn.: Seabury Press, 1962.

La Noue, George R. A Bibliography of Doctoral Dissertations Undertaken in American and Canadian Universities, 1940-1962, on Religion and Politics. New York: National Council of Churches, 1963.

Latourette, Kenneth Scott. The Gospel, the Church, and the World. Freeport, N.Y.: Books for Libraries, 1956.

Lecler, Joseph. The Two Sovereignties; A Study of the Relationship Between Church and State. New York: Philosophical Library, 1952.

Lee, Umphrey. The Historic Church and Modern Pacifism. New York, Nashville: Abingdon-Cokesbury, 1943.

Lefever, Ernest W. Ethics and United States Foreign Policy. New York: Meridian, 1957.

Lekachman, Robert. "The Secular Uses of the Religious Press." In The Religious Press in America, edited by Martin E. Marty. New York: Holt, Rinehart and Winston, 1963.

Levitt, Albert. Vaticanism: The Political Principles of the Roman Catholic Church. New York: Vantage, 1960.

Link, Eugene P. Labor-Religion Prophet: The Times and Life of Harry F. Ward. Boulder, Colo.: Westview, 1984.

Link, Henry. The Return to Religion. New York: Macmillan, 1937.

Littell, Franklin H. The Church and the Body Politic. New York: Seabury Press, 1969.

Loetscher, Lefferts A. The Broadening Church. Philadelphia: University of Pennsylvania Press, 1954.

Long, Edward Leroy, Jr. Conscience and Compromise. Philadelphia: Westminster, 1954.

Love, Thomas Teel. John Courtney Murray: Contemporary Church-State Theory. Garden City, N.Y.: Doubleday, 1965.

McAvoy, Thomas T., ed. Roman Catholicism and the American Way of Life. Fort Wayne, Ind.: University of Notre Dame Press, 1960.

Mackay, John A. "Church, State, and Freedom." Theology Today 8 (May-June 1951), 218-233.

Mackay, John A. "Religion and Government, Their Separate Spheres and Reciprocal Responsibilities." Theology Today 9 (July 1952), 204-222.

McKean, Dayton D. "The State, the Church, and the Lobby." In Religious Perspectives in American Culture, vol. 2 of Religion in American Life, edited by James W. Smith and A. Leland Jamison, 119-159. Princeton, N.J.: Princeton University Press, 1961.

McKinnon, C. "Are We Really Against Communism?" Catholic Mind
48 (May 1950), 276-283.

McMahon, Francis E. A Catholic Looks at the World. New York:
Vanguard, 1945.

McNeal, Patricia. "Catholic Conscientious Objection During
World War II." Catholic Historical Review 61 (April 1975),
222-242.

Manwaring, David R. Render Unto Caesar: The Flag-Salute
Controversy. Chicago: University of Chicago Press, 1962.

Maritain, Jacques. Man and the State. Chicago: University of
Chicago Press, 1956.

Marty, Martin E. The New Shape of American Religion. New
York: Harper and Row, 1958.

Maury, Philippe. Politics and Evangelism. Garden City, N.Y.:
Doubleday, 1959.

May, Henry F. Protestant Churches and Industrial America. New
York: Harper and Brothers, 1949.

Mead, Sidney E. "The Post-Protestant Concept and America's Two
Religions." Religion in Life 33 (Spring 1964), 191-204.

Menendez, Albert J. Church-State Bibliography. Silver Spring,
Md.: Americans United for Separation of Church and State,
1976.

Menendez, Albert J., ed. The Best of "Church & State", 1948-
1975. Silver Spring, Md.: Americans United for Separation
of Church and State, 1975.

Menes, Abraham. "Religious and Secular Trends in Jewish
Socialism." Judaism 1 (July 1952), 218-226.

Merkley, Paul. Reinhold Niebuhr: A Political Account.
Montreal: McGill-Queen's University Press, 1975.

Meyer, Carl S. "Friction Points in Church-State Relations in
the U.S." Concordia 28 (July 1957), 481-503.

Miller, William. Piety Along the Potomac: Notes on Politics
and Morals in the Fifties. Boston: Houghton Mifflin, 1964.

Miller, William. "Religion and the American Way of Life." In
Religion and the Free Society, edited by William Miller.
New York: Fund for the Republic, 1958.

Mills, C. Wright. The Power Elite. New York: Oxford
University Press, 1956.

Mitchell, David I. "American Christianity as I See it." Union Seminary Quarterly Review 11 (May 1956), 51-56.

Moehlman, Conrad Henry. The Wall of Separation Between Church and State: An Historical Study of Recent Criticism of the Religious Clause of the First Amendment. Boston: Beacon Press, 1951.

Moseley, James G. A Cultural History of Religion in America. Westport, Conn.: Greenwood, 1981.

Muehl, William. "Christian Faith and American Politics." Social Action 18 (November 1951), 1-35.

Muehl, William. Politics for Christians. New York: Association Press, 1956.

Muelder, Walter G. Foundations of the Responsible Society. New York: Abingdon, 1959.

Muelder, Walter G. Methodism and Society in the Twentieth Century. New York: Abingdon, 1961.

Murray, John Courtney. "The Church and Totalitarian Democracy." Theological Studies 13 (December 1952), 525-563.

Murray, John Courtney. "The Contemporary Orientation of Catholic Thought in Church and State in the Light of History." Theological Studies 10 (June 1949), 177-234.

Murray, John Courtney. We Hold These Truths: Catholic Reflections on the American Proposition. New York: Sheed and Ward, 1960.

National Council of Churches. Christian Faith in Action: Commemorative Volume. New York: National Council of Churches, 1951.

Neufeld, Elmer. "Christian Responsibility in the Political Situation." Mennonite Quarterly Review 32 (April 1958), 114-162.

Nichols, James Hastings. Democracy and the Churches. Philadelphia: Westminster, 1951.

Nichols, Roy Franklin. Religion and American Democracy. Baton Rouge: Louisiana State University Press, 1959.

Niebuhr, H. Richard. Christ and Culture. New York: Harper and Row, 1951.

Niebuhr, H. Richard. "The Idea of Covenant and American Democracy." Church History 23 (June 1954), 126-135.

Niebuhr, H. Richard. "The Protestant Movement and Democracy in the United States." In The Shaping of American Religion, vol. 1 of Religion in American Life, edited by James Ward Smith and A. Leland Jamison, 20-71. Princeton, N.J.: Princeton University Press, 1961.

Niebuhr, H. Richard. The Responsible Self: An Essay in Christian Moral Philosophy. New York: Harper and Row, 1963.

Niebuhr, Reinhold. The Children of Light and the Children of Darkness. New York: Scribner, 1944.

Niebuhr, Reinhold. Christianity and Power Politics. New York: Scribner, 1940.

Niebuhr, Reinhold. Christian Realism and Political Problems. New York: Scribner, 1953.

Niebuhr, Reinhold. "Do the State and Nation Belong to God or the Devil?" Being the Burge Memorial Lecture for the Year 1937. London: Student Christian Movement Press, 1937.

Niebuhr, Reinhold. The Irony of American History. New York: Scribner, 1952.

Niebuhr, Reinhold. Moral Man and Immoral Society. New York: Scribner, 1932.

Niebuhr, Reinhold. The Nature and Destiny of Man, A Christian Interpretation. Vol. 1, Human Nature; Vol. 2, Human Destiny. New York: Scribner, 1941, 1943.

Niebuhr, Reinhold. The Structure of Nations and Empires. New York: Scribner, 1959.

Niebuhr, Reinhold, and Heimert, Alan. A Nation So Conceived: Reflections on the History of America From Its Early Visions To Its Present Power. New York: Scribner, 1963.

Novak, Michael. The Rise of the Unmeltable Ethnics: Politics and Culture in the Seventies. New York: Macmillan, 1972.

Odegard, Peter H. Religion and Politics. New York: Oceana, 1960.

O'Flynn, R. "The Church and the Totalitarian State." Catholic Mind 38 (June 1940), 235-240.

O'Neill, James Milton. Catholics in Controversy. New York: McMullen Books, 1954.

Osmer, Harold H. U.S. Religious Journalism and the Korean War. Lanham, Md.: University Press of America, 1980.

Oxnam, G. Bromley. I Protest. New York: Harper and Brothers, 1954.

Pfeffer, Leo. Church, State, and Freedom. Boston: Beacon Press, 1953.

Pfeffer, Leo. Creeds in Competition: A Creative Force in American Culture. New York: Harper and Brothers, 1958.

Pike, James Albert. A Roman Catholic in the White House. Garden City, N.Y.: Doubleday, 1960.

Poling, Paul N., ed. God and the Nations. Garden City, N.Y.: Doubleday, 1950.

Powell, Theodore. The School Bus Law: A Case Study in Education, Religion and Politics. Middletown, Conn.: Wesleyan University Press, 1960.

Rasmussen, Albert T. "The Church and the Climate of Freedom." Social Action 23 (March 1957), 6-13.

Rausch, David A. "Our Hope: An American Fundamentalist Journal and the Holocaust, 1937-1945." Fides et Historia 12 (Spring 1980), 89-103.

Real, Michael R. "Trends in Structure and Policy in the American Catholic Press." Journalism Quarterly 52, no. 2 (1975), 265-271.

Redekop, John Harold. The American Far Right: A Case Study of Billy James Hargis and Christian Crusade. Grand Rapids: Eerdmans, 1968.

Regan, Richard J. American Pluralism and the Catholic Conscience. New York: Macmillan, 1963.

Reichley, A. James. Religion in American Public Life. Washington, D.C.: Brookings Institution, 1985.

Reisman, David. The Lonely Crowd. New Haven, Conn.: Yale University Press, 1950.

Reissig, Herman F. "A Christian Looks at the Atomic Age." Social Action 24 (October 1957), 3-11.

Rice, Dan. "Reinhold Niebuhr and Judaism." Journal of the American Academy of Religion 45 (March 1977), 72.

Rieff, Philip. "The Theology of Politics." Journal of Religion 32 (April 1952), 119-126.

Ringer, Benjamin B., and Glock, Charles Y. "The Political Role of the Church as Defined by its Parishioners." Public Opinion Quarterly 18 (Winter 1954-55), 337-347.

Robertson, D. B.   Reinhold Niebuhr's Works, A Bibliography.
Lanham, Md.: University Press of America, 1983.

Roelker, E. G.   "Citizen of the State, and the Faithful of the
Church." Ecclesiastical Review 107 (November 1949), 337-
352.

Rosenburg, Bernard, and White, David Manning, eds. Mass
Culture: The Popular Arts in America. Glencoe, Ill.: Free
Press, 1957.

Roy, Ralph Lord. Apostles of Discord: A Study of Organized
Bigotry and Disruption on the Fringes of Protestantism.
Boston: Beacon Press, 1953.

Roy, Ralph Lord. Communism and the Churches. New York:
Harcourt, Brace and World, 1960.

Roy, Ralph Lord. "Recent Attacks on Protestant Leaders."
Union Seminary Quarterly Review 8 (November 1952), 31-38.

Rudd, Myron S. "Toward an Understanding of the Landmark
Federal Decisions Affecting Relations between Church and
State." University of Cincinnati Law Review 36 (Summer
1967), 413-432.

Ruff, G. Elson. The Dilemma of Church and State.
Philadelphia: Muhlenberg Press, 1954.

Ryan, John A., and Bolan, F. J. Catholic Principles of
Politics. New York: Macmillan, 1940.

Ryan, John A.; Kingdon, Frank; and Goldstein, Sidney. The
Relation of Religion to Communism, Fascism and Democracy.
New York: American Sociological Society, 1938.

Sanders, Thomas Griffin. Protestant Concepts of Church and
State: Historical Backgrounds and Approaches for the Future.
New York: Holt, Rinehart and Winston, 1964.

Sanders, Thomas Griffin. "Protestantism, Catholicism and
POAU." Christianity and Crisis, 16 September 1957, 115-118.

Schapsmeier, Edward C., and Schapsmeier, Frederick H.
"Religion and Reform: A Case Study of Henry A. Wallace and
Ezra Taft Benson." Journal of Church and State 21 (Fall
1979), 525-535.

Seldes, George. The Catholic Crisis. New York: J. Messner,
1939.

Sharot, Stephen. "The Three-Generations Thesis and the
American Jews." British Journal of Sociology 24 (June
1973), 151-164.

Sharper, Philip. American Catholics: A Protestant-Jewish View. New York: Sheed and Ward, 1959.

Shea, G. W. "Catholic Orientations on Church and State." American Ecclesiastical Review 125 (December 1951), 405-416.

Shields, Currin. Democracy and Catholicism in America. New York: McGraw-Hill, 1958.

Shoemaker, Samuel Moor. Freedom and Faith. New York: Revell, 1949.

Singer, David G. "One Nation Completely Under God: The American Jewish Congress and the Catholic Church in the United States, 1945-1977." Journal of Church and State 26 (Fall 1984), 473-490.

Sklare, Marshall. Conservative Judaism--An American Religious Movement. Glencoe, Ill.: Free Press, 1955.

Smith, David H. The Achievement of John C. Bennett. New York: Herder and Herder, 1970.

Smith, James Ward, and Jamison, A. Leland, eds. Religious Perspectives in American Culture. Vol. 2 of Religion in American Life. Princeton, N.J.: Princeton University Press, 1961.

Smith, James Ward, and Jamison, A. Leland, eds. The Shaping of American Religion. Vol. 1 of Religion in American Life. Princeton, N.J.: Princeton University Press, 1961.

Smylie, James H. "Mackay and McCarthyism, 1953-1954." Journal of Church and State 6 (Fall 1964), 352-365.

Snape, Henry. "America and the Future of Christianity." Modern Churchman 46 (September 1956), 146-159.

Sorauf, Frank J. "Zorach v. Clauson: The Impact of a Supreme Court Decision." American Political Science Review 53 (September 1959), 777-791.

Spellman, Francis J. "Archbishop Declares His Principles: U.S. Diplomatic Relations With the Vatican." Catholic World 151 (April 1940), 93-96.

"Statement on Church and State." Christianity and Crisis, 5 July 1948, 89-90.

Stokes, Anson Phelps. Church and State in the United States. 3 vols. New York: Harper and Brothers, 1950.

Stone, Ronald H. Reinhold Niebuhr, Prophet to Politicians. Nashville: Abingdon, 1971.

Stumpf, Samuel Enoch. _A Democratic Manifesto: The Impact of Dynamic Christianity Upon Public Life and Government_. Nashville: Vanderbilt University Press, 1954.

Temple, William. _Christianity and Social Order_. London: Penguin Books, 1942.

Temple, William. _Citizen and Churchman_. London: Eyre & Spottiswoode, 1941.

Thomas, George F. "Political Realism and Christian Faith." _Theology Today_ 16 (July 1959), 188-202.

Thompson, Kenneth W. _Christian Ethics and the Dilemmas of Foreign Policy_. Durham, N.C.: Duke University Press, 1959.

Tillich, Paul. _The Protestant Era_. Chicago: University of Chicago Press, 1948.

Tillich, Paul. _The Theology of Culture_. New York: Oxford University Press, 1959.

Toulouse, Mark G. _The Transformation of John Foster Dulles: From Prophet of Realism to Priest of Nationalism_. Macon, Ga.: Mercer University Press, 1985.

Underwood, Kenneth. _Protestant and Catholic_. Boston: Beacon Press, 1957.

Universal Christian Conference on Life and Work, Second Oxford Conference. 1937. Reprint. Philadelphia: Fortress, 1966.

"Unwelcome Bedfellows Anywhere." _America_, 11 August 1945, 365-366.

Van Allen, Rodger. _The Commonweal and American Catholicism: The Magazine, the Movement and the Meaning_. Philadelphia: Fortress, 1974.

Van Dusen, Henry P. "World Church and World Order: Limitations and Possibilities." _Christianity and Crisis_, 4 April 1949, 33-34.

Van Dusen, Henry P., ed. _The Spiritual Legacy of John Foster Dulles: Selections from His Articles and Addresses_. Philadelphia: Westminster, 1960.

Van Hoogstrate, Dorothy Jane. _American Foreign Policy; Realists and Idealists: A Catholic Interpretation_. St. Louis: B. Herder, 1960.

Varg, Paul A. _Missionaries, Chinese, and Diplomats: The American Protestant Missionary Movement in China, 1890-1952_. Princeton, N.J.: Princeton University Press, 1958.

Venzke, Rodger R. <u>Confidence in Battle, Inspiration in Peace.</u>
<u>The United States Army Chaplaincy, vol. 5, 1945-1975</u>.
Washington, D.C.: Office of the Chief of Chaplains,
Department of the Army, 1977.

Visser 't Hooft, W. A. <u>The Kingship of Christ: An</u>
<u>Interpretation of Recent European Theology</u>. New York:
Harper and Brothers, 1948.

Visser 't Hooft, W. A., and Oldham, J. H. <u>The Church and its</u>
<u>Function in Society</u>. London: Allen, 1938.

Voorhis, Horace Jeremiah. <u>The Christian in Politics</u>. New
York: Association Press, 1951.

Wallfisch, M. Charles. "William O. Douglas and Religious
Liberty." <u>Journal of Presbyterian History</u> 58 (Fall 1980),
193-209.

Walker, Brooks R. <u>The Christian Fright Peddlers</u>. Garden City,
N.Y.: Doubleday, 1964.

Watson, Melvin. "The Church and Political Action." <u>Journal of</u>
<u>Religious Thought</u> 8, no. 2 (1951), 114-124.

Weigel, Gustave. "The Church and the Democratic State."
<u>Thought</u> 27 (Summer 1952), 165-184.

Wentz, Frederick K. "American Catholic Periodicals React to
Nazism." <u>Church History</u> 31 (December 1962), 400-420.

Wentz, Frederick K. "American Protestant Journals and the Nazi
Religious Assault." <u>Church History</u> 23 (December 1954), 321-
338.

Whitfield, Stephen J. "The Imagination of Disaster: The
Response of American Jewish Intellectuals to
Totalitarianism." <u>Jewish Social Studies</u> 42 (Winter 1980),
1-20.

Whyte, William H. <u>The Organization Man</u>. New York: Simon and
Schuster, 1956.

Wilson, John F. <u>Public Religion in American Culture</u>.
Philadelphia: Temple University Press, 1979.

Winter, Gibson. <u>The Suburban Captivity of the Churches: An</u>
<u>Analysis of Protestant Responsibility in the Expanding</u>
<u>Metropolis</u>. Garden City, N.Y.: Doubleday, 1961.

Wittner, Lawrence S. <u>Rebels Against War: The American Peace</u>
<u>Movement, 1941-1960</u>. New York: Columbia University Press,
1969.

Wolf, Donald Joseph. <u>Toward Consensus; Catholic-Protestant Interpretations of Church and State</u>. Garden City, N.Y.: Doubleday, Anchor Books, 1968.

Wolfe, James S. "The Religious Issue Revisited: Presbyterian Responses to Kennedy's Presidential Campaign." <u>Journal of Presbyterian History</u> 57 (Spring 1979), 1-18.

Wood, James E., Jr.; Thomson, E. Bruce; and Miller, Robert T. <u>Church and State in Scripture, History and Constitutional Law</u>. Waco, Tex.: Baylor University Press, 1958.

Wright, John Joseph. <u>National Patriotism in Papal Teaching</u>. Westminster, Md.: Newman Bookshop, 1943.

Yinger, J. Milton. <u>Religion and the Struggle for Power</u>. Durham, N.C.: Duke University Press, 1946.

Young, Michael. "Facing a Test of Faith: Jewish Pacifists During the Second World War." <u>Peace and Change</u> 3 (Summer/Fall 1975), 34-40.

8

Religion and the Nation: 1960 to the Present

David Harrington Watt

INTRODUCTION

The first edition of Richard E. Morgan's _The Politics of Religious Conflict_, published in 1968, argued that the underlying sources of church-state conflict in the United States were melting away, and predicted that church-state relations would likely prove less troublesome in future years than they had in the recent past. The second edition, which appeared in 1980, admitted with admirable candor that the prediction made in the first edition had proved premature. Church-state issues were still thorny: it now seemed likely that they would continue to be bothersome throughout the foreseeable future. The views Morgan expressed in 1968 and in 1980—and the intervening change of heart—represent broader shifts of informed opinion. In the early 1960s, few students of American society believed that church-state issues were particularly problematic; many assumed that in the future they would become less so. But most observers now agree that church-state issues have become, if anything, more discomforting. Indeed there is a sense in which this bibliographic volume—and the larger project of which it is a part—are products of that palpable thorniness.

We are not yet in a position to explain the shift with any great confidence. But already a number of works have appeared, treating a range of diverse topics, which shed light on the transformation. There are, first of all, a number of impressive scholarly works which can help us map the general contours of American religion between 1960 and 1985. There is also a growing body of scholarly work upon the relationship between religion and politics. And, finally, there is an increasingly sophisticated literature focusing upon the classic issues of church-state relations. As the pages that follow will indicate, these various studies suggest several plausible explanations of the continuing thorniness of church-state issues. It would be extremely unfortunate if these explanations of church-state tensions were allowed to harden into an orthodoxy or if they were judged to be so compelling that others were not sought out. They provide, however, a series of hypotheses to be tested: an agenda, as it were, for future research.

THE CHANGING SHAPE OF RELIGION IN AMERICA

Many of the best works treating the recent history of religion in America focus upon a particular group, rather than upon the general contours of American religion. Evangelical Protestants, Jews, mainline Protestants, the so-called "new religious movements," and Roman Catholics have all been studied with some care.

The best introductions to contemporary evangelicalism are *Evangelicalism and Modern America*, edited by George Marsden, and two books by James Davison Hunter—*American Evangelicalism* and *Evangelicalism: The Coming Generation*. R. Stephen Warner's "Theoretical Barriers" is an important, but neglected, discussion of the obstacles confronting scholars who seek to understand conservative Protestantism.

The selective and unannotated bibliography in Steven M. Cohen's *American Modernity and Jewish Identity* provides a concise guide to the remarkably sophisticated literature on the recent history of Judaism in America; the essays in *Understanding American Jewry*, edited by Marshall Sklare, discuss that literature in more detail. Samuel C. Heilman's "The Sociology of American Jewry" is a particularly useful introduction to the field. It is perceptive, intelligent, and—unlike most bibliographic essays—witty.

For a helpful overview of developments within the Jewish community in the 1960s and 1970s, see Chaim I. Waxman's *America's Jews in Transition*. The prominent role that the Orthodox community has played within American Judaism in recent years is discussed in Charles S. Liebman's "Orthodox Judaism Today," Samuel C. Heilman's "Constructing Orthodoxy," and "Varieties of Identity Transformation" by David Glanz and Michael I. Harrison. William Shaffir's exemplary *Life in a Religious Community* focuses upon a group of Lubavitcher Hassidim in Montreal, but many of his observations would apply to groups in the United States as well. "The Lubavitcher Movement" by Douglas Mitchell and Leonard Plotnicov examines Hassidic groups in Pittsburgh. Marshall Sklare's *Conservative Judaism* is a standard survey of that topic. Marc Lee Raphael's "History, Ideology, and Institutions" includes a concise survey of some of the recent developments in the Reform wing of Judaism.

The literature on mainline Protestantism is not as rich as that treating American Judaism. *Liberal Protestantism*—a useful anthology edited by

Robert S. Michaelsen and Wade Clark Roof—is probably the best place to begin. Roof's *Community and Commitment* (which focuses upon North Carolina Episcopalians), Dean R. Hoge's *Division in the Protestant House,* and Leonard I. Sweet's essay on "The 1960s" are also useful.

"New religious movements" is a convenient, if imprecise, term scholars use to describe groups ranging from the Hare Krishna movement to the Unification Church and from Scientology to the Children of God. Such movements have, of course, received a great deal of scholarly and journalistic attention. Particularly useful explorations include Eileen Barker's brief, but analytical, "New Religious Movements"; Robert J. Wuthnow's *The Consciousness Reformation; The New Religious Consciousness* edited by Charles Y. Glock and Robert N. Bellah; and the encyclopedic *Religious Movements in Contemporary America* edited by Irving I. Zaretsky and Mark P. Leone. "The Sociology of Contemporary Religious Movements" by Thomas Robbins and Dick Anthony is a brief, helpful bibliographic essay. *New Religious Movements* compiled by Diane Choquette provides a more comprehensive guide to the literature.

There are several useful explorations of how the Roman Catholic church has changed in the last twenty-five years. Philip Gleason's influential "Catholicism and Cultural Change" is a balanced and stimulating overview of the American Roman Catholic community in the 1960s. Jay P. Dolan's "A New Catholicism" and James Hennesey's "A Revolutionary Moment" both analyze recent developments within the context of the entire sweep of American Catholic history. Andrew M. Greeley's *The American Catholic* is another extremely valuable work. Greeley's "Sociology of American Catholics" is a lively, somewhat polemical, bibliographic essay. George A. Kelly's *The Battle for the Catholic Church* chronicles developments within American Catholicism since Vatican II, evaluating those developments from a conservative point of view. *Bare Ruined Choirs*—Garry Wills's account of Roman Catholicism in the 1950s and 1960s—is harsh in some of its judgments and idiosyncratic in some of its interpretations. It is nevertheless an important and provocative book.

Researchers trying to map the general contours of American religion in recent years might well begin by reading Sydney E. Ahlstrom's beautifully crafted, somewhat impressionistic, surveys, "The Radical Turn" and "The Traumatic Years," Daniel Bell's now slightly dated "Religion in the Sixties," Benton Johnson's provocative "A Sociological Perspective," and *Religion in America: 1950 to the Present* by Jackson W. Carroll and others. Two recent anthologies should also prove helpful. *The Sacred in a Secular Age,* edited by Phillip E. Hammond, draws together the insights of a number of sociologists of religion; most of the essays in that volume focus upon the contemporary

American scene. *Religion and America* edited by Mary Douglas and Steven M. Tipton draws its contributors from a broader range of disciplines but examines many of the same issues. The *Atlas of Religious Change in America* by Peter Halvorson and William M. Newman, and *Religion in America*, a volume published each year by the Gallup Opinion Index, both make available significant statistical data.

Researchers will also no doubt want to draw upon the religious press. They will find six indexes of great help: *The Index to Jewish Periodicals*, *The Catholic Periodical Index*, *The Catholic Periodical and Literature Index*, *Index to Religious Periodical Literature*, *Religion Index One: Periodicals*, and *The Christian Periodical Index*.

Religious Vitality and Change

Several themes of particular interest to students of church-state issues emerge from the literature. The first is the obvious and striking vitality displayed by religious traditions in the last quarter century. That vitality has been an obvious precondition for the thorniness of recent church-state issues: cultures in which religion plays only a very minor role are not likely to be racked by controversies over the proper relationship between religious communities and governmental structures. Indeed the assumption—so common in scholarly circles a quarter of a century ago—that American society was becoming relentlessly more secular was one of the reasons it was widely thought that church-state issues were becoming less problematic.

To be sure, the vitality of religion in contemporary America may be exaggerated and many scholars have stressed, instead, signs of the possible attenuation of religious zeal. Arthur Hertzberg's "Triumph of the Jews" finds, for instance, few signs of genuine religious zeal in the American Jewish community. Instead he highlights a spirit of social activism—lobbying efforts on behalf of the state of Israel and of Soviet Jewry, for example—which he argues has come to serve as a sort of substitute for religious faith. Herbert J. Gans's highly interesting "Symbolic Ethnicity" presents a rather different argument and its focus is not exclusively upon Jews. Its analysis is, however, congruent with Hertzberg's argument. The insights of both could plausibly be applied to other expressions of religion. Some observers would argue, for instance, that there is a sense in which the social activism of religious groups in the 1960s and the 1970s and the emergence of the new Christian right are both signs not of religious vitality, but rather of an increasingly secular outlook even among ostensibly religious organizations. Of course, the assumption that religious and worldly interests always stand in simple opposition to each other is suspect. In any case it is clear that among some American religious bodies—the Roman Catholic church and the mainline Protestant denominations, for example—there were some clear statistical indications of stagnation and even decline. Between 1965 and 1975, the United Church of Christ, and the United Methodist, the United Presbyterian, USA, and the Episcopal denominations all lost more than 10 percent of their members.[1]

Yet religious traditions have also displayed many signs of life in recent years. There was surely marked vitality as well as decline among Roman Catholics (see *The Renewal of American Catholicism* by David J. O'Brien). And some recent works such as "Past Imperfect" by William R. Hutchison and *All Faithful People* by Theodore Caplow and others argue that the extent of decline among mainline churches may have been exaggerated. Certainly there were many signs of religious vitality in American culture as a whole— and vitality in places where many observers were most surprised to find it: in the new religious movements, in Orthodox Judaism, and among conservative Protestants. As Peter L. Berger has recently noted, social observers now seem to be talking less and less about "the crisis of religion" and increasingly about "the crisis of secularity."[2]

Cultural Pluralism and Social Conflict

"Intergroup Relations and Tensions in the United States" by Lucy S. Dawidowicz, and Murray Friedman's "Intergroup Relations" are illustrative of a series of essays that have appeared annually in the *American Jewish Yearbook*. The essays constitute a remarkable chronicle of the shifting patterns of cultural, ethnic, and religious tensions in the United States. Reading through these essays, or through Albert Menendez's *Religious Conflict in America*, one is struck by how little, if at all, those tensions have diminished between 1960 and the present. Such strains were one of the reasons that church-state relations have been so complicated and difficult in our era.

To be sure, outright and open hostility to Jews seems to have moved to the margins of American culture and there seems to have been a marked decline in more subtle forms of anti-Semitism as well. Outright and open hostility towards, as well as latent prejudice against, Roman Catholics seems to have declined too. The causes of the declining Protestant suspicion of Roman Catholics are varied and complex. Many commentators have focused upon the role two Roman Catholic leaders played in bringing about the change. The first, of course, was John F. Kennedy: his campaign for the presidency brought Protestant fears concerning Catholic political power to a boiling point, but the skill with which Kennedy avoided even the appearance of partiality to his own church eventually quieted those fears. (For a useful discussion of this subject, see Lawrence Fuchs's *John F. Kennedy and American Catholicism*.) The other leader was John Courtney Murray, the Jesuit theologian who developed a sophisticated, original, and highly influential Roman Catholic approach to church-state relations. Murray's views are set out in *We Hold These Truths*. His thought is analyzed in studies by Donald E. Pelotte and Thomas T. Love. The structural roots of the declining fear of Roman Catholics—which surely include the increasing "Americanization" of Roman Catholics in the United States—have not yet been fully analyzed. Gleason's "Catholicism and Cultural Change" and Dolan's "A New Catholicism," both cited above, are probably the best places to begin a consideration of that assimilation.

Few observers would argue, however, that hostility to Jews and Roman Catholics has entirely disappeared from American society. *Anti-Semitism* by Harold E. Quinley and Charles Y. Glock summarizes the findings of a series of investigations sponsored by the Anti-Defamation League, stressing the continuing existence of anti-Semitic sentiment. *Vatican Imperialism* by Auro Manhattan illustrates the continuing suspicion of Roman Catholics in some quarters of American culture. Thus these older forms of religious conflict have survived, in a somewhat attenuated form, to the present day and continue to complicate church-state relations.

Moreover, and for our purposes perhaps more importantly, a newer set of religious antipathies and suspicions has emerged in recent decades. The most dramatic of these conflicts—those connected with the luxuriance of the new religious movements—and those conflicts' effects upon church-state issues have been examined with some care. They are analyzed in "Cults, Brainwashing, and Counter-Subversion" by Thomas Robbins and Dick Anthony; a collection of essays edited by David G. Bromley and James T. Richardson titled *The Brainwashing/Deprogramming Debate;* and three separate works by Anson D. Shupe and David G. Bromley—*Strange Gods*, "Social Responses to Cults," and *The New Religious Vigilantes*. The more strictly legal and constitutional issues raised by the new religious movements are examined in Leo Pfeffer's "The Legitimation of Marginal Religions in the United States," John Richard Burkholder's " 'The Law Knows No Heresy,' " William C. Shepherd's *To Secure the Blessings of Liberty*, and *Cults, Culture and the Law*, edited by Thomas Robbins and others.

Scholars have, by contrast, only just begun to explore the other varieties of religious conflict characteristic of recent American culture. That is unfortunate, for religious tensions have radiated in many different directions in our era; a narrow focus upon the tensions created by the new religious movements necessarily produces a skewed interpretation of what has been going on. In recent years, liberal Roman Catholics and their conservative coreligionists, mainline Protestants and evangelicals, fervent pietists and those denominated "secular humanists" have clashed repeatedly.

These tensions have been accompanied—as such tensions most often are—by widespread fears that religious traditions other than one's own were exercising an undue influence upon the American government. Madalyn Murray O'Hair's assessment of the churches' influence upon the state (presented in *Freedom Under Siege*) was an extreme expression of a not uncommon perception. As she read the situation, the American state was under the sway of organized religion: religious bodies used the state to oppress women, enforce censorship, promote ignorance, indoctrinate children, and regulate the sexual lives of the American people. Other Americans, of course, feared that the state was promoting "secular humanism." William A. Stanmeyer argued in *Clear and Present Danger* that "whole segments of our governing apparatus—the federal judiciary, educational administrators, the media elite and much of the government bureaucracy in charge of tax collection and educational regulation—are by and large hostile to Judeo-Christian principles and values" (p. 199). Of such conflicting perceptions are church-state conflicts made.

American Civil Religion

Throughout much of the nation's history conflicts between Americans with varying religious beliefs and practices were counterbalanced by a widely shared set of cultural assumptions, which came to be referred to in the 1960s as American civil religion. The precise meaning of this term was, for a decade or so, a subject of fierce debate: indeed one of the weaknesses of the concept of civil religion is that, unless it is used with extreme care, it becomes either too slippery or too brittle to be of much use. But the term points to an important reality: Americans have often interpreted events in their nation's history as part of a larger, transcendent scheme. These interpretations served both to legitimate the American nation-state and to offer a set of ideals against which American realities could be judged. They thereby produced a common faith that counterbalanced the differences between the nation's various religious communities.

The important point for our purposes is that in recent years American civil religion apparently began to lose its power to unite the American people. In some quarters of American culture allegiance to civil religion seems to have declined precipitously—killed off, it is variously said, by Vietnam, or Watergate, or by more fundamental realignments of the society. Yet it would be a mistake to assume—as some commentators have suggested—that American civil religion is *everywhere* in decline. In some quarters its themes and symbols are still evoked with great force and remarkable regularity: the speeches of President Reagan and those of the leaders of the new religious right both draw heavily on the rhetorical tradition of civil religion. The result of this complex, bifurcated pattern has been that civil religion, once such an effective damper upon interreligious conflict, itself seems to have become a divisive issue.

The classic explication of civil religion is, of course, Robert N. Bellah's 1967 essay, "Civil Religion in America." *Varieties of Civil Religion* edited by Bellah and Phillip E. Hammond, *The Religion of the Republic* edited by Elwyn A. Smith, and *American Civil Religion* edited by Russell E. Richey and Donald G. Jones, are three extraordinarily fine collections of essays which together contain much, even most, of the best work on the subject. There are two fine overviews of the scholarly literature on civil religion: Phillip E. Hammond's elegant essay, "The Sociology of American Civil Religion," neatly summarizes the development of the debate on the subject up to the middle 1970s; *American Civil Religion* by Gail Gehrig, while not as crisp, is more comprehensive. Hammond's essay and Gehrig's monograph both contain helpful discussions of the complexities involved in defining American civil religion; John A. Coleman's "Civil Religion" is a particularly influential approach to that question. John F. Wilson's *Public Religion in American Culture* and Richard K. Fenn's *Toward a Theory of Secularization* both ask, in effect, if the very concept of civil religion as it is normally used is not misleading—obscuring nearly as much as it illuminates.

Three books that do not focus on civil religion per se, but which shed considerable light on the corrosives it has faced in our era, are: Samuel Huntington's *American Politics*, Alasdair MacIntyre's much-discussed *After Virtue*, and *Habits of the Heart* by Robert N. Bellah and others. Works that explicitly discuss the apparent enfeeblement of American civil religion in recent years include Michael Novak's *Choosing Our King;* Conrad Cherry's "American Sacred Ceremonies," and Robert N. Bellah's *Broken Covenant.* "Spiritual Innovation and the Crisis of American Civil Religion" by Dick Anthony and Thomas Robbins is a particularly sophisticated essay, published in the early 1980s, which interprets the decline of civil religion as part of a "legitimation problem" of tremendous proportions faced by American institutions in general and the American state in particular. The observations of Anthony and Robbins may be usefully compared to the arguments Jürgen Habermas advanced in *Legitimation Crisis.*

THE RELATIONSHIP BETWEEN RELIGION AND POLITICS

Two of the most helpful overviews of recent developments within American political life are Walter Dean Burnham's *The Current Crisis in Ameri-*

can Politics and Samuel Huntington's *American Politics*. Robert Booth Fowler's *Religion and Politics* is the best general, book-length introduction to the interaction of religion and politics in the last quarter century; for a more concise introduction to the topic, see Benton Johnson's "Religion and Politics."

In the early 1960s many observers found it hard to believe, Johnson's essay notes, that religion exerted any real "independent influence upon public affairs." Even those observers who believed that religion still shaped American politics were inclined to believe that its influence was, essentially, residual: it would surely steadily diminish as the decades wore on. The role religious issues had played in the 1960 presidential contest seemed, to many observers, to be no more than a rule-proving exception.

That interpretation of American public life seems less plausible now than it did earlier. This is in part because a number of recent scholarly investigations have suggested a clear correlation between voting behavior and religious affiliation. It seems less plausible, too, because of the highly visible—and often extremely controversial—role religious leaders and religious bodies have played in American political life since 1960. The jailing of Martin Luther King, Jr. in Birmingham, Alabama, Daniel and Philip Berrigan's pouring blood on draft files, Jerry Falwell's referring, in a benediction at the 1984 Republican national convention, to Ronald Reagan and George Bush as "God's instruments in rebuilding America"—such phenomena vividly demonstrated the continuing relationship between religion and our national political life.[3] And, of course, they provoked heated debate upon the proper relation of church and state.

Political values

We now possess a rich literature on the correlations between religious affiliation and political values.[4] "Theology and Party Preference Among Protestant Clergymen" and "Theology and the Position of Pastors on Public Issues"—both by Benton Johnson—are two pioneering efforts to make such correlations. The correlations are also described in Michael Parenti's rather sweeping "Political Values and Religious Cultures." *Religion and the Presidential Election* by Paul Lopatto explores the interplay between religious affiliation and voting behavior in the 1960, 1980, and intervening elections. Joan Fee's "Political Continuity and Change," Andrew M. Greeley's "How Conservative Are American Catholics?" and *The American Catholic* all use survey data to evaluate the political attitudes of American Catholics. *Catholics and American Politics* by Mary T. Hanna, draws upon survey data as well, and also includes information garnered from interviews with Catholic politicians and church leaders. Interestingly enough, Hanna, Greeley, and Fee all argue that Roman Catholic voters have not moved as far to the right of the political spectrum as is commonly believed. Voting patterns within America's Jewish community are examined in William Heitzmann's *American Jewish Voting Behavior*. For discussions of the apparent shift of American Jews away from the left of the political spectrum see "Are American Jews Turning to the Right?" by Bernard Rosenberg and Irving Howe, and "Realignment of the Jewish Vote?" by Alan M. Fisher.

None of these studies forces us to conclude that religious faith and practice are the most important factor in deciding how Americans vote. Indeed, many specialists would assert that the correlations between religious affiliation and voting behavior in our era are weaker than in most others in American history. The studies do suggest however a limited, but quite real, religious factor in elections.

Social Protest in the 1960s and 1970s

There is no dearth of primary sources that shed light on religion and social protest in the 1960s and 1970s. But, perhaps in part because so much attention has been focused lately on the emergence of the new Christian right, the secondary literature on the religious social activists of the 1960s and 1970s is surprisingly thin. Thus we are not yet in a position to make a thorough analysis of just how crucial a role religious leaders and groups played in shaping either the civil rights or the antiwar movements. We are not yet able to say why—in sharp contrast to the 1940s and 1950s—so many clerics felt compelled to denounce the status quo with such vehemence. Nor are we yet able to assess all the effects that religious opposition to segregation and to America's involvement in Vietnam had upon American religion in particular or American culture in general. These are crucial matters: it would be unfortunate if investigators' enthusiasm for looking at the links between religion and conservative politics precluded new efforts to comprehend them.

Two extremely useful collections make available the official pronouncements of American Roman Catholic officials on the nation's social and economic order: *Renewing the Earth*, edited by David J. O'Brien and Thomas A. Shannon (which includes, as well, a helpful introduction and documents written by non-Americans) and a mammoth volume titled *Quest for Justice* edited by J. Briar Benestad and Francis J. Butler. There are no comparable collections for the central Protestant denominations in these years, but the public statements of the leading Protestant organizations and of the Protestant social activists are both readily available: see, for instance, *Conscience and Action*, edited by Carl F. Reuss, and *What the Religious Revolutionaries Are Saying*, edited by Elwyn A. Smith.

The roots of the social-activist stances of the National Council of Churches in the 1960s and 1970s are analyzed in Henry J. Pratt's *The Liberalization of American Protestantism*. Jeffrey K. Hadden's influential *The Gathering Storm in the Churches* uses survey data to explore Protestant clergymen's attitudes toward social activism. Most other interpretations of clerical involvement in social protest have a marked partisan orientation and must, therefore, be used with care. *Divine Disobedience* by Francine du Plessix Gray is, for instance, a collection of gracefully written essays that describes the views and actions of radical Catholics with great sympathy. For other sympathetic accounts of the activities of Roman Catholic leftists see David J. O'Brien's *The Renewal of American Catholicism*, and *With Clumsy Grace* by Charles A. Meconis. James Hitchcock's *The Decline and Fall of Radical Catholicism* and Michael Novak's "Blue-Bleak Embers" present conservative critiques of the Catholic left. Harvey Cox's "The 'New Breed'" offers a highly enthusiastic description of the views and activities of Protestant activist clergymen. William R. Garrett's "Politicized Clergy" is an informal, cynical, and somewhat hostile set of reflections upon the same group.

The Movement for Racial Justice

There are four bibliographies to which researchers may turn as they make their way into the literature on the civil rights movement: *The Negro in America*, compiled by Elizabeth W. Miller and Mary L. Fisher; *Blacks in America*, by James M. McPherson and others; *Afro-American History*, by Dwight L. Small; and *The Howard University Bibliography*, by Ethel L. Williams and Clifton F. Brown. The Miller and Fisher bibliography and the McPherson volume contain only brief descriptions of the cited works. The bibliography Small edited offers a full summary of each listed work. Nearly all of its references are to periodical literature; its coverage of scholarly journals is particularly strong. The Williams and Brown bibliography is the most recent and it focuses on religious matters; it therefore includes a wealth of relevant works not included in the other three. It is annotated very sparsely, but does direct the researcher to those libraries from which cited works may be obtained.

Two classic discussions of white Protestants' response to the civil rights movement are "Clergy Involvement in Civil Rights" and *The Gathering Storm* both by Jeffrey K. Hadden. They emphasize white clerics' devotion to the movement and white laypersons' misgivings concerning it. Henry Clark's "The National Council of Churches' Commission" explores the role that churchmen played in organizing the 1963 March on Washington and in securing the passage of the Civil Rights Act of 1964. The response of white Christians to the rise of black nationalism is discussed, briefly, in Hadden's essay; an array of primary sources that shed light on that topic are listed in *The Howard University Bibliography*, by Williams and Brown, cited above.

Those not already familiar with them will surely want to read *Why We Can't Wait* by Martin Luther King, Jr., the *Autobiography of Malcolm X* (Malcolm Little), and James Forman's *The Making of Black Revolutionaries*. Researchers interested in the views of black religious leaders in the late sixties and early seventies will want to read *The Black Messiah* and *Black Christian Nationalism*, both by Albert B. Cleage, Jr., and two books by James H. Cone: *Black Theology and Black Power* and *A Black Theology of Liberation*. Several distinguished biographies shed light upon the civil rights movement. Stephen B. Oates's recent and comprehensive *Let the Trumpet Sound* and David L. Lewis's balanced and insightful *King* provide useful perspectives on Martin Luther King's life, and on the civil rights movement in general. Peter Goldman's carefully researched, thoughtfully composed *The Death and Life of Malcolm X* focuses on the final, tumultuous years of Malcolm X's life. Henry C. Young's *Major Black Religious Leaders Since 1940* chronicles the lives and describes the thought of fourteen important figures. It is a very brief work, intended for a wide audience.

A rich and sophisticated body of sociological literature examines the relationship between religious commitment and political activism among American blacks. Gary T. Marx's pioneering "Religion: Opiate or Inspiration" and his *Protest and Prejudice* argued that religious commitment inhibited the development of black militance. Subsequent analysis suggests, however, that the linkage Marx postulated may have been overly simple. Larry L. Hunt and Janet G. Hunt's reexamination of the statistical data upon which Marx's argument rested led them to conclude that black religiosity produced activist as well as quietist outlooks. For the details of their argument see "Black Religion as *Both* Opiate and Inspiration." "Black Religion's Promethean Motif" by Hart M. Nelsen and others argues a case similar to that presented by the Hunts. *Black Church in the Sixties* by Hart M. Nelsen and Anne Kusener Nelsen explores these questions in great detail and with admirable sophistication. Gary R. Peck's "Black Radical Consciousness" provides a more concise discussion of the debate; it concludes with a useful proposal for future research.

The Antiwar Movement

Less scholarly attention has been given to clerical involvement in the antiwar movement than to the role of the clergy in the civil rights movement. James H. Smylie's "American Religious Bodies, Just War, and Vietnam" does, however, contain a very full description of the debate on the war that raged among theologians and religious leaders. Harold E. Quinley's "The Protestant Clergy and the War in Vietnam" (a work based on surveys of California ministers) notes the tremendous amount of attention clerics opposed to the war attracted and suggests that clerical sentiment was on the whole more dovish than that of the laity, but it also points toward a sizable body of ministers who supported the war effort. Richard John Neuhaus's "The War, the Churches, and Civil Religion" points toward a similar pattern.

There is a wealth of readily accessible primary material written by religious critics of the war—and by the critics of those critics. *Vietnam: Crisis of Conscience* by Robert McAfee Brown, Abraham J. Heschel, and Michael Novak was an important, widely circulated denunciation of U.S. policy in Vietnam. *American Catholics and Vietnam*, edited by Thomas E. Quigley, brought together the reflections of a number of Roman Catholics opposed to the war. Robert F. Drinan's *Vietnam and Armageddon* denounced American involvement in the war on the basis of Drinan's interpretation of the just war tradition. Philip Berrigan recorded his views in *Prison Journals of a Priest Revolutionary;* his brother Daniel presented his in *No Bars to Manhood.* Arguments for granting conscientious objector status to those opposed to particular wars, but not to all wars, are advanced in *The Conflict of Loyalties*, edited by James Finn; the case against the granting of conscientious objector status to such persons is presented in *Prophets Without Honor* by John A. Rohr. For a clerical defense of American policy in Vietnam see *A Chaplain Looks at Vietnam* by John O'Connor. For a critique of those who opposed the war see Paul Ramsey, "Vietnam." See, too, *The Just War*—a collection of essays written by Ramsey between 1961 and 1968. The footnotes in Smylie's "American Religious Bodies" (cited above) will lead the researcher to a number of other important sources.

Conservative Protestantism

Scholars and journalists have recently devoted a great deal of attention to the political views and behavior of conservative Protestants in general and to the new Christian right in particular. Much of their work has a clear polemical edge. Richard V. Pierard's *Unequal Yoke* is a critique, as well as an analysis, of conservative Protestantism's tendency to align itself with social and political conservatism. *Holy Terror* by Flo Conway and Jim Siegelman stresses the "threats" the movement poses to American politics and culture. Erling Jorstad's *Politics of Moralism* betrays little sympathy for the new religious right's goals or tactics.

Yet in spite of the strong passions the topic evokes, we now have a number of instructive works on the relations between American evangelicalism and American politics in our era. "Preachers of Paradox" by George Marsden, and Grant Wacker's "Searching for Norman Rockwell" are two especially sophisticated and balanced analyses of evangelical political attitudes. Those two articles, together with *New Christian Right* edited by Robert C. Liebman and Robert Wuthnow, and *New Christian Politics* edited by David G. Bromley and Anson D. Shupe, Jr., are the best starting points for investigating the topic. Other useful works include: Frances FitzGerald's dazzling examination of Jerry Falwell and his followers in her recent book *Cities on a Hill: Individualism and Social Ethics*, Dennis P. Hollinger's analysis of, and reflections upon, the editorials and articles published in *Christianity Today;* and "Born-Again Christians" by Kant Patel and others, which uses survey data to analyze the political views of the evangelical rank and file. Michael Linesch's "Right-Wing Religion" is weak on the religious aspects of his subject but strong on its political implications.

At present most scholars seem inclined to question the potency of the new Christian Right. Richard V. Pierard's exemplary study of relations between American presidents and Billy Graham argues, quite convincingly, that the presidents have influenced Graham's views more than he influenced theirs. *The New Religious-Political Right in America*, by Samuel S. Hill and Dennis E. Owen, argues that the movement is not likely "to alter the basic course of American public life." Anson D. Shupe and William A. Stacey's *Born Again Politics* argues that the attention journalists, scholars, and politicians have paid to the Moral Majority is grossly disproportionate to the grass roots support it enjoys. "The Christian Right" by Stephen D. Johnson and Joseph B. Tamney concludes—largely on the basis of interviews with 262 residents of a single midwestern community—that the Christian right "had no significant impact at all" on the 1980 presidential election. "The Election and the Evangelicals" by Seymour M. Lipset and Earl Raab reaches a similar conclusion.

Such readings of the actual influence of the new Christian right have much to recommend them. There is good reason to suppose, for example, that many conservative Protestants are essentially apolitical in outlook, and thus unlikely to focus much of their energy upon any sort of political crusade. (See R. Stephen Warner, "Theoretical Barriers.") Then too, there is abundant evidence of diversity of opinion among conservative Protestants upon many political questions: there are many moderate and a fair percentage of left of center voices to be heard in the evangelical chorus. Robert Booth Fowler's *A New Engagement*, makes that point quite forcefully; so does James Davison Hunter's "Religion and Political Civility." A particularly notable sign of the emergence of the liberal wing of evangelical subculture is *The Chicago Declaration* edited by Ronald J. Sider. But the *Declaration* only begins to suggest the range of moderate and liberal social thought to be found among evangelicals. Researchers might also want to consult Sherwood Eliot Wirt's *Social Conscience*, Jim Wallis's *Agenda*, and the sources listed in the bibliography of Fowler's *A New Engagement*.

Nevertheless, the current reaction against the exaggerated claims concerning the power of the new Christian right may well have gone too far. Most political scientists agree that the American political system is undergoing an important transformation. Some believe that we are in the midst of a party realignment similar to the one that occurred in the late 1920s and early 1930s. Others argue that we are witnessing instead the demise of traditional partisan politics and the emergence of a new sort of political system dominated by interest groups rather than parties. (See Everett Carll Ladd, "The Brittle Mandate.") In either case, evangelicals are likely to play an important role in shaping American political life. If we are moving from partisan to interest group politics, then the evangelical right, which has already managed to make its influence felt on several specific political issues, will most likely be one of the more important of those interest groups. If what we are seeing is a political realignment, then the evangelical right, one of the constituencies from which the Republican party of the 1980s draws most heavily, would seem to be a crucial element in one of the two partisan coalitions.

THE NATURE OF THE STATE AND THE CLASSIC ISSUES OF CHURCH-STATE RELATIONS

In recent years a number of scholars have investigated the nature of the modern state, exploring how it differs from earlier varieties of state, how it affects the lives of those it governs, and to what degree those who live under it may affect its decisions. "The Expansion of the State," a bibliographic essay by George M. Thomas and John W. Meyer, provides a useful entry point into the literature these investigations have produced. Particularly noteworthy explorations of these themes are Bob Jessop's *The Capitalist State*, Ralph Miliband's *The State*, Kenneth H. F. Dyson's *The State Tradition*, Eric Nordlinger's *On the Autonomy of the Democratic State*, and *Bringing the State Back In*, edited by Peter B. Evans and others. Thus far most researchers focusing upon American church-state issues in our era have taken little notice of these investigations. But a few works, such as Richard K. Fenn's *Liturgies and Trials* and Roland Robertson's "Considerations," which display considerable sensitivity to the issues raised by the investigations of the modern state, have now begun to appear. More such works would greatly enrich our understanding of church-state relations in our era.

Already, there are a number of impressive works exploring the form classic church-state issues have taken in recent American history. A wealth of help-ful material may be found in the articles, reviews, and notes column of the *Journal of Church and State*. Richard E. Morgan's *The Politics of Religious Conflict* concisely analyzes the structural sources of church-state tension. *Religion, State, and the Burger Court* by Leo Pfeffer—the influential advo-cate of a separationist approach to church-state questions—offers a sure-footed analysis of the Supreme Court's role in defining the relation of church and state in America. *Private Churches and Public Money* by Paul J. Weber and Dennis A. Gilbert examines the fiscal aspects of the issue, illustrating the inconsistencies of present practices and suggesting an alternative to them. Frank J. Sorauf's *The Wall of Separation* is a well-researched, carefully ar-gued, and clearly written study of church-state litigation. The body of the book focuses on the years between 1951 and 1971; an epilogue takes the story up to 1974. Its treatment of the various groups that have played a prominent role in church-state litigation in recent years—Americans United, the Ameri-can Civil Liberties Union, the American Jewish Congress, and the United States Catholic Conference, among others—is particularly valuable.

Implicit in much of the church-state literature is a theme that deserves more systematic attention: the way in which church-state questions have been complicated by the increasingly important role the American state plays in shaping American society in general and American religion in particular. The theme of expansion surfaces most frequently in connection with govern-mental attempts to regulate the activity of religious bodies. "Bureaucratic Governmental Regulation" by James Leo Garrett, Jr., examines, for instance, four specific instances of the conflicts between religious institutions and federal officials. Garrett's "Church-State Separation" argues that the Internal Revenue Service's reluctance to grant tax exemption to religious organiza-tions that attempt to influence public legislation seems to deny "the prophet-ic society-changing role of the churches"; "Government Restraint" by Wilfred Caron and others examines the same issue. Nearly all of the essays in *Gov-ernment Intervention in Religious Affairs*, edited by Dean M. Kelley, empha-size, in his words, "the increasing dominance of government and its propen-sity to press the churches back into ever smaller sanctums of time and space and subject" (p. 3).

Many of the explorations of this theme are somewhat polemical in nature and should therefore be used with care. (William Lee Miller's "Responsible Government," explicitly framed as a response to the excesses of those who stress "governmental intervention," is a useful corrective.) Those works point, however, to important realities: the state's role in shaping American society expanded dramatically in the twentieth century; that expansion played a crucial role in producing church-state tension in our era. Religious leaders and religious bodies did indeed reap huge harvests of state funding for their charitable endeavors and for their educational enterprises. They did indeed chafe under increasing governmental regulation. In our era, the state has probably been a more valuable ally—or a more dangerous adversary—than in any other era of American history. Religious leaders and religious bodies could not safely ignore it. Moreover, the American government has become more deeply enmeshed in the lives of its citizens. Consequently it has become an increasingly crucial battleground for cultural conflict: a battleground on which a number of emotionally charged issues, affecting the private as well as the public lives of the American people, have been hotly contested.

One final point. The expansion of the state suggests that we need to expand our definition of church-state relations. Throughout the most recent era of American history, religious persons and organizations were embedded in a society characterized by numerous mushrooming bureaucracies, by rising standards of education, and by increasing technological sophistication. It was a society built upon an economy that was no doubt imperfect and surely beyond the control of individual citizens, but that nevertheless produced considerable prosperity. It was also a society in which a variety of professionals—psychologists, social scientists, social workers, to name only the most obvious instances—performed tasks that the clergy had performed in earlier eras. It was, too, a less segmented society, that is, one in which the boundaries between various regions, and between racial, ethnic, and religious subcultures were increasingly permeable. Each of these features of modern American society profoundly shaped the religiosity of the American people. Each was profoundly linked to the American state. Future students of church-state relations will, surely, want to analyze these indirect, but critical, relations between church and state with great care.

NOTES

1. Jackson W. Carroll, Douglas W. Johnson, and Martin E. Marty, *Religion in America*, p. 15. Some commentaries, such as Sydney E. Ahlstrom's "Traumatic Years," suggest that the pattern of vitality and stagnation was of great importance in producing church-state tension. America, it can be argued, had a quasi-establishment in 1960. The last quarter century has seen the weakening of that quasi-establishment and the growing vitality, self-confidence, and assertiveness of "dissenting" groups. It is an interesting suggestion, which deserves systematic attention.

2. Two consistently perceptive—and occasionally brilliant—discussions of secularization are Richard K. Fenn's *Toward a Theory of Secularization* and Guy A. Swanson's "Modern Secularity."

3. Falwell's remark is quoted in James E. Wood, Jr., "Religion and Politics," p. 402.

4. We have, by contrast, only a few books that focus upon religion's influence upon the legislative process. E. Raymond Wilson's *Uphill For Peace* provides a detailed chronicle of the first registered Protestant lobbying organization—the Friends' Committee on National Legislation. James L. Adams's *The Growing Church Lobby in Washington* is a capable survey of the efforts of religious organizations to influence federal legislation. *Religion on Capitol Hill* by Peter L. Benson and Dorothy L. Williams provides a level-headed and discriminating analysis of the religious beliefs of American congresspersons and of how those beliefs affect their voting.

BIBLIOGRAPHY

Abrams, Ray H. Preachers Present Arms: The Role of the American Churches and Clergy in World Wars I and II with Some Observations on the War in Vietnam. rev. ed. Scottdale, Pa.: Herald Press, 1969.

Adams, James L. The Growing Church Lobby in Washington. Grand Rapids: Eerdmans, 1970.

Ahlstrom, Sydney E. "The Radical Turn in Theology and Ethics: Why It Occurred in the 1960's." Annals of the American Academy of Political and Social Science 387 (January 1970), 1-13.

Ahlstrom, Sydney E. "The Traumatic Years: American Religion and Culture in the '60s and '70s." Theology Today 36 (January 1980), 504-520.

Anthony, Dick, and Robbins, Thomas. "Spiritual Innovation and the Crisis of American Civil Religion." In Religion and America: Spiritual Life in a Secular Age, edited by Mary Douglas and Steven M. Tipton. Boston: Beacon Press, 1983.

Au, William A. The Cross, the Flag, and the Bomb: American Catholics Debate War and Peace, 1960-1983. Westport, Conn.: Greenwood, 1985.

Barker, Eileen. "New Religious Movements: Yet Another Great Awakening?" In The Sacred in a Secular Age, edited by Phillip E. Hammond. Berkeley: University of California Press, 1985.

Beckford, James A. "Politics and the Anti-Cult Movement." Annual Review of the Social Sciences of Religion 3 (1979), 169-190.

Bell, Daniel. "Religion in the Sixties." Social Research 38 (Autumn 1971), 447-497.

Bellah, Robert N. The Broken Covenant. New York: Seabury,
    1975.

Bellah, Robert N. "Civil Religion in America." Daedalus 96
    (Winter 1967), 1-21.

Bellah, Robert N. "Response to the Panel on Civil Religion."
    Sociological Analysis 37 (Summer 1976), 153-159.

Bellah, Robert N., and Hammond, Phillip E. Varieties of Civil
    Religion. San Francisco: Harper and Row, 1980.

Bellah, Robert N.; Madsen, Richard; Sullivan, William M.;
    Swidler, Ann; and Tipton, Steven M. Habits of the Heart:
    Individualism and Commitment in American Life. Berkeley:
    University of California Press, 1985.

Benestad, J. Briar, and Butler, Francis J., eds. Quest for
    Justice: A Compendium of Statements of the United States
    Catholic Bishops on the Political and Social Order, 1966-
    1980. Washington, D.C.: United States Catholic Conference,
    1981.

Benson, John M. "The Polls: Rebirth of Religion?" Public
    Opinion Quarterly 45 (Winter 1981), 576-585.

Benson, Peter L., and Williams, Dorothy L. Religion on Capitol
    Hill. San Francisco: Harper and Row, 1982.

Berger, Peter L. "From the Crisis of Religion to the Crisis of
    Secularity." In Religion and America: Spiritual Life in a
    Secular Age, edited by Mary Douglas and Steven M. Tipton.
    Boston: Beacon Press, 1983.

Berrigan, Daniel. No Bars to Manhood. Garden City, N.Y.:
    Doubleday, 1970.

Berrigan, Philip. Prison Journals of a Priest Revolutionary.
    New York: Holt, Rinehart and Winston, 1970.

Berson, Lenora E. The Negroes and the Jews. New York: Random
    House, 1971.

Blau, Joseph L. Judaism in America: From Curiosity to Third
    Faith. Chicago: University of Chicago Press, 1976.

Bodo, John R. "The Pastor and Social Conflict." In Religion
    and Social Conflict, edited by Robert Lee and Martin E.
    Marty. New York: Oxford University Press, 1964.

Bromley, David G., and Richardson, James T., eds. The
    Brainwashing/Deprogramming Debate. New York: E. Mellen,
    1983.

Bromley, David G., and Shupe, Anson D., Jr., eds. New
Christian Politics. Macon, Ga.: Mercer University Press,
1984.

Bromley, David G., and Shupe, Anson D., Jr., eds. Strange
Gods: The Great American Cult Scare. Boston: Beacon Press,
1981.

Brown, Robert McAfee; Heschel, Abraham J.; and Novak, Michael.
Vietnam: Crisis of Conscience. New York: Association Press,
1967.

Burkholder, John Richard. "'The Law Knows No Heresy': Marginal
Religious Movements and the Courts." In Religious Movements
in Contemporary America, edited by Irving I. Zaretsky and
Mark P. Leone. Princeton, N.J.: Princeton University Press,
1974.

Burnham, Walter Dean. The Current Crisis in American Politics.
New York: Oxford University Press, 1982.

Canavan, Francis. "The Impact of Recent Supreme Court
Decisions on Religion in the United States." Journal of
Church and State 16 (Spring 1974), 217-236.

Caplow, Theodore; Bahr, Howard M.; Chadwick, Bruce A.; Hoover,
Dwight W.; Martin, Laurence A.; Tamney, Joseph B.; and
Williamson, Margaret Holmes. All Faithful People: Change
and Continuity in Middletown's Religion. Minneapolis:
University of Minnesota Press, 1983.

Carnoy, Martin. The State and Political Theory. Princeton,
N.J.: Princeton University Press, 1984.

Caron, Wilfred; Dessingue, Deirdre; and Liekweg, John.
"Government Restraint on Political Activities of Religious
Bodies." In Government Intervention in Religious Affairs,
edited by Dean M. Kelley. New York: Pilgrim Press, 1982.

Carroll, Jackson W.; Johnson, Douglas W.; and Marty, Martin E.
Religion in America: 1950 to the Present. New York: Harper
and Row, 1979.

Cherry, Conrad. "American Sacred Ceremonies." In American
Mosaic: Social Patterns of Religion in the United States,
edited by Phillip E. Hammond and Benton Johnson. New York:
Random House, 1970.

Cherry, Conrad. "Nation, Church and Private Religion: The
Emergence of an American Pattern." Journal of Church and
State 14 (Spring 1972), 222-233.

Childs, John Brown. The Political Black Minister: A Study in
Afro-American Politics and Religion. Boston: G. K. Hall,
1980.

Choquette, Diane, comp. New Religious Movements in the United States and Canada: A Critical Assessment and Annotated Bibliography. Westport, Conn.: Greenwood, 1985.

Christenson, Larry. Social Action: Jesus Style. Minneapolis: Dimension, 1976.

Clark, Henry. "The National Council of Churches' Commission on Religion and Race: A Case Study of Religion in Social Change." In American Mosaic: Social Patterns of Religion in the United States, edited by Phillip E. Hammond and Benton Johnson. New York: Random House, 1970.

Cleage, Albert B., Jr. Black Christian Nationalism. New York: William Morrow, 1972.

Cleage, Albert B., Jr. The Black Messiah. New York: Sheed and Ward, 1968.

Coffin, William Sloane, Jr. Once to Every Man: A Memoir. New York: Atheneum, 1977.

Cohen, Steven M. American Modernity and Jewish Identity. New York: Tavistock Publications, 1983.

Coleman, John A. "Civil Religion." Sociological Analysis 31 (Summer 1970), 67-77.

Cone, James H. Black Theology and Black Power. New York: Seabury, 1969.

Cone, James H. A Black Theology of Liberation. New York: Lippincott, 1970.

Conway, Flo, and Siegelman, Jim. Holy Terror: The Fundamentalist War on America's Freedoms in Religion, Politics and Our Private Lives. Garden City, N.Y.: Doubleday, 1982.

Cox, Harvey. "The 'New Breed' in American Churches: Sources of Social Activism in American Religion." Daedalus 96 (Winter 1967), 135-150.

Cox, Harvey. The Secular City: Secularization and Urbanization in Theological Perspective. New York: Macmillan, 1965.

Dawidowicz, Lucy S. "Intergroup Relations and Tensions in the United States." In American Jewish Year Book, 1967, edited by Morris Fine and Milton Himmelfarb. New York: American Jewish Committee, 1967.

Dolan, Jay P. "A New Catholicism." Chap. 15 in The American Catholic Experience. Garden City, N.Y.: Doubleday, 1985.

Douglas, Mary, and Tipton, Steven M., eds. <u>Religion and America: Spiritual Life in a Secular Age</u>. Boston: Beacon Press, 1983.

Drinan, Robert F. <u>Vietnam and Armageddon: Peace, War and the Christian Conscience</u>. New York: Sheed and Ward, 1970.

Dyson, Kenneth H. F. <u>The State Tradition in Western Europe: A Study of an Idea and an Institution</u>. New York: Oxford University Press, 1980.

Ellwood, Robert S., Jr. <u>Religious and Spiritual Groups in Modern America</u>. Englewood Cliffs, N.J.: Prentice-Hall, 1973.

Evans, Peter B.; Rueschemeyer, Dietrich; and Skocpol, Theda, eds. <u>Bringing the State Back In</u>. New York: Cambridge University Press, 1985.

Falwell, Jerry. <u>Listen America</u>. Garden City, N.Y.: Doubleday, 1980.

Fee, Joan. "Political Continuity and Change." In <u>Catholic Schools in a Declining Church</u>, edited by Andrew M. Greeley, William C. McCready, and Kathleen McCourt. Kansas City, Mo.: Sheed and Ward, 1976.

Fenn, Richard K. <u>Liturgies and Trials: The Secularization of Religious Language</u>. New York: Pilgrim Press, 1982.

Fenn, Richard K. <u>Toward a Theory of Secularization</u>. [Storrs, Conn.]: Society for the Scientific Study of Religion, 1978.

Finn, James. "American Catholics and Social Movements." In <u>Contemporary Catholicism in the United States</u>, edited by Philip Gleason. Notre Dame, Ind.: University of Notre Dame Press, 1969.

Finn, James, ed. <u>The Conflict of Loyalties: The Case for Selective Conscientious Objection</u>. New York: Pegasus, 1968.

Fisher, Alan M. "Realignment of the Jewish Vote?" <u>Political Science Quarterly</u> 94 (Spring 1979), 97–116.

FitzGerald, Frances. <u>Cities on a Hill: A Journey Through Contemporary American Cultures</u>. New York: Simon and Schuster, 1986.

Forman, James. <u>The Making of Black Revolutionaries: A Personal Account</u>. New York: Macmillan, 1972.

Forster, Arnold, and Epstein, Benjamin R. <u>The New Anti-Semitism</u>. New York: McGraw-Hill, 1974.

Fowler, Robert Booth. A New Engagement: Evangelical Political
     Thought, 1966-1976. Grand Rapids: Eerdmans, 1982.

Fowler, Robert Booth. Religion and Politics in America.
     Philadelphia: The American Theological Library Association;
     Metuchen, N.J.: Scarecrow, 1985.

Friedman, Murray. "Intergroup Relations." In American Jewish
     Year Book, 1985, edited by Milton Himmelfarb and David
     Singer. New York: American Jewish Committee, 1985.

Fuchs, Lawrence. John F. Kennedy and American Catholicism.
     New York: Meredith, 1967.

Gallup Opinion Index. Religion in America. Princeton, N.J.:
     American Institute of Public Opinion, 1976, 1977-1978, 1978-
     1979, 1979-1980, 1981, and 1982.

Gans, Herbert J. "Symbolic Ethnicity: The Future of Ethnic
     Groups and Cultures in America." Ethnic and Racial Studies
     2 (January 1979), 1-20.

[Garrett, James Leo, Jr.] "Bureaucratic Governmental
     Regulation of Churches and Church Institutions." Journal of
     Church and State 21 (Spring 1979), 195-207.

[Garrett, James Leo, Jr.] "Does Church-State Separation
     Necessarily Mean the Privatization of Religion?" Journal of
     Church and State 18 (Spring 1976), 209-216.

Garrett, William R. "Politicized Clergy: A Sociological
     Interpretation of the 'New Breed.'" Journal for the
     Scientific Study of Religion 12 (December 1973), 383-399.

Gehrig, Gail. American Civil Religion: An Assessment. Storrs,
     Conn.: Society for the Scientific Study of Religion, 1981.

Gellhorn, Walter, and Greenawalt, R. Kent. The Sectarian
     College and the Public Purse: Fordham--A Case Study. Dobbs
     Ferry, N.Y.: Oceana, 1970.

Glanz, David, and Harrison, Michael I. "Varieties of Identity
     Transformation: The Case of the Newly Orthodox Jews."
     Jewish Journal of Sociology 20 (December 1978), 129-142.

Glazer, Nathan. American Judaism. 2d ed. Chicago: University
     of Chicago Press, 1972.

Gleason, Philip. "Catholicism and Cultural Change in the
     60's." Review of Politics 34 (October 1972), 91-107.

Glock, Charles Y., and Bellah, Robert N., eds. The New
     Religious Consciousness. Berkeley: University of California
     Press, 1976.

Goldman, Peter. The Death and Life of Malcolm X. New York: Harper and Row, 1973.

Graubard, Stephen R., ed. The State. New York: Norton, 1980.

Gray, Francine du Plessix. Divine Disobedience: Profiles in Catholic Radicalism. New York: Knopf, 1970.

Greeley, Andrew M. The American Catholic: A Social Portrait. New York: Basic, 1977.

Greeley, Andrew M. "American Catholicism 1950-1980." Chap. 8 in Come Blow Your Mind With Me. Garden City, N.Y.: Doubleday, 1971.

Greeley, Andrew M. "How Conservative Are American Catholics?" Political Science Quarterly 92 (Summer 1977), 199-218.

Greeley, Andrew M. "The Sociology of American Catholics." Annual Review of Sociology 5 (1979), 91-111.

Habermas, Jürgen. Legitimation Crisis. Boston: Beacon Press, 1973.

Hadden, Jeffrey K. "Clergy Involvement in Civil Rights." Annals of the American Academy of Political and Social Science 387 (January 1970), 118-127.

Hadden, Jeffrey K. The Gathering Storm in the Churches. Garden City, N.Y.: Doubleday, 1969.

Halpern, Ben. "Zion in the Mind of American Jews." In The Future of the Jewish Community in America, edited by David Sidorsky. New York: Basic, 1973.

Halvorson, Peter L., and Newman, William M. Atlas of Religious Change in America, 1952-1971. Washington, D.C.: Glenmary Research Center, 1978.

Hamilton, Michael P. The Vietnam War: Christian Perspectives. Grand Rapids: Eerdmans, 1967.

Hammond, Phillip E. "The Sociology of American Civil Religion: A Bibliographic Essay." Sociological Analysis 37 (Summer 1976), 169-182.

Hammond, Phillip E., ed. The Sacred in a Secular Age: Toward Revision in the Scientific Study of Religion. Berkeley: University of California Press, 1985.

Hanna, Mary T. Catholics and American Politics. Cambridge: Harvard University Press, 1979.

Harris, Louis, and Swanson, Bert E. Black-Jewish Relations in New York City. New York: Praeger, 1970.

Heilman, Samuel C. "Constructing Orthodoxy." In In Gods We Trust: Patterns in American Religious Pluralism, edited by Thomas Robbins and Dick Anthony. New Brunswick, N.J.: Transaction Books, 1981.

Heilman, Samuel C. "The Sociology of American Jewry: The Last Ten Years." Annual Review of Sociology 8 (1982), 135-160.

Heitzmann, William. American Jewish Voting Behavior: A History and Analysis. San Francisco: R & E Associates, 1975.

Hennesey, James. "A Revolutionary Moment." Chap. 21 in American Catholics: A History of the Roman Catholic Community in the United States. New York: Oxford University Press, 1981.

Hertzberg, Arthur. "The Triumph of the Jews." New York Review of Books, 21 November 1985, 18-22.

Hill, Samuel S., and Owen, Dennis E. The New Religious-Political Right in America. Nashville: Abingdon, 1982.

Hitchcock, James. The Decline and Fall of Radical Catholicism. New York: Herder and Herder, 1971.

Hitchcock, James. What is Secular Humanism? Ann Arbor, Mich.: Servant Books, 1982.

Hodgson, Godfrey. America in Our Time. Garden City, N.Y.: Doubleday, 1976.

Hoge, Dean R. Division in the Protestant House. Philadelphia: Westminster, 1976.

Hollinger, Dennis P. Individualism and Social Ethics: An Evangelical Syncretism. Lanham, Md.: University Press of America, 1983.

Hunt, Larry L., and Hunt, Janet G. "Black Religion as Both Opiate and Inspiration of Civil Rights Militance: Putting Marx's Data to the Test." Social Forces 56 (September 1977), 1-14.

Hunter, James Davison. American Evangelicalism: Conservative Religion and the Quandary of Modernity. New Brunswick, N.J.: Rutgers University Press, 1983.

Hunter, James Davison. Evangelicalism: The Coming Generation. Chicago: University of Chicago Press, forthcoming.

Hunter, James Davison. "Religion and Political Civility: The Coming Generation of American Evangelicals." Journal for the Scientific Study of Religion 23 (December 1984), 364-380.

Huntington, Samuel. _American Politics: The Promise of Disharmony_. Cambridge: Harvard University Press, 1981.

Hutcheson, Richard G., Jr. _Mainline Churches and the Evangelicals_. Atlanta: John Knox, 1981.

Hutchison, William R. "Past Imperfect: History and the Prospect for Liberal Protestantism." In _Liberal Protestantism: Realities and Possibilities_, edited by Robert S. Michaelsen and Wade Clark Roof. New York: Pilgrim Press, 1986.

Jessop, Bob. _The Capitalist State: Marxist Theories and Methods_. New York: New York University Press, 1982.

Johnson, Benton. "Religion and Politics in America: The Last Twenty Years." In _The Sacred in a Secular Age_, edited by Phillip E. Hammond. Berkeley: University of California Press, 1985.

Johnson, Benton. "A Sociological Perspective on the New Religions." In _In Gods We Trust: Patterns in American Religious Pluralism_, edited by Thomas Robbins and Dick Anthony. New Brunswick, N.J.: Transaction Books, 1981.

Johnson, Benton. "Theology and Party Preference Among Protestant Clergymen." _American Sociological Review_ 31 (April 1966), 200-208.

Johnson, Benton. "Theology and the Position of Pastors on Public Issues." _American Sociological Review_ 32 (June 1967), 433-442.

Johnson, Stephen D., and Tamney, Joseph B. "The Christian Right and the 1980 Presidential Election." _Journal for the Scientific Study of Religion_ 21 (June 1982), 123-131.

Jorstad, Erling. _The Politics of Moralism_. Minneapolis: Augsburg, 1981.

Kelley, Dean M. _Why Conservative Churches Are Growing_. New York: Harper and Row, 1972.

Kelley, Dean M., ed. _Government Intervention in Religious Affairs_. New York: Pilgrim Press, 1982.

Kelly, George A. _The Battle for the Catholic Church_. Garden City, N.Y.: Doubleday, 1979.

Kerrine, Theodore M., and Neuhaus, Richard John. "Mediating Structures: A Paradigm for Democratic Pluralism." _Annals of the American Academy of Political and Social Science_ 446 (November 1979), 10-18.

King, Martin Luther, Jr. Why We Can't Wait. New York: Harper
    and Row, 1964.

Krasner, Stephen D. "Approaches to the State: Alternative
    Conceptions and Historical Dynamics." Comparative Politics
    16 (January 1984), 223-246.

Ladd, Everett Carll. "The Brittle Mandate: Electoral
    Realignment and the 1980 Presidential Election." Political
    Science Quarterly 96 (Spring 1981), 1-26.

Lewis, David L. King: A Critical Biography. New York:
    Praeger, 1970.

Liebman, Arthur. Jews and the Left. New York: Wiley, 1979.

Liebman, Charles S. The Ambivalent American Jew.
    Philadelphia: Jewish Publication Society, 1973.

Liebman, Charles S. "Orthodox Judaism Today." Midstream,
    August-September 1979, 19-26.

Liebman, Robert C., and Wuthnow, Robert. The New Christian
    Right: Mobilization and Legitimation. Hawthorne, N.Y.:
    Aldine, 1983.

Lincoln, C. Eric. The Black Muslims in America. Boston:
    Beacon Press, 1961.

Linesch, Michael. "Right-Wing Religion: Christian Conservatism
    as a Political Movement." Political Science Quarterly 97
    (Fall 1982), 403-425.

Lipset, Seymour M., and Raab, Earl. "The Election and the
    Evangelicals." Commentary, March 1981, 25-31.

Littell, Frank H. "Religious Liberty in a Pluralistic
    Society." Journal of Church and State 8 (Autumn 1966), 430-
    444.

Little, Malcolm. The Autobiography of Malcolm X. New York:
    Grove, 1965.

Lopatto, Paul. Religion and the Presidential Election. New
    York: Praeger, 1985.

Lorentzen, Louise. "Evangelical Lifestyle Concerns Expressed
    in Political Action." Sociological Analysis 41 (Summer
    1980), 144-154.

Love, Thomas T. John Courtney Murray: Contemporary Church-
    State Theory. Garden City, N.Y.: Doubleday, 1965.

MacIntyre, Alasdair. After Virtue. 2d ed. Notre Dame, Ind.:
    University of Notre Dame Press, 1984.

McPherson, James M.; Holland, Laurence B.; Banner, James M.,
    Jr.; Weiss, Nancy J.; and Bell, Michael D. "The Civil
    Rights Revolution, 1954-1970." Part IX of Blacks in
    America: Bibliographic Essays. Garden City, N.Y.:
    Doubleday, 1971.

Manhattan, Auro. Vatican Imperialism in the Twentieth Century.
    Grand Rapids: Zondervan, 1965.

Marsden, George. "Preachers of Paradox: The New Religious
    Right in Historical Perspective." In Religion and America:
    Spiritual Life in a Secular Age, edited by Mary Douglas and
    Steven M. Tipton. Boston: Beacon Press, 1983.

Marsden, George, ed. Evangelicalism and Modern America. Grand
    Rapids: Eerdmans, 1984.

Marx, Gary T. Protest and Prejudice. rev. ed. New York:
    Harper and Row, 1969.

Marx, Gary T. "Religion: Opiate or Inspiration of Civil Rights
    Militancy Among Negroes." American Sociological Review 32
    (February 1967), 64-72.

Mead, Sidney E. The Nation with the Soul of a Church. New
    York: Harper and Row, 1975.

Mechling, Jay. Church, State, and Public Policy. Washington,
    D.C.: American Enterprise Institute for Public Policy, 1978.

Meconis, Charles A. With Clumsy Grace: The American Catholic
    Left, 1961-1975. New York: Seabury, 1979.

Menendez, Albert, comp. Religious Conflict in America: A
    Bibliography. New York: Garland, 1985.

Michaelsen, Robert S., and Roof, Wade Clark, eds. Liberal
    Protestantism: Realities and Possibilities. New York:
    Pilgrim Press, 1986.

Miliband, Ralph. The State in Capitalist Society. New York:
    Basic, 1969.

Miller, Elizabeth W., and Fisher, Mary L., comps. The Negro in
    America: A Bibliography. 2d ed. Cambridge: Harvard
    University Press, 1970.

Miller, William Lee. "Responsible Government, Not Religion, is
    the Endangered Species." In Government Intervention in
    Religious Affairs, edited by Dean M. Kelley. New York:
    Pilgrim Press, 1982.

Mitchell, Douglas, and Plotnicov, Leonard. "The Lubavitcher
    Movement: A Study in Contexts." Urban Anthropology 4
    (Winter 1975), 303-315.

Morgan, Richard E. The Politics of Religious Conflict: Church and State in America. 2d ed. Washington, D.C.: University Press of America, 1980.

Mueller, Carol. "In Search of a Constituency for the 'New Religious Right.'" Public Opinion Quarterly 47 (Summer 1983), 214-229.

Murray, Charles A. Losing Ground: American Social Policy, 1950-1980. New York: Basic, 1984.

Murray, John Courtney. We Hold These Truths. New York: Sheed and Ward, 1960.

Needleman, Jacob, and Baker, George, eds. Understanding the New Religions. New York: Seabury, 1978.

Nelsen, Hart M.; Madron, Thomas M.; and Yokley, Raytha L. "Black Religion's Promethean Motif: Orthodoxy and Militancy." American Journal of Sociology 81 (July 1975), 139-146.

Nelsen, Hart M., and Nelsen, Anne Kusener. Black Church in the Sixties. Lexington: University Press of Kentucky, 1975.

Nelsen, Hart M.; Yokley, Raytha L.; and Nelsen, Anne Kusener, eds. The Black Church In America. New York: Basic, 1971.

Neuhaus, Richard John. The Naked Public Square: Religion and Democracy in America. Grand Rapids: Eerdmans, 1984.

Neuhaus, Richard John. "The War, the Churches, and Civil Religion." Annals of the American Academy of Political and Social Science 387 (January 1970), 128-140.

Nordlinger, Eric. On the Autonomy of the Democratic State. Cambridge: Harvard University Press, 1981.

Novak, Michael. "Blue-Bleak Embers . . . Fall, Gall Themselves . . . Gash Gold-Vermilion." In Conspiracy: The Implications of the Harrisburg Trial for the Democratic Tradition, edited by John C. Raines. New York: Harper and Row, 1974.

Novak, Michael. Choosing Our King. New York: Macmillan, 1974.

Oates, Stephen B. Let the Trumpet Sound: The Life of Martin Luther King, Jr. New York: Harper and Row, 1982.

O'Brien, David J. The Renewal of American Catholicism. New York: Oxford University Press, 1972.

O'Brien, David J., and Shannon, Thomas A. Renewing the Earth: Catholic Documents on Peace, Justice and Liberation. Garden City, N.Y.: Image Books, 1977.

O'Connor, John. A Chaplain Looks at Vietnam. Cleveland, Ohio: World, 1968.

O'Hair, Madalyn Murray. Freedom Under Siege: The Impact of Religion on Your Liberty and Your Pocketbook. Los Angeles: J. P. Tarcher, 1974.

Page, Ann L., and Clelland, Donald A. "The Kanawha County Textbook Controversy: A Study of the Politics of Lifestyle Concern." Social Forces 57 (September 1978), 265-281.

Parenti, Michael. "Political Values and Religious Cultures." In American Mosaic: Social Patterns of Religion in the United States, edited by Phillip E. Hammond and Benton Johnson. New York: Random House, 1970.

Patel, Kant; Pliant, Denny; and Rose, Gary. "Born-Again Christians in the Bible Belt: A Study in Religion, Politics and Ideology." American Political Quarterly 10 (April 1982), 255-272.

Patterson, James T. America's Struggle Against Poverty, 1900-1980. Cambridge: Harvard University Press, 1981.

Peck, Gary R. "Black Radical Consciousness and the Black Christian Experience: Toward a Critical Sociology of Afro-American Religion." Sociological Analysis 43 (Summer 1982), 155-169.

Pelotte, Donald E. John Courtney Murray: Theologian in Conflict. New York: Paulist Press, 1976.

Pfeffer, Leo. God, Caesar, and the Constitution: The Court as Referee of Church-State Confrontation. Boston: Beacon Press, 1975.

Pfeffer, Leo. "Issues that Divide: The Triumph of Secular Humanism." Journal of Church and State 19 (Winter 1977), 203-216.

Pfeffer, Leo. "The Legitimation of Marginal Religions in the United States." In Religious Movements in Contemporary America, edited by Irving I. Zaretsky and Mark P. Leone. Princeton, N.J.: Princeton University Press, 1974.

Pfeffer, Leo. Religion, State, and the Burger Court. Buffalo, N.Y.: Prometheus Books, 1984.

Pfeffer, Leo. "What Hath God Wrought to Caesar: The Church as a Self-Interest Group." Journal of Church and State 13 (Winter 1971), 97-112.

Pierard, Richard V. "Billy Graham and the U.S. Presidency." Journal of Church and State 22 (Winter 1980), 107-127.

Pierard, Richard V. "The Christian Right: Suggestions for Further Reading." Foundations 25 (April-June 1982), 107-127.

Pierard, Richard V. The Unequal Yoke: Evangelical Christianity and Political Conservatism. Philadelphia: Lippincott, 1970.

Pratt, Henry J. "The Growth of Political Activism in the National Council of Churches." Review of Politics 34 (July 1972), 323-341.

Pratt, Henry J. The Liberalization of American Protestantism. Detroit: Wayne State University Press, 1972.

Quigley, Thomas E., ed. American Catholics and Vietnam. Grand Rapids: Eerdmans, 1968.

Quinley, Harold E. The Prophetic Clergy: Social Activism Among Protestant Ministers. New York: Wiley, 1974.

Quinley, Harold E. "The Protestant Clergy and the War in Vietnam." Public Opinion Quarterly 34 (Spring 1970), 43-52.

Quinley, Harold E., and Glock, Charles Y. Anti-Semitism in America. New York: Free Press, 1979.

Rader, Stanley R. Against the Gates of Hell: The Threat to Religious Freedom in America. New York: Everest House, 1980.

Ramsey, Paul. The Just War: Force and Political Responsibility. New York: Scribner, 1968.

Ramsey, Paul. "Vietnam: Dissent from Dissent." Christian Century, 20 July 1966, 909-913.

Raphael, Marc Lee. "History, Ideology, and Institutions: 1937-1983." Chap. 3 in Profiles in American Judaism. San Francisco: Harper and Row, 1984.

Ravitch, Diane. The Troubled Crusade: American Education, 1945-1980. New York: Basic, 1983.

Reichley, A. James. Religion in American Public Life. Washington, D.C.: Brookings Institution, 1985.

Reuss, Carl F., ed. Conscience and Action: Social Statements of the American Lutheran Church, 1961-1970. Minneapolis: Augsburg, 1971.

Richardson, Herbert, ed. Constitutional Issues in the Case of Reverend Moon. New York: E. Mellen, 1984.

Richardson, James T. "People's Temple and Jonestown: A
    Corrective Comparison and Critique." Journal for the
    Scientific Study of Religion 19 (September 1980), 239-255.

Richey, Russell E., and Jones, Donald G., eds. American Civil
    Religion. New York: Harper and Row, 1974.

Robbins, Thomas. "Church, State and Cult." Sociological
    Analysis 42 (Fall 1981), 209-226.

Robbins, Thomas, and Anthony, Dick. "Cults, Brainwashing, and
    Counter-Subversion." Annals of the American Academy of
    Political and Social Science 446 (November 1979), 78-90.

Robbins, Thomas, and Anthony, Dick. "The Sociology of
    Contemporary Religious Movements." Annual Review of
    Sociology 5 (1979), 75-89.

Robbins, Thomas, and Anthony, Dick, eds. In Gods We Trust:
    Patterns in American Religious Pluralism. New Brunswick,
    N.J.: Transaction Books, 1981.

Robbins, Thomas; Shepherd, William C.; and McBride, James, eds.
    Cults, Culture, and the Law: Perspectives on New Religious
    Movements. Chico, Calif.: Scholars Press, 1985.

Robertson, Roland. "Considerations from Within the American
    Context on the Significance of Church-State Tension."
    Sociological Analysis 42 (Fall 1981), 193-208.

Rohr, John A. Prophets without Honor: Public Policy and the
    Selective Conscientious Objector. Nashville: Abingdon,
    1971.

Roof, Wade Clark. "America's Voluntary Establishment: Mainline
    Religion in Transition." In Religion and America: Spiritual
    Life in a Secular Age, edited by Mary Douglas and Steven M.
    Tipton. Boston: Beacon Press, 1983.

Roof, Wade Clark. Community and Commitment: Religious
    Plausibility in a Liberal Protestant Church. New York:
    Elsevier, 1978.

Roof, Wade Clark, and Hadaway, Christopher Kirk.
    "Denominational Switching in the Seventies: Going Beyond
    Stark and Glock." Journal for the Scientific Study of
    Religion 18 (December 1979), 363-377.

Rosenberg, Bernard, and Howe, Irving. "Are American Jews
    Turning to the Right?" Dissent 21 (Winter 1974), 30-45.

Rothenberg, Stuart, and Newport, Frank. The Evangelical Voter:
    Religion and Politics in America. Washington, D.C.:
    Institute for Government and Politics, 1984.

Schaeffer, Francis A. _A Christian Manifesto_. Westchester,
Ill.: Crossway Books, 1981.

Schuchter, Arnold. _Reparations: The Black Manifesto and Its
Challenge to White Churches_. Philadelphia: Lippincott,
1970.

Shaffir, William. _Life in a Religious Community: The
Lubavitcher Chassidim in Montreal_. Toronto: Holt, Rinehart
and Winston, 1974.

Sharot, Stephen. _Judaism: A Sociology_. New York: Holmes and
Meier, 1976.

Shepherd, William C. _To Secure The Blessings of Liberty:
American Constitutional Law and the New Religious Movements_.
New York: Crossroad, 1985.

Shupe, Anson D., and Bromley, David G. _The New Religious
Vigilantes: Deprogrammers, Anti-Cultists and the New
Religions_. Beverly Hills, Calif.: Sage, 1980.

Shupe, Anson D., and Bromley, David G. "Social Responses to
Cults." In _The Sacred in a Secular Age_, edited by Phillip
E. Hammond. Berkeley: University of California Press, 1985.

Shupe, Anson D., and Stacey, William A. _Born Again Politics
and the Moral Majority: What Social Surveys Really Show_.
New York: E. Mellen, 1982.

Sider, Ronald J. _Rich Christians in an Age of Hunger_.
Downer's Grove, Ill.: InterVarsity Press, 1977.

Sider, Ronald, J., ed. _The Chicago Declaration_. Carol Stream,
Ill.: Creation House, 1974.

Sklare, Marshall. _Conservative Judaism: An American Religious
Movement_. New York: Schocken, 1972.

Sklare, Marshall, ed. _Understanding American Jewry_. New
Brunswick, N.J.: Transaction Books, 1982.

Small, Dwight L., ed. _Afro-American History: A Bibliography_.
Santa Barbara, Calif.: ABC-Clio, 1974.

Smith, Elwyn A., ed. _The Religion of the Republic_.
Philadelphia: Fortress, 1971.

Smith, Elwyn A., ed. _What the Religious Revolutionaries Are
Saying_. Philadelphia: Fortress, 1971.

Smylie, James H. "American Religious Bodies, Just War, and
Vietnam." _Journal of Church and State_ 11 (Autumn 1969),
383-408.

Sorauf, Frank J. The Wall of Separation: The Constitutional
    Politics of Church and State. Princeton, N.J.: Princeton
    University Press, 1976.

Stackhouse, Max L. The Ethics of Necropolis: An Essay on the
    Military-Industrial Complex and the Quest for a Just Peace.
    Boston: Beacon Press, 1971.

Stanmeyer, William A. Clear and Present Danger: Church and
    State in Post-Christian America. Ann Arbor, Mich.: Servant
    Books, 1983.

Stark, Rodney, and Bainbridge, William Sims. The Future of
    Religion: Secularization, Revival, and Cult Formation.
    Berkeley: University of California Press, 1985.

Swanson, Guy A. "Modern Secularity." In The Religious
    Situation: 1968, edited by Donald R. Cutler. Boston: Beacon
    Press, 1968.

Sweet, Leonard I. "The 1960s: The Crises of Liberal
    Christianity and the Public Emergence of Evangelicalism."
    In Evangelicalism and Modern America, edited by George
    Marsden. Grand Rapids: Eerdmans, 1984.

Thomas, George M., and Meyer, John W. "The Expansion of the
    State." Annual Review of Sociology 10 (1984), 461-482.

Thomas, Michael C., and Flippen, Charles C. "American Civil
    Religion: An Empirical Study." Social Forces 51 (December
    1972), 218-225.

Urban Bishops Coalition. To Hear and to Heed: The Episcopal
    Church Listens and Acts in the City. Cincinnati: Forward
    Movement Publications, 1978.

Van Allen, Roger. The Commonweal and American Catholicism.
    Philadelphia: Fortress, 1974.

Vogel, Manfred. "Some Reflections on the Jewish-Christian
    Dialogue in the Light of the Six-Day War." Annals of the
    American Academy of Political and Social Science 387
    (January 1970), 96-108.

Wacker, Grant. "Searching for Norman Rockwell: Popular
    Evangelicalism in Contemporary America." In The Evangelical
    Tradition in America, edited by Leonard I. Sweet. Macon,
    Ga.: Mercer University Press, 1984.

Wallis, Jim. Agenda for Biblical People. rev. ed. San
    Francisco: Harper and Row, 1984.

Warner, R. Stephen. "Theoretical Barriers to the Understanding
    of Evangelical Christianity." Sociological Analysis 40
    (Spring 1979), 1-9.

Waxman, Chaim I. _America's Jews in Transition_. Philadelphia: Temple University Press, 1983.

Waxman, Chaim I. "The Centrality of Israel in American Jewish Life: A Sociological Analysis." _Judaism_ 25 (Spring 1976), 175-187.

Weber, Paul J., and Gilbert, Dennis A. _Private Churches and Public Money: Church-Government Fiscal Relations_. Westport, Conn.: Greenwood, 1981.

Williams, Ethel L., and Brown, Clifton F., comps. _The Howard University Bibliography of African and Afro-American Religious Studies_. Wilmington, Del.: Scholarly Resources, 1977.

Wills, Gary. _Bare Ruined Choirs: Doubt, Prophecy and Radical Religion_. Garden City, N.Y.: Doubleday, 1972.

Wilson, Bryan R., ed. _The Social Impact of New Religious Movements_. New York: Rose of Sharon Press, 1981.

Wilson, E. Raymond. _Uphill for Peace: Quaker Impact on Congress_. Richmond, Ind.: Friends United, 1975.

Wilson, John F. _Public Religion in American Culture_. Philadelphia: Temple University Press, 1979.

Wimberly, Ronald C. "Testing the Civil Religion Hypothesis." _Sociological Analysis_ 37 (Winter 1976), 341-352.

Wimberly, Ronald C., and Christenson, James A. "Civil Religion and Church and State." _Sociological Quarterly_ 21 (Winter 1980), 35-40.

Wirt, Sherwood Eliot. _The Social Conscience of the Evangelical_. New York: Harper and Row, 1968.

Wolcott, Roger T. "Church and Social Action: Steelworkers and Bishops in Youngstown." _Journal for the Scientific Study of Religion_ 21 (March 1982), 71-79.

Wood, James E., Jr. "Religion and Politics--1984." _Journal of Church and State_ 26 (Autumn 1984), 401-411.

Wood, James E., Jr., ed. _Religion and Politics_. Waco, Tex.: Baylor University Press, 1983.

Worthing, Sharon L. "The State Takes Over a Church." _Annals of the American Academy of Political and Social Science_ 446 (November 1979), 136-148.

Wuthnow, Robert J. "Anti-Semitism and Stereotyping." In _In the Eye of the Beholder_, edited by Arthur G. Miller. New York: Praeger, 1982.

Wuthnow, Robert J. The Consciousness Reformation. Berkeley:
    University of California Press, 1976.

Young, Henry C. Major Black Religious Leaders Since 1940.
    Nashville: Abingdon, 1979.

Zaretsky, Irving I., and Leone, Mark P., eds. Religious
    Movements in Contemporary America. Princeton, N.J.:
    Princeton University Press, 1974.

9

Religion and Education: 1870 to the Present

John W. Lowe, Jr.

From colonial times, the relationship between church, state, and education has been close-knit. The development of its main features to the Civil War has been described in the preceding volume. That relationship, however, underwent fundamental change in the last quarter of the nineteenth century. Previously, education had primarily been a local responsibility, but the society's growing pluralism gave rise to controversies, in particular over Bible reading in the schools, which could not be resolved at that level. In consequence, a series of court cases, first in the state courts and eventually in the federal, established the role of the judiciary in affairs concerning church, state, and education. In the late nineteenth and the twentieth centuries, therefore, discussion of this topic entails extensive attention to legal cases. But these in turn reflect a series of issues such as the development of schools outside the public system, particularly Catholic parochial schools, new philosophies and methods of education, including curriculum changes, and various conceptions of the role of religion in the schools.

There is a wealth of written material on this subject. And in recent years active public interest in the issues has led as well to various programs and documentaries on radio and television, to articles in newspapers and popular magazines, and even to cassette and videotape presentations. Nevertheless, this essay will confine itself to written materials and must, in view of their volume, be extremely selective. Moreover, as a consequence of considering several major themes separately, such as federal concern for education, its alleged secularization, and the growth of independent schools, the essay will of necessity deemphasize their interrelatedness.

Several volumes give an overview of church-state-education issues in the United States. All include reference to the period before 1870, but are important for their discussion of the issues since 1870 as well. Robert Michaelsen's *Piety in the Public School* surveys the role of religion in education and deals extensively with the important Supreme Court cases after World War II. Paul A. Freund and Robert Ulich also survey the history of the issue from the legal side in *Religion and the Public Schools*. William W. Brickman and Stanley Lehrer's *Religion, Government, and Education* is a collection of essays by various authors which includes an extremely helpful chronological listing of items important to church-state-education relations from 1600 through 1961. Herbert M. Kliebard's *Religion and Education in America: A Documentary History*, while including items from the eighteenth and nineteenth centuries, provides a good compilation of relevant twentieth-century documents and court cases. Also useful is an edited volume by James E. Wood, Jr., *Religion, the State and Education*, which reprints several recent articles from the *Journal of Church and State*.

In education, as in other segments of American society, an important factor gaining in importance toward the end of the nineteenth century was the growing role of the federal government. A national Department of Education was established in March 1867. Initially an independent, subcabinet-level office, it was expected to collect data on education in the states and territories, disseminate information which would improve the schools, promote the cause of education, and present an annual report to Congress with recommendations for future actions. Later placed under the direction of the Department of Interior, and then, in 1939, under the Federal Security Agency, the office was given cabinet-level status in the formation of the Department of Health, Education, and Welfare in 1953, and finally made a separate cabinet position with the creation of the Department of Education in 1979. Its power has been increased throughout the years by acts of Congress and as a result of its influential activities.

With the creation of the department, the Commissioner for Education became a figure of some importance who, although without legislative power, could significantly influence opinion. William Torrey Harris, for example, who took office in 1889, published many articles, and these give an indication of the changed place of religion in the public schools. While Torrey had no objection to the schools permitting religious practices, he did not wish them to be the primary location of religious education. Such a point of view represented a marked change in the expected role of schools and reflected the fact that, as the goal of universal education had been implemented, Protestant influence in schools, expressed in practices such as daily prayer, had become contentious. Church-state conflict with regard to education often centered in Protestant responses to what were perceived as attempts to secularize the schools.

Some implications of secularization were explored in a highly publicized court case in 1872 involving issues of church, state, and education. In *Board of Education of Cincinnati v. Minor* (23 Ohio St. 211), the Supreme Court of Ohio declared Bible reading in the Cincinnati schools to be unconstitutional. (This case is discussed in volume 1 and well documented in *The Bible in the Public Schools.*) A common fear was that all religion might then be banned from the public schools. *Minor* also aroused a new awareness of the issues regarding education dividing Protestants and Catholics and of the possibility that the government might come to stand neutral where religious issues were concerned. This was one of many such cases heard in state courts.

In response to this general situation, several constitutional amendments were proposed in the 1870s that promoted universal, but nonsectarian, education (see Daniel Ullmann, *Amendments to the Constitution of the United States. Non-Sectarian and Universal Education*). Although the amendments never passed, they, together with the Bible reading cases, signaled the new era which began after the Civil War. The secularization of the schools in the subsequent decades has been discussed at length. An early attempt to explore that process by means of state documents is Samuel Windsor Brown's *The Secularization of American Education.* A later history, which built upon Brown's early work, is Burton Confrey's *Secularism in American Education.* Increased attention to the topic came after Supreme Court decisions of the 1940s.

PERSPECTIVES OF EDUCATIONAL PROFESSIONALS

With the professionalization of education early in this century, there began a new discussion of the relation of religion and public school education. Among many authors, for example, Elmer Ellsworth Brown, in *The Changing Relations of Education and Religion*, sought to look objectively at the historical relationship between church and school and analyze the changes that were taking place. A year later, in 1909, Raymond C. Knox, in *Religion in Education*, attempted to suggest a new relationship for religion and education. The National Education Association (NEA) also became involved, sponsoring an essay contest on the question and publishing the winning essays in *The Essential Place of Religion in Education.* In the context of World War I, Walter S. Athearn, in *Education and American Democracy*, and Benjamin S. Winchester, in *Religious Education and Democracy*, both argued that religion, education, and democracy were interrelated.

The Religious Education Association (REA), founded in 1903, was a continuing forum for discussion of the question of the relationship of religion and public education at conventions and in a journal, *Religious Education.* Publications by its general secretary, Henry F. Cope (on, for example, weekday religious education), present its view. The REA refused to support efforts to compel Bible reading in the schools but did support other relationships, such as a released-time plan and academic credit for Bible study in high schools.

In the late 1920s, new impetus was given to discussion of the problems and possibilities of religious education and public education (see the 1928 book by Jerome K. Jackson and Constantine F. Malmberg, *Religious Education and the State*). An important resource published in 1927 was *Religious Teaching in the Public Schools*, by Lamar Taney Beman. Having compiled a survey of all state laws pertaining to religion in the public schools, Beman was able to document the varying attitudes and methods prevalent in the states and the issues as states perceived them.

Discussion of church-state-education issues seems to have abated in the 1930s, perhaps because of the Great Depression and events leading to World War II. In the mid-1940s, however, this situation changed, with one result being William Clayton Bower's *Church and State in Education*. While Bower's book was essentially the last written on this issue from the viewpoint of progressive education, it also pointed to an urgency in dealing with the issues of church and state in education that would become apparent in Supreme Court decisions within a few years. It answered, in many ways, the arguments of William S. Fleming, an official of the National Reform Association, who in *God in Our Public Schools* advocated the teaching of nonsectarian religion in the public schools in order to return to them the biblical truths upon which he believed the United States had been founded. The American Council on Education also entered the debate, sponsoring a conference of educators on religion and education issues. In 1945 the addresses and reports of this conference were published as *Religion and Public Education*.

Following World War II, interest in the relationship between religion, education, and the state increased, in part because of the series of relevant Supreme Court decisions beginning with *Everson v. Board of Education of Ewing Township* (330 U.S. 1 [1947]) and *McCollum v. Board of Education* (333 U.S. 203 [1948]). Edward S. Corwin, in a notable article, "The Supreme Court as the National School Board," argued that local authority over public schools had been eroded by Supreme Court decisions. Other examples of exchanges on this issue are books by Renwick Harper Martin and Vivian Trow Thayer. The NEA, in *The State and Sectarian Education*, presented its view of the constitutional, statutory, and judicial bases of the church-state-education relationship. It also presented the findings of a survey of 5,100 school superintendents concerning existing religious education programs in the schools (*The Status of Religious Education in the Public Schools*). The American Council on Education, in *The Relation of Religion to Public Educa-*

tion. The Basic Principles, also surveyed current practices and analyzed both the meaning of public education and the arguments of opponents to religious instruction.

PERSPECTIVES OF RELIGIOUS PROFESSIONALS

Numerous writers have explored the role of religion in education from different religious viewpoints. Conservative and largely evangelical statements include Marjorie E. Adams, *God in the Classroom;* Christopher Hall, *The Christian Teacher and the Law;* Brian Hill, *Faith at the Blackboard: Issues Facing the Christian Teacher;* and George Van Alstine, *The Christian and the Public School.* Moderate to liberal views are found in David W. Beggs, III, and R. Bruce McQuigg, *America's Schools and Churches, Partners in Conflict:* Fellows of the Calvin Center for Christian Scholarship, *Society, State, & Schools; A Case for Structural and Confessional Pluralism;* James E. Loder, *Religion and the Public Schools;* Richard C. MacMillan, *Education, Religion, and the Supreme Court* and *Religion in the Public Schools;* Niels C. Nielsen, Jr., *God in Education: A New Opportunity for American Schools;* and John M. Swomley, *Religion, the State and the Schools.* An older Catholic viewpoint was offered in James M. O'Neill's *Religion and Education Under the Constitution.*

THE ROLE OF RELIGION IN THE PUBLIC SCHOOLS

In the postwar years, one line of argument held that religion could and should be taught in the public schools. Among examples of this literature, see Fount William Mattox (*The Teaching of Religion in the Public Schools*), and Clyde Lemont Hay (*The Blind Spot in American Public Education*). The evangelical position advocating religion in the public schools was detailed in *Christian Education in a Democracy,* by Frank E. Gaebelein. In *American Education and Religion: The Problem of Religion in the Schools,* F. Ernest Johnson published a number of speeches given at the Institute for Religion and Social Studies of the Jewish Theological Seminary. The book includes representative viewpoints from the three major faiths concerning religion in the public schools. Although Vivian Trow Thayer was typically an advocate of secular schools, in *Religion in Public Education* he dealt with trends and arguments for religious instruction and practices in the public schools. The American Jewish Committee, in *Religion in Public Education,* gave the Jewish view of the role of religion in education. The committee also published *Religion in Public Education. A Guide for Discussion,* by Philip Jacobsen.

The National Council of Churches of Christ stated its position in *Relation of Religion to Public Education.*

Surveys of the place of religion in the public schools also appeared in the postwar decades. In *The Function of the Public Schools in Dealing with Religion,* the American Council on Education reported the results of a survey of educators, clergy, and community leaders on the role of religion in education. Five years later, Nicholas C. Brown, in *The Study of Religion in the Public Schools,* reported on an American Council on Education conference which discussed introducing religious material into the curriculum at various levels and in relevant subjects. Among important books on church-state-education issues was Richard B. Dierenfield's *Religion in American Public Schools.* Dierenfield summarized the results of a survey among thousands of school districts on such areas as religious exercises and practices, religion in the curriculum, released-time programs, and parochial busing. Its importance to the discussion cannot be overestimated.

Over the last twenty-five years, vigorous theoretical and philosophical discussion of the relationships of church, state, and education has continued, especially among educators. The American Association of School Administrators reviewed what should or should not be done about religion in the schools in *Religion in the Public Schools.* Lawrence Byrnes, in *Religion and Public Education,* sought to clarify pedagogical and psychological aspects of teaching religion in the schools for teachers. A volume edited by Theodore R. Sizer, *Religion and Public Education,* gave the perspectives of various educators on the issue. Richard U. Smith in *Religion and the Schools: From Prayer to Public Aid* analyzed the ways that religion and public education interrelated, and provided specific illustrations. A group of educators generated *Public Schools and the First Amendment,* the report of a conference sponsored by Phi Delta Kappa and several schools of the University of Indiana.

The broader role of schools in moral or character education is also related to the issue of explicit religious teaching and practices. Early in our period, William Torrey Harris (*Morality in the Schools*) had not been sure that religious practices ought to take place in the schools, but he had felt strongly that the schools should teach morality. Moral education, indeed, had a place in the curriculum of most public schools in America until the 1930s when the approach changed and a new concept, character education, emerged. This new concept placed more emphasis upon the individual student's internalization of values. See examples of this literature by Harold S. Tuttle, Edward R. Bartlett, and Henry L. Smith and his collaborators.

Following World War II, interest returned to the concept of moral education, without losing some of this emphasis. See William C. Bower, *Moral and*

Spiritual Values in Education, the Educational Policies Commission's publication, *Moral and Spiritual Values in the Public Schools*, and the *Religious Education* issue for July-August 1951, which contains a symposium of views on moral education entitled "Moral and Spiritual Values in the Public Schools." Attention to moral education has continued into the current decade. See the book by Thomas C. Hunt and Marilyn M. Maxson, *Religion and Morality in American Schooling*, and Hunt's article, "Public Schools and Moral Education: An American Dilemma." Currently these issues are being explored through literature on values clarification and in terms of psychological theories of moral development (see Lawrence Kohlberg, *Essays on Moral Development*, and Sidney B. Simon and Sally Wendkof Olds, *Helping Your Child Learn Right From Wrong*). Where moral education should take place—in the home, the church, or the school—remains hotly contested.

PAROCHIAL EDUCATION AS ALTERNATIVE

Secularization of public education and the consequences that flowed from it were paralleled by the development of a separate Catholic parochial school system. For the origins of the modern system see Daniel F. Reilly, *The School Controversy, 1891–1893*. Among Catholics, opinion concerning public education polarized around accommodationist and isolationist positions. The leading early spokesman for the accommodationist position was Bishop John Ireland of St. Paul. In an address before the NEA in 1890, Ireland discussed the question: "State Schools and Parish Schools: Is Union Between Them Possible?" Ireland proposed that the public schools provide religious education, but that it be nonsectarian. (He later reversed his opinion, addressing the need for parochial schools in *Catholic Schools for Catholic Youth*.)

The leading advocate of the isolationist position, proposing a separate Catholic school system, was Bishop Bernard John McQuaid, of Rochester, New York. McQuaid's book, *Christian Free Schools*, published in 1872, did much to provoke the public versus parochial school debate. While initially he had wanted Protestants to join him in a campaign against nonreligious public schools, McQuaid led the successful argument for parochial schools at the Third Plenary Council of Baltimore in 1884. In the end, Pope Leo XIII sent Archbishop Satolli to mediate the issue among the Catholics. Satolli's presence, and further letters from Pope Leo, supported the development of a strong parochial school system. Archbishop John L. Spalding, however, continued to present the accommodationist position in his books, among them *Education and the Future of Religion*. The NEA also became involved in the debate with the publication of *The Two Sides of the School Question*, which attempted to present the issue nonjudgmentally. In the end, neither the accommodationist nor the isolationist position triumphed and the debate has continued, influencing public as well as parochial education.

The growth of the parochial schools is chronicled by such writers as Harold A. Buetow (*Of Singular Benefit: The Story of Catholic Education in the United States*); Richard J. Gabel (*In Hoc Signo?: A Brief History of Catholic Parochial Education in America*); Neil G. McCluskey (*Catholic Education in America: A Documentary History*); and Robert T. O'Gorman ("American and Catholic: The Education of a People Within the Public"). Issues facing parochial schools more recently are reviewed by C. Albert Koob (*What is Happening to Catholic Education?*); Neil G. McCluskey (*Catholic Viewpoint on Education* and *Catholic Education Faces Its Future*); and Russell B. Shaw (*Trends and Issues in Catholic Education*). Sister Raymond McLaughlin, in *A History of State Legislation Affecting Private Elementary and Secondary Schools in the United States, 1870–1945*, considers state legislation concerning Catholic schools. And Peter M. J. Stravinskas, in *Constitutional Rights and Religious Prejudice: Catholic Education as the Battleground*, examines parochial education in the context of the argument for constitutional rights and the struggle against religious prejudice.

Discussion within the Catholic community about the necessity for parochial schools continues. Apologists for Catholic schools include Roy J. Deferrari (*A Complete System of Catholic Education is Necessary*) and Jerome E. Diffley (*Catholic Reaction to American Public Education*). For the opposing view, see Mary Perkins Ryan (*We're All in This Together: Issues and Options in the Education of Catholics*), who argues that the parochial schools, having served their purpose, are no longer necessary, and James M. O'Neill (*The Catholic in Secular Education*), who supports public education and implores Catholics to become involved in public schools and colleges in order to strengthen them.

Although the Catholic parochial system is the largest parochial system in America, other religious schools exist. Some are denominational, others are independent, and still others, more recent in origin, may be loosely linked together as "Christian." An early description of one Protestant denomination's parochial system is Walter H. Beck's *Lutheran Elementary Schools in the U.S.* Paul A. Kienel's *The Christian School: Why it is Right for Your Child* is a defense of Protestant parochial schools, and in many ways foreshadows arguments for the current Christian school movement. Although there is no extensive Jewish parochial school system, the Jewish educational experience in America is described by two sources. Lloyd P. Gartner's *Jewish Education in the United States: A Documentary History* is the most complete. Israel S. Chipkin, in "Jewish Education in America," provides a brief description. A summary history of both private and parochial education in America is Otto F. Kraushaar's *American Nonpublic Schools.*

While less dramatic as an issue, governmental regulation of both private and parochial schools is of great importance. Fred Francis Beach and Robert F. Will, in *The State and Nonpublic Schools,* list state and federal regulations concerning all nonpublic schools. Helen M. Jellison, in *State and Federal Laws Relating to Nonpublic Schools,* has studied state constitutional provisions and federal programs operating in nonpublic schools. One of the few books which deals with the relationship between public and nonpublic schools is Donald A. Erickson, *Public Controls for Nonpublic Schools.* Erickson believes that nonpublic schools serve a function in America, and seeks to understand the interplay between public and nonpublic education.

AID TO PAROCHIAL SCHOOLS

One continuing source of tension in church-state-education relations is that of assistance to nonpublic, especially parochial and church-related, schools, a pattern now known as "parochaid." One form of such assistance is supplying textbooks to nonpublic schools. The Supreme Court ruled in *Cochran v. Louisiana State Board of Education* (281 U.S. 370 [1930]) that such aid was constitutional on the basis of the child benefit doctrine. In *Board of Education v. Allen* (392 U.S. 236 [1968]), the Supreme Court ruled that a New York law requiring tax subsidies for textbooks for parochial and private schools was constitutional. Because the Court applied the child benefit theory in both of these cases, there have been few subsequent challenges to parochaid with respect to textbooks and instructional materials. Another form of assistance ruled constitutional by the Supreme Court is busing of parochial school students, an issue decided in *Everson.*

The most controversial aspect of this issue is direct aid to parochial schools in the form of financial grants from tax revenues. The literature indicates that patterns of support varied widely by states until the 1950s. Since that period numerous publications have analyzed the issue and argued for different outcomes. *Freedom of Choice in Education* by Virgil C. Blum, argues for such aid as do his *Freedom in Education: Federal Aid for All Children* and *Catholic Education: Survival or Demise?* Another proponent of parochial aid is George A. Kelly, in *Government Aid to Nonpublic Schools: Yes or No?;* see also the National Catholic Welfare Conference publication, *The Constitutionality of the Inclusion of Church-Related Schools in Federal Aid to Education.*

Daniel J. Callahan's *Federal Aid and Catholic Schools* contains arguments both for and against parochaid in an attempt to explain the issue objectively. It also includes data on parochial aid in other countries. Another relatively objective study of the parochial aid issue is Martin A. Larson's *When Parochial Schools Close: A Study in Educational Financing*. Larson describes case studies of sixteen communities where parochial schools closed and the effect of the closings on public schools and tax structures.

While Blum and others have argued for parochaid, others have opposed it. In *What Price Parochaid?*, Gaston Cogdell strongly states the case against aid to parochial education. Marvin Schick presents Jewish views on the issue in *Governmental Aid to Parochial Schools*. In *Public Aid to Nonpublic Schools* an economist, Daniel J. Sullivan, concludes that not only is public aid to parochial and private schools undesirable, but it is also not economically feasible.

An alternative approach has looked to vouchers or tuition tax credits. In *Educational Vouchers: Concepts and Controversies*, George R. La Noue dealt with a specific plan for aid to parochial and other nonpublic schools by means of vouchers allowing parents to choose schools other than public for their children (see also John E. Coons and Stephen D. Sugarman, *Education by Choice*). More recently, Barbara M. Morris, in *Tuition Tax Credits: A Responsible Appraisal*, has sought to present the concept of tuition tax credits for parochial and private education in an objective manner, although she finally opposes them. The Reagan administration has publicly supported tuition tax credits or an educational voucher plan. In a strange reversal of their usual position, conservative Protestants involved in the Christian school movement urge aid to nonpublic schools in order to gain funds for the Christian schools. It is difficult to predict how this new coalition of conservative Protestants and Catholics may influence any potential legislation concerning tuition tax credits or vouchers.

LITIGATION OF SELECTED ISSUES IN THE CONTEXT OF EDUCATION

As the preceding discussion has made clear, litigation has played an important and growing role in defining the many separate issues concerning church, state, and education which have appeared before the courts since 1870. Chapter 10 of this volume should be consulted for broader literature on the development of church-state law. In the context of education, a valuable resource is Robert T. Miller and Ronald B. Flowers's *Toward Benevolent Neutrality: Church, State, and the Supreme Court*. Miller and Flowers comment on every major church-state case through 1982, including all church-state-education cases. In their introduction, they address the neutrality doctrine espoused by the Supreme Court, as well as tests suggested by the Supreme Court to determine the constitutionality of cases. Other useful resources include former Congressman Robert F. Drinan's book, *Religion, the Courts, and Public Policy*. An analysis of how law has evolved on this subject is Frank J. Sorauf's *The Wall of Separation: The Constitutional Politics of Church and State*. An educator's view of the Supreme Court rulings is given by Thayer S. Warshaw, *Religion, Education and the Supreme Court*. All emphasize the importance of legal issues in the last quarter century.

Perhaps the most sustained issue in the courts has been the use of the Bible in public schools. In the nineteenth century, state courts adjudicated many challenges to Bible reading, among them *Minor*, discussed above. The debate over Bible reading in the schools emerged anew in the twentieth century. But although some states, beginning with Pennsylvania in 1913, decided to legislate Bible reading in the schools, others refused. Equally checkered was the outcome of challenges in the state courts. In 1957 the first challenge to Bible reading in the schools was brought before the federal courts. In the final stages of litigation in *Abington Township School District v. Schempp* (374 U.S. 203 [1963]), the U.S. Supreme Court paired the case with *Murray v. Curlett*, which challenged the mandatory recitation of the Lord's Prayer in Maryland's public schools. In its historic decision, the Court declared that both compulsory Bible reading and prayer were unconstitutional according to the establishment clause of the First Amendment to the Constitution and applied to the states under the Fourteenth Amendment.

An excellent source for the history of the Bible reading issue, including the Schempp decision, is Donald E. Boles, *The Bible, Religion, and the Public Schools*. Boles fully discusses Bible reading practices and includes information on court cases and decisions. See also David L. Barr and Nicholas Piediscalzi's *The Bible in American Education: From Sourcebook to Textbook*. Arthur B. Frommer's edited volume, *The Bible and the Public Schools*, concentrates largely on the Schempp case. Justice William O. Douglas, who voted with the majority in the Schempp case, defends the Court's actions in this case and the *Engel v. Vitale* prayer case (370 U.S. 421 [1962]) in *The Bible and the Schools*.

After World War II, as evidenced in *Murray v. Curlett*, the use of the Lord's Prayer (or other prayers) in the public schools was no less controversial than Bible reading. Concerted opposition to prayer began in the late 1950s, although the issue had been raised earlier. Kenneth M. Dolbeare and Phillip E. Hammond, in *The School Prayer Decisions: From Court Policy to Local Practice*, review earlier prayer cases through the lens of *Engel* and *Murray v. Curlett*, the crucial decisions. (In *Engel*, the Supreme Court ruled that a prayer mandated by the New York State Board of Regents was unconstitutional, basing its argument on the establishment clause of the First Amendment.)

The two prayer decisions evoked several responses. Representative publications are Charles Wesley Lowry's *To Pray or Not to Pray!*, which makes a case for prayer in the schools, and Charles E. Rice's *The Supreme Court and Public Prayer*, which argues that despite the Court's decisions, public prayer is still permissible.

The prayer decisions also stimulated numerous congressional representatives and senators to propose prayer amendments. A useful overview of these amendments is Richard K. Seckinger's "School Prayers and Bible Reading by Constitutional Amendment: An Analysis of 152 Congressional Proposals." Joseph A. Fisher, in "The Becker Amendment: A Constitutional Trojan Horse," discusses the amendment proposed by Representative Frank J. Becker, a strong proponent of prayer in the schools, and the consequences of its potential passage. Also useful are H. M. Engel's "School Prayer Issue, a Perverse Paradox," and a more recent essay by Ethan M. Fishman, "School Prayer: Principle and Circumstance in American Politics," which explores the issue from a Jewish perspective. The most recent development has taken the form of proposals for a moment of silence (usually interpreted as prayer) in the public schools. The issue has been greatly politicized by President Ronald Reagan who, while promising a prayer amendment, has delayed in proposing one. Several state courts have already ruled the moment of silence unconstitutional, but through 1986 no case has reached the Supreme Court.

Another highly divisive issue has concerned the teaching of evolution. By the latter part of the nineteenth century, the theory of evolution had become accepted in the biology curriculum of the public schools. Nevertheless, in 1920, John T. Scopes was brought to trial for breaking a Tennessee law forbidding the teaching of evolution. The infamous "Scopes Monkey Trial" gained worldwide attention when William Jennings Bryan agreed to represent the state, while Clarence Darrow defended Scopes. For this case, see especially Willard B. Gatewood, Jr., *Controversy in the Twenties. Fundamentalism, Modernism, and Evolution*, which sets out the religious factions involved in the Tennessee trial and other background to the evolution controversy. More recently cast as creationism versus evolution, the issue has preoccupied educators, with new cases coming before courts in Arkansas and California. For the California struggle, see Harvey Siegel, "Creationism, Evolution, and Education: The California Fiasco," and Donald H. Layton, "Scientists Versus Fundamentalists: The California Compromise." On the Arkansas case, see Marcel C. LaFollette's *Creationism, Science, and the Law: The Arkansas Case*, which includes reference and supplementary materials. The issue remains under contention in challenges to textbooks which include evolution but not creationism. With cases currently before state courts it is possible that one or more will eventually reach the Supreme Court.

Compulsory school attendance is another long-standing church-state-education issue. In a 1925 decision, *Pierce v. Society of Sisters* (268 U.S. 510), the Supreme Court struck down Oregon's mandatory public school attendance law, which made no exceptions for children attending religious or other private schools, on grounds that it restricted rights of private property. In passing, the Court stated that parents should be able to direct the education of their children. This has been widely interpreted as ensuring to parents their right to educate their children in private schools, among them religious schools. For interpretation of this case, see Stephen Arons, "The Separation of School and State: *Pierce* Reconsidered"; Donald P. Kommers and Michael J. Wahoske, *Freedom and Education: Pierce v. Society of Sisters Reconsidered;* and David B. Tyack, "The Perils of Pluralism: The Background of the Pierce Case." Compulsory school laws have also affected other religious minorities. The Amish, especially, have challenged compulsory education laws in, among other states, Pennsylvania, Wisconsin, and Iowa. In Iowa, a difficult compromise was reached, described by Harrell R. Rodgers, Jr., in *Community Conflict, Public Opinion and the Law: The Amish Dispute in Iowa.* Amish conflicts with education are also treated in Albert N. Keim's *Compulsory Education and the Amish: The Right Not to Be Modern.*

The practice of compulsory flag salute in schools was challenged by several religious groups, particularly the Jehovah's Witnesses. In 1940, the Supreme Court decided in *Minersville School District v. Gobitis* (310 U.S. 586) that requiring the flag salute was constitutional. Three years later the Court explicitly reversed itself in *West Virginia State Board of Education v. Barnette* (319 U.S. 624) and declared the required flag salute unconstitutional on First and Fourteenth Amendment grounds. David R. Manwaring, *Render Unto Caesar: The Flag Salute Controversy,* gives a useful history of this issue.

Censorship of books has also recently become a contested issue. In the name of religious belief, parents have demanded that certain textbooks or library books be banned. The issue is discussed by Michelle M. Kamhi in "Censorship vs. Selection—Choosing the Books Our Children Shall Read," C. L. McNearney in "The Kanawha County Textbook Controversy," and E. H. Welch in "Textbook Crisis in West Virginia." *Compelling Belief: The Culture of American Schooling,* by Stephen Arons, includes a chapter on censorship along with other issues. Resources on the flag salute, censorship, and additional topics such as holiday celebrations, the wearing of religious garb by teachers, and the use of religious exercises such as baccalaureate services are listed in the bibliography under the subheading "Other Issues in Public Education."

INCLUDING RELIGION IN THE PUBLIC SCHOOL CURRICULUM

In striking down Bible reading, the Schempp case suggested that religion might be studied, if not practiced, in the public schools. For constructive responses, see Robert Michaelsen, "Beyond the Ground Rules: Next Steps in the Study of Religion in the Public Schools," and Thayer S. Warshaw, "Teaching About Religion in Public Schools: Eight Questions." See more detailed proposals by James S. Ackerman and Jane Stouder Hawley, Thayer S. Warshaw, and John R. Whitney, which describe ways in which the Bible might be included in English literature classes. Publications by Lawrence C. Little and J. Susan Austin concern social studies curricula. See also Nicholas Piediscalzi and William E. Collie's *Teaching About Religion in Public Schools*. Claire Cox, *The Fourth R: What Can Be Taught About Religion in the Public Schools*, takes seriously the Supreme Court's refusal to allow religion in the schools. She presents the problems, suggests the potential, and proposes future means for instruction about religion to be included in public education.

Recent efforts to incorporate the study of religion within school curricula should be compared with an earlier attempt to foster a new program of religious education in the schools through cooperation with recognized religious groups. Religious classes were to be offered in the schools, with pupils excused from their regular courses. Begun in Gary, Indiana, early in this century, the plan was later called the "released-time program."

In one of the first education cases ruled on by the Supreme Court, the released-time program in Champaign, Illinois, which used public school facilities, was ruled unconstitutional. *McCollum v. Board of Education* (333 U.S. 203 [1948]) affected only released-time programs held on school property; the question of programs off school property was decided four years later in *Zorach v. Clauson* (343 U.S. 306 [1952]). The Court ruled that since they were not held on school premises, New York City's programs were constitutional.

Released-time and dismissed-time programs have given rise to another form of weekday religious education known as shared time. Shared-time programs allow a child to attend the public schools for part of each school day and then attend classes at a religious school for the remainder. *Dual Enrollment in Public and Nonpublic Schools*, edited by James E. Gibbs, describes many different variations on this arrangement, as does *Shared-time Programs: An Exploratory Study*, by the NEA. Shared-time programs have not been widely accepted because of problems involved with scheduling and transportation. In addition, neither proponents of public schools nor those of parochial schools see shared time as a desirable strategy.

The use of school premises by students for meetings of their own choosing, including religious meetings, has also led to litigation. A Supreme Court decision in *Lubbock Independent School District v. Lubbock Civil Liberties Union* (459 U.S. 1155 [1983]), and the Court's denial of rehearing in *Bender v. Williamsport* (106 S.Ct. 2003 [1986]) have failed to settle the issue. In 1984 Congress passed an equal access law, making it unlawful for public schools to discriminate against any meetings of students in the schools. The law allows schools to prohibit meetings of all student groups, and does not permit students to set up illegal groups.

HIGHER EDUCATION

For numerous historic reasons, higher education in the United States—college and graduate studies—has developed independently of primary and secondary education. Yet there are points of connection between them on issues related to state controls and funding. One major issue in church-state relations in higher education has been the presence of religion on state university campuses. Numerous authors have addressed this issue. Henry E. Allen, for example, in *Religion in the State University*, reports the proceedings of a conference of state university administrators on the responsibility of such schools to provide for the religious needs of students.

A good general introduction to the question of whether religion should be taught on state university campuses is by Howard H. Hintz, *Religion and Public Higher Education*. A Catholic viewpoint on the issue is provided by Richard Butler, *God on the Secular Campus*. From his experience as a Newman chaplain, Butler discusses the interaction of religion and secular higher education. The philosophical aspects of the issue can be found in Erich A. Walter, *Religion and the State University*. One study, *Religion in State Teachers Colleges*, looks specifically at this particular type of college. Several volumes survey selected colleges and universities or discuss higher education in general. Dean R. Hoge, in *Commitment on Campus: Changes in Religion and Values Over Five Decades*, chose a dozen colleges and traced the changes in their attitudes about religion from 1920 until 1970. Robert Michaelsen considers religion study in ten colleges in *The Study of Religion in American Universities*. See also Paul Ramsey and John F. Wilson, *The Study of Religion in American Colleges and Universities*.

In 1981, the Supreme Court ruled in *Widmar v. Vincent* (454 U.S. 263) that religious groups could not be denied free exercise of their religious beliefs on state university campuses. Religious freedom both as to study and practice seems to be assured in higher education.

State funding of religion in higher education has been raised as an issue on several occasions. Among the many commentaries are Walter Gelhorn and R.

Kent Greenawalt's *The Sectarian College and the Public Purse*, and Philip R. Moots and Edward M. Gaffney, Jr.'s *Church and Campus: Legal Issues in Religiously Affiliated Education*. The issue of public funds for religiously affiliated colleges and universities continues to be raised in the context of federally insured loan programs, federal programs for funding areas of the curriculum, and federal loans and grants for construction of buildings and dormitories.

APPROACHES TO THE HISTORY OF EDUCATION

In recent years, educational historians have turned from attempts to write simple histories of schools and schooling to consider the social context of education. A recent history which exemplifies this broader aspiration is Robert L. Church's *Education in the United States: An Interpretive History*. Others, like Henry J. Perkinson, *The Imperfect Panacea: American Faith in Education, 1865–1965*, review education for its importance to blacks, the city, the government, or those seeking economic opportunity in America. A history of the struggles to establish education in the cities is found in David B. Tyack's *The One Best System: A History of American Urban Education*—which also investigates religion's role in urban education. In light of such objectives, some historians have offered more ideological interpretation of the history of education. Clarence J. Karier, Paul Violas, and Michael B. Katz, in *Roots of Crisis: American Education in the Twentieth Century*, see education as a means of control of the poor by the upper and middle classes. Katz expands this view in *Class, Bureaucracy, and Schools: The Illusion of Educational Change in America*. A Marxist interpretation of education is offered by Samuel Bowles and Herbert Gintis, in *Schooling in Capitalist America*. A final example is Joel H. Spring's *Education and the Rise of the Corporate State*, which argues education was controlled by business and changed to meet the needs of rising corporations in America.

Other historians of education explore personal and professional influences upon education. Lawrence Cremin's *The Transformation of the School: Progressivism in American Education, 1876–1957*, provides a comprehensive look at the progressive education movement and how it changed American education. The influence of leading educators is suggested in Merle Curti's *The Social Ideas of American Educators*. Part II of this book concerns education since the Civil War. Edgar B. Wesley's *NEA, the First Hundred Years: The Building of the Teaching Profession* focuses upon the organization and professionalization of teaching.

Certain periodicals and organizations give continuing attention to church-state-education relations. Publications of the NEA should be checked since religion in education was a prominent topic in the early years of the association. Its current periodical, *Education*, also contains information and articles on these questions. The publications of the REA, especially the periodical *Religious Education*, also include numerous articles and information on church and state in education. For the past several decades, the National Council on Religion and Public Education has been actively involved in discussing church-state-education issues. See especially the council's periodical, *Religion and Public Education*.

Other helpful periodicals are the *Journal of Church and State, Church and State, LIBERTY*, and *Teachers College Record*. Law reviews, though often written in technical language, frequently offer helpful articles on court decisions and legislation concerning church-state issues in education. Publications of the American Jewish Committee, the American Civil Liberties Union, the J. M. Dawson Institute of Church-State Studies, and the National Council of Churches often speak to church-state-education issues. And finally, many denominations and religious bodies in America issue statements concerning religion and education which may be useful to researchers.

BIBLIOGRAPHY

GENERAL RESOURCES

Brickman, Willam W., and Lehrer, Stanley, eds. Religion, Government, and Education. New York: Society for the Advancement of Education, 1961.

Freund, Paul A., and Ulich, Robert. Religion and the Public Schools. Cambridge: Harvard University Press, 1965.

Kliebard, Herbert M., ed. Religion and Education in America: A Documentary History. Scranton, Pa.: International Textbook Company, 1969.

Michaelsen, Robert. Piety in the Public School. New York: Macmillan, 1970.

Wood, James E., Jr. Religion, the State, and Education. Waco, Tex.: Baylor University Press, 1984.

SECULARIZATION AND THE PUBLIC SCHOOLS

The Bible in the Public Schools: Arguments in the Case of John D. Minor et al. vs. The Board of Education of the City of Cincinnati et al. (Superior Court of Cincinnati) With the Opinions and Decision of the Court. Cincinnati: Robert Clarke & Co., 1870.

Brown, Samuel Windsor. The Secularization of American Education as Shown by State Legislation, State Constitutional Provisions and State Supreme Court Decisions. New York: Teachers College, Columbia University, 1912.

Confrey, Burton. <u>Secularism in American Education: Its</u>
   <u>History</u>. Washington, D.C.: Catholic University of America
   Press, 1931.

Harris, William Torrey. "The Division of Schools Funds for
   Religious Purposes." <u>Atlantic Monthly</u> 38 (August 1876),
   171-184.

Harris, William Torrey. "The Separation of the Church from the
   Tax-Supported School." <u>Educational Review</u> 26 (October
   1903), 222-235.

Ullmann, Daniel. <u>Amendments to the Constitution of the United</u>
   <u>States. Non-Sectarian and Universal Education</u>. New York:
   Baker & Godwin, printers, 1876.

PERSPECTIVES OF EDUCATIONAL PROFESSIONALS

American Council on Education. <u>The Relation of Religion to</u>
   <u>Public Education. The Basic Principles</u>. American Council on
   Education Studies, ser. 1, no. 26. Washington, D.C.:
   American Council on Education, 1947.

American Council on Education. <u>Religion and Public Education</u>.
   American Council on Education Studies, ser. 1, no. 22.
   Washington, D.C.: American Council on Education, 1945.

Athearn, Walter S. <u>Education and American Democracy</u>. Boston:
   Pilgrim Press, 1917.

Beman, Lamar Taney. <u>Religious Teaching in the Public Schools</u>.
   New York: H. W. Wilson, 1927.

Bower, William Clayton. <u>Church and State in Education</u>.
   Chicago: University of Chicago Press, 1944.

Brickman, William W. "Public and Religious Education as
   Copartners in the Formation of American Society, 1875-1964."
   <u>Religious Education</u> 59 (July-August 1964), 294-305.

Brown, Elmer Ellsworth. <u>The Changing Relations of Education</u>
   <u>and Religion</u>. Hartford: Hartford Seminary Press, 1908.

Cope, Henry F. <u>Education for Democracy</u>. New York: Macmillan,
   1920.

Corwin, Edward S. "The Supreme Court as the National School
   Board." <u>Law and Contemporary Problems</u> 14 (Winter 1949), 3-
   22.

Fleming, William S. <u>God in Our Public Schools</u>. Pittsburgh:
   National Reform Association, 1942.

Hubner, Sister Mary of Saint Michael. _Professional Attitudes Toward Religion in the Public Schools of the United States Since 1900_. Washington, D.C.: Catholic University of America Press, 1944.

Jackson, Jerome K., and Malmberg, Constantine F. _Religious Education and the State_. Garden City, N.Y.: Doubleday, Doran, 1928.

Knox, Raymond C. _Religion in Education_. New York: Columbia University Press, 1909.

McCarthy, Martha M. _A Delicate Balance: Church, State, and the Schools_. Bloomington, Ind.: Phi Delta Kappan Educational Foundation, 1983.

Martin, Renwick Harper. _Our Public Schools, Christian or Secular_. Pittsburgh: National Reform Association, 1952.

National Education Association. _The Essential Place of Religion in Education_. Ann Arbor, Mich.: National Education Association, 1916.

National Education Association. _The State and Sectarian Education_. Washington, D.C.: National Education Association, 1946.

National Education Association. _The Status of Religious Education in the Public Schools_. Washington, D.C.: National Education Association, 1949.

Thayer, Vivian Trow. _The Attack Upon the American Secular School_. Boston: Beacon Press, 1951.

Thayer, Vivian Trow. "Sectarian Attacks upon Public Education." In _Public Education and its Critics_, 30-72. New York: Macmillan, 1954.

Winchester, Benjamin S. _Religious Education and Democracy_. New York: Abingdon, 1917.

PERSPECTIVES OF RELIGIOUS PROFESSIONALS

Adams, Marjorie E., ed. _God in the Classroom_. South Pasadena, Calif.: National Educators Fellowship, 1970.

Beggs, David W., III, and McQuigg, R. Bruce, eds. _America's Schools and Churches: Partners in Conflict_. Bloomington: Indiana University Press, 1965.

Fellows of the Calvin Center for Christian Scholarship, Calvin College. Society, State, & Schools: A Case for Structural and Confessional Pluralism. Grand Rapids: Eerdmans, 1981.

Hall, Christopher. The Christian Teacher and the Law. Oak Park, Ill.: Christian Legal Society, 1975.

Hill, Brian. Faith at the Blackboard: Issues Facing the Christian Teacher. Grand Rapids: Eerdmans, 1982.

Loder, James E. Religion and the Public Schools. New York: Association Press, 1965.

McMillan, Richard C. Religion in the Public Schools: An Introduction. Macon, Ga.: Mercer University Press, 1983.

McMillan, Richard C., ed. Education, Religion, and the Supreme Court. Danville, Va.: Association of Baptist Professors of Religion, 1979.

Morrison, Charles Clayton. The Separation of Church and State in America. Indianapolis: International Convention of Disciples of Christ, 1947.

Nielsen, Niels C., Jr. God in Education: A New Opportunity for American Public Schools. New York: Sheed and Ward, 1966.

O'Neill, James M. Religion and Education Under the Constitution. New York: Harper & Brothers, 1949.

Swomley, John M. Religion, the State and the Schools. New York: Pegasus, 1968.

Van Alstine, George. The Christian and the Public School. Nashville: Abingdon, 1982.

THE ROLE OF RELIGION IN THE PUBLIC SCHOOLS

American Association of School Administrators. Religion in the Public Schools. New York: Harper & Row, 1964.

American Council on Education. The Function of the Public Schools in Dealing with Religion. Washington, D.C.: American Council on Education, 1953.

American Jewish Committee. Church, State, and the Public Schools. Institute of Human Relations Press Pamphlet Series no. 5. New York: Institute of Human Relations Press, 1963.

American Jewish Committee. Religion in Public Education. rev. ed. New York: American Jewish Committee, 1957.

Blanshard, Paul. Religion and the Schools: The Great
Controversy. Boston: Beacon Press, 1963.

Brown, Nicholas, C., ed. The Study of Religion in the Public
Schools. An Appraisal. Washington, D.C.: American Council
on Education, 1958.

Byrnes, Lawrence. Religion and Public Education. New York:
Harper & Row, 1975.

Conway, Don. "Religion and Public Education in the States."
International Journal of Religious Education 32 (March
1956), 34-40.

Costanzo, Joseph F. This Nation Under God: Church, State, and
Schools in America. New York: Herder and Herder, 1964.

Dierenfield, Richard B. Religion in American Public Schools.
Washington, D.C.: Public Affairs Press, 1962.

Gaebelein, Frank E. Christian Education in a Democracy. New
York: Oxford University Press, 1951.

Hay, Clyde Lemont. The Blind Spot in American Public
Education. New York: Macmillan, 1950.

Henry, Virgil. The Place of Religion in Public Schools. A
Handbook to Guide Communities. New York: Harper & Brothers,
1950.

Jacobsen, Philip. Religion in Public Education. A Guide for
Discussion. New York: American Jewish Committee, 1960.

Johnson, Alvin W., and Yost, Frank H. Separation of Church and
State in the United States. Minneapolis: University of
Minnesota Press, 1948.

Johnson, F. Ernest. American Education and Religion: The
Problem of Religion in the Schools. New York: Institute for
Religious and Social Studies, 1952.

Mattox, Fount William. The Teaching of Religion in the Public
Schools. Nashville: Bureau of Publications, George Peabody
College for Teachers, 1948.

Moehlman, Conrad Henry. School and Church: The American Way.
New York: Harper & Brothers, 1944.

National Council of Churches of Christ. Relation of Religion
to Public Education. New York: National Council of Churches
of Christ, 1960.

Public Schools and the First Amendment: Proceedings of a
    Conference Sponsored by Phi Delta Kappa [and] School of
    Education, Indiana University [and] School of Continuing
    Studies, Indiana University. April 20-21, 1982,
    Indianapolis, Indiana. Bloomington, Ind.: Phi Delta Kappa,
    1983.

"Religion in American Public Schools: Symposium." Religious
    Education 64 (March-April 1969), 83-128.

"Religion in the Public Schools: Symposium." Religious
    Education 59 (November-December 1964), 443-479.

Sizer, Theodore R., ed. Religion and Public Education.
    Boston: Houghton Mifflin, 1967.

Smith, Richard U. Religion and the Schools: From Prayer to
    Public Aid. Washington, D.C.: National School Public
    Relations Association, 1970.

Thayer, Vivian Trow. Religion in Public Education. New York:
    New York Society for Ethical Culture, 1946.

Williams, J. Paul. The New Education and Religion. New York:
    Association Press, 1945.

Moral and Character Education in the Public Schools

Bartlett, Edward R. "The Character Education Movement in the
    Public Schools." In Studies in Religious Education, edited
    by Philip Henry Lotz and L. W. Crawford, 450-471.
    Nashville: Cokesbury, 1931.

Bower, William C. Moral and Spiritual Values in Education.
    Lexington: University of Kentucky Press, 1952.

Educational Policies Commission. Moral and Spiritual Values in
    the Public Schools. Washington, D.C.: National Education
    Association, 1951.

Harris, William Torrey. Morality in the Schools. Boston:
    Christian Register Association, 1889.

Hunt, Thomas C. "Public Schools and Moral Education: An
    American Dilemma." Religious Education 74 (July-August
    1979), 350-372.

Hunt, Thomas C., and Maxson, Marilyn M. Religion and Morality
    in American Schooling. Washington, D.C.: University Press
    of America, 1981.

Kohlberg, Lawrence. Essays on Moral Development. San
    Francisco: Harper & Row, 1981.

McCluskey, Neil G. _Public Schools and Moral Education: The Influence of Horace Mann, William Torrey Harris, and John Dewey_. New York: Columbia University Press, 1958.

"Moral and Spiritual Values in the Public Schools: Symposium." _Religious Education_ 46 (July-August 1951), 195-256.

Simon, Sidney B., and Olds, Sally Wendkof. _Helping Your Child Learn Right From Wrong: A Guide to Values Clarification_. New York: McGraw-Hill, 1977.

Smith, Henry L.; McElhinney, Robert S.; and Steele, George R. _Character Redevelopment Through Religious and Moral Education in the Public Schools of the United States_. Bloomington: Bureau of Cooperative Research, Indiana University, 1937.

Taylor, Marvin J. _Religious and Moral Education_. New York: Center for Applied Research in Education, 1965.

Tuttle, Harold S. _Character Education by State and Church_. New York: Abingdon, 1930.

PAROCHIAL EDUCATION AS ALTERNATIVE

Beach, Fred Francis, and Will, Robert F. _The State and Nonpublic Schools_. Washington, D.C.: U.S. Department of Health, Education, and Welfare, 1958.

Beck, Walter H. _Lutheran Elementary Schools in the U.S._ St. Louis: Concordia, 1939.

Buetow, Harold A. _Of Singular Benefit: The Story of Catholic Education in the United States_. New York: Macmillan, 1970.

Chipkin, Israel S. "Jewish Education in America." In _Orientation in Religious Education_, edited by Philip Henry Lotz, 501-518. New York: Abingdon-Cokesbury Press, 1950.

Deferrari, Roy J. _A Complete System of Catholic Education is Necessary_. Boston: St. Paul Editions, 1964.

Diffley, Jerome E. _Catholic Reaction to American Public Education_. Notre Dame, Ind.: University of Notre Dame Press, 1959.

Erickson, Donald A., ed. _Public Controls for Nonpublic Schools_. Chicago: University of Chicago Press, 1969.

Gabel, Richard J. _In Hoc Signo?: A Brief History of Catholic Parochial Education in America_. Port Washington, N.Y.: Kennikat, 1973.

Gartner, Lloyd P., ed. <u>Jewish Education in the United States:</u>
<u>A Documentary History</u>. New York: Teachers College Press,
1969.

Ireland, John. <u>Catholic Schools for Catholic Youth</u>. New York:
Wagner, 1915.

Ireland, John. "State Schools and Parish Schools: Is Union
Between Them Possible?" <u>Journal of the Proceedings and</u>
<u>Addresses of the NEA</u> 29 (1890), 179-185..

Jellison, Helen M., ed. <u>State and Federal Laws Relating to</u>
<u>Nonpublic Schools</u>. Washington, D.C.: U.S. Department of
Health, Education, and Welfare, 1975.

Kienel, Paul A. <u>The Christian School: Why it is Right for Your</u>
<u>Child</u>. Wheaton, Ill.: Victor, 1974.

Koob, C. Albert, ed. <u>What is Happening to Catholic Education?</u>
Washington, D.C.: National Catholic Education Association,
1966.

Kraushaar, Otto F. <u>American Nonpublic Schools</u>. Baltimore:
Johns Hopkins University Press, 1972.

McCluskey, Neil G. <u>Catholic Education Faces Its Future</u>.
Garden City, N.Y.: Doubleday, 1969.

McCluskey, Neil G. <u>Catholic Viewpoint on Education</u>. Garden
City, N.Y.: Hanover House, 1959.

McCluskey, Neil G., ed. <u>Catholic Education in America: A</u>
<u>Documentary History</u>. New York: Bureau of Publications,
Teachers College, Columbia University, 1964.

McLaughlin, M. R. <u>Religious Education and the State: Democracy</u>
<u>Finds a Way</u>. Washington, D.C.: Catholic University of
America Press, 1967.

McLaughlin, Sister Raymond. <u>A History of State Legislation</u>
<u>Affecting Private Elementary and Secondary Schools in the</u>
<u>United States, 1870-1945</u>. Washington, D.C.: Catholic
University of America Press, 1946.

McQuaid, Bernard John. <u>Christian Free Schools</u>. Rochester,
N.Y.: A. C. Burrough, 1872.

McQuaid, Bernard John. <u>The Public School Question</u>. Boston:
Free Religious Association, 1876.

National Education Association. <u>The Two Sides of the School</u>
<u>Question</u>. Boston: Arnold, 1890.

O'Gorman, Robert T. "American and Catholic: The Education of a
     People Within the Public." In <u>The Church in the Education
     of the Public: Refocusing the Task of Religious Education</u>,
     edited by Jack L. Seymour, Robert T. O'Gorman, and Charles
     R. Foster. Nashville: Abingdon, 1984.

O'Neill, James M. <u>The Catholic in Secular Education</u>. New
     York: Longmans Green, 1956.

Reilly, Daniel F. <u>The School Controversy, 1891-1893</u>.
     Washington, D.C.: Catholic University of America Press,
     1943.

Ryan, Mary Perkins. <u>We're All in This Together: Issues and
     Options in the Education of Catholics</u>. New York: Holt,
     Rinehart and Winston, 1972.

Shaw, Russell B., ed. <u>Trends and Issues in Catholic Education</u>.
     New York: Citation, 1969.

Spalding, John L. <u>Education and the Future of Religion</u>. Notre
     Dame, Ind.: Ave Maria, 1901.

Stravinskas, Peter M. J. <u>Constitutional Rights and Religious
     Prejudice: Catholic Education as the Battleground</u>.
     Milwaukee: Catholic League, 1983.

AID TO PAROCHIAL SCHOOLS

Blum, Virgil C. <u>Catholic Education: Survival or Demise?</u>
     Chicago: Argus, 1969.

Blum, Virgil C. <u>Freedom in Education: Federal Aid for All
     Children</u>. Garden City, N.Y.: Doubleday, 1965.

Blum, Virgil C. <u>Freedom of Choice in Education</u>. rev. ed.
     Glen Rock, N.J.: Paulist Press, 1963.

Callahan, Daniel J., ed. <u>Federal Aid and Catholic Schools</u>.
     Baltimore: Helicon, 1964.

Cogdell, Gaston. <u>What Price Parochaid?</u> Washington, D.C.:
     Americans United for Separation of Church of State, 1968.

Coons, John E., and Sugarman, Stephen D. <u>Education by Choice:
     The Case for Family Control</u>. Berkeley: University of
     California Press, 1978.

Federal Council of the Churches of Christ in America. <u>Federal
     Aid to Sectarian Education?</u> New York: Federal Council of
     Churches, 1947.

Gabel, Richard J.   Public Funds for Church and Private Schools.
    Washington, D.C.: Catholic University of America Press,
    1937.

Golding, Joanne.   "State Aid to Non-Public Schools: A Legal-
    Historical Overview." Journal of Church and State 19
    (Spring 1977), 231-240.

Jones, Harry W.   "The Constitutional Status of Public Funds for
    Church Related Schools." Journal of Church and State 6
    (Winter 1964), 61-73.

Keesecker, Ward W.   Legislation Concerning Free Textbooks.
    U.S. Office of Education, 1935, Pamphlet no. 59.
    Washington, D.C.: U.S. Government Printing Office, 1935.

Kelly, George A., ed.   Government Aid to Nonpublic Schools: Yes
    or No? New York: St. John's University Press, 1972.

La Noue, George R.   Educational Vouchers: Concepts and
    Controversies. New York: Teachers College Press, 1972.

Larson, Martin A.   When Parochial Schools Close: A Study in
    Educational Financing. Washington, D.C.: R. B. Luce, 1972.

McGarry, Daniel D., and Ward, Leo.   Educational Freedom and the
    Case for Government Aid to Students in Independent Schools.
    Milwaukee: Bruce Publishing Company, 1966.

Morris, Barbara M.   Tuition Tax Credits: A Responsible
    Appraisal. Upland, Calif.: Barbara Morris Report, 1983.

National Catholic Welfare Conference.   The Constitutionality of
    the Inclusion of Church-Related Schools in Federal Aid to
    Education. Washington, D.C.: National Catholic Welfare
    Conference, 1961.

National Catholic Welfare Conference.   School Bus
    Transportation Laws in the United States. Washington, D.C.:
    National Catholic Welfare Conference, 1946.

National Education Association. Research Division.   State Aid
    to Private Schools: Constitutional Provisions, Statutes,
    Court Decisions. Washington, D.C.: National Education
    Association, 1943.

Powell, Theodore.   The School Bus Law: A Case Study in
    Education, Religion, and Politics. Middletown, Conn.:
    Wesleyan University Press, 1960.

Proffitt, Maris Marion.   State Provisions for Free Textbooks
    and Instructional Materials. U.S. Office of Education,
    Bulletin, 1944, no. 1. Washington, D.C.: U.S. Government
    Printing Office, 1944.

Schick, Marvin, ed. _Governmental Aid to Parochial Schools--_
   How Far? New York: National Jewish Commission on Law and
   Public Affairs, 1968.

Sullivan, Daniel J. _Public Aid to Nonpublic Schools._
   Lexington, Mass.: D. C. Heath, 1974.

Walinsky, Adam. "Aid to Parochial Schools." _New Republic_,
   7 October 1982, 18-21.

LITIGATION OF SELECTED ISSUES IN THE CONTEXT OF EDUCATION

General Sources

Boles, Donald E. _The Two Swords: Commentaries and Cases in_
   Religion and Education. Ames: Iowa State University Press,
   1967.

Drinan, Robert F. _Religion, the Courts, and Public Policy._
   New York: McGraw-Hill, 1963.

Fellman, David, ed. _The Supreme Court and Education._ 3d ed.
   New York: Teachers College Press, 1976.

Griffiths, William Edward. _Religion, the Courts and the Public_
   Schools: A Century of Litigation. Cincinnati: W. H.
   Anderson, 1966.

Reutter, E. Edmund, Jr. _Schools and the Law._ Dobbs Ferry,
   N.Y.: Oceana, 1964.

Miller, Robert T., and Flowers, Ronald B. _Toward Benevolent_
   Neutrality: Church, State, and the Supreme Court. rev. ed.
   Waco, Tex.: Baylor University Press, 1982.

Sorauf, Frank J. _The Wall of Separation: The Constitutional_
   Politics of Church and State. Princeton, N.J.: Princeton
   University Press, 1976.

Warshaw, Thayer S. _Religion, Education and the Supreme Court._
   Nashville: Abingdon, 1979.

Zollman, Carl Frederich Gustav. _American Church Law._ St.
   Paul: West Publishing, 1933.

Bible Reading in the Public Schools

Barr, David L., and Piediscalzi, Nicholas, eds. _The Bible in_
   American Education: From Sourcebook to Textbook. Chico,
   Calif.: Scholars Press, 1982.

Bennett, John R. The Bible in the Schools. Opinion of Judge
    John R. Bennett, in the Case of Weiss, et al. vs. the School
    Board of Edgerton. Edgerton, Wisc.: F. W. Coon, printer,
    1889.

Boles, Donald E. The Bible, Religion and the Public Schools.
    3d ed. Ames: Iowa State University Press, 1965.

Crooker, Joseph Henry. The Bible in the Public Schools, or Dr.
    Bascom and the Supreme Court. Madison, Wis.: State Journal
    Printing Company, 1890.

Decision of the Supreme Court of the State of Wisconsin
    Relating to the Reading of the Bible in the Public Schools.
    Opinions by Justices Lyon, Cassoday and Orton. Madison,
    Wisc.: Democrat Printing Company, 1890.

Douglas, William O. The Bible and the Schools. Boston: Little,
    Brown, 1966.

Frommer, Arthur B., ed. The Bible and the Public Schools. New
    York: Frommer/Pasmantier Pub. Corp., 1963.

Hood, William R. The Bible in the Public Schools, Legal Status
    and Current Practice. Washington, D.C.: U.S. Government
    Printing Office, 1923.

Keesecker, Ward W. The Legal Status of Bible Reading and
    Religious Instruction in the Public Schools. U.S. Office of
    Education, Bulletin no. 14. Washington, D.C.: U.S.
    Government Printing Office, 1930.

McAtee, W. A. Must the Bible Go? A Review of the Decision of
    the Supreme Court of Wisconsin, in the Edgerton Bible Case.
    Madison, Wisc.: Tracy, Gibbs, & Co., 1890.

People ex rel. Ring v. Board of Education. 245 Illinois
    Reports 334 (1910).

Weiss v. The District Board of Edgerton. 76 Wisconsin Reports
    177 (1890).

Westbrook, Richard B. Shall the Bible Be Read in Our Public
    Schools? Philadelphia: J. B. Lippincott, 1890.

Prayer in the Public Schools

Dolbeare, Kenneth M., and Hammond, Phillip E. The School
    Prayer Decisions: From Court Policy to Local Practice.
    Chicago: University of Chicago Press, 1971.

Engel, H. M. "School Prayer Issue, a Perverse Paradox."
    Catholic World 211 (June 1970), 125-127.

Fisher, Joseph A.   "The Becker Amendment: A Constitutional
    Trojan Horse." Journal of Church and State 11 (Autumn
    1969), 427-455.

Fishman, Ethan M.   "School Prayer: Principle and Circumstance
    in American Politics." Religious Education 77 (May-June
    1982), 269-278.

Laubach, John H.   School Prayers: Congress, the Courts, and the
    Public. Washington, D.C.: Public Affairs Press, 1969.

Lowry, Charles Wesley. To Pray or Not to Pray! Washington,
    D.C.: University Press of Washington, 1963.

Muir, William K. Prayer in the Public Schools: Law and
    Attitude Change. Chicago: University of Chicago Press,
    1967.

Rice, Charles E. The Supreme Court and Public Prayer. The Need
    for Restraint. New York: Fordham University Press, 1964.

Seckinger, Richard K. "School Prayers and Bible Reading by
    Constitutional Amendment: An Analysis of 152 Congressional
    Proposals." Religious Education 60 (September-October
    1965), 362-367.

The Teaching of Evolution in the Public Schools

Allen, Leslie H., ed. and comp. Bryan and Darrow at Dayton:
    The Record and Documents of the "Bible Evolution Trial."
    1925. Reprint. New York: Russell & Russell, 1967.

Gatewood, Willard B., Jr., ed. Controversy in the Twenties:
    Fundamentalism, Modernism, and Evolution. Nashville:
    Vanderbilt University Press, 1969.

Keith, Bill. Scopes II: The Great Debate: Creation vs.
    Evolution. Shreveport, La.: Huntington House, 1982.

LaFollette, Marcel C., ed. Creationism, Science, and the Law:
    The Arkansas Case. Cambridge, Mass.: MIT Press, 1983.

Larson, Edward J. Trial and Error: The American Controversy
    Over Creation and Evolution. New York: Oxford University
    Press, 1985.

Layton, Donald H. "Scientists Versus Fundamentalists: The
    California Compromise." Phi Delta Kappan 54 (June 1973),
    696-697.

Scopes v. Tennessee. 289 S.W. 363 (1927).

Siegel, Harvey. "Creationism, Evolution, and Education: The California Fiasco." Phi Delta Kappan 63 (October 1981), 95-101.

Zetterberg, J. Peter, ed. Evolution versus Creationism: The Public Education Controversy. Phoenix: Oryx Press, 1983.

Compulsory School Attendance

Arons, Stephen. "The Separation of School and State: Pierce Reconsidered." Harvard Education Review 46 (February 1976), 76-104.

Keim, Albert N., ed. Compulsory Education and the Amish: The Right Not to Be Modern. Boston: Beacon Press, 1975.

Kommers, Donald P., and Wahoske, Michael J., eds. Freedom and Education: Pierce v. Society of Sisters Reconsidered. Notre Dame, Ind.: Center for Civil Rights, University of Notre Dame Law School, 1978.

Rodgers, Harrell R., Jr. Community Conflict, Public Opinion and the Law: The Amish Dispute in Iowa. Columbus, Ohio: Charles E. Merrill, 1969.

Tyack, David B. "The Perils of Pluralism: The Background of the Pierce Case." American Historical Review 74 (October 1968), 74-98.

Other Issues in Public Education

Arons, Stephen. Compelling Belief: The Culture of American Schooling. New York: McGraw-Hill, 1983.

Boyer, W. W. "Baccalaureate in Brodhead: A Study of Interfaith Tension." School and Society 88 (April 9, 1960), 183-186.

Culligan, G. "Bah, Humbug: Christmas Poses Dilemma for the Schools." American Education 3 (December 1966), 14-17.

Kamhi, Michelle M. "Censorship vs. Selection--Choosing the Books Our Children Shall Read." Educational Leadership 39 (December 1981), 211-215.

Kerlinger, F. N. "Religious Displays and Public Education." School and Society (April 21, 1962), 196-198.

McNearney, Clayton L. "The Kanawha County Textbook Controversy." Religious Education 70 (September-October 1975), 519-540.

Manwaring, David R. Render Unto Caesar: The Flag Salute Controversy. Chicago: University of Chicago Press, 1962.

"Religious Garb in the Public Schools: A Study in Conflicting
    Liberties." University of Chicago Law Review 22 (Summer
    1955), 888-895.

Sherwin, J. Stephen. "Christmas in the Schools." School and
    Society 85 (November 9, 1957), 331-333.

Torpey, William George. "Wearing Distinctive Garb." In
    Judicial Doctrines of Religious Rights in America. Chapel
    Hill: University of North Carolina Press, 1948.

Welch, E. H. "Textbook Crisis in West Virginia." Educational
    Forum 41 (November 1976), 26, 30-32.

INCLUDING RELIGION IN THE PUBLIC SCHOOL CURRICULUM

Curricular Alternatives

Ackerman, James S., and Hawley, Jane Stouder. On Teaching The
    Bible as Literature. Bloomington: Indiana University Press,
    1968.

Austin, J. Susan. "Religion in Elementary School Social
    Studies: A Vehicle for Attitudinal Change." Religious
    Education 71 (September-October 1976), 474-487.

Cox, Claire. The Fourth R: What Can Be Taught About Religion
    in the Public Schools. New York: Hawthorn Books, 1969.

Engel, David E., ed. Religion in Public education: Problems
    and Prospects. New York: Paulist Press, 1974.

Gloger, Sheldon. "The Bible in the Science Program."
    Religious Education 68 (January-February 1973), 126-132.

Healey, R. M. "An Interim Report on the Study of Religion in
    Public Schools." Journal of Church and State 20 (Autumn
    1978), 469-489.

Little, Lawrence C., ed. "Religion in Public School Social
    Studies Curricula." Religious Instruction Association, Fort
    Wayne, Ind., 1970. Photocopy.

Little, Lawrence C., ed. Religion in the Social Studies.
    Report of the Committee on Religion in Social Studies
    Curriculum of the Pittsburgh Public Schools. New York:
    National Conference of Christian and Jews, 1966.

Michaelsen, Robert. "Beyond the Ground Rules: Next Steps in
    the Study of Religion in the Public Schools." Religious
    Education 68 (March-April 1973), 212-217.

Panoch, James V., and Barr, David L. Religion Goes to School:
    A Practical Handbook for Teachers. New York: Harper & Row,
    1968.

Piediscalzi, Nicholas. "The Separation of Church and State:
    Public Education Religion Studies." Religious Education 75
    (November-December 1980), 631-639.

Piediscalzi, Nicholas, and Collie, William E., eds. Teaching
    About Religion in Public Schools. Niles, Ill.: Argus
    Communications, 1977.

Taylor, Lynn. Religion and Culture in Education: Open Door for
    the Fourth R. Lawrence: University of Kansas Publications,
    1977.

Warshaw, Thayer S. "The Bible as Textbook in Public Schools."
    Religious Education 77 (May-June 1982), 279-299.

Warshaw, Thayer S. Handbook for Teaching the Bible in
    Literature Classes. Nashville: Abingdon, 1978.

Warshaw, Thayer S. "Teaching About Religion in Public Schools:
    Eight Questions." Phi Delta Kappan 49 (November 1967), 127-
    133.

Whitney, John R. "Introducing Religious Literature in
    Pennsylvania Secondary Schools." Religious Education 63
    (March-April 1968), 89-96.

Programs for Released, Dismissed, and Shared Time

Allred, Vincent C. Legal Aspects of Released Time.
    Washington, D.C.: National Catholic Welfare Conference,
    1946.

Cope, Henry F. Weekday Religious Education. New York: Doran,
    1922.

Davis, Mary Dabney. Weekday Religious Instruction: Classes for
    Public-School Pupils Conducted on Released School Time.
    U.S. Office of Education, 1933, Pamphlet no. 33.
    Washington, D.C.: U.S. Government Printing Office, 1933.

Davis, Mary Dabney. Week-Day Classes in Religious Education
    Conducted on Released School Time for Public School Pupils.
    U.S. Office of Education, Bulletin 1941, no. 3. Washington,
    D.C.: U.S. Government Printing Office, 1941.

Drinan, Robert F. "McCollum Decision: Three Years After."
    America 80 (March 5, 1949), 593-595.

Duker, Sam. "The Issue of Shared Time." Educational Forum 29
    (January 1965), 235-241.

Friedlander, Anna Fay. The Shared Time Strategy. St. Louis: Concordia, 1966.

Gibbs, James E., Jr., et al. Dual Enrollment in Public and Nonpublic Schools. Washington, D.C.: U.S. Department of Health, Education, and Welfare, Office of Education, 1965.

Gove, Floyd S. Religious Education on Public School Time. Cambridge: Graduate School of Education, Harvard University, 1926.

Keesecker, Ward W. Laws Relating to the Releasing of Pupils from Public Schools for Religious Instruction. U.S. Office of Education, 1933, Pamphlet no. 39. Washington, D.C.: U.S. Government Printing Office, 1933.

McCollum, Vashti Cromwell. One Woman's Fight. Boston: Beacon Press, 1961.

McKibben, Frank M., ed. Report and Interpretation of the First National Conference on Weekday Religious Education. New York: National Council of Churches, 1956.

National Education Association. Research Division. Shared-time Programs: An Exploratory Study. Washington, D.C.: National Education Association, 1964.

Patric, Gordon. "The Impact of a Court Decision: Aftermath of the McCollum Case." Journal of Public Law 6 (1957), 455-463.

Sorauf, Frank J. "Zorach v. Clauson: The Impact of a Supreme Court Decision." American Political Science Review 53 (September 1959), 777-791.

Wirt, William M. "The Gary Public Schools and the Churches." Religious Education 11 (June 1916), 221-226.

HIGHER EDUCATION

Allen, Henry E., ed. Religion in the State University. Minneapolis: Burgess, 1950.

Butler, Richard. God on the Secular Campus. Garden City, N.Y.: Doubleday, 1963.

Cunninggim, Merrimon. The Protestant Stake in Higher Education. Washington, D.C.: Council of Protestant Colleges and Universities, 1961.

Gauss, Christian, ed. The Teaching of Religion in American Education. New York: Ronald Press, 1951.

Gelhorn, Walter, and Greenawalt, R. Kent. _The Sectarian College and the Public Purse_. Dobbs Ferry, N.Y.: Oceana, 1970.

Hazen Foundation and American Council on Education. _College Reading and Religion: Being Reports of a Survey of College Reading Materials_. New Haven: Yale University Press, 1948.

Hintz, Howard H. _Religion and Public Higher Education_. Brooklyn: Brooklyn College Press, 1955.

Hoge, Dean R. _Commitment on Campus: Changes in Religion and Values Over Five Decades_. Philadelphia: Westminster, 1974.

Holbrook, Clyde A. _Religion, a Humanistic Field_. Englewood Cliffs, N.J.: Prentice Hall, 1963.

Kimber, Harry H. _The Teaching of Religion in State Universities_. Ann Arbor: University of Michigan, 1960.

McLean, Milton D., ed. _Religious Studies in Public Universities_. Carbondale: Southern Illinois University Press, 1967.

Michaelsen, Robert. _The Study of Religion in American Universities_. New Haven: Society for Religion in Higher Education, 1965.

Michaelsen, Robert. _The Scholarly Study of Religion in the College or University_. New Haven: Society for Religion in Higher Education, n.d.

Moots, Philip R., and Gaffney, Edward M., Jr. _Church and Campus: Legal Issues in Religiously Affiliated Education_. Notre Dame, Ind: University of Notre Dame Press, 1979.

Ramsey, Paul, and Wilson, John F. _The Study of Religion in American Colleges and Universities_. Princeton, N.J.: Princeton University Press, 1970.

Religion in State Teachers Colleges. New Haven: Yale University Divinity School, 1951.

Smith, Harry E. _Secularization and the University_. Atlanta: John Knox, 1968.

Underwood, Kenneth Wilson. _The Church, the University, and Social Policy_. 2 vols. Middletown, Conn.: Wesleyan University Press, 1969.

Walter, Erich A., ed. _Religion and the State University_. Ann Arbor: University of Michigan Press, 1964.

Wilder, Amos N., ed. _Liberal Learning and Religion_. New York: Harper & Brothers, 1951.

APPROACHES TO THE HISTORY OF EDUCATION

Bowles, Samuel, and Gintis, Herbert. Schooling in Capitalist America: Educational Reform and the Contradiction of Economic Life. New York: Basic, 1976.

Church, Robert L. Education in the United States: An Interpretive History. New York: Free Press, 1976.

Cremin, Lawrence. The Transformation of the School: Progressivism in American Education, 1876-1957. New York: Knopf, 1961.

Curti, Merle. The Social Ideas of American Educators. Patterson, N.J.: Littlefield, Adams, 1959.

Karier, Clarence J.; Violas, Paul; and Katz, Michael B. Roots of Crisis: American Education in the Twentieth Century. Chicago: Rand McNally, 1973.

Katz, Michael B. Class, Bureaucracy, and Schools: The Illusion of Educational Change in America. New York: Praeger, 1971.

Katz, Michael B., ed. Education in American History: Readings on the Social Issues. New York: Praeger, 1973.

Perkinson, Henry J. The Imperfect Panacea: American Faith in Education, 1865-1965. New York: Random House, 1968.

Seymour, Jack L.; O'Gorman, Robert T.; and Foster, Charles R. The Church in the Education of the Public: Refocusing the Task of Religious Education. Nashville: Abingdon, 1984.

Spring, Joel H. Education and the Rise of the Corporate State. Boston: Beacon Press, 1972.

Tyack, David B. The One Best System: A History of American Urban Education. Cambridge: Harvard University Press, 1974.

Wesley, Edgar B. NEA, the First Hundred Years: The Building of the Teaching Profession. New York: Harper & Brothers, 1957.

FURTHER BIBLIOGRAPHIC SOURCES

Brickman, William W. "Selected Bibliography on the History of Church-State Relations in Education in the United States." New York University School of Education, New York, 1959. Photocopy.

Cohen, Iva. "Church, State and Education: A Selected
    Bibliography." 2d rev. ed. American Jewish Committee,
    Library of Jewish Information, New York, 1954. Photocopy.

Drouin, Edmond G., comp. The School Question: A Bibliography
    on Church-State Relationships in American Education, 1940-
    1960. Washington, D.C.: Catholic University of America
    Press, 1963.

Little, Lawrence C. Religion and Public Education: A
    Bibliography. Pittsburgh: University of Pittsburgh, 1966.

Menendez, Albert J. "Church, State, and Education." In Church-
    State Relations: An Annotated Bibliography. New York:
    Garland Publishing, 1976.

Menendez, Albert J. Religious Conflict in America: A
    Bibliography. New York: Garland Publishing, 1985.

Politella, Joseph. Religion in Education: An Annotated
    Bibliography. Oneonta, N.Y.: American Association of
    Colleges for Teacher Education, 1956.

Pope, James D. "Moral, Spiritual and Religious Values in
    Public Education." University of Florida Education Library
    Bibliography no. 31, Gainesville, 1958. Photocopy.

10

Religion and Law in the United States: 1870 to the Present

Winnifred F. Sullivan

In contrast to the period covered by the first volume of this work, questions of religion and law since 1870 have been increasingly dominated by the Supreme Court. The result has been both a nationalization and a constitutionalization of the issues. Moreover, since Reconstruction there has been an enormous increase in the pervasiveness of government in people's lives, an intensified litigiousness, particularly over civil rights, and a proliferation of new religions and new religious sects in American society. All of these trends have caused a growth in the number and variety of religion cases in both the state and federal courts. This essay will reflect briefly on the ways in which religion and the American legal system, primarily as it functions in the courts, have encountered one another during this period. Other essays in this volume address the church-state issue more broadly as an intellectual and cultural phenomenon as well as addressing issues concerning church and state as they arise specifically in the context of education and of the family. These latter specific applications overlap with this essay, and those essays should be consulted in conjunction with this one. I have not included works in the bibliography which deal solely with church-state law as it relates to education or family issues.

Literature concerning church, state, and law ranges from philosophical works on the interrelationship between law and religion to articles detailing the specific applications of the Internal Revenue Code and is addressed to three different audiences: lawyers and judges, scholars, and laypeople. I have tried to reflect this unwieldy diversity in the essay and bibliography that follow.

Most articles in law reviews and books by lawyers and legal scholars are concerned with articulating an understanding of the law at a particular moment in time for the purposes of representing a client. As far as a practicing lawyer is concerned, law review articles may become dated very quickly.

There are, therefore, a great many of them and few are enduring classics. To an historian, however, these articles may be very useful in understanding legal history. I have, therefore, tried to cite law review articles which illustrate changes in the law. My citation of relevant law review articles is by no means exhaustive. There are hundreds of them.

Two cases from the 1870s address questions which are early precursors of issues which continued to be significant for the entire period: *Reynolds v. United States*[1] and *Board of Education of Cincinnati v. Minor.*[2] *Reynolds*, the first religious freedom case to reach the Supreme Court, concerned a conflict between a duty to conform to secular laws and a duty to obey unorthodox religious commands, and raised not only the issue about the appropriate scope of the First Amendment free exercise clause provision[3] but also demonstrated the dependence of the criminal law on religious moral teaching. The Cincinnati case was one of many establishment cases which focused on the appropriate relationship between religious tradition and national culture.

In 1878 the Supreme Court considered the case of Joshua Reynolds, who had been convicted of bigamy in the Territory of Utah. He had appealed, claiming the protection of the First Amendment on the ground, among others, that as a male member of the Church of Jesus Christ of Latter-day Saints he had a duty to practice polygamy. Failure to do so would result in damnation; therefore he was justified in violating the law. Mr. Chief Justice Waite, for the Supreme Court, affirmed the decision of the Utah court, finding that the First Amendment prohibition against infringement of the free exercise of religion extended only to opinion, not to action which might be subject to criminal prosecution.

The language of the Court in *Reynolds* is intolerant and hostile to the Mormon church, reflecting the political and theological environment in which the case was brought. The "secular regulation" rule established by *Reynolds*, however, was good law until 1943, when it began to break down. Religious exemptions from compliance with laws of general application, especially criminal laws, are, nevertheless, in fact quite rare, tending to be examples of ad hoc recognition of eccentric religious practices by small religious communities with a claim to historical justification.[4]

In the course of his opinion, Chief Justice Waite quoted Thomas Jefferson's characterization of the First Amendment religion clauses as "building a wall of separation between Church and State." The "wall" metaphor employed by Jefferson has provided a focus for, but has also often obscured, the national debate over the historical meaning of the First Amendment which has raged with greater or lesser intensity since the *Reynolds* decision.

Several years before *Reynolds* was decided, the Supreme Court of Ohio was asked to address the question as to whether Bible reading in public schools was required by the Ohio Constitution. After declaring a commitment to religious freedom, the Ohio Constitution stated:

Religion, morality and knowledge, however, being essential to good government, it shall be the duty of the general assembly to pass suitable laws to protect every religious denomination in the peaceable enjoyment of its own mode of public worship, and to encourage schools and the means of instruction.[5]

Further on it continued:

The general assembly shall make provisions, by taxation or otherwise, as, with the income arising from the school trust fund, will secure a thorough and efficient system of common schools throughout the state.[6]

A group of taxpayers had sued to reinstate in the Cincinnati schools the reading of the Protestant Bible which had been discontinued because of Catholic and Jewish protest. In a lengthy opinion dismissing the suit, Justice Welch discussed the necessity of a doctrine of "hands off" as a solution to the problem of church and state:

Let the state not only keep its own hands off, but let it also see to it that religious sects keep their hands off each other. Let religious doctrines have a fair field, and a free intellectual, moral, and spiritual conflict. The weakest—that is, the intellectually, morally, and spiritually weakest—will go to the wall, and the best will triumph in the end. This is the golden truth which it has taken the world eighteen centuries to learn, and which has at last solved the terrible enigma of "church and state."[7]

The debate over the appropriate role of publicly endorsed religion in this country has focused on religion in education and has been loud and rancorous. Cases concerning public schools form a large percentage of the religion cases considered by the Supreme Court, and there are constant legislative efforts to promulgate laws either aiding or forbidding aid to religious schools and either enforcing or prohibiting prayer in public schools. Most recently, the Supreme Court declared unconstitutional an Alabama statute authorizing a moment of silence for meditation or voluntary prayer at the beginning of the school day because it was the stated intention of the Alabama legislature to foster religion.[8]

By the end of the nineteenth century, notwithstanding a considerable amount of continued bigotry and prejudice especially against Catholics, a public consensus, reflected in the opinions in *Reynolds* and the Ohio Bible case, had been reached supporting the ideals of the First Amendment religion clauses as to both religious freedom and no establishment. Americans were proud of their tradition of church-state separation, and Protestant theology had developed so as to incorporate the principles of the First Amendment. The First Amendment had become, one might say, not only a constitutional principle, but also an article of faith.

In 1898, the English observer, Lord Bryce, wrote:

It is accepted as an axiom by all Americans that the civil power ought to be not only neutral and impartial as between different forms of faith, but ought to leave these matters entirely on one side, regarding them no more than it regards the artistic or literary pursuits of the citizens. There seem to be no two opinions on this subject in the United States.[9]

Application of this axiom to the myriad confrontations between religion and government over the following century has proved more difficult, and has produced both a mountain of legal cases and of scholarly articles analyzing them and an increasingly varied number of different situations to which the principle needs to be applied. (Two good introductions to American church-state law are David Fellman, *Religion in American Public Law* and Richard E. Morgan, *The Supreme Court and Religion.*)

The courts, at their best shrines to human impartiality and rationality, have been and continue to be ill-equipped for discourse with individuals or groups (like Joshua Reynolds and the Mormon church) motivated by a divinely compelled duty to a belief concerning the ultimate meaning of life. Often acutely aware of their incompetence, they have tended to try to avoid ruling on what they consider to be purely theological issues, but have not entirely succeeded in leaving them "on one side."

In the late nineteenth and early twentieth centuries, the large Protestant denominations exercised great national political power. Examples of their influence include framing public responses to such issues as prohibition and gambling, and involvement in welfare issues. Legal cases involving religious issues, however, were largely local, being decided in state and lower federal courts, interpreting state constitutions and laws.[10] (*Reynolds* was an exception as it arose in a territory and therefore within the jurisdiction of the federal court.) These cases ranged over the many areas in which churches and individuals practicing their religion came into contact with state and local governments as well as the spectrum of internal disputes within congregations and religious bodies which were brought into the courts. Their resolution varied from state to state as the histories and religious complexion of the states varied.[11] An enormous body of primary legal material is available for this period: state constitutions and statutes, state legislative histories, transcripts of court proceedings and published opinions as well as contemporary articles and treatises on church law.[12] Very little scholarly analysis of this material has been done.

A church as an institution functioning in the community interacted with local, state, and federal governments at many points. Churches might be incorporated under state laws providing for the incorporation of religious bodies. They were required to comply with a range of local, state, and federal regulations governing taxation, employment, and building codes. There were often special zoning ordinances for their benefit. Clerics frequently had special privileges—exemption from jury duty, exemption from taxation, special rates on public transportation, privilege to keep confidential disclosures made by a member of their congregations.

One of the most frequent disputes bringing churches into courts was intra-church disputes concerning the ownership of church property after a split in the congregation. One of these, *Watson v. Jones,*[13] reached the Supreme Court in 1872. The congregation of a Presbyterian church in Louisville, Kentucky, had been split by a difference in the national Presbyterian church over the Civil War. A minority of the congregation, loyal to the Confederacy and objecting to a resolution of the national church condemning slavery, had control of the property. The majority filed suit in federal court and eventually appealed to the Supreme Court. The Court rejected the English rule of implied trust urged by the minority which would have required the Court to determine which group was true to Presbyterian doctrine; instead the Court announced a rule requiring an American court to determine only who had the power under the rules of the particular church organization to decide such matters. Distinguishing English precedent on the ground that England had an established church and did not recognize religious freedom, the Court said:

The law knows no heresy, and is committed to the support of no dogma, the establishment of no sect. The right to organize voluntary religious associations to assist in the expression and dissemination of any religious doctrine, and to create tribunals for the decision of controverted questions of faith within the association, and for the ecclesiastical government of all the individual members, congregations and officers within the general association, is unquestioned.[14]

Thus, the rule of the association governs, and the court does not inquire as to the truth of religious doctrine. That rule, unique to American courts, has more or less prevailed since, although there has been controversy over its application to particular situations. *Watson v. Jones* was brought in a federal court because it was a suit between citizens of different states (known as diversity jurisdiction). It applied federal common law so was not necessarily applied by the state courts. In *Presbyterian Church in the United States v. Mary Elizabeth Blue Hull Memorial Presbyterian Church*, the principle enunciated in *Watson* was constitutionalized and applied to the states.[15]

Intrachurch disputes continue to flourish, of course, as can be seen in a July 1986 article in the *Chicago Tribune* concerning a dispute over the choice of pastor. According to the article, such intrachurch disputes are brought into the Circuit Court of Cook County on an average of twice a week.[16]

State regulation of churches and religious practitioners has created innumerable conflicts, some of which were later resolved by the Supreme Court. Sunday closing laws were challenged by Sabbatarians, among others, as an establishment of religion. Faith healing by Christian Science practitioners led to medical licensing laws. Exemption of churches and ministers from various forms of taxation was challenged as an establishment of religion.

To a large extent, legal rules about religious issues have reflected the Protestant character of American society in shaping the relationship between religion and government. Jefferson's "wall" metaphor has fit in nicely with an individualistic, democratic, and private style of religion. One reason why Protestants could be so enthusiastic about separation of church and state was that, in a sense, their church was not separate. A generalized Protestant establishment supported and gave expression to Protestant values. Mormon and Catholic traditions, among others, were seen to be undemocratic and un-American. First Amendment law has been largely forged by minority religious groups seeking elbowroom for their religious life-style in a dominantly Protestant society.[17]

The period of this essay is divided dramatically by the decision in 1940 by the Supreme Court in *Cantwell v. Connecticut*.[18] The Court in that case determined that the enactment of the Fourteenth Amendment had had the effect of applying the First Amendment religion clauses, until then understood as addressed only to the federal government, to the states.[19] The great preponderance of the Supreme Court's efforts to put into practice the religion clauses of the First Amendment follow that decision, as most cases have arisen in a state law context.

The effect of *Cantwell* was not only to increase the number of Supreme Court cases but to focus all courts, state and lower federal courts, on the First Amendment and, specifically, on the Supreme Court's interpretation of the First Amendment. Since 1940, therefore, when the Supreme Court became the most important expositor of church-state law in the United States, public discussion of the issues has been framed in categories drawn from the language and history of the First Amendment religion clauses. Thus the Court and its critics have tended to divide religion cases into "freedom" or "establishment" cases. Interest groups have tended to divide into "separationists" or "accommodationists" depending on their reading of the intentions of the framers of the First Amendment and the relative importance each assigns to the two clauses. Separationists tend to regard "no establishment" as the dominant principle. Accommodationists assert the supremacy of religious freedom. These categories have become loaded with emotional baggage because they represent serious divisions within American society as to the appropriate relationship between church and state. At the extreme they are cloaks for serious and bitter prejudice.

Since *Cantwell* not only has there been this further centralization or nationalization of legal conflicts involving church-state issues, but there has also been a parallel rise in the importance of professional advocates. In the most marginal local conflicts between religion and government one finds briefs filed by national groups which make a full-time effort with professional legal staffs to monitor and influence interpretation of the First Amendment.

Traditionally, these groups have fallen into the two camps mentioned above, separationist and accommodationist. Although there is some blurring of these lines on particular issues, their importance in characterizing and presenting church-state issues has been considerable. Individual lawsuits are forums for rehashing clashes over national public policy through the filing of amicus briefs. The dialogue on church and state is dominated and often obscured by purportedly objective works written by partisans of one or the other. (Helpful works on this issue include Richard E. Morgan, *Politics of Religious Conflict* and Frank J. Sorauf, *The Wall of Separation.*)

The separationists, under the rallying cry of "no establishment," include ascendant Protestants afraid of the Vatican's political influence and therefore hostile to parochial education, Jews who believe that protection for a place in American society free from persecution demands a rigid separation, and secularists opposed to religion in general. The major active separationist groups with professional legal staffs include the National Council of Churches, Protestants and Other Americans United for the Separation of Church and State (known as Americans United), the Religious Liberty Association (supported by the Seventh Day Adventists), the American Jewish Congress, the American Jewish Committee of the Anti-Defamation League, and the American Civil Liberties Union.

Accommodationists have traditionally included Catholics and a range of minority religious groups. Accommodationist groups include the United States Catholic Conference, Citizens for Educational Freedom (a lay Catholic group), and fundamentalist Protestant groups.

This debate is carried on also among academics, who have argued the separationist or accommodationist position based on differing readings of

the history of the First Amendment and of the influences which affected its
drafting and adoption.[20] The difference centers on the relative importance to
be given to the political and religious motives for the First Amendment. Is the
wall intended to protect the church from the state or the state from the
church? Separationists tend to argue the latter; accommodationists the former. Separationists also tend to emphasize the importance of neutrality and
equality as constitutional principles, while accommodationists tend to advocate the special status of religion in American society. Neither views the wall
as impregnable, but each views it as assailable only from one side. Separationists are comfortable with any regulation of churches which results from
laws of general application. Accommodationists tend to advocate an actively
supportive role toward religion, on the ground that it encourages public
morality.

Separationists tend to ignore or underestimate the real importance and
influence of religion in people's lives, both private and public, and to be
blindly absolutist in their insistence upon separation as they see it: keeping
religion private. It can also be argued that the active support of religion by
government tends to foster a nondenominational, flavorless civic religion, the
function of which is to support the status quo rather than to ask prophetic
questions about the meaning of life. In two recent cases Chief Justice Burger
has appealed to historic religious practice to excuse government endorsement of sectarian practices. In *Lynch v. Donnelly*,[21] the display of a crèche
on public property was approved as evocative of the historical background of
a public holiday, rather than as government support of religion. In *Bowers v.
Hardwick*,[22] historic religious tradition was cited as a reason to condemn
sodomy. In neither case was there an inquiry by the Court into the religious
values which underlay the practice or any consideration of the effect on both
religious and nonreligious people of governmental endorsements of a religious tradition.

In *Bowers*, as in *Reynolds*, religious tradition is invoked to validate a moral
proscription enacted as a criminal law. A much-debated question is the extent to which it is appropriate in a secular pluralistic society to penalize
violations of behavior considered immoral within one religious tradition, but
which may or may not be a threat to a secular society in a purely utilitarian
sense.[23] A broader question is the general philosophical relationship between
religion and law. The historical dependence of law on religion, both in its
content and institutionally, is obvious. To what extent modern American law
should acknowledge that dependence and how it can do so in a nonsectarian
way are more difficult questions.

In recent years there has been some shifting or softening of rigid separa-
tionist/accommodationist positions. The extremes are still represented by
the strident secularists on the one hand and by fundamentalist Protestants on

the other, but the middle is less predictable as traditionally separationist Protestant groups have become alarmed for one reason or another by increasing secularization and government bureaucratic involvement in religious affairs and traditional opponents, like Americans United and the Bishops Conference, are occasionally finding themselves on the same side.[24] Perhaps in a secular society the religion of the majority is becoming a minority group demanding protection from the religious freedom clause.

The Supreme Court's artificial division of religion cases into establishment cases and religious freedom cases has led to irreconcilable conflicts and tensions between interpretation of the two clauses because the same case often presents both an establishment and a freedom issue depending on how the question is framed. Government action advancing religion may have the effect of discriminating among religious or aiding religion over irreligion and therefore presenting both freedom and establishment questions. On the other hand, a free exercise claim of exemption from the application of secular laws, if granted, may result in an establishment issue. Although efforts have been made periodically to read the two clauses together as embodying one principle,[25] the Court begins consideration of a First Amendment religion case by labeling it either an establishment or a freedom of religion case and then on the basis of two separate lines of precedent, proceeds to apply different legal standards.

The first establishment case was *Everson v. Board of Education of the Township of Ewing.*[26] A New Jersey statute reimbursing the parents of both public and parochial school students for bus fare was challenged on the ground that such support for sectarian education violated the First Amendment. Justice Black's frequently quoted opinion for the majority announced an uncompromising loyalty to a Jeffersonian separation of church and state:

The "establishment of religion" clause of the First Amendment means at least this: Neither a state nor the Federal Government can set up a church. Neither can pass laws which aid one religion, aid all religions, or prefer one religion over another. Neither can force nor influence a person to go to or remain away from church against his will or force him to profess a belief or disbelief in any religion. No person can be punished for entertaining or professing religious beliefs or disbeliefs, for church attendance or nonattendance. No tax in any amount, large or small, can be levied to support any religious activities or institutions, whatever they may be called, or whatever form they may adopt to teach or practice religion. Neither a state nor the Federal Government can, openly or secretly, participate in the affairs of any religious organizations or groups and *vice versa.*[27]

In spite of this statement, the decision was in favor of the statute on the ground that children, not churches, were benefited by it.

In establishment cases, the Court now purports to apply a three-part test:

First, the statute must have a secular legislative purpose; second, its principal or primary effect must be one that neither advances nor inhibits religion, *Board of Education v. Allen*, 392 U.S. 236, 243 (1968); finally, the statute must not foster "an excessive government entanglement with religion."[28]

This test has been applied primarily in school cases as the Court has attempted to determine how much aid to parochial schools is permitted and in what form. Other establishment issues include Sunday closing laws, school prayer, legislative and military chaplains, religious symbols in public places, and laws requiring accommodation by private employers to the religious practices of their employees.

Although the Warren Court was certainly not consistent in its analysis of establishment cases, the Burger Court has quite clearly drawn back from the strict separation announced by Justice Black and has modified the *Lemon* test in favor of an "accommodationist" position toward religion. Accommodation is allegedly mandated by a historical bias toward religion first mentioned by Justice Douglas in his opinion in *Zorach v. Clauson*,[29] which upheld a released-time program for religious study by public school students off school property:

We are a religious people whose institutions presuppose a Supreme Being. . . . When the state encourages religious instruction or cooperates with religious authorities by adjusting the schedule of public events to sectarian needs, it follows the best of our traditions. For it then respects the religious nature of our people and *accommodates* the public service to their spiritual needs. To hold that it may not would be to find in the Constitution a requirement that the government show a callous indifference to religious groups.[30] (emphasis added)

The Burger Court has upheld a tax exemption for church property, *Walz v. Tax Commission of the City of New York*,[31] and paid legislative chaplains in *Marsh v. Chambers*,[32] both on "historical" grounds: that has been our tradition. The most important recent "victory" for the forces of accommodation has been *Lynch v. Donnelly*,[33] in which the Court held that a crèche displayed as part of a civic Christmas display did not violate the establishment clause under the *Lemon* test because its secular purpose was to depict the historical origins of a national holiday, because it did not have the effect of advancing religion any more than having religious paintings in state-owned museums, and because there was no evidence of administrative entanglement.

It is ironic to note that "accommodation" in the *Lynch* case was achieved by determining that religion was not involved. This can be viewed as an offense to rather than as an advance of religious freedom. Justice Brennan dissented:

To suggest, as the Court does, that such a symbol is merely "traditional" and therefore no different from Santa's house or reindeer is not only offensive to those for whom the crèche has profound significance, but insulting to those who insist for religious or personal reasons that the story of Christ is in no sense a part of "history" nor an unavoidable element of our national "heritage."[34]

See also Justice Blackmun's dissent in *Lynch*.[35] Indeed, these dissents raise one of the central problems with accommodation: whose view of religion is being accommodated?

Free-exercise cases begin with *Reynolds* and its distinction between religious belief and religious action, a distinction reinforced by a Protestant theological emphasis on the private relationship between any person and God. The "secular regulation" rule, which had the advantage of being clear in its application and of avoiding the establishment and equal protection pitfalls of special exemptions for certain religious practices, has broken down. We now have a balancing test, under which the state must show a compelling interest if a regulation is a burden to religious practice.

The secular regulation rule first started to break down in a series of cases brought by the Jehovah's Witnesses under both the free speech and free exercise clauses of the First Amendment. In *West Virginia State Board of Education v. Barnette*,[36] the Supreme Court held that school children with conscientious scruples against saluting the flag had a First Amendment right not to do so, modifying the *Reynolds* rule. In *Sherbert v. Verner*,[37] the Court first announced the compelling state interest test when it declared unconstitutional the application of state laws which denied unemployment compensation to a Sabbatarian who was fired for refusing to work on a Saturday.

The most recent and widely criticized decision by the Supreme Court in the free-exercise area is *Wisconsin v. Yoder*,[38] in which the Amish were held to be exempt from state compulsory education laws. It is difficult not to conclude that the Amish received special treatment because of their quaint and purportedly exemplary life style. The Supreme Court of California allowed a similar exemption for the Native American Church from laws prohibiting the use of narcotics.[39] The opinion is rhapsodic, with repeated and patronizing references to the good influence of religion on Indians, but the principle is obscure.

Principled resistance to government policy based on religious conviction also raises issues of religious freedom, and, at least in theory, has tended to broaden rather than narrow a free-exercise exemption. Whereas *Yoder* and *Woody* are clearly nostalgic exceptions for small religious communities, more comparable to the ancient royal prerogative of dispensation, as Philip Kurland has suggested,[40] the draft cases are based on traditional American respect for individual conscience and public political dissent. Conscientious objection, draft resistance, refusal to pay war taxes, and sheltering of illegal aliens by the Sanctuary movement, all test the limits of a constitutional mandate for religious freedom to act according to conscience and demonstrate the difficulty of granting such exemptions.

Although it is undoubtedly true, as Kurland has repeatedly asserted,[41] that government-sponsored religious persecution is basically unknown in this country, there are at least two dramatic examples of coercion of belief by the American government: the aftermath of *Reynolds* was a government persecution of the Mormons leading to a forced recantation of the polygamy doctrine; and the government colluded with and actively supported religious missionaries in an attempt to Christianize American Indians. It is interesting that after many suits advocating Indian rights it is only recently that religious freedom has been used as a legal argument to support Indian claims. A 1973 casebook, *Law and the American Indian*, by Monroe E. Price (Indianapolis: Bobbs-Merrill) makes no mention of religion. In 1978 Congress passed the American Indian Religious Freedom Act,[42] which addressed such issues as access to sacred areas and burial sites, use of prohibited substances such as peyote for sacramental purposes, and protection of religious events from intrusion by tourists or other onlookers. Invocation of the First Amendment in Indian claims suits is now common.

Religious cults have recently raised new religious freedom issues. Accusations of forced conversions and brainwashing have led to attempts to "deprogram" converts. Vociferous efforts have been made on both sides of the issue. Lawyers and legislators, backed by mental health experts, have attacked these cults, while others, strongly defending the First Amendment right of these religious movements, argue that they are being discriminated against simply because of their unorthodoxy.[43]

Many religious freedom cases blend into free speech and association issues. Thus, both free speech and religious freedom are involved in challenges to licensing laws for people engaged in religious proselytizing and to the right of children not to salute the flag.[44]

In spite of intense debate in the Supreme Court and among academic commentators about the origins of the First Amendment and about the correctness of the Supreme Court opinions interpreting the First Amendment, most of which tend to advocate a separation of church and state, a de facto establishment, or public presumption about the benefit of religion, exists in this country. This presumption takes several legal forms. Churches are tax-exempt. Legislatures, prisons, and the armed forces have chaplains paid by the government. Students at the service academies are required to attend chapel. Both churches and individual religious expression are tolerated or positively aided at the local level. Examination of state or local statutes will reveal hundreds of accommodations to religion, some of which may well be unconstitutional but which have not been tested: low-speed laws in church zones, exemption for ministers from jury duty, zoning restrictions, penalties for disturbing religious services, reduced rates on public transportation for clergy, and exemption of the Bible from attachment, for example. A majority of Americans seems to be comfortable with a general policy of separation of church and state combined with general support for religion. This schizophrenia is reflected in the law.

Recurring questions for the courts (which underlie both free exercise and establishment issues) have been how to define religion and whether courts may inquire into the good faith of religious beliefs used to justify some action. The Supreme Court directly addressed the issue in *United States v. Ballard*,[45] in which Guy, Edna, and Donald Ballard were prosecuted for perpetrating a fraud through the use of the mails to solicit contributions for the propagation of a religious cult known as "I Am" based on the teachings of a fifth-century French bishop who miraculously guided them. In evaluating a First Amendment defense, the trial judge ruled that the jury was not to consider the truth or falsity of the Ballards' beliefs but only the sincerity of those beliefs. The Ballards were convicted. On appeal the Ninth Circuit reversed, rejecting the trial court's distinction between truth or falsity, and sincerity or insincerity. The Supreme Court reversed again, approving the trial judge's instruction to the jury. Justice Jackson dissented, arguing forcefully that it was impossible to separate what is believed from what is believable, and urging that the courts "have done with this business of judicially examining other people's faiths."[46]

The need to define religion arises whenever laws make special classifications for religion: laws regulating tax exemptions, religious practices in prisons, and conscientious objector status with respect to the draft board, among others. When directly confronted with a need to define religion, courts have naturally tended to the broadest possible coverage. A dramatic example of this tendency can be seen in the draft cases (which involve the interpretation of the Selective Service Act rather than the First Amendment). The Selective Service Act requires that a conscientious objector "by reason of religious training and belief" be conscientiously opposed "to participation in war in any form." In *United States v. Seeger*,[47] Mr. Seeger struck out "belief in a Supreme Being" on his application for conscientious objector status. The

Court found that his belief occupied a parallel place to a belief in God. In *Welsh v. United States*,[48] the Court interpreted the Selective Service Act's exemption to cover Mr. Welsh, who had struck the word "religion" from his application and asserted that his beliefs had been formed by reading in the fields of history and sociology.

The problem of defining religion arises frequently in the context of what accommodation prison officials must make to the religious customs of their inmates. A lengthy legal fight resulted in Black Muslims being recognized as a religious body in prison and being granted rights to worship according to their teaching.[49] In *Africa v. Commonwealth of Pennsylvania*,[50] an appeal had been taken from a trial court holding that prison officials were not required to provide Mr. Africa with the diet of raw foods he asserted was required by his religion. The Court of Appeals, in a lengthy and cautious opinion, concluded that Mr. Africa's organization, MOVE, was not a religion because it did not deal with "ultimate ideas."[51]

The problem of defining religion for legal purposes has been extensively addressed in law review articles. One suggestion has been that religion be defined differently for different purposes. Thus, for example, while it may be appropriate to be as liberal as possible when granting conscientious objector status because of the high stakes and a national policy which seeks to exclude unenthusiastic soldiers, special privileges in prison may lead to uncontrollable fraud.

An interesting perspective on the problem of defining religion can be seen in the context of new religious movements. Thomas Robbins, in a recent essay, argues that it is

unlikely that certain movements, such as Synanon or Scientology, would have defined themselves as churches or even as "religious" movements were it not for the legal protection the Constitution affords such groups.[52]

In contrast to certain prison cults, clearly organized solely for the purpose of obtaining special privileges, Robbins suggests that these other movements originally organized with legitimate social purposes have changed their self-definition in order to obtain a special social and legal status.

It is interesting when investigating church-state issues as they arise in court to note whether the case involves an individual who asserts a right based on religious freedom or a religious institution which either asserts a right for itself or brings into court an internal dispute. American courts are often more sympathetic to an individual who acts out of conscience than to an institution which threatens a rival authority. Michael Smith argues in a recent article that the personal attitudes of Supreme Court justices toward organized religion have affected their decisions.[53]

Whether religious institutions have the freedom to exercise political rights has been raised recently in a suit against the United States Conference of Catholic Bishops (USCCB) asserting that the conference has forfeited its right to a tax exemption by engaging in political activity against abortion. The argument made by the abortion rights advocates is that it is a violation of the equal protection clause of the Fourteenth Amendment for churches to use tax-exempt funds for political purposes when they themselves must pay taxes on the funds they use. The USCCB has been held in contempt and fined $50,000 a day for refusing to turn over its records.[54]

There is a certain frustration in attempting to understand the peculiarly American interaction between religion and law in the United States. The constitutional ideals espoused by the First Amendment and endlessly worried over by commentators are often difficult to relate to the daily clashes between and among religious interests and legal agencies and processes. Increased government, feverish litigation over civil rights generally, and an uneasiness in the community about religion[55] combine to produce complex interrelationships. A vast literature analyzes and dissects the Supreme Court cases interpreting the First Amendment. Much is partisan. Hundreds of law review articles debate the fine points of these cases. The most important legal commentary on the Supreme Court cases is included in the bibliography. There is far less analysis of state and lower federal court opinions and of the actual working relationship between religion and local governments and federal, state, and local agencies.

Repeatedly, legal cases concerning religion raise larger questions concerning the relationship of religion and society, both institutionally and individually. Each situation presents a new and concrete need to resolve these questions. The common law tradition allows a progressive modification of legal rules tailored to each situation, but the larger principles governing these cases have, in the religion area, often been absent or obscure. The result is an interesting but unsatisfactory body of American law.

NOTE ON LEGAL RESEARCH

An enormous quantity of material is available to the legal historian interested in religion and law in the United States since 1870: state constitutions, state and federal statutes and legislative history, published opinions for most state and federal appellate courts, and records of federal and state administrative agencies. Articles analyzing the legal significance of this material are accessible through the *Guide to Legal Periodicals* and more recently the *Current Law Index*, available both in hard copy and on computer. Much of this material is available in any good law library.

There are a number of guides to assist a nonlawyer in doing legal research. Three of the best are: Morris L. Cohen and Robert C. Berring, *How to Find the Law* (St. Paul: West Publishing Co., 1983); Elias Stephen, *Legal Research* (Berkeley: Nolo Press, 1982); and Peter Jan Honigsberg, *Cluing Into Legal Research: A Simple Guide to Finding the Law* (Berkeley: Golden Rain Press, 1979).

NOTES

1. 98 U.S. 145 (1878).

2. 23 Ohio State Reports 211 (1872).

3. The First Amendment to the United States Constitution provides: "Congress shall make no law respecting an establishment of religion or prohibiting the free exercise thereof."

4. See, for example, *Wisconsin v. Yoder*, 406 U.S. 205 (1972) (exemption of Amish from compulsory education laws); *People v. Woody*, 61 Cal. 2d 716 (1964) (exemption of Native American Church from criminal prosecution for use of peyote).

5. 23 Ohio Reports, p. 241.

6. Ibid.

7. Ibid., pp. 250–251.

8. *Wallace v. Jaffree*, 86 L.Ed. 2d 29, 44 (1985). The sponsor of the bill had stated that the only purpose of the statute was "to return voluntary prayer" to the public schools.

9. James Bryce, *The American Commonwealth*, 2d ed. (New York: Macmillan, 1924), p. 766.

10. Each of the state constitutions has its own version of the First Amendment religion clauses, usually spelled out in greater detail. See C. J. Antieau, *Religion Under the State Constitutions*.

11. See, for example, Orville H. Zabel, *God and Caesar in Nebraska*, for a history of the legal relations between church and state in Nebraska from 1854 to 1954.

12. I have listed examples of contemporary treatises in the bibliography that follows. The list is by no means exhaustive. A person working on nineteenth- and early twentieth-century church-state law is advised to examine the materials in relevant historical archives.

13. 80 U.S. (Wall.) 679 (1872).

14. Ibid., pp. 728–729.

15. 393 U.S. 440 (1969).

16. *Chicago Tribune*, July 10, 1986, sec. 2., p. 3.

17. Will Herberg argues that, over time, there developed, in a sense, an establishment, or Americanizing, of religion in three "flavors," Protestant, Catholic, or Jewish, but that all supported the status quo (*Protestant-Catholic-Jew* [Garden City, N.Y.: Doubleday, 1955]).

18. 310 U.S. 296 (1940).

19. The appropriateness of that determination has been strongly questioned, given the wording of the First Amendment and the history of the enactment of the Fourteenth Amendment. Few would disagree, however, that it is a closed issue.

20. See for example Michael W. McConnell, "Accommodation of Religion," and Norman Redlich, "Separation of Church and State: The Burger Court's Tortuous Journey." Mark DeWolfe Howe, *The Garden and the Wilderness*, is a classic in this debate.

21. 465 U.S. 668 (1984).

22. 106 S. Ct. 2841, 2844 (1986).

23. See Basil Mitchell, *Law, Morality and Religion,* and works listed in the Jurisprudence section of the bibliography for discussion of the debate between Lord Devlin and H. L. A. Hart on this subject.

24. See, for example, *Ohio Civil Rights Commission v. Dayton Christian Schools,* No. 85–488.

25. See, for example, Philip B. Kurland, *Religion and the Law.*

26. 330 U.S. 1 (1947).

27. Ibid., pp. 15–16.

28. *Lemon v. Kurtzman,* 403 U.S. 602, 613 (1971).

29. 343 U.S. 306 (1952).

30. Ibid., pp. 313–314.

31. 397 U.S. 664 (1970).

32. 463 U.S. 783 (1983).

33. 465 U.S. 668 (1984).

34. Ibid., pp. 711–712.

35. Ibid., p. 726.

36. 319 U.S. 624 (1943).

37. 374 U.S. 398 (1963).

38. 406 U.S. 205 (1972).

39. *People v. Woody,* 61 Cal. 2d 716 (1964).

40. Kurland, "The Irrelevance of the Constitution: The Religion Clauses of the First Amendment and the Supreme Court," p. 17.

41. See, for example, the preface to Kurland, *Church and State.*

42. 42 *United States Code* § 1996.

43. See Thomas Robbins, William C. Shepherd, and James McBride, eds., *Cults, Culture and the Law,* for a full discussion of the legal, theological, psychological, and sociological aspects of this issue.

44. See *Cantwell* and *Barnette,* respectively.

45. 322 U.S. 78 (1944).

46. Ibid., p. 95.

47. 380 U.S. 163 (1965).

48. 398 U.S. 333 (1970).

49. *Pierce v. La Vallee,* 293 F. 2d 233 (2d Cir. 1961).

50. 662 F.2d 1025 (3rd Cir. 1981).

51. Ibid., p. 1033.

52. Thomas Robbins, "New Religious Movements on the Frontiers of Church and State," in Robbins, Shepherd, and McBride, eds., *Cults, Culture, and the Law*, p. 8.

53. Michael E. Smith, "The Special Place of Religion in the Constitution."

54. *Abortion Rights Mobilization, Inc. v. Baker*, Slip Opinion, May 8, 1986 (S.D.N.Y.).

55. Whether or not there is indeed a current worldwide religious revival is a matter of scholarly debate, but Roland Robertson suggests that the new trends in religion, both new religious movements as well as the growth of fundamentalism and liberation theology, can all be understood from a global perspective. As people come to see themselves as citizens of the world as well as of countries, he argues, a world civil religion is emerging to explain the individual's relation to the world and to challenge his respective national government (Robertson, "The Relativization of Societies, Modern Religion, and Globalization," in Robbins, Shepherd, and McBride, eds., *Cults, Culture and the Law*).

BIBLIOGRAPHY

CHURCH AND STATE: GENERAL

Beth, Loren P. The American Theory of Church and State.
  Gainesville: University of Florida Press, 1958.

Buzzard, Lynn R. Law and Theology: An Annotated Bibliography.
  Oak Brook, Ill.: Christian Legal Society, 1979.

"Church-State: Religious Institutions and Values--A Legal
  Survey." Notre Dame Lawyer 33 (May 1958), 416-462; 35 (May
  1960), 405-442; 37 (August 1962), 649-719; 39 (June 1964),
  427-497; 41 (June 1966), 681-785; 43 (June 1968), 684-780.

Decker, Raymond G. "Religion and Law in the United States: A
  Prognosis." Capital University Law Review 8 (Fall 1979), 357-
  370.

Drinan, Robert F. Religion, the Courts, and Public Policy. New
  York: McGraw Hill, 1963.

Fellman, David. Religion in American Public Law. Boston:
  Boston University Press, 1965.

Hammar, Richard R. Pastor, Church and Law. Springfield, Mo.:
  Gospel Publishing House, 1983.

Howard, A. E. Dick; Baker, John W.; and Derr, Thomas S. Church,
  State, and Politics. Washington, D.C.: Roscoe Pound-American
  Trial Lawyers Foundation, 1981.

Johnson, James T., ed. The Bible in American Law, Politics, and
  Political Rhetoric. Philadelphia, Pa: Fortress, 1985.

La Noue, George R. A Review of Church-State Legal Developments
  1961-62. New York: National Conference of Christians and
  Jews, 1962.

"Law and Religion: Proceedings of the Annual Judicial Conference of the Tenth Judicial Circuit of the United States." Federal Rules Decisions 34 (1963), 37-71.

McGrath, John J. Church and State in American Law: Cases and Materials. Milwaukee: Bruce Publishing Co., 1962.

Mechling, Jay, ed. Church, State and Public Policy. Washington, D.C.: American Enterprise Institute, 1978.

Muelder, Walter G. "Protestants, Catholics and 'Free Exercise.'" Cumberland Law Review 8 (Spring 1977), 77-104.

Murray, John C. We Hold These Truths. New York: Sheed and Ward, 1960.

Pfeffer, Leo. Church, State and Freedom. 2d ed. Boston: Beacon Press, 1967.

Religion and the Public Order (Institute of Church and State, Villanova University School of Law) nos. 1-5 (1963-65, 1968-69).

Sanders, Thomas G. Protestant Concepts of Church and State. New York: Holt, Rinehart and Winston, 1964.

Stokes, Anson P. Church and State in the United States. 3 vols. New York: Harper and Brothers, 1950.

"The Uneasy Boundary: Church and State." Annals of the American Academy of Political and Social Science 446 (November 1979).

Valparaiso University. Colloquy on Law and Theology. St. Louis, Mo.: Lutheran Academy for Scholarship, 1960.

Wilson, John F., ed. Church and State in American History. 2d ed. Boston: Beacon Press, 1986.

SUPREME COURT

Abraham, Henry J. Freedom and the Court. New York: Oxford University Press, 1967.

Curry, Patricia E. "James Madison and the Burger Court: Converging Views of Church-State Separation." Indiana Law Journal 56 (Summer 1981), 615-636.

Griswold, Erwin N. "Absolute is in the Dark--A Discussion of the Approach of the Supreme Court to Constitutional Questions." Utah Law Review 8 (Summer 1963), 167-182.

Howe, Mark DeWolfe, comp. Cases on Church and State in the United States. Cambridge: Harvard University Press, 1952.

Katz, Wilbur G. Religion and American Constitutions. Evanston, Ill.: Northwestern University Press, 1964.

Katz, Wilbur G., and Southerland, Harold P. "Religious Pluralism and the Supreme Court." Daedalus 96 (Winter 1967), 180-192.

Kauper, Paul G. Religion and the Constitution. Baton Rouge: Louisiana State University Press, 1964.

Kurland, Philip B. Religion and the Law: Of Church and State and the Supreme Court. Chicago: Aldine Publishing Co., 1962.

Kurland, Philip B., ed. Church and State: The Supreme Court and the First Amendment. Chicago: University of Chicago Press, 1975.

Louisell, David W. "The Man and the Mountain: Douglas on Religious Freedom." Yale Law Journal 73 (May 1964), 975-998.

Marty, Martin E. "Of Darters and Schools and Clergymen: The Religion Clauses Worse Confounded." Supreme Court Review (1978), 171-190.

Mauney, Constance. "Religion and First Amendment Protections: An Analysis of Justice Black's Constitutional Interpretation." Pepperdine Law Review 10 (January 1983), 377-420.

Morgan, Richard E. The Supreme Court and Religion. New York: Free Press, 1972.

Oaks, Dallin, ed. The Wall Between Church and State. Chicago: University of Chicago Press, 1963.

O'Brien, F. William. Justice Reed and the First Amendment: The Religion Clauses. Washington, D.C.: Georgetown University Press, 1958.

Redlich, Norman. "Separation of Church and State: The Burger Court's Tortuous Journey." Notre Dame Law Review 60, no. 5 (1985), 1094-1149.

Smith, Michael E. "The Special Place of Religion in the Constitution." Supreme Court Review (1983), 83-123.

Smith, Rodney K. "Justice Potter Stewart: A Contemporary Jurist's View of Religious Liberty." North Dakota Law Review 59, no. 2 (1983), 183-210.

Tussman, Joseph. The Supreme Court on Church and State. New
    York: Oxford University Press, 1962.

West, Ellis M. "Justice Tom Clark and American Church-State
    Law." Journal of Presbyterian History 64 (Winter 1976), 387-
    405.

                              STATES

American Jewish Congress. Digest and Analysis of State Attorney
    General Opinions Relating to Freedom of Religion and
    Separation of Church and State. New York: Commission on Law
    and Social Action, 1959.

Antieau, C. J. Religion under the State Constitutions.
    Brooklyn, N.Y.: Central Book Co., 1965.

"Blasphemy." Columbia Law Review 70 (April 1970), 694-733.

Casad, Robert C. "Compulsory High School Attendance and the Old
    Order Amish: A Commentary on State v. Garber." University of
    Kansas Law Review 16 (April 1968), 423-435.

"The Lord Buildeth and the State Taketh Away--Church
    Condemnation and the Religion Clauses of the First Amendment."
    University of Colorado Law Review 46 (Fall 1974), 43-58.

Pratt, John Webb. Religion, Politics and Diversity: The Church-
    State Theme in New York History. Ithaca, N.Y.: Cornell
    University Press, 1967.

"The Right Not to Be Modern Men: The Amish and Compulsory
    Education." Virginia Law Review 53 (May 1967), 925-952.

Zabel, Orville H. God and Caesar in Nebraska: A Study of the
    Legal Relationship of Church and State, 1854-1954.
    University of Nebraska Studies, n.s., no. 14. Lincoln: The
    University at Lincoln, 1955.

                         FIRST AMENDMENT

Choper, Dean. "The Religion Clauses of the First Amendment:
    Reconciling the Conflict." University of Pittsburgh Law
    Review 41 (Summer 1980), 673-701.

Giannella, Donald. "Religious Liberty, Nonestablishment and
    Doctrinal Development: Part I. The Religious Liberty
    Guarantee." Harvard Law Review 80 (May 1967), 1381-1431.

Giannella, Donald. "Religious Liberty, Nonestablishment and Doctrinal Development: Part II. The Nonestablishment Principle." Harvard Law Review 81 (January 1968), 513-590.

Howe, Mark DeWolfe. The Garden and the Wilderness. Chicago: University of Chicago Press, 1965.

Kurland, Philip B. "The Irrelevance of the Constitution: The Religion Clauses of the First Amendment and the Supreme Court." Villanova Law Review 24 (November 1978), 3-27.

McCoy, Thomas R., and Kurtz, Gary A. "A Unifying Theory for the Religion Clauses of the First Amendment." Vanderbilt Law Review 39 (March 1986), 249-274.

Marnell, William H. The First Amendment: The History of Religious Freedom in America. Garden City, N.Y.: Doubleday, 1964.

Rushing, Ernest L. "The Expanded Jurisprudence of the Religion Clauses: Will the Sanctuary Movement Benefit?" Gonzaga Law Review 21 (Fall 1985), 177-197.

FREE EXERCISE

Clark, Morris J. "Guidelines of the Free Exercise Clause." Harvard Law Review 83 (December 1969), 327-365.

Dodge, Joseph M., II. "The Free Exercise of Religion: A Sociological Approach." Michigan Law Review 67 (February 1969), 679-728.

Fernandez, Ferdinand F. "The Free Exercise of Religion." Southern California Law Review 36 (June 1963), 546-595.

Galanter, Marc. "Religious Freedoms in the United States: A Turning Point?" Wisconsin Law Review 1966, no. 2, 217-296.

Katz, Wilbur G. "Freedom of Religion and State Neutrality." University of Chicago Law Review 20 (Spring 1953), 426-440.

Kelley, Dean, ed. Government Intervention in Religious Affairs. New York: Pilgrim Press, 1982.

Konvitz, Milton R. Religious Liberty and Conscience. New York: Viking, 1968.

Marcus, Paul. "The Forum of Conscience: Applying Standards Under the Free Exercise Clause." Duke Law Journal 1973, no. 6, 1217-1272.

"Medical Care, Freedom of Religion, and Mitigation of Damages." Yale Law Journal 87 (June 1978), 1466-1487.

"Protecting Religious Exercise: The First Amendment and Legislative Responses to Religious Vandalism." Harvard Law Review 97 (December 1983), 547-564.

"Religious Exemptions Under the Free Exercise Clause: A Model of Competing Authorities." Yale Law Journal 90 (December 1980), 350-376.

Religious Freedom Reporter (Oak Park, Ill: Center for Law and Religious Freedom of the Christian Legal Society), monthly from January 1981.

"The Religious Rights of the Incarcerated." University of Pennsylvania Law Review 125 (April 1977), 812-875.

Saltzman, Penelope W. "Potter v. Murray City: Another Interpretation of Polygamy and the First Amendment." Utah Law Review 1986 (May 1986), 345-371.

Shetreet, Shimon. "Exemptions and Privileges on Grounds of Religion and Conscience." Kentucky Law Journal 62 (Winter 1974), 377-420.

Smith, Elwyn A. Religious Liberty in the United States. Philadelphia: Fortress, 1972.

Torpey, William G. Judicial Doctrine of Religious Rights in America. Chapel Hill: University of North Carolina Press, 1948.

U.S. Commission on Civil Rights. Religion in the Constitution: A Delicate Balance. Washington, D.C.: U.S. Commission on Civil Rights, 1983.

U.S. Commission on Civil Rights. Religious Discrimination: A Neglected Issue. Washington, D.C.: U.S. Commission on Civil Rights, 1979.

ESTABLISHMENT

Antieau, C. J. Freedom From Federal Establishment. Milwaukee: Bruce Publishing Co., 1964.

Blakely, William A. American State Papers Bearing on Sunday Legislation. Washington, D.C.: Religious Liberty Association, 1911.

Corwin, Edward S. "The Supreme Court as National School Board."
    Law and Contemporary Problems 14 (Winter 1949), 3-22.

Esbeck, Carl H. "Establishment Clause Limits on Governmental
    Interference with Religious Organizations." Washington and
    Lee Law Review 41 (Spring 1984), 347-420.

Levy, Leonard W. Religion and the First Amendment. New York:
    Macmillan, 1986.

Paulsen, Michael A. "Religion, Equality and the Constitution:
    An Equal Protection Approach to Establisment Clause
    Adjudication." Notre Dame Law Review 61, no. 3 (1986), 311-
    371.

Ripple, Kenneth F. "The Entanglement Test of the Religious
    Clauses--A Ten-Year Assessment." University of California Los
    Angeles Law Review 27 (August 1980), 1195-1239.

Schwartz, Alan. "No Imposition of Religion: The Establishment
    Clause Value." Yale Law Journal 77 (March 1968), 692-737.

Serritella, James A. "Tangling with Entanglement: Toward a
    Constitutional Evaluation of Church-State Contacts." Law and
    Contemporary Problems 44 (Spring 1981), 143-167.

Shortt, Bruce N. "The Establishment Clause and Religion-Based
    Categories: Taking Entanglement Seriously." Hastings
    Constitutional Law Quarterly 10 (Fall 1982), 145-185.

Sperow, Janice L. "Rajneeshpuram: Religion Incorporated."
    Hastings Law Journal 36 (July 1985), 917-968.

Steinberg, David E. "Church Control of a Municipality:
    Establishing a First Amendment Institutional Suit." Stanford
    Law Review 38 (May 1986), 1363-1409.

Van Alstyne, William. "Trends in the Supreme Court: Mr.
    Jefferson's Crumbling Wall--A Comment on Lynch v. Donnelly."
    Duke Law Journal 1984, no. 4, 770-787.

ACCOMMODATIONIST

Brady, Joseph H. Confusion Twice Confounded: The First
    Amendment and the Supreme Court. South Orange, N.J.: Seton
    Hall University Press, 1954.

Buzzard, Lynn R. Freedom and Faith: The Impact of Law on
    Religious Liberty. Westchester, Ill.: Crossway Books, 1982.

Cord, Robert L. _Separation of Church and State_. New York:
Lambeth Press, 1982.

Goldberg, George. _Reconsecrating America_. Grand Rapids:
Eerdmans, 1984.

Kelley, Dean M., ed. _Government Intervention in Religious
Affairs_. New York: Pilgrim Press, 1982.

McConnell, Michael W. "Accommodation of Religion." _Supreme
Court Review_ (1985), 1-59.

                         SEPARATIONIST

Blanshard, Paul. _Religion and the Schools: The Great
Controversy_. Boston: Beacon Press, 1963.

Church and State (Silver Springs, Md.: Americans United for
Separation of Church and State), monthly from May 15, 1948.

Lowell, C. Stanley. _Embattled Wall: Americans United, An Idea i
a Man_. Washington, D.C.: Americans United, 1966.

McCollum, Vashti C. _One Woman's Fight_. Boston: Beacon Press,
1951.

Rubenstein, Isadore H. _Law on Cults_. Chicago: Ordain Press,
1981.

Swancara, Frank. _Obstruction of Justice by Religion_. Denver:
W. H. Courtright Publishing Co., 1936.

                       DEFINING RELIGION

Bowser, Anita. "Delimiting Religion in the Constitution: A
Classification Problem." _Valparaiso University Law Review_ 11
(Winter 1977), 163-226.

Boyan, A. Stephen, Jr. "Defining Religion in Operational and
Institutional Terms." _University of Pennsylvania Law Review_
116 (January 1968), 479-498.

Choper, Jesse H. "Defining 'Religion' in the First Amendment."
University of Illinois Law Review 1982, no. 3, 579-613.

"Defining Religion: Of God, the Constitution and the D.A.R."
University of Chicago Law Review 32 (Spring 1965), 533-559.

Freeman, George C., III. "The Misguided Search for the
    Constitutional Definition of Religion." <u>Georgetown Law
    Journal</u> 71 (August 1983), 1519-1565.

Merel, Gail. "The Protection of Individual Choice: A Consistent
    Understanding of Religion Under the First Amendment."
    <u>University of Chicago Law Review</u> 45 (Summer 1978), 805-843.

"Toward a Constitutional Definition of Religion." <u>Harvard Law
    Review</u> 91 (March 1978), 1056-1089.

"Transcendental Meditation and the Meaning of Religion Under the
    Establishment Clause." <u>Minnesota Law Review</u> 62 (June 1978),
    887-948.

Weiss, Jonathan. "Privilege, Posture and Protection: 'Religion'
    in the Law." <u>Yale Law Journal</u> 73 (March 1964), 593-623.

Whelan, Charles M. "'Church' in the Internal Revenue Code: The
    Definitional Problems." <u>Fordham Law Review</u> 45 (March 1977),
    885-928.

Worthing, Sharon L. "'Religion' and 'Religious Institutions'
    Under the First Amendment." <u>Pepperdine Law Review</u> 7 (Winter
    1980), 313-353.

JURISPRUDENCE

Berman, Harold J. <u>The Interaction of Law and Religion</u>.
    Nashville: Abingdon, 1974.

Devlin, Patrick. <u>The Enforcement of Morals</u>. London: Oxford
    University Press, 1965.

Hart, H. L. A. <u>The Morality of the Criminal Law</u>. London:
    Oxford University Press, 1965.

Henkin, Louis. "Morals and the Constitution: The Sin of
    Obscenity." <u>Columbia Law Review</u> 63 (March 1963), 391-414.

Hughes, Graham. "Morals and the Criminal Law." <u>Yale Law Journal</u>
    71 (March 1962), 662-683.

Mitchell, Basil. <u>Law, Morality and Religion in a Secular
    Society</u>. London: Oxford University Press, 1965.

Neuhaus, Richard J. "Law and the Rightness of Things."
    <u>Valparaiso University Law Review</u> 14 (Fall 1979), 1-13.

Rostow, Eugene V. "The Enforcement of Morals." <u>Cambridge Law
    Journal</u> (November 1960), 174-198.

"Symposium on Law and Christianity." Vanderbilt Law Review 10
   (August 1957), 879-966.

"Symposium on Law and Christianity." Oklahoma Law Review 12
   (February 1959), 45-146.

"Symposium: Religion and Law." Capital University Law Review 8
   (Fall 1979), 345-464.

                            CONTEMPORARY

Desmond, Humphrey J. The Church and the Law. Chicago:
   Callaghan & Co., 1898.

Goddard, Edwin C. "The Law in the United States in the Relation
   to Religion." Michigan Law Review 10 (January 1912), 161-177.

Jones, Alonzo T. "Due Process of Law" and the Divine Right of
   Dissent. New York: National Religious Liberty Association,
   1892.

Lee, G. T. Church and State: Can We Save the Country By
   Legislation? Minneapolis: Augsburg, 1927.

Roberts, William H. Laws Relating to Religious Corporations.
   Philadelphia: Presbyterian Board of Publication, 1896.

Zollmann, Carl. American Civil Church Law. New York: Columbia
   University Press, 1917.

                         INTRACHURCH DISPUTES

Abuhoff, Daniel. "Title VII and the Appointment of Women Clergy:
   A Statutory and Constitutional Quagmire." Columbia Journal of
   Law and Social Problems 13, nos. 3 and 4 (1977), 256-302.

Bennett, Roger W. "Church Property Disputes in the Age of
   'Common-Core Protestantism': A Legislative Facts Rationale for
   Neutral Principles of Law." Indiana Law Journal 57 (Winter
   1982), 163-187.

Bernard, Kent S. "Churches, Members, and the Role of the Courts:
   Toward a Contractual Analysis." Notre Dame Lawyer 51 (April
   1976), 545-573.

Duesenberg, Richard W. "Jurisdiction of Civil Courts Over
   Religious Issues." Ohio State Law Journal 20 (Summer 1959),
   508-548.

"Judicial Intervention in Disputes over the Use of Church Property." Harvard Law Review 75 (April 1962), 1142-1186.

Loring, H. Helmut. "The Power of Courts Over the Internal Affairs of Religious Groups." California Law Review 43 (May 1955), 322-324.

SOCIOLOGY/HISTORY

Manwaring, David R. Render Unto Caesar: The Flag Salute Controversy. Chicago: University of Chicago Press, 1962.

Morgan, Richard E. Politics of Religious Conflict. New York: Pegasus, 1968.

Nagel, Stuart, and Erikson, Robert. "Editorial Reaction to Supreme Court Decisions on Church and State." Public Opinion Quarterly 30 (Winter 1966-67), 647-655.

Pfeffer, Leo. "Amici in Church-State Litigation." Law and Contemporary Problems 44 (Spring 1981), 83-110.

Rogers, Harrell R., Jr. Community Conflict, Public Opinion and the Law: The Amish Dispute in Iowa. Columbus: Charles E. Merrill Publishing Co., 1969.

Sorauf, Frank J. The Wall of Separation. Princeton, N.J.: Princeton University Press, 1976.

Weber, Paul J., and Gilbert, Dennis A. Private Churches and Public Money: Church-Government Fiscal Relations. Westport, Conn.: Greenwood, 1981.

REGULATION

Cafardi, Nicholas P. "Bequests for Masses: Doctrine, History and Legal Status." Duquesne Law Review 20 (Spring 1982), 403-427.

Cox, Kenneth. "The F.C.C., the Constitution and Religious Broadcast Programming." George Washington Law Review 34 (December 1965), 196-218.

Curry, James E. Public Regulation of the Religious Use of Land; A Detailed and Critical Analysis of a Hundred Court Cases. Charlottesville, Va.: Michie, 1964.

Figinski, M. Albert. "Military Chaplains--A Constitutionally
   Permissible Accommodation Between Church and State." Marylan
   Law Review 24 (Fall 1964), 377-416.

Hermann, Klaus J. "Time Considerations on the Constitutionalit
   of the United States Military Chaplaincy." American
   University Law Review 14 (December 1964), 24-37.

Loevinger, Lee. "Religious Liberty and Broadcasting." George
   Washington Law Review 33 (March 1965), 631-659.

Rabinowitz, Stephen L. "Goldman v. Secretary of Defense:
   Restricting the Religious Rights of Military Servicemembers."
   American University Law Review 34 (Spring 1985), 881-926.

TAXATION

Bittker, Boris I. "Churches, Taxes and the Constitution." Yal
   Law Journal 78 (July 1969), 1285-1310.

"Constitutionality of State Property Tax Exemptions for
   Religious Property." Northwestern University Law Review 66
   (March-April 1971), 118-145.

Davidson, Joel E. "Religion in Politics and the Income Tax
   Exemption." Fordham Law Review 42 (December 1973), 397-424.

Kelley, Dean M. Why Churches Should Not Pay Taxes. New York:
   Harper and Row, 1977.

Robertson, D. B. Should Churches Be Taxed? Philadelphia:
   Westminster, 1968.

Taff, Roger H. "Tax Benefits for the Clergy: The
   Unconstitutionality of Section 107." Georgetown Law Journal
   62 (March 1974), 1261-1272.

Tanner, Andrew D. The Question of Tax Exemption for Churches.
   New York: National Conference of Christian and Jews, 1963.

Van Alstyne, Arvo. "Tax Exemption of Church Property." Ohio
   State Law Journal 20 (Summer 1959), 461-507.

Weber, Paul J., and Gilbert, Dennis A. Private Churches and
   Public Money. Westport, Conn.: Greenwood, 1981.

CONSCIENTIOUS OBJECTION

Berrigan, Daniel. The Trial of the Catonsville Nine. Boston: Beacon Press, 1970.

Brodie, Abner, and Southerland, Harold P. "Conscience, the Constitution, and the Supreme Court: The Riddle of United States v. Seeger." Wisconsin Law Review 1966, no. 2, 306-330.

"The Conscientious Objector and the First Amendment: There but for the Grace of God . . ." University of Chicago Law Review 34 (Autumn 1966), 79-105.

Cook, David D. "War Tax Refusal Under the Free Exercise Clause." Wisconsin Law Review 1980, no. 4, 753-781.

Cornell, Julien. The Conscientious Objector and the Law. New York: John Day Company, 1943.

Kellogg, Walter G. The Conscientious Objector. New York: Boni and Liveright, 1919.

Rabin, Robert L. "When is a Religious Belief Religious: United States v. Seeger and the Scope of Free Exercise." Cornell Law Quarterly 51 (Winter 1966), 231-249.

Schlissel, Lillian. Conscience in America: A Documentary History of Conscientious Objection in America, 1757-1767. New York: E. P. Dutton, 1968.

Sibley, Mulford Q., and Jacob, Philip E. Conscriptions of Conscience: The American State and the Conscientious Objector, 1940-1947. Ithaca, N.Y.: Cornell University Press, 1952.

Tatum, Arlo, ed. 11th ed. Handbook for Conscientious Objectors. Philadelphia: C.C.C.O., 1971.

TRIAL PRACTICE

Biggs, J. Crawford. "Religious Belief as Qualification of a Witness." North Carolina Law Review 8 (December 1929), 31-43.

Chadbourn, James H. "Impeaching a Witness by Showing Religious Belief." North Carolina Law Review 9 (December 1930), 77-82.

Dominick, Susan E. "Trial Court Allowed to Bar Wearing of Clerical Collar by Priest-Attorney in Jury Trial." Vanderbilt Law Review 29 (January 1976), 267-276.

"The Priest-Penitent Privilege in South Carolina--Background and Development." South Carolina Law Quarterly 12 (Spring 1960), 440-453.

"A Reconsideration of the Sworn Testimony Requirement: Securing Truth in the Twentieth Century." Michigan Law Review 75 (August 1977), 1681-1707.

Reese, Seward. "Confidential Communications to the Clergy." Ohio State Law Journal 24 (Winter 1963), 55-88.

Stoyles, Robert L. "The Dilemma of the Constitutionality of the Priest-Penitent Privilege--the Application of the Religion Clauses." University of Pittsburgh Law Review 29 (October 1967), 27-63.

Taylor, Thomas W. "The New North Carolina Priest-Penitent Statute." North Carolina Law Review 46 (February 1968), 427-433.

AMERICAN INDIANS

Doyle, John T. "Constitutional Law: Dubious Intrusions--Peyote, Drug Laws, and Religious Freedom." American Indian Law Review 8, no. 1 (1980), 79-96.

Ensworth, Laurie. "Native American Free Exercise Rights to the Use of Public Lands." Boston University Law Review 63 (January 1983), 141-179.

Gould, Diane B. "The First Amendment and the American Religious Freedom Act: An Approach to Protecting Native American Religion." Iowa Law Review 71 (March 1986), 869-891.

Kenneth, Philip. "John Collier and the Crusade to Protect Indian Religious Freedom, 1920-1926." Journal of Ethnic Studies 1 (Spring 1973), 22-38.

Stambor, Howard. "Manifest Destiny and American Indian Religious Freedom: Sequoyah, Badoni and the Drowned Gods." American Indian Law Review 10, no. 1 (1982), 59-89.

Suagee, Dean B. "American Indian Religious Freedom and Cultural Resources Management: Protecting Mother Earth's Caretakers." American Indian Law Review 10, no. 1 (1982), 1-58.

U.S. Federal Agencies Task Force. American Indian Religious Freedom Act Report, P.L. 95/341. Washington, D.C.: U.S. Federal Agencies Task Force, 1979.

CHRISTIAN SCIENCE

The Buswell Case.   Boston: Christian Science Publishing Society,
    1900.

Campbell, Irving E.   "Christian Science and the Law."   Virginia
    Law Register 10 (August 1904), 285.

Damore, Leo.   The 'Crime' of Dorothy Sheridan.   New York: Arbor
    House, 1978.

Rubenstein, Isadore H.   A Treatise on the Legal Aspects of
    Christian Science.   Chicago: Crandon Press, 1935.

Smith, Clifford P.   Christian Science: Its Legal Status.
    Boston: Christian Science Publishing Society, 1914.

CULTS

Delgado, Richard.   "Religious Totalism: Gentle and Ungentle
    Persuasion Under the First Amendment."   Southern California
    Law Review 51 (November 1977), 1-98.

Homer, David R.   "Abduction, Religious Sects and the Free
    Exercise Guarantee."   Syracuse Law Review 25 (Spring 1974),
    623-645.

Robbins, Thomas; Shepherd, William C.; and McBride, James, eds.
    Cults, Culture and the Law.   Chico, Calif.: Scholars Press,
    1985.

Shepherd, William C.   To Secure the Blessing of Liberty:
    American Constitutional Law and the New Religious Movements.
    Chico, Calif.: Scholars Press, 1985.

Spendlove, Gretta.   "Legal Issues in the Use of Guardianship
    Procedures to Remove Members of Cults."   Arizona Law Review
    18, no. 4 (1976), 1095-1139.

11

Women and Religion in America, 1870–1920

Elizabeth B. Clark

WOMEN'S ROLE IN THE INSTITUTIONAL CHURCH

Many historians have treated nineteenth-century women's religious movements as ancillary to secular feminism. Yet to identify organized movements
like suffrage as secular—or religious movements as insufficiently feminist—
can be misleading. In the material on women's role in organized religion we
see that the same desires were moving women toward fuller participation in
the church as in society, desires to speak and be listened to, to vote in
governing bodies, and to bring their values to bear on institutional policies. A
survey of titles in this first section will show that the questions of public
speaking, preaching, and ordination were crucial issues for women. Although
women far outnumbered men in congregations, and were by far more active
in the life of the church, most major denominations denied them ministerial
positions and even the right to speak publicly throughout the century.

Excellent introductions to the study of nineteenth-century women in the
institutional church are *Women of Spirit: Female Leadership in the Jewish
and Christian Traditions*, edited by Rosemary Radford Ruether and Eleanor
McLaughlin, and *Women and Religion in America*, Volume 1, *The Nineteenth
Century*, edited by Rosemary Radford Ruether and Rosemary Skinner Keller.
Both are collections of writing from the best recent work on women's participation in the churches, a question which has concerned scholars of religion
more than historians, and both cover the range of women's experiences. The
two-volume set *Women in New Worlds*, edited by Hilah F. Thomas, Rosemary
Skinner Keller, and Louise L. Queen, also contains a tremendous amount of
valuable work on women in the Methodist tradition, addressing both denominational history and the broader story of women's religiosity in American
society.

Although women could not rise above lay work in most denominations, their spirituality expressed itself informally outside the institutional church in a number of ways. Both Martha Tomhave Blauvelt and Barbara Epstein trace the beginnings of the nineteenth-century phenomenon of "feminization," or the identification of piety with women, to women's enthusiastic participation in great numbers in the evangelical revivals which swept the country at the turn of the century. It was in the revival movement that women first developed the passive role of worshiper into a more active ministry of prayer, public speaking, and exhortation to conversion, giving them an appetite for greater participation.

The Second Great Awakening was the seedtime for women's struggle for religious authority, but the battle for their full acceptance into the clergy still loomed. In "The Struggle for the Right to Preach" Barbara Brown Zikmund outlines the arguments of both supporters and opponents of women's ministry. Their effectiveness at religious work, the broad scope of the pastoral work they were already performing, and most of all the conviction of being called to preach were powerful arguments for women's ordination. The question also lent itself to the larger debate over the nature of scriptural authority. Advocates of woman's rights argued against orthodox literalists that the Bible was a historical document, one which must be interpreted in light of prevailing social conditions. More conservative mainstream denominations—Episcopalians, Presbyterians, Lutherans, and even the Methodists—did not come around until late in the century. By then, fear of waning Protestant supremacy in a newly pluralist culture gave new respectability to women's claims.

But within the Quaker, Universalist, and Unitarian traditions women's position was established much earlier. The natural convergence of their liberal teachings, which shared little of early evangelicalism's distaste for the political world, and the woman's suffrage movement is well illustrated in the lives of many early woman's rights activists. Lucretia Mott, Olympia Brown, and Antoinette Brown Blackwell were all first-generation feminists whose deep religious conviction of the moral equality of all human beings underlay their leadership roles in both their religious communities and the suffrage movement.

For many women, because they were denied formal positions in the established churches, the creative energy of faith ran in different directions. Two in particular stand out, with very different tendencies. The woman's foreign and domestic mission movement was a huge, crossdenominational operation which provided women with a powerful and autonomous sphere within the churches. And the proliferation of new religions and renewals of piety within those already established created alternative spheres for the articulation of more female-oriented systems of religious belief and for women's spiritual leadership.

WOMEN PROPHETS, SPIRITUALISM, AND NEW RELIGIONS

Many women spent their church lives seeking to make their way in the established denominations, or to penetrate male-dominated church authority from within. Others—a large number of women over the course of the century—found more congenial spiritual homes and more active involvement outside the orthodox fold. Barbara Brown Zikmund's "The Feminist Thrust of Sectarian Christianity" and Mary Farrell Bednarowski's "Outside the Mainstream" lay down the outlines of alternative religious experience for women. Bednarowski, discussing marginal groups like Shakers, Spiritualists, Christian Scientists, and Theosophists, finds that four common attitudes helped make such religious environments more hospitable to women: a perception of divinity that emphasized female as well as male qualities; little or no adherence to doctrines of original sin; the denial of the need for a traditional ordained clergy; and a critical view of family and marriage, one which did not value domesticity as women's sole identity. Such a constellation gave women far greater opportunity for personal and professional advancement in spiritual causes. Zikmund sees this sectarianism as feminist, particularly in the first half of the century. For her, in the acceptance of female leadership, feminine religious imagery, and often a communitarian lifestyle, sectarian groups self-consciously set their faces against the Protestant ethos. Unlike the "soft feminism" of mainstream evangelicalism which embroidered a secondary role, sectarian Christianity practiced a radical restructuring of gender roles within a Christian community.

Although the female individual who rose to prominence in the world of religion was certainly the exception, the nineteenth century produced a number of women prophets who were at least notorious in their own land. Mother Ann Lee (for whom see volume 1, chapter 11), Phoebe Palmer, the table-rapping Fox sisters, Ellen Gould White, Mary Baker Eddy, the Theosophist Madame Blavatsky, and Aimee Semple McPherson were among the best known of the women who parlayed their spiritual gifts into careers—careers not just in the sense of financial remuneration, although some succeeded there as well, but of an engrossing, lifetime work. Public acceptance of these women grew over time. Mother Ann Lee, a product of the eighteenth century, could only have gained a following within the confines of a sectarian community. By the middle of the next century, by contrast, Palmer, the Foxes, and others had staked out at least fringe positions within middle-class society, and many reputable people dabbled in their spiritual arts. Certainly Christian Science, although not strictly a Protestant denomination, was never removed from the world as the Shakers were: Mary Baker Eddy commanded a sizeable following and a religious empire with offices in Boston rather than farms in Sabbathday Lake, Maine. In part this greater acceptance reflected the growing identification of women with the spiritual, the expansion of women's sphere of competence to include public pronouncements on moral issues, and women's own exploitation of their spiritual identities. The work of both Theodore Hovet and Nancy Hardesty on women in the holiness movement suggests that they were using the opening revivalism offered for their special talents at prayer and exhortation to make inroads within denominationalism by establishing female-oriented religious programs.

Women's ability to establish themselves in new religions also speaks tellingly of a curious middle-class ethos and epistemological confusion. At least within the elite of this self-conscious class in this devout period, there was a surprising latitude in religious belief. The expansive religious impulse, humanitarian reformism, and the new scientism combined to bring into at least temporary prominence spiritually oriented movements far afield from Protestantism which attracted scoffers and followers among middle-class men and women both. Many different types of reform were interrelated both philosophically and in their overlapping memberships. Thomas Wentworth Higginson in *Cheerful Yesterdays* (1898. Reprint, New York, 1968) reports a friend's comment, "Not know the Briggs girls? I should think you would certainly know them. Work in the Globe Mills; interested in all the reforms; bathe in cold water every morning; one of 'em is a Grahamite" (p. 119). Health diets, water cures, abolitionism, feminism, seances, were all in some measure part of a cultural urge to discover laws of God and nature which governed the human body and human society alike, and which would assert themselves once artificial habits and injurious social customs were discarded. In this environment alternative spiritual modes and new religions had a good deal of play.

Both R. Laurence Moore and Mary Farrell Bednarowski's interesting works on spiritualism show how it fit into this welter of reform activities. Matrons as hardheaded as Elizabeth Cady Stanton and as devout as Harriet Beecher Stowe were intrigued with the medium's art. Despite its deviant quotient, spiritualism fell within the pale of middle-class respectability, and functioned as part of a larger movement to liberalize Christianity. Spiritualism provided women with expanded career opportunities as well. Although there were male mediums, the larger number were female, and the role of medium became associated in the public mind with women as drawing on the female qualities of sensitivity, receptivity, and passivity. Certainly mediums never gained the professional status or respect they aspired to, although there were several organizations like the Mediums Mutual Aid Society, established in

Boston in 1860. The practice of spiritualism nevertheless brought women success, public acclaim, and opportunities for travel and adventure.

Spiritualism was without any rigorous theology or philosophy, and some saw it as a rival force to denominationalism. Other "Christian spiritualists" were members of mainstream denominations as well, but all fell on the liberal side, and were united in opposition to Calvinist-tinged orthodoxy. As Moore pictures it, spiritualism partook of both the past and future, giving a backward nod to a wonder-working deity while believing itself within the scope of empirical science. Bednarowski suggests that the movement was an attempt to fuse science and religion, circumventing the problem of science making religion obsolete. But spiritualism was assaulted by orthodoxy and rejected by science, which did not accept its claims to empiricism. This mismatch brings up, not the specter of religion warring with science, but the more intriguing one of religion courting science and being spurned. For most of the Protestant reformers of the nineteenth century were not hostile to science: in fact they welcomed and sought to use it to a surprising degree. This is true not just for the radical fringe, but for activists as staid as the ladies of the Women's Christian Temperance Union (WCTU). Far from being antimodernist, even temperance women saw social science as an ally in their fight to improve social conditions, and adopted its techniques enthusiastically. Patricia Hill has suggested (see next section) that this ready acceptance of empiricism and professionalization ultimately undermined women's base of authority, an analysis which could apply here as well. Certainly science in this period did not defer to or seek to integrate moral or religious tenets, as reform did those of science.

Several other new faiths sprang up in mid-century as well, with organizational structures resembling more traditional religion than spiritualism. Among them, Christian Science, Theosophy, Adventism, and Pentecostalism were all inspired by or led by women. Christian Science was the most influential of these and, like Adventism, was particularly connected with issues of health and healing. Both Donald Meyer in *The Positive Thinkers* and Gail T. Parker in *Mind Cure in New England* put Christian Science into the generic category of "mind cure," or the several therapeutic faiths which proclaimed the power to heal the body through right thinking. The two works together illustrate the two poles of interpretation of women's religious experiences. Meyer's book, written in 1965, is skeptical, even contemptuous of the role mind cure played for nineteenth-century women. He suggests that its virtue was that it made "the weak feel strong while remaining weak" (p. 121), and sees it as the refuge of the neurotic. For Meyer, the "megalomaniac ideologies of self help . . . invited the feminization of American life," leaving men as powerless as women (p. 123). Meyer is at least right that Christian Science provided a refuge for unhappy adherents of the female culture of sickness and debility, but is a little quick to dismiss mind cure as simply a manifestation of female pathology. Parker's interpretation of mind cure is more sympathetic, as is the rest of the work on new religions, much of which stresses their potential for developing a feminist agenda. Feminist or not, however, it is clear from the female following they generated that these religions were addressing problems in ways congenial to nineteenth-century American women, at least of the middle classes. Again, the emphasis on self-controlled health is revealing, and may reflect women's outrage at the male medical establishment's treatment of women patients, and its policy of protective custody and fostering the myths of female sickliness and frailty. Bednarowski suggests in "Outside the Mainstream" that what Christian Science offered women was a way to control or subsume their own bodies, the source of their weakness and second-class status.

Christian Science's emphasis on mental power and dismissal of the material world as illusory set it apart from social reform movements in important ways: in its focus on the inner life to the exclusion of the outer, it was a throwback to a time before the merging of social, moral, and religious objectives involved virtually all churches in reform and mission work. Others of the new religions were more outward looking. Theosophy combined spiritualism (belief in reincarnation, karma) with fervent doctrines of equality of race, class, and gender. Matilda Gage, for example (see last section of this essay), was a leading suffragist who was also deeply concerned with questions of church and state. After suffering a major defeat within the suffrage association, Gage turned to Theosophy and numerology, devoting her last eight years to a study of the number five and the color blue. Clearly, however, the same philosophical underpinnings supported both suffrage and Theosophy for Gage, and her new focus on occultism was not as abrupt a shift as we might conclude. For Gage, a skilled legal advocate, as for many activist women of her generation of all religious persuasions, good political governance was inseparable from adherence to underlying "natural" laws of spiritual origin, and the discovery and implementation of those principles was as critical to women's emancipation as the vote.

This said, it is important to recognize the differences within women's religious understandings, for they did not all tend in the same direction. Certainly the Methodist temperance worker from Evanston held in her mind a God far more recognizable by her ancestors than Gage's deity, a "universal Divine principle" (Bednarowski, "Outside the Mainstream," p. 221), an impersonal, gender-free composite of Eastern religion and radical egalitarianism. The interpretation of God's will in the nineteenth century balanced between a demand for obedience and a license for human happiness for theologians and lay people alike. Spiritualists, Theosophists, and their liberal peers had not rejected God, but they construed divinity so fully in terms of the individual's search for self-fulfillment that even the mildest creed began to erode; ultimately their passionate individualism made it impossible to sustain a common cause.

WOMAN'S WORK FOR WOMAN: MISSIONS AND MISSIONIZING

The Foreign Mission Movement

Although it is a relatively new field, there has been a rush of good writing about women's mission activity in recent years. The classic work is R. Pierce Beaver's *American Protestant Women in World Mission*, the first book to recognize the woman's mission movement as a separate entity, and one that remains central to its study. This development of women's independent missionary careers took some time. Despite the revival role of woman as converter, exhorter, and moral uplifter, Barbara Welter shows in "She Hath Done What She Could" that before the Civil War the role of "missionary wife" was the only one available to women. This submissive part had little to distinguish it from "wife," except that climate and primitive conditions usually conspired to make it more unpleasant: as with their peers at home, many missionary wives made their greatest mark through a "cheerful and holy demise" which could be eulogized and marketed.

After the Civil War, woman's mission work flourished. Women in most denominations formed and controlled their own organizations, establishing for themselves a sphere of power in which they were largely unaccountable to church authority. Keller's "Lay Women in the Protestant Tradition" and Virginia Lieson Brereton and Christa Ressmeyer Klein's "American Women in Ministry" are two good accounts of women's rise to lay leadership: the latter in particular has full references to all the classic works. Keller makes the point that, to the extent that women gained a footing in church authority, it was not by rising within the established church hierarchy, but rather by founding and maintaining their own highly successful auxiliary organizations. Joan Jacobs Brumberg's *Mission for Life* recognizes the ambiguity inherent in the separatist nature of the missionary movement: although powerful within their own organizations, women's strength was never used to challenge the church's male hierarchy directly. Ultimately, this failure to confront the leadership was costly, when in the 1910s and 1920s church boards reabsorbed women's mission organizations, which lost their autonomy in consequence.

But Brumberg and others find that mission work nevertheless provided women with important experience and impetus for broader participation in religious and quasi-religious activities. Recent works are sensitive to complexity of motive, showing how the development and control of missionary organizations gave women a tremendous opportunity to use their own administrative talents while at the same time fulfilling their sincerely felt Christian responsibility to evangelize. The earlier view of missionaries as insensitive cultural imperialists has been tempered by a sympathy for their real desire to do good. The Christian spirit merged with women's growing impulse toward public life to form one of the largest and most active of women's movements: in fact, "the two ideas fused in a growing conviction that worldwide female uplift was identical with worldwide Christian evangelization, that the 'pure religion of Jesus' provided not only spiritual salvation but a 'Magna Carta of womanhood'" (Irwin T. Hyatt, p. 67). The common phrase "woman's work for woman" captured the essence of women's missionary calling: to improve the conditions under which godless women lived, and thereby, their own. Even Barbara Welter, who suggests that women only rose into prominence as missionaries as the profession lost status for men, agrees that the experience was largely positive, both for the individual and as an entry for women into public life. The political and organizational skills developed while administering church and reform groups stood many women in good stead later in more overtly political causes.

Although this development away from male authority is seen as basically positive, Brumberg and Brereton both point out that the "respectable" or "pragmatic" feminism of the evangelical women estranged them from another group—the political feminists. Women in the mission movement eschewed the idea of formal equality under the law and rejected the growing woman's rights movement, including the demand for suffrage by their sisters in the WCTU. The split between traditionalists and political feminists became increasingly clear as the woman's suffrage movement grew, but its roots are discernible even in the structure and philosophy of the pre-war reform movements. Carolyn DeSwarte Gifford's penetrating comparison between Catherine Beecher and Angelina Grimke shows how groups she calls conservative and radical reformers disagreed sharply over Christian teachings, the nature of women, and especially over the idea of a woman's sphere, an idea which the Grimkes rejected and the evangelicals at least in theory accepted. Mission work was an outlet for energy which made it possible for individual women to expand their own spheres without confronting their legal and institutional disabilities as a class or group. The tenets of evangelical womanhood—submissiveness to church authority, service to others—contrasted sharply with the growing assertion of status by advocates of women's rights. Lori D. Ginzberg's important work points out that the ideology of female benevolence obscured what were actually class interests, and that standards of feminine morality were also used to encourage conformity and denigrate more radical women's activities.

In fact, evangelical women were not oblivious to the oppression of women, but rather than in themselves or their own society they saw it in the degraded state of the women they sought to convert. Brumberg emphasizes the frequency of language about the bondage and oppression of heathen women, language so emphatic that it is difficult to doubt that evangelical women saw something of their own plight symbolized there. And it was clear that the missionary women saw themselves providing heathen women with the tools to raise themselves up, especially the ability to read. In evangelical missionizing we see an alternative type of feminism, one equally concerned with the status and condition of women. But two quite different political cultures underlie the split between the evangelist's and the feminist's methods and goals.

Finally, Jane Hunter's *Gospel of Gentility* and Patricia Hill's *The World Their Household* are both highly rewarding, and together offer views of both sides of the ocean. Hunter's book focuses on the lives and work of American women in China, putting American missionaries in the context of Western imperialism and America's mission to civilize the heathen East. Hunter is less sanguine than others about the opportunities mission work offered women. She rejects Page Smith's contention that mission work allowed women to achieve equal professional status with men. She finds inferior pay and status for women, and a gender code which even on the other side of the world restricted activities, particularly for missionary women with children. Nonetheless, she does see mission work as a career choice, if a conservative one: in her eyes, missionaries were socially conservative women who exiled themselves to perform in the name of Christian service jobs like teaching and nursing that many more innovative women were performing at home. Such a career choice was more easily explicable within the canons of domesticity in the context of foreign service.

Hill's book concentrates more on the relationship between the mission movement and American culture from the Civil War to 1920, showing that, far from remaining static, mission work changed with the times. Initially women were thought to be fitted to evangelize by their innate piety and penchant for prayer, valuable tools for the work of conversion. Since women could not be ordained, though, their roles had to be defined in ways contrasting to those of male missionaries. The stress on good deeds and service to others which defined women's work at home shaped their mission work as well. Female missionaries often became involved in education and medical and health care as well as religious instruction. Missionaries were heroines, often household names, to the women they left behind. Organization at home was quite decentralized, and members of each local mission society (often known as "mite societies") sent their pennies and letters to women abroad with whom they felt a deep personal connection, and for whom they prayed daily. It was this level of involvement that attracted so many women to mission work, especially important at a time when there were few other opportunities.

As Hill portrays it, women's missions were ultimately weakened by their own success. Support for woman's work abroad swelled into the early years of the twentieth century. Both Hill and Brumberg make important connections between missionizing and the culture of print, showing how wide public dissemination of letters, accounts, and journals from abroad in missionary organizations' periodicals, as well as fiction about women in the Far East, helped popularize the cause. By the First World War, though, forces of progress which were manifest in society as a whole had also changed women's culture and the mission movement. Mission organizations at home became more centralized and businesslike: no longer funded by "mites," they were a sophisticated and economically sound venture run by professionals. Mission women in the field, too, had come to think of themselves as professional women in many ways. Prayer was no longer at the center of their mission; rather, their energies ran to the founding and administration of schools, colleges, and hospitals. These women were not fundamentalists resisting modernity, but rather they embraced progressive social science tactics in an effort to make their discipline a science.

According to Hill, in the course of this development the source of the movement's success, the pennies and prayers of women at home, was lost. Women were urged to recognize that "a conception of religion as a precious personal consolation must give way to that of religion as the great transforming force of life" (p. 166). The new mission movement required only a periodic contribution, not the deeply personal support and commitment of earlier days. It no longer played on or encouraged a vision of distinctive female spirituality, and indeed that vision had little resonance in the culture by the First World War. Leaders of the mission movement helped to discard the ideal of woman's special spiritual nature without realizing that piety itself was significantly rooted in that cultural context and would not survive as woman's defining characteristic in the less gender-differentiated, more public world of the professional. The picture Hill draws may be the most valuable to date in explaining what happened to female piety as the canons of domesticity eroded. The lesson is not that faith is a hothouse flower, but that spirituality too has an important cultural dimension and may be constructed in different ways in different societies. By the 1920s, mission work no longer attracted the support of vast numbers of women. Many who would have been drawn to it a generation earlier chose instead literary clubs, nursing, teaching, or other newly respectable options.

Domestic Missions and the Social Gospel

Unfortunately, there is less to say about the role of Protestantism in domestic reform at the end of the century because the role religion played in women's Progressive Era reform movements other than temperance remains obscure. The pattern obvious on the surface is one of secularization: women moved from church-centered societies to clubs, colleges, jobs, or reforms like temperance which were organized outside the church. In many cases historians of women have not looked behind the secular organization to the religious influences still in play; and historians of the social gospel have in most cases not extended their work to include women's reforms, which cannot be understood by analogy to men's. Certainly women's public activities after the Civil War spread far beyond evangelizing. The tract societies of the early part of the century and the heavy emphasis on conversion were no longer dominant, and their place was filled by social activism and concern for the health, well-being, and morals of the evangelized classes.

The overtly secular nature of reform in this period is somewhat misleading. Despite trends away from church-centered activities, nineteenth-century America was still a deeply Protestant culture. During the eighteenth century conservatives expressed their concern for the fate of the poor in an industrializing society through a paternalism which was overwhelmed by the nineteenth century's optimistic belief in an unlimited capacity for production. The problems of the poor and the working classes persisted nonetheless, and the evangelical reformer of the later nineteenth century sought to address poverty and intolerable living conditions, not with the individual patronage or largesse of agrarian paternalism, but with the pioneering social work techniques of nascent agencies. The impulse toward social work sprang directly from the religious and cultural hegemony and the compassionate perfectionism of nineteenth-century Protestantism, and many women reformers were deeply influenced by their religious affiliations. In addition, the domestic missionizing of denominational groups and organizations, of which the Salvation Army is a primary example, has not been given enough recognition, and even those who have written on the subject have largely ignored women.

Timothy L. Smith's *Revivalism and Social Reform in Mid-Nineteenth Century America* and Norris Magnuson's *Salvation in the Slums* are two of the works which recognize the radical social reform component in evangelical societies, whose concern for all aspects of the lives of the poor and working class and systematic critique of the capitalist wage labor system qualified them as Christian socialists. Magnuson observes that often evangelicals' reform efforts are dismissed because their "emotional preaching, emphasis on individual conversion, and isolation from contemporary society are thought to have made them irrelevant" (p. 165), and feels that the scope of their concerns has been unfairly dwarfed. The urban missions which many denominations ran for the benefit of the impoverished were often staffed by deaconesses whose life's work and calling, like settlement house staffers', was social work in its early form, before professionalization excluded many of the people who had first practised it.

Anne Firor Scott's *The Southern Lady* and John P. McDowell's *The Social Gospel in the South* are two of the fullest descriptions of female reform, but the two books have divergent tendencies: Scott's southern lady is in the process of secularization, moving away from the church and toward clubs and secular political activities, while her contemporary in McDowell's book is moved by religious ideals to participate in a myriad of social reform movements, disproving the received wisdom that the South was untouched by social gospelism. Mary E. Frederickson's "Shaping a New Society" best reconciles these competing visions by showing the significance of the convergence between women's Christian ideals and their growing focus on social conditions. She suggests that many Methodist women in the South shifted their interest from foreign to home missions as they came to understand the full consequences for America of their evangelical philosophy. Recognizing that entrepreneurs and industrialists were constructing a society with radical, inbuilt inequalities, Methodist women set out to reduce the imbalance, creating in the process a critical ideology which sought to restrain capitalism from running roughshod over workers, and promoted as a corrective a kind of Christian communalism. Although Frederickson concludes that the effort achieved mixed results, she envisions Christian reform in this period as a political counterculture, acting as a counterweight against unrestrained economic development.

This was a powerful position, and the role of women reformers in this movement toward restraint of economic power has been underplayed. The wide-ranging programs of groups like domestic missions and the WCTU must be understood within the context of efforts by farmers, the labor movement, and other progressive activists to redress the balance of power between owners and workers. These efforts failed, of course, in the sense that Christian communalism was never established as the prevailing model of social relations. But they were successful to the extent that by the First World War protective regulation and relief programs were widely acknowledged as among the proper functions of government. Well before the New Deal, liberal political philosophy had come to encompass welfare responsibilities as well as the tradition of individual liberty, a transformation to which organized women's groups contributed significantly.

THE TEMPERANCE MOVEMENT

Temperance was the largest and most influential of the women's reform movements, and its development is emblematic of the development of women's volunteer work and women's politics generally. Over its long history, the movement underwent a metamorphosis from its early evangelical orientation to the establishment of a national society, organized on secular lines, with a broad social and political agenda. Yet until the late 1960s, scholars largely dismissed nineteenth-century temperance activists, both men and women, as an unbalanced group pursuing trivial, idiosyncratic ends outside the scope of the true reform tradition. The historiography of the 1960s sought to revise this interpretation by placing temperance within the social control model popular at the time, as best represented in Joseph R. Gusfield's thesis that the temperance movement was a bid for cultural dominance, a means for groups representing an older order to impose their own values on the diversifying nineteenth-century society and so retain their status in the American social hierarchy.

With the discrediting of the social control model has come the beginning of a fuller understanding of the temperance movement. Recent work has recognized the genuine humanitarian concerns of many temperance activists, and also the worth of the movement itself. Alcoholism was common and destructive, especially among the poor: nineteenth-century reformers saw clearly the continuing cycle of drink and poverty to which many working-class families were condemned. Women, economically dependent and without legal standing, had a particular stake in this tragedy. A husband's alcoholism could destroy the family's security, their home, and sometimes their very lives.

Once again, women entered the reform arena through domesticity, using their role as the custodians of family welfare to mount an assault on the drinking habits of the American male. Ian R. Tyrrell's article gives a good account of women's part in the movement in the years before the Civil War, and of the way in which "women reformers began to depict the drink problem as a glaring and critical example of the sexual subordination of women" (p. 140). As in the social purity movement, women began to cast the consumption of alcohol in terms of sexual antagonism, and behind the condemnation of drink lay a critique of the whole structure of gender relations.

In their early years—the 1830s and 1840s—women's temperance societies followed traditional patterns: they were organized through churches, usually as auxiliaries to men's groups. Women played no public role, and they relied on moral suasion rather than political means to effect their ends. Female temperance work retained an evangelical flavor throughout the century in the personal visits to afflicted homes, the persuasion of the reluctant sinner, the sudden conversion and signing of the abstinence pledge, and the joyful public testimony to the good news. The choice to drink or not was always cast in the familiar paradigm of sin and virtue even though the understanding of the problem quickly became social rather than religious, an example of the continuing power of religious forms.

But by the 1850s women were supplementing prayers and exhortation with more political methods. Maine's passage in 1851 of the nation's first prohibition law gave a heady taste of the power of the state to effect immediate and sweeping social change well beyond the slow and painstakingly uncertain personal conversion to abstinence. Although still without a national organization, temperance women moved slowly both toward political means and political rights: they became engaged in legislative petitioning and in lobbying for local and state laws, and it was in this period that cautious support for women's suffrage began to grow.

Women's temperance showed a more militant face during the Woman's Crusade of 1873 to 1875, the saloon-bashing period when women sought to stop the sale of liquor in public places through picketing or holding revival meetings in bars until saloon keepers agreed to close down. Behavior like this seemed even to the activists themselves far outside the prescribed role of the true woman: one activist admitted that "a woman knocking out the head of a whiskey barrel with an ax to the tune of Old Hundred, is not the ideal woman sitting on a sofa, dining on strawberries and cream and sweetly warbling 'The Rose that All Are Praising'" (Tyrrell, p. 144). But the public image of the virtuous woman leading lost men and boys back to a moral life was so powerful that, except for the liquor industry (which later organized a vigorous lobby against the woman's vote), there was little outcry. Almost certainly the strong persistence of revivalistic and evangelistic forms and themes even as temperance became oriented toward social problems helped women to win public acceptance. But it may be important that the crusade started in the small towns of the Midwest, and worked best in areas where religious networks operated: in many cases the crusade relied on existing benevolent and missionary societies for its initial organization. The leaders and most active crusaders seem to have been well connected within the elite of the small towns—wives of professionals and ministers who relied on their family standing to make their influence felt. Indeed, without backing from churches and community leaders, it is hard to imagine that such behavior from women would have been tolerated.

Jack S. Blocker's "Separate Paths" and "*Give to the Winds Thy Fears*" as well as Jed Dannenbaum's *Drink and Disorder* examine the crusaders' attitudes toward law and legislation in light of the lawlessness of their own actions. Both find that they were deeply disenchanted with or alienated from the law. Blocker suggests that women felt betrayed by male legislators and police who continued to license grogshops and would not enforce prohibitory laws even where they were enacted. The crusade was an effort to circumvent male-dominated legal channels, and to impart moral standards to governance through direct action. Blocker documents criticisms by suffragists of crusaders which hint at fascinating divisions: suffragists like Stanton gave unqualified support to the crusade as breaking new ground in women's public participation, but deplored the tendency to circumvent the law by direct moral appeal rather than seeking to make the law work. This suggests that crusaders were acting as witnesses from the position of the Christian outsider, while the more politically astute suffragists made their appeals from the vantage point of the moral insider. Dannenbaum also cites women's feelings of helplessness in the legal and political worlds as an impetus for the crusade, and in this joins with Paula Baker's important argument in "The Domestication of Politics." That article sets out a chronology of women's entrance into the male world of politics, an entrance made necessary in part by the declining effectiveness of the local, religious networks of the antebellum community in the new economic and social conditions which prevailed after the war. Temperance work in all its manifestations was an important step in uniting men's and women's political worlds.

Militant tactics proved to be of limited effectiveness, and after two years the crusade petered out. There followed the period of the temperance movement's unambiguous politicization. The crusade provided the impetus for the formation of the largest woman's organization of the nineteenth century, the WCTU, whose national political character represented a very different model of influence from local, church-based organizations. Until recently the WCTU has received little attention, some of it unkind. But recent books by Ruth B. Bordin, Barbara Epstein, and Jed Dannenbaum have all drawn valuable pictures of the organization.

Early on the Union underwent an emblematic struggle for power between the first president, Annie Wittenmyer, a conservative advocate of moral suasion who opposed political rights for women or involvement in political struggles, and Frances Willard from Illinois, who represented the prosuffrage faction which was stronger in the West. Willard's victory and her twenty-year reign moved the WCTU toward a broad social agenda and the endorsement of political means to effect it. Among the departments within the WCTU were the "Politics Department," established to orchestrate participation in national politics, and the "Suffrage Department," whose job was to promote the woman's ballot.

The WCTU was highly organized at local, state, and national levels, giving unprecedented numbers of women political experience. Under Willard, the WCTU's policy was a brand of "gospel socialism" which took temperance women into areas as diverse as child care, prison reform, and labor legislation, challenging the social and economic relations of industrial capitalism as immoral. In the 1880s and 1890s Willard even involved the WCTU deeply in national politics: Blocker's "The Politics of Reform" describes the wheelings and dealings of the WCTU's unsuccessful attempt to ally itself with the Populist party and force on them planks endorsing prohibition and woman's suffrage. Clearly the WCTU expressed a political consciousness far removed from the moral suasion of the earlier, unorganized evangelical temperance. And despite the fact that the membership was more conservative than the leadership, the network of temperance newspapers, conventions, and lecture circuits kept the members informed on the political front. The WCTU introduced far more women to politics than the more radical women's rights movement, raising their awareness about women's issues and about broader social problems.

Despite this, the temperance movement has been characterized or criticized by women's historians as espousing only a limited feminism. As Barbara Epstein sees it, the WCTU never broke with its evangelical background to endorse the radical stands of feminists like Stanton, and was weakened by the contradictions inherent in gospel socialism, at least when the gospel was conventional, Victorian domesticity. While the WCTU's platform encompassed some feminist concerns for equality, they were expressed in the concepts of moral stewardship, so that ultimately temperance women claimed to be seeking the vote, not as citizens or equals, but as guardians of the public virtue. Their suffrage campaign slogan was "Home Protection," because they hoped to vote in a raft of temperance and purity laws which would make the American home a model embodying Willard's ideal of marriage as "the white life for two." In the eyes of many historians this was a failing which kept the WCTU from dealing effectively with the systemic social problems caused by intemperance and woman's unequal status. The temperance movement never resolved dilemmas such as the religious and legal prohibition on divorce, for example: to support divorce would offend religious sensibilities, both among the membership and within the religious community. In fact the Union supported the ban on divorce, though waveringly, and opposed other major realignments of power within the family. Yet without the legal right to diforce a woman could be at the mercy of a drunken husband for a lifetime. For Epstein and others this adherence to the ideal of the Victorian family limited the scope of reform, and prevented temperance women from acknowledging the roots of their subordination within the structure of the family.

Both Barbara Epstein and Paul Johnson characterize the early temperance movement as a campaign against masculine culture, and an attempt to restructure gender relations through women's insistence on men behaving soberly, respectfully, and responsibly within the home, using personal appeal as well as the importance of reputation and community approval as goads. Epstein sees gender antagonism as the framework for the entire movement, and the paradigm for women's religious experience in the nineteenth century in general.

But in its later years Epstein and Johnson see the focus of temperance encompassing class antagonism as well. Despite its working-class adherents, temperance was a critical prop of middle-class culture, one of the traits by which the middle class defined itself. Although temperance offered new forms of power to working-class women, the ideal of sexual respect and female dominance in the home developed by Charles Grandison Finney threatened the patriarchal structure which persisted in working-class families. Furthermore, the working class was being swelled by immigrant populations, and the neighborhood bar often became a focus of their transplanted culture. Temperance women attacked these institutions in a conflict which Perry R. Duis characterizes as a middle-class notion of privacy and respectability pitted against the leisure patterns of the working class and their use of public space. Because working-class cultures were not contained within the sphere of temperance women's moral influence, though, legislative solutions like curtailed hours, Sunday closings, and prohibition became the most effective tools of reform. Temperance women enthusiastically campaigned for repressive social measures of all kinds, and it was in this period that the ideology of government as the agent of moral reform became vital. Johnson's excellent review exposes the paradox of temperance studies. From the vantage point of women, temperance was a good thing, giving them more control over family life and extending their scope well into the public realm. For working-class men, though, coercive temperance reform was more likely to be intrusive, or to destroy customary patterns of friendship and relaxation, as well as infringe on individual rights.

While the differences between the WCTU and suffrage groups like the National Woman Suffrage Association (NWSA) were real, the characterization of evangelical suffrage as second-class feminism rests on valuations based in a distinct political theory. The mainstream of contemporary feminism has been secular, with a liberal, individualist rights orientation that rejects the more communitarian, regulatory structures supported by Christian feminists in the nineteenth century. The question of who was *really a* feminist and who was not may be important in constructing the history of the women's movement today, but the search for liberal antecedents prejudices the results from the start. Ellen DuBois suggests that the fact that the WCTU officially endorsed woman's suffrage, and spent much of the rest of the century working toward that goal, shows that the feminists finally set the agenda for the woman's movement, a political agenda which temperance workers and evangelists adopted somewhat against their will. Rather than seeing the WCTU's program as a deviant brand of liberal feminism, it is time to take temperance and other evangelical reforms on their own terms. What the historiography patronizes as "domestic feminism" may have valued social programs over a more abstract theory of individual rights. However, such a preference was a rational choice, particularly in an industrializing society. The broad social agenda of the temperance movement appealed to women not just as a more cautious variant of liberal feminism, but because it responded to the problems of poverty, intemperance, and the financial insecurity of the wage-labor system in a way that a rights-based movement did not. For the evangelicals, "freedom" for a divorced mother of six was known by its other names, immiseration and abandonment.

In addition, the truly radical components of Willard's movement have been underestimated even by sympathetic chroniclers like Ruth Bordin. Willard, like Catherine Booth and other Christian reformers, was a socialist with a far-ranging critique of capitalism. Christian reform movements functioned as a political counterculture, both in their criticism of existing social structures and their compassionate responsibility for the dispossessed. Willard and her peers *did* value natural rights, including individual rights. But unlike Stanton, their final emphasis was not on the inviolable perfection of each individual's rights, but on the exercise of rights within the community. They understood that at times the rights of individuals and of the community came into conflict, a dilemma which liberalism never acknowledged, and offered an ideology of communitarian rights as their solution.

Increasingly after Willard's death in 1898 the WCTU began to play down politics and emphasize moral reform, advocating such repressive legislative solutions as curfews and censorship laws. The Departments of Politics and Suffrage lost ground to the Department of Social Purity, whose vision of total reform gave rise to men's and boys' auxiliaries like the Society of the White Cross and Knights of the Silver Crown. More than most reform movements, women's temperance remained true to its evangelical origins. But by the twentieth century the ideal of moral purity, or "the white life for two," which had been so important a part of the middle-class evangelical ethos in the 1800s, had lost much of its power and no longer functioned as a norm. The WCTU declined in importance as a result.

FEMINISM, POLITICS, AND POWER

The movement for woman's rights, by contrast with all other nineteenth-century women's movements, did not have clear origins in the church, and was often at odds with it. In fact, there was a deeply anticlerical strain within suffragism which has led most historians to regard it as the first secularized woman's movement. Feminists' hostility to established churches was not unwarranted. A few individual clergymen strongly supported woman suffrage from the movement's inception. Sometimes a minister would preach a sermon friendly to woman's rights, or offer his church as a meeting place, as the Methodist minister at Seneca Falls did to the first woman's rights convention in 1848. (Even that offer was ambivalent: when the first women arrived the door was locked, and they had to climb through a window.) But Protestant orthodoxy as a whole was staunchly opposed to woman's rights, and the evils of the movement were staple sermon fare for years. Clergymen relied on ridicule, exhortation, and scriptural citation to nip dangerous thoughts of equality in the bud and reinforce woman's domestic and apolitical image. Horace Bushnell's diatribe, *Women's Suffrage: The Reform Against Nature* (New York, 1869), spoke for most of his colleagues on women's essential unfitness for political life.

Woman's rights activists did not turn the other cheek. Donna A. Behnke's book chronicles the joining of issues between Christianity and feminism, the great issue in the antebellum suffrage movement. Woman's rights advocates saw the orthodox church as the chief pillar of patriarchy. In their declarations and resolutions they repeatedly attacked its role in creating and perpetuating a sexist ideology, and passed resolutions calling for freedom from repressive Protestant dogma.

Much of the historiography, then, traces no lines of descent from churchwomen to feminists. The exception is the group of works by Alice Rossi, Donald W. Dayton, Lucille Sider Dayton, Nancy Hardesty, Barbara Brown Zikmund, and Beverly Wildung Harrison. Rossi's is the earliest development of their common argument: that evangelicalism in the form of Finneyite revivalism, the holiness movement, and sectarian religion created a feminist tradition which directly influenced many who later became prominent advocates of woman's rights. Both Rossi and Harrison suggest that, with few exceptions, American feminists were cut of different cloth than their European sisters: Americans were not in the tradition of secular, Enlightenment

skepticism, but moral crusaders embarked on a more conservative search fo
a vaguely Christian utopia. This would include even women like Elizabet
Cady Stanton, one of the most radical women of her day and openly antag
onistic toward the established church. Despite Stanton's antipathy towar
religion, Rossi stresses that her social ideals were formed while growing t
adulthood in an evangelical culture, and that that cultural milieu was critica
to her development as a social activist. All of these historians emphasize th
friendliness of the revival environment to women: Finney's commonsens
approach to religion and biblical interpretation, the individual, experientia
nature of the conversion experience for which the individual prepared her
self, the incitement to public testimony—all this worked toward the develop
ment of a feminist consciousness. Certainly many activists never stoppe
seeking to reconcile Christianity with political equality for women: An
toinette Brown Blackwell, one of the first ordained female ministers, intro
duced a resolution at the women's rights convention of 1852 acknowledging
that the Bible, properly interpreted, was the guarantor of women's full equal
ity, and that there was "neither male nor female in Christ Jesus."

This thrust, however, provoked a conflict which exposed several compet
ing strains of rights theories. All agreed that women had rights, but all did no
agree on their source: the Founding Mothers' debates about whether their
rights were sacred or secular in origin, guaranteed by God or by government
by script or by overarching, unwritten moral principle, were carried on over
years, and resembled the colonists' quest for a theory of rights which pre
ceded the Revolution. What these debates do reveal, though, is that for many
feminists faith was the backbone of political conviction. Despite evan
gelicalism's hospitality to women's participation, many of the early suf
fragists had strong affiliations to liberal groups like Quakers and Unitarians
who provided them with the theology as well as the experience of female
equality. Maureen Fitzgerald argues persuasively that even Stanton formed
the values which underlay her lifelong political work within the tradition of
liberal Protestantism, values like the moral equality of the sexes, the worth of
the individual, and the imperative for full self-development as a human being

There is a growing body of work, then, which is redefining the suffrage
movement as coming in part out of a spiritual tradition. It is important to
understand the sharply anticlerical strain within antebellum suffrage, not as
antireligious, but as anti-institutional. Antebellum suffragists echoed abolitionists' condemnation of unjust and coercive institutions, and shared their
belief in a natural order, God's order, which would reassert itself once the
artifice of custom and corrupt human governance was lifted. This vision lay
behind suffragists' attacks on both the clerical orthodoxy of mainstream
Protestantism, and their attacks on the male legal and political order which

xcluded women and legislated such abominations as slavery and the sale of liquor. Woman's rights advocates pursued these attacks on church and state as of a piece, understanding the two as intertwined.

Suffrage never fully detached itself from larger social movements, but neither did it stand still. Paula Baker's excellent article, "The Domestication of Politics," traces women's movement into formal political activities, and shows that, over the course of the nineteenth century, separate men's and women's political spheres merged into one, as women moved to participate more fully in the public realm. Although historians often assess this development as the secularization of women's movements, religion continued as a moving force for activists well into the twentieth century, whether as an inspiration or a burr. All suffragists, from Stanton to Willard, dedicated themselves to a struggle against the combined powers of church and state, and were unable to conceive of governance, either the kind they despised or desired, in other terms. Still, religious attitudes did change; faith became diffused in works; and government on earth became more real and more immediate to most suffragists than the government of God.

Progress also meant fragmentation, and issues of church and state were frequently at the bottom of quarrels. The two dominant suffrage groups, the National Woman Suffrage Association (NWSA) and the American Woman Suffrage Association (AWSA), often worked at odds with each other from their founding in the late 1860s until their union in 1890. Ellen DuBois's *Feminism and Suffrage*, the major work in the field, is an excellent discussion of the politics of the split, largely over the question of whether the constitutional guarantee of black suffrage should take precedence over woman suffrage.

But the struggle over tactics was symptomatic: deep fissures underlay the woman's movement, differences of religion, culture, political belief. The AWSA represented a group which was by and large more conservative than its rival. The leadership, laced with former abolitionists, acquiesced in the exclusion of women from the Fifteenth Amendment, but continued to work through established channels, political parties, and the organized churches. Women in the AWSA tended to have a more orthodox orientation, and they leaned toward appeals to state and local governments rather than direct involvement in national politics. The AWSA also had closer ties with the WCTU and its platform of moral reform.

The AWSA's attempt to secure suffrage state by state was anathema to the NWSA, whose position was that the national government and constitution were the only proper guarantors of the right to vote, and that nothing less than full national citizenship would suffice. Many members also expressed concern over the repressive nature of the WCTU's program for reform, believing that, possibly with the collusion of the AWSA, the WCTU intended to turn America into a Christian nation, altering the established balance between church and state. Stanton and Matilda Gage understood the struggle to contain the power of the Protestant church over civic life to be as critical a condition of women's freedom as the struggle against patriarchy: in fact they were one, and Stanton was not betraying her priorities when she said that she would rather never vote than see the government in the hands of religious bigots. Stanton clearly grasped the evangelical suffragists' ambitious desire to turn the government into an instrument of moral policy.

The *National Citizen and Ballot Box*, the newspaper edited by Gage, reflected the NWSA's preoccupation with religion. Gage was the foremost female church historian of her day. She shared with Stanton and others the passionate conviction that orthodox religion had used Saint Paul's views on women to shape an oppressive ideology of female subordination that was woman's strongest prison, and the greatest obstacle to equal rights. Stanton and Gage were ardent suffragists, but unlike most of their allies they saw inequality as systemic and not easily cured even by the liberal measure of giving women the ballot. Both women proposed a more radical reconstruction of family and of institutions to end the "four-fold bondage of women" at the hands of the church, state, capitalist, and home. Gage's masterwork, *Woman, Church, and State,* published in 1893, remains one of the few scholarly investigations of that three-way relationship, and strikingly prefigures the work of contemporary feminist theologians like Mary Daly. Gage saw practices such as celibacy and witch-hunts as part of the church's policy to degrade women by perpetuating the image of a lustful and wicked female sexuality. For Gage, women's glory had been in the pre-Christian matriarchal societies; they had suffered their own Fall in their degradation after the establishment of Christianity. Equally prescient were Gage's descriptions of the psychology of oppression, of women's passivity and inability to exert themselves, their morbid dependence on men for their identities.

Throughout the 1870s and 1880s, Stanton and Gage continued to urge on others the connections between religion and oppression, both at suffrage conventions and in their writings. By the end of this period, though, their anticlericalism was becoming less acceptable even to the women of the NWSA. Both Stanton's and Gage's apprehensions about the church were intensifying during the period when many were coming to see the church in a more benevolent light. The dynamic of religion in the suffrage movement has not been explored, but several explanations for this change present themselves. The 1880s experienced a resurgence of revivalism in America, and it may be that an increasing number of women became involved in the organized churches. Many denominations had dropped their aggressive stance against women's rights, and some, particularly the Methodists but also clergy from other denominations, had become strong supporters of the woman's vote. A new generation of women peopled the suffrage movement as well, a generation which had not struggled with the more rigid orthodoxy of prewar America. Despite the fact that Gage and Stanton both found Frances Willard's gospel socialism to be a dangerous influence, fewer of their followers were moved by their diatribes on the church, finding them irrelevant or even harmful to public support of the cause of suffrage.

This new attitude led to a reconciliation between the two branches of the movement, and in 1890 they merged to form the National American Woman Suffrage Association (NAWSA). Stanton came to accept the situation, even accepting the post of president. Gage did not, and she left to form the Woman's National Liberal Union on a platform calling for separation of church and state, opposing prayer in the schools, and condemning the religious ideology which was the foundation of woman's subordination. It was resolved at the organizing convention held in Washington, D.C. in February 1890

That every Church is the enemy of liberty and progress and the chief means of enslaving women's conscience and reason, and, therefore, as the first and most necessary step towards her emancipation, we should free her from the bondage of the Church. . . . That Christianity is false and its foundations a myth which every discovery of science shows to be as baseless as its former belief that the earth is flat (*Report of the Convention for Organization* [Syracuse, 1890]).

Although Gage was vilified by some of her former allies, others supported her and followed her out of the NAWSA. Still others, disillusioned by the duplicitous way Susan B. Anthony had effected the merger, left the movement altogether. These events leave no doubt that a central feature of the woman's movement was a dialogue on the relationship of church and state to each other and to the female citizenry, a dialogue which is ignored in institutional histories of church-state relations.

Meanwhile, Elizabeth Cady Stanton, too, although continuing in the NAWSA, was increasingly preoccupied with the church's threat to women's autonomy. 1895 saw the publication of the first volume of *The Woman's Bible*, an exegesis of biblical texts in line with feminist interpretations prepared by a mixed committee of freethinkers and believers under Stanton's guidance. Their motives ranged from seeking to restore what Stanton called "the White Man's Bible" as a source of authority to seeking to undermine it completely. DuBois's essay introducing Part 3 of her edition of Stanton and Anthony's writings details the political context in which the *Woman's Bible* was received. DuBois makes it clear that, for the first time, Stanton's seeming obsession with religion

took her well outside the mainstream of suffrage. She ran up against the
growing power within the movement of the WCTU, whose "Christian feminists" believed that, far from degrading them, Christianity had elevated women
to an exalted status. The *Woman's Bible* was the culmination of a tradition of
radical biblical exegesis that had begun with abolitionists and was carried on
by feminists; it foreshadowed the woman-centered interpretation of today's
feminist theology. But it was rejected by the NAWSA, whose members resolved in 1895 that as a "non-sectarian" group they had no connection with the
project, a public repudiation. Given the outcry against Stanton on its publication, that decision was politic, if nothing else. But for all the seeming increase
in piety, religion never again became the center of burning controversy in the
woman's rights movement. In part this was a reflection of churches' diminishing opposition to woman's rights, and of women's greater acceptance of the
role of the church, as those who describe the evangelization of the suffrage
movement imply. But it also suggests the church's diminishing role in political
discourse, and its loosened grip on public life.

The paradox of suffrage is that although as an organized movement it was
almost wholly contained in the East, a number of western states gave women
the vote well before the Nineteenth Amendment was passed in 1920. Alan P.
Grimes and Beverly Beeton are the two main sources on non-Mormon suffrage in the West, and both conclude that suffrage in those states owed little
to the ideology of equality. Grimes uses status anxiety analysis to argue that
woman suffrage has to be seen in the context of a large nativist movement to
restore or maintain a "Puritan" moral standard: women's votes were enlisted
by progressives who sought to tame the western territories using temperance
laws and restrictions on immigration, and believed that the woman's vote
would further their cause.

Grimes's analysis is now somewhat dated, and his concept of the "Puritan
ethic," an overworked and underdefined tag, is not very helpful. But his book
shows clearly the part racism played in the campaign for the vote. Suffragists
were embittered by their exclusion from the Fifteenth Amendment, and by
many years of watching vote men who were less educated, less informed, less
committed to an ideal of citizenship than they. Grimes quotes Anthony's vivid
description of the antisuffrage coalition of liquor manufacturers, drunks,
"Mexican greasers," religious bigots, colored men, impassive Scandinavians
on their great, glassy horses—in short, "this vast mass of ignorant, unedu-
cated, degraded population." By contrast, the prosuffrage group included
"native born white men, temperance men, cultivated, broad, generous men,
just men, men who think," Methodists, Presbyterians, Episcopalians (Grimes,
pp. 86–87). Like the Rev. Josiah Strong, a supporter of suffrage whose *Our
Country* was published in 1885, Anthony could sum up America's ills as

'Romanism, Mormonism, Immigration, Socialism, Urbanization, and Intemperance" (Grimes, p. 112), certain that she was appealing to a wide audience. Doubtless the "degraded population" perceived woman suffrage as a threat: though little work has been done on this, James Kennealy's article discusses Catholic opposition to woman suffrage in Massachusetts on the grounds that women's votes could create a climate unfavorable to Catholicism and to working-class culture.

Aileen S. Kraditor's important book, *The Ideas of the Woman Suffrage Movement, 1890–1920*, shows the ideological shifts which underlay the new antagonism between middle-class Protestant women and working-class, immigrant men. In 1860 Stanton gave a speech to the American Anti-Slavery Society which outlined a theory of rights, not in conflict, but mutually dependent. When any group was deprived of its rights, all suffered: liberty was not perfect until each citizen was protected equally. By the 1880s, the mission of some suffragists appeared to have become an attempt not to secure rights for all, but to pry open the constitutional settlement of the founders just long enough for native-born, white, Protestant women to slip in, slamming the door behind them. This attitude allowed white southern women to ally with the suffrage association out of common fears of the growing power of non-white groups. The new concept of competing rights still embodied a certain aspect of classic republican thought, harking back to a small, homogeneous community, but social conditions made that vision elitist rather than democratic in the late nineteenth century. In their elitism, suffragists followed the founders better than they knew. But in an interesting way they also showed their kinship with the evangelical suffragists: despite their antagonism toward religious institutions, many members of the NWSA were defending the integrity of a culture that was inherently Protestant in its values and traditions, and resisting the cultural pluralism created by the mix of ethnic and religious groups.

Mormon women also found themselves in the position of using the ballot to protect their culture, but in their case the church was embattled in a bitter conflict with the federal government. More than on any other topic, the literature on Mormonism is vast, and can only be presented selectively in this bibliography. But some of the most fundamental questions of church and state have arisen out of attempts to regulate Mormon Utah, the only theocratic polity to have mounted a sustained challenge to the United States government.

The place of polygamy and woman suffrage in this conflict is a matter of debate. In the eyes of nineteenth-century critics of Mormonism and some twentieth-century writers, it was Protestant outrage at the Mormon system of plural marriage that fueled the anti-Mormon campaign. Certainly polygamy stuck in the craws of many Protestants for whom monogamy was the foundation of a virtuous republican society. Congress made two attempts to outlaw plural marriage before the final, successful Edmunds-Tucker Act of 1887. Leonard J. Arrington and Jon Haupt's "Intolerable Zion," Charles A. Cannon's "The Awesome Power of Sex," and the works by David Brion Davis, Stuart W. Hyde, and Gail Farr Casterline analyze the images of unrestrained lust and sexuality in anti-Mormon literature of the day, myths of sadism and debauchery which reveal both their makers' own fears of loss of civic and personal virtue, and the secret lascivious pleasure of the righteous voyeur. Davis examines the extraordinary disjunction between the straitlaced Mormon practices and lurid Gentile accounts as part of the nativist fear that groups like the Mormons, Freemasons, Catholics, and other foreign bodies were engaged in plots to subvert republican government and substitute religious despotism.

But Arrington is the best known of those who argue that practices like polygamy, though repugnant, were only a superficial example of Mormonism's incompatibility with American ideals. He maintains that the hierarchical, cooperative community of economic life in Utah was fundamentally at odds with the freewheeling, competitive, speculative nature of American capitalism. In addition, the theocratic government of the Mormon state demanded absolute loyalty, so that national citizenship was a distant second commitment. Henry J. Wolfinger suggests that the clash between the federal government and the Mormon hierarchy was finally unavoidable, a fundamental conflict between civil and ecclesiastical authority.

This was the context in which Mormon women were enfranchised in 1869, two months after woman suffrage was enacted in Wyoming. The conflict between the patriarchal Mormon ideal with its theology of woman's inequality and the fact of the woman's vote raises questions about the ideology behind this particular piece of politics. Most writers have answered that, as in the rest of the West, ideology had little to do with it. Grimes and Beeton both conclude that the vote came to women not in spite of polygamy, but because of it. Outsiders, critics of polygamy, were convinced that woman's natural monogamous nature would assert itself to vote out the brutish custom: Mormon men were equally convinced that their wives would follow their lead and support the church, showing the world that they were not the enslaved, degraded creatures of myth, thereby thwarting efforts to pass antipolygamy legislation and improving Utah's chances for statehood. By this reading, women became the pawn of both sides in the government's protracted war on Utah.

More recent work by Lawrence Foster, Thomas G. Alexander, Jean Bickmore White, Judith Rasmussen Dushku, and Heather Symmes Cannon, though, concentrates on Mormon women's real, principled desire and struggle for political rights. These writers see in the strengthening sisterhood of polygamy, the politically active Woman's Relief Society, the newspaper *The Woman's Exponent* which actively endorsed and reported on suffrage news from around the country, and the existence of state and local suffrage organizations, an awareness of feminist ideals and political theory. Mormon women's own activism has been overlooked in the past, in part because many scholars were unable to reconcile a desire for equal rights with Mormon women's defense of polygamic marriage. This juxtaposition of suffrage and polygamy was another issue on which the eastern rights movement split. Marilyn Warenski provides evidence that the NWSA supported the Mormon women's suffrage; Stanton and Anthony both testified on their behalf in the congressional hearing for the Edmunds-Tucker Act, which nevertheless succeeded in repealing woman suffrage in Utah as well as in outlawing polygamy. Their support makes sense in view of their emphasis on equal rights and disinclination to legislate morality. But as Kathleen Marquis shows, moral outrage got the better of the evangelical suffragists. Many belonged to the Anti-Polygamy Society, an organization closely tied to the WCTU which sought to wipe out the second of the "twin relics of barbarism," slavery and polygamy. Once disabused of the notion that Mormon women would immediately vote to invalidate their marriages and bastardize their children by outlawing polygamy, many moral reformers were bitter and relentless in their drive to repeal suffrage for such unnatural and degraded women.

Mormon wives, paradoxically, defended themselves and their marriage customs against charges of lust, debauchery, and unnatural womanhood by the tenets of Victorianism. They considered themselves to be no less repositories of virtue than Gentile women.

Were we the stupid, degraded, heartbroken beings that we have been represented, silence might better become us; but as women of God . . . in the purest, noblest sense of refined womanhood . . . we not only speak because we have the right, but justice and humanity demand that we should (Cannon, "Practical Politicians," p. 164).

They were not prepared to cede their virtue or their vote to the righteous crusade of their Protestant countrywomen: as one woman said, "The women of this country want to crush us, but it will be diamond cut diamond" (Marquis, p. 105). Marilyn Warenski's recent *Patriarchs and Politics* contains a particularly sympathetic account of the dilemma of Mormon women who, despite belonging to a rigidly patriarchal society, actively resisted the assaults of antipolygamists and legislators on their right to vote. Mormon women regained the lost vote by provision of the state constitution on Utah's entry into the Union, more than twenty years before the Nineteenth Amendment. But by that time the Mormon elders had repudiated the practice of plural marriage, and the fitness of the "unnatural" Mormon plural wife to vote was no longer at issue.

Back in the East, the official suffrage organization had come under the leadership of moderate suffragists like the Christian reformer Anna Howard Shaw, a Methodist minister who had gotten her start in temperance work and was a fervent opponent of projects like the *Woman's Bible*. Shaw, who retained close ties to the WCTU, served as the NAWSA's vice-president from 1892 to 1904, and as president from 1904 to 1915. Much of this period is known to students of suffrage as "the doldrums," because little was gained in the fight for state and national suffrage laws. Shaw has been acknowledged as a poor administrator, and the movement's organizational disarray may account for NAWSA's ineffectiveness. Or perhaps moral superiority translated into a political activism which could not take the sharp, confrontational stands or aggressive approach to legislative lobbying necessary to political success. The WCTU in this period had retreated from active political involvement back into social purity work: all in all neither the radical agenda of Stanton and Gage nor the gospel socialism of Frances Willard had survived to offer women a comprehensive social program that included, but went well beyond, the vote.

Nor did the revitalization of the suffrage movement from 1910 to 1920 come about through any radical religious impulse. Leaders like Carrie Chapman Catt, Harriet Stanton Blatch, and Alice Paul (though Paul was a Quaker) had all been influenced by the new militancy of English suffragists, who were conducting political warfare with the modern weapons of propaganda and demonstrations, public opinion and the media. The American suffrage campaign was modernized under these women, whose revolution in tactics augured the successful suffrage amendment of 1920. Suffrage continued to make its bows to the domestic woman, using imagery of motherhood and purity to dispel fears of the woman voter unsexed. Indeed, ERA marchers in the 1970s still wore white in homage to their foremothers, whose parading ranks of white-clad women came to symbolize the movement. But the woman's movement became more a bid for equal political standing than an attempt to impose female moral standards on a flawed world.

Women who were young in the 1910s and 1920s by and large repudiated the reforming tendencies of their mothers and grandmothers, and ceased to identify themselves as women through the attributes of piety and purity: the dominant cultural image of the period was the flapper, whose provocative style and wild behavior were a revolution of her own and a radically different way of seeing herself in the world. Individual women's religious experience continued to transform and sustain them. But the reigning social construction of womanly piety, the identification of women as naturally spiritual, had lost its monopoly. Above all, the thrust of woman's culture in the teens and twenties seems to have emphasized woman's sameness to man, not her special qualities or virtues: the new woman, unlike the true woman, neither gained her strength and public position from a spiritual identity, nor was confined to activities in that sphere.

BIBLIOGRAPHY

1. WOMEN'S ROLE IN THE INSTITUTIONAL CHURCH

Barfoot, Charles H. "Prophetic vs. Priestly Religion: The Changing Role of Women Clergy in Classical Pentecostal Churches." Religious Research Review 22, no. 1 (1980), 2-17.

Bass, Dorothy C. "Memoirs of Eminently Pious Women: A Study in the Evangelical Religion of New England, 1790-1840." Paper delivered at the Third Berkshire Conference on the History of Women, Bryn Mawr, Pa., 1976. (On deposit at the Schlesinger Library, Radcliffe College.)

Beckwith, R. T. "Office of Woman in the Church, to the Present Day." Churchman 83 (August 1969), 170-183.

Blauvelt, Martha Tomhave. "Women and Revivalism." In Women and Religion in America, vol. 1, The Nineteenth Century, edited by Rosemary Radford Ruether and Rosemary Skinner Keller, 1-45. San Francisco: Harper & Row, 1981.

Boyd, Lois A. "Presbyterian Ministers' Wives: A Nineteenth-Century Portrait." Journal of Presbyterian History 59, no. 1 (1981), 3-17.

Boyd, Lois A. "Shall Women Speak? Confrontation in the Church, 1876." Journal of Presbyterian History 56, no. 4 (1978), 281-294.

Boyd, Lois A., and Brackenridge, Douglas R. Presbyterian Women in America: Two Centuries of a Quest for Status. Westport, Conn.: Greenwood, 1983.

Boylan, Anne M. "Evangelical Womanhood in the Nineteenth Century: The Role of Women in Sunday Schools." Feminist Studies 4, no. 3 (1978), 62-80.

Boylan, Anne M. "The Role of Conversion in Nineteenth-Century Sunday Schools." American Studies 20, no. 1 (1979), 35-48.

Brauer, Ruth. "Tracing Women's Services in the Missouri Synod." Concordia Historical Institute Quarterly 36, no. 1 (1963), 5-13.

Brown, Earl K. "Women in Church History: Stereotypes, Archetypes, and Operational Modalities." Methodist History 18, no. 2 (1980), 109-132.

Calvo, Janis. "Quaker Women Ministers in Nineteenth-Century America." Quaker History 63 (Autumn 1974), 75-93.

Dayton, Donald, and Dayton, Lucille Sider. "Women as Preachers: Evangelical Precedents." Christianity Today, 23 May 1975, 4-8.

Epstein, Barbara. "Religious Conversions in the Nineteenth Century: Men's and Women's Diverging Experiences." Chap. 2 in The Politics of Domesticity: Women, Evangelism, and Temperance in Nineteenth-Century America. Middletown, Conn.: Wesleyan University Press, 1981.

Ewens, Mary. "The Leadership of Nuns in Immigrant Catholicism." In Women and Religion in America, vol. 1, The Nineteenth Century, edited by Rosemary Radford Ruether and Rosemary Skinner Keller, 101-149. San Francisco: Harper & Row, 1981.

Ewens, Mary. "Removing the Veil: The Liberated American Nun." In Women of Spirit: Female Leadership in the Jewish and Christian Traditions, edited by Rosemary Radford Ruether and Eleanor McLaughlin. New York: Simon & Schuster, 1979.

Ewens, Mary. The Role of the Nun in Nineteenth-Century America. New York: Arno Press, 1978.

Fraser, Dorothy Bass. "Women With a Past: A New Look at the History of Theological Education." Theological Education 8, no. 4 (1972), 213-224.

Gorrell, Donald K. "Ordination of Women by the United Brethren in Christ, 1889." Methodist History 18, no. 2 (1980), 136-143.

Greaves, Richard L., ed. Triumph Over Silence: Women in Protestant History. Westport, Conn.: Greenwood, 1985.

Harkness, Georgia. "Pioneer Women in the Ministry." Religion in Life 39, no. 2 (1970), 261-271.

Hitchings, Catherine F. Universalist and Unitarian Women Ministers. Boston: Universalist Historical Society, 1975.

Jeffrey, Julie Roy. "Am Beginning to Feel Quite Civilized." Chap. 4 in _Frontier Women: The Trans-Mississippi West, 1840-1880_. New York: Hill & Wang, 1979.

Keller, Rosemary Skinner. "Creating a Sphere for Women in the Church: How Consequential an Accommodation?" _Methodist History_ 18, no. 2 (1980), 83-94.

Keller, Rosemary Skinner; Queen, Louise L.; and Thomas, Hilah F., eds. _Women in New Worlds: Historical Perspectives on the Wesleyan Tradition_, vol. 2. Nashville: Abingdon, 1982. (Vol. 1, 1981, ed. Thomas et al.)

Kolmer, Elizabeth. "Catholic Women Religious and Women's History: A Survey of the Literature." _American Quarterly_ 30, no. 5 (1978), 639-651.

Letsinger, Norman H. "The Status of Women in the Southern Baptist Convention in Historical Perspective." _Baptist History and Heritage_ 12, no. 1 (1977), 37-44.

Linton, Ruth C. "Paradox and Paradigm: Women and Sunday Schools in the Early Nineteenth Century." _Working Papers from the Regional Economic History Research Center_ 5, nos. 2-3 (1982), 119-130.

McBeth, Harry Leon. "The Role of Women in Southern Baptist History." _Baptist History and Heritage_ 12, no. 1 (1977), 3-25.

McLaughlin, Eleanor. "The Christian Past: Does It Hold a Future for Women?" _Anglican Theological Review_ 57, no. 1 (1975), 36-56.

Melder, Keith. "Mask of Oppression: The Female Seminary Movement in the United States." _New York History_ 55, no. 3 (1974), 261-279.

Micks, Marianne H. "Exodus or Eden? A Battle of Images." _Anglican Theological Review Supplementary Series_ 1973 (1), 126-139.

Miller, Page Putnam. "Women in the Vanguard of the Sunday School Movement." _Journal of Presbyterian History_ 58, no. 4 (1980), 311-325.

Mitchell, Norma Taylor. "From Social to Radical Feminism: A Survey of Emerging Diversity in Methodist Women's Organizations, 1869-1974." _Methodist History_ 13, no. 3 (1975), 21-44.

Noll, William T. "Women as Clergy and Laity in the Nineteenth Century Methodist Protestant Church." _Methodist History_ 15, no. 2 (1977), 107-121.

Oates, Mary J. "Organized Voluntarism: The Catholic Sisters in Massachusetts, 1870-1940." American Quarterly 30, no. 5 (1978), 652-680.

Penfield, Janet Harbison. "Women in the Presbyterian Church: An Historical Overview." Journal of Presbyterian History 55, no. 2 (1977), 107-123.

Price, Marian Gail. "A Study of Some of the Effects of Nineteenth-Century Revivalism on the Status and Accomplishments of Women in the Evangelical Covenant Church of America." Ph.D. diss., Boston University School of Education, 1977.

Reuther, Rosemary Radford, and Keller, Rosemary Skinner, eds. Women and Religion in America, vol. 1, The Nineteenth Century. San Francisco: Harper & Row, 1981.

Reuther, Rosemary Radford, and McLaughlin, Eleanor, eds. Women of Spirit: Female Leadership in the Jewish and Christian Traditions. New York: Simon & Schuster, 1979.

Rowe, Kenneth E. "The Ordination of Women: Round One: Anna Oliver and the General Conference of 1880." Methodist History 12, no. 3 (1974), 60-72.

Spencer, Ralph W. "Anna Howard Shaw." Methodist History 13, no. 2 (1975), 33-51.

Sweet, Leonard. The Minister's Wife: Her Role in Nineteenth-Century American Evangelism. Philadelphia: Temple University Press, 1983.

Thomas, Hilah F., and Keller, Rosemary Skinner, eds. Women in New Worlds: Historical Perspectives on the Wesleyan Tradition, vol. 1. Nashville: Abingdon, 1981. (Vol. 2, 1982, ed. Keller et al.)

Tucker, Cynthia Grant. A Woman's Ministry: Mary Collson's Search for Reform as a Unitarian Minister, a Hull House Social Worker, and a Christian Science Practitioner. Philadelphia: Temple University Press, 1984.

Wasson, Margaret. "Texas Methodism's Other Half." Methodist History 19, no. 4 (1981), 206-223.

Zikmund, Barbara Brown. "The Struggle for the Right to Preach." In Women and Religion in America, vol. 1, The Nineteenth Century, edited by Rosemary Radford Ruether and Rosemary Skinner Keller, 193-241. San Francisco: Harper & Row, 1981.

Zikmund, Barbara Brown. "Where Two or Three Are Gathered
    Together: Denominationalism and the Role of Women." In The
    American Religious Experiment: Piety and Practicality,
    edited by Clyde L. Manschreck and Barbara Brown Zikmund.
    Chicago: Exploration Press, 1976.

            2. WOMEN PROPHETS, SPIRITUALISM, AND NEW RELIGIONS

Bednarowski, Mary Farrell. "Nineteenth Century American
    Spiritualism: An Attempt at a Scientific Religion." Ph.D.
    diss., University of Minnesota, 1973.

Bednarowski, Mary Farrell. "Outside the Mainstream: Women's
    Religion and Women Religious Leaders in Nineteenth-Century
    America." Journal of the American Academy of Religion 48
    (June 1980), 207-231.

Bednarowski, Mary Farrell. "Spiritualism in Wisconsin in the
    Nineteenth Century." Wisconsin Magazine of History 59, no.
    1 (1975), 2-19.

Burfield, Diana. "Theosophy and Feminism: Some Explorations in
    Nineteenth-Century Biography." In Women's Religious
    Experiences, edited by Pat Holden. Totowa, N.J.: Barnes &
    Noble Books, 1983.

Chapel, Gage William. "Christian Science and the Nineteenth-
    Century Women's Movement." Central States Speech Journal 26
    (1975), 142-149.

Cunningham, Raymond J. "From Holiness to Healing: The Faith
    Cure in America, 1872-1892." Church History 43, no. 4
    (1974), 499-513.

Davis, Rodney O. "Prudence Crandall, Spiritualism, and
    Populist-Era Reform in Kansas." Kansas History 3, no. 4
    (1980), 239-254.

Delp, Robert W. "American Spiritualism and Social Reform,
    1847-1900." Northwest Ohio Quarterly 44, no. 4 (1972), 85-
    99.

Dieter, Melvin E. The Holiness Revival of the Nineteenth
    Century. Metuchen, N.J.: Scarecrow, 1980.

Fox, Margery Q. "Power and Piety: Women in Christian Science."
    Ph.D. diss., New York University, 1973.

Fox, Margery Q. "Protest in Piety: Christian Science
    Revisited." International Journal of Women's Studies
    (Canada) 1, no. 4 (1978), 401-416.

Fuller, Robert C. Mesmerism and the American Cure of Souls.
    Philadelphia: University of Pennsylvania Press, 1982.

Gottschalk, Stephen. The Emergence of Christian Science in
    American Religious Life. Berkeley: University of California
    Press, 1973.

Hansen, Penny. "Woman's Hour: Feminist Implications of Mary
    Baker Eddy's Christian Science Movement, 1885-1910." Ph.D.
    diss., University of California, Irvine, 1981.

Hardesty, Nancy; Dayton, Lucille Sider; and Dayton, Donald W.
    "Women in the Holiness Movement: Feminism in the Evangelical
    Tradition." In Women of Spirit: Female Leadership in the
    Jewish and Christian Traditions, edited by Rosemary Radford
    Ruether and Eleanor McLaughlin. New York: Simon & Schuster,
    1979.

Hovet, Theodore. "Phoebe Palmer's 'Altar Phraseology' and the
    Spiritual Dimension of Woman's Sphere." Journal of Religion
    63, no. 3 (1983), 264-280.

Humez, Jean, ed. Gifts of Power: The Writings of Rebecca Cox
    Jackson, Black Visionary and Shaker Eldress. Amherst:
    University of Massachusetts Press, 1981.

Jones, Charles Edwin. A Guide to the Study of the Holiness
    Movement. Metuchen, N.J.: Scarecrow, 1974.

Jones, Charles Edwin. Perfectionist Persuasion: The Holiness
    Movement and American Methodism, 1867-1936. Metuchen, N.J.:
    Scarecrow, 1974.

Judah, J. Stillson. The History and Philosophy of the
    Metaphysical Movements in America. Philadelphia:
    Westminster, 1967.

Leach, William. True Love and Perfect Union: The Feminist
    Reform of Sex and Society. New York: Basic, 1980.

Lears, T. J. Jackson. No Place of Grace: Antimodernism and the
    Transformation of American Culture, 1880-1920. New York:
    Pantheon, 1981.

Lindley, Susan Hill. "The Ambiguous Feminism of Mary Baker
    Eddy." Journal of Religion 64, no. 3 (1984), 318-331.

McLoughlin, William G. "Aimee Semple McPherson: 'Your Sister
    in the King's Glad Service.'" Journal of Popular Culture 1,
    no. 3 (1967), 193-217.

Marty, Martin E. "In the Mainstream." Reviews in American
    History 2, no. 3 (1974), 408-413.

Meyer, Donald. The Positive Thinkers: Religion as Pop
  Psychology from Mary Baker Eddy to Oral Roberts. Garden
  City, N.Y.: Doubleday, 1965.

Moore, R. Laurence. In Search of White Crows: Spiritualism,
  Parapsychology, and American Culture. New York: Oxford
  University Press, 1977.

Moore, R. Laurence. "Spiritualism." In The Rise of Adventism,
  edited by Edwin S. Gaustad. New York: Harper & Row, 1974.

Moore, R. Laurence. "Spiritualism and Science: Reflections on
  the First Decade of Spirit Rappings." American Quarterly
  24, no. 4 (1972), 474-500.

Moore, R. Laurence. "The Spiritualist Medium: A Study of
  Female Professionalism in Victorian America." American
  Quarterly 27, no. 2 (1975), 200-221. Reprinted in Women's
  Experience in America: An Historical Anthology, edited by
  Esther Katz and Anita Rapone. New Brunswick, N.J.:
  Transaction Books, 1980.

Nethercot, Arthur H. The First Five Lives of Annie Besant.
  Chicago: University of Chicago Press, 1960.

Nethercot, Arthur H. The Last Four Lives of Annie Besant.
  Chicago: University of Chicago Press, 1963.

Noorbergen, Rene. Ellen G. White: Prophet of Destiny. New
  Canaan, Conn.: Keats, 1972.

Numbers, Ronald. Prophetess of Health: A Study of Ellen G.
  White. New York: Harper & Row, 1976.

Parker, Gail T. "Mary Baker Eddy and Sentimental Womanhood."
  New England Quarterly 43, no. 1 (1970), 3-18.

Parker, Gail T. Mind Cure in New England From the Civil War to
  World War I. Hanover, N.H.: University Press of New
  England, 1973.

Peel, Robert. Mary Baker Eddy: The Years of Discovery. New
  York: Holt, Rinehart and Winston, 1966.

Peel, Robert. Mary Baker Eddy: The Years of Trial. New York:
  Holt, Rinehart and Winston, 1971.

Peel, Robert. Mary Baker Eddy: The Years of Authority. New
  York: Holt, Rinehart and Winston, 1977.

Rea, Walter T. The White Lie. Turlock, Calif.: M & R
  Publications, 1982.

Setta, Susan. "Denial of the Female--Affirmation of the
Feminine: The Father/Mother God of Mary Baker Eddy." In
Beyond Androcentrism: New Essays on Women and Religion,
edited by Rita M. Gross. Missoula, Mont.: Scholars Press,
1977.

Silberger, Julius. Mary Baker Eddy: An Interpretive Biography
of the Founder of Christian Science. Boston: Little, Brown,
1980.

Skultans, Vieda. "Mediums, Controls, and Eminent Men." In
Women's Religious Experience, edited by Pat Holden. Totowa,
N.J.: Barnes & Noble Books, 1983.

Stein, Stephen J. "Retrospection and Introspection: The Gospel
According to Mary Baker Eddy." Harvard Theological Review
75, no. 1 (1982), 97-116.

Synan, Vinson. The Holiness-Pentecostal Movement in the United
States. Grand Rapids: Eerdmans, 1971.

Tucker, Cynthia Grant. A Woman's Ministry: Mary Collson's
Search for Reform as a Unitarian Minister, a Hull House
Social Worker, and a Christian Science Practitioner.
Philadelphia: Temple University Press, 1984.

Williams, Richard E. Called and Chosen: The Story of Mother
Rebecca Jackson and the Philadelphia Shakers. Metuchen,
N.J.: Scarecrow, 1981.

Wisbey, Herbert A. Pioneer Prophetess: Jemima Wilkinson, the
Publick Universal Friend. Ithaca, N.Y.: Cornell University
Press, 1964.

Zikmund, Barbara Brown. "The Feminist Thrust of Sectarian
Christianity." In Women of Spirit: Female Leadership in the
Jewish and Christian Traditions, edited by Rosemary Radford
Ruether and Eleanor McLaughlin. New York: Simon & Schuster,
1979.

3. WOMAN'S WORK FOR WOMAN: MISSIONS AND MISSIONIZING

a. The Foreign Mission Movement

Agnew, Theodore. "Reflections on the Women's Foreign
Missionary Movement in Late Nineteenth-Century American
Methodism." Methodist History 6, no. 2 (1968), 3-16.

Baxter, Annette K. "Myths, Mediums, and Money: The
Transformations of Evangelicalism." Reviews in American
History 9, no. 4 (1981), 481-486.

Beaver, R. Pierce. <u>American Protestant Women in World Mission:
A History of the First Feminist Movement in North America</u>.
rev. ed. Grand Rapids: Eerdmans, 1980.

Brereton, Virginia Lieson, and Klein, Christa Ressmeyer.
"American Women in Ministry: A History of Protestant
Beginning Points." In <u>Women of Spirit: Female Leadership in
the Jewish and Christian Traditions</u>, edited by Rosemary
Radford Ruether and Eleanor McLaughlin. New York: Simon &
Schuster, 1979.

Brumberg, Joan Jacobs. <u>Mission For Life</u>. New York: Free
Press, 1984.

Brumberg, Joan Jacobs. "Zenanas and Girlless Villages: The
Ethnology of American Evangelical Women, 1870-1910."
<u>Journal of American History</u> 69, no. 2 (1982), 347-371.

Calkins, Grace G. "Rooted in Missions: 1865-1920." Chap. 1 in
<u>Follow Those Women: Church Women in the Ecumenical Movement</u>.
New York: United Church Women, National Council of Churches,
1961.

Campbell, Penelope. "Presbyterian West-African Missions: Women
as Agents of Social Change." <u>Journal of Presbyterian
History</u> 56, no. 2 (1978), 121-132.

Donovan, Mary Sudman. "Zealous Evangelists: The Woman's
Auxiliary to the Board of Missions." <u>Historical Magazine of
the Protestant Episcopal Church</u> 51, no. 4 (1982), 371-383.

Duncan, Janice K. "<u>Ruth Rover</u>: Vindictive Falsehood or
Historical Truth?" <u>Journal of the West</u> 12, no. 2 (1973),
240-253.

Falls, Helen E. "Baptist Women in Mission Support in the
Nineteenth Century." <u>Baptist History and Heritage</u> 12, no. 1
(1977), 26-36.

Gingerich, Melvin. "The Mennonite Woman's Missionary Society."
<u>Mennonite Quarterly Review</u> 37, no. 2 (1963), 113-125; no. 3
(1963), 214-233.

Hill, Patricia R. "Heathen Women's Friends: The Role of
Methodist Episcopal Women in the Woman's Foreign Mission
Movement, 1869-1915." <u>Methodist History</u> 19, no. 3 (1981),
146-154.

Hill, Patricia R. <u>The World Their Household: The American
Woman's Foreign Mission Movement and Cultural
Transformation, 1870-1920</u>. Ann Arbor: University of
Michigan Press, 1985.

Hummel, Margaret Gibson. <u>The Amazing Heritage</u>. Philadelphia:
Geneva Press, 1970.

Hunt, Alma. *History of Woman's Missionary Union*. Nashville: Convention Press, 1964.

Hunter, Jane. *The Gospel of Gentility: American Women Missionaries in Turn-of-the Century China*. New Haven: Yale University Press, 1984.

Hyatt, Irwin T., Jr. *Our Ordered Lives Confess: Three Nineteenth-Century American Missionaries in East Shantung*. Cambridge: Harvard University Press, 1976.

Ives, Hilda Libby. *All In One Day*. Portland, Me.: Bond Wheelwright, 1955.

Jacobs, Sylvia. "Their 'Special Mission': Afro-American Women as Missionaries to the Congo, 1894-1937." In *Black Americans and the Missionary Movement in Africa*, edited by Sylvia Jacobs. Westport, Conn.: Greenwood, 1982.

Johnstone, Margaret Blair. *When God Says "No": Faith's Starting Point*. New York: Simon & Schuster, 1954.

Keller, Rosemary Skinner. "Lay Women in the Protestant Tradition." In *Women and Religion in America*, vol. 1, *The Nineteenth Century*, edited by Rosemary Radford Ruether and Rosemary Skinner Keller, 242-293. San Francisco: Harper & Row, 1981.

Keller, Rosemary Skinner; Queen, Louise L.; and Thomas, Hilah F., eds. *Women in New Worlds: Historical Perspectives on the Wesleyan Tradition*, vol. 2. Nashville: Abingdon, 1982. (Vol. 1, 1981, ed. Thomas et al.)

Knauer, Louise T. "Foot Soldiers in the Kingdom of God: Backgrounds and Motivations of Single Women Missionaries." Paper delivered at the Third Berkshire Conference on the History of Women, Bryn Mawr, Pa., 1976. (On deposit at the Schlesinger Library, Radcliffe College.)

Lollis, Lorraine. *The Shape of Adam's Rib: A Lively History of Woman's Work in the Christian Church*. St. Louis: Bethany Press, 1970.

McAfee, Sara J. *History of the Woman's Missionary Society in the Colored Methodist Episcopal Church*. rev. ed. Phenix City, Ala.: Phenix City Herald, Harold E. Poor, Sr., 1945.

Magalis, Elaine. *Conduct Becoming to a Woman*. N.p.: Education and Cultivation Division, Board of Global Ministries, United Methodist Church, 1973.

Meyer, Ruth Fritz. *Women on a Mission: The Role of Women in the Church . . . Including a History of the Lutheran Women's Missionary League During Its First Twenty-Five Years*." St. Louis: Concordia, 1967.

Smith, Page. <u>Daughters of the Promised Land</u>. Boston: Little,
    Brown, 1970.

Tatum, Noreen Dunn. <u>A Crown of Service: A Story of Woman's
    Work in the Methodist Episcopal Church South, 1878-1940</u>.
    Nashville: Parthenon Press, 1960.

Thomson, Sandra. "Women's Work for God: The Nineteenth Century
    Mission Experience." Paper delivered at the Third Berkshire
    Conference on the History of Women, Bryn Mawr, Pa., 1976.
    (On deposit at the Schlesinger Library, Radcliffe College.)

Torbet, Robert G. <u>Venture of Faith: The Story of the American
    Baptist Foreign Mission Society and the Woman's American
    Baptist Foreign Mission Society</u>. Philadelphia: Judson,
    1955.

Verdesi, Elizabeth Howell. <u>In But Still Out: Women in the
    Church</u>. Philadelphia: Westminster, 1976.

Welter, Barbara. "She Hath Done What She Could: Protestant
    Women's Missionary Careers in Nineteenth-Century America."
    <u>American Quarterly</u> 30, no. 5 (1978), 624-638.

Wills, David W., and Newman, Richard, eds. <u>Black Apostles at
    Home and Abroad: Afro-Americans and the Christian Mission
    from the Revolution to Reconstruction</u>. Boston: G. K. Hall,
    1982.

Wyatt-Brown, Bertram. "Conscience and Career: Young
    Abolitionists and Missionaries." In <u>Anti-Slavery, Religion
    and Reform: Essays in Memory of Roger Anstey</u>, edited by
    Christine Bolt and Seymour Drescher, 183-203. Folkestone,
    England: W. Dawson; Hamden, Conn.: Archon Books, 1980.

b. Domestic Missions and the Social Gospel

Blair, Karen J. <u>The Clubwoman as Feminist: True Womanhood
    Redefined, 1868-1914</u>. New York: Holmes & Meier, 1980.

Bordin, Ruth B. "Emma Hall and the Reformatory Principle."
    <u>Michigan History</u> 48, no. 4 (1964), 315-332.

Brandenstein, Sherilyn. "The Colorado Cottage Home." <u>Colorado
    Magazine</u> 53, no. 3 (1976), 229-242.

Brenzel, Barbara. "Domestication as Reform: A Study of the
    Socialization of Wayward Girls, 1856-1905." <u>Harvard
    Educational Review</u> 50, no. 2 (1980), 196-213.

Clement, Priscilla Ferguson. "Families and Foster Care:
    Philadelphia in the Late Nineteenth Century." <u>Social
    Services Review</u> 53, no. 3 (1979), 406-420.

Conway, Jill. "Women Reformers and American Culture, 1870-
    1930." Journal of Social History 5, no. 2 (1971-72), 164-
    177.

Davis, Allen F. American Heroine: The Life and Legend of Jane
    Addams. New York: Oxford University Press, 1973.

Davis, Allen F. Spearheads for Reform: The Social Settlements
    and the Progressive Movement, 1890-1914. New York: Oxford
    University Press, 1967.

Deweese, Charles W. "Deaconesses in Baptist History: A
    Preliminary Study." Baptist History and Heritage 12, no. 1
    (1977), 52-57.

Dougherty, Mary Agnes. "The American Deaconess Movement, 1888-
    1918." Ph.D. diss., University of California, Davis, 1979.

Dougherty, Mary Agnes. "The Methodist Deaconess: A Case of
    Religious Feminism." Methodist History 21, no. 2 (1983),
    90-98.

Falls, Helen E. "The Vocation of Home Missions, 1845-1970."
    Baptist History and Heritage 7, no. 1 (1972), 25-32.

Frederick, Peter J. "Vida Dutton Scudder: The Professor as
    Social Activist." New England Quarterly 43, no. 3 (1970),
    407-433.

Frederickson, Mary E. "Shaping a New Society: Methodist Women
    and Industrial Reform in the South, 1880-1940." In Women in
    New Worlds: Historical Perspectives on the Wesleyan
    Tradition, vol. 1, edited by Hilah F. Thomas and Rosemary
    Skinner Keller. Nashville: Abingdon, 1981. (Vol. 2, 1982,
    ed. Keller et al.)

Gifford, Carolyn DeSwarte. "Women in Social Reform Movements."
    In Women and Religion in America, vol. 1, The Nineteenth
    Century, edited by Rosemary Radford Reuther and Rosemary
    Skinner Keller, 294-340. San Francisco: Harper & Row, 1981.

Ginzberg, Lori D. "Women and the Work of Benevolence: Morality
    and Politics in the Northeastern United States, 1820-1885."
    Ph.D. diss., Yale University, 1984.

Hook, Alice. "The YWCA in Cincinnati: A Century of Service,
    1868-1968." Cincinnati Historical Society Bulletin 26, no.
    2 (1968), 119-136.

Lee, Elizabeth Meredith. As Among the Methodists: Deaconesses
    Yesterday, Today and Tomorrow. New York: Women's Division
    of Christian Service, Board of Mission, Methodist Church,
    1963.

McDowell, John P. _The Social Gospel in the South: The Woman's Home Mission Movement in the Methodist Episcopal Church, South, 1886-1939_. Baton Rouge: Louisiana State University Press, 1982.

McLoughlin, William G. "Billy Sunday and the Working Girl of 1915." _Journal of Presbyterian History_ 54, no. 3 (1976), 376-384.

Magnuson, Norris. _Salvation in the Slums: Evangelical Social Work, 1865-1920_. Metuchen, N.J.: Scarecrow, 1977.

Meeker, Ruth Esther. _Six Decades of Service, 1880-1940: A History of the Woman's Home Missionary Society of the Methodist Episcopal Church_. Cincinnati: Steinhauser, 1969.

Minow, Martha. "Two Women: Autonomy and Caretaking in a New Century." _Reviews in American History_ 13, no. 2 (1985), 240-244.

Mitchinson, Wendy. "The YWCA and Reform in the Nineteenth Century." _Social History_ (Canada) 12, no. 24 (1979), 368-384.

Murdoch, Norman H. "Female Ministry in the Thought and Work of Catherine Booth." _Church History_ 53, no. 3 (1984), 348-362.

Oates, Mary J. "Organized Voluntarism: The Catholic Sisters in Massachusetts, 1870-1940." _American Quarterly_ 30, no. 5 (1978), 652-680.

Ohlmann, Erich H. "An Ulterior Motive for Baptist Home Missions." _Foundations_ 22, no. 2 (1979), 125-139.

Phillips, J. O. C. "The Education of Jane Addams." _History of Education Quarterly_ 14 (Spring 1974), 49-67.

Pivar, David. _Purity Crusade: Sexual Morality and Social Control, 1868-1900_. Westport, Conn.: Greenwood, 1973.

Rosenberg, Carroll. _Religion and the Rise of the American City: The New York City Mission Movement, 1812-1870_. Ithaca, N.Y.: Cornell University Press, 1971.

Rothman, Sheila. "The Protestant Nun." Chap. 2 in _Woman's Proper Place: A History of Changing Ideals and Practices, 1870 to the Present_. New York: Basic, 1978.

Rousmaniere, John P. "Cultural Hybrid in the Slums: The College Woman and the Settlement House, 1889-1894." _American Quarterly_ 22, no. 1 (1970), 45-66. Reprinted in _Women's Experience in America: An Historical Anthology_, edited by Esther Katz and Anita Rapone. New Brunswick, N.J.: Transaction Books, 1980.

Scott, Anne Firor. The Southern Lady: From Pedestal to
    Politics, 1830-1930. Chicago: University of Chicago Press,
    1970.

Sedlak, Michael W. "Young Women and the City: Adolescent
    Deviance and the Transformation of Educational Policy, 1870-
    1960." History of Education Quarterly 23 (Spring 1983), 1-
    28.

Smith, Timothy L. Revivalism and Social Reform in Mid-
    Nineteenth Century America. New York: Abingdon, 1957.

Stapleton, Carolyn L. "Belle Harris Bennett: Model of Holistic
    Christianity." Methodist History 21, no. 3 (1983), 131-142.

Sutherland, John F. "The Origins of Philadelphia's Octavia
    Hill Association: Social Reform in the 'Contented' City."
    Pennsylvania Magazine of History and Biography 99, no. 1
    (1975), 20-44.

Tatum, Noreen Dunn. A Crown of Service: A Story of Woman's
    Work in the Methodist Episcopal Church South, 1878-1940.
    Nashville: Parthenon Press, 1960.

Tucker, Cynthia Grant. A Woman's Ministry: Mary Collson's
    Search for Reform as a Unitarian Minister, a Hull House
    Worker, and a Christian Science Practitioner. Philadelphia:
    Temple University Press, 1984.

Weiner, Lynn. "'Our Sister's Keepers': The Minneapolis Woman's
    Christian Association and Housing for Working Women."
    Minnesota History 46, no. 5 (1979), 189-200.

Weiser, Frederick S. Love's Response: A Story of Lutheran
    Deaconesses in America. Philadelphia: Board of Publication,
    United Lutheran Church in America, 1962.

4. THE TEMPERANCE MOVEMENT

Baker, Paula. "The Domestication of Politics: Women and
    American Political Society, 1780-1920." American Historical
    Review 89, no. 3 (1984), 620-647.

Blocker, Jack S., Jr. "Annie Wittenmyer and the Woman's
    Crusade." Ohio History 88, no. 4 (1979), 419-422.

Blocker, Jack S., Jr. "Give to the Winds Thy Fears": The
    Woman's Temperance Crusade, 1873-1874. Westport, Conn.:
    Greenwood, 1985.

Blocker, Jack S., Jr. "The Politics of Reform: Populists, Prohibition and Woman Suffrage, 1891-1892." Historian 34, no. 4 (1972), 614-632.

Blocker, Jack S., Jr. Retreat From Reform: The Prohibition Movement in the United States, 1890-1913. Westport, Conn.: Greenwood, 1976.

Blocker, Jack S., Jr. "Separate Paths: Suffragists and the Woman's Temperance Crusade." Signs 10, no. 3 (1985), 460-476.

Bordin, Ruth B. "The Baptism of Power and Liberty: The Woman's Crusade of 1873." Ohio History 87, no. 4 (1978), 393-404.

Bordin, Ruth B. Woman and Temperance: The Quest for Power and Liberty, 1873-1900. Philadelphia: Temple University Press, 1981.

Bordin, Ruth B. "Women March for Temperance: The Woman's Crusade in Adrian." Michigan Chronicle 15 (Winter 1980), 16-23.

Caldwell, Dorothy J. "Carry Nation, A Missouri Woman, Won Fame in Kansas." Missouri Historical Review 63, no. 4 (1969), 461-488.

Clark, Norman. Deliver Us From Evil: An Interpretation of American Prohibition. New York: W. W. Norton, 1976.

Clark, Roger W. "Cincinnati Crusaders for Temperance: 1874." Cincinnati Historical Society Bulletin 32, no. 4 (1974), 185-198.

Conway, Jill. "Women Reformers and American Culture, 1870-1930." Journal of Social History 5, no. 2 (1971-72), 164-177.

Dannenbaum, Jed. "The Crusade Against Drink." Reviews in American History 9, no. 4 (1981), 497-502.

Dannenbaum, Jed. Drink and Disorder: Temperance Reform in Cincinnati From the Washingtonian Revival to the WCTU. Urbana: University of Illinois Press, 1984.

Dannenbaum, Jed. "The Origins of Temperance Activism and Militancy Among American Women." Journal of Social History 15, no. 2 (1981), 235-252.

DuBois, Ellen. "The Radicalism of the Woman Suffrage Movement: Notes Toward the Reconstruction of Nineteenth-Century Feminism." Feminist Studies 3, no. 3 (1975), 63-71.

Duis, Perry R. The Saloon: Public Drinking in Chicago and Boston, 1880-1920. Urbana: University of Illinois Press, 1983.

Earhart, Mary. Frances Willard: From Prayers to Politics. Chicago: University of Chicago Press, 1944.

Epstein, Barbara. The Politics of Domesticity: Women, Evangelism, and Temperance in Nineteenth-Century America. Middletown, Conn.: Wesleyan University Press, 1981.

Evans, Sara M., and Boyte, Harry C. Free Spaces: The Sources of Democratic Change in America. New York: Harper & Row, 1986.

Franklin, J. L. "The Fight for Prohibition in Oklahoma Territory." Social Science Quarterly 49, no. 4 (1969), 876-885.

Giele, Janet Zollinger. "Social Change in the Feminine Role: A Comparison of Woman's Suffrage and Woman's Temperance, 1870-1920." Ph.D. diss., Radcliffe College, 1961.

Gifford, Carolyn DeSwarte. "For God and Home and Native Land: The W.C.T.U.'s Image of Woman in the Late Nineteenth Century." In Women in New Worlds: Historical Perspectives on the Wesleyan Tradition, vol. 1, edited by Hilah F. Thomas and Rosemary Skinner Keller. Nashville: Abingdon, 1981. (Vol. 2, 1982, ed. Keller et al.)

Gusfield, Joseph R. "Social Structure and Moral Reform: A Study of the Woman's Christian Temperance Union." American Journal of Sociology 61 (November 1955), 221-232.

Gusfield, Joseph R. Symbolic Crusade: Status, Politics, and the American Temperance Movement. Urbana: University of Illinois Press, 1966.

Hohner, Robert A. "Prohibition Comes to Virginia: The Referendum of 1914." Virginia Magazine of History and Biography 75, no. 4 (1967), 473-488.

Isetts, Charles A. "A Social Profile of the Women's Temperance Crusade: Hillsboro, Ohio." In Alcohol, Reform, and Society: The Liquor Issue in Social Context, edited by Jack S. Blocker, Jr., 101-110. Westport, Conn.: Greenwood, 1979.

Jessup, Jacquie. "The Liquor Issue: A Bibliography." In Alcohol, Reform, and Society: The Liquor Issue in Social Context, edited by Jack S. Blocker, Jr., 259-279. Westport, Conn.: Greenwood, 1979.

Jimerson, Randall; Blouin, Francis X.; and Isetts, Charles A.,
    eds. <u>Guide to the Microfilm Edition of Temperance and
    Prohibition Papers</u>. Ann Arbor: University of Michigan,
    1977.

Johnson, Paul. "Bottoms Up: Drinking, Temperance, and the
    Social Historians." <u>Reviews in American History</u> 13, no. 1
    (1985), 48-53.

Lee, Susan Earls Dye. "Evangelical Domesticity: The Origins of
    the Woman's National Christian Temperance Union Under
    Frances E. Willard." Ph.D. diss., Northwestern University,
    1980.

Lee, Susan Earls Dye. "Evangelical Domesticity: The Woman's
    Temperance Crusade of 1873-74." In <u>Women in New Worlds:
    Historical Perspectives on the Wesleyan Tradition</u>, vol. 1,
    edited by Hilah F. Thomas and Rosemary Skinner Keller.
    Nashville: Abingdon, 1981. (Vol. 2, 1982, ed. Keller et
    al.)

Levine, Harry G. "Temperance and Women in 19th Century United
    States." In <u>Research Advances in Alcohol and Drug Problems</u>,
    vol. 5, edited by Oriana Kalaut, 25-67. New York: Plenum
    Press, 1980.

Lupton, Mary Jane. "Ladies' Entrance: Women and Bars."
    <u>Feminist Studies</u> 5, no. 3 (1979), 571-588.

Mezvinsky, Norman. "The White Ribbon Reform, 1874-1920."
    Ph.D. diss., University of Wisconsin, 1959.

Mitterling, Doris, and Brennan, John. "A Guide to the Colorado
    WCTU Papers, 1878-1975." University of Colorado Library,
    <u>Western Historical Collections</u> 1976 (June), 1-32.

Morton, Marian J. "Temperance, Benevolence, and the City: The
    Cleveland Non-Partisan Woman's Christian Temperance Union,
    1874-1900." <u>Ohio History</u> 91 (1982), 58-73.

Paulson, Ross Evans. <u>Women's Suffrage and Prohibition: A
    Comparative Study of Equality and Social Control</u>. Glenview,
    Ill.: Scott Foresman, 1973.

Timberlake, Joseph. <u>Prohibition and the Progressive Movement,
    1900-1920</u>. Cambridge: Harvard University Press, 1963.

Turner, James Ross. "The American Prohibition Movement, 1865-
    1897." Ph.D. diss., University of Wisconsin, 1972.

Tyrrell, Ian R. "Women and Temperance in Antebellum America,
    1830-1860." <u>Civil War History</u> 28, no. 2 (1982), 128-152.

Wesser, Robert F.   "Women Suffrage, Prohibition, and the New
    York Experience in the Progressive Era."   In An American
    Historian: Essays to Honor Selig Adler, edited by Milton
    Plesur.   Buffalo: State University of New York Press, 1980.

Whitaker, Francis M.   "A History of the Ohio Woman's Christian
    Temperance Union, 1874-1920."   Ph.D. diss., Ohio State
    University, 1971.

Whitaker, Francis M.   "The Ohio W.C.T.U. and the Prohibition
    Amendment Campaign of 1883."   Ohio History 83, no. 2 (1974),
    84-102.

5.   FEMINISM, POLITICS, AND POWER

a.   General

Bacon, Margaret Hope.   As the Way Opens: The Story of Quaker
    Women in America.   Richmond, Ind.: Friends United Press,
    1980.

Bacon, Margaret Hope.   Lucretia Mott Speaking: Excerpts from
    the Sermons and Speeches of a Famous Nineteenth Century
    Quaker Minister and Reformer.   Wallingford, Pa.: Pendle Hill
    Publications, 1980.

Bacon, Margaret Hope.   "Quaker Women and the Charge of
    Separatism."   Quaker History 69 (Spring 1980), 23-26.

Bacon, Margaret Hope.   Valiant Friend: The Life of Lucretia
    Mott.   New York: Walker & Co., 1980.

Bacon, Margaret Hope.   "A Widening Path: Women in the
    Philadelphia Yearly Meeting Move Toward Equality, 1681-
    1929."   In Friends in the Delaware Valley, edited by John M.
    Moore.   Haverford, Pa.: Friends Historical Association,
    1981.

Baker, Paula.   "The Domestication of Politics: Women and
    American Political Society, 1780-1920."   American Historical
    Review 89, no. 3 (1984), 620-647.

Banks, Olive.   Faces of Feminism: A Study of Feminism as a
    Social Movement.   New York: St. Martin's, 1981.

Beeton, Beverly.   "Woman Suffrage in the American West, 1869-
    1896."   Ph.D. diss., University of Utah, 1976.

Behnke, Donna A.   Religious Issues in Nineteenth-Century
    Feminism.   Troy, N.Y.: Whitston Publishing Co., 1982.

Buhle, Mari Jo. Women and American Socialism, 1870-1920.
    Urbana: University of Illinois Press, 1981.

Cazden, Elizabeth. Antoinette Brown Blackwell: A Biography.
    Old Westbury, N.Y.: Feminist Press, 1983.

Dayton, Donald W. "The Evangelical Roots of Feminism." Chap.
    8 in Discovering an Evangelical Heritage. New York: Harper
    & Row, 1976.

Dayton, Lucille Sider, and Dayton, Donald W. "'Your Daughters
    Shall Prophesy': Feminism in the Holiness Movement."
    Methodist History 14, no. 2 (1976), 67-92.

DuBois, Ellen. Feminism and Suffrage: The Emergence of an
    Independent Women's Movement in America, 1848-1869. Ithaca,
    N.Y.: Cornell University Press, 1978.

DuBois, Ellen. "The Radicalism of the Woman Suffrage Movement:
    Notes Toward the Reconstruction of Nineteenth-Century
    Feminism." Feminist Studies 3, no. 3 (1975), 63-71.

DuBois, Ellen, ed. Elizabeth Cady Stanton and Susan B.
    Anthony: Correspondence, Writings, Speeches. New York:
    Schocken, 1981.

Fitzgerald, Maureen. "Religion in the Life and Thought of
    Elizabeth Cady Stanton." M.A. thesis, University of
    Wisconsin, 1985.

Fraser, Dorothy Bass. "The Feminine Mystique, 1890-1910."
    Union Seminary Quarterly Review 27, no. 4 (1972), 225-239.

Gadt, Jeanette Carter. "Women and Protestant Culture: The
    Quaker Dissent From Puritanism." Ph.D. diss., University of
    California, Los Angeles, 1974.

Gage, Matilda J. Woman, Church and State: The Original Expose
    of Male Collaboration Against the Female Sex. 1893.
    Reprint. With an introduction by Sally Roesch Wagner.
    Watertown, Mass.: Persephone Press, 1980.

Gething, Judith R. "Christianity and Couverture: Impact on the
    Legal Status of Women in Hawaii, 1820-1920." Hawaiian
    Journal of History 11 (1977), 188-220.

Giele, Janet Zollinger. "Social Change in the Feminine Role: A
    Comparison of Woman's Suffrage and Woman's Temperance, 1870-
    1920." Ph.D. diss., Radcliffe College, 1961.

Ginzberg, Lori D. "Women and the Work of Benevolence: Morality
    and Politics in the Northeastern United States, 1820-1885."
    Ph.D. diss., Yale University, 1984.

reene, Dana. "Quaker Feminism: The Case of Lucretia Mott."
Pennsylvania History 48, no. 2 (1981), 143-154.

reene, Dana, ed. Lucretia Mott: Her Complete Speeches and
Sermons. New York: E. Mellen, 1980.

reene, Dana, ed. Suffrage and Religious Principle: Speeches
and Writings of Olympia Brown. Metuchen, N.J.: Scarecrow,
1983.

riffith, Elisabeth. In Her Own Right: The Life of Elizabeth
Cady Stanton. New York: Oxford University Press, 1984.

rimes, Alan P. The Puritan Ethic and Woman Suffrage. New
York: Oxford University Press, 1967.

ardesty, Nancy. Women Called to Witness: Evangelical Feminism
in the 19th Century. Nashville: Abingdon, 1984.

ardesty, Nancy; Dayton, Lucille Sider; and Dayton, Donald W.
"Women in the Holiness Movement: Feminism in the Evangelical
Tradition." In Women of Spirit: Female Leadership in the
Jewish and Christian Traditions, edited by Rosemary Radford
Ruether and Eleanor McLaughlin. New York: Simon & Schuster,
1979.

arkness, Georgia. Woman in Church and Society. Nashville:
Abingdon, 1972.

arrison, Beverly Wildung. "The Early Feminists and the
Clergy: A Case Study in the Dynamics of Secularization."
Review and Expositor 72 (Winter 1975), 46.

ersh, Blanche Glassman. "'Am I Not a Woman and a Sister?'
Abolitionist Beginnings of Nineteenth-Century Feminism." In
Antislavery Reconsidered: New Perspectives on the
Abolitionists, edited by Lewis Perry and Michael Fellman.
Baton Rouge: Louisiana State University Press, 1979.

ersh, Blanche Glassman. The Slavery of Sex: Feminist-
Abolitionists in America. Urbana: University of Illinois
Press, 1978.

udson, Winthrop S. "Early Nineteenth-Century Evangelical
Religion and Women's Liberation." Foundations 23, no. 2
(1980), 181-185.

enneally, James J. "Catholicism and Woman Suffrage in
Massachusetts." Catholic Historical Review 53, no. 1
(1967), 43-57.

enneally, James J. "Eve, Mary, and the Historians: American
Catholicism and Women." In Women in American Religion,
edited by Janet Wilson James. Philadelphia: University of
Pennsylvania Press, 1980.

Kraditor, Aileen S. The Ideas of the Woman Suffrage Movement, 1890-1920. New York: Columbia University Press, 1965.

Larson, T. A. "Woman Suffrage in Western America." Utah Historical Quarterly 38, no. 1 (1970), 7-19.

Larson, T. A. "The Women's Rights Movement in Idaho." Idaho Yesterdays 16, no. 1 (1972), 2-15, 18-19.

Leach, William. True Love and Perfect Union: The Feminist Reform of Sex and Society. New York: Basic, 1980.

Lewis, Helen M. The Woman Movement and the Negro Movement: Parallel Struggles for Equal Rights. Charlottesville: University Press of Virginia, 1949.

McGovern, James R. "Anna Howard Shaw: New Approaches to Feminism." Journal of Social History 3, no. 2 (1969-70), 135-153.

Massey, Marilyn Chapin, and Massey, James A. "Feminists on Christianity: Some Nineteenth-Century Parallels." In Beyond Androcentrism: New Essays on Women and Religion, edited by Rita M. Gross. Missoula, Mont.: Scholars Press, 1977.

May, Elaine Tyler. "Expanding the Past: Recent Scholarship on Women in Politics and Work." Reviews in American History 10, no. 4 (1982), 216-233.

Melder, Keith. Beginnings of Sisterhood: The American Woman's Rights Movement, 1800-1850. New York: Schocken, 1977.

Minow, Martha. "In Her Own Right." Harvard Law Review 98 (1985), 1084-1099.

Mitchell, Norma Taylor. "From Social to Radical Feminism: A Survey of Emerging Diversity in Methodist Women's Organizations, 1869-1974." Methodist History 13, no. 4 (1975), 21-44.

Neu, Charles E. "Olympia Brown and the Woman's Suffrage Movement." Wisconsin Magazine of History 43, no. 4 (1960), 277-287.

Paulson, Ross Evans. Women's Suffrage and Prohibition: A Comparative Study of Equality and Social Control. Glenview, Ill.: Scott Foresman, 1973.

Rossi, Alice. "Pioneers on a Moral Crusade: Feminism and Status Politics." Part 2 of The Feminist Papers. New York: Columbia University Press, 1974.

Ruether, Rosemary Radford. "The Subordination and Liberation of Women in Christian Theology: Saint Paul and Sarah Grimke." Soundings 61, no. 2 (1978), 168-181.

Scott, Anne Firor. The Southern Lady: From Pedestal to Politics, 1830-1930. Chicago: University of Chicago Press, 1970.

Sinclair, Andrew. The Better Half: The Emancipation of the American Woman. New York: Harper & Row, 1965.

Smylie, James H. "The Woman's Bible and the Spiritual Crisis." Soundings 59, no. 3 (1976), 305-328.

Spretnak, Charlene, ed. The Politics of Women's Spirituality: Essays on the Rise of Spiritual Power Within the Feminist Movement. Garden City, N.Y.: Doubleday, Anchor, 1982.

Stanton, Elizabeth Cady. The Woman's Bible. 1895-98. Reprint. Introduction by Barbara Welter. New York: Arno Press, 1972.

Stern, Madeleine. "The First Feminist Bible: The 'Alderney' Edition, 1876." Quarterly Journal of the Library of Congress 34 (January 1977), 23.

Sumners, Bill. "Southern Baptists and Women's Right to Vote, 1910-1920." Baptist History and Heritage 12, no. 1 (1977), 45-51.

Swidler, Arlene. "Brownson and the 'Woman Question.'" American Benedictine Review 19, no. 2 (1968), 211-219.

Ullman, Claire F. "The Quaker Spirit and the Ethic of Feminism: The Influence of Quaker Religious Beliefs on the American Woman's Rights Movement, 1848-1860." Senior thesis, Harvard University, 1984. (On deposit at Widener Library, Harvard University.)

Wagner, Sally Roesch. "That Word is Liberty: A Biography of Matilda Joslyn Gage." Ph.D. diss., University of California, Santa Cruz, 1978.

Zikmund, Barbara Brown. "The Feminist Thrust of Sectarian Christianity." In Women of Spirit: Female Leadership in the Jewish and Christian Traditions, edited by Rosemary Radford Ruether and Eleanor McLaughlin. New York: Simon & Schuster, 1979.

b. Mormonism and Woman Suffrage

Aaron, Richard I. "Mormon Divorce and the Statute of 1852: Questions for Divorce in the 1980s." Journal of Contemporary Law 8 (1982), 5-45.

Alexander, Thomas G. "An Experiment with Progressive Legislation: The Granting of Woman Suffrage in Utah in 1870." Utah Historical Quarterly 38, no. 1 (1970), 20-30.

Arrington, Leonard J., and Haupt, Jon. "Intolerable Zion: The Image of Mormonism in Nineteenth-Century American Literature." Western Humanities Review 22 (Summer 1968), 243-260.

Beeton, Beverly. "The Hayes Administration and the Woman Question." Hayes Historical Journal 2, no. 1 (1978), 52-56.

Beeton, Beverly. "Woman Suffrage in Territorial Utah." Utah Historical Quarterly 46, no. 2 (1978), 100-120.

Bennion, Sherilyn Cox. "The Woman's Exponent: Forty-Two Years of Speaking for Women." Utah Historical Quarterly 44, no. 3 (1976), 222-239.

Brudnoy, David. "A Decade in Zion: Theodore Schroeder's Initial Assault on the Mormons." Historian 37, no. 2 (1975), 241-256.

Cannon, Charles A. "The Awesome Power of Sex: The Polemical Campaign Against Mormon Polygamy." Pacific Historical Review 43, no. 1 (1974), 61-82.

Cannon, Heather Symmes. "Practical Politicians." In Mormon Sisters: Women in Early Utah, edited by Claudia L. Bushman. Cambridge, Mass.: Emmeline Press, 1976.

Casterline, Gail Farr. "'In the Toils' or 'Onward for Zion': Images of the Mormon Woman, 1852-1890." M.A. thesis, Utah State University, 1974.

Clayton, James. "The Supreme Court, Polygamy and the Enforcement of Morals in Nineteenth-Century America: An Analysis of Reynolds v. United States." Dialogue: A Journal of Mormon Thought 12, no. 4 (1979), 46-61.

Davis, David Brion. "Some Themes of Counter-Subversion: An Analysis of Anti-Masonic, Anti-Catholic, and Anti-Mormon Literature." Mississippi Valley Historical Review 47, no. 2 (1960), 205-224.

Davis, Ray Jay. "Plural Marriage and Religious Freedom: The Impact of Reynolds v. United States." Arizona Law Review 15 (1973), 287-306.

Davis, Ray Jay. "The Polygamous Prelude." American Journal of Legal History 6, no. 1 (1962), 1-27.

Dushku, Judith Rasmussen. "Feminists." In Mormon Sisters: Women in Early Utah, edited by Claudia L. Bushman. Cambridge, Mass.: Emmeline Press, 1976.

Flowers, Ronald B. "The Supreme Court's Interpretation of the Free Exercise Clause." Religion in Life 49, no. 3 (1980), 322-335.

Foster, Lawrence. "From Frontier Activism to Neo-Victorian Domesticity: Mormon Women in the Nineteenth and Twentieth Centuries." Journal of Mormon History 6 (1979), 3-21.

Godfrey, Kenneth W. "The Coming of the Manifesto." Dialogue: A Journal of Mormon Thought 5, no. 3 (1970), 11-25.

Holsinger, M. Paul. "Henry M. Teller and the Edmunds-Tucker Act." Colorado Magazine 48, no. 1 (1971), 1-14.

Holsinger, M. Paul. "Senator George Graham Vest and the 'Menace' of Mormonism, 1882-1887." Missouri Historical Review 65, no. 1 (1970), 23-36.

Hyde, Stuart W. "The Anti-Mormon Drama in the United States." Western Humanities Review 9 (Spring 1955), 177-182.

Kern, Louis. An Ordered Love: Sex Roles and Sexuality in Victorian Utopias. Chapel Hill: University of North Carolina Press, 1981.

Larson, Gustive O. The "Americanization" of Utah for Statehood. San Marino, Calif.: Huntington Library, 1971.

Larson, T. A. "Emancipating the West's Dolls, Vassals, and Hapless Drudges: The Origins of Woman Suffrage in the West." In Essays in Western History in Honor of T. A. Larson, edited by Roger Daniels. Laramie: University of Wyoming, 1971.

Linford, Orma. "The Mormons and the Law: The Polygamy Cases." Utah Law Review 9 (1964), 308-370; (1965), 543-591.

Madsen, Carol Cornwall. "Emmeline B. Wells: 'Am I Not a Woman and a Sister?'" Brigham Young University Studies 22, no. 2 (1982), 161-178.

Magrath, C. Peter. "Chief Justice Waite and the 'Twin Relic': Reynolds v. United States." Vanderbilt Law Review 18 (1965), 507-543.

Marquis, Kathleen. "'Diamond Cut Diamond': Mormon Women and the Cult of Domesticity in the Nineteenth Century." University of Michigan Papers in Women's Studies 2, no. 2 (1975), 105-124.

Mikkelsen, D. Craig. "The Politics of B. H. Roberts." Dialogue: A Journal of Mormon Thought 9, no. 2 (1974), 25-43.

Walker, Ronald W., and Allen, James B. "B. H. Roberts and the Woodruff Manifesto." Brigham Young University Studies 22, no. 3 (1982), 363-366.

Warenski, Marilyn. _Patriarchs and Politics: The Plight of Mormon Women_. New York: McGraw Hill, 1978.

Weisbrod, Carol, and Sheingorn, Pamela. "_Reynolds v. United States_: Nineteenth-Century Forms of Marriage and the Status of Women." _Connecticut Law Review_ 10 (1978), 828-858.

White, Jean Bickmore. "Gentle Persuaders: Utah's First Women Legislators." _Utah Historical Quarterly_ 38, no. 1 (1970), 31-49.

White, Jean Bickmore. "Woman's Place is in the Constitution: The Struggle for Equal Rights in Utah in 1895." _Utah Historical Quarterly_ 42, no. 4 (1974), 344-369.

White, William G., Jr. "The Feminist Campaign for the Exclusion of Brigham Henry Roberts from the Fifty-Sixth Congress." _Journal of the West_ 17, no. 1 (1978), 45-52.

Wolfinger, Henry J. "An Irrepressible Conflict." _Dialogue: A Journal of Mormon Thought_ 6, nos. 3/4 (1971), 124-131.

Wolfinger, Henry J. "A Re-examination of the Woodruff Manifesto in the Light of Utah Constitutional History." _Utah Historical Quarterly_ 39, no. 4 (1971), 328-349.

Index

Abbott, Kenneth A., 110–11
Abbott, Lyman, 151
Abell, Aaron I., 69, 73, 75, 163, 200
Abernathy, Mollie C., 198
Abington Township School District v. Schempp, 311, 314
Abolitionism, 5–6
Abrahams, Edward, 155
Abrams, Ray H., 162, 227–28
Accommodationist/separationist debate, 345–47, 348–49
Ackerman, James S., 314
Adams, James L., 280 n.4
Adams, Marjorie E., 305
Addams, Jane, 68–69, 83, 84, 164
Adler, Felix, 120
Adventists, 377
Africa v. Commonwealth of Pennsylvania, 352
Afro-Americans. *See* Blacks
Agricultural Adjustment Act (AAA), 199, 200
Ahlstrom, Sydney E., 6, 16, 161, 265, 279 n.1
Ahmann, Matthew, 239
Aid to education, 309–10, 315–16, 347–48
Aiken, John R., 77
Alexander, Thomas G., 155, 398–99
Allen, Board of Education v., 309, 348
Allen, Henry E., 315

American Association of School Administrators, 306
American Bible Society, 155, 158
American Board of Commissioners for Foreign Missions, 158
American Civil Liberties Union, 278, 317, 345
American Council on Education, 304–5, 306
American dream. *See* American Way of Life; Melting pot
American Economic Association, 88
American Home Mission Society, 158
American Indian Religious Freedom Act (1978), 350
American Jewish Committee, 305, 317, 345
American Jewish Congress, 157, 278, 345
American Missionary Association, 41
American Protective Association, 110
American Red Cross, 155
American Sunday School Union, 158
American Tract Society, 155, 158
American Way of Life, 107, 109–10, 123
American Woman Suffrage Association (AWSA), 393–94
Americanism and Catholicism, 153–54, 235, 268
Americans for Democratic Action, 196–97

Americans United for Separation of Church and State, 239, 278, 345, 347
Anabaptists, 228
Anderson, Charles H., 116
Andrews, James Osgood, 48–49
Angel, Marc D., 119–20
Anglicans, 34
Anthony, Dick, 265, 268, 270
Anthony, Susan B., 395, 396–97, 399
Anti-Catholicism, 238–40, 267–68, 345
Anti-Defamation League, 268, 345
Anti-Polygamy Society, 399
Anti-Saloon League, 85, 86, 87
Anti-Semitism, 110, 193, 203, 267–68
Anti-Slavery Society, 158
Antieau, C. J., 354 n.10
Antiwar movement, 274–75, 350, 351–52
Arden, G. Everett, 116
Argersinger, Peter H., 80
Arons, Stephen, 313
Arrington, Leonard J., 398
Ashdown, Paul G., 10
Association of Catholic Trade Unions, 199, 201
Athearn, Walter S., 303
Atkins, Glenn Gaius, 145
Augustana Synod, 115, 116
Austin, J. Susan, 314
AWSA. *See* American Woman Suffrage Association

Badger, Reid, 109
Bailey, Hugh C., 84
Bailey, Kenneth K., 41, 84, 198
Bainton, Roland H., 228
Baker, Paula, 387, 393
Baker, Robert A., 154
Balancing test in American law, 349
Baldwin, James Mark, 89
Ballard, United States v., 234, 351
Bannister, Robert C., 111
Baptists, 2, 9, 40, 43, 84, 111, 161
Bardolph, Richard, 114
Barker, Eileen, 265
Barnes, Howard A., 6

Barnette, West Virginia State Board of Education v., 234, 313, 349
Barr, David L., 311
Barry, Colman J., 117, 239
Barth, Gunther P., 112
Barth, Karl, 226
Bartlett, Edward R., 306
Barton, Bruce, 198
Barton, Michael, 12
Barton, William E., 15
Bashford, James W., 149
Batten, Samuel Zane, 72
Beach, Fred Francis, 309
Beals, Carleton, 80
Beard, Augustus Field, 41–42
Beaver, R. Pierce, 379
Beck, Walter H., 308
Becker, Frank J., 312
Bednarowski, Mary Farrell, 375, 376, 377, 378
Beecher, Catherine, 380
Beeton, Beverly, 396, 398
Beggs, David W., III, 305
Behnke, Donna A., 391
Beijbom, Ulf, 115
Beisner, Robert L., 151
Belknap, Michael R., 231
Bell, Daniel, 265
Bellah, Robert N., 15, 265, 270
Bellamy, Edward, 68, 79, 81
Bellows, Barbara L., 39
Beman, Lamar Taney, 304
Bender v. Williamsport, 315
Benestad, J. Briar, 272
Benjamin, Walter W., 76
Benkart, Paula K., 110–11
Bennett, John C., 227, 229, 233
Bennett, William W., 38
Benson, Peter L., 280 n.4
Berger, Peter L., 242, 267
Beringer, Richard E., 4, 5, 8, 13, 14
Berman, Hyman, 76
Bernstein, Louis, 157
Berrigan, Daniel, 271, 275
Berrigan, Philip, 271, 275

Berring, Robert C., 354
Berthoff, Rowland T., 108, 122
Beth, Loren P., 236–37
Betten, Neil, 75
Bicha, Karel D., 80
Bigham, Darrel E., 165
Billington, Ray Allen, 110
Bingham, June, 233
Birmingham, Stephen, 121
Bishops' Program of Social Reconstruction (National Catholic War Council), 199, 200
Black, Isabella, 112
Black Muslims, 352
Blacks: and black nationalism, 114–15; and the churches, 35–39, 41–42, 198; and the clergy, 42, 198, 205; decline of religion among, 114; and education, 316; emancipation of, 41–42; migration of, 113–15; and military chaplains, 11–12; and the New Deal, 205; and political activism, 274; in the twenties and thirties, 204, 205; and urbanization, 113–15. *See also* Civil rights movement
Blackwell, Antoinette Brown, 374, 392
Bland, Jean, 86–87
Blanshard, Paul, 238–39
Blantz, Thomas E., 201
Blassingame, John W., 11, 42
Blatch, Harriet Stanton, 400
Blau, Joseph L., 81, 120, 121
Blauvelt, Martha Tomhave, 374
Blavatsky, Elena Petrovna, 375
Blied, Benjamin J., 9
Bliss, William D. P., 70
Blocker, Jack S., 87, 387, 388
Blum, Virgil C., 309, 310
Board of Education, McCollum v., 304, 314
Board of Education of Cincinnati v. Minor, 302–3, 311, 340
Board of Education of Ewing Township, Everson v., 234, 304, 347
Board of Education v. Allen, 309, 348

Bode, Frederick A., 44
Bodo, John R., 237
Boles, Donald E., 311
Boles, John B., 6, 47
Book of Common Prayer, Episcopal, 12–13, 40
Booth, Catherine, 390
Borchert, James, 113
Borden, Morton, 15
Bordin, Ruth B., 87, 387, 390
Bos, A. David, 75
Boswell, E. M., 12
Bower, William Clayton, 304, 306–7
Bowers v. Hardwick, 346
Bowles, Samuel, 316
Boyce, James Petigru, 49
Boyer, Paul S., 109
Brackenridge, R. Douglas, 198
Brandeis, Louis, 205
Brauer, Jerald C., 48
Brent, Charles Henry, 149
Brereton, Virginia Lieson, 379, 380
Bretall, Robert W., 233
Brewer, Paul D., 154
Brickman, William W., 302
Briggs, John W., 118
Brinkley, Alan, 74, 194
Broadus, John Albert, 49
Brock, Peter, 164
Broderick, Francis L., 74, 163, 200, 201
Brody, David, 205
Bromley, David G., 268, 276
Brown, Bruce T., 10
Brown, Clifton F., 114, 273, 274
Brown, Elmer Ellsworth, 303
Brown, Lawrence L., 198
Brown, Nicholas C., 306
Brown, Olympia, 374
Brown, Robert McAfee, 239, 275
Brown, Samuel Windsor, 303
Brown, William Adams, 145, 146
Browne, Henry J., 75
Brown scare, 193–94
Bruce, Dickson D., Jr., 8
Bruere, Martha Bensley, 86

Brumberg, Joan Jacobs, 379–80, 381,
  382
Brusher, Joseph F., 75
Bryan, William Jennings, 81–82, 187,
  190, 191, 312
Brydon, G. MacLaren, 12–13
Bryson, Lyman, 229
Buck, Paul H., 45
Buenker, John D., 68, 82, 83, 84–86
Buetow, Harold A., 308
Buhle, Paul, 231
Bureaucratization of religion: and Ca-
  tholics, 153–54; and ecumenism, 158;
  and evangelicalism, 161; and Jews,
  157; and the liquor question, 160–61;
  and missionary work, 382; and pol-
  itics, 160–62; and Protestants, 154–56,
  158, 160; and voluntary societies, 158
Burg, David F., 109
Burke, John J., 145, 163
Burkett, Randall K., 114, 205
Burkholder, John Richard, 268
Burner, David, 189
Burnham, John C., 83, 86
Burnham, Walter Dean, 270–71
Buroker, Robert L., 110
Bush, George, 271
Bushnell, Horace, 6, 7, 391
Business boosterism, 197–98
Butler, Francis J., 272
Butler, Richard, 315
Byrnes, Lawrence, 306

Cable, George W., 41–42
Cahensly, Peter Paul, 117
Calhoun, John C., 3
Callahan, Daniel J., 239, 309–10
Calvin Center for Christian Scholarship,
  305
Campbell, Rex R., 113
Cannon, Charles A., 398
Cannon, Heather Symmes, 398–99
Cannon, James, 87
Cantwell v. Connecticut, 234, 344–45

Capers, Ellison, 48–49
Caplow, Theodore, 267
Caron, Wilfred, 278
Carpenter, Joel A., 191
Carroll, Jackson W., 265, 279 n.1
Carter, Dan T., 47
Carter, Paul A., 48, 68, 71, 144, 195, 198,
  227
Cashman, Sean Dennis, 188
Cass, Michael M., 39
Casterline, Gail Farr, 398
Catholic Total Abstinence Union, 86–87
Catholic Worker Movement, 74, 199, 201
Catholics: and Americanism, 153–54,
  235, 268; antipathy to, 238–40, 267–
  68, 345; and the antiwar movement,
  275; and Blanshardism, 238–39; and
  the bureaucratization of religion, 153–
  54; and church-state relations, 235–
  36, 237; and the Civil War, 9; conservative, 118–19, 200; and cultural pluralism, 267–68; decline of, 266–67;
  and ecumenism, 239; and education,
  305, 307–8, 315; and faith of candidates for executive office, 238, 240;
  and foreign policy, 202–3; French,
  116; German, 117, 200; and immigration, 116–19, 154; and industrialization, 72, 73–74, 75–76; Irish, 116–17;
  Italian, 118; and Jews, 204; and labor
  issues, 73–74, 75–76, 199, 201; liberal,
  153–54, 199–200; and the liquor question, 86–87, 188; and litigation, 345;
  and McCarthyism, 231; and military
  chaplains, 12; and missionary work,
  149–50, 151–52; and modern America,
  265, 266–68; and the New Deal, 199,
  201; and pacifism, 202–3; and
  pietism/liturgicalism, 161; Polish,
  117–18; and politics, 201–2; and Protestants, 110, 149–50, 189–90, 238–39,
  267, 345; and racism, 204; and the
  social gospel, 72, 73–74, 75–76, 227;
  and social reform, 199–202, 205–6,
  272, 273; and socialism, 200; in the

South, 49; and U.S. relations with the Vatican, 238, 239–40; and urbanization, 116–19; and World War I, 162, 163. *See also* Parochial education; *names of organizations*

Catt, Carrie Chapman, 400

Cauthen, Kenneth, 145

Cavert, Samuel McCrea, 156

Cayton, Horace, 113

Censorship of books, current controversy over, 313

Center for the Study of Democratic Institutions, 234

Central Conference of American Rabbis, 157

Chadwin, Mark L., 228

Chalmers, David M., 192

Chambers, Marsh v., 348

Chandler, Alfred D., 84–85, 159

Chaplains, military, 1–2, 11–13, 228

Chatfield, E. Charles, 84, 164

Cherny, Robert W., 81

Cherry, Conrad, 270

Cheshire, Joseph Blount, 8

Child benefit doctrine (legal), 309

Child Labor Amendment, 71

Child Labor Committee, 84

Children of God, as new religious movement, 265

Children's Bureau, 69

Chinese, 112–13, 147–48

Chipkin, Israel S., 308–9

Choquette, Diane, 265

Christian Commission, 12

Christian Realism, 233–34

Christian right, 275–77. *See also* Fundamentalism

Christian school movement, 310

Christian Scientists, 344, 375–76, 377–78

Christian socialism, 70, 74

Chu, George, 112

Church, Robert L., 316

Church Association for the Advancement of the Interest of Labor, 69

Church and State (journal), 317

Church-state relations: and Catholics, 235–36, 237; church views about, 237–38; definition of, 1–2, 279; and democracy, 233–42; and Jews, 240; and the melting pot, 242; and nature of the state, 277–79; and scholarship/academia, 236–37; in the South, 33–34; thorniness of, 263–64, 266, 269; and two-sword doctrine, 238; and wall of separation principle, 234–35, 278, 340, 344, 347. *See also* Constitution, First Amendment of

Cianfarra, Camille Maximilian, 240

Citizens for Educational Freedom, 345

Civil religion, 14–16, 269–70, 346

Civil Rights Act (1964), 273–74

Civil rights movement, 46, 162, 273–74

Civil War: and civil religion, 14–16; and the Confederacy, 9–10, 13–14, 16, 37–38; and effect on churches in the South, 39–40; and God's will, 13–14; Lincoln's religious role in, 14–16; and millennialism, 6–8; and nationalism, 2–3, 15–16; pacifism during the, 13; Protestants during the, 2–3, 8–9, 39–42; and Union occupation of the South, 10–11

Clark, Dennis, 117

Clark, Elmer T., 114

Clark, Henry, 273–74

Clark, John Bates, 88

Clark, Mark, 239

Clark, Norman H., 86–87, 188

Clauson, Zorach v., 235, 314, 348

Cleage, Albert B., Jr., 274

Clebsch, William A., 6

Clergy: and the antebellum period, 35; and the antiwar movement, 274–75; black, 42, 198, 205; and the Confederacy, 9–10; and feminism, 391; and imperialism, 151; in the post–war South, 36, 40, 42, 48–49; and the Lost Cause, 36–38; mission of northern to South, 40–41; Protestant, 9–10, 144, 272–73; in Reconstruction, 42; and so-

(Clergy, cont.)
cial reform, 273; and southern social ethic, 35; and World War II, 227–28. *See also* Military chaplains; Rabbinate

Clymer, Kenton J., 149

Coats, Alfred W., 88

Coben, Stanley, 110

Cochran v. Louisiana State Board of Education, 309

Coffin, Henry Sloane, 228

Cogdell, Gaston, 310

Cogley, John, 234, 239

Cohen, Morris L., 354

Cohen, Naomi W., 121

Cohen, Steven M., 264

Cole, Charles C., Jr., 5, 6

Cole, Stewart G., 190

Coleman, John A., 270

Coletta, Paolo E., 81–82, 191

Collie, William E., 314

Colonization Society, 158

Commager, Henry S., 111

Commission on a Just and Durable Peace (Federal Council of Churches), 228–29

Commonwealth of Pennsylvania, Africa v., 352

Communism, 230–33

Compulsory school attendance, 313, 349–50

Cone, James H., 274

Confederacy, 9–10, 13–14, 16, 37–38

Confrey, Burton, 303

Congregationalists, 69, 71, 161

Connecticut, Cantwell v., 234, 344–45

Connelly, Thomas L., 39

Conscientious objectors. *See* Antiwar movement

Conservatives: Catholic, 118–19, 200; and education, 305, 309, 310; and industrialization, 70; Jewish, 119–20, 157; and missionary work, 381; and modern America, 275–77; Protestant, 198, 232, 275–77; and the social gospel, 70, 77–78; and women, 374

Constitution: and Child Labor Amendment, 71; Eighteenth Amendment of, 85, 193; and Equal Rights Amendment, 400; Fifteenth Amendment of, 393, 396; First Amendment of, 311, 312, 313, 340–53; Fourteenth Amendment of, 311, 313, 353; Nineteenth Amendment of, 189, 396, 399–400; proposed amendments to, 71, 303, 312, 400; Twenty-first Amendment of, 188–89. *See also* Liquor question

Conway, Flo, 275

Conway, John S., 239

Conwell, Russell, 77–78

Conzen, Kathleen Neils, 117

Cooke, Bernard, 239

Coons, John E., 310

Cope, Henry F., 303

Corcoran, Theresa, 77

Cornelison, Isaac Amada, 145

Corporate state, 67–68, 69, 77

Corporatism, 79, 83–84

Cort, John C., 231

Corwin, Edward S., 304

Coughlin, William, 74, 191, 194, 200

Country Life Movement, 84

Cox, Claire, 314

Cox, Harvey, 11, 273

Crahan, Margaret E., 149

Creationism. *See* Evolutionary theory

Cremin, Lawrence A., 316

Cronin, John, 239

Cronon, Edmund David, 114, 205

Crosby, Donald F., 231

Cross, Robert D., 111, 118–19, 153, 154, 200

Crunden, Robert M., 68–69, 70, 71–72, 83, 84–85

Cuddy, Edward, 192

Cullman, Oscar, 237

Cults, religious, 350

Cultural pluralism, 267–68, 267–69

Cunninggim, Merrimon, 236–37

Curlett, Murray v., 311

Curran, Robert E., 119

Current Law Index, 353
Curti, Merle, 316

Dabney, Robert Lewis, 37, 48–49
Dabney, Virginius, 87
Dalin, David H., 204–5
Dallek, Robert, 161
Daly, Mary, 394
Daniel, W. Harrison, 8, 9, 11, 12, 13, 39–40
Danish Lutheran church, 116
Dannenbaum, Jed, 387
Darrow, Clarence, 312
Davis, Allen F., 84–85
Davis, David Brion, 110, 398
Davis, J. Treadwell, 9
Davis, Jefferson, 8
Davis, John W., 189
Davis, Lawrence B., 111
Davis, Moshe, 120
Dawidowicz, Lucy S., 267
Dawson, Christopher, 226, 227
Dawson, Joseph Martin, 236–37
Day, Dorothy, 74, 199, 200, 201
Dayton, Donald W., 78, 391
Dayton, Lucille Sider, 391
Declaration on Religious Freedom (Second Vatican Council), 236
Defenders of the Christian Faith, 193
Deferrari, Roy J., 308
Degler, Carl N., 46
Department of Education, U.S., 302
DeSantis, Vincent P., 231
DeSaulniers, Lawrence B., 201
Dewey, John, 68–69, 84
Dierenfield, Richard B., 306
Dietz, Peter, 75
Dietz, William, 199
Diffley, Jerome E., 308
DiMaggio, Paul, 159
Dinnerstein, Leonard, 49, 110, 111
Disciples of Christ, 13, 161
Dismissed-time program, 314

Doctrine: child benefit (legal), 309; of the spirituality of the church, 3–4, 34, 42–45; two-sword, 238
Dohen, Dorothy, 162
Doherty, William T., Jr., 198
Dolan, Jay P., 73, 117, 119, 153, 265, 268
Dolbeare, Kenneth M., 311–12
Dombrowski, James, 70
Donald, David Herbert, 48
Donnelly, Lynch v., 346, 348–49
Dorn, Jacob, 71
Douglas, Mary, 265–66
Douglas, William O., 235, 311
Douglass, H. Paul, 41–42
Dowie, James Iverne, 115
Drake, St. Clair, 113
Dressner, Richard B., 70
Drinan, Robert F., 275, 311
Drury, Clifford M., 228
DuBois, Ellen, 390, 393, 395–96
DuBois, W.E.B., 42
DuBose, William Porcher, 36
Duis, Perry R., 389
Dulles, John Foster, 228–29, 233
Duncan, Richard R., 10
Dunn, Joe P., 228
Dunning, William Archibald, 45
Durnbaugh, Donald F., 202
Dushku, Judith Rasmussen, 398–99
Dynes, Russell R., 88
Dyson, Kenneth H. F., 277

Earhart, Mary, 87
Eastern Orthodox church, 230
Eaton, Clement, 48
Eaton, John, 41
Ebersole, Luke Eugene, 232
Economics, 88
Ecumenism, 155–56, 158, 230, 239. *See also names of organizations*
Eddy, Mary Baker. *See* Christian Scientists
Eddy, Sherwood, 196, 197
Edmunds-Tucker Act (1887), 398, 399

Education: aid to, 309–10, 315–16, 347–48; and the post–Civil War period, 41; and Bible reading, 311, 314, 341; and blacks, 316; and Catholics, 301, 305, 307–8, 315; and censorship of books, 313; commissioner for, 302; and compulsory school attendance, 313, 349–50; and conservatives, 305, 309, 310; constitutional amendments about, 303, 312; and evangelicalism, 305; and evolutionary theory, 312–13; and fundamentalism, 191; higher, 315–16; history of, 316–17; and Jews, 305, 308–9, 310, 312; and liberals, 305; litigation about, 301–3, 304–5, 310–13, 341–42, 347–50; and missionary work, 41; moral, 306–7; parochial, 301, 307–10, 315–16; periodicals, 316–17; and prayer, 311–12, 341–42; professional perspectives about, 303–5, 316; and progressivism, 316; and Protestants, 302, 308–10; role of religion in public, 301–7, 314–15, 341, 342, 347, 348; and saluting the flag, 313, 349; and urbanization, 316; U.S. Department of, 302. *See also names of legal cases*
Education (journal), 317
Educational Policies Commission, 306–7
Eighmy, John Lee, 5, 43, 84, 198
Eight-Hour League, 69
Einhorn, David, 72
Eisendrath, Maurice N., 157
Elliott, Stephen, 48–49
Ellis, John Tracy, 163, 237, 239
Ely, Richard T., 69, 70–71, 88
Endy, Melvin B., Jr., 14, 16
Engel, H. M., 312
Engel v. Vitale, 235, 311–12
Ensley, Philip C., 76
Entz, Margaret, 164
Episcopalians, 40, 149, 161, 267, 374
Epstein, Barbara L., 374, 387, 388–89
Equal access law (education), 315
Equal Rights Amendment, 400

Erickson, Donald A., 309
Ernst, Eldon G., 76, 156
Espelie, Ernest M., 115
Establishment of religion clause. *See* Constitution: First Amendment of; Litigation
Ethical Culture Society, 120
Evangelical Alliance, 70, 150, 155
Evangelicalism: and the antebellum South, 33–35; and the bureaucratization of religion, 161; and the Confederacy, 37–38; and conservatives, 275–77; and education, 305; and fundamentalism, 190; and industrialization, 77–78, 84; and the liquor question, 385–91; and missionary work, 147, 148, 380–82; and modern America, 264, 275–77; and Protestants, 33–35, 37–39, 42–43, 144, 155–56, 158, 187, 275–77; and slavery, 33–34; and the social gospel, 43–44, 67–69, 70, 76, 77–78, 81–82, 84, 383–84; and women, 374, 375, 376, 380–82, 383–85, 391
Evans, Clement, 38
Evans, Hiram Wesley, 192
Evans, Peter B., 277
Everett, John Rutherford, 88
Everson v. Board of Education of Ewing Township, 234, 304, 347
Evolutionary theory, 152, 190–91, 312–13
Expansion, U.S.: and missionary work, 143, 145, 146–53

Fain, Elaine, 192
Faith of candidates for executive office, 238, 240
Falk, Stanley, 121
Falwell, Jerry, 271, 276
Farish, Hunter D., 47
Farmers' Alliance, 78, 79
Farrell, John C., 84
Fascism, 193–94
Faulkner, William, 36

Faunce, William H. P., 145

Fauset, Arthur Huff, 114

Federal Council of Churches of Christ in America, 71, 156, 158, 163, 228–29, 230

Fee, Joan, 271–72

Feingold, Henry L., 203

Feinstein, Marnin, 121

Feldblum, Esther, 241

Feldman, Egal, 72–73

Fellman, David, 342

Fellowship for a Christian Social Order, 196

Fellowship of Reconciliation, 202

Feminism, 391–400. *See also* Women

Fenn, Richard K., 270, 277, 279 n.2

Fennero, Matthew John, 197

Fevold, Eugene L., 116

Findlay, James F., 78

Fine, Sidney, 71–72

Finn, James, 275

Finney, Charles Grandison, 389, 392

Finnish Lutheran church, 115, 116

First Amendment. *See* Constitution; Litigation

Fishburn, Janet F., 72

Fisher, Alan M., 272

Fisher, Joseph A., 312

Fisher, Mary L., 273

Fishman, Ethan M., 312

Fite, Gilbert C., 164

FitzGerald, Frances, 276

Fitzgerald, Maureen, 392

Fitzgerald, Oscar P., 48–49

Flag salute cases, 313, 349

Flaherty, William B., 75–76

Fleischman, Harry, 197

Fleming, William S., 304

Flowers, Ronald B., 310–11

Flynn, George Q., 200–201, 203

Flynt, J. Wayne, 44, 84

Fogarty, Gerald P., 119, 153, 154

Ford, Henry, 191, 198

Foreign Missions Conference of North America, 156

Forell, George W., 238

Forman, Charles, 229

Forman, James, 274

Fosdick, Harry Emerson, 165, 197

Foster, Lawrence, 398–99

Fowler, James W., 197

Fowler, Robert Booth, 271, 276, 277

Fox, Daniel M., 88

Fox, Mary Harrita, 76

Fox, Richard Wightman, 197, 233

Fox, Steven A., 157

Fox sisters, 375

Frazier, E. Franklin, 42, 113

Frederickson, George M., 5

Frederickson, Mary E., 384

Free exercise clause. *See* Constitution: First Amendment of; Litigation

Freedmen's Bureau, 41

Freeman, Douglas Southall, 37

French Catholics, 116

Freund, Paul A., 302

Friedman, Lawrence J., 5

Friedman, Murray, 267

Friedman, Saul S., 203

Frommer, Arthur B., 311

Fuchs, Lawrence H., 240, 267–68

Fundamentalism, 187, 190–91, 193–94, 275–77

Furfey, Paul Hanley, 201

Furniss, Norman K., 190

Gabel, Richard J., 308

Gabriel, Ralph Henry, 88

Gaebelein, Frank E., 305

Gaffney, Edward M., Jr., 315–16

Gage, Matilda J., 378, 394, 395, 400

Gailor, Thomas F., 48–49

Gallup Opinion Index, 266

Gans, Herbert J., 266

Garrett, James Leo, Jr., 278

Garrett, William R., 273

Gartner, Lloyd P., 120–21, 308

Garvey, Marcus, 114, 205

Gaston, Paul M., 45, 46

Gatewood, Willard B., Jr., 191, 312

Gavin, Donald, 73
Gehrig, Gail, 270
Gelhorn, Walter, 315–16
Genovese, Eugene D., 42
George, Henry, 68, 79, 81
German Catholics, 117, 200
Gersh, Harry, 241
Gibbons, James Cardinal, 73, 75, 152, 163
Gibbs, James E., 314
Giddings, Franklin, 84
Gifford, Carolyn DeSwarte, 380
Gilbert, Dennis A., 278
Gintis, Herbert, 316
Ginzberg, Lori D., 381
Girardeau, John L., 48–49
Girouard v. United States, 234
Glad, Paul W., 81–82
Gladden, Washington, 69, 70–71, 74, 75, 82–83
Glanz, David, 264
Glanz, Rudolph, 121
Glazer, Nathan, 120, 121, 122, 123, 240–41
Gleason, Philip, 73–74, 117, 123, 200, 265, 268
Glock, Charles Y., 265, 268
Gobitis, Minersville School District v., 234, 313
Goen, C. C., 2–3
Goldberg, Robert Alan, 193
Goldstein, Sidney, 227
Goodwyn, Lawrence, 187
Gordon, George A., 77–78
Gordon, John Brown, 38
Gordon, Milton M., 123
Goren, Arthur A., 120
Gorman, P. J., 231
Gorrell, Donald K., 71, 154–55
Gossett, Thomas F., 111
Grady, Henry, 45
Graham, Billy, 276
Graham, Robert A., 240
Grange movement, 79
Grantham, Dewey W., 83

Gravely, William, 5–6, 41
Gray, Francine du Plessix, 273
Greeley, Andrew M., 265, 271–72
Green, Fletcher Melvin, 5, 13
Greenawalt, R. Kent, 315–16
Greene, Victor R., 117–18
Greene, William B., 88–89
Griffen, Clyde, 83
Griffin, Clifford S., 5
Grimes, Alan P., 396, 398
Grimke, Angelina, 380
Guide to Legal Periodicals, 353
Gurock, Jeffrey S., 121
Gusfield, Joseph R., 85, 160–61, 385
Gushwa, Robert L., 228
Gutman, Herbert, 76

Haas, Francis J., 201
Habermas, Jürgen, 270
Hackey, Thomas E., 203
Hackney, Sheldon, 46
Hadden, Jeffrey K., 273
Haldeman, Isaac M., 77
Hall, Christopher, 305
Hall, G. Stanley, 89
Hall, Jacquelyn Dowd, 44, 198
Haller, Mark H., 111
Halpern, Ben, 121
Halsey, William M., 119
Halvorson, Peter L., 266
Hammond, Phillip E., 265–66, 270, 311–12
Handlin, Oscar, 111, 116–17, 120, 121, 122, 123, 237
Handy, Robert T., 67–68, 70–71, 108, 122, 155–56, 187, 229–30, 237
Hanna, Mary T., 271–72
Hansen, Marcus, 111
Hardesty, Nancy, 376, 391
Hardman, J.B.S., 76
Hardwick, Bowers v., 346
Hare Krishna movement, 265
Harper, Richard Conant, 111
Harrell, David Edwin, Jr., 13

Harrington, Michael, 201
Harris, William Torrey, 302, 306
Harrison, Beverly Wildung, 391–92
Harrison, Ira E., 114
Harrison, Michael I., 264
Hartmann, Edward G., 110
Hartz, Louis, 107, 108
Harvey, Charles E., 71, 156
Hatch, Nathan O., 108
Haupt, Jon, 398
Haven, Gilbert, 41
Hawley, Jane Stouder, 314
Hay, Clyde Lemont, 305
Hayes, Samuel P., 68, 80, 82
Haygood, Atticus G., 41–42
Heilman, Samuel C., 264
Hein, David, 16
Heilman, Samuel C., 264
Heitzmann, William, 272
Hellor, Maximilian, 157
Henderson, Steven T., 154
Hennesey, James, 265
Henri, Florette, 113
Henry, James O., 12
Henry, Patrick, 242
Hentoff, Nat, 164
Herberg, Will, 107, 123, 242, 354 n.17
Herron, George D., 70
Hertzberg, Arthur, 266
Hertzberg, Steven, 121
Heschel, Abraham J., 275
Hickey, James C., 10
Hicks, John D., 80, 186
Higginson, Thomas Wentworth, 376
Higham, John, 110, 122, 191–92
Higher education, 315–16
Hill, Brian, 305
Hill, D. H., 38
Hill, Patricia R., 377, 381–82
Hill, Robert A., 205
Hill, Samuel S., Jr., 3–4, 8, 47, 49, 276
Hillquit, Morris, 204–5
Hintz, Howard H., 315
Hitchcock, James, 273
Hoare, F. R., 226

Hofstadter, Richard, 68, 80, 82, 85, 111,
  144, 152, 186–87, 191, 192–93
Hoge, Dean R., 264–65, 315
Hoge, Moses Drury, 48–49
Hoglund, A. William, 115
Holifield, E. Brooks, 35
Hollinger, Dennis P., 276
Home Missions Council, 156
Honeywell, Roy J., 11
Honigsberg, Peter Jan, 354
Hoopes, Townsend, 229
Hoover, Herbert, 202
Hoover, J. Edgar, 231
Hopkins, C. Howard, 48, 69, 72, 145, 155
Horowitz, Helen Lefkowitz, 110
Horst, Samuel, 13
House Committee on Un-American Ac-
  tivities (HUAC), 231
Hovet, Theodore R., 376
Howard, O. O., 41
Howe, Frederic C., 83, 84
Howe, Irving, 120, 204, 272
Howe, Julia Ward, 7
Howe, Mark DeWolfe, 355 n.20
Hoyt, Frederick B., 202
Hudson, Winthrop S., 108, 144, 151, 234
Huggins, Nathan I., 72
Hughes, Charles Evans, 84–85
Hunnicutt, Benjamin Kline, 161
Hunt, Janet G., 274
Hunt, Larry L., 274
Hunt, Thomas C., 307
Hunter, James Davison, 264, 276
Hunter, Jane, 381
Huntington, Samuel, 270, 270–71
Hutchison, John A., 232
Hutchison, William R., 71–72, 108, 144,
  145, 148, 267
Huthmacher, J. Joseph, 82
Hyatt, Irwin T., 380
Hyde, Stuart W., 398

Immigration: and the American Way of
  Life, 107, 109–11, 123; and Catholics,
  116–19, 154; Chinese, 112–13; and

(Immigration, cont.)
Jews, 72–73, 119; and the melting pot, 111, 123, 242; and pacifism, 202, 203; and Protestant core culture, 107–12, 122–23; and racism, 109, 111; and radicalism, 110; Scandinavian Lutheran, 115–16
Immigration Restriction League, 111
Imperialism, 143, 145, 146–53
Implied trust (English rule of), 343
Indians, American, 349, 350
Industrialization: and Catholics, 72, 73–74, 75–76; and conservative Christianity, 70; and corporatism, 79, 83–84; and evangelicalism, 77–78, 84; and Jews, 72–73; and labor issues, 71–72, 74–77; and the liquor question, 79, 85–87; and populism, 79–82; and progressivism, 70–72, 78, 82–85; and the social gospel, 69–72; and social reform, 67–89; and the social sciences, 87–89; and socialism, 70; in the South, 84
Interchurch World Movement, 71, 76, 156, 195
Internal Revenue Service, 278
International Christian Workers Association, 77–78
Intrachurch disputes (legal), 344
Ireland, John, 73, 152, 154, 307
Irish Catholics, 116–17
Isolationism, 202, 225
Israel, Jerry, 149
Italian Catholics, 118

J. M. Dawson Institute of Church-State Studies, 317
Jacklin, Thomas M., 198–99
Jackson, Andrew, 37
Jackson, Jerome K., 304
Jackson, Kenneth T., 192–93
Jacobsen, Philip, 305
Jacoway, Elizabeth, 41
Jaffree, Wallace v., 354 n.8

Jalkanen, Ralph J., 116
Jefferson, Thomas. See Wall of separation principle
Jehovah's Witnesses, 155, 234, 313, 349
Jellison, Helen M., 309
Jensen, Billie Barnes, 70
Jensen, Richard, 80–82, 161
Jessop, Bob, 277
Jewish Theological Seminary (New York City), 157
Jews: and the bureaucratization of religion, 157; and Catholics, 204; and church-state relations, 240; and the Civil War, 9; conservative, 119–20, 157; and education, 305, 308–9, 310, 312; and immigration, 72–73, 119; and industrialization, 72–73; and isolationism, 202; and labor issues, 72–73, 76; and McCarthyism, 231; and military chaplains, 12; and modern America, 264, 266, 267, 268; and the New Deal, 205; and pacifism, 203; and the rabbinate, 157; Reform, 72–73, 119–21, 157; as separationists, 345; Sephardic, 119–20, 121; and the social gospel, 72–73, 76; and socialism, 204; and sociology, 241; in the South, 49; in the twenties and thirties, 204–5; and urbanization, 119; and Zionism, 121, 157, 241. See also Anti-Semitism
Jick, Leon A., 120
Johnson, Benton, 265, 271
Johnson, Daniel M., 113
Johnson, Donald, 165
Johnson, Douglas W., 279 n.1
Johnson, F. Ernest, 229, 305
Johnson, Niel M., 192
Johnson, Paul, 389
Johnson, Stephen D., 276
Jones, Charles C., Jr., 33
Jones, Donald G., 9, 41, 270
Jones, Edgar D., 15
Jones, Howard Mumford, 109
Jones, J. William, 37–38
Jones, Jacqueline, 41

Jones, Maldwyn A., 111
Jones, Samuel, 82–83
Jones, Watson v., 343–44
Jordan, Philip D., 70, 110–11
Jorstad, Erling, 275
Joseph, Ted, 164–65
Journal of Church and State, 237, 317
Juhnke, James C., 164

Kaganoff, Nathan M., 49
Kamhi, Michelle M., 313
Karier, Clarence J., 316
Karl, Barry D., 186
Karp, Abraham J., 121–22
Katz, Michael B., 316
Kauffman, Christopher J., 200, 203
Keane, John, 152
Kedro, Milan J., 11
Kegley, Charles, 233
Keim, Albert N., 228, 229, 235, 313
Keller, Rosemary Skinner, 373, 379
Kelley, Dean M., 278
Kelly, George A., 265, 309
Kemper, Donald J., 204
Kenneally, James J., 397
Kennedy, John F., 240, 267–68
Kerr, K. Austin, 86
Kibby, Leo P., 12
Kienel, Paul A., 308
Killen, David P., 119
King, Martin Luther, Jr., 271, 274
Kingdom of God theology, 72
Kingdon, Frank, 227
Kinzer, Donald L., 110
Klein, Christa Ressmeyer, 379
Kleppner, Paul, 80–82, 160, 161
Kliebard, Herbert M., 302
Knights of Columbus, 203
Knights of Labor, 73
Knox, Raymond C., 303
Koenker, Ernest B., 238
Kohlberg, Lawrence, 307
Kohler, Kaufmann, 72
Kommers, Donald P., 313
Koob, C. Albert, 308

Korman, Gerd, 110
Korn, Bertram W., 9, 12
Kraditor, Aileen S., 110, 397
Kraushaar, Otto F., 308–9
Kraut, Benny, 120
Kreider, Robert, 202
Ku Klux Klan, 187, 189, 191–93, 195, 200
Kurland, Philip B., 350
Kuykendall, John W., 5, 35
Kuzniewski, Anthony J., 118
Kyvig, David E., 188–89

Labor issues: and Catholics, 73–74, 75–76, 199, 201; and industrialization, 71–72, 74–77; and Jews, 72–73, 76; and the social gospel, 71–72
Lacy, Creighton, 155
Ladd, Everett Carll, 277
LaFarge, John, 204
LaFollette, Marcel C., 312
LaFollette, Robert, 84–85
Lai, H. M., 112
Langer, William, 146
La Noue, George R., 310
Larson, Martin A., 310
Latourette, Kenneth Scott, 229
Layton, Donald H., 312
League of Christian Socialists, 71
Lears, T. J. Jackson, 48, 122
Lecler, Joseph, 236–37
Lee, Elizabeth, 110–11
Lee, Mother Ann, 375
Lee, Robert E., 37–38
Lee, Rose Hum, 112–13
Lee, Umphrey, 228
Lehrer, Stanley, 302
Lemon v. Kurtzman (tripartite test), 348
Leo XIII, Pope, 153–54, 235, 307
Leone, Mark P., 265
Leuchtenburg, William E., 162, 186
Levine, Lawrence W., 42, 191
Lewis, David L., 274
Liberals: Catholic, 153–54, 199–200; and education, 305; and fundamentalism,

(Liberals, cont.)
190; and Methodism, 144; and mis-
sionary work, 148; Protestant, 143–46,
190, 194–99; religious, 143–46; in the
twenties and thirties, 185–86, 194–99;
and women, 374
LIBERTY (journal), 317
Liberty League, 188–89
Lichtman, Allan J., 189–90
Lieberson, Stanley, 113
Liebman, Arthur, 204
Liebman, Charles S., 122, 264
Liebman, Robert C., 276
Light, Ivan H., 112
Lincoln, Abraham, 6, 14–16, 45
Lincoln, C. Eric, 113
Linder, Robert D., 78
Lindmark, Sture, 115
Lindner, Eileen W., 81
Linesch, Michael, 276
Link, Arthur S., 84, 164
Link, Eugene P., 197
Link, Henry, 241
Lippy, Charles H., 8, 49
Lipset, Seymour M., 276
Liquor question: and the bureaucratiza-
tion of religion, 160–61; and evan-
gelicalism, 386; and industrialization,
79, 85–87; and the law, 387; and pol-
itics, 386–91; and Protestants, 43,
160–61, 187–90; in the South, 43; and
stewardship ideal, 188; and the temperance movement, 385–91; and
women, 87, 385–91
Lisenby, William Foy, 189–90
Litigation: and the accommoda-
tionist/separationist debate, 345–47,
348–49; and aid to education, 347–48;
and the antiwar movement, 350, 351–
52; and Bible reading, 341; and Catholics, 345; and civil religion, 346;
and the definition of religion, 351–52;
and education, 301–3, 304–5, 310–13,
341–42, 347–48; and English law, 343;
and intrachurch disputes, 344; and

Jews, 345; and new religious move-
ments, 352; and ownership of church
property, 343–44; and politics, 353;
Protestant influence on, 342–43, 344;
and religious cults, 350; and school
prayer, 341–42; and state and local
governments, 342–44; and state reg-
ulation of religion, 344. See also
names of law cases
Littell, Franklin H., 241
Little, Lawrence C., 314
Litwack, Leon F., 42
Lloyd, Henry Demarest, 68, 79
Loder, James E., 305
Lodge, Henry Cabot, 146
Long, Huey, 191, 193, 194
Lopatto, Paul, 271
Lost Cause, 35–39
Louisiana State Board of Education,
Cochran v., 309
Love, Thomas Teel, 236, 268
Loveland, Anne C., 5, 35
Lowry, Charles Wesley, 312
Lubbock Independent School District v.
Lubbock Civil Liberties Union, 315
Luce, Henry R., 228
Luker, Ralph E., 44, 72
Lutherans, 115–16, 161, 195, 238, 374
Lyman, Stanford M., 112
Lynch v. Donnelly, 346, 348–49

McAdoo, William Gibbs, 189
Macartney, Clarence, 190
McAvoy, Thomas T., 116, 118–19, 239,
242
McBeth, Leon, 191
McBride, James, 355 n.43
McCarthy, Carlton, 38
McCarthy, G. Michael, 189–90
McCarthyism, 231–32, 234
McCluskey, Neil G., 308
McCollum v. Board of Education, 234–
35, 304, 314
McConnell, Francis J., 76, 196, 197, 227

McConnell, Michael W., 355 n.20
McCormick, Richard L., 159–60
McDonnell, James R., 77
McDowell, John Patrick, 44, 72, 384
MacFarland, Charles S., 156
McFeely, William S., 41
McGlynn, Edward, 73
McGowan v. State of Maryland, 235
McGuffin, John B., 148
Machen, J. Gresham, 190
McIlwaine, Richard, 48–49
Macintosh, Douglas Clyde, 197
MacIntyre, Alasdair, 270
Mackay, John, 232, 237–38
McKean, Dayton D., 232
McKee, Delber L., 112
MacKenzie, Kenneth M., 148–49
McKeown, Elizabeth, 163
McKim, Randolph Harrison, 38
McKivigan, John R., 5
McLaughlin, Eleanor, 373
McLaughlin, Raymond, 308
Maclear, James Fulton, 5, 6
McLoughlin, William G., Jr., 78, 83, 163–64
MacMillan, Richard C., 305
MacNab, John B., 110–11
McNamara, Robert F., 153
McNeal, Patricia, 202–3, 228
McNearney, Clayton L., 313
McPheeters, Samuel, 11
McPherson, Aimee Semple, 375
McPherson, James M., 48, 273
McQuaid, Bernard John, 153, 307
McQuigg, R. Bruce, 305
Maddex, Jack P., 4, 35
Madison, James, 237
Magnuson, Norris, 78, 383–84
Malcolm X (Malcolm Little), 274
Malmberg, Constantine F., 304
Manhattan, Auro, 268
Manifest destiny, 150–52
Mann, Arthur, 109
Manwaring, David R., 235, 313
Marchand, C. Roland, 164

Marcus, Sheldon, 194
Maritain, Jacques, 236–37
Marquis, Kathleen, 399
Marsden, George M., 77–78, 108, 190, 191, 264, 275–76
Marsh v. Chambers, 348
Marszalek, John, 198
Martin, Renwick Harper, 304
Martin, Tony, 114
Marty, Martin E., 123, 279 n.1
Marx, Gary T., 274
Mary Elizabeth Blue Hull Memorial Presbyterian Church, Presbyterian Church in the United States v., 344
Maryland [State of], McGowan v., 235
Massee, J. C., 190
Mathews, Basil, 155
Mathews, Donald G., 8, 35
Mathews, Shailer, 163–64, 197
Mathieson, Robert R., 78
Mattox, Fount William, 305
Maurin, Peter, 199, 201
Maxson, Marilyn M., 307
Maxwell, William Quentin, 12
May, Ernest R., 151
May, Henry F., 47, 69–71, 108, 122, 145–46
Mays, Benjamin E., 113
Mead, Sidney E., 68, 107, 108, 158, 242
Meconis, Charles A., 273
Mediums Mutual Aid Society, 376–77
Melting pot, 111, 123, 242
Men and Religion Forward Movement, 69
Menendez, Albert J., 239, 267
Menes, Abraham, 231
Mennonites, 13, 155, 164–65, 202, 228, 238
Merkley, Paul, 233
Merwick, Donna, 117
Merz, Charles S., 160–61, 187
Methodist Episcopalians, 2, 9
Methodist Episcopalians, South, 38
Methodist Federation for Social Service, 154–55

Methodists: and bureaucratization, 154–
    55; and the Civil War, 2, 6, 9; and
    liberal theology, 144; and the liquor
    question, 43, 84, 378; missionary ac-
    tivities of, 40, 148–49; and pietism,
    161; in the post–Civil War South, 40,
    43–44; schisms in, 2; and Social
    Creed of the Churches, 71, 85, 154–
    55; and the social gospel, 43–44; and
    women, 373, 374, 378, 384, 395
Meyer, D. H., 108–9
Meyer, Donald B., 145, 196, 202, 377–78
Meyer, Isidore S., 121
Meyer, John W., 277
Meyer, Paul R., 70
Michaelsen, Robert S., 264–65, 301–2,
    314, 315
Miliband, Ralph, 277
Military chaplains, 1–2, 11–13, 228
Millar, Moorhouse F. X., 200
Millennialism, 5, 6–8, 108
Miller, Elizabeth, W., 273
Miller, F. P., 228
Miller, Randall W., 49
Miller, Robert Moats, 71, 145, 192, 195–
    96, 197, 198, 204
Miller, Robert T., 237, 310–11
Miller, Sally M., 110
Miller, Stuart Creighton, 112
Miller, William, 242
Miller, William D., 74, 201
Miller, William Lee, 278
Mills, C. Wright, 242
Minersville School District v. Gobitis,
    234, 313
*Minor, Board of Education of Cincin-
    nati v.*, 302–3, 311, 340
Miscamble, Wilson D., 203
Missionary Education Movement of the
    United States and Canada, 156
Missionary work: bureaucratization of,
    382; and Catholics, 149–50, 151–52; in
    China, 147–48; and conservatives,
    381; and economic expansion, 147–
    48, 152–53; and education, 41; and

evangelicalism, 147, 148, 380–82; for-
    eign, 147–48, 379–83; and imperi-
    alism, 143, 145, 146–53; and liberals,
    148; motivation for, 147–48, 380; and
    pacifism, 202; and political feminists,
    380–81; post-World War II, 229–30;
    and Protestants, 40–41, 110–11, 112;
    and religious toleration, 150; and So-
    cial Darwinism, 152; and the social
    gospel, 383–85; in the South, 5, 40–41,
    44; and urbanization, 384; and wom-
    en, 44, 374, 379–85. *See also names of
    denominations*
Missouri Synod (Lutheran), 192
Mitchell, Basil, 355 n.20
Mitchell, Douglas, 264
Moberg, David, 78
Moehlman, Conrad Henry, 236–37
Monzell, Thomas I., 117
Moody, Dwight L., 77, 147
Moore, Deborah Dash, 204–5
Moore, Edmund A., 189
Moore, R. Laurence, 376, 377
Moorhead, James H., 6, 7, 16, 48
Moots, Philip R., 315–16
Moral education, 306–7
Moral Majority. *See* Fundamentalism
Morgan, J. Graham, 88–89
Morgan, Richard E., 263, 278, 342, 345
Morgenthau, Hans J., 16
Mormons, 155, 340–42, 344, 346, 349,
    350, 397–400
Morris, Barbara M., 310
Morris, Robert C., 41
Morrison, Charles Clayton, 227
Morrow, Ralph E., 41
Mortensen, Enok, 116
Mott, John R., 153, 155, 156
Mott, Lucretia, 374
Mount, Graeme S., 149
Moynihan, Daniel P., 123
Muehl, William, 232
Muelder, Walter G., 154–55
Mulder, John M., 164
Murphy, Edgar Gardner, 44

Murray, John Courtney, 235–36, 239, 267–68
Murray, Robert K., 110, 192
Murray v. Curlett, 311
Muste, A. J., 164, 194, 196, 197
Myers, Robert Manson, 33

Nash, George H., 75
Nash, Roderick, 186
National American Woman Suffrage Association (NAWSA), 395–96, 400
National Catholic War Council, 163, 200
National Catholic Welfare Conference, 200, 309
National Conference of Catholic Bishops, 163
National Conference of Catholic Charities, 73
National Council of Churches in the U.S.A. (NCC), 230, 273, 306, 317, 345
National Council of Congregational Churches, 69, 71
National Council on Religion and Public Education, 317
National Education Association (NEA), 303, 307, 316–17
National Industrial Recovery Act (NIRA), 199, 200
National Union for Social Justice, 74, 194
National Woman Suffrage Association (NWSA), 389, 393, 397, 399
Nationalism, 2–3, 15–16, 226–27
Native American Church, 349, 350
NAWSA. *See* National American Woman Suffrage Association
Nee, Brett de Bary, 112
Nee, Victor G., 112
Nelli, Humbert S., 118
Nelsen, Anne Kusener, 274
Nelsen, Hart M., 274
Nelson, E. Clifford, 116
Nelson, John K., 202
Neuchterlein, James A., 198
Neufeld, Elmer, 238

Neuhaus, Richard John, 275
New Deal, 199, 201, 205
Newman, Richard, 114
Newman, William M., 266
New religious movements, 265, 268, 352, 374, 376–79
New South, 16, 45, 46
Nicholl, Grier, 70
Nichols, James Hastings, 234
Nicholson, Joseph W., 113
Nicklason, Fred, 81
Nicolson, John, 11
Niebuhr, H. Richard, 197, 229
Niebuhr, Reinhold, 71, 194–99, 203, 227, 229, 232–34
Nielsen, Niels C., Jr., 305
Noble, David W., 83
Nordlinger, Eric, 277
Norris, J. Frank, 190
North, Frank Mason, 155
Northern Protestants: and abolitionism, 5–6; and civil religion, 14–16; and guilt, 14; and millennialism, 5, 6–7; and missionary work, 40–41; and social reform, 33–35; and societal stewardship, 5–6; and the South, 33–35, 40–41
Norton, Herman A., 11
Norwegian Lutheran church, 116
Norwood, Frederick A., 9
Novak, Michael, 123, 233, 239, 242, 270, 273, 275
NWSA. *See* National Woman Suffrage Association
Nyholm, Paul P., 116

Oakes, James, 14
Oates, Stephen B., 274
O'Brien, David J., 73, 75, 201, 267, 272, 273
O'Connell, Denis, 152
O'Connor, John, 275
O'Gorman, Robert T., 308
O'Hair, Madalyn Murray, 269
Oldham, J. H., 226

Olds, Sally Wendkof, 307
Old School/New School (Presbyterian Church), 2
O'Leary, Cornelius, 75
O'Neill, James M., 305, 308
Osofsky, Gilbert, 114
Osterweis, Rollin G., 39
Otey, James Hervey, 48–49
Outlawry of War movement, 202
Owen, Dennis E., 276
Ownership of church property, legal question, 343–44
Oxford pledge movement, 202
Oxford Universal Christian Conference on Life and Work (1937), 227, 229
Oxnam, G. Bromley, 231–32

Pacifism, 13, 163–65, 202–3, 228
Page, Kirby, 164, 196
Palmer, Benjamin Morgan, 48–49
Palmer, Phoebe, 375
Palsson, Mary Dale, 49
Pankratz, Herbert L., 164
Pantojas García, Emilio, 149
Parenti, Michael, 271
Parker, Gail T., 377, 378
Parkhurst, Charles, 69
Parochial education, 301, 307–10, 315–16, 347–48
Partin, Robert, 12
Patel, Kant, 276
Patten, Simon N., 88
Paul, Alice, 400
Peabody, Francis Greenwood, 88–89
Pearson, Ralph L., 71
Peck, Garry R., 274
Pelley, William Dudley, 193
Pells, Richard H., 186
Pelotte, Donald E., 268
Pendleton, William Nelson, 48–49
Pennington, Edgar Legare, 9, 12
Pentecostalists, 377
People's party, 78, 79–82. See also Populism
People v. Woody, 350, 354 n.4

Perkinson, Henry J., 316
Perlman, Selig, 76
Perman, Michael, 47
Persons, Stow, 109
Peterson, Horace, C., 164
Petryshyn, J., 197
Pfeffer, Leo, 1, 236–37, 239, 268, 278
Philpott, Thomas L., 109
Piediscalzi, Nicholas, 311, 314
Piehl, Mel, 74, 201
Pierard, Richard V., 275, 276
Pierce, George Foster, 48–49
Pierce v. Society of Sisters, 313
Pike, James Albert, 240
Pine Street Church incident (St. Louis, Missouri), 11
Ping Chiu, 112
Piper, John F., Jr., 162–63
Pitts, Charles F., 12
Pittsburgh Platform, 72
Pius XI, Pope, 199, 200, 201
Pleck, Elizabeth H., 113–14
Plotnicov, Leonard, 264
Poling, Paul N., 229
Polish Catholics, 117–18
Political feminists, 380–81
Politics: and blacks, 274; and the bureaucratization of religion, 160–62; and Catholics, 201–2; and the liquor question, 386–91; and litigation, 353; and Protestants, 189–90, 193–99, 275–77; and religion, 9–11, 80–81, 270–77; and women, 391–400
Pollack, Norman, 80
Pollard, Edward A., 35
Pomerantz, Linda, 113
Pope, Liston, 74–75
Populism, 78, 79–82, 85, 87, 187, 388
Porter, Anthony Toomer, 48–49
Potter, David M., 152–53
Potts, David B., 88–89
Powell, Theodore, 235
Powell, Walter, 159
Pratt, Henry J., 273
Pratt, J. W., 151

Prayer, school, 311–12, 341–42
Presbyterian Church in the United States v. Mary Elizabeth Blue Hull Memorial Presbyterian Church, 344
Presbyterians: and bureaucratization, 155; and church-state relations, 237–38; and the Civil War, 2, 4, 8–9, 10, 11; General Assembly of, 156; and pietism/liturgicalism, 161; schisms in, 2; and *Watson v. Jones* case, 343–44; and women, 374
Press, religious, 266
Preston, William, 110
Price, Monroe E., 350
Primer, Ben, 160
Prison Reform Association, 84
Progressivism: and education, 316; and industrialization, 70–72, 78, 82–85; and the liquor question, 85, 86; and Protestants, 109, 144, 194–95; and the social gospel, 71–72, 78, 82–85
Prohibition. *See* Liquor question
Protestant Episcopalians, 9
Protestants: and the brown scare, 193–94; and the bureaucratization of religion, 154–56, 158, 160; and business boosterism, 197–98; and Catholics, 110, 149–50, 189–90, 238–40, 267–68, 345; and Christian Realism, 232–34; and the civil rights movement, 273–74; and the Civil War, 2–3, 8–9; and the clergy, 144, 272–73; and communism, 230–33; conservative, 232, 275–77; core culture of, 107–12, 122–23; decline of, 266–67; and ecumenism, 155–56; and education, 302, 308–310; and evangelicalism, 144, 155–56, 158, 161, 187, 275–77; and fundamentalism, 187, 190–91; and immigration, 107–12, 122–23; and liberalism, 143–46, 190, 194–99; and the liquor question, 160–61, 187–90; litigation, influence of, 342–43, 344; and millennialism, 108; and missionary work, 110–11, 112; and modern America, 264–65, 266–67; polarization of, 232–33; and politics, 189–90, 193–99, 275–77; and populism, 187; and Progressivism, 109, 144, 194–95; and racism, 109, 110, 111, 112, 115, 122; schisms among, 2–3, 33, 77; and the social gospel, 144, 156, 194–96; and social reform, 272–73; and socialism, 194–95; and urbanization, 107–12, 122–23; and voluntary societies, 158; and women, 394, 397; and World War I, 162–64. *See also* Anti-Semitism; Northern Protestants; Southern Protestants; *names of denominations*
Protestants and Other Americans United for Separation of Church and State (POAU), 238–39, 345
Purcell, Edward A., Jr., 186, 201–2

Quadragesimo Anno (Pius XI), 199, 200
Quakers, 161, 202, 228, 374, 392
Quandt, Jean B., 83, 84
Queen, Louise L., 373
Quigley, Thomas E., 275
Quimby, Rollin W., 11
Quinley, Harold E., 268, 275
Quinn, D. Michael, 155

Raab, Earl, 276
Rabbinate, 157
Rabbinate Council of America, 157
Rabbinical Assembly of America, 157
Raboteau, Albert J., 42
Racism, 109, 110, 111, 112, 115, 122, 204
Rader, Benjamin G., 88
Raleigh, John Henry, 109
Ramsey, Paul, 275, 315
Randall, James G., 48
Raphael, Marc Lee, 157, 204–5, 264
Raskob, John J., 189
Rausch, David A., 241
Rauschenbusch, Walter, 69, 70–71, 77, 195, 196
Reagan, Ronald, 271, 310, 312

Reconstruction: black churches in, 41–42; northern clergy mission to blacks in, 40–41; revisionist views of, 45–47

Redekop, John Harold, 232

Redlich, Norman, 355 n.20

Reed, James Eldin, 150–51

Reform Jews, 72–73, 119–21, 157

Reilly, Daniel F., 307

Reilly, Michael C., 149

Reimers, David M., 111, 198, 204

Released-time program, 314, 348

Religion: civil, 14–16, 269–70; decline/vitality of, 266–67, 269–70, 279 n.1; definition of, 351–52; entanglement test, 348; return to, 229–30, 241–42; and science, 377; state regulation of, 344; and World War I, 143, 145, 163–65. *See also* Southern religion; *names of sects and denominations*

Religion and Public Education (journal), 317

Religious Education Association (REA), 303–4, 317

Religious Education (journal), 303, 306–7, 317

Religious Liberty Association, 345

Religious toleration, 150

Rerum Novarum (Pope Leo XIII), 73, 75, 199

Reuss, Carl F., 272–73

Reuter, Frank T., 150

Reynolds v. United States, 340–42, 346, 349, 350

Ribuffo, Leo P., 193–94

Rice, Charles E., 312

Richardson, James T., 268

Richardson, Joe M., 41

Richey, Russell E., 158–59, 270

Rideout, Lionel U., 110–11

Riesman, David, 242

Riess, Steven, 161

Rightmyer, Nelson Waite, 10

Riley, William Bell, 190

Ringgold, Samuel, 10

Rischin, Moses, 120, 121

Robbins, Thomas, 265, 268, 270, 352, 355 n.43

Robertson, Roland, 277, 356 n.55

Robinson, Jo Ann Oviman, 197

Rockefeller, John D., Jr., 156

Rodgers, Harrell R., Jr., 313

Rohr, John A., 275

Romero, Sidney J., 12

Roof, Wade Clark, 264–65

Roohan, James E., 73

Roosevelt, Franklin Delano. *See* New Deal

Roosevelt, Theodore, 82–83, 84–85, 161

Rose, Willie Lee, 42

Rosenberg, Bernard, 242, 272

Rosenberg, Stuart E., 120

Rosenblum, Herbert, 157

Ross, Dorothy, 88, 89

Ross, Robert W., 203

Rossi, Alice, 391–92

Roy, Ralph Lord, 232

Roy, William G., 159

Rudd, Myron S., 235

Ruether, Rosemary Radford, 373

Russell, C. Allyn, 190

Ryan, Abram Joseph, 36

Ryan, John A., 74, 163, 199, 200, 203, 227

Ryan, Mary Perkins, 308

Rydell, Robert W., 109

Sabine, David B., 12

St. James Church (Wilmington, North Carolina), 10–11

Salvation Army, 383–84

Sandeen, Ernest R., 190

Sanders, Thomas Griffin, 237, 239

Sandmeyer, Elmer C., 112

Sanitary Commission, 12

Saveth, Edward Norman, 111

Saxton, Alexander P., 112

Scandinavian Lutherans, 115–16

Schecter, Solomon, 157

Scheiber, Harry N., 165

Scheiner, Seth M., 114

Schempp, Abington Township School District v., 311, 314
Schick, Marvin, 310
Schisms, 2–3, 77
Schlabach, Theron F., 155
Schlesinger, Arthur M., 68
Schlesinger, Arthur M., Jr., 186
Schmitt, Karl M., 149–50
Science, relation to religion of, 377
Scientology, 265
Scopes trial. *See* Evolutionary theory
Scott, Anne Firor, 44, 384
Scudder, Vida, 77
Seager, Robert H., 110–11
Seaton, Douglas P., 201
Seckinger, Richard K., 312
Second Inaugural Address (Lincoln), 16
Second Vatican Council, 236
Secular regulation rule, in U.S. law, 340, 349
Seeger, United States v., 351–52
Seidler, Murray B., 164, 197
Selective Service Act, 351–52
Sennett, Richard, 109–10
Sephardic Jews, 119–20, 121
Seventh Day Adventists, 345
Shaffir, William, 264
Shakers, 375
Shankman, Arnold, 198
Shannon, Thomas A., 272
Shapiro, Yonathan, 121
Shared-time program, 314
Sharot, Stephen, 242
Sharpe, Dores R., 71
Shaw, Anna Howard, 400
Shaw, Russell B., 308
Sheerin, John B., 163
Shepard, John, Jr., 12
Shepherd, William C., 268, 355 n.43
Sherbert v. Verner, 349
Shields, Currin, 234
Shover, John L., 75, 189–90
Shupe, Anson D., Jr., 268, 276
Shuster, George N., 239
Sider, Ronald J., 276–77

Siegel, Harvey, 312
Siegelman, Jim, 275
Silver, James W., 8, 11, 13
Simon, Sidney B., 307
Simonhoff, Harry, 9
Simpson, John A., 39
Sinclair, Andrew, 85, 187
Singleton, Gregory H., 191
Sizer, Theodore R., 306
Skaardal, Dorothy B., 115
Sklare, Marshall, 241, 264
Slave religion, 42
Slavery, 2–6, 16, 33–35
Small, Albion, 68–69
Small, Dwight L., 273
Smith, Al, 189, 201, 240
Smith, Albert Edward, 197
Smith, David H., 233
Smith, Elwyn Allen, 9, 270, 272–73
Smith, Gerald L. K., 193
Smith, H. Shelton, 4–5, 35
Smith, Henry L., 306
Smith, John Abernathy, 156
Smith, Michael E., 352, 356 n.53
Smith, Page, 381
Smith, Richard U., 306
Smith, Timothy L., 5, 70, 78, 123, 159, 383–84
Smylie, James H., 70, 232, 274–75
Smylie, Robert F., 202
Social Creed of the Churches (Methodist), 71, 85, 154–55
Social Darwinism, 152
Social gospel: and Catholics, 72, 73–74, 75–76, 227; and Christian socialism, 70, 74; and conservatives, 70, 77–78; and the corporate state, 67–68, 69, 77; and evangelicalism, 67–69, 70, 76, 77–78, 81–82, 84, 383–84; and the Federal Council of Churches, 71; and industrialization, 69–72; and Jews, 72–73, 76; and labor issues, 71–72; and the liquor question, 85–87; and missionary work, 383–85; and nationalism, 227; and populism, 79–82;

(Social gospel, cont.)
and progressive social Christianity,
70–71; and Progressivism, 71–72, 78,
82–85; and Protestants, 43–44, 144,
156, 194–96, 198–99; revival of, 227;
and the South, 43–44, 154, 198–99;
and women, 383–85. *See also* Social
reform
Socialism, 70, 74, 194–95, 200, 204
Social reform: and Catholics, 199–202,
205–6, 272, 273; and the clergy, 273;
and industrialization, 67–89; and modern America, 266–67, 272–75; and
Protestants, 4–5, 6, 33–35, 47–48,
272–73; and the South, 33–35, 42–45;
and stewardship of society, 5–6; and
women, 376–78, 383–91. *See also* So-
cial gospel
Social Reform Union, 70
Social sciences, 87–89, 377. *See also*
names of social sciences
Society of Christian Soldiers, 70
Society of Sisters, Pierce v., 313
Sociology, 79, 88–89, 159–60, 241
Soden, Dale E., 44
Soldier's Tract Association (Methodist
Episcopal Church, South), 38
Solomon, Barbara M., 111
Sorauf, Frank J., 235, 278, 311, 345
Southern Baptist Convention, 154, 191
Southern Baptist Temperance League,
84
Southern Methodist Temperance
League, 84
Southern Protestants: and blacks, 41–
42, 198; and the Civil War, 39–42; and
the clergy, 9–10; and the Confederacy, 7–9; and conservatives, 198;
and evangelicalism, 33–35, 37–39, 42–
43; and guilt about the Civil War, 14,
16; and industrialization, 84; and the
liquor question, 43; and millennialism,
6–8; and moral crusades, 43–44; and
republicanism, 44–45; and the social
gospel, 43–44, 198–99; and social reform, 4–5, 6, 33–35, 47–48; and wom-
en, 198. *See also* Civil War; *names of
denominations*
Southern religion: and black churches,
41–42; and Catholics, 49; and Civil
War impact on, 39–40; clergy in, 48–
49, 198; and the Confederacy, 7–10,
37–38; evangelicalism in, 33–35, 42;
home missions, 44; and liquor question, 43; and Lost Cause, 35–39; millennialism in, 5, 6–8; as new field of
inquiry, 47–49; relation with state,
33–34; and revivals, 13; role of guilt
in defeat, 14; and slavery, 3–4, 33–34;
and social ethic, 33–34, 35, 43–45;
and social gospel, 43–45, 154, 198–99;
spirituality of the church (doctrine),
3–4, 34, 42–45; and Union occupation,
10–11, 40. *See also names of
denominations*
Southern Sociological Congress, 84
Sowle, Patrick, 13
Spain, Rufus B., 43
Spalding, John L., 307
Spear, Allan H., 114
Speer, Robert E., 155, 156
Spellman, Francis Cardinal, 239
Spiritualism, 376–77, 378
Spiritualists, 375, 379
Spirituality of the church, doctrine of
the, 3–4, 34, 42–45
Spivak, John L., 194
Spring, Joel H., 316
Sproat, John G., 109
Stacey, William A., 276
Stampp, Kenneth M., 46
Stanmeyer, William A., 269
Stanton, Elizabeth Cady, 376, 387, 390,
392–97, 399, 400
State, evolution of the, 277–79
Stephen, Elias, 354
Stewardship, ideal of, 5–6, 188
Stiles, Robert, 38
Stokes, Anson Phelps, 48, 236
Stone, Ronald H., 197, 233

Storch, Neil T., 154
Stowe, Harriet Beecher, 7, 376
Stowe, Walter H., 40
Straton, John Roach, 190
Stravinskas, Peter M. J., 308
Strong, Donald S., 203
Strong, Josiah, 69, 70, 150–51, 396–97
Student Volunteer Movement, 153, 155, 158
Stumpf, Samuel Enoch, 234
Suffrage, women's, 393–400
Sugarman, Stephen D., 310
Sullivan, Daniel J., 310
Sunday, Billy, 163–64
Suomi Synod, 116
Supreme Court. *See* Constitution; Education; Litigation; *names of law cases*
Swanson, Guy A., 279 n.2
Swanson, Merwin, 84
Swatos, William H., 88–89
Swedish Lutheran church, 115
Sweet, Leonard I., 9, 264–65
Sweet, William Warren, 9, 121
Swomley, John M., 305
Szasz, Ferenc Morton, 71–72, 78, 191

Tamney, Joseph B., 276
Tappan, Lewis, 5–6
Tavard, Georges, 239
Tax Commission of the City of New York, Walz v., 348
Taylor, George Boardman, 49
Taylor, James B., 49
Taylor, Philip A. M., 111
Tcherikower, Elias, 76
Teachers College Record (journal), 317
Teaford, Jon C., 15, 159
Teichroew, Allan, 164–65
Temkin, Sefton D., 120
Temperance. *See* Liquor question
Temperance Society, 158
Temple, William, 226–27
Testem Benevolentiae (Pope Leo XIII), 153–54, 235
Thayer, Vivian Trow, 304, 305

Theosophists, 375, 377, 378, 379
Thernstrom, Stephan, 109–10
Thomas, Donna, 200
Thomas, Emory M., 8, 13
Thomas, George M., 277
Thomas, Hilah F., 373
Thomas, John L., 68, 81
Thomas, Norman, 164, 194, 197
Thomas, Samuel J., 154
Thompson, Ernest Trice, 9
Thompson, James J., Jr., 198
Thomson, E. Bruce, 237
Thornwell, James Henley, 4–5, 34
Thurow, Glen E., 15–16
Timberlake, James H., 86
Tindall, George B., 82
Tipton, Steven M., 265–66
Todd, Edward N., 10
Tomasi, Silvano M., 118
Torbet, Robert G., 9
Toulouse, Mark G., 229
Trachtenberg, Alan, 109, 122
Trauner, Joan B., 112
Trueblood, Elton, 16
Truman, Harry, 239
Tsai, Shih-shan H., 113
Tuition tax credits, 310
Tull, Charles J., 74, 194
Tumin, Melvin M., 110
Turner, Henry M., 42
Tuttle, Harold S., 306
Tuveson, Ernest Lee, 6, 108
Two-sword doctrine (Lutheran), 238
Tyack, David B., 313, 316
Tyng, Stephen, 77–78
Tyrrell, Ian R., 385

Ulich, Robert, 302
Ullmann, Daniel, 303
Unification Church, 265
Union of American Hebrew Congregations, 157
Union of Orthodox Jewish Congregations, 157
Union of Orthodox Rabbis, 157

Union Reform League, 70
Unitarians, 120, 374, 392
United Church of Christ, 267
United Methodist Church, 267
United Nations, 229
United Presbyterian Church, U.S.A., 267
United States Conference of Catholic Bishops, 163, 278, 345, 347, 353
United States, Girouard v., 234
United States, Reynolds v., 340–42, 346, 349, 350
United States v. Ballard, 351
United States v. Seeger, 351–52
United States, Welsh v., 352
United Synagogue of America, 157
Universalists, 374
Universal Negro Improvement Association, 114, 205
University of Indiana, 306
Urbanization: and the American Way of Life, 107, 109–10, 123; and blacks, 113–15; and Catholics, 116–19; and the Chinese, 112–13; and education, 316; and Jews, 119; and missionary work, 384; and Protestant core culture, 107–12, 122–23; and Scandinavian Lutheran immigrants, 115–16. *See also* Industrialization
Urofsky, Melvin I., 49, 121, 157, 205

Vallandigham, Clement L., 12
Van Alstine, George, 305
Vander Velde, Lewis G., 9
Vanderbilt, Kermit, 109
Van Dusen, Henry P., 144, 145, 228, 229
Van Dyke, Henry, 151
Varg, Paul A., 147–48
Vatican, U. S. relations with, 238, 239–40
Vecoli, Rudolph J., 111, 118
Venzke, Rodger R., 228
Verner, Sherbert V., 349
Vietnam, 274–75
Vincent, Theodore G., 114
Vincent, Widmar V., 315

Violas, Paul, 316
Visser't Hooft, W. A., 71, 226
Vitale, Engel v., 235, 311–12
Volstead Act (1920), 85, 187
Voluntary societies, 158
Vorspan, Max, 120

Wacker, Grant, 275–76
Wagner Act (1935), 199
Wahoske, Michael J., 313
Wakelyn, Jon L., 49
Walasky, Paul William, 110–11
Walker, Brooks R., 232
Walker, Clarence E., 9
Walker, Jimmy, 205
Walker, Randolph Meade, 198
Wall of separation principle, 234–35, 278, 340, 344, 347. *See also* Constitution: First Amendment of the; Litigation
Wallace v. Jaffree, 354 n.8
Wallis, Jim, 277
Walnut Street Presbyterian Church (Louisville, Kentucky), 10
Walter, Erich A., 315
Walz v. Tax Commission of the City of New York, 348
Wangler, Thomas E., 119, 151–52, 153
Ward, Harry, 194, 196, 197, 227
Ward, Lester Frank, 88
Warenski, Marilyn, 399
Warner, R. Stephen, 264, 276
Warner, Sam Bass, 109
Warshaw, Thayer S., 311, 314
Washington, Booker T., 198
Washington, Joseph R., 114
Watson, Alfred A., 10–11
Watson v. Jones, 343–44
Waxman, Chaim I., 264
Weber, Max, 160
Weber, Paul J., 278
Weber, Timothy P., 78, 190
Weeks, Louis, 10
Weigel, Gustave, 237, 239

Weinstein, James, 68, 82
Welch, E. H., 313
Welsh v. United States, 352
Welter, Barbara, 379, 380
Wentz, Frederick K., 228
Werly, John M., 191
Wesley, Edgar B., 316
West Virginia State Board of Education v. Barnette, 234, 313, 349
White, David Manning, 242
White, Ellen Gould, 375
White, Jean Bickmore, 398–99
White, Ronald C., 48, 72
Whitney, John R., 314
Whittingham, William Robinson, 10
Whyte, William H., 241–42
Widmar v. Vincent, 315
Wiebe, Robert H., 68, 82
Wight, Willard E., 8, 12
Wiley, Bell Irvin, 11, 12
Will, Robert F., 309
Willard, Frances, 87, 390, 393, 395, 400
Williams, Dorothy L., 280 n.4
Williams, Ethel L., 114, 273, 274
Williams, Michael, 162
Williams, William Appleman, 152–53
Williamson, Joel, 42
Williamsport, Bender v., 315
Wills, Garry, 265
Wilmer, Richard Hooker, 40, 48–49
Wilmore, Gayraud S., 114
Wilson, Charles Reagan, 8, 13, 39
Wilson, E. Raymond, 280 n.4
Wilson, John F., 270, 315
Wilson, John R. M., 202
Wilson, R. Jackson, 89
Wilson, Woodrow, 83, 84, 156, 161, 164
Winchester, Benjamin S., 303
Wingo, Barbara C., 189–90
Winrod, Gerald B., 193
Winter, Gibson, 242
Wirt, Sherwood Eliot, 277
Wisconsin v. Yoder, 349–50, 354 n.4
Wise, Isaac, 72
Wise, Stephen, 157, 205

Wittenmyer, Annie, 387
Wittke, Karl, 111
Wittner, Lawrence S., 228
Wolf, William J., 16
Wolfe, James S., 240
Wolfinger, Henry J., 398
Woman's Crusade, 386
Woman's National Liberal Union, 395
Woman's Relief Society, 399
Women: and conservatives, 374; and evangelicalism, 374, 375, 376, 380–82, 383–85; and God's will, 378–79; and the institutionalized church, 373–74; and liberalism, 374; and the liquor question, 87, 385–91; and missionary work, 41, 44, 374, 379–85; and Mormonism, 397–400; and new religions, 374, 376–79; ordination of, 373–74; and politics, 380–81, 391–400; prophets, 375–76; and the social gospel, 383–85; and social reform, 376–78, 383–91; and southern Protestants, 198; and spiritualism, 376–77, 378; spirituality of, 374, 382–83
Women's Christian Temperance Union (WCTU), 87, 377, 380, 384, 387–91, 393–94, 396, 399, 400
Wood, James E., Jr., 237, 302
Woodrum, Eric, 160
Woodson, Carter G., 42, 113
Woodward, C. Vann, 46, 47, 48
Woody, People v., 350, 354 n.4
World Council of Churches, 230
World order movement, 229
World's Columbian Exposition, 109
World War I, 143, 145, 162–65
World War II, 225, 227–29
Wright, Edward Needles, 13
Wuthnow, Robert J., 265, 276
Wyatt-Brown, Bertram, 5–6, 14, 35

Yans-McLaughlin, Virginia, 118
Yellowitz, Irwin, 204–5
Yoder, Wisconsin v., 349–50, 354 n.4

Yorke, Peter, 75
Young, Brigham, Jr., 155
Young, Henry C., 274
Young, Michael, 228
Young Men's Christian Association, 153,
    155, 158

Zaretsky, Irving I., 265
Zikmund, Barbara Brown, 374, 375, 391
Zionism, 121, 157, 241
Zola, Gary P., 157
Zorach v. Clauson, 235, 314, 348
Zuber, Richard L., 13

Contributors

JAMES D. BEUMLER is a graduate of Union Theological Seminary and a doctoral candidate in religion at Princeton University. He is the author of "Social Teachings of the Presbyterian Church," published in *Church and Society*, and is currently at work on a study of religion and social criticism in the 1950s.

ELIZABETH B. CLARK teaches legal history at Cardozo Law School and is completing her doctoral dissertation—a study of religion and the suffrage movement in the nineteenth century—in the Department of History at Princeton University.

WILLIAM F. DEVERELL is a doctoral candidate in American history at Princeton University, working under James M. McPherson. A graduate of Stanford University, he is preparing a doctoral dissertation on the transition from a frontier to a post-frontier society in nineteenth-century California.

RICHARD D. HORN is a graduate student in history at Princeton University and holds degrees from Harvard, Dartmouth, and Princeton. A specialist in twentieth-century intellectual history, he is currently working on a study of Sidney Hook, pragmatism, and liberalism.

JOHN W. LOWE, JR., is a doctoral candidate in the joint Doctor of Education program in Religion and Education of Union Theological Seminary and Teachers College, Columbia University. He has degrees from Juniata College, Bethany Theological Seminary, and Teachers College. His doctoral dissertation examines the compulsory Bible reading law of Pennsylvania of 1913. He has also been a pastor and religious educator with involvement in education in many capacities.

MARK S. MASSA is a graduate of the University of Chicago and the Weston School of Theology. He holds the Ph.D. from Harvard University and teaches at Fordham University in New York City.

RICHARD HUGHES SEAGER holds degrees from the University of Wisconsin and Harvard Divinity School. He has recently completed a doctoral study in religion at Harvard University with a specialization in religion in the United States and modern Europe. His dissertation is a study of the Chicago World's Parliament of Religions of 1893.

GARDINER H. SHATTUCK, JR., holds the Ph.D. from Harvard University and the M.Div. from General Theological Seminary. He is rector of the Church of the Ascension, Cranston, R.I. His dissertation on the religious life of the Civil War armies will be published by Mercer University Press.

WINNIFRED F. SULLIVAN is a graduate of the University of Chicago Law School and a member of the Illinois Bar. She has studied at the Catholic Theological Union in Chicago and is now a student in the Ph.D. program at the University of Chicago Divinity School.

DAVID HARRINGTON WATT is an assistant professor in the Religion Department at Temple University. He is currently completing a history of American evangelicalism in the middle decades of the twentieth century.

JOHN F. WILSON is Collord professor of religion at Princeton University, where he also directs the Project on the Church-State Issue in American Culture. The project is funded by the Lilly Endowment. He is a specialist in American religious history, and his publications include work on Puritanism in seventeenth-century England, Jonathan Edwards, the church-state issue, and civil religion in American society. He is the author of *Pulpit in Parliament* and *Public Religion in American Culture.*

DATE DUE